RESEARCH IN ORGANIZATIONS
Issues and Controversies

RESEARCH
IN ORGANIZATIONS
Issues
and Controversies

Edited by

Richard T. Mowday
University of Oregon

Richard M. Steers
University of Oregon

Goodyear Publishing Company, Inc.
Santa Monica, California

Library of Congress Cataloging in Publication Data

Main entry under title:

Research in organizations.

    1. Organizational research—Addresses, essays,
lectures.   2. Management research—Addresses, essays,
lectures.   I. Mowday, Richard T.   II. Steers,
Richard M.
HD30.4.R47   658'.007'2   78-25809
ISBN 0-87620-760-3

Current Printing (last digit):

10 9 8 7 6 5 4 3 2 1

Printed in the United States of America

Composition and Design: Sandy Bennett
Cover Design: Marshall Licht

To
Mary and Sheila

Contents

            BEHAVIORAL RESEARCH   287

        19. Some Unintended Consequences of Rigorous Research   290
            Chris Argyris

        20. Fads, Fashions, and Folderol in Psychology   305
            Marvin D. Dunnette

        21. The Yin and Yang of Progress in Social Psychology:
            Seven Koan   318
            William J. McGuire

        22. The Experimenting Organization: Problems
            and Prospects   331
            Barry M. Staw

Preface

Courses on research methodology have long been considered an integral part of the curriculum in graduate programs in organizational behavior and theory. The importance of a thorough understanding of the methods of research for students preparing for active research careers is apparent. While the early writing of management theorists was often characterized by anecdotal accounts of organizational experiences, the current literature on organizations increasingly reflects the use of sophisticated multivariate field studies and complex experiments in studying organizational phenomena. The scientific method has become vital to the study of organizations and the field is beginning to develop its own research traditions. Although researchers interested in organizations remain less likely than those in other fields to discuss issues associated with their research methods, they are steadily recognizing that organizations present unique research problems and that various methodologies may be employed.

There also appears to be a growing recognition that a knowledge of research methods may be useful for students preparing for careers as practicing managers. One reason research methods may be useful is that empirically-based knowledge about organizations has grown at a phenomenal rate in recent years and as a result, the manager can expect to be continually exposed to a number of theories and research findings having relevance for organizations. If the manager is to be a sophisticated consumer of this information, he or she must have some understanding of the research process through which the information was generated. Clearly, some research and theory is of higher quality than others, and managers must have the necessary skill to evaluate the research findings and decide which of them apply to their own organizations. Healthy skepticism toward organizational research by managers is to be preferred to indiscriminate acceptance of research findings. The importance of a healthy skepticism was well summarized by the late Premier of France, Georges Pompidou:

> There are three ways for a politician to ruin his career: chasing women, gambling, and trusting experts. The first is the most pleasant and the second the quickest, but trusting experts is the surest.*

*Benveniste, Guy. *The Politics of Expertise*. Berkeley, Calif.: Glendessary Press, 1972, p. 3.

The problem faced by managers may be similar to that faced by politicians. Behavioral science "experts" or management consultants should probably not be trusted by managers any more than political experts should be trusted by politicians. Skepticism based on a good understanding of the research process is perhaps the manager's best defense against accepting and applying inappropriate managerial techniques.

A second reason for increasing the exposure of managers to research methods is that the ability to evaluate the research literature critically is often inadequate. In many cases, techniques or practices that managers may want to apply in their own organization may not have been thoroughly studied. The manager who wants to implement job enrichment, for example, may discover only limited evidence concerning the application of this technique to other similar organizations. In this situation, the manager may want to experimentally implement job enrichment and evaluate its consequences before going ahead with more widespread and costly implementation throughout the organization. Managers may therefore benefit from a knowledge of research methods in experimenting with new managerial practices and effectively evaluating their consequences for employee attitudes and behavior.

A final reason why managers may benefit from a greater knowledge of the research process concerns the basic similarity between the problems faced by managers and those encountered by researchers. Although the roles of the manager and the research scientist are often viewed as very different, many of the day-to-day problems managers must deal with are similar to those faced by researchers. For example, the manager may have a problem of high absenteeism in one department. Once the problem is identified and the need to take corrective action recognized, the manager must collect reliable and valid information about the problem. The manager may often have hunches about the problem which are analogous to the hypotheses of the researcher. Managers may be more likely to act on their hunches, however, resulting in an inefficient (and costly) process of trial and error in learning about the problem. If the managers were trained in more systematic data collection procedures like those commonly employed by the researcher, their problem solving effectiveness may be increased substantially.

A knowledge of the research process is likely to prove useful to students with diverse career goals and at several educational levels. The intended audience for this book therefore includes not only doctoral students but also managers and students preparing for careers as managers. The goal is to present readings that fill a void in the literature on research in organizations. Although there are a number of excellent introductory texts on research methodology (some devoted exclusively to research on organizations), there are few suitable collections of readings available that highlight specific aspects of the research process and allow students to study these aspects in depth. In addition, it is often desirable for students to be exposed to the ideas of more than one author, particularly in an area where there is a great deal of controversy surrounding different strategies and techniques.

This book is primarily intended as a supplement to existing introductory texts on research methodology. The coverage of the readings was designed to be sufficiently broad, however, so that the book may be used alone in courses on organizational research. The book may also be a useful addition to advanced courses on organizational behavior and theory in which research methods is a major, but not the primary, focus of the class. Although readings were selected from a number of different areas of the literature, the selections have a decidedly organizational focus. The readings may therefore prove useful where instructors prefer to use a psychologically- or sociologically-based text on research methods in courses on organizational research.

In the process of preparing this collection of readings we have solicited the views of several colleagues. The comments of Barry M. Staw, Jeanne B. Herman, Lyman W. Porter, and Eugene F. Stone on an early outline of the book were extremely useful. Their willingness to share readings they have found useful in teaching courses on research methodology and their encouragement of our efforts are greatly appreciated. Mary Beth Corrigan, Dorothy Wynkoop, Thom McDade, and Daniel Spencer provided valuable assistance in the often tedious process of preparing a collection of readings of this type. In addition, the cheerful and patient efforts of Linda Schreiber from Goodyear on the production of the book has made this project more enjoyable than might otherwise have been the case. Finally, we are indebted to the authors who agreed to allow their work to be reprinted on these pages.

Richard T. Mowday
Richard M. Steers

PREFACE

Contributors

Argyris, Chris
Bakan, David
Bruyn, Severyn T.
Campbell, Donald T.
Cartwright, Dorwin
Champoux, Joseph E.
Clegg, C. W.
Cook, Thomas D.
Dunnette, Marvin D.
Ellsworth, Phoebe C.
House, Robert
Jackson, P. R.
Kimberly, John R.
Lawler, Edward E., III
Mackenzie, Kenneth D.
McGrath, Joseph E.
McGuire, William J.
Orne, Martin T.
Peters, William S.
Pfaffenberger, Roger
Rosenthal, Robert
Rosnow, Ralph L.
Seashore, Stanley E.
Staw, Barry M.
Wall, T. D.
Webb, Wilse B.
Weick, Karl E.

RESEARCH IN ORGANIZATIONS
Issues and Controversies

Nature of
Scientific Inquiry

It is possible to draw a parallel between the way investigators approach a particular research problem and the way employees approach their work environment. Members of organizations develop beliefs about relationships between different aspects of their work environment and the causes of events which transpire in the work setting. They observe events which occur around them and formulate explanations for what they have observed. For example, an employee may observe that the supervisor of a particularly ineffective work group is unconcerned about the well-being of his employees and insensitive to their feelings about matters related to work. From these observations the employee may conclude that the way supervisors respond to the feelings of their employees is related to the level of employee performance in the work group. If the employee observing these events is also a supervisor, he or she may conclude that the way to increase the effectiveness of his or her own work group is to demonstrate a concern for the feelings and well-being of employees.

This process that people follow to make greater sense out of their work environments is not too different from one followed by researchers interested in learning more about organizations (cf. Ross, 1977). Both observe events in the work setting and seek to provide explanations for these events. Such explanations provide the basis for subsequent predictions about what is likely to result when certain events occur (Stone, 1978). In this regard, people in general can be regarded as naive scientists trying to bring greater cognitive order to their experiences.

What tends to distinguish most people from formally trained researchers, however, is the systematic process followed by the latter in gathering facts and utilizing rigorous standards for assessing whether explanations of observed events are in fact accurate. The scientific method is one such systematic process and is composed of several prescribed steps: (1) identification of a research question; (2) formulation of hypotheses or predictions about the question in advance of study; (3) design of a study to test the hypotheses; (4) observation of variables; (5) examination of relationships between the variables observed; and (6) drawing conclusions about the research question based on observed relationships. Moreover, this process is viewed as a continuing cycle in which the conclusions reached on the basis of one study may lead to a reformulation of the original hypotheses or to new research questions for future investigation. One additional feature of the scientific method is that the procedures followed by a researcher are public, and thus the conclusions reached can be independently verified or evaluated by other researchers.

Besides using a systematic process, scientists are also thought to differ from others in terms of their personal characteristics and the norms they adopt to regulate their behavior. A number of *norms* have been identified which are commonly viewed as guiding the researcher in the pursuit of knowledge. The list presented by West (cited by Mitroff, 1974) is perhaps the most complete.

1. Faith in rationality
2. Emotional neutrality toward ideas and research findings
3. Belief in the universal right of all people to claims of discovery and possession of knowledge
4. Individualism or the unwillingness to be swayed by the majority
5. Belief in the larger interests of the scientific community in which property rights are limited to credit for discovery and secrecy is considered an immoral act
6. Disinterestedness in personal prestige or self-interest
7. Impartiality in the production and evaluation of new knowledge
8. Suspension of judgment in the absence of conclusive evidence
9. Absence of bias in evaluating the work of others
10. Belief that the production of new knowledge by research is the most important of all activities
11. Resistance to restraint or control over scientific investigation

In evaluating the steps of the scientific method and the norms which are thought to guide the scientist in research endeavors, it is important to distinguish between prescriptive guidelines for conducting research and descriptions of the process as it is typically carried out. Generally, these statements about the nature of scientific inquiry are less descriptive of the actual research process than the normative standards the researcher may continually strive to achieve. Mitroff (1974) has carefully analyzed what he terms the "storybook" image of science and finds serious deficiencies in the extent to which it describes research as it is commonly practiced.

A blue-ribbon committee of the American Psychological Association (Garner, Hunt, and Taylor, 1959) has also seriously questioned the stereotype of the research process commonly held by both scientists and the general public. Rather than finding research to be a logical process, they found that it is more often a "messy looking affair" that includes a great deal of "floundering about in the real world" (page 169). Moreover, when they considered the characteristics of the most productive researchers in psychology, they found those researchers to be narrow in their interests, preoccupied with their own ideas, and unsystematic in both their reading of the literature and methods of research.

These conclusions question the accuracy of the commonly held view of the scientific method. Furthermore, questions have been raised about the utility of certain norms thought to govern researchers in their pursuit of the larger goal of advancing knowledge in a given area. How many discoveries can be attributed to researchers who were willing to emotionally advance their ideas in the absence of existing empirical support or in the face of considerable criticism from their colleagues? This is an interesting question and certainly one that suggests that the norms that should govern the behavior of researchers are a controversial topic for discussion.

The readings in this section discuss the nature of scientific inquiry from somewhat different perspectives. The first selection by McGrath presents a cogent discussion of the choices facing a researcher investigating organizational phenomena. Proceeding from the belief that the strategic choices made by the researcher between alternative methodologies make a real difference in the potential rewards of a study, McGrath provides a useful discussion of the tradeoffs involved in selecting one method over another. Although various fields often develop characteristic methods for studying various problems (for example, the survey or correlational study is used in research on organizations), this selection suggests that the researcher choose a method appropriate to the question being asked and the state of existing knowledge about the question.

The selection by MacKenzie and House then takes a more macro view of research in suggesting a strategy for paradigm development that is most efficient in generating and accumulating research knowledge. Their work has been heavily influenced by Kuhn's (1970) writing on scientific paradigms and Platt's (1964) method of strong inference in research. Rather than limit their attention to the choices confronting a researcher in a particular study, they suggest that research design be viewed in the broader perspective of a research program extending over a number of studies and aimed toward the ultimate development and testing of theory. Their concern is both with the design of individual studies that build upon previous research and lines of research that efficiently accumulate knowledge.

Finally, the paper by Cartwright provides an interesting basis for comparing the ideas of MacKenzie and House with an actual line of research that has extended over a number of years. Cartwright presents a case study of research on the "risky-shift" phenomenon in group decision making. He traces the origin of the research to a single Master's thesis and follows its development by other researchers. A high degree of interconnectedness is evident in the line of research whose paradigmatic nature is related to the shared assumptions and methods of different researchers. The important issue raised by Cartwright concerns the potential negative consequences of research paradigms and how these negative consequences may be minimized.

REFERENCES AND SUGGESTED READINGS

Cronbach, L. J. "The Two Disciplines of Scientific Psychology," *American Psychologist,* **12** (1957), pp. 671–684.

Dubin, R. "Theory Building in Applied Areas." In M. Dunnette (ed.), *Handbook of Industrial and Organizational Psychology.* Chicago: Rand McNally, 1976.

Garner, W. R., Hunt, H. F., and Taylor, D. W. "Education for Research in Psychology," *American Psychologist,* **14** (1959), pp. 167–179.

Kaplan, A. *The Conduct of Inquiry.* San Francisco: Chandler, 1964.

Kuhn, T. S. *The Structure of Scientific Revolutions* (2nd ed.). Chicago: University of Chicago Press, 1970.

Meehl, P. E. "Theory-testing in Psychology and Physics: A Methodological Paradox," *Philosophy of Science,* **34** (1967), pp. 103–115.

Mitrofff, I. I. *The Subjective Side of Science.* Amsterdam: Elsevier, 1974.

Platt, J. "Strong inference," *Science,* **146** (1964), pp. 347–353.

Ross, L. "The Intuitive Psychologist and His Shortcomings: Distortions in the Attribution Process." In L. Berkowitz (ed.), *Advances in Experimental Social Psychology* (vol. 10). New York: Academic Press, 1977.

Stone, E. *Research Methods in Organizational Behavior.* Santa Monica, Calif.: Goodyear, 1978.

1   Toward a "Theory of Method" for Research on Organizations

Joseph E. McGrath

INTRODUCTION

Organization research is a meeting ground (and, hopefully, a melting pot) for the sociologist, the economist, the political scientist, the operations researcher, the mathematician, the social psychologist, and the engineer. Men from each of these fields, and others, have contributed much to our current state of knowledge about the nature and dynamics of organizations.

But because the field of organization research is inherently as well as historically an interdisciplinary field, it is marked by great diversity in concepts, terms, and methods of study. Since the men who do organization research come from a variety of backgrounds, they tend to bring with them different tools, different concepts, and different methodological approaches. Consider, for example . . . Seashore and Bowers (1962) in their studies of organizational effectiveness; or consider the differences between Guetzkow's (1962) and Jensen's (1962) approaches to the study of internation tensions; similarly, notice the differences between . . . Likert's (1961) and Homans' (1950) empirically derived organization theories. Even when these sets of studies deal with the "same" problem in the field of organization research, the methodological differences among them seem about as great as the differences between the methodologies of totally separate scientific disciplines.

Such diversity has both positive and negative effects on the field. On the plus side, diversity of concepts and methods insures a dynamic, searching, pluralistic growth for the field, which probably offers a substantial safeguard against conceptual stagnation. On the other hand, diversity of theoretical concepts—and above all, diversity in the use of methods—leads to considerable malcommunication within the field, which doubtless decreases the efficiency with which we can advance our knowledge.

Furthermore, it is apparent that every methodology has some limitations in terms of what it *cannot* do (or cannot do efficiently), as well as some advantages in terms of what it *can* do. Hence, methods are not totally interchangeable, and the choice of methodology in any given case should be made on the basis of the possibilities and limitations of that methodology *vis-à-vis* the research problem to which it is to be applied.

This [article] is written on the assumption that differences in research methodology *do* make a difference in the yield of research. In other words, when we choose one methodology over others in a study of organization, we are thereby affecting the kinds and amount of information which we can obtain from results of that study. If this

From W. W. Cooper, H. L. Leavitt, and M. W. Shelly (eds.), *New Perspectives in Organizational Research*, pp. 533-557. Copyright © 1964 by John Wiley & Sons, Inc. Reprinted by permission of John Wiley & Sons, Inc.

assumption is true, it follows that we should choose the methodology that we will use in a given case on the basis of the kinds of information we are seeking (i.e., the nature of the problem we are studying), and we should choose so as to maximize the amount of information which we will gain about that problem. It also follows that when we choose our methodology for reasons of personal preference, familiarity, or operational expediency, we are changing the nature of the problem about which we will be gaining information, as well as altering the amount of information which we can gain from our study.

If we are to make "rational" choices of methodology, so as to maximize the amount of information relevant to our purposes, we must be able to do at least two things. First, we must be able to compare alternative approaches in terms of their relative effectiveness in providing the desired information. This, in turn, requires ability to specify what we mean by "research information," and how we will assess the efficiency of a research approach for generating such information. In short, if we are to make rational choices of method, we need a "theory of method" to guide us in those choices.

This [article] is an attempt to take some first steps toward the development of such a "theory of method" for the study of organizations. Our presentation falls naturally into three stages which constitute the three sections of the [article]. First, we will consider methodologies that have and/or can be applied to the study of organizations, and attempt to place them in a framework within which they can be related to one another. Secondly, we will attempt to define certain key concepts—"research information," "information potential" and "information yield"—and from them formulate what we mean by "comprehensiveness," "efficiency," and "effectiveness" of a study.[1] Then, in the final section, we will try to apply these concepts to compare and contrast different methodologies, and will consider some of the implications of these comparisons for programmatic planning of organization research.

It should be pointed out here that we doubt if any of the concepts presented in this [article] will in themselves be new or startling to the reader. Nor will our conclusions likely offer the reader profound new insights. The contribution which this [article] makes, if any, lies in its attempt to formulate some well-recognized concepts and distinctions in a fairly systematic and rigorous way. Hence, this [article] will not particularly add to "what we know," but, hopefully, it will add to our appreciation of the import of "what we know" for "what we do," when we set out to do research on organizations.

A CLASSIFICATION OF DATA-COLLECTION METHODS USED IN ORGANIZATION RESEARCH

Many streams of endeavor contribute to the current field of organization research, and studies based on many different methodological approaches form part of the body of knowledge of that field. The methodology used in studies of organizations ranges from carefully delimited, laboratory-controlled studies, such as those on communication networks by Bavelas (1950), Leavitt (1951), Guetzkow and Simon (1955), and others, to broad and sweeping conceptual analyses of large organizations, and even total societies (e.g., Homans, 1950; Merton, 1940; Parsons, 1960). Organization research includes intensive case studies of single organizations (e.g., W. F. Whyte, 1948; Selznick, 1949), broad surveys of many organizations of a single type,[2] journalistic analyses based on anecdotal evidence (e.g., W. H. Whyte, 1956; Riesman, 1950), true "field experiments" which involve experimental manipulations of an entire large-scale organization (e.g., Morse and Reimer, 1956; Seashore and Bowers, 1962), man-computer simulation studies (e.g., Guetzkow, 1962; Rome and Rome, 1960), all-computer simulations and use of formal mathematical models. At a superficial glance, it would appear that the only common feature of all of these approaches is that they are—or are intended to be—applicable to the study of some aspect of organizations.

We can begin to see some common elements among these methodologies, however, when we consider each of them in terms of the nature of the setting within which data-collection takes place and in terms of the extent to which activities of the investigator intrude upon, or are responsible for, the nature of that setting. Viewed in these terms, in fact, most of the types of methodology used in organization research seem to fit within one of four major classes. We will label these four classes of research settings as field studies; experimental simulations; laboratory experiments; and computer simulations.

Field Studies

Field studies are those research investigations which take place within "natural" or "real life" social situations. This category includes all types of empirical investigations which use data from real, existing organizations. Within this category we include a number of types of research which are heterogeneous in many respects. For example, one kind of "field study," as the term is used here, is those "studies" which consist only of casual or anecdotal observations. Another kind of field study would be the systematic and intensive case study of existing or past organizations, including those done primarily through analysis of records and documents (e.g., Selznick, 1949; Alger, 1962). Broad surveys are also included,[3] as are both the so-called natural experiments and the carefully planned, deliberately-executed field experiments (e.g., Seashore and Bowers, 1962; Morse and Reimer, 1956; Coch and French, 1948).

The kinds of research here included within the over-all category of field studies show marked variations in method. They are listed here in a generally increasing order of rigor of procedure. At the same time, they are here classed together on the basis of one crucial common feature. All of these types of field studies are investigations which obtain their data directly from real, existing organizations of the kind to which results are intended to apply. That is, all field studies are direct studies of (members of) the class of phenomena with which the investigation is concerned, namely, real "flesh-and-blood" organizations. One important feature of data obtained from a "real-life" situation is that the humans in that situation are operating under natural (not necessarily stronger) motivational forces, since the phenomena being studied are a part of their actual lives.

Experimental Simulations

The term "experimental simulations" is used here to refer to empirical investigations which attempt to create a relatively faithful representation of "an organization" under quasi-laboratory conditions, set that simulated organization "in motion," and study the operation of that organization as it is expressed in the behavior of humans who are assigned roles within it (e.g., Guetzkow, 1962; Rome and Rome, 1960). This category is roughly equivalent to Guetzkow's category of "man-computer simulations" (Guetzkow, 1962).

In such studies, many features of the structure and process of the organization are simulated, often by the use of computers, to study the process and consequences of behavior of human subjects who operate the simulated system. These studies are distinguished from laboratory experiments (Class 3 in our present classification) in several respects. First, the stimulus situation within which the individual is operating is more or less continuous in an experimental simulation, in contrast to the laboratory experiment which usually consists of a series of discrete trials. Secondly, as a part of the continuous nature of experimental simulations, participants' reponses at any particular point in time partly determine (along with the "rules of the game") the stimulus situation in which they will be operating at subsequent points in time. Finally, experimental simulations differ from laboratory studies in that they attempt to simulate or model properties of "real-life" organizations, which is the key defining property of this class of methods in the present schema.

However, experimental simulations vary considerably in terms of the degree of fidelity of the simulation involved. They also vary in terms of the complexity of the simulation, and in terms of whether the particular simulation is intended to represent a generic type of organization or some particular type of organization. All three of these distinctions go together to determine whether the simulation presents the participants with a "bare-bones," fairly abstract representation of only the key processes felt to be important (e.g., Guetzkow's internation simulation, 1962) or whether it attempts to provide them with a content-enriched stimulus situation which "seems" very similar to the "real" situation. Experimental simulations also vary in terms of how much of the total operation of the organization is simulated and how much is left to determination by the performance of the human participants.

Laboratory Experiments

Laboratory experiments are those studies in which the investigator does not attempt to recreate "reality" in his laboratory, but rather tries to abstract variables from real life situations and represent them in a more fundamental form. His purpose is to study the operation of these more fundamental processes under highly controlled conditions. He is not so much interested in making his laboratory situation a "greenhouse" for the study of some particular class of organizations. Rather, he is interested in studying fundamental processes which presumably underlie the behavior of humans in a broad range of organizational (and other) settings.[4]

Perhaps the essential features of laboratory experiments as they relate to the field of organization research can best be presented by using the studies of communication networks (Bavelas, 1950; Christie, et al., 1952; Guetzkow and Simon, 1955; Leavitt, 1951; Shaw, 1955; and others) as illustrations of this class of method. The communication net studies isolate one fundamental feature common to *all* organizations, namely, the pattern of communication linkages between organizational components and study the effects of variations in this pattern under laboratory conditions. Neither the specific nets studied (four and five node nets, of various patterns ranging from highly centralized to highly decentralized) nor the tasks being performed (symbol-identification problems, simple arithmetic problems, etc.) were meant to "simulate" real organizational structures or real organizational tasks. Rather, the purpose of the communication net studies was to determine how variations in highly abstract and basic patterns of communication influenced certain basic kinds of human activities (e.g., transmission and reception of messages, deductive problem-solving, organizational planning) and certain classes of human reactions (felt satisfaction, attraction to the group, job satisfaction), which presumably operate in *all* human organizations.

This attempt to create and study generic structures or processes is one of several features which distinguish laboratory experiments from experimental simulations as discussed previously. Other distinguishing features are the frequent use of a series of discrete, independent "trials," for which the stimulus conditions are entirely preprogrammed by the investigator, rather than using a continuous stimulus situation which is partly determined by prior responses of participants. This pattern of procedure gives the laboratory experimenter greater control over the stimulus situation and reduces confounding between different stages of performance, although it also reduces the continuity and the "felt realness" of the situation for the participant.

Computer Simulations

This class of methods should more properly be called "mathematical models." It is here referred to as computer simulations, both in order to contrast it with experimental simulations (Class 2 in the present schema) and because the special kind of logical or mathematical model which we call computer simulations is frequently used in the study of organizations. Guetzkow (1962) designates this class of studies as "all-computer" studies. Computer simulations are also sometimes referred to as "Monte Carlo" studies, because they generally utilize the procedure of random selection from predetermined probability distributions as a means of "simulating" specific behaviors of parts of the system on specific occasions.

Computer simulations are distinguished from experimental simulations because they are closed or logically complete models of the class of phenomenon being simulated. *All* variables, including the "dependent variables" or "output variables" which result from operation of the system, are built into the formulation of the simulation model itself. Thus, the model does not involve or require performance by human participants. Performance or output variables are "contained" within the model, most often as stochastically determined consequences of the computerized "operation" of the simulated organization.

Computer simulations can represent either a generic class or a particular class of organizations. Computer simulations vary considerably in the "richness" and complexity with which they simulate the (class of) organizations being studied. They vary, in particular, in the extent to which the simulation tries to represent "depth" characteristics of the human components of the organization (e.g., values, attitudes, norms, conformity pressures) as well as their superficial "output" characteristics. They also vary, of course, in the "validity" or "reasonableness" of the assumptions by means of which such representations of human behavior are inserted into the model.

Models do not necessarily have to make use of computers to belong in the computer simulation class as here defined. In fact, an interesting example of a simple and low-cost model, which "runs" without the use of any major computational aids but which nevertheless has all of the essential characteristics of this class of research methods, is presented in Guetzkow (1962). The essential feature of this class of research is that *all* structures and processes which are to be dealt with in the investigation are represented in the simulation model itself either as parameters, as operating rules, or as stochastic processes.

Relations Between the Four Classes of Methods

These four classes of methods appear to be more or less ordered along a continuum which has several facets. The ordering continuum can be thought of as proceeding from concrete (at the field study end) to abstract (at the computer simulation end). Alternatively, we can label the ends of the continuum as realism versus artificiality, or we can label them as going from "open" to "closed" settings, or from "loose" to "controlled" conditions.[5]

Regardless of how we designated the underlying continuum, the four different classes of methods which we have identified along that continuum differ markedly from one another in terms of the advantages which they offer the researcher and in terms of the limitations which they impose upon him. At the field study end of the continuum, for example, the investigator has the substantial advantages of "felt realism" and of the operation of inherent motivational forces. As pointed out previously, this does not necessarily mean that human participants are operating at higher levels of motivation. Rather, it means that they are operating under more "natural" kinds of motivations, since the study itself is an integral part of their lives. These advantages of the field study are gained at the cost of less precision, less control, and less freedom to manipulate variables whose effects may be of central concern. Research methods at the other end of the continuum—laboratory experiments and computer simulations—have as their major advantages precisely those characteristics which are the major disadvantages of the field study: precision, control of variables, and considerable freedom to manipulate variables of central concern. However, they also have the complementing disadvantage of lack of realism.

These and many other advantages and disadvantages of various research settings make it very clear that the four classes of methods are not at all interchangeable. Rather, they seem to offer complementary approaches, and the choice of the best approach in a given case must reckon with the *relative* importance of realism, precision of measurement, opportunities to manipulate variables, and many other features of the research situation. Our purpose here is to work toward development of some guide rules for making these comparisons, hence for making our choices of method more nearly "rational."

Development of such guide rules requires that we establish a network of basic methodological concepts—a theory of method—in terms of which we will "calculate" the relative efficiency, comprehensiveness, and effectiveness of various research approaches, so that their relative usefulness to us in a given case can be determined with some rigor. Accordingly, we will interrupt our consideration of different classes of research methods temporarily to establish some basic tools for methodological comparisons in the next section of this presentation. Then, in the final section . . . we will return to a comparison of advantages and disadvantages of different research settings armed with more adequate tools for making such comparisons.

SOME CONCEPTS FOR ASSESSING THE ADEQUACY OF RESEARCH METHODS

The Nature of a Research Problem

Research has to do with identification and measurement of variables thought to be relevant to a certain problem or phenomenon and determination of the interrela-

tionships among those variables. When we do research, we ask three basic questions:
(1) What are the important or relevant variables (conditions, parameters, properties,
etc.) of the phenomenon I wish to study? (2) How does each of them vary (in nature);
what range of values can each of them assume? (3) How do they covary; is the value of
one variable predictable from (or predictive of) the value of one or more other variables?

Let us consider a "research problem" as a set of variables, descriptive of some
phenomenon which is of interest to us, whose covariations we are going to attempt to
describe. The variables in such a set include: (1) properties of the class of object or
entity being studied (e.g., individuals, organizations, etc.), including properties that
have to do with relations between parts; (2) properties of the environment, situation,
or setting within which that class of objects exists (including suprasystems to which
the objects are organic, their physical environments, their tasks); and (3) properties of
the action or behavior of the objects in relation to the environment.

A variable of any of the above types is *relevant* to the research problem if its variation has an (appreciable) effect on, or is (detectably) affected by, variations in one or
more of the other variables of the set.

We will assume that, in any given case, there are a *finite* number of relevant variables in the set to be studied. (Variables which are determinable mathematical functions
of one another—such as the radii and diameters of a given set of circles—are considered
collectively as a unitary variable.) *All* of the relevant variables are always present at
some value (including "zero" or "absent") in a research situation, whether their presence is recognized by the researcher or not. Hence, the research problem always concerns the total set of variables V. We cannot reduce the number of relevant variables in
the situation; we can only limit the scope of our study by restricting variation of some
of them, or reduce the precision of our study by ignoring variation of some of them.

Alternative Treatments of Variables

We must do something about each of the relevant variables in a research problem.
Basically, any one variable can be treated in one of four mutually exclusive ways:

Treatment W. We can *control* a certain variable V_j so that all of its values except
one, k_i, are *prevented* from occurring. We can do this in several ways: by selective sampling of cases, by arrangement of conditions, etc.

Treatment X. We can *manipulate* a certain variable V_j so that a certain value k_i is
required to occur. This operation can also be performed by a number of techniques,
including design or assembly of parts, induction of conditions, and so forth.[6]

Treatment Y. We can deal with a given variable V_j by *permitting it to vary freely
and measuring* the values of it which do occur. Such measurement can take various
forms, including the use of physical instruments, the use of human observers, the use
of self-reports by the objects of study.

Treatment Z. We can *ignore* a variable V_j by permitting it to vary freely, but failing to determine what values *do* occur. This treatment is applied to all variables which
are *in* the relevant set V, but which are not dealt with by Treatments X, Y, or Z.

In any given research situation, *every* relevant variable is handled by one and only
one of these four treatments. These four ways of treating variables are used with differential frequency in studies conducted in different types of research settings. For
example, Treatments W and X are the hallmarks of laboratory studies and are used sel-

dom or not at all in field studies. The use of Treatment Z is more or less inevitable in field studies, but its use can be minimized in the laboratory.

These four ways of treating variables have different implications for the scope, precision, and effectiveness of study design, because they have different effects on the amount of research information which inheres in a study design and the amount of information which can be extracted from that study. So, before returning to a discussion of research settings and their uses, let us consider the concepts of research information, information potential, and information yield within a research design.

Research Information, Information Potential, and Information Yield

Research information has to do with the specification of relationships between variables. We have gained research information when we ascertain *whether or not* the occurrence of a particular value of a variable V_1 is predictive of (or predictable from) the value(s) which obtain for variable V_2 (V_3, $\cdots$, V_N). As a convention, we will say that we gain research information from determination of *whether or not* two (or more) variables vary together, while we will say that we gain *positive research information* when we discover that two such variables *do*, in fact, vary together predictably.

The amount of information which *can* be gained about any given situation is a function of the amount of "uncertainty," or *potential information*, which is inherent in that situation. The *potential information* contained in a situation depends on the number of (relevant) variables and the number of values which each variable can assume. If there are V variables relevant to a situation, and each has k values, then for *any given instance* (trial, event, etc.) of that situation there are k^v possible combinations of values of the variables involved. That term k^v represents the *total information potential* of a situation.[7]

We gain *positive research information* to the extent that we reduce the number of possible combinations of values of variables k^v by ascertaining that two or more variables vary concomitantly. That is, we gain *positive research information* when we can predict that the occurrence of a certain value k_1 of variable V_1 will be accompanied by the occurrence of a certain value k_i (or a *restricted* range of values, less than the total range) of another variable V_2, *under conditions where values of V_2 other than the predicted value(s) are free to occur* (insofar as the study operations are concerned). Hence, we gain positive research information *when and only when* something that is *free to happen* predictably *does not*.

On the other hand, when we *reduce the potential information* of a situation by deliberately precluding the occurrence of certain values of a variable (as we do when we "experimentally control" a variable, as in Treatment W), we have not gained any research information by so doing. Rather, when we *alter* what values of a variable can occur—either by preventing some values from occurring (as in experimental control of a variable, Treatment W), or by insuring that a certain value of the variable does occur (as in experimental manipulation, Treatment X)—we *reduce* the potential information which our study situation contains below that which is contained in the "real-world" situation. For example, if one variable is controlled at a single value, its range of occurrence is reduced from k to 1 value, and the total information potential is reduced from k^v to k^{v-1}. If there are five variables, each with ten possible values, k^v = 100,000, k^{v-1} = 10,000, a reduction by $9/10$ in this particular case.

This reduction of potential information represents a restriction of the scope of our study and a limitation on the generality of our findings. We can represent the scope or generality of a given study in terms of the ratio of the information potential of the study to the information potential of the "real-world" situation to which it refers (and to which its results are intended to apply) k^{v-w}/k^v, where w refers to the number of variables which were *made to occur* at one particular value.

The total potential information in a study situation sets the upper limit for the total research information which that study *can* yield, just as the amount of uncertainty associated with a message limits the amount of information which the message can convey. Within this limit, study procedures affect the extent to which that potential information is realized as research information. By definition, research information involves statements about the covariation (or lack of it) between two or more variables, at least one of which is free to vary "at will." Determination of such covariation, or its absence, requires: (1) that at least one of the variables being related be free (insofar as our study procedures are concerned) to take on any of a range of values, *and* (2) that we identify (measure) what value of all of the variables being related *actually obtained* in each of a given set of instances. When we permit a variable V_j to vary freely, but do not determine what values it assumes (Treatment Z), we do *not* reduce the information potential inherent in the situation (i.e., the number of alternative combinations of values of variables which can occur), but we greatly reduce the information which we can *extract* from the situation (i.e., the *information yield* of our study). Variables which are uncontrolled but unmeasured (Treatment Z) generate *noise* in our data. Extending the previous illustration: If we have five variables, each with ten values, $k^v = 100,000$. If one of the five variables is controlled at a single value, but a second variable is ignored, the total information potential of the *study* remains $k^{v-1} = 10,000$; but the accountable or specifiable information is reduced to k^{v-2}, which equals 1,000. If *accountable* information is considered *information yield*, and effects of variables which are uncontrolled but ignored are considered *noise*, the ratio $k^{v-(w+z)}/k^{v-w}$ expresses the *precision* of a study in terms of the ratio of *accountable information* (*information yield*) to *potential information*.[8]

Efficiency, Comprehensiveness, and Effectiveness

One might consider that the *efficiency* of a study is reflected in its precision as defined above; that is, the ratio of accountable information to potential information, $k^{v-(w+z)}/k^{v-w}$. One might further view the *comprehensiveness* of a study in terms of its scope or generality, expressed as the relation between information potential of the study and information potential of the referent situation, k^{v-w}/k^v, as previously discussed. However, we should probably view the *over-all effectiveness* of a study by comparing its *information yield* to the *total potential information of the referent situation*. Hence effectiveness of a study can be expressed as $k^{v-(w+z)}/k^v$. In this view, we lose "comprehensiveness" when we control variables (i.e., restrict their range of values, by Treatments W or X); we lose "efficiency" when we ignore variables (i.e., let them vary but fail to measure them, Treatment Z); and we lose "effectiveness" when we do *either* of these.

Since different types of research settings vary in their relative uses of Treatments W, X, Y, and Z, as previously noted, these settings also differ, in an orderly way, in the extent to which they are limited in comprehensiveness, efficiency, and effectiveness. We shall examine these differences in the next section.

COMPARISON OF RESEARCH METHODS

Let us return now to consideration of the four classes of research settings previously described. As already noted, these four classes of research settings differ in the extent to which they utilize the four treatments of variables (see Table 1). Hence, they differ in their potential information and their information yield. Let us consider the four classes of methods comparatively, in terms of the way they use the four different treatments of variables, and the consequences of that use.

TABLE 1   Relative Frequency of Use of Different Treatments of
Variables in the Four Classes of Research Settings

| Classes of Research Settings | Alternative Treatments of Variables | | | |
	Treatment W Excluded by Control	Treatment X Made to Occur by Experimental Manipulation	Treatment Y Varying Freely and Measured	Treatment Z Varying Freely but Ignored
Field studies	Low or no use	Low or no use	High or low use, gross measurement	Very high use
Experimental simulations	Medium to high use	Moderate use	High or low use, moderately precise measurement	High use
Laboratory experiments	High use	High use	High or low use, precise measurement	Low use
Computer simulations	Very high use	Very high use	Not possible	Not possible

Treatment W: Experimental Control

The use of Treatment W, control of a variable by experimental means, tends to increase as we move along the continuum of methods from field studies to computer simulations. This occurs in two ways. First, the laboratory or computer investigator uses Treatment W deliberately to hold certain of the relevant variables in the problem at a single, constant value so that they will not confound effects of other variables which are of more central concern to him. In doing so, he deliberately reduces the scope or comprehensiveness of his study—he cuts down the potential information in it—as a price for excluding "noise" from it. However, the laboratory or simulation investigator also often uses Treatment W *unwittingly*. That is, in the process of simulating or recreating the class of phenomena being studied, he is likely to overlook important features of the real life situation which he is modeling. Hence, he applies Treatment W to these variables by holding them at a single constant value ("zero" or "excluded"). These exclusions also reduce the information potential of the study, even though they are not done on the basis of deliberate choice by the investigator. In the field study, the investigator usually does not have an opportunity to control variables, either deliberately or unwittingly. Hence he avoids both the problems and the advantages involved in use of Treatment W.

The use of Treatment W has positive and negative effects on a study design. On the positive side, to control a variable (Treatment W), rather than permitting it to vary freely without measuring it (Treatment Z), prevents a loss of efficiency in the study by reducing the "noise." On the other hand, to control a variable at a single value (Treatment W), rather than making it occur at each of a series of specific values (Treatment X) or letting it vary but measuring its variation (Treatment Y), reduces the information potential of the study below the information potential of the referent situation and thus reduces the scope or comprehensiveness of the study.

Results of a study only refer to the specific combinations of conditions used. They might or might not hold if one or more of those variables to which Treatment W has been applied had been held at some *different* value. Such a situation would occur in all cases where a variable that is held constant has *interactive* effects with other variables in the problem. It is often said that systems in general, and organizations in particular, are complexes of *interactive* variables. If so, then we need to be very careful not to violate that concept of organizations by choosing to control key *interactive* variables at a single value in order to make our study design more feasible.

We should also be concerned, it would seem, about selection of the *particular value* at which we will control a variable to which we have decided to apply Treatment W. If we *must* limit a relevant variable to a single value, hence limit the applicability of our results to combinations of conditions which include that value, we probably ought to choose the natural modal value of that variable as it occurs in the referent situation rather than some value which gives us "baseline" information, or a "cleaner" (looking) design, or a study plan that is easy to implement.

As a rather simple illustration, suppose we wish to simulate or do experiments pertaining to an organization whose subsystems have a mixture of male and female members. We might want to do a laboratory study of the effects of group communication processes on the performance effectiveness of such groups. A study using uniformly male groups (or uniformly female groups), or using a constant ratio of males and females in each group, would seem on the surface to offer a "cleaner" design (and perhaps a design that is easier to implement). However, such designs may very well not be as useful as a design which determines male-female composition of groups on a random basis. Sex differences (and especially *sex composition* differences) may very well *interact with* communication patterns in affecting task performance. That is, the "best" communication pattern for task effectiveness may be quite different in all-male, all-female, and mixed-sex groups. If this were true, results obtained from study of all-male groups just simply would not apply to mixed-sex groups even if all other features of the study were well executed. In fact, trying to apply results of such a study to real life organizations which have mixed-sex work groups would *systematically* lead us to the *wrong* answer (i.e., we would be led to select as optimal a communication pattern which was definitely *not* optimal for task effectiveness).

If we found it necessary to do our experiment with groups of only one sex composition, we would be better off using the composition pattern that is modal for those groups (or organizations) to which we want to apply our findings. If we used randomly composed groups, or groups with male-female proportion which was most predominant in the referent organizations, we still would not gain information about other sex composition patterns, of course. Nor would we avoid the problems posed by the interaction effects of the variable we chose to control. But at least we would obtain results which, when applied, would lead us to be *systematically right* in our choice of optimal communication patterns.

Treatment X: Experimental Manipulation

In Treatment X, we use experimental manipulation to insure that a certain value k_i of variable V_j will occur on a certain occasion (or trial). Most often, we are manipulating circumstances so that different values of V_j occur on different trials according to a predetermined schedule. If only one value of a variable is used for *all* trials, Treatment X becomes identical with Treatment W, and has the same restrictive effects on the study design. If the variable is manipulated so that every one of its possible values occurs on some trials, then Treatment X does not place any limitation on the information potential of the study. In most cases, however, experimental manipulations use more than one, but less than all values of the variable; hence they lead to some restriction in scope.

The use of Treatment X tends to increase as we go from field studies to computer simulations. Furthermore, there tends to be an increase in the number of values of a variable which are utilized when a variable is manipulated. For example, when a field study does manage to include an experimentally manipulated variable it is almost always necessary to limit the manipulation to two, or at the most, three, levels of the variable (including control groups) (e.g., Seashore and Bowers, 1962; Morse and Reimer, 1956). In laboratory experiments, on the other hand, it is often possible to vary systematically one or more variables at each of a series of values. To the extent that this can be done, we can then determine the functional relationships between the manipulated variables and other "free-but-measured" variables (Treatment Y).

On the other hand, while the field study is seldom able to manipulate any variables, or to manipulate them at many levels, the manipulations which sometimes can be achieved in field settings are often very powerful. Partly, this power comes from the fact that manipulations of conditions in a field study—whether due to "natural" causes or to experimental plan—affect the very lives of the participants in the study. Manipulations in the laboratory, on the other hand, are often relatively weak, both for ethical reasons and because of the inherent artificiality of the motivational conditions under which participants are operating.

One of the special advantages of the computer simulation lies in the facility which it provides for systematic manipulation of many variables at each of many values. In fact, the computer simulation can generate combinations of conditions which do not exist in the real world, but whose effects may be of vital importance for theoretical development. For example, a computer simulation might be developed to represent an organization whose "human components" perform with perfect efficiency and rationality—a situation not found in nature—to study upper limit conditions for performance of that organization. (Sometimes, computer simulations seem to build such assumptions about human perfection into their models, without recognizing that they are dealing with hypothetical upper limits.)

Treatment Y: A Necessary Condition for Obtaining Research Information

The number of variables handled by Treatment Y does not necessarily increase or decrease as we proceed along the continuum of methods from field studies to the laboratory situation. However, the precision with which variables can be measured tends to increase. Precision of measurement is used here to refer both to sensitivity (the number of values of a variable which can be distinguished) and to reliability (the stability of results from independent measures) of the measurement process.

Treatment Y does not exist in the computer situation, for the same reason that Treatment Z is not a part of that class of research settings. Treatment Y refers to permitting a variable to vary freely and measuring its variation; Treatment Z refers to permitting a variable to vary freely but not measuring it. Since no variable is operating outside the control of the investigator in a "closed model" such as a computer simulation, neither Treatment Y nor Treatment Z is possible within it. Even the "output" variables of a computer simulation do not vary freely, but rather are *wholly determined* by the values and relationships built into the model. Thus, even though the complexity of the model and the stochastic nature of some of the variables in it may prevent us from clearly specifying the output of its "operation" in advance, that output is nevertheless determined fully, albeit in a complex manner.

Hence, while the computer simulation entirely eliminates "noise" because it does not permit Treatment Z, it also entirely eliminates *information*, in the sense in which that term is here defined, because it does not permit Treatment Y. Returning to our earlier definition, we can gain research information when and only when something that is free to happen does not happen. That condition is never met by a computer simulation or any logically closed formal model.

Since the presence of Treatment Y is a necessary condition for obtaining research information, maximizing its use would seem to be an unqualified desideratum. However, such a generalization could lead to substantial inefficiency in the collection of empirical data. For example, there may be a particular value of a variable which seldom occurs in nature but which is of key theoretical significance. To obtain information on how that value affects other variables by use of an "all-Treatment Y" approach might be prohibitively costly. We would need to obtain a rather large sample of data for all frequently occurring values in order to obtain even a meager sample of cases which include the value of particular concern. The substitution of Treatment X in such a situation greatly increases efficiency by controlling the rate at which we sample values of (independent) variables. It permits us to substitute *systematic* for *representative* sampling, hence to provide an adequate amount of data for all values of concern within a minimum total amount of data.

Treatment Z: Uncontrolled Variables

The uncontrolled and unmeasured operation of a variable (Treatment Z) generates "noise" within a study design. All variables which are neither controlled, manipulated, nor measured are, necessarily, noise-producing variables. The "use" of Treatment Z in a study is always more or less unwitting, either as a result of lack of knowledge about the phenomena being studied or as a result of lack of knowledge about appropriate scientific procedures.

By their very nature, field studies are likely to contain variables handled by Treatment Z (i.e., variables which have been ignored), because field study situations preclude much use of control (W) and manipulation (X), and are likely to contain more variables than can be measured effectively (Y). The major advantage of laboratory studies is their ability to minimize uncontrolled variables (i.e., minimize use of Treatment Z). They do so by applying Treatments W and X, and sometimes Y, to variables which might have received Treatment Z in a field setting. Experimental simulations also share this advantage with the laboratory setting, but to a lesser degree because of the greater complexity and and continuity-of-situation which they contain. Computer simulations essentially eliminate Treatment Z. They have no "noise."[9]

Comprehensiveness, Efficiency, and Effectiveness

Comparisons of the research methods in terms of their comprehensiveness, efficiency, and effectiveness are implicit in the foregoing discussion. Any procedure which reduces the number of combinations of values of variables which can occur in the study situation reduces the comprehensiveness of that study. Use of Treatment W, and use of Treatment X so that only a small number of values of a variable occur during the study, both lead to a reduction of information potential and hence to a reduction of comprehensiveness. Since the use of both W and X increases as we move from field study to experimental simulation to laboratory study, comprehensiveness decreases at the same time. Generally, comprehensiveness decreases still further in the computer simulations because of the extensive use of Treatment W (often in the form of simplifying assumptions designed to make the model feasible for computer programming). But it is *possible* for a computer simulation to offset the reduction of comprehensiveness somewhat by systematically "playing" many values of many variables (i.e., using Treatment X rather than Treatment W).

At the same time, permitting a variable to go unmeasured and uncontrolled (Treatment Z) introduces noise into the design, which will tend to confound information from other variables, and hence reduce the efficiency of the study. Since the use of Treatment Z decreases as we move from the field study to other settings, it follows that field studies are generally less efficient than experimental simulations, which in turn are less efficient than laboratory experiments. Computer simulations eliminate noise in the present sense of the term, but they do so in a manner which also eliminates information. Hence, no meaningful statement of efficiency, in the present sense, can be made about the computer simulation.

Thus, within the framework of the present set of concepts, field studies are relatively comprehensive but inefficient. As study designs they retain almost all of the potential information which exists in the real life situation, but they also contain much noise which reduces the effective information yield. Laboratory experiments, on the other hand, are relatively efficient but low in comprehensiveness. They minimize noise, and hence convert much of the potential information in the study design into information yield. But they do so by restricting the information potential of the study design far below the information potential of the real-world situation to which the study is related. Experimental simulations seem to lie between field studies and laboratory experiments in both comprehensiveness and efficiency. Computer simulations are often relatively low in comprehensiveness, while the concept of efficiency does not apply since they yield no research information in the present use of that term.

We might summarize these comparisons by commenting that field studies may learn a little about a lot, whereas laboratory experiments may learn a lot about a little. In the same vein, computer simulations may learn "everything" about nothing.

But we have not yet commented on the relative *effectiveness* of these four classes of methods. Previously, we defined effectiveness of a research setting such that a loss in *either* scope or efficiency constitutes a loss in effectiveness. No overall comparison of these four classes of methods in terms of their relative effectiveness can be made from the present context, since methods high in efficiency tend to be low in comprehensiveness and *vice versa*.

It might be argued that experimental simulations provide the most effective setting since they offer an optimal balance of scope and efficiency. To make such a conclusion, however, we would need to be able to formulate the metric properties of our continuum of methods, and accurately place the four classes of methods along that continuum; and this we clearly cannot do with our present "weak" model. Thus, we cannot reasonably conclude that experimental simulations are inherently more effective research settings than other methods. However, they do seem to provide a research context which lets us avoid an extreme loss of *either* scope or efficiency.

Ultimately, effectiveness depends in a large measure on the specific research procedures which we use in a given case and the rigor with which we apply them. Hence, we can assess the relative effectiveness of specific studies, rather than of classes of study settings, because studies using any of the four types of settings can be executed well or poorly in terms of the rigor of procedures. However, the type of study setting used does place *limits* on the comprehensiveness and efficiency of *any* study done in that kind of setting, hence, effectiveness of a study is not entirely independent of the type of research setting by means of which it is done.

Implications for Programmatic Research

It should be pointed out that use of the different classes of research settings implies different levels of prior knowledge about the problem to be studied. The investigator needs to know a lot more (or assume he knows a lot more) about the phenomena he is studying in order to work with the methods at the laboratory and computer end of the continuum. As we proceed down the continuum from field studies to laboratory and computer studies, our results become more and more a function of the structure which we impose on the situation (by our Treatment W and Treatment X operations). Consequently, the empirical "truth" of the results which we obtain (as they apply to the real life phenomena which we are studying) becomes more and more dependent upon the empirical "truth" of the structure which we have imposed.

On the field study end of the continuum, however, the investigator needs to know (or assume) less about the phenomena before he starts. He imposes less of a structure or a theory upon the situation. However, it should never be assumed that the field investigator does not also impose some theory as he selects and measures variables. Furthermore, although in one sense the data from the field study is necessarily "true," the investigator needs to know (or assume) a lot about what was and was not operating in his field situation in order for his *interpretations* to be "true." Hence, the field study investigator imposes a "strong" structure *after*, rather than before, he collects his data.

Obviously, then, the choice of methods along this continuum is not to be done in a haphazard way, on the basis of personal preference, or on the basis of mere expediency. We might view the continuum of methods as a two-way street.[10] If we are starting research on a relatively unexplored phenomenon, it would seem to be best to start far over at the field study end of the continuum. As we learn more about the problem, we can then work with methods further along the continuum, with which we can gain more precise information. Then, having explored the problem with precision and in depth, and perhaps having formulated and thoroughly manipulated a formal model, we can return toward the field study end of the street to find out how closely our representations fit the phenomena of the real world. This "path" of programmatic research is illustrated in Figure 1.

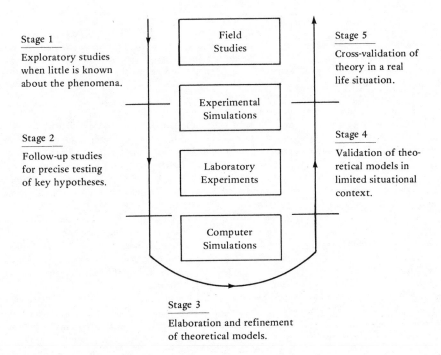

Stage 1

Exploratory studies
when little is known
about the phenomena.

Field
Studies

Stage 5

Cross-validation of
theory in a real
life situation.

Experimental
Simulations

Stage 2

Follow-up studies
for precise testing
of key hypotheses.

Laboratory
Experiments

Stage 4

Validation of theo-
retical models in
limited situational
context.

Computer
Simulations

Stage 3

Elaboration and refinement
of theoretical models.

FIGURE 1   Diagram of a Five-Stage Logical Path for Programmatic Research

This is, of course, an idealized description of what everyone knows to be the best way to do programmatic research. What is not specified here, and perhaps cannot be answered in the general case, is how to allocate time and effort among the various classes of methods, both on the "way down" and on the "way back" on this two-way street. In any actual case, for example, choice of methods must be determined on the basis of available resources, as well as on the basis of our present stage of knowledge about the problem. Methods differ considerably in the cost of running a given number of "cases." The more artificial and more abstract methods of the laboratory and computer generally have a far lower cost per case.

But the ever present need to compromise our idealized research plan on pragmatic grounds does not in any way lessen the need for a full and careful reckoning of the advantages and limitations of methodological alternatives. Only by such a reckoning of the relative information which can be derived from different approaches to a given problem can we possibly be in a position to know how "costly" a given compromise would be. It must be recognized, of course, that the present formulation of a "theory of method" for the study of organizations is only a first step toward that aim. A much more thorough and precise formulation will be needed before we can truly "calculate" the relative losses and gains to be achieved by the choice of one approach over another. Still, it is hoped that this partial and tentative formulation may take us closer to the point where our choices of method for organization research can be done more often in a rational and efficient manner.

NOTES

1. Many of the ideas presented in this [article] were developed in a research program designed to review and integrate research methodology used in studies of complex man-machine systems, sponsored by the Psychological Sciences Division, Office of Naval Research. See McGrath, Nordlie, and Vaughan (1960).

2. For example, Comrey, et al. (1952) . . .

3. For example, Pepinski, et al. (1962) . . .

4. In a sense, all laboratory experiments of human behavior, as individuals and as groups, are relevant to the field of organization research. A few of the many laboratory experiments which seem to have made important direct contributions to organization research, besides the communication net studies, include: studies on communication, development of norms, and pressures for conformity in informal groups (Back, 1951; Festinger, 1952; Kelley, 1951; Schachter, 1951; Thibaut, 1950); and studies of cohesiveness and group pressures as they affect productivity (Schachter, Ellertson, McBride and Gregory, 1951; Berkowitz, 1954).

5. It is obvious from the prior discussion that the methodologies being considered vary along a continuum rather than in a categorical manner. For example, the "field experiment," which is here classified as a field study, often shades into the experimental simulation class. Similarly, experimental simulations which are highly abstract representations of generic classes of organizations may become nearly indistinguishable from the laboratory experiment. The four-category classification of methods is used for convenience and clarity of presentation.

6. There are several important special cases of Treatment X. One of the more interesting ones, which is widely used under the name of "Monte Carlo technique," is the random selection of a value k_i for a given variable V_j on a given "trial," out of a predetermined probability distribution of values for V_j. Here, although there is some indeterminancy for any given trial, the distribution of values over a series of trials is predictable in advance, the accuracy of the prediction being a function of the number of trials in the series.

7. This formulation assumes that there are a *finite* number of relevant variables in a situation, and that each has a *finite* range and a *finite* number of possible alternative values.

8. This is equivalent to the ratio of "signal" to "signal-plus-noise." It is an expression of the effects of unsystematic confounding of a variable.

9. One might argue that computer simulations contain "noise" because they deliberately introduce random variation by the use of stochastic processes. Such variation is noise of a different sort than meant here. Although it produces indeterminancy for a given trial, the distribution of values for the total set of trials is predictable in advance. As noted previously (see footnote 6), these "Monte Carlo" procedures are really a special case of Treatment X.

10. To extend the analogy of the "two-way street," our prior discussion of variations within each class of methods (see footnote 3) suggests that the four classes of methods here defined are *neighborhoods*, rather than specific addresses, along that street. Within each neighborhood, the specific methods range so that some (such as field experiments) are on the borderline between adjacent neighborhoods.

REFERENCES

Alger, C. F. "The External Bureaucracy in U.S. Foreign Affairs," *Administrative Science Quarterly,* 7 (1962), pp. 50–78.

Back, K. W. "Influence Through Social Communication," *Journal of Abnormal and Social Psychology,* 46 (1951), pp. 9–23.

Bavelas, A. "Communication Patterns in Task Oriented Groups," *Journal of the Acoustical Society of America,* 22 (1950), pp. 725–730.

Berkowitz, L. "Group Standards, Cohesiveness and Productivity," *Human Relations,* 7 (1954), pp. 509–519.

Christie, L. A., et al. *Communication and Learning in Task Oriented Groups* (Cambridge, Mass.: Research Laboratory of Electronics, 1952).

Coch, L., and J. R. P. French. "Overcoming Resistance to Change," *Human Relations*, 1, No. 4 (1948), pp. 512–532.

Comrey, A. L., J. M. Pfiffner, and H. P. Beem. "Factors Influencing Organizational Effectiveness I: The U.S. Forest Survey," *Personnel Psychology*, 5 (1952), pp. 307–325.

Festinger, L., H. B. Gerard, B. Hymovitch, H. H. Kelley, and B. Raven. "The Influence Process in the Presence of Extreme Deviates," *Human Relations*, 5 (1952), pp. 327–346.

Guetzkow, H. *Simulation in Social Science* (Englewood Cliffs, N.J.: Prentice-Hall, 1962).

——, and H. A. Simon. "The Impact of Certain Communication Nets Upon Organization and Performance in Task-Oriented Groups," *Management Science*, 1 (1955), pp. 233–250.

——, R. A. Brody, and M. J. Driver. *An Experimental Approach to the n-County Problem* (St. Louis, Mo.: Washington University, 1961).

Homans, G. C. *The Human Group* (New York: Harcourt, Brace, 1950).

Jaques, E. *The Changing Culture of a Factory* (London: Tavistock, 1951).

Jensen, J. *The Postwar Disarmament Negotiations: A Study in American-Soviet Bargaining Behavior* (Ann Arbor, Mich.: University of Michigan, 1962).

Kelley, H. H. "Communication in Experimentally Created Hierarchies," *Human Relations*, 4 (1951), pp. 39–56.

Leavitt, H. J. "Some Effects of Certain Communication Patterns on Group Performance," *Journal of Abnormal and Social Psychology*, 46 (1951), pp. 38–50.

Likert, R. *New Patterns of Management* (New York: McGraw-Hill Book Co., 1961).

McGrath, J. E., P. G. Nordlie, and W. S. Vaughan. *A Systematic Framework for Comparison of System Research Methods* (Arlington, Va.: Human Sciences Research, Technical Note HSR-59/7, Contract No. Nonr 2525-(00), 1960).

Merton, R. K. "Bureaucractic Structure and Personality," *Social Forces*, 18 (1940), pp. 560–568.

Morse, N. C., and E. Reimer. "The Experimental Change of a Major Organizational Variable," *Journal of Abnormal and Social Psychology*, 52 (1956), pp. 120–129.

Parsons, T. *Structure and Process in Modern Society* (Glencoe, Ill.: The Free Press, 1960).

Pepinsky, Pauline N., et al. "The Research Team and Its Organizational Environment," Paper presented at AFSDR Conference on Research on Organization Behavior, Athens, Ga., May 1962.

Riesman, D. *The Lonely Crowd* (New Haven, Conn.: Yale University Press, 1950).

Rome, S. C., and B. K. Rome. *The Leviathan Technique for Large-Group Analysis* (Santa Monica, Calif.: System Development Corp., 1960).

Schachter, S. "Deviation, Rejection, and Communication," *Journal of Abnormal and Social Psychology*, 46 (1951), pp. 190–207.

——, N. Ellertson, D. McBride, and D. Gregory. "An Experimental Study of Cohesiveness and Productivity," *Human Relations*, 4 (1951), pp. 229–238.

Seashore, S. E., and D. G. Bowers. *Communications and Decision Processes as Determinants of Organizational Effectiveness*, AFOSR Contract No. AF 49 (638)-1032 (Ann Arbor, Mich.: Institute for Social Research, University of Michigan, 1962).

Selznick, P. *TVA and the Grass Roots* (Berkeley: University of California Press, 1949).

Shaw, M. E. "Communication Patterns in Small Groups," *Research Review* (1955), pp. 11–12.

Thibaut, J. W. "An Experimental Study of the Cohesiveness of Underprivileged Groups," *Human Relations*, 3 (1950), pp. 251–278.

Whyte, W. F. *Human Relations in the Restaurant Industry* (New York: McGraw-Hill Book Co., 1948).

Whyte, W. H., Jr. *The Organization Man* (New York: Simon and Schuster, 1956).

2 Paradigm Development in the Social Sciences: A Proposed Research Strategy

Kenneth D. Mackenzie
Robert House

The purpose of this article is to suggest a paradigm development strategy for the development of cumulative growth of knowledge in the social sciences. Such a research strategy is needed in the social sciences because of its efficiency in generating knowledge.

Kuhn (1970) argues that science is a series of peaceful periods interrupted by intellectually intense revolutions. During the peaceful interludes scientists are guided by a paradigm—a set of theories, standards, methods, and beliefs which are accepted by most scientists in a field. Masterman points out that Kuhn "with that quasi-poetic style of his, . . . uses 'paradigm' in not less than twenty-one different senses in his (1962 book)" (Masterman, 1970, p. 61). Paradigms help organize the processes of science. They provide direction for its development and help sort out facts in terms of their relevance. In the absence of a paradigm, all facts are more or less relevant and this gives the appearance of randomness to those gathering the facts. The cumulation of knowledge requires an organizing framework upon which the facts and ideas are organized.

Byrne (1971) presented the results of an extensive program of research based on his interpretation of the term paradigm. By paradigm he means a specific body of research, accepted by a group of scientists and consisting of specific procedures, measuring devices, empirical laws, and a specific set of theoretical superstructures. Some of Byrne's research illustrates our approach.

Most social sciences are still in the preparadigm or paradigm development stage, and they are likely to remain in this stage indefinitely unless more persons begin to think carefully about their paradigm development strategy. Elms (1975) points to the crisis of confidence in current paradigms in social psychology.

This article supplements earlier work by House (1972) and Mackenzie (1976 a and b) and attempts to articulate and reconcile their hunches about the nature of paradigm development. Paradigm research consists, in part, of integrating data into a common theoretical framework, inducing general laws to explain the data, deducing hypotheses from the general laws, and subjecting these hypotheses to empirical test.

Our suggested paradigm development strategy is the strong inference approach. This strategy is based upon: (1) deductive nomological reasoning, (2) crucial experiment, (3) experimenter control strategies, and (4) strong inference. These four bases are discussed in sufficient detail to employ them in the paradigm development strategy.

From the *Academy of Management Review*, 1978, 3(1), 7-23. Reprinted by permission.

DEDUCTIVE NOMOLOGICAL REASONING

Theoretical frameworks are integrated networks of lawlike statements. The Greek origin of the word "law" is "nomos." Deductive nomological explanations are explanations by deductive subsumption under general laws. Discovery of such general laws and development of deductive law governed (nomological) theories are major characteristics of paradigm research. Traditionally, deductive systems are viewed in terms of three parts:

1. The phenomenon to be accounted for, called the *explanandum phenomenon*,
2. The statements describing the phenomenon, called the *explanandum sentences*, and
3. The statements specifying the explanatory information, called the *explanans sentences*.

The set of explanans sentences forms the explanans.

There are two subsets of the explanans: (1) the set of general laws, $L_1, L_2, \ldots, L_r$, and (2) the special conditions, $C_1, C_2, \ldots, C_k$, that are assertions about particular facts. The laws are subdivided into two types of principles, called internal principles and bridge principles (Hempel, 1966). Bridge principles "indicate how the processes envisaged by the theory are related to empirical phenomena with which we are already acquainted, and which the theory may then explain, predict, or retrodict" (Hempel, 1966, pp. 72-73). They permit a theory to have explanatory power and permit it to be tested empirically. The special conditions, $C_1, C_2, \ldots, C_k$, usually mean the set of assumptions under which a theory is expected to be valid. These conditions are usually in the form of antecedent conditions for an experiment.

A deductive nomological explanation, then, weaves the internal and bridge principles ($L_1, L_2, \ldots, L_r$) and the special conditions or assumptions ($C_1, C_2, \ldots, C_k$) by deductive logic in order to produce the explanandum sentence. Or, following Hempel and Oppenheim (1948), a deductive nomological explanation can be described by:

$$L_1, L_2, \ldots, L_r \qquad \text{Explanans sentence}$$
$$\underline{C_1, C_2, \ldots, C_k}$$
$$E \qquad \text{Explanandum sentence}$$

If E has been observed and the explanans sentences are provided afterwards, we have an *explanation* for E. But if E is deduced from the explanans sentences, then we have a *prediction*. Clearly, the requirements for explanation are those appropriate for prediction. Deductive nomological explanations are not "cut and dried." There are often unstated, tacitly assumed premises that do not enter the logical deduction explicitly. These *auxiliary hypotheses* are often hard to define. Some rest upon deeper laws that are yet unknown, some lie in hidden assumptions, and some are a part of the system of measurement. For example, a phenomenon may be unobserved because of imprecise instruments or it may be obscured by hidden assumptions about the causality. Some assumptions are, for the present state of knowledge, counterfactual. The problems of working with counterfactual conditionals in economic theory are discussed by Cyert and Grunberg in their critique of the views of Milton Friedman (1953) in Cyert and March (1963).

The possible existence of auxiliary assumptions creates difficulties when judging outcomes of experiments. Suppose that there is a hypothesis, H. We argue that if H is true, then there is a test implication, I, that is true. The purpose of the experiment is to establish whether or not I is, in fact, true. A *modus tollens* form of argument for rejection of H has this general line of reasoning: (1) if H is true, then so is I. But (2) if the evidence shows that I is not true, we conclude that (3) H is not true given the explanans sentences and logic of deduction. The argument for acceptance is less conclusive. If we argue that (1) if H is true, then so is I, obtaining evidence that (2) I is true does not imply, logically, (3) that H is true. If we conclude that H is true on the basis that I is true, we are committing the *fallacy of affirming the consequent*, which is deductively invalid. A conclusion can be false even if its premises are true. Presumably, too, for a given H one can derive a long series of test implications $I_1, I_2, \ldots, I_n$ that are all true. This still does not imply that logically H is true. Thus, the process of obtaining many enumerations of a hypothesis cannot lead to a deductively valid test of a hypothesis. On the other hand, a rejection using modus tollens may not be a genuine rejection because of auxiliary hypotheses. In fact, it is possible to use a modus tollens argument to reject a rejection. But the result is not an acceptance of H. It is simply not a rejection.

One conclusion is that one can conditionally reach deductively valid rejections of a hypothesis but not achieve a deductively valid affirmation of a hypothesis. Nonrejections and further development lead to a synthesis and growth of the deductive nomological network. We can draw a "tree" of these relationships, called a *strong inference tree*. Mackenzie (1976) provides extensive descriptions of such a tree for his research on group structures.

CRUCIAL EXPERIMENTS

A second part of our strong inference strategy is conducting crucial experiments whenever possible. Crucial experiments—defined in terms of decisions made by the experimenter in gathering and transforming information—represent an ideal method for developing a strong inference tree, but it is not always possible to run one.

Arranging for a crucial experiment is not always easy because of the many decisions that must be made concerning bridging principles and special conditions. Many auxiliary hypotheses are built into the analysis because of the nature of any experiment. The description here follows that of Mackenzie and Barron (1970).

Abstractly, let $\{\Omega\}$ refer to the universe of potential observations. Then let $\{\Omega_E\}$ denote the class of potential observations under the chosen experiment. Ω_E is a special case of $\{\Omega\}$. The selection of Ω_E from $\{\Omega\}$ is a decision. Or let us suppose that there is some transformation τ_0 such that $\Omega_E = \tau_0 \Omega$. If we plan to use Ω_E to obtain data, a decision must be reached for what aspects of the events in Ω_E the experimenter wishes to record. Let $\{D\}$ denote the class of recorded observations. The particular set chosen, say D, is the result of a decision. Abstractly, there is some transformation τ_1 that describes how we record D out of Ω_E, or $D = \tau_1 \Omega_E$. For example, in a communications network experiment, D can be the set of all transmitted messages among the subjects. This D is a subset because there are many other ways of extracting or recording information from Ω_E. These recorded observations, D, then are coded to convert them into symbols. Let D_R be the class of all recorded observations arising from D. We can say that there is a transformation τ_2, called coding, that converts D into raw data, D_R. Or, $D_R = \tau_2 D$. Coded data then get transformed again into various measures. Let $\{M\}$ denote the possible classes of measures. The particular set of measures, M, is used as a transformation of the raw data, D_R. Or, $M = \tau_3 D_R$. Normally, there is a class of models that transforms the measures into data that is ready for hypothesis testing, D_{HT}. The particular models define how one transforms M into data that are ready for a hypothesis test called D_{HT}. Thus, we can write $D_{HT} = \tau_4 M$. Finally, there are many methods and techniques for making a hypothesis test. These hypotheses testing methods convert, D_{HT}, into results, $\{E\}$. These results are seen to be a result of the method of hypothesis testing, denoted by the transformation τ_5. In short, a result $E = \tau_5 D_{HT}$.

Four points are immediately obvious from the foregoing description of the decision processes of the experiment. First, the most important is that the results, $\{E\}$, are dependent upon the set of transformations, including the last one, τ_5. Second, the τ_5 are not limited to statistical hypothesis testing. In particular, there is a procedure, called strong inference, for which some advocate that the existence of a single counter example, despite mountains of "confirming" results, is sufficient to reject a theory. Third, mistakes can be made at any stage of the analysis. Messick (1975) discusses problems with meaning and values in measurement. Focusing only on possible misinterpretations of results after employing a τ_5 is a mistake because it overlooks other major sources of problems. Fourth, there are many types of errors: working on the wrong problem; using the wrong code; picking the wrong model; and combining errors such as selecting the wrong experimental situation, recording the wrong information, and using incorrect measures, model, and statistical test. One is not limited to type I and II errors of elementary statistics. The dependence of any results on the prior decisions is clear and unavoidable in principle (Pinkham, 1975).

To arrive at a decision about a result, a long sequence of decisions has been made. The result, E, does not stand by itself, but is understood within the context of these decisions (the set τ_0, τ_1, τ_2, τ_3, τ_4, and τ_5). These transformations depend upon the theory and the purposes of the experimenter. The $\{\tau_j\}$, $j = 0, \ldots, 5$, include the explanans and unstated auxiliary hypotheses. To the extent that the $\{\tau_j\}$, $j = 0, \ldots, 5$, are defined explicitly, the experimenter has reduced the number of auxiliary assumptions. But it is probably impossible not to include some auxiliary hypotheses, no matter what precautions are taken. For example, the choice of τ_0 and τ_1 may be dictated by experimental conventions in a field. These conventions involve auxiliary assumptions. Similarly, the choice of code, measures, model, and hypothesis testing involves other auxiliary assumptions. For example, most measures assume constructs, and these are not always fully understood. Probably the transformation involving the most deliberate listing of assumptions is τ_5, the method of hypothesis testing.

Let us suppose that there are two rival theories T and T' for which the $\{\tau_j\}$, $j = 0$, $1, \ldots, 5$, are consistent, and that under T we expect E and under T' we expect E' using this set of $\{\tau_j\}$. Then, a *crucial experiment* is the event:

$$\{\tau_j\}, j = 0, 1, \ldots, 5, (T, E), (T', E')$$

where E and E' are mutually exclusive. This definition is similar to the one given earlier except that it provides more detail about how one obtains E and E' from the transformations.

This reformulation of a crucial experiment makes it clear that the results are dependent upon a series of prior decisions. These prior decisions can be viewed as "controls." The choice of the code, τ_2, can control the results. Accordingly, in paradigm development, we are concerned with all of the τ_j. We consider statistical hypotheses testing procedures as the end point of a longer sequence of decisions. While they are important, they are only a part of the process of paradigm development.

EXPERIMENTER CONTROL STRATEGIES

For the purpose of discussion, let us consider three types of "controls." The first is the degree to which the scientist manipulates antecedent conditions. This type of control concentrates on manipulating the environment to match the set of assertions or special conditions, $C_1, C_2, \ldots, C_k$. The second type of control manipulates the degree to which measurement requirements are imposed on a situation. The imposition of measurement requirements refers to the types of $\{\tau_j\}$ that are imposed. For example, an extremely high degree of imposition of measurement requirements produces data that are already at D_{HT}. Observer observations, where only τ_1 is controlled, are an example of a low degree of imposition of measurement requirements. The greater the degree of imposition of measurement requirements, the smaller the discretion of the analyst to apply ex post facto transformation in order to obtain results.

A third type of control is the degree to which one has structured the explanans—that is, the extent to which one can state the internal and bridging principles and the special conditions in such a way that one can deductively derive the explanandum. A high degree of structuring of the explanans does not imply that the theory is correct. Rather it refers to the extent to which one can explicate the reasoning upon which one bases the prediction. Many scientists conduct "experiments" in which there is almost no structure to the explanans. Such exercises often employ elaborate controls on antecedent conditions and imposition of units. The person who follows the procedures of experimental design in applied research will often conduct such experiments.

These three dimensions can be employed to describe a typology of strategies for a scientist. For the sake of discussion, assume that each dimension can be characterized in terms of low, medium, and high degree of control. Any strategy then is conceived of as a 3-tuple described by the amount of control on each of the three dimensions of control. It helps to visualize this in terms of locations in a cube whose three dimensions correspond to the degree to which the three types of control are applied, as seen in Figure 1.

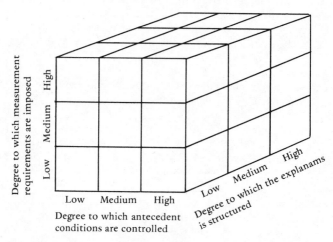

FIGURE 1   A Representation of Typologies of Research Strategies by Degree and Type of Control

Generally, if we think of the cube of Figure 1 in terms of sections rather than subcubes, it is easier to understand the range of possible behaviors for each research strategy. For example, laboratory experiments refer to the section where there is a high degree of control over antecedent conditions. In this diagram, there are nine possible classifications of type of experiment, depending upon the degree to which measurement requirements are imposed and the degree to which the explanans is structured. Crucial experiments occur where there is a high degree of control on all three dimensions. Many experiments in social psychology involve low controls on the structure of the explanans and varying degrees of controls on imposition of measuring units. Many experiments in decision making require a high degree of imposition of measurement requirements by limiting behavior to the choice of a strategy. Others who attempt to gather protocols may have only a low degree of imposition of measurement requirements.

Naturalistic observations, a strategy preferred by many because it reduces the chance of artificially "tying" dimensions of behavior in a laboratory where they would not be tied in a more natural setting and vice versa, involve portions of the front face of the cube. Willems and Raush (1969) describe naturalistic observations in terms of a low degree of structure to the explanans and the exclusion of joint combinations of medium and high degree of control on the other two dimensions. Naturalistic observations are often explorations into a phenomenon. Gadlin and Ingle (1975) discuss the use and misuse of the laboratory experiment in psychology, particularly when method seems to dominate and precede content.

Field experiments can be characterized by: (1) medium degrees of control of the degree to which antecedent conditions are controlled, and (2) medium to high degree to which measurement units are imposed. Field experiments, which can range widely over the degree to which the explanans is structured, are a compromise between naturalistic observations and laboratory experiments. This compromise often is necessary because of real constraints on using pretest and posttest control groups. Confounding factors in a business setting, that may not be present in a laboratory, include: the presence of external incidents, changes that are a function of time and not manipulation, the possibility that testing can affect responses, the possibility that the subjects or the observer's perceptions can change. In addition, many variables may be changing together. Controlling selection of subjects often is difficult, and subjects can drop out of the experiments. There are also the problems of: (1) ethical treatment of subjects, especially when not all are volunteers; (2) high cost of obtaining information; and (3) unique situations being studied that may not be capable of replication. We think of field experiments as investigations rather than as exploration or crucial experiments. But Lippitt (1975) used strong inference in her study of committee formation by university administrators. Clearly, a large range of scientists' behavior can be classified as field experiments.

The three way classification of research strategies by the degree and type of control places a perspective on the range of scientific research strategies. Not only do different strategies require different degrees of different types of control, but it often is argued that this diversity is a good thing because it provides multi-method replication and thus minimizes reliance on any single set of auxiliary hypotheses or bridging rules. Examining this three way classification of research strategies places our proposed paradigm development strategy into a wider perspective than just a laboratory setting. The choice of controls, and hence the particular research strategy, will vary with the theory and purpose of the study. The stages in the paradigm development will likewise depend on and affect the choice of research strategies as the paradigm develops.

STRONG INFERENCE

A fourth characteristic of paradigm research is the frequent use of what Platt (1964) calls strong inference—an ideal approach for the development of cumulative knowledge through theory building. We argue that, while the prerequisites for conducting strong inference research do not obtain in all social science disciplines, a strong inference "attitude" in the paradigm development stage is clearly appropriate. For this reason we shall describe our interpretation of the strong inference approach.[1]

Strong inference research is based on the assumptions that: (1) all theories, no matter how good at explaining a set of phenomena, are ultimately incorrect and consequently will undergo modification over time (Kuhn, 1970); and (2) the fate of the better theories is to become explanations that hold for some phenomena in some limited conditions. These assumptions are expressed by two quotations:

> A good theory is one that holds together long enough to get you to a better theory communication by W. A. H. Ruston in Platt, 1964).

> A good theory is one that holds together long enough to get you to a better theory (Hebb, 1969. p. 21).

These assumptions are further illustrated in modern physicists' challenge of the unrestricted range of application of classical mechanics, or in biochemists' dispute over what is to count as living (Cunningham, 1973). A guiding principle of the strong inference research strategy is the Popperian position that pursuit of knowledge is more efficient when scientists deliberately set out to disprove theories, or seek rejections, than when they attempt to assemble proof for theories. Such attempts to disprove theories not only reflect the tradition of scientific skepticism but also focus the investigator on a different set of variables than do attempts to prove theories. Dubin (1969) makes the distinction between research directed at proving a theory and research directed at *improving* a theory. He points out that research directed at improving a theory causes the researcher to focus:

> . . . particularly on the deviant cases and nonconforming results that do not accord with the predictions made by the hypotheses of his theoretical model. It is from the evidence contained *in the deviant cases* that the insights come on the basis of which the extant theory is improved by *reformulating* it to generate predictions that will encompass all the data, including those initially considered deviant (1969, p. 234, emphasis ours).

Dubin argues that none of the advantages of the theory-proving orientation are lost by the theory-improving orientation. Opportunities are enhanced for theory modification and therefore, for growth and improvement of the theory. Churchman (1968, 1971) calls for construction of a counterperspective to one's view in order to flush out into the open one's basic assumptions and tacit restrictions. His ideas are useful in generating instances of deviant cases which are so important to theory construction.

If it is assumed that all theories will undergo modification over time, successful attempts at disproving them are contributions to knowledge, in that such disproof facilitates identification of the specific aspects of the theory that are erroneous, or the boundaries within which the theory holds. Thus, attempts to disprove a theory constitute one of the most efficient processes whereby knowledge can be discovered. This process is illustrated in an experiment on the effects of seeking confirming evidence versus seeking disconfirming evidence as a means of discovering valid hypotheses.

Wason (1960) instructed subjects to infer a mathematical rule from a set of numbers. He then observed the process by which the subjects arrived at their conclusions. A greater proportion of subjects who systematically eliminated alternative rules by seeking disconfirming evidence (counter examples) discovered the appropriate rule than subjects who sought confirming evidence. Subjects who sought disconfirming evidence also discovered the appropriate rule in fewer trials than subjects who sought confirming evidence.

Wason's experiment simulates in the most pure form a scientific problem in which the variables are unknown and in which evidence has to be used to refute a support hypothesis. Those subjects indicating a disposition to refute rather than to vindicate assertions and to tolerate the distress of negative results made more rapid progress. This disposition to refute and an orientation toward focusing on deviant cases evidence what we call the "strong inference attitude." The strong inference approach is a natural result of such an attitude.

THE STRONG INFERENCE APPROACH

The strong inference approach consists of the following steps. A substantial amount of time and effort is invested in conceptualizing a theory of a given set of phenomena in such a way that the theory resolves previous anomalies and/or explains important issues in the area of inquiry. The emphasis is on development of well-defined concepts and deductive nomological theory. In the absence of an initial theory that appears to the investigator to be adequate to guide research, initial work frequently begins with exploratory investigation, literature review, or sheer speculation. After development of a tentative theory, strong inference research usually involves development of research technology, i.e., experimental designs, measurement instruments, and criteria for the rejection of hypotheses. Here the emphasis is on development of bridging principles and transformations required to link empirical observations to the concepts expressed in the explanandum sentence. Research is then directed at identifying counter examples to the theory's most fundamental predictions. Identification of clear counter examples requires the theorist to reexamine the theory as it was originally stated. Such identification requires scientists to specify the transformation to be used and the criteria of acceptance to be applied. If counter examples are found, either a fundamentally new theory is advanced, or the initial theory is reformulated in such a way that the reformulation accounts for the counter examples. The more fundamental the counter examples, the more fundamental the revision of the theory.

Failure to identify clear counter examples of the obvious and fundamental predictions of the theory establishes tentative credibility of the theory in the eyes of the scientists, but does not end the process of theory building. Failures to reject the theory are not considered confirmation. Rather, the theory is considered "not yet" invalidated and is considered tentatively to be useful. A "not no, yet" result stimulates new attempts to produce a rejection. After attempts to reject the basic propositions of the theory have failed, more subtle and less fundamental predictions of the theory may be stated and attempts may be made at identifying clear counter examples of these predictions. By focusing on counter examples, the researcher concentrates energy on improvement of the theory. Extensions, *improvements*, and refinements of the theory are made by identification of such counter examples. Clear counter examples to the theory's predictions not only call those predictions into question, but also may call into question the more fundamental propositions. Thus, each counter example requires the researcher to reconsider the credibility placed on even the earlier successful predictions of the theory, since prior successful predictions may be sample specific, or they may be based on faulty methodology.

The strong inference process can be linked to the construction of a logical tree whose trunk represents the basic propositions of the theory. The objective is to grow the tree by careful nurturing and pruning. A major emphasis is placed on conceptualization of a cumulating series of interrelated studies and on careful formulation of competing hypotheses and the criteria of clear counter examples. Predictions are derived from the propositions, and studies are designed in an attempt to disprove them. A series of contingency statements is made before the studies are conducted, indicating the branch, or branches, of the logical tree to be followed, contingent on the outcome of the initial round of studies. The potential outcomes of each study are compared. The studies with potential to eliminate the largest number of predictions and answer the greatest number of questions are conducted first.

If the result of the first series of studies is not inconsistent with this theory, one has more specific information about the theory. As a result, the theory can be made less crude or more fine. If the experimenter feels that she or he can still reject the theory using a different research design, it should be tried. If the results are inconsistent with the theory, the theory must be changed. After the change, the researcher repeats the steps to construct the first branches out of this new base. These branches on the same level are called *outward* growths. Outward growths represent: (1) the domain of the theory, i.e., the populations and range of variables for which the theory makes accurate predictions; and (2) the kinds of predictions that can be derived validly from the propositions of the theory at that level. Those branches leading from other branches, but which apply under a more restricted range, are *upward* growths. The process of strong inference starts at the base and proceeds upwards and outwards by asking questions and making predictions that lead to more specificity about the theory or its mechanisms. Rejections are used to prune the strong inference tree by cutting back "dead" branches. In this process, the branches in question may have been allowed to grow from a conceptually incorrect branch. A branch may be theoretically irrelevant, and such growth must be weeded out from the proper branches in the main tree; thus, pruning and weeding often result in a reorganization of the tree.

A failure to reject adds a twig or a leaf. Every rejection raises questions, and consistent rejections allow one to chop off branches. The goal of strong inference is to produce a theory. This is done best by pruning and weeding because it is wasteful to expend resources following clearly false leads, no matter how attractive they may seem.

The planning phase of a strong inference strategy provides the intellectual framework for theory building. The strong inference plan is a tentative deductive nomological explanation. But this explanation need not be static or rigid. New information may suggest rerouting to a lower level branching point, or it may suggest entirely new branches. For example, suppose that an early study indicated taking Branch A as an alternative explanation and excluding Branch B. Suppose also that a later study indicated findings contrary to the first one. These suggest a problem with the methodology of one of the two studies or the existence of new variables not specified at the outset. Such a sequence would require backtracking to the initial decision point where Branches A and B parted, specifying new laws or bridge principles to account for the findings of the second study, and recycling the effort.

Strong inference planning is likely to cut down the number of investigations required, by providing a framework for arraying all relevant, available information and evaluating the potential payoff of alternatives that can be eliminated by the next study. While failures to disprove the theory are comforting, less is likely to be learned from them than from successful disproofs because they do not help identify where the theory made erroneous predictions. Identification of erroneous predictions helps identify invalid propositions within the theory, inadequate conceptualization of the theoretical variables and their relationships, and boundary conditions beyond which the theory does not make valid predictions. If multiple, mutually exclusive, hypotheses are advanced, failure to disprove one hypothesis results in elimination of one or more of the other hypotheses. Disproof of one hypothesis results in further support for counter hypotheses. Thus, attempts to disprove these hypotheses constitute advances in the state of knowledge, regardless of the outcome of the study. Strong inference planning also can be used to coordinate the efforts of a set of research efforts, even if the scientists are separated geographically. The strong inference strategy is considered by Platt (1964) as the most efficient means of developing reliable theory.

PARADIGM DEVELOPMENT RESEARCH

The major values of the strong inference research strategy are its efficiency and the fact that it permits research to be cumulative. For a research strategy to be truly a strong inference strategy, a guiding paradigm must exist.

Few areas of inquiry in the social sciences have developed to the paradigm stage of development. What then should be the strategy of the researcher who is interested in theory building? The starting point is development of the paradigm. Specifically, one begins with a general idea or a rather crude conceptual framework, a set of explanandum sentences, with full recognition of the need for its refinement.

This is followed by research concerned with refinement of the transformations necessary to test the theory. These transformations concern development of instruments or a research technology with which to develop and test initial theories and specification of clear criteria for the acceptance or rejection of predictions derived from their theories. Thus, we argue for development of a conceptual framework, operational definitions, measurement instruments, experimental apparatuses, and rejection criteria as the starting point of paradigm development research. Once these are developed, we have what Byrne (1971) defines as a paradigm, and the necessary prerequisite knowledge and technology for strong inference research.

QUESTION RAISING AND HYPOTHESIS TESTING

One method frequently employed in both the paradigm building and strong inference stages of a research program is that of question-raising rather than hypothesis testing. While the search for counter examples is usually cast in the form of tests of hypotheses, the intent of proving or disproving the hypotheses is actually secondary to the intent to generate descriptive data with which to build an improved theory. Dubin states that:

. . . a moment's reflection on some of the landmark contributions to the social sciences makes clear that among them will be found essentially descriptive studies (studies not guided by hypotheses but rather by research questions). Such a list would include Myrdal's *An American Dilemma*, Thomas and Znaniecki's *The Polish Peasant in Europe and America*, Stouffer and his associates' *The American Soldier*, Sherif's work on the autokinetic effect, Asch's research on social pressures in small groups, and Bales' categorization of interactions within small groups (1969, p. 227).

In a recent paper concerning human information processing, Simon (1974) raises objections to the traditional form of experimental design and argues for experimental designs for the purpose of parameter estimating rather than hypothesis testing. He points out that the more orthodox approach to experimentation—testing for significance of differences between experimental treatments—yields "a one-bit" message that there is a relationship between the independent and the dependent variable.

In strong inference research, attempts are made to design studies that go beyond hypothesis testing to shed additional light about the phenomena under question. As Simon (1974) observes, one such question concerns parameter estimation. Other research questions that are frequently raised concern the effects of interacting variables, the range over which predictions can be extended, and the magnitude of forces operating on theoretical variables. If the researcher sets out with the assumption that the theory is incorrect, the question most likely to yield the most information is one which, when answered, will indicate exactly where the theory is weak. Such a question necessarily *eliminates* one or more propositions of the theory or some part of the domain of the theory. Since attempts to disprove the theory focus the researcher's attention on avenues of elimination, such attempts are more likely to yield data with which to reformulate the theory, if it is indeed rejected.

Successive failures to reject a theory, regardless of how satisfying to the researcher, seldom provoke additional questions or insights. Thus, the researcher who seeks to improve the theory after failing to reject one or more hypotheses must rely on information or insights from sources other than his or her investigation. Such sources may include second thoughts developed on reflection, opinions of colleagues, or data published by other investigators. Because such sources soon run dry, their usefulness is both unpredictable and limited. In contrast, failures to confirm the theory almost assuredly raise new questions, thereby opening avenues for subsequent investigation.

The strategy of seeking to refute hypotheses is essentially a strategy of raising and eliminating questions. Its advantage over attempts to prove a theory through hypothesis testing can be illustrated with a hypothetical problem. Suppose two people are engaged in a game. The object for person A is to identify a specific number between 1 and 100 that person B has in mind, in the minimum time possible. If person A asks "Is the number x?", he or she is testing a hypothesis. If the hypothesis is incorrect, only one number has been eliminated. If A continues by testing hypotheses about other numbers, as many as 99 questions may have to be asked before identifying the correct number. Each question yields only a one-bit information message. But suppose A asks "Is the number above 50?" and then proceeds to narrow the range of possible numbers by halving the remaining possible numbers with each additional question. By this process of elimination the correct number always can be identified within seven questions. Each question disconfirms a range of alternatives and thus adds much more information than conventional hypothesis testing because its answer directs further search. Although conventional hypothesis testing tells one if a theory is or is not supported, it does not direct further search upon failure to confirm. *In short, one of the main advantages of strong inference is that it increases the amount of information per step in the research process.*

TWO EXAMPLES OF PARADIGM DEVELOPMENT RESEARCH

In addition to our own work, several social science research programs include many of the characteristics of paradigm development research. These include studies by: McClelland and Atkinson and their associates concerning the achievement motive; Maier (1970) concerning social processes involved in problem solving; Rokeach (1960) concerning dogmatism; Deutsch and his associates (1973) concerning conflict and conflict resolution; and Hovland and his associates concerning persuasive communication. Two such paradigm development programs will be briefly described.

A little known, but impressive series of studies was conducted by Miner (1965). Based on his observation of the role requirements of managers in a large bureaucractic organization, plus his prior training in psychology, he postulated that individuals whose motivations correspond to the requirements of the roles they fill will be more successful in those roles. He hypothesized that there are "certain components (motives) which contribute to what amounts to a common variant . . . , which operates across a great many managerial positions . . . ." This constituted Miner's explanandum sentence. An auxiliary hypothesis was " . . . are presumed to occur with relative high frequency, and across a considerable range of positions and organizations (1965, p. 42)." The specific role requirements which were identified theoretically were presumed to be among those which occur with high frequency in business firms organized in accordance with the Scalar principle. Miner stated that:

> It is entirely possible that the theory is applicable to managerial, or administrative jobs in educational, governmental, medical, military and other types of organizations, but it was not devised with these positions in mind. The initial tests, at least, should be carried out within the particular segment of society for which it was originally constructed (1965, p. 42).

Here we see Miner's first transformation of the theory, selection of the test sample for the purpose of specifically testing the theory in question. Observation of role and behavior in a hierarchical organization led Miner to conclude that managerial roles in hierarchical organizations demand their incumbents to have a generally positive orientation towards the use of power as a means of attaining success.

To test the theory, a special sentence completion test was constructed. The test was assumed to be a measure of the degree to which the respondent desires to compete for and exercise power over people. Several hypotheses were postulated: (1) that the measure of power motivation, the Miner Sentence Completion Scale (MSCS), should yield both concurrent and predictive validity when compared against such success indexes as organizational level, promotion rate, ratings of effectiveness in managerial work, and rated potential for promotion; (2) that if motivational changes are induced by management education, such changes will be enforced by the role requirements and the reward system of the organization and will thus be sustained; (3) that management education efforts should be differentially effective depending on the personality characteristics of the participant in the education effort; and (4) that different occupational groupings tend to attract individuals having different levels of interest in the exercise of power and that these differences will be reflected in the MSCS scores.

These hypotheses represent the test implications of the theory. Miner's research progressed through a series of stages. He began with a test of the concurrent validity of the MSCS scale and tested the hypothesis that there would be a significant association between the MSCS and various criteria of success: job grade level, performance rating, and potential rating. Having established significant correlations between the scale and the criteria, he raised the possibility that success may serve to precipitate motivational changes and that these in turn contribute to the concurrent validity which had been found, or conceivably some external factor might be responsible for both the motivation and the success. He called for evidence that those who possess the various motives measured tend *subsequently* to perform particularly well on the various organizational criteria. Miner stated that:

> . . . certainly, if a positive association between motivational variables and behavior in the managerial role cannot be demonstrated under these conditions, the theory is deficient (1965, p. 60).

Here he stated a criterion for refutation of the theory.

A test of the predictive validity of the MSCS revealed significant correlations between the MSCS and subsequent criteria of managerial success. Miner then tested the possibility that in a somewhat different type of business organization the relationships might not appear. Shifting from the initial sample of managers in an organization producing heavy equipment, he tested the concurrent validity of his scale with a population of male and female managers in a large department store. Results revealed that three subscales of the MSCS held up across samples.

Miner then raised a series of questions concerning the MSCS scale.

> Does the MSCS really measure the motivational variables that it is devised to measure? Is it really motivation of this particular kind, motivation that is congruent with managerial role requirements that produces the success? Or is it possible that the MSCS yields the results it does due to the influence of component variables which are not those the test was constructed to measure. Or perhaps some external factor, highly correlated with the MSCS accounts for the findings which have been obtained (1965, p. 90).

A variety of analyses were conducted in a number of different samples. Correlations between the MSCS and age, intelligence, concept mastery, attitudes toward various stimuli, grades in undergraduate school, and education achievement were computed.

From a strong inference viewpoint, these tests can be considered attempts to rule out competing hypotheses concerning interpretation of the scale. Miner reported several additional tests of the theory. He measured the degree to which a course developed to increase attitudes measured by the MSCS scale, did indeed effect a change in responses to the scale in the predicted dimension as compared with the control group of subjects who did not participate in the educational program. He then tested whether the change produced by the experimental treatment was retained long enough for managerial performance to be affected materially.

Following these validation studies, which can be considered tests of the adequacy of the theory to predict within the specified domain of the theory, several additional studies were conducted to answer descriptive research questions. These concern the effects of motivational education among college students and the retention of change resulting from such education, the degree to which female students respond as well, the relationship between change and the climate in the organization, a search for organizational and personality predictors of change, and a test of the hypothesis that occupations tend to attract individuals having different levels of power of motivation. Since the original publication of the research described above (1965), additional studies have been conducted to identify the boundary conditions of the theory (Miner, 1968; Miner, 1971; Miner, 1974; and Rizzo et al., 1974). These results generally confirm the proposition that power motivations significantly predict success in hierarchical situations and fail to predict success in nonhierarchical situations in experimental laboratories, consulting firms and nonbureaucratic schools.

Another example of paradigm development research is reported by Byrne (1969, 1971). His specific research focused on the effect of the expression of attitude statement on subsequent affective responses directed toward the source of such statements. He began with the tentative empirical generalization that people with similar attitudes are attracted to one another. At that time a substantial amount of common sense observation and empirical data supported this generalization.

Byrne states two assumptions:

A meaningful and positive increase in knowledge is possible only if identical or equivalent operations serve as connecting links across experiments (1971, p. 47).

. . . in the initial stages of paradigm research, a preliminary theory is useful and perhaps essential in guiding and organizing experimental efforts.

The theoretical underpinning of the research conducted by Byrne and his associates was that:

Attraction toward X is a function of the relative number of rewards and punishments associated with X (1971, p. 49).

The initial study concerned development of an instrument with which to vary the degree of similarity between an experimental subject and a hypothetical other subject. Upon finding that with the use of a newly developed instrument he was able to replicate prior studies, Byrne raised a question about the possible interpretation of the results. He stated that the lack of attraction between dissimilar others in a subject could be due to perceptions of dissimilarity, or due to the perception of deviancy of the other from cultural norms. To deal with this problem Byrne constructed a new scale by which bogus strangers could be made to express attitudes similar or dissimilar to those of the subjects, without at the same time expressing either conforming or deviant beliefs. He then found that attraction is a function of similarity of attitudes, but raised a further question regarding this function. Was it the number of similar attitudes, the number of dissimilar attitudes, or the ratio of similar to dissimilar attitudes? Here we see an example of question raising rather than hypothesis testing and research directed at parameter estimating similar to that advocated by Simon (1974).

Subsequent experimentation revealed that attraction was clearly a function of the ratio of dissimilar to similar attitudes. Byrne then stated that:

With the stimulus identified as proportion of similar attitudes, data from a variety of investigations could be meaningfully combined even though attitude scales of various length had been used (1969, p. 53–54).

He then proposed a theoretical formulation to account for the relationship between similarity and attraction, stating that:

The empirical attraction is interpreted as a special case of reward and punishment. Specifically, it is proposed that attitude statements are affect arousing; the motive involved is the learned drive to be logical and to interpret correctly one's stimulus world (1971, p. 70).

Byrne then derived implications from the attraction literature rather than from the classical conditioning or other learning paradigms. The relationship between attraction and stimulus information was conceptualized as a law of interaction: attraction toward X is a positive linear function of the sum of the weighted positive reinforcements (number times magnitude) associated with X divided by the total number of weighted positive and negative reinforcements associated with X. Byrne and Rhamey (1966) conducted an experiment to determine the effect of differential weights of the magnitude of positive and negative reinforcers. A subsequent study (Byrne and Griffitt, 1966) showed that the Byrne-Rhamey coefficients were applicable in subsequent experiments. Further studies showed that similar attitude statements by others may be used as positive reinforcers and dissimilar attitudes as negative reinforcers. Based on a review of prior studies, the utility of the law of attraction was shown with respect to studies of topic importance, personal evaluations, physical attractiveness, emotional disturbance, and race.

Several hypotheses were derived from the model, asserting the interrelationship of the three elements of the model: independent variables (any stimulus with reinforcement properties), intervening variable (any implicit affective) response), and dependent variable (any evaluative response such as attraction). Thus Byrne's initial model of interpersonal attraction was broadened to explain attraction not only to other persons, but also to things and experiences.

Byrne then reported a series of studies conducted by himself and his associates, designed to test several of the major hypotheses derived from the theory. Several hypotheses were supported, thus leading to increased confidence in the theory. In addition, Byrne (1971) reviewed a wide range of practical applications of the theory and suggested several avenues for its extension. These include using the theory to explain such phenomena as how attitudes are formed (or valence of an object is developed) with respect to tasks, job candidates, spending funds for facilities for the disabled, aptitudes and performance of others, educational activities, and persons accused of crimes.

Byrne's research reflects clearly the iterative process of formulating theory, testing predictions, raising questions, pruning branches, and supplanting them.

DISCUSSION AND CONCLUSIONS

Two essential characteristics qualify a research strategy as a paradigm development strategy: (1) commitment to theory building and (2) commitment to a program of research. A commitment to theory building has characterized most major contributors to the social sciences. Theory building efforts, to be effective, require a long term commitment, considerable ingenuity, and flexibility. Theory building which is restricted to a single setting can become sterile, ingrained, and increasingly arcane. While crucial experiments are important in the social sciences, much is to be learned from applying the knowledge gained in the laboratory to outside settings. Application is not the sole justification for basic research, but it is certainly helpful in generating counter examples to a theory.

One of the authors recently formed a corporation to apply and develop theories of group structures which originated in a laboratory. This extension forced him to consider other related issues and to develop a technology to bridge the gap from laboratory groups to real world organizations. The confrontation between his theories and the complex problems of these organizations has been a continuing source of stimulus to improve the theories. One result is alteration of the program for developing the theory. It is necessary to move back and forth between the two settings. Problems from the practical world and from pure theory interact and supplement each other.

Paradigm development research necessarily implies commitment to a program of research. Theories seldom are built from a single study or even from a small number of studies. We contend that almost all major contributions to the social sciences have resulted from a series of studies which have culminated over time in a reformulation of earlier concepts and research findings.

In all these research programs the initial theories were reformulated through subsequent research. Improvements in the theories resulted not only from conventional hypothesis testing but also from inquiry into questions raised for the purpose of adding descriptive information with which to refine and extend theoretical positions that had received prior support.

In one sense, the programmatic approach advocated here is counter to the "success ethic" whereby researchers act if they are "piece workers" grinding out a quota of "successes" per unit time, with bonuses for above average productivity. In the approach recommended here, one attempts to produce rejections instead of "successes." A virtue is made out of success in producing rejections. The error of working on the wrong problem (examining twigs on a dead branch) is considered more serious than accepting a false hypothesis (calling a twig "alive" when it is not), or rejecting a true hypothesis (calling a twig "dead" when it is alive). Because the error of working on the wrong problem (a type 3 error) is rarely mentioned, even in conversations, and because conventional statistics does not treat this important error, seeking rejections is likely to be efficacious in generating better theory. It would seem that "piece work" based upon producing rejections is potentially better paid than "piece work" based upon producing successes, assuming of course that the goal is to develop theories, not merely a larger number of publications.

Our proposed research strategy for developing paradigms, which requires commitment to build theory and commitment to a program of research, is a recipe for serious scholars. Recent trends in evaluation of faculty, which reward short term exploitation—in the stop and go trends in research funding, the lack of resources to engage in paradigm development, and the declining fraction of nontenured research positions—create institutional barriers against our strategy. This pressure will intensify as many universities convert to teaching institutions and seek contract research whose goals are dictated by the funding agency rather than by the requirements of the research problem. But serious scholars always have had to overcome and rise above their institutions. They have had to be determined, flexible, and ingenious. Above all they have needed the dual commitment to developing theory and to establishing a program of research. Our strategy is not an easy one and is not intended for the fainthearted. We argue that it is, over the long term, more efficient and more exciting.

NOTE

1. The authors have some disagreements about the use of strong inference. House, whose main interests have been in field experiments, where there are lower degrees of experimenter control, argues that statistical significance is usually sufficient to make a decision to accept tentatively or to reject empirical hypotheses. Mackenzie, whose main interests have been in laboratory experiments, where there are higher degrees of experimenter control, argues that statistical significance is insufficient as a criterion for the decision of whether to tentatively accept or reject an empirical hypothesis. Mackenzie seeks to conduct crucial experiments that are capable of producing counter examples to the theory. He recognizes the existence of measurement errors and uses two criteria for counting a datum as a counter example: (1) after allowing for measurement error, a result is a counter example if it still lies within the set of results that disconfirm the stated result; and (2) it is possible to replicate the conditions producing the counter example to provide more of them.

While both subscribe to the paradigm development strategy outlined in this article, they disagree on the need to structure the explanans. Mackenzie is an inveterate tree builder and likes to do research whenever he can proceed as if there is a high degree of structuring the explanans. House is more willing to proceed with field experiments where there is a lower degree of structure on the explanans. The goals are identical but they have tactical disagreements on details for implementing paradigm development strategies. These differences are evident to any reader who studies House's work on leadership and Mackenzie's work on a theory of group structures.

REFERENCES

Byrne, D. "Attitudes and Attractions," in L. Berkowitz (Ed.), *Advances in Experimental Social Psychology* (New York: Academic Press, 1969), Vol. 4, pp. 36–90.

Byrne, D. *The Attraction Paradigm* (New York: Academic Press, 1971).

Byrne, D., and W. Griffitt. "A Development Investigation of the Law of Attraction," *Journal of Personality and Social Psychology*, Vol. 4 (1966), pp. 699–702.

Byrne, D., and R. Rhamey. "Magnitude of Positive and Negative Reinforcement as a Determinate of Attraction," *Journal of Personality and Social Psychology*, Vol. 2 (1965), pp. 884–889.

Churchman, C. W. *The Systems Approach* (New York: Delacorte Press, 1968).

Churchman, C. W. *The Design of Inquiring Systems* (New York: Basic Books, 1971).

Cunningham, F. *Objectivity in Social Science* (Toronto, Ontario, Canada: University of Toronto Press, 1973).

Cyert, R. M., and J. G. March. *A Behavioral Theory of the Firm* (Englewood Cliffs, N.J.: Prentice-Hall, 1963).

Deutsch, M. *The Resolution of Conflict: Constructive and Destructive Processes* (New Haven, Conn.: Yale University Press, 1973).

Dubin, R. *Theory Building* (New York: The Free Press, 1969).

Elms, A. C. "The Crisis of Confidence in Social Psychology," *American Psychologist*, Vol. 30, No. 10 (1975), pp. 967–976.

Friedman, M. *Essays in Positive Economics* (Chicago, Ill.: University of Chicago Press, 1953).

Gadlin, H., and G. Ingle. "Through the One-Way Mirror: The Limits of Experimental Self-Reflection," *American Psychologist*, Vol. 30, No. 10 (1975), pp. 1003–1009.

Hebb, D. O. "Hebb on Hocus-Pocus: A Conversation with Elizabeth Hall," *Psychology Today*, Vol. 3 (1969), pp. 20–28.

Heckhausen, H. *The Anatomy of Achievement Motivation* (New York: Academic Press, 1966).

Hempel, C. G. *Philosophy of Natural Science* (Englewood Cliffs, N. J.: Prentice-Hall, 1966).

Hempel, C. G., and P. Oppenheim. "Studies in the Logic of Explanation," *Philosophy of Science*, Vol. 15 (1948), pp. 135–178.

House, R. J. "Strong Inference in the Social Sciences: An Explanation and an Illustration from Leadership Research," *Studies in Managerial Process and Organizational Behavior* (J. H. Turner, 1961) (Glenview, Ill.: Scott, Foresman, 1972), pp. 403–410.

Kuhn, T. S. *The Structure of Scientific Revolutions* (Chicago, Ill.: University of Chicago Press, 1970).

Lippitt, M. E. *Development of a Theory of Committee Formation* (Ph.D. dissertation, The University of Kansas, 1975).

Mackenzie, K. D. *A Theory of Group Structures, Vol. I: Basic Theory* (New York: Gordon and Breach Science Pubs., 1976). (a)

Mackenzie, K. D. *A Theory of Group Structures, Vol. II.: Empirical Tests* (New York: Gordon and Breach Science Pubs., 1976). (b)

Mackenzie, K. D., and F. H. Barron. "Analysis of a Decision Making Investigation," *Management Science*, Vol. 17, No. 4 (1970), pp. B-226-B-241.

Maier, N. R. F. *Problem Solving and Creativity in Individuals and Groups* (Belmont, Calif.: Brooks/Cole, 1970).

Masterman, M. "The Nature of a Paradigm," in I. Lakatos and A. Musgrave (Eds.), *Criticisms and the Growth of Knowledge* (Cambridge: Cambridge University Press, 1970).

Messick, S. "The Standard Problem: Meaning and Values in Measurement and Evaluation," *American Psychologist*, Vol. 30, No. 10 (1975), pp. 955–966.

Miner, J. B. *Studies in Managerial Education* (New York: Springer, 1965).

Miner, J. B. "The Managerial Motivation of School Administrators," *University Council for Educational Administration Quarterly* (Winter, 1968), pp. 57–72.

Miner, J. B. "Personality Tests as Predictors of Consulting Success," *Personnel Psychology*, Vol. 24 (1971), pp. 191–204.

Miner, J. B. "Motivation to Manage Among Women: Studies of Business Managers and Educational Administrators," *Journal of Vocational Behavior*, Vol. 5 (1974), pp. 197–208.

Miner, J. B. "Motivation to Manage Among Women: Studies of College Students," *Journal of Vocational Behavior*, Vol. 5 (1974), pp. 241–251.

Pinkham, G. N. "Some Doubts About Scientific Data," *Philosophy of Science*, Vol. 42 (1975), pp. 260–269.

Platt, J. R. "Strong Inference," *Science*, Vol. 146, No. 3642 (1964), pp. 347–353.

Rizzo, J. R., J. B. Miner, D. N. Harlow, and J. W. Hill. "Role Motivation Theory of Managerial Effectiveness in a Simulated Organization of Varying Degrees of Structure," *Journal of Applied Psychology*, Vol. 59 (1974), p. 31.

Rokeach, M. *The Open and Closed Mind.* (New York: Basic Books, 1960).

Simon, H. A. "How Big is a Chunk?" *Science,* Vol. 183 (1974), pp. 482–488.

Towne, C. H. "Quantum Electronics and Surprise in Development of Technology: The Problem of Research Planning," in D. Byrne, *The Attraction Paradigm* (New York: Academic Press, 1971).

Wason, P. C. "On the Failure to Eliminate Hypotheses in a Conceptual Task," *The Quarterly Journal of Experimental Psychology* (1960), pp. 129–139.

Willems, E. P., and H. L. Raush. (Eds.). *Naturalistic Viewpoints in Psychological Research* (New York: Holt, Rinehart and Winston, 1969).

3 Determinants of Scientific Progress: The Case of Research on the Risky Shift[1]

Dorwin Cartwright

This article reports the results of an investigation of the conditions affecting the quality of research. More specifically, it is concerned with the problems encountered when one attempts to evaluate an entire field of research, as opposed to the more limited work of a single investigator. The study was undertaken as an outgrowth of the

From D. Cartwright, "Determinants of Scientific Process," *American Psychologist*, 1973, *28*(3), pp. 222–231. Copyright 1973 by the American Psychological Association. Reprinted by permission.

author's experience as a member of the Social Science Research Committee of the National Institute of Mental Health.

Anyone familiar with the work of committees of this kind will agree that they rarely encounter serious difficulty in reaching consensus about the merits of any proposal submitted to them, as long as they restrict their attention to such matters as the clarity of its objectives, the sophistication of its methodology, the feasibility of its design, or the competence of the investigator who would carry out the research. The criteria for making technical judgments of this sort are reasonably straightforward and generally are accepted throughout the research community. But it is equally clear that the task of evaluation becomes much more troublesome whenever questions are raised about the potential significance of the project, for these questions require an assessment of the larger field of which the contemplated work is but a small part. And since there are few established criteria for evaluating an entire field of investigation, the critical issue of research significance tends to be relegated to the realm of intuition and subjective judgment.

In considering the kinds of criteria that would be most useful for the planning of future research, it seemed that they should be derived from the experience of past research. And it was decided to undertake an evaluative study of the work produced in one of the areas of investigation falling under the purview of the Social Science Research Committee in order to identify the factors that had facilitated or impeded its fruitful course of development. There are, of course, dangers in generalizing from a single case, but it was hoped that such a study might constitute a first step toward a more comprehensive analysis of the conditions affecting the conduct of research.

Of the many topics considered by the Review Committee in recent years, that of "group decisions involving risk" appeared to be especially well suited for our purposes. During the past decade, this topic has engaged the intense interest of numerous social scientists here and abroad. The obtained findings have been publicized widely and have generated theoretical controversy. The rate of productivity has accelerated rapidly and is currently at a high level. And yet, the resulting body of literature is of a size permitting a comprehensive review in a reasonably short period of time.

Two interrelated but somewhat different approaches were adopted in this investigation, one focusing on the substantive content of the research itself and the other on the setting in which the research took place. The study began with a systematic review of the published and unpublished literature in order to identify the dependable findings that had been produced, to examine critically the theoretical explanations proposed, to evaluate the research methods and strategies employed, and to arrive at some judgment about the most promising directions for future work. The conclusions from this part of the study, it was believed, would be of value both to members of the Review Committee and to investigators planning new research on the topic. These have been presented in a separate article (Cartwright, 1971), and will not be discussed here.

The second approach was essentially that of a case study in the history of science. The materials for this analysis consisted of the relevant literature, correspondence with the more active investigators, and personal interviews with those whose work had had the greatest impact on the research of others. The primary objective here was to attain a better understanding of the factors affecting the formation and growth of a field of investigation and of the ways in which the intellectual and social environment of research influences its course of development. It was thought that the results of such a study would suggest tentative guidelines for those responsible for the formulation of research policy. And it was hoped that the experience gained from this exploratory investigation would be helpful to others who might conduct similar studies of other fields of research.

THE CONCEPT OF A "LINE OF INVESTIGATION"

The bibliography assembled for the project contains 196 items directly related to the topic of group decisions involving risk and represents the work of 187 investigators[2] from eight different countries. Even a cursory examination of this literature reveals that it has a degree of coherence that is rather remarkable in view of the wide geographical and institutional dispersion of those who produced it. The research is self-contained and internally structured in the sense that nearly every study addresses a problem and employs methods which were explicitly derived from earlier investigations concerned with the same topic. And in fact, it can be shown that 182 of the 196 items, taken together, form a well-defined *line of investigation* through which each study can be traced back to a single "source," an experiment conducted by Stoner (1961). The tree-like structure of this line of investigation is reflected in its accelerating rate of growth. The average number of items added to it each year rose from 4, to 8, to 23, for the successive three-year periods beginning with 1961, and reached 40 for the period 1970–1971.

In the absence of comparable data for other areas of research, it is not possible to say how typical this line of investigation may be, but it is clear that its high degree of structure cannot be attributed to the influence of a single dominant research figure nor to the coordinated activities of a previously existing "invisible college" of investigators. Stoner's original study was an unpublished master's thesis which was initially brought to the attention of social scientists through the publications of two members of his thesis committee (Marquis, 1962; Wallach, Kogan, and Bem, 1962) who replicated his basic results and advanced rather different explanations for them. These publications, in turn, induced several others to conduct research whose results then stimulated still other investigators to follow up on their work. Interest in the field was heightened further by the publication of a popular social psychology textbook by Brown (1965), which devoted an entire chapter to this research and proposed an ingenious explanatory scheme to account for the major results known at the time. For the most part, then, recruitment was accomplished through the publication of articles and books, and although there eventually developed an informal communication network among the more active investigators, most interaction took place through the media of scientific publication. The effects of this impersonal and time-consuming mode of collaboration on the conduct of research will be considered later.

In order to understand the nature of this line of investigation and why it came into existence, it is necessary to examine some of the salient features of Stoner's original study. Its basic objective was to ascertain the validity of a generalization drawn from the conventional wisdom of the time[3] that groups, by demanding conformity to norms, tend to stifle creativity, innovation, and the willingness to take risks. To test this assertion, Stoner employed an instrument known as the Choice Dilemmas Questionnaire (CDQ) which had previously been developed by Kogan and Wallach[4] to measure the risk-taking dispositions of individuals. Using a repeated-measures design, he first administered the CDQ to a collection of individuals, then formed them into groups and asked each group to arrive at a "group answer" for each item by means of a unanimous group decision. A comparison of the scores earned by individuals and groups (composed of the same people) revealed that, contrary to conventional wisdom, groups were significantly "riskier" than individuals. This shift in mean CDQ scores from the individual to the group condition is known now generally as the "risky shift."

The immediate response to the announcement of this finding was to check on its replicability. Several investigators independently repeated Stoner's experiment, and all obtained essentially the same results. These studies, and numerous subsequent ones in several different countries, soon demonstrated quite conclusively that the risky shift is thoroughly dependable, occurring in groups composed of subjects of both sexes, over a wide range of ages, and from a variety of occupations. Social scientists rarely have been blessed with so robust a phenomenon.

It is not difficult to understand, then, why work on this topic became so popular. But if one is to account for the way in which the research proceeded, it is essential to realize that the founders of this line of investigation did not simply establish the "reality" of the risky shift. They also did at least three other important things: they provided a particular *interpretation of its significance*; they formulated a neat *theoretical problem* of how to explain its occurrence; and they demonstrated the utility of certain *research procedures* that other investigators could employ with relative ease. These three features of the early work established the theoretical and methodological context for all later research. And taken together, they constitute something analogous to what Kuhn (1962) has called a paradigm.

In the following discussion, we shall borrow this term from Kuhn and speak of the "risky-shift paradigm." In doing so, it is possible that we may be using the same word for two somewhat different things, since Kuhn's paradigms refer to much more comprehensive and highly developed fields of research than the one considered here. We believe, however, that the striking parallels between Kuhn's cases and this one can be conveyed best in this manner. These will become more evident as we examine some of the ways in which the initial studies in this line of investigation influenced its subsequent course of development.

Significance of the Risky Shift

The finding that CDQ scores are dependably different for groups and individuals was interpreted uniformly in the early literature as supporting the flat generalization that groups are riskier, or less conservative, than individuals. Considerable emphasis was placed on both the theoretical and practical significance of this general conclusion. It was held to be theoretically important because it appeared to be inconsistent with widely accepted theories of social conformity. And it was said to have the practical implication that decision making should be assigned to groups, rather than to individuals, only when risk taking is socially desirable. (More than one article, for example, pointed to the dangers in having a committee decide whether or not to embark upon nuclear warfare.) The fact that the reasoning in support of these assertions was neither well developed nor especially persuasive went almost unnoticed, and this interpretation of the significance of the basic phenomenon was adopted implicitly by nearly all of those who engaged in this research.

The Theoretical Problem

Although the early studies succeeded in demonstrating the existence of the risky shift, they did not provide an unequivocal explanation for its occurrence. Several possible explanations were immediately forthcoming. Some investigators held, for example, that group decisions are riskier than those of individuals because responsibility for the consequences of a decision is diffused among the members of the group. Others attributed the effect to the disproportionate influence exerted by those members who are generally more willing to take risks. And still others proposed that a group discussion serves to activate widely held cultural values that favor the taking of risks. Eventually, there were more than a dozen competing explanations, the exact number depending on how one treats minor differences. It is clear, then, that the discovery of the risky shift presented a challenge to the theoretical ingenuity of numerous social scientists. And this challenge was especially appealing because the basic problem was so neatly circumscribed and of such a nature that a solution appeared to be attainable by means of a few well-designed experiments. Interest was further heightened by the tendency of individual investigators to become proponents of particular explanations. And indeed, some felt that they were involved in a race to be the first to establish the "true" explanation of the risky shift.

Standard Research Procedures

The persisting influence of Stoner's original study can also be seen in the methods employed by those who contributed to this line of investigation. His operational definition of the risky shift has remained the dominant one throughout. The CDQ, or some variant of it, has been by far the most widely used instrument for measuring the risk-taking dispositions of individuals and groups. Nearly all of the studies have been conducted in the laboratory on groups with no history or future, whose sole purpose was to provide data for the experimenter. And most have used a factorial design, with repeated measures, in order to assess the effects of various experimental treatments on shifts in risk scores. Alternative methods, such as the observation of groups in naturalistic settings or the use of a between-subjects design, have rarely been employed. There are undoubtedly many reasons for this fixation on such a limited set of methods, but the major ones would seem to be mainly pragmatic. These procedures are remarkably easy to use. They are relatively inexpensive. And they produce results that could be dependably replicated by others.

FUNCTIONS AND FATE OF THE
RISKY-SHIFT PARADIGM

The risky-shift paradigm—consisting of a particular interpretation of a thoroughly dependable phenomenon, an enticing theoretical problem, and certain standard research procedures—was set forth in the earliest publications and adopted by nearly all subsequent investigators, usually without any explicit consideration of alternatives. Its influence on the course of development of this line of investigation can best be understood, we believe, through an examination of the functions that it served.

Among the more important of these would seem to be the sense of security it engendered by providing investigators with a shared framework within which research projects could be formulated readily without the risk of getting bogged down in a morass of difficult theoretical and methodological issues. At the same time, its interpretation of the meaning of the risky shift gave a broader significance even to rather mundane studies which otherwise might not seem to have much intrinsic importance. Its identification of problems that were both manageable and significant made work on this topic especially attractive. And its promise of social "relevance" must have been at least partly responsible for the unusually high level of participation of younger people in this line of investigation.[5]

But the paradigm did more than simply stimulate research. It also served to give the work a sharp focus and a marked degree of internal interdependence. By mobilizing a standard set of techniques for the solution of a rather narrow array of problems, it created a situation in which the results of each study could be compared directly, and often quantitatively, with others generated by the same paradigm. From this interdependent and focused effort there resulted an impressive body of firmly established facts having to do with the nature of the risky shift, several interesting phenomena associated with it, and some of the conditions that determine its occurrence.

As time went by, however, it gradually became clear that the cumulative impact of these findings was quite different from what had been expected by those who produced them. Instead of providing an explanation of why "groups are riskier than individuals," they in fact cast serious doubt on the validity of the proposition itself. And since this proposition was such a central part of the risky-shift paradigm, they undermined confidence in the very paradigm that led to their discovery. In order to understand more fully the exact nature of this paradoxical outcome, it is necessary to look a bit more closely at the methods that produced these "embarrassing" findings.[6]

As mentioned above, most of the research in this line of investigation has employed the CDQ to measure a postulated "disposition to take risks." This instrument contains twelve items, each of which requires the respondent (either an individual or a group) to select the minimum probability of success that would justify undertaking a particular hypothetical "risky" course of action, and these twelve probabilities are summed, or averaged, to give a single score for the CDQ as a whole. Since smaller probabilities are assumed to reflect a greater willingness to take risks, smaller total scores are said to indicate a stronger risk-taking disposition on the part of the respondent.

Now there has never been any doubt since the completion of the earliest studies that CDQ scores are dependably smaller after group discussion than before. This is the "risky shift." But as research proceeded, it became progressively clear that the use of a single score to summarize responses to the twelve items conceals some very important information about differences among items and actually leads to quite dubious generalizations. Consider, for example, the following well-established facts: (1) Each item of the CDQ yields its own characteristic mean shift from individual to group conditions. And although these shifts are remarkably stable across a great variety of experimental settings, they differ substantially both in direction and magnitude for the different items. Some items consistently produce risky shifts; a few regularly generate cautious ones; and some fail to bring about significant shifts of either kind. (2) The distribution of the total set of choices made by specific groups on specific items shows that most of these decisions produce no shifts at all or only quite small ones. Items with a mean shift toward risk simply yield a larger number of risky than conservative shifts, whereas those with a mean shift toward caution display the opposite tendency. (3) New items similar in form to the original ones have been constructed which consistently generate cautious shifts.

A major outcome of the concerted effort to find an explanation of the risky shift has thus been the accumulation of data demonstrating that groups are not invariably riskier than individuals. And since it is now known that choice dilemmas can be constructed that will yield consistent mean shifts toward caution, it is clear that an instrument like the CDQ could be designed to produce results that would lead, by customary reasoning, to the conclusion that groups are actually *more conservative* than individuals.

Further embarrassment for the risky-shift paradigm was provided by research intended to demonstrate the existence of a risky shift for decisions other than those asked for in the CDQ. Several studies have required a choice among alternative "gambles" differing presumably in the amount of risk they entail. Some have simulated "real-life" risk-taking situations faced by investors, juries, or consumers. And some have posed dilemmas involving the taking of ethical risks. The results of this work can best be described as mixed; sometimes there is a risky shift, sometimes a cautious one, and sometimes none whatsoever. And, in contrast to research with the CDQ, the findings often are not replicable. Taken together, they certainly do not support the simple assertion that groups make riskier decisions than individuals. The most important effect of these studies, however, may well have been to make manifest certain ambiguities in the concept of "risk" which investigators had been able to ignore while concentrating exclusively on the CDQ.

The course of development of this line of investigation shows a marked similarity to that of "normal science" as described by Kuhn. Just as in his examples, a dominant paradigm served to stimulate research whose results had the effect of revealing the inadequacies of the paradigm itself. And, as in normal science, the end result was the creation of a state of crisis. The severity of this crisis is most evident in a certain theoretical disorientation that is beginning to overtake the field. It is now evident that the persistent search for an explanation of "the risky shift" was misdirected and that any adequate theory will have to account for a much more complicated set of data than originally anticipated. But it is not clear how theorizing should proceed, since serious questions have been raised as to whether, or in what way, "risk" is involved in the effects to be explained. Dissatisfaction with the theoretical framework given by the risky-shift paradigm is mounting, and various attempts recently have been made to redefine the conceptual meaning of the basic phenomena by treating them as instances of social influence, attitude change, social comparison, coalition formation, rational decision making, and once again, conformity. It is not yet possible, however, to predict which, if any, of these orientations ultimately will provide a theoretical home for the accumulated findings.

THE PROBLEM OF EVALUATION

Since the most dramatic outcome of this work was a demonstration of the inadequacies of its underlying premises, one might be tempted to argue that the whole enterprise was useless. But such a dismal conclusion surely would be too severe, for it would fail to recognize the importance of the many detailed findings that were established by this research. These results constitute a body of closely interrelated "hard facts" whose validity does not depend on the theoretical preconceptions of those who discovered them. The assumptions implicit in the risky-shift paradigm were entirely compatible with the social-psychological thinking of the time, and the fact that the research it generated was able to force a basic reexamination of these assumptions attests to its quality. If Kuhn's thesis about the role of crises in the development of science is at all applicable here, it would suggest that the fate suffered by this paradigm should be taken as evidence of genuine progress.

The conclusion that the work in this line of investigation had positive consequences does not, of course, imply that its paradigm was the best possible one. It is quite easy, in retrospect, to imagine many different approaches that might have been adopted. The original laboratory experiments could have led immediately to studies in naturalistic settings in order to discover whether the findings actually generalize to "real" groups of various kinds. Instead of relying so heavily on the CDQ, a systematic comparison could have been made of alternative measuring instruments. A more intensive investigation of the nature of risk itself could have been completed before devoting so much attention to the effects of groups on risk-taking behavior. And rather than simply dismissing conformity theory, a more careful examination could have been made of its ability to account for the basic findings. Any of these or other strategies might have produced better results.

Speculation about the possible advantages of alternative courses of research must be tempered, however, by questions as to why they never came into being. Any historically given line of investigation is a social product which reflects the scientific judgments of those who fashioned it. And since such judgments always derive from a particular intellectual and social setting and are basically shaped by it, retrospective criticisms that ignore the contemporary context of research are bound to be of limited value.

The influence of the research environment of the early 1960s on the emergence of the risky-shift paradigm can be seen quite clearly if we compare the impact of Stoner's experiment with that of some other quite good ones conducted at about the same time. These studies all dealt with the same general topic and employed equally straightforward methods, and it might seem that any one of them could have founded a new line of investigation. But only Stoner's did. The critical feature of the "unsuccessful" studies appears to have been simply that they found no consistent difference in the risk taking of individuals and groups. As seen from the perspective of the dominant thinking of the time, this finding was not at all startling. It posed no special problem, seemed to have no unusual practical or theoretical implications, and therefore attracted no special attention. Stoner's risky shift, on the other hand, was surprising in that it appeared to be inconsistent with both common sense and accepted theory. And because it was anomalous, it required an explanation. There is, to be sure, a certain irony in the fact that the resulting research eventually showed there to be no universal risky shift, but it does not follow that a line of investigation based on these other studies would have made a significantly greater contribution to knowledge.

Rather than attempt to specify a superior paradigm that could have gained acceptance, it would seem more informative to examine the research actually done and ask how it might have been improved. In reviewing the many studies concentrated in this one area of research, it is difficult not to conclude that, given the resources employed, progress somehow should have been more rapid. And now that we know the results of this work, we can understand why it was not more effective. The basic premise of the risky-shift paradigm—that groups are invariably riskier than individuals—had to be abandoned and the central research problem had to reformulated. But even though these requirements are now clear, the fact remains that the risky-shift paradigm survived intact for nearly 10 years and continued to shape the conduct of research until well after the evidence demonstrating its inappropriateness had become overwhelming. Let us try to identify some of the factors responsible for this conceptual rigidity.

First, there is the matter of *labeling*. Stoner's original finding could have been given any of a great variety of names, and it is interesting to try to imagine what the subsequent course of development might have been if some other label, such as "the shift in risk taking" or "the group discussion effect" had been chosen instead. There seems little doubt that the research would have been different. The term *risky shift* placed the phenomena in the domain of risk taking rather than other possible ones, such as group problem solving, group decision making, social influence, or attitude change. And it carried the implicit implication that groups are, indeed, invariably riskier than individuals. Once the term had become firmly established in the vocabulary of social psychology, investigators were not inclined to question whether these connotations were warranted. Their thinking about the phenomenon thus was unnecessarily limited, and its continued use served to delay the conceptual reorientation that was needed.

Just how hard it is to change a label after it has come into common usage can be seen in the fact that most authors still describe their research as being concerned with "the risky-shift effect" even though they acknowledge that groups often display a shift toward caution. The field continues to be identified as "risky-shift research." Its findings are still indexed under this heading. And the term will undoubtedly find its way into textbooks for many years to come. It will probably not disappear completely until a new term comes to take its place.

A second inhibiting factor has to do with *motivation*. Most of those who participated in this line of investigation were attracted to it by the theoretical puzzle posed by the discovery of a striking new phenomenon. Their primary motivation for engaging in this research stemmed from their desire to establish an explanation for its occurrence. And since nearly all investigators shared this motivation, a social situation was created in which interest centered almost exclusively on the conditions responsible for the shift, and hardly at all on the properties of the shift itself. We have seen that the resulting research inadvertently did produce findings that should have raised questions about the nature of the phenomenon that was to be explained. But since these findings generally were not regarded as central to the main task at hand, they tended to be overlooked, treated as experimental error, or set aside for later consideration. And although these protective mechanisms are entirely understandable, we must conclude that the concentrated search for explanations was premature and that it resulted in a good deal of misdirected effort.

Our analysis of this motivational situation would not be complete, however, without some discussion of the effects of controversy on the conduct of research. Most of the investigators who worked on this topic quickly became proponents of a particular explanation of the risky shift and spent a good deal of effort in its defense. Much of their research was therefore designed to demonstrate the superiority of their preferred explanation or, more often, the inadequacies of the others. And although this controversy never became especially acrimonious, it undoubtedly contributed to the persistence of the unwarranted proposition that groups are riskier than individuals, since it would have had little point without this assumption. But we should not conclude that the controversy had only deleterious consequences, for it activated a search for detailed evidence that would permit a definitive choice among the competing explanations, and it was this evidence concerning the microstructure of the alleged risky shift that eventually forced investigators to revise their thinking about the nature of the central research problem. The experience provided by this single case suggests that the long-term effects of controversy often may be both subtle and complex and that one should view with skepticism any simple generalization about the role of controversy in the development of science.

The third inhibiting factor concerns *methodology*. The CDQ, which played such a critical part in the entire course of development, was conceived by most investigators as a *test* whose scores constituted measures of a hypothetical risk-taking disposition of individuals and groups. In keeping with this psychometric orientation, it was generally assumed that the risky shift was due to an alteration in this presumably unitary disposition, and it became standard practice to treat total test scores as the primary dependent variable in most research. Many investigators did not even report findings separately for items, and those who did tended to ignore, or to minimize, the substantial differences occurring in the responses to different items, often on the assumption that they could be attributed to a certain internal unreliability of the test. This fixation on total test scores thus diverted attention away from the most critical information contained in the data and thereby delayed the attainment of a proper understanding of the true nature of the so-called risky shift.

Perhaps an even more serious consequence of this psychometric orientation was that it steered research away from the concrete processes actually responsible for the shifts in observed test scores. The assumption that these shifts reflected dispositional changes led investigators to look for conditions that might affect the postulated disposition itself and to overlook the possibility that changes in test scores merely summarize changes in responses to their constituent elements. The research thus lacked concreteness and remained one step removed from reality. Several years elapsed before anyone undertook a serious analysis of the properties of the dilemmas described in the various items of the CDQ. Little attention was paid to the content of the discussions that brought about the changes in responses to the individual items. And investigators were remarkably slow in recognizing the effects of the initial distribution of choices within a group on its final decision. The typical experiment in all of this research has been one in which a factorial design is used to assess the effects of two or more treatments on CDQ scores and thus, by implication, on the hypothetical disposition to take risks. One cannot but be impressed by the ingenuity displayed in the construction of these treatments, but the fact remains that this black-box approach was, by its very nature, incapable of providing direct information about the processes underlying the global shift in test scores. And there can be little doubt that the flight from concreteness engendered by this psychometric orientation seriously reduced the effectiveness of much of the research.

The fourth factor affecting the rate of progress in this line of investigation has to do with the *media of communication*. We noted earlier that most of the communication among those working in this field took place through articles and books. This mode of communication is remarkably time consuming, for the average lag between the completion of a piece of research and its appearance in print is not less than two years. And if we add to this the time required to plan and execute an experiment that was inspired by a previously published one, we see that the average temporal gap between successive studies must exceed three years. It would seem, then, that the 10-year history of this line of investigation permitted at most only three or four generations of studies. And this observation suggests that, given this cumbersome mode of communication, the rate of progress actually achieved should not be criticized too severely. But it also suggests that the field would have benefited from the development of a more effective system of communication.

One additional comment should be made about the role of journals in the scientific enterprise. Although the available evidence is not conclusive, it appears that the editorial practices of journals may have contributed inadvertently to the inflexibility of thinking in this field. Editors, in seeking advice about the manuscripts submitted to them, naturally turn to those who may be expected to know most about the topic. And this procedure seems to have been commonly followed in the editing of manuscripts on the risky shift, for there is reason to suspect that most of them were referred by perhaps a half-dozen individuals who were active leaders in the field. The resulting evaluations undoubtedly benefited from the reviewers' intimate knowledge of the previous work on the topic and their general competence as researchers. But this practice also had the unintended effect of creating a situation in which reviewers and authors tended to share the same paradigm and thus tended to view the research in essentially the same way. It seems, therefore, that the editorial process was not especially well designed to raise questions about the conceptual and methodological assumptions that were implicitly adopted by all of those who were under the influence of the paradigm. And it appears that the use of a more diverse and less involved group of reviewers would have hastened the discovery of the obstacles that were hampering progress. The possibility that journal editing has similar inertial effects on other fields of research deserves further investigation.

SUMMARY AND CONCLUSIONS

This completes my case history of research on the risky shift, and I turn now to a brief consideration of some of the conclusions that may be drawn from it.

1. Two concepts have been central to this analysis. The term *line of investigation* was selected to emphasize the high degree of interconnectedness displayed by the work on the risky shift. And the term *paradigm* has been used to refer to the complex set of beliefs and assumptions that investigators implicitly adopted in their research on this topic. It seems unlikely that all fields of research can be said to form a line of investigation in the meaning of this term, but I believe that it would be useful in the analysis of other cases to investigate the ways in which studies are linked together and to attempt to characterize the properties of the resulting network. The use of graph theory should be helpful for this purpose. It may turn out that there are only a few common types of organization and that the research conducted in each type has its own particular set of characteristics. Similar questions could be raised about paradigms. The risky-shift paradigm was much more specific than the grander ones that are said to influence the work of entire disciplines. Its applicability did not extend beyond this particular line of investigation, although its content undoubtedly was influenced by the more general paradigms shared by all social psychologists. This observation suggests that there may be hierarchies of paradigms. In any event, a comparative study of the nature of paradigms in a variety of fields should provide useful insights about their role in the creation of scientific knowledge.

2. This case study has identified, we believe, certain important benefits which result when research is organized into a line of investigation and is guided by a single paradigm. The gains to be derived from a highly focused and sustained attack on a single problem are substantial. And the cumulative impact generated by the use of a limited number of standard methods should not be underestimated. There are, to be sure, dangers in such a heavy concentration of resources, but in this particular case at least, it would appear that the long-run gains outweighed the costs.

3. This analysis has also shown, however, that paradigms may exert subtle, though profound, influences that are detrimental to the course of development of research. The processes governing the formation of paradigms are therefore of critical importance. But even so, one should remain skeptical about the possibility of deliberately creating paradigms for new fields of research, since a paradigm, by its very nature, cannot be imposed on a community of scholars.

4. A more immediately promising approach would seem to be one in which an attempt is made to reduce the negative consequences of a paradigm once it has gained acceptance. My analysis suggests that the risky-shift paradigm engendered certain self-protective processes that unnecessarily delayed progress in this line of investigation. These had to do with labeling, motivation, methodology, and the media of communication. If the research community were to become more sensitive to these processes, policies then might be devised to counteract them, and individual investigators could be alerted to their possible effects on the conduct of their own research.

5. One of the more interesting questions raised by this case study has to do with the ways in which a field responds to a state of crisis. Although it is too soon to know what the long-term reactions to the demise of the risky-shift paradigm will be, two types of response are already apparent. Some investigators have withdrawn from the field in the belief that further work would be useless, while others have begun a vigorous search for alternative formulations of the basic problem. The ultimate significance of the research in this line of investigation will depend to a considerable degree on which of these responses becomes dominant. There is a real possibility that interest in the topic will gradually subside and that the accumulated findings will simply fade into the history of social psychology. Such an outcome would not be unprecedented, for this has been the fate of many quite popular research enterprises of the past. There is also the possibility, however, that the search for a new conceptualization will be successful and that the better established findings will become an enduring part of a more comprehensive paradigm of the future. Since so little is known about the processes activated by a state of crisis, it is not possible to predict what the outcome will be, but a careful documentation of these processes, as they unfold, should provide a better understanding of this critical stage in the development of research.

6. No overall evaluation of the accomplishments of this line of investigation would be complete without considering one disturbing fact. After 10 years of research, Stoner's original problem remains unsolved. We still do not know how the risk-taking behavior of "real life" groups compares with that of individuals. Should the decision about nuclear war be assigned to a committee or to an individual? Should decisions about surgery be left to a group of surgeons? Is it better to have a jury or an individual decide whether a possibly dangerous person is to be set free? The answers to such questions are not much clearer now than they were 10 years ago. The results of research on the risky shift do suggest, however, that there is probably no universal answer to these questions and that the problem should be stated differently. This is not a trivial conclusion, since a problem that is not formulated properly inevitably results in much wasted effort. And even though one may regret that more research was not done on natural groups in realistic settings, there can be little assurance that such research would have made a greater contribution to our understanding of the nature of group decisions involving risk.

NOTES

1. A slightly modified version of this article was presented at a symposium in honor of Robert B. MacLeod, Cornell University, June 2, 1972. The research reported here was supported by Contract HSM-42-69-55 with the National Institute of Mental Health.

2. The fact that there are nearly as many authors as items is due to the operation of two opposing tendencies. Most publications have more than one author, but the names of several authors appear repeatedly.

3. See, for example, the popular book by Whyte (1956).

4. For a full discussion of the nature of this instrument, see Kogan and Wallach (1964).

5. Although a strict comparison of the age distributions for different topics has not been attempted, it is clear that a large proportion of the research has been conducted by students and younger faculty members. Of the 182 items in the compiled bibliography, at least 30 can be identified explicitly as graduate theses or student projects, and many report investigations that are direct extensions of doctoral dissertations.

6. A more complete account of this research is given in Cartwright (1971).

REFERENCES

Brown, R. *Social Psychology*. New York: Free Press, 1965.

Cartwright, D. "Risk Taking by Individuals and Groups: An Assessment of Research Employing Choice Dilemmas," *Journal of Personality and Social Psychology*, 1971, *20*, 361–378.

Kogan, N., and Wallach, M. A. *Risk Taking: A Study in Cognition and Personality*. New York: Holt, Rinehart and Winston, 1964.

Kuhn, T. S. *The Structure of Scientific Revolutions*. Chicago: University of Chicago Press, 1962.

Marquis, D. G. "Individual Responsibility and Group Decisions Involving Risk," *Industrial Management Review*, 1962, *3*, 8–23.

Stoner, J. A. F. "A Comparison of Individual and Group Decisions Involving Risk," Unpublished master's thesis, Sloan School of Management, Massachusetts Institute of Technology, 1961.

Wallach, M. A. Kogan, N., and Bem, D. J. "Group Influence on Individual Risk Taking," *Journal of Abnormal and Social Psychology*, 1962, *65*, 75–86.

Whyte, W. H., Jr. *The Organization Man*. New York: Simon and Schuster, 1956.

Issues in Research Design

The most important work of the researcher is often the least visible, tangible, or glamorous. When we consider the task of the researcher, we frequently limit our attention to such visible activities as the hours spent in the laboratory or in collecting questionnaires. In reading a published account of research, our attention is often directed toward the results section rather than less glamorous descriptions of background details concerning how the results were achieved. Overemphasis on these visible activities of the researcher, however tends to obscure the fact that the researcher's most important work may take place long before he or she goes into the field or gets to the point of analyzing data.

The thought given by the researcher to decisions concerning choices of a research question, of an appropriate site in which to study the question, and of a suitable method of study, probably constitutes the most critical, although less visible and tangible, aspects of the research process. If such strategic choices are made wisely, the collection and analysis of data may represent little more than the straightforward implementation of these prior decisions.

The selections in this section highlight important aspects of the research process which occur (or should occur) before the researcher goes into the field. The first article by Webb addresses issues surrounding the choice of a research question. This may be the most important issue faced by a researcher, yet it remains perhaps the least understood step in the research process. Research that makes a major contribution to a field is often distinguished from poor research less on the basis of adequate research methodology than by the importance of the research question addressed. As McGuire (Section 6) points out in paraphrasing Abraham Maslow: "That which is not worth doing is not worth doing well." Webb differentiates factors that typically influence the choice of a research question from considerations that are likely to guide the researcher to ask important research questions. He reveals that two of the three factors leading to the choice of an important research question are characteristics of the researcher and not of the question being addressed.

For the new student or novice in research, identifying important research questions—or often *any* research questions for that matter—is a formidable task. Webb points out a fundamental prerequisite to this task is a thorough understanding of one's chosen area of study and knowledge about what has been done in the past. Consequently, as students gain greater knowledge about a field, the identification of research questions should become progressively easier. Beyond exposing students to knowledge about an area of study, however, there is often little help we can provide in stimulating the creativity necessary to define important research questions. Webb explains that the researcher's skepticism or dissatisfaction with the literature is important in this regard.

Once a research question has been identified, the researcher is required to identify a method of study appropriate for answering the question. In most instances, the researcher must decide on experimental methods in the laboratory or field research in actual organizations. In some instances, the nature of the research question itself may dictate the type of methodology possible. A researcher inquiring into an area previously unstudied, for example, may find the absence of existing knowledge about the topic requires a case study, observational study, or other exploratory method that is designed to identify the important variables for study. More often, the researcher will have several potential methods that may be appropriate and must make a decision about which method is most appropriate for the research question being addressed.

It is important in the early stages of research for the researcher to anticipate potential problems that may be associated with the method of study under consideration. The selection by Cook and Campbell deals with such problems in an extensive discussion of common threats to validity in research. These threats provide a useful set of criteria the researcher can use in evaluating a particular method of study. For example, the researcher should anticipate the extent to which the chosen method guards against threats to internal validity (for example, what alternative explanations for the results may be possible?) and evaluate the extent to which the results may be generalizable to settings other than the one in which the research is conducted. Considering these issues *before* a study is actually undertaken is likely to greatly enhance the value of the research results.

A related issue that must be considered by the researcher concerns selecting a setting in which the research is to be conducted. In many instances, selection of a research setting or sample is dictated by expediency. As Nunnally (1960) has suggested, we often have a specific sample in mind, but in a pinch our spouses, secretaries, students, or just about anyone will do. The important consideration for the researcher is often the willingness of a particular sample to participate in the study. Beyond these considerations, few guidelines are usually available to the researcher in selecting a research setting. The article by Ellsworth suggests several factors the researcher must consider in choosing a sample. The primary consideration is whether or not the research setting allows for a fair test of the hypotheses. In addition, Ellsworth indicates the choice of a research setting should be related to the types of research settings which have been used in similar studies in the past, the nature of the variables being studied, the scope of the hypotheses, and plausible alternative hypotheses that can be raised for the results.

In organizational research, once a setting has been chosen it is not always possible to randomly sample respondents. Ethical considerations and legal restrictions (for example, Department of Health, Education, and Welfare guidelines) often require that potential subjects be given the choice of whether or not they wish to participate in the study. In studies conducted in organizational settings, the researcher should explain the general purpose of the study to employees and then request their voluntary participation in the study. The selection by Rosenthal and Rosnow raises important questions about the consequences of our reliance on voluntary subjects. The problem associated with the use of volunteer subjects is straightforward; individuals who are likely to volunteer for a study may differ in systematic ways from those who do not volunteer. The differences which may exist between volunteers and nonvolunteers may limit the external validity of research results. Rosenthal and Rosnow review a number of individual and situational characteristics associated with the act of volunteering for research. In addition, they make several suggestions concerning ways to increase the rate of volunteering by subjects. The problems that may be caused by reliance on volunteer subjects in organizational research may often be beyond the ability of the researcher to solve. Even though these problems are not easily overcome, the researcher needs to be aware of the implications of using volunteers who may affect the results of the research.

REFERENCES AND SUGGESTED READINGS

Lundberg, C. C. "Hypothesis Creation in Organizational Behavior Research," *Academy of Management Review*, 1 (1976), pp. 5-12.

Nunnally, J. "The Place of Statistics in Psychology," *Educational and Psychological Measurement*, 20 (1960), pp. 641-650.

Rosenthal, R. and Rosnow, R. L. (eds.). *Artifact in Behavioral Research*. New York: Academic Press, 1969.

Webb, E. J., Campbell, D. T., Schwartz, R. D., and Sechrest, L. *Unobtrusvie Measures: Nonreactive Research in the Social Sciences*. Chicago: Rand McNally, 1966.

4 The Choice of the Problem[1]

Wilse B. Webb

The matter of how to judge the goodness or badness of a result, particularly when this result is a theoretical formulation, has received considerable attention in recent years. Today in psychology, such decisions are increasingly necessary. Our subject matter has become quite boundless: muscle twitches and wars, the sound of porpoises and problems of space, the aesthetic qualities of tones and sick minds, psychophysics and labor turnover. The range of organisms involved in the studies of these problems extends from pigeons to people, from amoeba to social groups. Further, the techniques of measurement have been honed and sharpened by electronic tubes, computing machines, mathematical niceties, and imaginative testing procedures. Too often, in this lush environment, we as researchers may find after some months of toil and research that our findings, although in accord with nature and beautifully simple, are utterly petty and we ourselves are no longer interested in them much less anyone else being interested.

This problem of carefully selecting and evaluating a problem does not involve the researcher alone. In our complex beehive of today, this is a question for the teacher of research, the thesis and dissertation director, the research director of laboratories or programs, and the dispensers of research funds—in a small way, department chairmen and deans, and in a large way, the guardians of the coffers of foundations and government agencies.

We are not without criteria, of course. Either implicitly or explicitly we seek justification for what we do. Certainly when grants are involved we seek for some reasons to justify the getting or the giving of money. For our consideration, I have rummaged around and turned up six widely used bases for doing an experiment: curiosity, confirmability, compassion, cost, cupidity, and conformability—or, more simply, "Am I interested?" "Can I get the answer?" "Will it help?" "How much will it cost?" "What's the payola?" "Is everyone else doing it?"

I believe you will find that these are the things that enter our minds when we evaluate a student's problem, dispense a sum of research money, or decide to put ourselves to work. To anticipate myself, however, I will try to establish the fact that these bases, used alone or in combination although perhaps correlated positively with a "successful" piece of research, will probably have a zero or even negative correlation with a "valuable" piece of research.

Before proceeding to examine these criteria, however, let me introduce a clarifying footnote. Although I am concerned about selecting a problem beyond the routine and "successful" experiment—and here I shall use completely indiscriminately (with apologies to the philosophers) such terms as "good," "valued," "enduring," "worthwhile"—I

From W. B. Webb, "The Choice of the Problem," *American Psychologist*, 1961, *16* (5), pp. 223–227.

do not wish to disparage the necessary place of routine experiments, i.e., well-conducted experiments which fill in and extend those more creative ones. I think that even the most cursory consideration of the history of science reveals that the "original" or the "important" experiment almost inevitably pushes out from routine work that has preceded it and is further dependent upon the supportive routine experiments for their fruition into the field. Most definitely, I would contend that it is far more important to do a routine experiment than no experiment at all.

But back to the problem before us: Are our reasons for experimenting sufficient guidelines to decide about experiments? The first of these, *curiosity*, is the grand old man of reasons for experimentation and hence, justification for our experimentation. In the days when knighthood was in flower, this was the most familiar emblem on the scientist's shield. It was enough to seek an answer to "I wonder what would happen if . . . ." This was sometimes formalized with the dignified phrase, "knowledge for knowledge's sake."

Today this is not a strong base of operation. Perhaps costs have outmoded whimsey; perhaps the glare of the public stage has made us too self-conscious for such a charming urge. Or, perhaps more forebodingly, we are less curious—or, perhaps a combination of these has made curiosity less defensible. More critically, when we look more closely at this justification for doing, or proposing to do an experiment, it does not turn out to be one. Clearly a person can be curious about valuable things, trivial things, absurd things, or evil things. I think we would all find it a little difficult to judge the relative merits of two pieces of completed research by trying to decide which of the two experimenters was the most curious. Perhaps wisely, then, it seems more and more difficult to convince deans or directors of research, or dispensers of funds that a problem is worth investigating because we, personally, happened to be puzzled by it.

The criterion of *confirmability* as a criterion of worthiness of the pursuit of a topic has two sides: a philosophic one and a pragmatic one. Philosophically, this criterion reached its glory in the '30s and '40s when the voice of a logical positivist was heard throughout the land. In no uncertain terms, they told us that the criterion for a problem was "that the question asked could be answered." On the pragmatic side, this criterion is interpreted to mean: "Pick variables which are likely to be statistically significant." Undoubtedly, the philosophical point of view has done much to clear up our experimental work by hacking through a jungle of undefined and ambiguous terms. From the pragmatic point of view, this has been a much valued criterion for the graduate student with several kids and who must finish his thesis or dissertation to get out and start earning a living. However, it is just this criterion that may be voted the most likely to result in a pedestrian problem. It demands problems which have easily measurable variables and clearly stated influences. It discourages the exploration of new, complex, or mysterious areas. To exercise this criterion alone would force one to choose an experiment of measuring age as related to strength of grip on the handle of the dynamometer against exploring variables associated with happiness. Both may be quite worthwhile, but the latter has less of a chance of being approached so long as we exercise the criterion of confirmability alone.

The problem of *costs* must enter into considerations of undertaking an experiment. In the real, live world, determining the value of a thing is very simple. Find out how much it costs. Clearly, anything that costs a lot is very valuable. A car or house which costs more than another car or another house is naturally worth more. One pays for what one gets and one gets what one pays for. This thinking carries over into the world of scientific affairs. Space probes are obviously important because they cost a lot; a project which can get a large grant must be a good one or else it would not cost so much.

Certainly this is very faulty reasoning. That methodologies differ in their costs is quite obvious; the more expensive the methodology, the more valuable and important the activity is not a direct derivative. Einstein undoubtedly used less equipment than his dentist but we may suspect that Einstein attacked the more valuable problem. Departments of Philosophy are far less expensive than Departments of Veterinary Medicine but I do not believe them to be necessarily less valuable.

It is quite true that when a large sum of money is expended on a particular project that some decisions have been made that the desirability or the value of that project justifies the expenditure of this large sum. Money may serve as a crude index of where to look for decision bases that justify large expenditures but cannot serve as judgment bases themselves. If a person says, "To do this piece of research will cost x amount of money and will occupy x amount of my life," he has merely brought his problem into focus and has raised the critical question more clearly, i.e., is such an expenditure worth it? He has not solved the problem of how valuable his experiment is, but raised the question—some other criterion must be sought for an answer to that question.

A somewhat new criterion has entered into thinking today: *compassion*. As we have moved into the applied world, this rather new criterion has come into increasing use—at least this seems true of psychology. A person asks himself as he begins an experiment, "Will the results make things better?" and implicitly assumes that an affirmative answer will make his experiment or his project more valuable. The problem then is assessed in terms of its solutions or answers resulting in a patient's improvement, a reduction in prejudice, a happier or a healthier world, etc. A variation on this question, as it is asked in the market place and in some of the other sciences directly, is in a slightly cruder form: "Will this be useful; what service will this finding perform?"

H. G. Wells has a comment on this guideline for performance in his book *Meanwhile*:

The disease of cancer will be banished from life by calm, unhurrying, persistent men and women working with every shiver of feeling controlled and suppressed in hospitals and in laboratories .... Pity never made a good doctor, love never made a good poet, desire for service never made a discovery.

In one sense of the word, this criterion is a form of the old, applied vs. basic issue that plagues all sciences that live with one foot in technology and the other foot in theory. I cannot begin to resolve this issue here. I can, however, I believe, say this: it is quite possible for a piece of research undertaken in compassion or for utility to be quite valuable, enduring, well thought of, etc. It is also quite possible that it be trivial, superficial, limited, useless, etc. The same may be said for any given piece of basic research in which utility or compassion was never an issue. I am not one who believes that because a piece of research has no relevant use, it then by definition is valuable; or that a finding because it is useful is worthless. If these statements may be granted, it would appear then that some more fundamental criteria must be applied.

Cupidity is a variation on the criterion of compassion. Here, however, the "payoff" is not for others but for oneself. Very simply the research is evaluated in terms of whether it will get one a promotion, favorable publicity, peer applause. Well, sometimes, undoubtedly what is good for you is good for others, and hence of general value.

However, the contrary is just as likely to be true: namely, what is good for you is not necessarily good for others at all. For example, making the natural assumptions that deans cannot read and department chairmen do not, the greater the number of papers, then the greater the probability of promotion. This results in a whirling mass of fragmented, little, anything printables to be constantly turned out instead of mature, integrated, programmatic articles. In being good to yourself you have done little or no good for others. The most casual recall would suggest that the impelling motives behind most significant advances in thought have not been cupidity, rather to the contrary such advances seemed to be more "selfless" than "selfish."

The last of my "useful" criteria is that of *conformity*. In these days of togetherness, it is not at all surprising to find conformity and its cousin, comfortableness, serving as guidelines for determining the should or should not of experimentation. We mean, by conformity, the choice of the currently popular problem, i.e., one within an ongoing and popular system, for example, operant conditioning, statistical learning theory; or a currently popular area of investigation, for example, sensory deprivation, or the Taylor Manifest Anxiety Scale.

As with all of our preceding criteria for deciding about a research project, conformity clearly has its merits. It would be foolish to turn one's back on new methods or a recent breakthrough of ideas which have been developed and certainly the interactive stimulation of mutual efforts in the same area are helpful factors in research. These, however, seem to be more means than ends to be sought for. One must be cautioned against becoming overenamored by the availability of a method at the expense of thoughtfulness or being charmed by the social benefits of working in an active area at the expense of the scientific implications of such work. More simply, some things that a lot of people are doing are quite worthwhile, and some are quite ridiculous.

Unfortunately, however, the assiduous cultivation of all these virtuous goals may still, it would seem, even in combination result in the most pedestrian of problems. We must then search further for means of assuring ourselves that the problem is a good one. The usual criteria do not seem to answer.

I am going to say that there are three fundamentals which form the basis for good experiments or good problems. None of these are new. By disclaiming originality, however, I can claim that they are profound and that their presence or absence makes a significant effect in the value of the problem to an individual. Two of these are characteristics of the person, and one of the problem. The most common tags for my trio are: knowledge, dissatisfaction, and generalizability. The first two of these, of course, refer to the individual himself and the third to the problem itself.

I think that there is very general agreement that one can only work effectively in an area when he has a thorough understanding of this general area of concern. It is quite often that the significant finding comes from a fusion of quite a number of simple studies or a perception of gaps in the detailed findings or the methodologies and procedures of others. I am quite sure that the vaunted, creative insight of the scientist occurs more frequently within a thorough knowledge of one's area than as a bolt from the blue.

In a quite mechanical sense, a failure to obtain all knowledge possible about one's problem area is to fail to profit from the errors of thought of the past, if they be errors, or the knowledges obtained, if such knowledges are correct. Either represents an arrogance of a witless kind. Moreover, in this very practical sense, unless these backgrounds are well assessed by the worker, one may find oneself both discovering a most well-known discovery and be in the embarrassing position of arriving at the party dressed in full regalia a day late. Or perhaps, more tragic for the world of ideas, such a person without knowledge may remain unheard, being incapable of gaining the attention of competent workers through an ineptitude of expression or lack of relation to the field.

Secondly, however, to avoid the sins of conformity, suggested previously—for specialized knowledge groups can become more ingroupish than a band of teenagers—a healthy opposition must be present. I have designated this as dissatisfaction. Other terms to be used are skepticism, negativism, or perhaps more charmingly, iconoclasm.

It is, of course, quite possible that I am very wrong in emphasizing the necessity of an opposing set to the existent knowledges and methodologies in one's time. Clearly the most convenient position would be to invoke the concept of "genius" or "insight," leading to important problems as a result of broad surveys of the literature, or efficiency in employing procedures. This, however, would hardly be useful as a guideline. One can hardly suggest to a person that they strain and have an insight, or try hard and be a genius.

There is, on the other hand, considerable empirical evidence, or at least examples, to substantiate the fact that original discoveries contain an element of active revolution. Skipping lightly through psychological history, we can point to Hemholtz's classical rate of nerve conduction experiments which flew in the face of established knowledge about immediate conductivity, Freud defied the reign of conscious thought, Watson negated mentalism, Köhler set against the tide of trial and error learning, in recent times Harlow has spoken not so much for positive adient motivation as against avoidant motives as the prime mover of man.

Logically, and psychologically (and happily they conjoin occasionally) this seems to make good sense. A significant research problem is a creative act. One can hardly be creative if one is avidly listening to the voice of others. We have good evidence from such experimentations as the Luchin's jar experiments that developed sets can clearly block solutions to problems. More simply, if one agrees with everything that everyone else says, one's role is automatically limited to feeding the fires, applauding the words or, at best, carrying the word. None of these are actions that lead to truly important research activities.

We may have, however, great knowledge and object quite violently to the items of this knowledge and proceed to conduct small experiments to substantiate our objections and still be doing little more than picking at a pimple on the face of one's science, to use a vulgar analogy. A further critical requirement must be recognized—a critical requirement that is most difficult to capture in words: to be an important result, one's findings require "extensity." Another word used here is that one's results must be generalizable. Poincaré, in his *Methods of Science*, states most clearly the reasoning underlying this requirement:

> What, then, is a good experiment? It is that which informs us of something besides an isolated fact. It is that which enables us to foresee, i.e., that which enables us to generalize . . . . Circumstances under which one has worked will never reproduce themselves all at once. The observed action then will never recur. The only thing that can be affirmed is that under analogous circumstances, analogous action is produced.

A further quotation from the same book amplifies this point of view:

> . . . it is needful that each of our thoughts be as useful as possible and this is why a law will be the more precious the more general it is. This shows us how we should choose. The most interesting facts are those which may serve many times.

Very simply, this boils down to being able to evaluate the probable consequence of your findings with the question which goes something like this: "In how many and what kind of specific circumstances will the relationships or rules that hold in this experiment hold in such other instances?" If the answer to this is only in instances almost exactly replicable of this particular circumstance, the rules that we obtain are likely to be of little consequence. If, however, the rule applies to what apparently is a vast heterogeneity of events in time and space, in varieties of species and surrounds, this rule is likely to have great value. Stated otherwise, the extent to which our variables and situations are unique and rare in contrast to universal and common largely determines the extent to which the findings are likely to be considered trivial or tremendous in their implications.

My summary can be quite simple:

Research today is both complex and costly. Guidelines are needed to sort among these complexities to enhance our chances of a sound investment, be this personal, financial, or temporal.

Six criteria may be, and often are, applied to judge a project's "success" potential: curiosity, confirmability, cost, compassion, cupidity, and conformability. There is probably a good probability that studies meeting the guidelines will "pay off" in some form of coinage—perhaps small change.

However, for a study to be an enduring and critical one for the history of ideas or to enter into that stream three further items seem involved:

1. You must know thoroughly the body of research and the techniques of experimentation which are related to a given problem area. Naiveté may be a source of joy in an artistic field but is not the case in valued research efforts.

2. You should be able to disbelieve, be dissatisfied with, or deny the knowledge that you have. (This is no paradox in relation to our first statement. Recognize that the first requirement is propaedeutic to this one. This is an active, not a passive state; this is to know and then know differently, rather than a know-nothing state.) Valued research seems to grow from dissatisfactions with the way things are, rather than agreeable perpetuation of present ways of proceeding.

3. You should, very simply, look for the forest beyond the tree, test the generality of your proposed finding. If your finding is referent to a rat in a particular maze, a patient on a particular couch, or a refined statistical difference, then that rat, that patient, or a captive statistician may listen to you. This would be a skimpy and disappointing audience to my way of thinking.

It is quite likely that we cannot all become geniuses. We can at least try to be less trivial. Learn as much as we can, believe in new ways, seek as great extensity in our variables as we can.

NOTE

1. An abridged version of the Presidential Address to the Southern Society for Philosophy and Psychology given at the fifty-second Annual Meeting in Biloxi, Mississippi, April 15, 1960.

5 From Abstract Ideas to Concrete Instances: Some Guidelines for Choosing Natural Research Settings

Phoebe C. Ellsworth

Some people, including many social scientists, are most comfortable when negotiating in the realm of abstract ideas. They think in terms of conceptual variables and constructs, such as "attitude," "commitment," and "frustration," examining the research literature for relationships among variables and exceptions to these relationships, seeking logical consequences not previously considered, generating hypotheses, and arranging abstract concepts and relationships into theories intended to account for past and future observations. This kind of thinking is justifiably admired by scientists, and it is essential for the development of theory.

Those who think in this abstract manner tend to do research of the hypothesis-testing variety. Having generated predictions that provide the impetus for research, their next task is to find empirical realizations of their conceptual variables in order to test these predictions (Carlsmith, Ellsworth, and Aronson, 1976). The more general the concepts, the more concrete instances there are to choose from. And yet, within many of the broad provinces of social science, very few of the available paths are followed; the abstract ideas turn out, in practice, to encompass only a very narrow range of empirical realizations. The mental dexterity demonstrated in dealing with abstractions often seems to vanish at the translation stage, as the old standard treatments and measures are used and reused with little consideration of their suitability for the task at hand (Webb, Campbell, Schwartz, and Sechrest, 1966, chap. 1).

Of course, not all researchers think this way; many start with a concrete situation or behavior and study it (see Sidman, 1960, for an excellent defense of this less prestigious approach.)[1] They do not face the problem of finding the concrete instance that best embodies the abstract idea, since they have started with the instance. The suggestions presented here are not intended for them. Other researchers have managed to excel at both levels. The dissonance theorists, for example, working in the service of an abstract set of hypotheses, have happily exploited the psychological laboratory, the small group of religious zealots (Festinger, Schachter, and Back, 1950), the discount house (Doob, Carlsmith, Freedman, Landauer, and Tom, 1969), and the race track (Knox and Inkster, 1968). But many social psychologists are untrained and uncertain when it comes to choosing a concrete version of an abstract question, and they cling to the settings and techniques that have been used before. Courses on research methods

From P. Ellsworth, "From Abstract Ideas to Concrete Instances," *American Psychologist*, 1977, *32*(8), pp. 604–615. Copyright 1977 by the American Psychological Association. Reprinted by permission.

generally do not pay much attention to the problem of finding concrete instances that fit abstract questions, and while the research literature contains many examples of the ingenious use of natural settings, it is difficult to know how to profit from these examples unless they represent the same variables one wants to study. We can admire, but we cannot emulate. The purpose of this article, then, is to provide a few tentative suggestions and rough guidelines for the location of natural instances of conceptual variables.

I should say at the outset that I am not interested in devising ways of finding settings in which hypotheses are likely to be *confirmed*. The aim of research is to arrange or locate a setting in which a hypothesis can be tested, or a question fairly asked. Selecting a setting on the basis of the adequacy of the test of the hypothesis, however, implies that the investigator will believe a disconfirmation. If he[2] won't, it is no kind of test. A theory or a hypothesis is useful only insofar as it is falsifiable (Popper, 1961), and thus the aim of the scientist is to find a context in which the hypothesis can be falsified to his satisfaction. The only time that it is useful to seek a setting in order to confirm a hypothesis is when everyone believes that the hypothesis is wrong or the predicted outcome impossible. In general, the goal of the hypothesis tester is to find a context in which the hypothesis may or may not be confirmed and in which he would believe a disconfirmation. A secondary goal is to pick a context that is informative enough to generate ideas about why the hypothesis was disconfirmed.

CHOICE OF A SETTING BASED ON PROGRESS SO FAR

At the early stages of research, the investigator may not yet have a hypothesis, but simply a general area of interest. Some areas of interest imply definite concrete settings: One may be interested in trials, mental patients, blind people, or policemen. In these cases the selection problem is simple; for the initial exploratory stages the researcher may simply pick the courtroom, hospital, institute for the blind, or police station that is most convenient, first checking around a little to make sure that the convenient instance is not a notoriously peculiar one.

Other general areas of interest are abstract: One may be interested in persuasion, deindividuation, helplessness, or role conflict, again without yet having a specific hypothesis. In this case, there is often a much wider range of settings to choose from. Persuasion, for example, can be studied in courtrooms, in mental hospitals, in institutes for the blind, or in police stations. Before moving into the field, the researcher will already have thrown out certain possible instances of his concepts as irrelevant, and in this process the concepts themselves are refined.

So far, I have been more or less assuming that the investigator is interested in an abstract concept but that he is at the exploratory stages of research in an area. When this is the case, the investigator has maximal freedom in his choice of instances, since when nothing is known the information gain is bound to be great, no matter what the starting point. Virgin territory is rare, however, and additional considerations come into play in the secondary growth of follow-up studies. At this stage, the investigator must ask, How has this topic, or phenomenon, been studied before? Unfortunately, many investigators regard this question as the equivalent of the question: How does one study this topic? and they model their contexts as closely as possible on those of their predecessors. For some purposes this is advantageous, for others (such as direct replication) even necessary, but for other purposes it may be disadvantageous. In any case, the decision should not be an automatic one.

All settings have unfavorable quirks and characteristic sources of error, and often one's aim in asking about previous research is to select an instance that is free of the problems of the earlier instances. In what is perhaps the typical case for the social psychologist, the answer to this question will be "in the laboratory," and the characteristic disadvantages will be demand characteristics (Orne, 1962), evaluation apprehension (Rosenberg, 1969), use of subject populations that restrict the range of variation on the dimensions being studied, and treatments that are weak. Some topics, such as interpersonal distance regulation, may have a history of research in nonlaboratory settings and may need the advantages of the laboratory, such as the opportunity it provides to uncorrelate normally correlated variables. No single instance is a perfect embodiment of a set of abstract concepts, and in choosing a way of operationalizing a research question, the investigator always compromises, sacrificing some methodological advantages for the sake of others.

In choosing a new context in which to ask a question that has been asked before, one aim is to achieve a compromise that is as different as possible from the type of compromise typical of that line of research. Thus, if the techniques used in the past allowed great precision of measurement and careful, parametric specification of the treatment levels at the price of a restricted range of both treatments and subjects (as in the case with most psychological research on attitudes, to cite the usual example), a new instance that is characterized by treatments falling outside the previously studied range and by a heterogeneity of subjects is desirable, even if it means that the assessment of treatments and outcomes is relatively crude.

There are some properties that are desirable in any research setting. In brief, one wants an instance that is capable of disconfirming the hypothesis, that allows for fairly precise specification of both independent and dependent variables, that is free of serious confounds, and that is informative, allowing the investigator to collect supplementary data that will be helpful in understanding the results. These criteria apply to both laboratory and field research, and they are rarely or never completely satisfied in a single instance. In choosing a setting, however, it is often wise to look out from one's own small corner, to consider the whole history of research on the topic, and to try to choose a new instance that will help the field as a whole to approximate the fulfillment of these criteria more closely.

It often—perhaps usually—happens that one is working within a tradition but that the specific question addressed is a new one, without even a single laboratory study devoted to it. In this case, the choice of an instance should still be responsive to the needs of the general research tradition, but it should also, and primarily, be responsive to the question itself. The investigator's first task (in any research) is to understand what it is that he is asking.

THE SUBSTANTIVE QUESTION: VARIABLES

Most hypotheses can be reduced to the basic form, "Whenever X occurs, Y will happen." X may be very simple, as in the hypothesis, "Whenever fear is aroused, behavior change will be facilitated" (Janis and Feshbach, 1953); moderately complex, as in the hypothesis "Whenever fear is aroused *and* the recommended behavior is easy and totally effective, behavior change will be facilitated" (Leventhal, Singer, and Jones, 1965); or highly complex, as in hypotheses involving very specific higher order interactions among many variables (for examples of such hypotheses in the area of fear arousal and behavior change, see Janis, 1967; Leventhal, 1970). In any case, the investigator's problem is to find an instance of X where Y is measurable. The simpler and more general X is, on the whole, the wider the range of settings the investigator has to choose from. As X becomes more clearly defined and more complex, many settings are ruled out. As I pointed out earlier, generating a list of settings may in itself reveal one's hidden assumptions about X.

The choice of setting for the general hypothesis "Whenever X occurs, Y will happen" is determined by X. The investigator does not look for settings in which both X and Y occur, for to do so would be to load the research, making it more like an exercise in "finding," in McGuire's (1973) sense of the term. The aim is to find a setting that provides a good realization of X, and the *possibility* of Y. In considering Y, one simply wants to assume that no extraneous factors are preventing Y from occurring or the investigator from measuring it. Thus, if the hypothesis is that fear of tetanus leads to getting a tetanus shot, there should be some place in the region where tetanus shots are given and where the records of who gets tetanus shots are available to the investigator; if the hypothesis is that fear leads to affiliation, the setting should include other people; if the hypothesis is that fear leads to compliance, the setting should provide a request or command. Otherwise, one concentrates on finding the most nearly perfect X.

Some hypotheses require a natural field setting because they are about that kind of setting; other, more abstract hypotheses may lead to the field because they involve variables not easily translated into laboratory terms. On the independent-variable side, the example most often given is the high-impact variable (Carlsmith, Ellsworth, and Aronson, 1976). If the question or hypothesis concerns powerful or highly arousing events or strong feelings, the psychological laboratory is usually not the most appropriate place to test it. While considerable ingenuity has been devoted to creating laboratory treatments that approximate the impact of analogous real-world events (e.g., Ax, 1953; Milgram, 1973), relatively little has been devoted to choosing settings where nature provides the powerful manipulation. If one is interested in fear, conflict, grief, or love, the laboratory may be one of the least appropriate settings, because the possible and permissible range of these variables is at best restricted to fairly low levels. Other independent variables such as subtle inconsistencies of information, evaluation, apprehension, and distraction may be easy to study in the laboratory. In general, variables for which precise control is more important than impact are particularly suited to the laboratory.

The ethical requirement of weak treatments, with its attendant restriction of range, creates one major limitation on the kinds of questions that can be studied successfully in the laboratory. Time constraints impose a second restriction. In general, laboratory studies are limited to studying the acute or reactive form of variables such as self-esteem, liking, or commitment. Chronic self-esteem, lasting friendship, or long-term commitment may have quite different effects from their reactive counterparts—they may not even involve the same underlying psychological processes; thus laboratory results based on acute manipulations may have very limited generality.

Occasionally, laboratory experimenters make an effort to get around this problem by adding pencil-and-paper tests designed to measure the chronic version of their manipulated variable, as in Aronson and Mettee's (1968) research on self-esteem. While this is some improvement over ignoring the problem altogether, it still usually suffers from the other problem of restriction of range in the homogeneous, college-student sample. If the investigator intends his hypothesis and results to apply to the chronic version of the variable or if he does not distinguish between acute and chronic, the study of an appropriate natural population is desirable and often necessary, at least as a supplement.

Weakness and brevity are perhaps the major restrictions typical of treatments administered in the laboratory. On the dependent-variable side, the problem is one of sweetness and light. Subjects who know that they are being observed by psychologists are motivated to look healthy, normal, tolerant, and intelligent, to turn the other cheek when attempts are made to provoke them to anger, and to judge others as they would be judged (Carlsmith, Ellsworth, and Aronson, 1976; Rosenberg, 1969). Hypotheses that involve socially undesirable behavior may often be better tested outside of the laboratory, ideally in a situation where subjects do not know that they are being observed by a social scientist.[3]

These substantive reasons for choosing a setting are first of all questions of construct validity, and a careful definition of the constructs involved is probably the best guideline to the choice of a setting. The chronic, process version of a variable may resemble the acute, reactive form in name only. An occasion of lowered self-esteem may have nothing to do with a lifetime of low self-esteem. Construct validity may be just as much a problem in cases where the problem is apparently a simple question of restricted range. Semantics aside, there is no a priori reason to assume that the same processes or consequences are characteristic of the "same" variable at different intensities: Mild anger may be qualitatively distinct from rage. For any given variable, of course, the question is an empirical one. Acute anxiety may resemble chronic anxiety in many important ways; faint anxiety may be linearly related to intense anxiety. The problem is that in most cases we haven't a particle of evidence that this is true, and thus to conduct research on the unconsidered assumption that the name of the variable guarantees that it is the thing we are interested in is foolhardy at best.

The second substantive reason for choosing a natural setting is that one ultimately wishes to apply one's results to similar settings; this is the problem of generality. In some ways, the standard philosophy-of-science line treats all hypotheses as universal hypotheses; we start out phrasing a hypothesis in very abstract terms, as though we expected it to be universally true. This leads to a concern for unconfounding variables and testing the abstract hypothesis in the purest way possible: The most nearly perfect X is the one that best fits the abstract conceptualization. For the researcher who only wants to generalize to a limited range of settings, this may not be the best strategy. It may be better for this purpose to sacrifice some of X's purity for the sake of a setting that falls within this range (Cook and Campbell, 1976). Much of the research in the field of psychology and the law, for example, suffers from the problem of these conflicting goals. In a classroom simulation study, the experimenter can prepare materials in which race of the offender, type of crime, past record, income, and amount of bail set are completely independent, as the "scientific study" of their relative contributions seems to require, but such an exercise does not accomplish very much if the experimenter intends to generalize to jury decision making. The noninteractive, large-group setting, the hypothetical nature of the case, and the homogeneous student-subject population make generalization to real juries extremely risky. Of course, if the researcher is interested in how people—any people—combine somewhat colorful information in a cognitive task, the classroom setting may be perfectly appropriate. It is often difficult to have it both ways. Again, it is a matter of choosing a setting that reflects the investigator's concerns: Is the question about abstract conceptual variables, or is it about juries?

There is no reason, incidentally, that a study has to be a laboratory study *or* a field study. Clearly there are a great many research questions that are most clearly illuminated by a series of studies, some of which take place in the laboratory, and others in natural settings. This point is frequently made and needs no further elaboration here. In addition, however, a single experiment may have *both* laboratory and field components. There is no general reason that the treatment and the measures must occur in the same context. The experimenter may take advantage of one of nature's powerful or long-term treatments to select subjects and may then bring these subjects into the laboratory to observe their behavior in a situation that is as controlled and structured as he wishes. Rubin's research on romantic love (e.g., Rubin, 1970) is a good example of this strategy; realizing that he was not likely to be able to create true love, Rubin chose couples who had been together for several months and observed their interaction in the laboratory, where very precise measurements were possible. Similarly, it may be possible to induce a treatment in the laboratory and then send the subjects back out into life, observing their behavior over a longer period of time than is possible in the usual laboratory experiment. This strategy has been followed by Janis (1975), who exposes overweight subjects to his independent variables in the laboratory and then uses weight loss as a long-term behavioral measure of the effects of these variables.

THE FORMAL QUESTION: RELATIONSHIPS

The substantive aspects of the experimenter's question lead him to find instances that seem to typify his conceptual variables. Additional guidelines for the choice of a setting are imposed by the form of the question or hypothesis. The form of the hypothesis defines the plausible rival hypotheses (Campbell and Stanley, 1966) and thus the necessary control groups. In choosing a natural setting, it is important to find a setting which has not only a treatment that fits the construct but also an appropriate control group. The nature of the requisite control groups should be clearly defined and a setting chosen in which these groups exist and in which their behavior can be measured in the same terms as that of the treatment group. Thus, if the hypothesis says that the mere presence of X will lead to Y, it is important to choose a setting that also includes some subjects who get no X at all. The contrast is between some (perhaps undefined) amount of X and a total absence of X. If the hypothesis says that Y increases with X, then a setting that includes a zero-baseline group may be less relevant than a setting that provides a *range* of X great enough to allow for the discrimination of enough levels to test the monotonic hypothesis. If there are plausible rival hypotheses, it is important to try to find a setting in which these hypotheses can also be tested or ruled out. Obviously, no setting can provide complete control or assessment of all alternative explanations, but often some settings are much better in this respect than others. Again, if there is a tradition of research that has been strong on one type of control and weak on another, the investigator may aim for a new setting that is strong on the latter type.

There are many different ways of defining the form of a question, and occasionally the line between form and substance is arbitrary or vague. Basically, I am talking about the abstract properties of the relationship among variables. Statements such as "When X, then Y" or "When more X, then more Y" impose certain formal requirements for adequate experimental design regardless of the particular Xs and Ys involved. A given question may be categorized within a number of different formal frameworks, each of which may have implications for the most appropriate method of seeking an answer. Some of these frameworks are discussed in the following sections.

First, one may consider the scope of the hypothesis or question: It may be universal, existential, general, or particular. A particular hypothesis states that on this occasion, a particular event will happen. The setting is defined by the question, and the main problems involve the measurement of the event. For example, one might predict that "on the day that P's mother dies, P will have a psychotic breakdown." Such hypotheses are rare in psychology, and are confirmed more rarely yet, as we are still far from the ability to specify all the variables operating in the individual case.

An example of a universal hypothesis is the hypothesis that all people recognize certain facial expressions as characteristic of certain emotions (Ekman, Sorenson, and Friesen, 1969). An existential hypothesis simply states that a phenomenon can exist, once, without regard for frequency: There is a philosopher's stone, a female genius, a culture in which a frown is recognized as a sign of delight. This last example points up the intimate relationship between universal and existential hypotheses: The disconfirmation of a universal hypothesis is the confirmation of an existential one. If the hypothesis is that X is universal, its disconfirmation is the demonstration of the existential hypothesis that not-X exists. In choosing a setting in which to prove an existential hypothesis, one searches for a setting in which it is most likely that X will occur, since the single occurrence of X is the proof of the hypothesis. The strategy for testing a universal hypothesis is conceptually the same: One looks for a setting in which not-X is likely to occur. If a single not-X instance can be found, the hypothesis is disconfirmed. (That an existential hypothesis can be confirmed but never disconfirmed, while a universal hypothesis can be disconfirmed but never confirmed, is cogently argued by Popper [1961] and provides a further indication of the misconception of "finding" confirmatory settings [McGuire, 1973], at least for universal hypotheses.) To take a concrete example, in seeking a context in which to test the universal hypothesis that facial expressions are associated with specific emotion labels, Ekman, Sorenson, and Friesen (1969) chose to study a New Guinea highlands tribe that had had minimal contact with Europeans. This was a setting in which not-X was likely to occur: It was very different from all other settings in which the expression-labeling relationship had been demonstrated, and it also ruled out many rival hypotheses that might have accounted for the relationship observed in other settings, but especially that of a shared, arbitrary code acquired via contact with Europeans or their communications media. In practice, choosing a setting that maximizes the probability of not-X may be equivalent to choosing a setting which maximizes the influence of all plausible, nonuniversal causes of X. It is a favorite technique of anthropologists in response to the glib universal statements of psychologists: One culture that lacks the Oedipus complex is sufficient to reduce that hypothesis from a universal one to a merely general one.

In fact, most hypotheses in social science are general, stating that on the whole, X is true. Many such hypotheses may be stated in the abstract *as though* they were universal, but typically the issue of universality is not a primary concern of the researcher; the investigator who has demonstrated that "residential proximity leads to marriage" is likely to greet travelers' tales of exogamous social groups with a tolerant smile, but not to abandon his research. For many researchers, the scope of the phenomenon is not a matter of explicit concern, beyond the rough assumption that it is reasonably general within some vaguely defined universe.

The issue of universality does arise, at least implicitly, when a hypothesis is disconfirmed or a finding fails to be replicated. The fact that most researchers take these events as a sign that something must be modified indicates that universality is at least an unspoken concern. Following a disconfirmation, an investigator can revise the theory (perhaps hoping that the new version will be universally true), can limit the conditions in which the relationship is expected to obtain (hoping that the universality of the hypothesis can be maintained if the universe is restricted), or can discount the failure (hoping that the failure really has no implication for the original statement, which is still universally true). Theoretically then, once the hypothesis is refined and all the conditions are specified, the hypothesis—now greatly qualified—may approximate universality.

But exogamy among the Bozo tribe is still not much of a concern—researchers are often willing to pay lip service to the appropriate limiting condition without much thought. The scope of the phenomenon usually becomes a matter of serious concern only when it is restricted in theoretically interesting ways. Thus, the researcher who predicts that fear leads to affiliation may not be concerned about situations in which affiliation is physically impossible, or by vague reports of the inhabitants of some tropical isle who isolate themselves when afraid, or even by another researcher who fails to replicate this effect in a setting similar to his own; he becomes concerned mainly when the failure to replicate is associated with some conceptual variable claimed to limit the scope of the theory. Then he searches for (or creates) a setting in which it is possible for this usurper variable to vary, so that he can discover whether or not that particular variable imposes a general restriction on the theory. So, for example, if it is claimed that fear will not lead to affiliation if the person is ashamed of his fear, the researcher may study the responses of older and younger children to a frightening situation (predicting that younger children will be less ashamed of their fear and will affiliate more), or males and females (predicting that at any given age, fear is considered less shameful for females, who should therefore affilate more), or people with common versus uncommon phobias (predicting that those with uncommon phobias will feel more deviant and ashamed, and will therefore affiliate less). The choice of settings in which to test the validity of the vaguely general hypotheses characteristic of social scientists is often determined by the plausible rival hypotheses advanced by other social scientists.

Another way of classifying the form of a hypothesis is in terms of the necessity and/or sufficiency of the independent variable. A hypothesis may claim that X is necessary to produce Y, that X is sufficient to produce Y, or both. A necessity hypothesis directs the investigator's attention to settings characterized by the dependent variable Y; since he is predicting that whenever there is Y, X must be present, the disconfirming instance he seeks is one characterized by Y but not X.[4] Looking for settings characterized by X may not fulfill this objective, since X, while necessary for Y, may not be sufficient, and thus the occurrence of X without Y does not disconfirm the hypothesis in the same say that the occurrence of Y without X does. A sufficiency hypothesis directs the investigator's attention to settings characterized by X;[5] there should be no such settings in which Y does not occur (although there may be settings in which Y occurs without X, since other things besides X may also be sufficient to produce Y).

If the hypothesis is that X is both necessary and sufficient to produce Y, then any occurrence of X or Y alone is grounds for rejecting the hypothesis. In testing the hypothesis that X is both necessary and sufficient for the occurrence of Y, one must choose a setting in which it is possible for both X and Y to be either present or absent. The investigator is predicting that of the four possible observable combinations (and they must be possible, or else the test is not a good one)—X and Y, X but no Y, Y but no X, no X and no Y—only the first and last will actually occur. If the investigator hypothesizes that a certain *amount* of X is necessary and sufficient to produce Y—in other words, if he has a threshold hypothesis—any amount less than that threshold can serve as a conceptual zero, and he need not seek a setting that permits a total absence of X.

In general, the researcher who has a presence-absence hypothesis or a well-specified threshold hypothesis looks for a setting in which two clearly differentiated groups can be measured—one of which is above threshold on X and one of which is below (or at absolute zero). In practice, other control groups or measurement occasions will no doubt be necessary to control for plausible rival hypotheses, but in essence the question is a two-group question; often it is embodied in some sort of pretest-posttest design, especially in field settings where nonrandom assignment is common and thus some check on the equivalence of groups is required. Logically, a question involving an X threshold that is not zero takes the same form, but in practice the investigator may not be able to specify the critical level of X in advance and so may seek a situation in which many groups can be tested at different levels of X. In analyzing the data, he will look for a sharp discontinuity in the function and, if brave and confident, may conduct a two-group follow-up study in which he tries to predict the discontinuity precisely.

If, on the other hand, the investigator's hypothesis involves continuous variables, taking the form "the more X, the more Y" or "the more X, the less Y"—in other words, if it is a degree hypothesis—the two-group setting is less appropriate. Instead, the investigator seeks a setting in which a wide range of X is present, so that he can choose Xs at many different levels. The natural setting may be especially useful in this case, as in the case of chronic variables, in that the laboratory is typically ill-suited to produce the heterogeneity of X values necessary for a strong test of a degree hypothesis. If the hypothesized relationship is nonmonotonic, the need for a wide range of X values is even more pressing.

PLAUSIBLE RIVAL HYPOTHESES
AND FORMAL CONTROL

Throughout this article the notion of control has appeared, now implicitly, now explicitly, as a kind of leitmotif. One's choice of controls—whether control groups or control observations on the same group (I intend to cover both by my use of the term *control group*)—is equivalent to one's choice of a falsifiability criterion for the hypothesis. For any kind of hypothesis-testing research, the availability of an appropriate control group or groups should be a major consideration in the choice of a natural setting. It is my hunch that many investigators devote a great deal of effort and creativity to finding a setting or population that provides a good embodiment of the treatment variable and that they then cast about hurriedly at the last minute for some sort of control group. The control group is exactly as important as the treatment group in research, and in fact it is impossible to separate the value of one from the value of the other.

Quasi-experimental designs require particular attention to the achievement of appropriate control groups, since the absence of random assignment raises serious dangers of noncomparability of groups and consequent uninterpretability of results. Many studies could be improved by the use of multiple control groups; the more different kinds of control groups (or control observations), the greater the number of rival hypotheses that can be rendered implausible, and the stronger the case for the causal relationship the experimenter has in mind.

But this utopian ideal has serious economic costs. When faced with the realization that 5 or 8 or 10 different control groups (as well as several versions of the treatment group) may be necessary for the best possible test of the hypothesis, the researcher

may throw up his hands in despair and decide that his creative impulses are better satisfied elsewhere. Given these constraints, the question then becomes, *Which* control
groups are the most important for a good test of my hypothesis? This question may be
addressed by imagining the treatment group behaving just as predicted, and then imagining the plausible rival hypotheses most likely to be raised by others to explain one's
results and to refute one's conclusions. What kind of information would be necessary
to eliminate these alternative explanations? What kind of control observations or control groups would provide that information? The unthinking choice of the most handy
no-treatment baseline group may result in information that is not particularly useful.

Just as in the case of the original hypothesis, the likely alternatives or plausible
rival hypotheses can be examined either substantively or formally. It is impossible to
provide a general listing of alternatives based on the content of the question; these will
be different for every question, and only the investigator can decide which of the substantive alternatives create real threats to his interpretation of the results.

Assessment of formal alternatives is a less difficult matter. There is only a finite
number of general formal relationships that can account for an observed correlation
between X and Y. When we say that correlation between X and Y does not imply causation, we usually mean that the correlation does not imply the particular causal relationship "X causes Y"; most correlations reflect some kind of causal relationship, and
the problem facing the investigator is to distinguish the causal relationship he favors
from the alternatives. Köbben (1970) has provided a succinct and valuable outline of
the possible causal relationships between two variables, and this outline is the basis of
the guidelines that follow.

In essence, what follows is a list of the formally possible rival hypotheses for the
situation in which "X causes Y" is the actual hypothesis. It is meant as a checklist or
set of guidelines that can be applied to a hypothesis as a means of defining the most
important control conditions. For any given hypothesis, some of the suggested rivals
may be completely *implausible*; the investigator will not be able to think of any credible alternative that takes that particular form. In this case, he will typically decide
that no control group is necessary to test that particular set of alternatives. Some
hypotheses, in their initial form, are not specific enough so that all of the alternatives
can be distinguished from the main hypothesis. Sometimes an investigator is mainly
interested in prediction and doesn't care about determining the contributing processes
with any precision. The investigator must decide not only which alternatives are plausible, but which ones matter. My hope is that some of the alternatives listed, when
embodied in a form that makes them pertinent to the investigator's substantive question, may seem important, and it is these that will direct the search for control groups.
Finally, I should point out that one person's "plausible alternative" may be another's
central question. For simplicity's sake, I start with the notion that the hypothesis of
interest is "X causes Y" and that the others are disconcerting rivals, but for a particular investigator, "X causes Y" may be an alternative that he will want to rule out or
examine by using an appropriate control group.

I should point out that the arguments presented below will have to be altered and
elaborated slightly to accommodate different types of causal statement. While I do not
wish to get involved in philosophical discussions of causality, to leave the matter
entirely up to the reader's common sense is to leave the matter ambiguous. When I use
phrases such as "X causes Y"—and I use them rather loosely—I mean, roughly, that X
is sufficient to produce Y, and that in some cases of non-X, non-Y obtains. (For those
who think in these terms, the guidelines may serve as an aid to deciding which kinds of

non-X are relevant.) If the hypothesis is that X is *necessary* for Y, then the central hypothesis is that not-X produces not-Y, and the alternatives must be rephrased accordingly. If the hypothesis is that X is necessary and sufficient for Y, a slightly different but also fairly obvious set of rephrasings is in order.

Finally, the hypotheses are generally discussed in terms of discrete variables or levels, rather than continuous ones, and some adjustments are necessary to handle hypotheses of degree.

Assume that you wish to test, examine, explore, or question the statement "X causes Y." Randomized assignment is impossible; you may or may not have a baseline control group; and for the time being, you are anticipating positive results.[6] You think forward to the moment when you have achieved these results and imagine the captious criticisms of your colleagues. If your foresight has been accurate, you will have collected information relevant to these objections before they are raised. The hypothesis is

$$X \rightarrow Y.$$

The first possible alternative is

$$Y \rightarrow X.$$

In a true experiment, with random assignment, this cannot be a confound, since the experimenter knows what caused X *in that situation*: he did. In quasi-experimental designs this may or may not be a plausible rival hypothesis. Clearly, if Y is an increase in heart rate and X is an earthquake, plausibility is low. In general, we can weaken the plausibility of this kind of confound by choosing settings in which (1) the temporal relations are such that X clearly precedes Y, and/or (2) we already know what causes X (e.g., shifting of the earth's crust) or at least know enough to know that it has nothing to do with Y. In some settings, particularly situations involving simultaneous measurement of chronic attributes, the "Y causes X" alternative may create a greater threat. Does considerate behavior lead to popularity or does popularity lead to considerate behavior? (Of course either of these hypotheses may be the one entertained, and the other the rival; the formal problems of control are the same.) If this kind of rival hypothesis is plausible, you want to find a situation in which either (1) you can introduce or at least define variables controlling X, or (2) you can sort out the temporal ordering. In the specific case, you can create popularity or considerate behavior, or you can find a situation in which either considerate behavior or popularity clearly preceded the other. (The last of these four possibilities taxes the ingenuity and may in fact be impossible.) If the hypothesis is that popularity leads to considerate behavior, one might arrange for a random sample of freshman women to be sought after, deferred to, courted, and included as stars in all important social activities and see if they are especially considerate (compared to their peers and their earlier selves) at the end of a year. If the hypothesis is that considerateness leads to popularity, one might study transfer students or new employees who have not yet had a chance to build up a reputation of popularity in their setting.

Perhaps somewhat more common, especially in natural settings, is the possibility that

$$X \rightleftharpoons Y.$$

This is the vicious (or possibly benign) circle of functional interdependence, perhaps more characteristic of continuous variables than discrete ones. Failure leads to depression and depression leads to failure; popularity leads to charity and charity leads to popularity; money leads to power and power leads to money, and so on. When this hypothesis takes the equivalent form of

$$X \rightleftharpoons \overline{Y},$$

it is the homeostatic hypothesis. In some cases the investigator may not be particularly concerned about this type of rival hypothesis: If all he wants to show is that X results in Y, without caring one way or the other about whether Y also leads to X, he need not bother to control for this alternative. He need only worry about finding a situation in which he can *begin* with an X that was not caused by Y (so as to rule out the possibility that X only enhances Y when Y is present to begin with). This may involve happy people who suddenly fail, considerate people who just moved into town, or poor people who are given power, for example. If, however, the investigator either wants to reject the circular alternative or to demonstrate it, he should find situations that are characterized by non-Y-produced X and situations that are characterized by non-X-produced Y. In addition, he will probably want to follow up these settings over extended periods of time, observing the relative fluctuations in X and Y, or, if the Xs are events in the past, to use some sort of lagged correlational procedure for analysis. Other good settings are settings in which intervention is possible: If at one time one can inhibit or prevent X and observe the effects on Y, and at another time (or in an equivalent setting) one can inhibit Y and observe X, one is in a good position to differentiate the one-way, cause-effect model from the two-way model. In fact, one can differentiate all three possibilities outlined so far, since the controls that work for the functional interdependence hypothesis also work for the $Y \rightarrow X$ alternative.

Next we come to the familiar third-variable correlation:

If a simple correlational study is performed, X and Y are observed to co-occur, but to conclude that $X \rightarrow Y$ would be erroneous. Domineering mothers may produce shy sons, but it is also possible that weak or absent fathers cause mothers to become more assertive and at the same time cause sons to behave in a dependent manner for lack of a strong male model. Finding appropriate settings in which to rule out this type of alternative requires considerable care and imagination because, although the problems of conclusion drawing are formal ones, requiring settings with and without Z and predicting variability in Y accounted for by X to the same extent in each, one cannot do this without first considering the substantive question of which Zs are plausible contenders, given one's particular question. Clearly there are myriad possible Zs for any hypothesis, and given limited time and resources, the difficulty lies in distinguishing the plausible ones. Again, presenting the hypothesis to one's friends and foes as though it had already been confirmed by the data is often a useful way of eliciting large numbers of both plausible and implausible Zs. Having decided upon the plausible ones, one has several options: (1) to choose a control setting in which Z is absent (or at an improbable level), in which case if Z is essential, X and Y should also be low or absent; (2) to choose a setting in which Z is at a constant level, in which case if Z is essential, X and Y should not vary; (3) to choose settings with and without Z (this of course is necessary if one's hypothesis *is* that Z causes both X and Y); (4) to choose a setting in which it is possible to interefere with Z and examine the effects on X and Y; (5) to choose a setting in which Z is absent and X can be introduced; and (6) to choose any old setting where all three could be present and partial out Z statistically. This last option is less satisfactory, as pointed out by Campbell and Stanley (1966) in their discussion of ex post facto designs, since many important Zs are extraordinarily complex, and partialing out a portion may still leave many spurious correlations. The third-variable correlation problem is one that should generally be considered carefully no matter what form of hypothesis one is testing, as it almost always invalidates any other hypothesis.

The fourth possibility is of less universal concern:

$$X \to Z \to Y.$$

That is, X only leads to Y via an intervening variable Z. Many investigators, especially those with practical concerns, may not regard this as a serious problem, and indeed during the early stages of hypothesis formation and research, the hypothesis may not be so sharply delineated that the $X \to Z \to Y$ possibility can even be considered a definite "rival." Instead, the investigator may predict that $X \to Y$ and not yet be concerned with the exact processes by which this occurs. Thus, for many researchers, this hypothesis may be more in the way of a refinement or an explanation than an alternative.

If, however, the investigator wishes to rule out (or demonstrate) the $X \to Z \to Y$ hypothesis, he must seek settings (1) in which X does not produce Z (and predict that Y will or will not still follow); or (2) in which something else besides X—preferably a variety of something elses—produces Z (and then if Y still follows, X is really of very secondary importance); or (3) in which X and Z can be prevented independently. As in the case of third-variable correlations, some ingenuity may be necessary to do justice to the range of possible Zs. Any Zs that are perfectly correlated with X may be of minor concern, merely involving a definitional problem of the boundaries between X and Z. The situation where Z is neither directly manipulable nor directly measurable is not uncommon in theory-testing research and is usually dealt with by showing that a variety of otherwise unrelated $X \to Y$ demonstrations can be predicted by postulating Z, and erased by using Xs that are similar in all respects except that they are unlikely, according to theory, to produce the hypothetical Z.

The next possibility if that X is not enough:

$$\left.\begin{array}{c} X \\ \\ Z \end{array}\right\} \to Y.$$

That is, X *and* Z together lead to Y. With discrete variables or a threshold hypothesis, this is a simple interaction; with continuous variables or a hypothesis of degree, it may also reflect two main effects.

In some ways the practical problems of choosing a setting to control for this alternative are similar to those raised by the problem of third-variable correlation. The interaction possibility is more likely to lead the investigator to falsely conclude that X has nothing to do with Y, if he happens to pick a situation with an uncongenial level of Z. However, the problems of choosing a setting are similar, and many of the same settings that can rule out third-variable correlations can rule out interaction effects as well. Again, the first and most difficult step is to guess at the important Zs. The essence of the formal control is to find or create settings or occasions in which X occurs alone,

Z occurs alone, X and Z occur together, and—for symmetry and to control for the possibility that X and Z aren't even the right variables—settings in which neither X nor Z occurs; the factorial design is the design for testing interactions. If the third-variable hypothesis is the right one, Y should occur when Z occurs even if X is blocked; if the interaction hypothesis is correct, Y should not occur unless both X and Z are present.

All of these alternative hypotheses have been causal hypotheses, under the loose definition of cause given earlier.

X and Y may also vary together without being causally related at all (or at least not at any level less cosmic than the trepidation of the spheres). Historical trends may coexist with no close interrelationships, and produce significant correlation coefficients when data are analyzed longitudinally. Thus, the development and proliferation of communism may be highly correlated with the development and proliferation of the automobile, with no functional relationship between them. Adding a cross-sectional setting to a longitudinal analysis may clarify the issues involved, as will choosing a smaller unit of time or space in which one of the variables changes drastically. If the other shows corresponding changes as more and more of these smaller settings are examined, the hypothesis of independence becomes correspondingly less and less plausible.

Finally, Y may be a logical implication of X, or in fact Y may *be* X by any other name. That is, being a woman doesn't *cause* having ovaries, nor does being a later-born child cause one to have an older sibling. Here again, one tries to think of settings in which the hypothesis might not be confirmed. If one can conceive of none at all, it is probably a good idea to ask whether there really is an empirical hypothesis.

More and more, we are coming to recognize that interrelations may be causal but much more complicated than we can assess with our usual methods (McGuire, 1973). There may be a plethora of Xs, Ys, and Zs locked together in a system in which all the simple types of relationship so far discussed are represented, perhaps represented more than once. It is in just these instances that the typical laboratory experiment is weakest; so much is held constant that there is no opportunity for this sort of complex causation to manifest itself.

Once again, we should point out that one person's hypothesis may be another person's rival. For some questions, the simple $X \to Y$ structure may be an alternative explanation. In any case, one starts with the relationship of interest and then scans the logical rivals to see which are plausible rivals in the particular instance; then one chooses one's setting in such a way as to control for or measure the strongest contenders.

Obviously, the same set of procedures may be followed, with minor modifications, if one's hypothesis takes the form $X \to \overline{Y}$ or $\overline{X} \to Y$.

If one is arguing that X is necessary and sufficient for Y, one is predicting not only that $X \to Y$, but also that $\overline{X} \to \overline{Y}$. In order to make this stronger dual statement, it may be necessary to add $\overline{X}$ control groups across the various rival hypotheses described above.

Still further modifications will be necessary to set up appropriate controls for hypotheses involving multiple independent variables and/or multiple levels of the independent variable, but the logic is the same. Likewise, some adjustments will be necessary if the hypothesis is one of degree and the variables are continuous; here a correlational analysis is an essential addition to the procedure.

In sum, the decision to move to a natural setting is often laudable, but rarely enough. It is but one of a whole series of decisions about the essence of one's question and the logic of its exploration. While finding good test settings in the field raises a somewhat different set of issues than creating good test settings in the laboratory, the essential logic remains unchanged.

NOTES

1. It is clear that this distinction has much in common with the distinction between deductive and inductive science. The validity, value, and very possibility of each of these approaches are admirably disputed elsewhere, and in the present article I express no opinion at all on this controversy.

2. The pronouns *he, his,* and *him* are used throughout this article to refer to both sexes.

3. When I say "ideally" I am speaking solely in methodological terms. Unfortunately, the "best" methods are not always the most ethical ones.

4. Logically, of course, the researcher could also go out and look for situations *without X* (predicting that no *Y* will occur), but this strategy is typically less efficient.

5. Or situations *without Y* (see footnote 4).

6. Ideally, of course, this exercise should be applied to all possible patterns of significant results, not merely to the hypothesized pattern.

REFERENCES

Aronson, E., and Mettee, D. R. "Dishonest Behavior as a Function of Different Levels of Self-esteem." *Journal of Personality and Social Psychology,* 1968, *9,* 121–127.

Ax, A. F. "The Physiological Differentiation Between Fear and Anger in Humans," *Psychosomatic Medicine,* 1953, *15,* 433–442.

Campbell, D. T., and Stanley, J. C. *Experimental and Quasi-experimental Designs for Research.* Chicago: Rand McNally, 1966.

Carlsmith, J. M., Ellsworth, P. C., and Aronson, E. *Research Methods in Social Psychology.* Reading, Mass.: Addison-Wesley, 1976.

Cook, T. D., and Campbell, D. T. "The Design and Conduct of Quasi-experiments and True Experiments in Field Settings." In M. Dunnette (ed.), *Handbook of Industrial and Organizational Research.* Chicago: Rand McNally, 1976.

Doob, A. N., Carlsmith, J. M., Freedman, J. L., Landauer, T. K., and Tom, S., Jr. "Effect of Initial Selling Price on Subsequent Sales," *Journal of Personality and Social Psychology,* 1969, *11,* 345–350.

Ekman, P., Sorenson, E. R., and Friesen, W. V. "Pan-cultural Elements in Social Displays of Emotion," *Science,* 1969, *164,* 86–88.

Festinger, L., Schachter, S., and Back, K. *Social Pressures in Informal Groups.* New York: Harper, 1950.

Janis, I. L. "Effects of Fear Arousal on Attitude Change." In L. Berkowitz (ed.), *Advances in Experimental Social Psychology* (Vol. 3). New York: Academic Press, 1967.

Janis, I. L. "The Effectiveness of Social Support for Stressful Decision." In M. Deutsch and H. Hornstein (eds.), *Applying Social Psychology.* New York: Basic Books, 1975.

Janis, I. L., and Feshbach, S. "Effects of Fear-arousing Communications on Attitude Change," *Journal of Abnormal and Social Psychology,* 1953, *48,* 78–92.

Knox, R. E., and Inkster, J. A. "Post Decision Dissonance at Post Time," *Journal of Personality and Social Psychology,* 1968, *8,* 319–323.

Köbben, A. "Cause and Intention." In R. Naroll and R. Cohen (eds.), *A Handbook of Method in Cultural Anthropology.* Garden City, N.Y.: Natural History Press, 1970.

Leventhal, H. "Findings and Theory in the Fear Communications." In L. Berkowitz (ed.), *Advances in Experimental Social Psychology* (Vol. 5). New York: Academic Press, 1970.

Leventhal, H., Singer, R. P., and Jones, S. "The Effects of Fear and Specificity of Recommendation Upon Attitudes and Behavior," *Journal of Personality and Social Psychology,* 1965, *2,* 20–29.

McGuire, W. J. "The Yin and Yang of Progress in Social Psychology," *Journal of Personality and Social Psychology,* 1973, *26,* 446–456.

Milgram, S. *Obedience to Authority: An Experimental View*. New York: Harper & Row, 1973.

Orne, M. "On the Social Psychology of the Psychological Experiment," *American Psychologist*, 1962, *17*, 776–783.

Popper, K. R. *The Logic of Scientific Discovery*. New York: Science Editions, 1961.

Rosenberg, M. J. "The Conditions and Consequences of Evaluation Apprehension." In R. Rosenthal and R. L. Rosnow (eds.), *Artifact in Behavioral Research*. New York: Acadmic Press, 1969.

Rubin, Z. "Measurement of Romantic Love," *Journal of Personality and Social Psychology*, 1970, *16*, 265–273.

Sidman, M. *Tactics of Scientific Research*. New York: Basic Books, 1960.

Webb, E. J., Campbell, D. T., Schwartz, R. D., and Sechrest, L. *Unobtrusive Measures*. Chicago: Rand McNally, 1966.

6 Four Kinds of Validity

Thomas D. Cook
Donald T. Campbell

In reading back numbers of the major journals devoted to industrial and organizational psychology we have been struck by the relative paucity of field experiments. By "experiment" we understand any experimenter-controlled or naturally occurring event (a "treatment") which intervenes in the lives of respondents and whose probable consequences can be empirically assessed. By "field" we understand any setting which respondents do not perceive to have been set up for the primary purpose of conducting research. Our hope is that this . . . [reading] might contribute to increasing the number of field experiments in future research.

TESTING CAUSAL RELATIONSHIPS

Experiments are vehicles for testing causal hypotheses. It is traditionally assumed that there are three necessary conditions for assuming with any confidence that the relationship between two variables is causal and that the direction of causation is from *A* to *B*. The first relates to temporal antecedence and states that a cause must precede

T. D. Cook and D. T. Campbell, "The Design and Conduct of Quasi-Experiments and True Experiments in Field Settings," from M. D. Dunnette (ed.), *Handbook of Industrial and Organizational Psychology*, pp. 224–246. Copyright © 1976 Rand McNally College Publishing Company. Reprinted by permission.

an effect in time. It is normally simple to meet this condition if the investigator knows when respondents experienced a treatment. In quasi-experiments, the investigator can combine such knowledge with his knowledge of respondents' pretest and posttest performance, and he can associate the introduction of a treatment with some measure of change in the dependent variable. The investigator who conducts a true experiment knows that a proper randomization procedure will ensure, probabilistically, the pretest equivalence of his various experimental groups. Hence, if there are posttest differences related to the treatments, he knows that these probably took place after the treatments were introduced.

A second necessary condition for confidently inferring a causal relationship from A to B is that the treatment or treatments have to covary with the effect, for if the potential cause and effect are not related, the one could not have been a cause of the other. Statistics are used for testing whether there is covariation, and arbitrary criteria have been developed for deciding whether there is or is not "real" covariation in the data (e.g., $p < .05$). Thus, statistics function as gatekeepers. Unfortunately, they are fallible gatekeepers even when they are properly used, and they fail to detect both true and false patterns of covariation. Since statistics lead to such important decisions, it would seem wise to explicate the threats that lead to false conclusions about covariation. These will be called threats to *statistical conclusion validity*.

The third necessary condition for causal inference is that there must be no plausible alternative explanations of B other than A. This condition is the most difficult to meet in two distinct senses. The first, which is particularly a problem with quasi-experiments, concerns the viability of alternative interpretations which imply that an apparent causal relationship from A to B may, in fact, be due to third variables which caused the change in B. For instance, one might introduce a new machine into a factory and note whether it was associated with an increase in productivity. If it were, one might want to attribute the increase to the machine. However, it is always possible that the increase might have nothing to do with the machine itself and might be due to a seasonal increase in productivity that occurs at that time of every year. This is only one example of such third variables, and we shall later present a systematic list of third variables under the heading of threats to *internal validity*.

Threats to internal validity suggest that a hypothesized causal relationship might be spurious. This is different from a second meaning of "alternative interpretation" which assumes that A-as-manipulated and B-as-measured are indeed causally related but which casts doubt on whether the empirical operations represent the A and B constructs which the investigator has tried to designate by his names for A and B. Most of the theoretical controversies in psychology are of this nature—controversies, for example, about whether a relationship between being paid more money and higher productivity should be explained as a consequence of the high payment creating feelings of inequity, or violating expectations, or threatening one's self-concept, or whatever. The issue in such studies is *not* about the internal validity issue of whether the payment manipulation caused a change in the index of productivity. Rather, it is about how the payment should be labeled in theory-relevant and generalizable terms. To give another example, for some persons the interpretative problem in the famous Roethlisberger and Dickson (1939) experiments at the Hawthorne plant is one of labeling what caused the women to increase productivity and is not one of determining whether the treatment increased productivity. Was the causal variable the fact of change irrespective of its nature, or the feedback about one's behavior given by the new changes, or improved work-group cohesiveness, or a new perception of management interest, or whatever?

We shall later discuss threats to *construct validity*, and these should be understood as threats to the correct labeling of the cause and effect operations in abstract terms that come from common linguistic usage or from formal theory. Actually, the problem of construct validity is broader than this and obviously applies to attempts to label any aspect of an experiment including the nature of the setting, the nature of the persons participating, and so forth.

It is worth noting that "internal validity" has been misused in the past to refer both to doubts about whether a causal relationship from A to B can be reasonably inferred and to doubts about how the cause and effect should be labeled. This confusion may arise because alternative interpretations have to be ruled out in establishing both internal and construct validity. However, internal validity involves ruling out alternative interpretations of the presumed causal *relationship* between A-as-manipulated and B-as-measured, and construct validity involves ruling out alternative interpretations of how A and B are referred to in hypothetical terms. Since the very rationale for experiments is to test whether the relationship of two variables is causal, the alternative interpretations that have to be ruled out as a *necessary* condition for inferring cause are alternative interpretations of the relationship (i.e., threats to internal validity) and not alternative interpretations of the cause and effect operations (i.e., threats to construct validity).

The good experiment (1) makes temporal antecedence clear; (2) is sensitive and powerful enough to demonstrate that a potential cause and effect could have covaried; (3) rules out all third variables which might alternatively explain the relationship between the cause and effect; and also (4) eliminates alternative hypotheses about the constructs involved in the relationship. At least one further step is useful. To infer a causal relationship at one moment in time, using one research setting, and with one sample of respondents, would give us little confidence that a demonstrated causal relationship is robust. A concern with the generalizability of findings across times, settings, and persons will be called a concern for *external validity* and we shall shortly list the major threats to this kind of validity.

The preceding discussion should not be taken to imply that, as a means of inferring cause, experiments are unique. A science like astronomy has progressed without experimentation, in part because it has been blessed with reliable observational methods and quantitative theories that have predicted precise locations in space, precise orbits, and precise time intervals for crossing space. The numerical precision of predictions has meant, first, that predictions could be tested with a high degree of accuracy, and second, that different theories making different numerical predictions could be pitted against each other. This is not to say that all the validity problems are answered in astronomy or that the investigator can give up the required task of trenchantly thinking through as many alternative hypotheses as possible, and consciously pitting each of them against the data to see if they can be ruled out. Our point should only be taken to mean that there will typically be fewer validity threats where measurement is as reliable as in astronomy and theories are as precise.

Unfortunately, the social sciences are not yet blessed with such powerfully precise theories, such reliable measurement, or such recurrent cyclical orders in the observational data. Imagine observing a difference in a worker's performance between a pretest which he takes before beginning a special course and a posttest which he takes after completing the course. What are the chances of predicting how much of this difference can be explained in terms of the course itself, spontaneous maturation by the worker, gains in test-taking skill between the pretest and posttest, unique historical events which affected the dependent variable between the pretest and posttest, or any combination of these forces? Moreover, even if we could predict specific numbers to be associated with each of the explanations above, how confident would we be that we could measure the relevant performance reliably enough to discriminate between the theories? The answer to this would depend, of course, on the size of the predicted differences in gain and on the particular kind of performance test. We believe, however, that there are few non-experimental settings in the social sciences where precise predictions can be successfully used to test competing hypotheses about cause.

Though the preceding discussion implies that experiments are better than non-experiments for testing causal propositions, it should not be taken to imply that experiments are infallible means of testing all the questions associated with causal hypothesis-testing. The following list of threats to internal, statistical conclusion, external, and construct validity, and the discussion of the interrelationship of these kinds of validity should make patently obvious the fallibility of experimentation. Improvements in design need to be made, can be made, and should be made in order to facilitate better causal inferences. But we would delude ourselves if we believed that a single experiment, or even a research program of several years' duration, would definitely answer the major questions associated with confidently inferring a causal relationship, naming its parts, and specifying its generalizability.

INTERNAL VALIDITY

The threats to internal validity are:

History. "History" is a threat when an observed effect might be due to some event which took place between the pretest and posttest and when this event is not the treatment of research interest.

Maturation. This is a threat when an observed effect might be due to the respondent's growing older, wiser, stronger, etc. between pretest and posttest and when this maturation is not the treatment of research interest.

Testing. This is a threat when an effect might be due to effects associated with taking a test different numbers of times.

Instrumentation. This is a threat when an effect might be due to a change in the measuring instrument between pretest and posttest and is not due to the treatment's differential impact at each time interval.

Statistical Regression. This is a threat when an effect might be due to respondents being classified into experimental groups at, say, the pretest on the basis of pretest scores or correlates of pretest scores. When this happens, and measures are unreliable, high pretest scorers will score relatively lower at the posttest and low pretest scorers will score higher at the posttest. It would be wrong to attribute such differential "change" to a treatment. It is due to statistical regression.

Selection. This is a threat when an effect may be due to the difference between the kinds of persons in experimental groups rather than to the different treatments each group has received.

Mortality. This is a threat when an effect may be due to the different kinds of persons who dropped out of particular treatment groups during the course of an experiment. This results in a selection artifact, since the experimental groups are composed of different kinds of persons at the posttest.

Interactions with Selection. Many of the foregoing threats to internal validity can interact with selection to produce forces that might spuriously appear as treatment effects. Perhaps the most common such force is the *selection-maturation* interaction which results when experimental groups are composed of different kinds of persons who are maturing at different speeds. Such group differences in growth rates typically occur, for example, when middle-class and lower-class children are compared at two different time intervals on some test of cognitive knowledge.

Ambiguity About the Direction of Causal Influence. It is possible to imagine a situation in which all plausible third variable explanations of an *A-B* relationship have been ruled out and where it is not clear whether *A* causes *B* or *B* causes *A*. This is an especially salient threat to internal validity in simple correlational studies where it will often not be clear whether, for example, less foreman supervision causes higher productivity or whether higher productivity causes less supervision. This particular threat is not salient in most experiments since the order of temporal precedence is clear. Nor is it a problem in those correlational studies where one direction of causal influence is relatively implausible (e.g., it is more plausible to infer that a decrease in the environmental temperature causes an increase in fuel consumption than it is to infer that an increase in fuel consumption causes a decrease in outside temperature). But it is a problem in all other correlational studies.

The use of randomized experiments provides an appropriate safeguard against all the foregoing threats to internal validity. But the five following threats may jeopardize the validity of randomized experiments as well as quasi-experiments. They represent additions to the list of threats provided by Campbell and Stanley (1963, 1966). The first three of them have the effect of equalizing the experimental and control groups, while the last two may create a spurious difference.

Diffusion or Imitation of the Treatment. If the treatments involve widely diffused information programs or if the experimental and control groups can communicate with each other, the controls may learn the information and, thereby, receive the treatment. The experiment thus becomes invalid because there is no functional difference between the treatment and the control groups in the treatments that they have experienced. In many quasi-experiments it is desirable to have units that are as similar as possible in all aspects except for the treatment. One way of doing this is to sample physically adjacent units. But this very propinquity can lead to the treatment being experienced by all the units. For example, if one of the New England states were used as a control group to study the effects of changes in the New York abortion law, any true effects of the new law would be obscured if New Englanders went freely to New York for abortions.

Compensatory Equalization of Treatment. When the experimental treatment provides goods generally believed to be desirable, there may emerge administrative and constituency reluctance to tolerate the focused inequality that results. Thus in nationwide educational experiments, such as Follow Through, the control schools, particularly if equally needy, tended to be given Title I funds in amounts equivalent to those coming to the experimental schools. Several other experimental evaluations of compensatory education have met the same problem. It exemplifies a problem of administrative equity that must certainly occur among units of an industrial organization, and it explains some administrators' reluctance to employ random assignment to treatments which their constituencies consider valuable.

Compensatory Rivalry. Where the assignment of persons or organizational units to experimental and control conditions is made public (as it usually must be in experiments in industrial and organizational psychology), conditions of social competition are generated. The control group, as the natural underdog, is motivated to a rivalrous effort to reduce or reverse the expected difference. This result is particularly likely where intact units (such as departments, plants, work crews, etc.) are assigned to treatments, or if members of the control group stand to lose if a treatment were successful. For instance, Saretsky (1972) has pointed out that performance contracting would threaten the job security of schoolteachers and has reviewed evidence suggesting that the academic performance of children taught by teachers in the control groups of the OEO Performance Contracting Experiment was better during the experiment than it had been in past years. The net effect of atypically high learning gains by controls would be to diminish the difference in learning between control students taught by their regular teachers and experimental children taught by outside contractors who were paid according to the gains made by children. Saretsky describes this special effort by the controls as a "John Henry effect" in honor of the John Henry who, when he knew his work as a railroad steel driver was to be compared with that of a steam drill, worked so hard that he outperformed the drill but then died of overexertion. Compensatory rivalry is in many ways like compensatory equalization. However, the latter results from administrators anticipating problems from the groups that receive less desirable treatments, while the former results from the way that members of these groups react to their treatments or non-treatments.

Resentful Demoralization of Respondents Receiving Less Desirable Treatments. When an experiment is obtrusive, the reaction of a no-treatment control group can be associated with resentment and demoralization, as well as with compensatory rivalry. This is because controls are often relatively deprived when compared to experimentals. In an industrial setting the controls might retaliate by lowering productivity and company profits. This situation is likely to lead to a posttest difference between treatment and no-treatment groups and it might be quite wrong to attribute the difference to the treatment. It would be more apt to label the no-treatment as the "resentment" treatment. (Of course, this phenomenon is not restricted to control groups. It can occur whenever treatments differ in desirability and respondents are aware of the difference.)

Local History. Random assignment to treatments controls for the contemporaneous irrelevant sources of change that are listed under "history." But this only holds under two conditions: first, that these irrelevant events are shared by experimentals and controls alike, and second, that these events do not occur in individual data-collection sessions which are unique to experimentals or controls. Where one collects data by groups, for example, randomly assigning all experimental persons to one group session will mean that any idiosyncratic events that took place in the session are confounded with the experimental treatment and may be responsible for effects. The cure for this, where feasible, is to administer the treatment to individuals or to many small groups, randomizing experimental and control sessions as to special location and time. In this latter procedure, the appropriate degrees of freedom are based on the number of groups, not persons. The likelihood of a local history explanation is often higher in quasi-experiments than in true experiments because in the former case the treatments are likely to be confounded with differences in the universe of respondents. Thus, the different treatments will be associated with all the unique historical experiences that each group has. Local history is equivalent to the interaction of selection and history in that the same events happen in different settings at different times, or in that some events happen in one kind of setting but not in others.

Estimating the internal validity of a relationship is a deductive process in which the investigator has to be his own most trenchant critic and has to systematically think through how each of the above factors may have influenced his data. Then, he has to examine the data to test which relevant threats can be ruled out. When all of them can be, it will be possible to make confident conclusions about whether a relationship is causal. When all of them cannot, perhaps because the appropriate data are not available or because the data indicate that a particular threat may indeed have operated, then the investigator has to conclude that a demonstrated relationship between two variables may or may not be causal. Sometimes, he will have to *act as if* the relationship were causal because practical decisions have to be made and it is possible that the relationship might be causal. At other times, the alternative interpretations may seem implausible enough to be ignored and the investigator will be inclined to dismiss them. He can dismiss them with a great deal of confidence when the alternative interpretation seems unlikely on the basis of findings from a research tradition with a large number of relevant and replicated findings. Often, however, it will be difficult to obtain higher inter-judge agreement about the plausibility of a particular alternative interpretation. Moreover, theory-testers place great emphasis on testing theoretical predictions that seem so implausible that neither common sense nor other theories would make the same prediction. There is in this an implied confession that the "implausible" is sometimes true and that "implausible" alternative interpretations should reduce but not eliminate our doubt about whether a relationship is causal.

The major difference between true experiments and quasi-experiments has to do with internal validity. When respondents are randomly assigned to treatment groups, each group is similarly constituted (no selection, maturation, or selection-maturation problems); each experiences the same testing conditions and research instruments (no testing or instrumentation problems); there is no deliberate selection of high and low scorers on any tests except under conditions where respondents are first matched according to, say, pretest scores and are then randomly assigned to treatment conditions (no statistical regression problem); each group experiences the same global pattern of history (no history problem); and if there are treatment-related differences in who drops out of the experiment, this is interpretable as a consequence of the treatment and is not due to selection. Thus, randomization takes care of most, but not all, the threats to internal validity.

With quasi-experimental groups, the situation is quite different. Instead of relying on randomization to rule out most internal validity threats, the investigator has to make them all explicit and then rule them out one by one. His task is, therefore, more laborious. It is also less enviable since his final causal inference will not be as strong as if he had conducted a true experiment.

STATISTICAL CONCLUSION VALIDITY

Experiments are conducted to make decisions. The investigator wants to decide whether his treatment has had some effect, has had no effect, or whether a decision cannot be made on the basis of the information on hand. Sometimes, effects are specified as points (e.g., the treatment is effective if productivity increases by 10 percent or if absenteeism is less than 2 percent of all working days per employee), and such point specifications reflect a concern with the magnitude of an effect as opposed to its mere existence.

Typically, however, we are interested in the mere existence of effects, which we infer from statistically significant differences either between specific statistics in a treatment group or between specific statistics in a treatment group relative to other treatment groups or to a no-treatment control group. We shall deal in this chapter with the threats that preclude valid conclusions about the existence of treatment effects, and this should not be taken to imply that we consider it unimportant to estimate the magnitude of effects. Rather, we consider this important once an effect can be reasonably inferred.

Arbitrary statistical traditions have developed for drawing conclusions about covariation from sample data. The most widely known of these is probably the cutting point $\rho < .05$. Relationships below the 5 percent level are treated as though they were "true" while those above it are treated as though they were "false." However, we can be wrong in concluding that the population means of various treatment groups truly differ even when the probability level is less than .05 and we can be wrong in concluding that they do not differ when the probability level is above that level. Drawing false positive or false negative conclusions about causal hypotheses is the essence of internal validity, and this was a major justification for Campbell (1969) adding "instability" to his list of threats to internal validity. "Instability" was defined as "unreliability of measures, fluctuations in sampling persons or components, autonomous instability of repeated or equivalent measures," and these are obviously threats to drawing correct conclusions about a treatment's effect. What precipitated the need for this addition was the viewpoint of some sociologists who had argued against using tests of significance unless the comparison followed random assignment to treatments (see Winch and Campbell, 1969, for further details).

The status of statistical conclusion validity as a special case of internal validity can be further illustrated by considering the distinction between bias and error. Bias refers to factors which systematically affect the value of means; error refers to factors which increase variability and decrease the chance of obtaining statistically significant effects. If we erroneously conclude from a quasi-experiment that A causes B, this might either be because threats to internal validity bias the relevant means or because, for a specifiable percentage of possible comparisons, differences as large as those found in a study would be obtained by chance. If we erroneously conclude that A does not affect B (or cannot be demonstrated to affect B), this can either be because threats to internal validity bias means and obscure true differences or because the uncontrolled variability obscures true differences. Statistical conclusion validity is concerned, not with sources of systematic bias, but with sources of error variance and with the appropriate use of statistics and statistical tests.

Before proceeding to a taxonomy of threats to statistical conclusion validity, we should perhaps briefly mention four points. This first concerns the logical impossibility, but practical necessity, of concluding that a treatment has had no measured effects. It is a standard statement in the literature on experimental design that the null hypothesis cannot be proven. This is because there is always the possibility, however remote, that statistics have failed to detect a true difference, and because we cannot know what would have resulted in an experiment if the treatment had been more powerful, or sources of random error had been controlled, or suppressor variables had been measured, or an analysis with greater statistical power had been used. However, in many practical situations failure to reject the null hypothesis can be taken as sufficient for believing that the treatment-as-implemented makes so small a difference that it would not be worth worrying about even if it had made a statistically significant difference.

Notwithstanding· this, there are other more theory-relevant situations where we can consider accepting the null hypothesis only if the experimental design was demonstrably sensitive enough in the ways described below that it maximized the chances of obtaining a true difference, and only if we can also be assured that all the theory-derived conditions that facilitate a particular effect were present in the experimental design that resulted in no differences.

The second point concerns the problem that one can falsely conclude that there is covariation just as one can falsely conclude that there is no covariation. Our discussion has thus far focused on the latter problem since field settings do not permit as much control over error variance as the laboratory, and so true differences are more likely to be obscured in the field. However, elementary statistics textbooks teach us that the control possibilities of the laboratory are of no help in avoiding Type I errors, concluding that there is covariation when there is not.

Third, a special problem of statistical conclusion validity arises in designs where there are two (or more) experimental groups and when there are pretest-posttest differences within each group, but there are no differences between these differences. At first glance, it would seem that there is and is not statistical covariation at the same time. However, the within-group comparisons test whether any change at all has taken place but fail to specify the locus of such change—it might be due to the treatment or to testing or to maturation or to history. The between-group comparison tests whether there is any more change in one experimental group than another. This specifies the locus of cause more adequately (since randomization rules out the possibility of maturation, etc.), but risks the underestimation of treatment effects if different treatments have an impact of comparable magnitude or if performance in the control group is raised by a John Henry effect (Saretsky, 1972). The within-group and between-group comparisons are thus tests of different things, and it is only an apparent contradiction if one of them indicates an effect but the other does not. Unfortunately, though, neither of them inevitably measures a treatment's effects alone: the one measures the effects of a treatment plus other factors, while the other measures only those treatment effects that are over and above what is found in other treatment or control groups. For purposes of making confident conclusions about cause, the between-group comparisons are obviously much stronger than the within-group comparisons.

Finally, much of this . . . [reading] deals with quasi-experiments but none of it deals in detail with how to conduct inferential statistical tests of the null hypothesis. Sometimes, we give references to sources in which appropriate tests can be found, and at other times we give references to the best approximate tests that, to our knowledge, are available. But it is a sad fact that research on the statistical evaluation of quasi-experiments has not reached the stage of definitiveness that currently characterizes the state of the statistical art for randomized experiments. In particular, no adequate statistical tests yet exist for the most frequently used quasi-experimental design in which non-equivalent groups, whose pretest performance levels vary, receive different treatments. Even with time-series analyses (in which observations are made at multiple times before and after a treatment), there is no definitiveness yet despite much vigorous and enlightened research that we shall mention later which promises well for the not-so-distant- future.

However, it should not be forgotten that inferential statistics are useful for testing only one of many threats to valid inference—that of chance. If they loom larger than this in the minds of many research workers, we suspect that this is because the researchers received their statistical training in such a way that they concentrated on true experiments in which randomization takes care of most other threats to validity. It may also be because we learn to value criteria that reduce uncertainty, and statistical tests do this because they determine the "eyeball" differences that do and do not require interpretation. In any event, we shall provide references about appropriate and approximate statistical tests, but shall not examine the tests in any detail.

Here, now, is our taxonomy of threats to statistical conclusion validity.

Statistical Power. The likelihood of making an incorrect no-difference conclusion (Type II error) increases when sample sizes are small, α is set low, one-sided hypotheses are incorrectly chosen and tested and most kinds of distribution-free statistics are used for hypothesis-testing. The likelihood of making incorrect difference conclusions (Type I error) increases if α is set high.

Fishing and the Error Rate Problem. Type I errors will result when multiple comparisons of mean differences are possible and no cognizance is taken of the fact that a certain proportion of the comparisons will be different by chance. Ryan (1959) has distinguished between the error rate per comparison ("the probability that any one of the comparisons will be incorrectly considered to be significant"), the error rate per experiment ("the expected number of errors per experiment"), and the error rate experiment-wise ("the probability that one or more erroneous conclusions will be drawn in a particular experiment"). The last two are the most important, and Ryan has illustrated one method of adjusting for the error rate per experiment. This involves computing a new t value which has to be reached before significance at a given α level can be claimed. The new t is obtained by taking the desired α (e.g., .05) and dividing it by the number of possible comparisons so as to give a proportion (p) that will be lower than .05. Then, the t value corresponding to this adjusted p is looked up in the appropriate tables, and it will, of course, be higher than the t values normally associated with $\alpha = .05$. This higher value reflects the stringency required for obtaining a true level of statistical significance when multiple tests are made. A second method for dealing with the error rate problem involves using the conservative multiple comparison tests of Tukey or Scheffé which are discussed in most moderately advanced statistics texts. And when there are multiple dependent variables in a factorial experiment, a multivariate analysis of variance strategy can be used for determining whether any of the significant univariate F tests within a particular main or interaction effect are due to chance rather than to the manipulations.

The Reliability of Measures. Measures of low reliability (conceptualized either as "stability" or "test-retest") cannot be depended upon to register true changes because they will inflate error terms. Some ways of controlling for this, *where possible*, are to use longer tests for which items have been carefully selected for their high intercorrelation, and to decrease the interval between tests and retests. Or, large units of analysis can be used (e.g., groups instead of individuals), though the reliability gain will be partly offset by fewer degrees of freedom. Or, standard corrections for unreliability can be used.

The Reliability of Treatment Implementation. The way a treatment is implemented may differ from one person to another if different persons are responsible for implementing the treatment. There may also be differences from occasion to occasion when the same person implements the treatment. This lack of standardization within and between persons will inflate error variance and decrease the chance of obtaining true differences. The threat can be most obviously controlled by making the treatment and its implementation as standard as possible across occasions of implementation.

Random Irrelevancies in the Experimental Setting. Some features of an experimental setting other than the treatment will undoubtedly affect scores on the dependent variable and will inflate error variance. This threat can be most obviously controlled by choosing settings free of extraneous sources of variation, or by choosing experimental procedures which force respondents' attention on the treatment and lower the saliency of environmental variables, or by measuring sources of extraneous setting variance that are common to the various treatment groups and using them in the statistical analysis.

Random Heterogeneity of Respondents. The respondents in an experiment can differ with respect to the major dependent variables. Sometimes, certain kinds of respondents will be more affected by a treatment than others, and this—as we shall soon see—is a matter of external validity. But irrespective of whether this happens, the error term for testing treatment effects, including interactions, will be inflated the more respondents are heterogeneous with respect to variables that affect the dependent variable. This threat can obviously be controlled by selecting homogeneous respondent populations (at some cost in external validity), or by blocking on these respondent characteristics, or by choosing within-subject error terms as in pretest-posttest designs. The extent to which within-subject error terms reduce the error terms depends on the correlation between each subject's scores: the higher the correlation, the greater the reduction in the error term.

EXTERNAL VALIDITY

Some of the concerns that Campbell and Stanley mentioned under external validity are here treated under the separate heading of construct validity. Those aspects that focus on generalizing to, or across, times, settings, and persons are retained under external validity, while those that have to do with interpreting operationalized treatments and measures in generalized terms (i.e., as abstract concepts) are grouped under construct validity. In the last analysis, as Bracht and Glass (1968) pointed out, external validity has to do with the correspondence between available samples, the populations they represent, and the populations to which generalization is required.

We have chosen to include under construct validity issues having to do with generalization to, or across, effect constructs. This is because in much research we want to know whether we can generalize from, say, a relationship between a new educational program and learning the alphabet to a relationship between the program and reading; or we might want to know whether a guaranteed annual income affects family stability as well as motivation to remain in the work force. The issue of whether the construct A causally affects the constructs $B, C, D,$ and E involves an attempt to specify how far the effects of A can be generalized, and as such it seems both conceptually related to external validity and conceptually distinct from the construct validity question of whether A affects multiple measures of B alone. However, the distinction becomes clouded since it is not unknown to discover empirically that the various planned measures of B are differently related to A, though it was originally thought that they would be similarly related. Such an unexpected data pattern suggests that more than one outcome construct was involved in the research. Moreover, another way of extending construct validity requires multiple outcome constructs, some of which should be affected by a treatment if the outcome is B and others of which should not be affected if the outcome is not C. For instance, a theory might predict an increase in the quantity of task performance but not its quality; or a theory of specific belief change might predict a change in belief measures but no change in overt behavioral measures that would at first sight seem related to the beliefs. The difficulty of classifying multiple outcome constructs under traditional validity headings might have prompted Snow (1974) to list it separately under "referent generality." But in the last analysis it is more important to note the multiple outcome issue and to know how to deal with it than it is to be able to classify it neatly under one of our validity labels.

Interaction of Treatments and Treatments. This threat occurs if respondents experience more than one treatment. We do not know in such an instance whether we could generalize any findings to the situation where respondents received only a single treatment. The solution to this problem is either to give only one treatment to respondents, or, wherever possible, to conduct separate analyses of the treatments which respondents received first and those which they received later.

Interaction of Testing and Treatment. To which kind of testing situations can a cause-effect relationship be generalized? In particular, can it be generalized beyond the testing conditions that were originally used to probe the hypothesized cause-effect relationship? This is an especially important question when the pretesting of respondents is involved and might condition the reception of the experimental stimulus. We would want to know whether the same result would have been obtained without a pretest, and a posttest-only control group is necessary for this. Similarly, if repeated posttest measurements are made, we would want to know whether the same results would be obtained if respondents were posttested once rather than at each delay interval. The recommended solution to this problem is to have independent experimental groups at each delayed test session.

Interaction of Selection and Treatment. To which categories of persons can a cause-effect relationship be generalized? Can it be generalized beyond the groups used to establish the initial relationship—to various racial, social, geographical, age, sex, or personality groups? In particular, whenever the conditions of recruiting respondents are systematically selective, we are apt to have findings that are only applicable to volunteers, exhibitionists, hypochondriacs, scientific do-gooders, those with nothing else to do with their time, etc. One feasible way of reducing this bias is to make cooperation in the experiment as convenient as possible. For example, volunteers in a TV studio audience experiment, who have to come downtown to participate, are much more likely to be atypical than are volunteers in an experiment carried door-to-door. Or, an experiment involving executives is more likely to be ungeneralizable if it takes a day's time than if it takes only ten minutes, for only the latter experiment is likely to include busy persons who have little free time.

Interaction of Setting and Treatment. Can a causal relationship obtained in a factory be obtained in a bureaucracy, in a military camp, on a university campus? The solution here is to vary settings and to analyze for a causal relationship within each. This threat is of particular relevance to organizational psychology since its settings are at such disparate levels as the organization, the small group, and the individual. When can we generalize from any one of these units to the other? The threat is also relevant because of the volunteer bias as to which organizations cooperate. The refusal rate in getting the cooperation of industrial organizations, school systems, etc. must be nearer 75 percent than 25 percent, especially if we include those that were never contacted because it was considered certain they would refuse. The volunteering organizations will often be the most progressive, proud, and institutionally exhibitionist. For example, Campbell

(1956), although working with Office of Naval Research funds, could not get access to destroyer crews and had to settle for high-morale submarine crews. Can we extrapolate from such situations to those where morale, exhibitionism, pride, or self-improvement needs are lower?

Interaction of History and Treatment. To which periods in the past and future can a particular causal relationship be generalized? Sometimes, an experiment takes place on a very special day (e.g., when a president dies), and the researcher is left wondering whether he would have obtained the same cause-effect relationship under more mundane circumstances. But even when circumstances are relatively more mundane, we still cannot logically extrapolate findings from the present to the future. Yet, while logic can never be satisfied "common-sense" solutions for short-term historical effects lie either in replicating the experiment at different times (for other advantages of consecutive replication see Cook, 1974a), or in conducting a literature review to see if there is prior evidence which does not refute the causal relationship.

Generalizing Across Effect Constructs. One very often hears the comment: "I wonder what would have happened if we had measured such and such a variable? Would the treatment have affected it, I wonder?" This issue is perhaps most critical when considering the unanticipated negative side effects that a treatment might have. For instance, does this new popular television program for children both teach *and* decrease reading? Does the new technological innovation increase productivity *but* decrease job satisfaction and so threaten turnover in the long run? Does a guaranteed annual income in an experiment lead to reduced labor force participation *and* patterns of conspicuous consumption by the poor that make it difficult for politicians to vote for such an income because they think that their constituencies will think it wasteful? The issue is not restricted to such negative side effects, however. Someone studying how a persuasion campaign affects beliefs might also wonder how it affects overt behaviors, while someone studying how an open floor arrangement affects communication patterns in a bureaucracy might also wonder how it differentially affects the promotion prospects of the gregarious and the shy. Of course, there is no end to the list of variables that a treatment might influence. The problem is to anticipate in advance as many secondary effects as are useful for theory building (by helping to elucidate the range of variables that are and are not affected by a treatment) or are useful for policy-guidance. In this respect, it is useful for experimenters to share their research question with a heterogeneous sample of persons before beginning the actual experiment. The more different the implications of the research from person to person or from interest group to interest group, the more useful will be the net of dependent variables that is collected (Cook, 1974b; Rossi, Boeckmann, and Berk, 1974).

Assessing external validity, unlike internal validity, is an inductive process. We cannot extrapolate with any logical certainty from the persons, settings, and times of a study to *all* persons, settings, and times, or even to specified limited future settings, persons, and times.

However, this is not to say that we have no techniques for increasing external validity. One infrequently used way involves *random sampling* from designated universes in order to obtain representative samples, a procedure that takes advantage of the outstanding achievement of survey research. But in quasi-experiments one has different populations of respondents in the various treatment conditions, none of which are randomly representative of any specifiable population other than themselves. Even with true experiments, randomization for assuring experimental-control group equivalence is usually much easier than randomization for achieving the representativeness of each sample from some universe of interest. This is because the persons or organizations that agree to be randomly assigned to experimental conditions, or that for political reasons can be so assigned, are typically a biased sample of all the persons or organizations in a particular universe of interest. Unfortunately, universes of convenience are much more likely than universes of interest.

A more practical model of external validity involves the deliberate creation within the research design of *heterogeneous groups* of persons, settings, and times. It would thereby be possible to estimate whether a particular cause-effect relationship holds over a wide range of the units in question, although one would not know whether the units were representative of anything in particular. One would merely attempt to test the range of variables across which a causal relationship could be inferred. Thus, generalizing *across* would replace generalizing *to*; and "quasi-representativeness" would replace the more "formal representativeness" of the random sampling model.

Another practical model requires *generalization to modal instances*. This occurs whenever groups of respondents, work settings, and conditions of testing can be specified that are modal for a given problem area. Imagine, for example, someone who wanted to develop a theory of piecework. External validity would be low if this person studied piecework on a sample of psychotherapists who were paid according to the quality of their therapy—with quality being perhaps assessed by supervisors from therapists' notes. We actually know of such a work setting, and it is obviously very different from the industrial settings where most piecework in the United States presumably goes on. That is, the kinds of persons who take on factory work are very different from those who become therapists; the quantity of output is more easily and objectively assessed in industrial settings than in therapy; and continuous feedback about his performance is typically accessible to the industrial worker in a way that it is not to the therapist. A theory of piecework which has been tested in the settings where most piecework takes place will apply to more persons and settings than a theory which has been tested on the few psychotherapists in the nation who are paid on a piecework basis.

A final model is really a special case of the preceding and it involves impressionistically *generalizing to target instances* even if these are not modal in the sense discussed above. For example, there may be investigators interested in psychotherapists who are paid on a piecework basis, and they may have no aspirations beyond generalizing to such a small and particular body of persons. Much consulting work has this narrower focus and the major concern has to be to make sure that the research respondents, settings, and testings are comparable (on an impressionistic basis at least) to the target respondents, settings, and testings. (Of course, generalization to target instances would be more accurate with randomly drawn samples of instances than with purposive samples. But it is often not practical to draw random samples of persons from meaningful universes, and it is difficult in most situations to conceive of populations of settings and times.)

The relative feasibility of these four models of external validity can be gained by examining the piecework example in more detail. The random sampling model would require developing a list of the universe of pieceworkers. While this would be possible within a firm or agency, it would be very difficult to accomplish across all the pieceworkers in the United States or beyond. Hence, while client-focused research may sometimes permit use of the random sample model, theory-focused research will not because there is no reason why theories should be limited to certain firms or agencies.

The heterogeneity model requires that the investigator think through the range of settings, times, tests, and persons across which piecework is practiced. Then, he has to sample as diverse units as possible. The difficulties here, of course, are that it is expensive to track down heterogeneous samples (especially when geography is one element of heterogeneity), and that it is difficult to gain access to multiple settings. The specific target model is easy to follow in client-focused work, where generalization to local instances is required. But if the investigator wants to explore how widespread a theory-relevant relationship is, then the model requires him to explicate the impressionistically modal instances—the kinds of persons most likely to be on piecework, the settings where this most typically occurs, the ways output or satisfaction are most typically measured, etc. Then, he has to find one or several research sites where the local conditions correspond with his analysis of the most typical conditions. Major difficulties here involve knowing what is typical and knowing where the typical can be found without laborious pilot-testing. Mostly, there will have to be a reliance on what experience says is typical.

The random sampling model is the most powerful for inferential purposes, and the heterogeneity and the modal target models are probably the next most powerful in that order. However, feasibility seems to us to be negatively correlated with inferential power, and it is this—together with the basically inductive nature of external validity—that makes external validity the Achilles heel of the behavioral sciences. These are not the only reasons. In any single experiment there are many subgroups of persons, settings, times, and effect constructs across which we could potentially generalize, but typically few of them can be examined. For instance, if we restrict ourselves just to generalizing across persons, they can differ by sex, age, SES, place of residence, intelligence, extroversion, anxiety, and so on. Even if we could sample to include considerable heterogeneity on all these dimensions—which we mostly cannot—it would still be difficult to take account of all of them in the data analysis so as to specify in which particular subgroups a causal relationship can be inferred. While this will be possible for some groups, it will not be possible for all of them, and for the person variables that cannot be separately examined the most that we could do would be to test whether a relationship holds *despite* such person-related sources of heterogeneity. That is, we would relegate the heterogeneity to the error-term instead of examining each of its sources as a factor in the experimental design. This difficulty is compounded, of course, once one realizes that settings may be as multidimensional as persons.

The difficulties associated with external validity should not blind experimenters to the very real steps they can make toward increasing generalizability. For instance, one can often deliberately choose to perform an experiment at three or more sites in each of which different kinds of persons live or work. Or, if one can randomly sample, it is useful to do this even if the population involved is not meaningful, for random sampling insures heterogeneity. Thus, in their experiment on the relationship between beliefs and behavior about open housing, Brannon et al. (1973) chose a random sample of all white households in the metropolitan Detroit area. While few of us are interested in generalizing to such a population, the sample was nonetheless considerably more heterogeneous than that used in most research, even despite the homogeneity on the attributes of race and geographical residence. It is especially worth remembering that our four methods of increasing external validity can be used in combination in the experiment, as has been achieved in some survey research experiments on improving survey research procedures (Schuman and Duncan, 1974). Usually, random samples of respondents are chosen in such experiments, but the interviewers are not randomly chosen—they are merely impressionistically modal of all experienced interviewers. Moreover, the physical setting of the research is limited to one target setting that is of little interest to anyone who is not a survey researcher—the respondent's living room—and the range of outcome variables is usually limited to those that survey researchers typically study—that is, those that can be assessed using paper and pencil. However, great care is normally taken that these questions cover a wide range of possible effects, thereby insuring considerable heterogeneity in the effect constructs studied.

Our pessimism about external validity should not be overgeneralized, for a consciousness of targets of generalization, of the kinds of settings in which a target class of behaviors most frequently occurs, and of the kinds of persons who most often experience particular kinds of natural treatments, will, at the very least, prevent the designing of experiments that many persons shrug off willy-nilly as "irrelevant." And it is sometimes possible to conduct multiple replications of an experiment at different times, in different settings, and with different kinds of experimenters and respondents.

CONSTRUCT VALIDITY

Construct validity is what experimental psychologists mean by "confounding"—the possibility that the operational definition of a cause or effect can be construed in terms of more than one construct, all of which are stated at the same level of reduction. Confounding means that what one investigator interprets as a causal relationship between A and B another investigator might interpret as a causal relationship between A and Y or between X and B or even between X and Y, and later experiments might support one or the other of these reinterpretations. The reference to the level of reduction is important because it is always possible to "translate" sociological terms into psychological terms, or psychological terms into biological terms. For example, participative decision making could become conformity to membership group norms on the one level, or some correlate of, say, the ascending reticular activating system on the other. Each of these levels of reduction is useful in different ways and none is more legitimate than any other. But such "translations" from one level to another do not involve the confounding of rival explanation that is at issue here.

Before we continue our abstract characterization, some well-known, concrete examples of construct validity problems may help. In medical experiments on the effects of drugs, the psychotherapeutic effect of the doctor's helpful concern was confounded with the chemical action of the pill. Also, the doctor's and the patient's belief that the pill should have helped were confounded with the chemical action as potential causes of patients' later reports of improvement. The placebo control group and the double-blind experimental design were introduced to unconfound these. In industrial relations research, the Hawthorne effect is another such confound; if we assume for the moment that productivity was increased, was this due to an increase in illumination or to the demonstrated administrative concern over improved working conditions or to feedback to the women about how well they were doing their work?

High construct validity requires rigorous definition of potential causes and effects so that manipulations or measures can be tailored to the constructs they are meant to represent. But since single exemplars of constructs never give a perfect fit, researchers should use multiple exemplars of each contruct wherever possible. These should demonstrably share common variance attributable to the target construct and should also differ from each other in unique ways that are irrelevant to the target construct. Such "multiple operationalism" allows tests of whether a particular cause-effect relationship holds even though a variety of different theoretical irrelevancies are present in each operation. One need not, therefore, be in the situation where a particular irrelevancy is associated with every exemplar of a construct, thereby confounding the construct and the irrelevancy.

Four other points are worth making about assessing construct validity. First, the proposed independent variables should demonstrably vary what they are meant to vary, and measuring this is usually called "assessing the 'take' of the independent variable." Second, the independent variables should not covary *with measures of related but different constructs*. For instance, a manipulation of "communicator expertise" should be correlated with reports from respondents about the communicator's level of knowledge but should not be correlated with attributions about his trustworthiness, likability, or power. Third, the proposed dependent variables should tap into the factors that they are meant to measure. Normally, some form of inter-item correlation can demonstrate this. And fourth, the dependent variables should not be dominated by irrelevant factors that make them measures of more or less than was intended. Without all or some of these data-bound processes, the interpretation of manipulations and measures can appear somewhat arbitrary.

The similarity and difference between external and construct validity can be seen at this point. External validity involves drawing samples that represent populations, and construct validity also seems to involve selecting a sample of measures or manipulations that represent the abstract construct (the "population," as it were). But while it is sometimes possible to conceptualize populations for external validity purposes and to draw up a list of all the instances in the population, it is often not possible to get high agreement among persons about the conceptualization of abstract constructs like, say, "aggression," and it is never possible to draw up a list of all possible instances of aggression from which a random sample of measures could be drawn. Moreover, when we decide on a measure or manipulation there will inevitably be some sources of equivocality concerning their fit with their referent construct, and we always have to settle for imperfect representations of construct. The researcher's task is to minimize the imperfection, which he does by the processes listed in the previous paragraph and by insuring that he has multiple operationalized manipulations and measures so that he can test whether different versions of the same construct—each of which hopefully has different imperfections—are similarly related.

We can illustrate these points by considering a possible experiment on the effects of supervisory distance. Suppose we operationalized "close supervision by a foreman" as standing within comfortable speaking distance of workers. This would exclude longer distances where speaking was not possible but from which workers might nonetheless perceive they were being supervised. Hence, the treatment might be more exactly characterized as "supervision from speaking distances" as opposed to "close supervision" or "supervision" in general. Indeed, it might be dangerous to generalize from the treatment to the construct, especially if supervision has different consequences if it comes from speaking rather than from seeing but not speaking distances. It would be much more useful for construct validity, therefore, if supervisory distance were systematically varied by means of planned manipulations, or if it inadvertently varied across a wide range because each foreman differed in his behavior from day to day. The systematic variation of distance would allow us to test whether we can generalize from one supervisory distance to another (and hence to the general construct), while the naturally occurring heterogeneity in the treatment implementation would allow us to conclude whether supervisory distance affects outcomes despite the error-inflating heterogeneity that is attributable to variation in the theoretical irrelevancy of actual physical distance.

The foremen might also differ from each other, or might themselves differ from day to day, in whether they supervise with a smile, in an officious manner, or inadvertently during some other task. Neither the smile, the officousness, nor the inadvertence would seem to be necessary components of "supervision," and a researcher would hope that such behaviors were equally frequent across instances where supervisory distance was manipulated or that they could be measured and used in analyses to ascertain whether the closeness of supervision had similar effects despite the heterogeneity introduced by the theoretical irrelevancy of a foreman's smile, officiousness, or inadvertence. If effects could not be generalized across all of these irrelevancies, important contingencies would be specified that determine the particular type of supervision that causes a particular effect, thereby implying a restriction in generality. But the restriction would add accuracy and better specify the causal construct as, say, "close supervision with a smile" rather than "close supervision."

The kind of specification we have just been discussing concerns variables that are manipulated contemporaneously with the intended treatment. It is more difficult to spell out the implications for construct validity of "developmental sequences," which are the processes that causally follow from the treatment and mediate its consequences. For example, close supervision by a foreman might mean that workers can ask for, and receive, task-relevant feedback that increases the quality or quantity of their performance. Alternatively, workers might feel resentment that their freedom is being curtailed by the supervision, and so might work less. The feedback and resentment process are consequences that presumably depend on who the foreman or worker is, how past relations have been in the particular work environment, etc. The researcher is, therefore, faced with the dilemma: Should the treatment be specified as, say, "closeness of supervision and task-relevant feedback," for this is the construct that led to the observed effects even though it was not the planned cause and is less general than the original construct? We are presently inclined not to include developmental sequences under the heading of construct validity since they do not have to do with the correspondence between referent constructs and either a treatment or a measure. Instead, they have to do with treatment consequences that are often situation or person-bound and that often lead to theoretical reformulations (i.e., one might rephrase research questions in terms of the determinants and consequences of resentment rather than closeness of supervision, for resentment would seem to be a more reliable determinant of productivity than supervisory style). However, the elucidation of "developmental sequences," is well worthwhile in its own right.

It is a mistake to think that construct validity should only be a concern of the theoretician. Many treatments in applied research are complex packages of variables rather than indicators of apparently unidimensional constructs. Hence, it will sometimes be difficult to reproduce the total package, and some effects might not be as easy to replicate as they would be if the causal components of a treatment could be specified. A concern with construct validity can also indicate whether the most policy-relevant questions have been asked in a research project. For instance, "Sesame Street" was evaluated in an experiment where children were visited on a weekly or monthly basis in the home and were encouraged to view the show by research staff members who left behind toys, books, and balloons which advertised the series (Ball and Bogatz, 1970; Bogatz and Ball, 1971). Such face-to-face encouragement probably cost between $100 and $200 per child per six-month viewing season over and above the costs of developing and distributing the program, and it probably is not a process that is, to the extent we understand it, as widespread nationally as viewing without encouragement from a research staff (Cook, Appleton, Conner, Shaffer, Tamkin, and Weber, 1975). Since viewing the show without encouragement costs only between $1 and $2 per child per season, and since most children in the United States view the show this way, viewing would seem to be a more policy-relevant construct than encouragement. It would, therefore, be useful to know whether the effects of viewing without encouragement are similar to those attributable to viewing with encouragement. While it is true that the applied researcher's major goal is, *and should be*, to make an impact on some neatly labeled outcome, it is nonetheless possible and desirable for him or her to conduct internal analyses of the experimental data which might help specify a causal construct more adequately. It is even better, of course, if the research is designed so that there is a high initial correspondence between the treatment and the policy-relevant variable to which generalization is desired.

Here, then, is a list of threats to construct validity. They all have to do either with the operations failing to incorporate all the dimensions of the construct, which we might call "construct underrepresentation," or with the operations containing dimensions that are irrelevant to the target constructs, which we might call "surplus construct irrelevancies." The list concentrates on the fit between operations and their referent constructs rather than on the fit between constructs and the way that the research problem is conceptualized. Getting the initial question "right" is not the same as the construct validity issue of getting one's operations to reflect one's research constructs. The list that follows is about the latter:

Inadequate Pre-Operational Explication of Constructs. The choice of operations should depend on the result of a conceptual analysis of the essential features of a construct. By consulting dictionaries (social science or otherwise) and the past literature on a topic, one would find, for example, that "attitude" is usually defined as a stable predisposition to respond, and that this stability is understood either as consistency across response modes (affective, cognitive, and behavioral) and/or as stability across time (responses to the same attitude measure taken at different times should correlate positively). Such an analysis immediately suggests that it would not be adequate to measure preferences or beliefs at a single session and to label this as "attitude," which is unfortunately done all too often. To give another example, many definitions of aggression include both the intent to harm others and the fact that harm results from actions. This is to distinguish between (1) the black eye one boy gives another as they collide coming round a blind bend; (2) the black eye that one boy gives another to get his candy (instrumental aggression) or to harm him (non-instrumental); and (3) the verbal threat by one child to another that he will give him a black eye unless the other boy gives him some candy. Since intent and physical harm are stressed in the definition, only (2) above is adequate as an example of the construct "aggression," though it will not be adequate for the minority of persons who prefer a more idiosyncratic definition of the term. A precise explication of constructs is vital for high construct validity since it permits tailoring the manipulations and measures to whichever definitions emerge from the explication.

Mono-Operation Bias. Many experiments are designed to have only one exemplar of a particular possible cause, and some have just one measure to represent some of the possible effect constructs. Since single operations both underrepresent constructs and contain irrelevancies, construct validity will be lower in single exemplar research than in research where each construct is multiply operationalized in order to triangulate on the referent. There is usually no excuse for single operations of effect constructs, since it is not costly to gather additional data from alternative measures of the targets. There is more excuse for having only one manipulation of a possible causal construct since increasing the total number of treatments in a factorial design. This can lead either to very large sample research or to small sizes within each cell of the design should it not be possible to increase the total sample size. Moreover, if one lets irrelevancies in the treatment presentation vary spontaneously from occasion to occasion, this threatens statistical conclusion validity, even though any treatment effects that emerge *despite* the inflated error are presumably not due to those irrelevancies that differed from occasion to occasion. There is really no substitute, where possible, for deliberately varying two or three exemplars of a treatment. Thus, if one were interested in the expertise of a communicator, one might have one distinguished male professor from a distinguished university, one distinguished female research scientist from a prestigious research center, and the most famous science journalist in Western Germany. Then, the variance due to the difference between these sources can be examined to test whether the different combinations of irrelevancies (sex, affiliation, nationality, or academic standing) differently affected responses and whether each expert—or the three combined—caused the expected outcome. If sample size did not permit analyzing separately by source, the data could be combined from all three and the investigator could then test whether expertise was effective despite the irrelevant sources of heterogeneity.

Mono-Method Bias. To have more than one operational representation of a construct does not necessarily imply that all irrelevancies have been made heterogeneous, and this is never the case when all the manipulations or measures use the same means of presenting treatments or recording responses. Thus, if all the experts in the previous hypothetical example had been presented to respondents in writing, it would not logically be possible to generalize to experts who are seen or heard and it would be more accurate to label the treatment as "experts presented in writing." Attitude scales are often presented to respondents without apparent thought (1) to using methods of recording other than paper-and-pencil; (2) to varying whether the attitude statements are positively or negatively worded; (3) to varying whether the positive or negative end of the response scale appears on the right or the left of the page. On these three points depends whether one can rule out if the measure has been of "personal private attitude" or "paper-and-pencil non-accountable responses" or "acquiescence" or "response bias."

Hypothesis-Guessing within Experimental Conditions. The internal validity threats called "resentful demoralization" and "compensation rivalry" were assumed to result because persons receiving no treatment, or less desirable treatments, compared themselves to persons receiving the most desired treatments, making it unclear whether there were any treatment effects of any kind. It is also possible for reactive research to result in real but uninterpretable treatment effects, especially when persons in these groups compare themselves to others and guess how they are supposed to behave (in many situations it is not difficult to guess what is desired, especially perhaps in education, or in industrial organizations). Furthermore, a hypothesis can be guessed without social comparison processes operating so that, informing respondents only of their own treatment and isolating them from others, does not by itself get around the problem of hypothesis-guessing. The problem can best be avoided by making hypotheses hard to guess (if there are any), by decreasing the general level of reactivity in the experiment, or by deliberately giving different hypotheses to different respondents. But these solutions are at best partial since respondents are not passive and may generate their own treatment-related hypotheses that are independent of experimenters' attempts to dampen hypothesis-guessing. However, having a hypothesis does not necessarily imply either the motivation to comply with it (or to "sabotage" it) or the ability to alter one's behavior in the direction indicated by the hypothesis. Despite the widespread discussion of treatment confounds that are presumed to result from wanting to give data that will please the researcher—which we suspect is a result of discussions of the Hawthorne effect—there is neither widespread evidence of the Hawthorne effect in field experiments (see reviews by D. Cook, 1967, and Diamond, 1974) nor is there evidence of an analogue orientation in laboratory contexts (Weber and Cook, 1972). However, we still lack a sophisticated and empirically corroborated theory of the conditions under which (1) hypothesis-guessing occurs, (2) is treatment-specific, and (3) is translated into behavior that (4) could lead to erroneous conclusions about the nature of a treatment construct.

Evaluation Apprehension. Weber and Cook (1972) reviewed considerable data from laboratory experiments in social psychology which indicated that subjects behaved in the manner attributed to them by Rosenberg (1969). That is, they were apprehensive about being evaluated by experimenters who were experts in personality adjustment and task performance, and so the respondents attempted to present themselves as both competent and psychologically healthy. It is not clear how widespread such an orientation is in social science experiments (as opposed to psychology experiments) in field settings, with treatments that last a long time, and with populations that do not especially value the way that social scientists or their sponsors evaluate them. Nonetheless, it is entirely plausible to assume that some past treatment effects may be due to respondents in the most desirable treatment groups presenting themselves to experimenters so as to be evaluated favorably. Yet this is rarely the target construct around which experiments are designed. It is a confound.

Experimenter Expectancies. There is some literature (Rosenthal, 1972) which indicates that an experimenter's expectancies can bias the data that he obtains. When this happens, it will not be clear whether the causal treatment is the treatment-as-labeled or the experimenter's expectations. This threat can be decreased by having experimenters who have no expectations or false expectations, or by analyzing the data separately for experimenters with different kinds or levels of expectancy. Experimenter expectancies are thus a special case of treatment-correlated irrelevancy.

Confounding Levels of Constructs and Constructs. Experiments typically involve the manipulation of several discrete levels of an independent variable that is continuous. Thus, one might conclude from an experiment that A does not affect B when in fact A-at-level-1 does not affect B, or A-at level-4 does not affect B, whereas A-at-level-2 might affect B, as might A-at-level-3. Obviously, this threat is a problem when A and B are not linearly related, and it is especially prevalent, we assume, when treatments have only a weak impact. Thus, low levels of A are manipulated but conclusions may be drawn about A without qualification about the strength of the manipulation. The best control for this threat is to conduct parametric research in which many levels of A are varied and many levels of B are measured.

Generalizing Across Time. We often do not know how long a treatment would affect a cause. If the effect were short-lived, it would be less useful to state that A caused B than it would to state that A caused B and effects persisted for n weeks, or that A did not seem to cause B at first but after n weeks a "sleeper effect" was observed. Generalizing across time is particularly important with constructs like attitude that are sometimes defined in terms of "consistency in responding" to specific attitude objects. If we conducted an experiment, observed posttest differences that were related to a treatment, but had no delayed follow-up measures, we could not be certain of having obtained any consistency in responding over time because we would not have measured attitude often enough to test this. Generalizing across time can also be a problem with the treatment, of course. Would a guaranteed income lasting for three years be similar to one lasting ten years or for life?

Interaction of Procedure and Treatment. Sometimes the respondents in the treatment and control groups will learn new information or undergo new experiences as part of the context in which treatments are embedded, and this may influence how treatments are reacted to. For example, respondents in the New Jersey Income Maintenance Experiment were guaranteed a fixed minimum income of various levels for three years. Thus, each respondent may have been reacting, not just to the payment but to the knowledge that this payment would only last three years. Was the manipulated cause a specified level of income maintenance payments or the provision of these payments for three years?

Construct validity is like external validity both in its inferential character and in the means necessary for reducing validity threats. If one wants to generalize across settings, persons, etc., one has to take heterogeneous instances of settings and persons. Similarly, if one wants to corroborate a generalization from one operational exemplification of a treatment or effect to the referent construct, one needs multiple operationalizations. Or, to switch to another model of external validity, if one has a target setting or target population of persons to whom one wants to generalize, one can carefully think through these settings and populations and can try to obtain as representative a sample as possible. In a similar vein, by a careful explication of constructs and reliable measures of the "take" of the independent variable, one can isolate some single operational definitions that are better approximations of the target construct than are others.

Field research affords poor prospects for achieving high construct validity of the cause. This is because it is costly to implement multiple operationalizations of a single causal concept and because multiple operationalization is a better means of enhancing construct validity than is the careful tailoring of a single operation to a referent construct. The prospects are brighter for the high construct validity of outcomes, because investigators typically have a much greater latitude for multiple measurement than for multiple manipulation. This means that they can measure using multiple methods (observation, interviews, questionnaires, etc.) and that within each method, they can have multiple items or observational categories. In many respects it is only the ingenuity and conceptual skill of investigators that stand between research operations and a high degree of construct validity of outcomes.

SOME RELATIONSHIPS AMONG THE FOUR KINDS OF VALIDITY

We have previously noted how internal and statistical conclusion validity are more like each other than they are like external and construct validity. We have also noted how these last two are, in their turn, like each other in several distinct ways. We want now to mention three other relationships among the different kinds of validity.

First, some ways of increasing one kind of validity will decrease another kind. For instance, internal validity is best served by carrying out true experiments, but the organizations willing to tolerate this are probably less representative than organizations willing to tolerate passive measurement; statistical conclusion validity is increased if the experimenter can rigidly control the stimuli impinging on respondents, but this procedure can decrease both external and construct validity; increasing the construct validity of effects by multiple operationalizing each of them is likely to increase the tedium of measurement and cause attrition from the experiment or a decrease in measurement reliability for individual tests. These countervailing relationships suggest that crucial parts of planning any experiment have to be an explication of the priority-ordering among the four kinds of validity, a search for ways of avoiding all unnecessary trade-offs between one kind of validity and another, and a search for ways of minimizing the loss entailed by the necessary trade-offs. However, since some trade-offs are inevitable, we think it unrealistic to expect that a single piece of research will effectively answer all of the validity questions surrounding even the simplest causal relationship.

Second, the general primacy of internal validity should be noted. Since experiments are conducted to make causal statements, internal validity assumes a particular importance because it relates to whether a relationship—of whatever strength—is unambiguously causal or not. The primacy of internal validity does not stand out where true experiments are concerned because the random allocation procedure rules out almost all the pertinent threats. But there is no randomized assignment of treatments in quasi-experiments, and the investigator's major task is to rule out the internal validity threats one by one . . . .

Third, the priority-ordering of the other threats varies with the kind of research being conducted. For persons interested in theory-testing it is almost as important to show that A causes B (a problem of construct validity) as it is to show that something *causes* something (a problem of internal validity). Moreover, most theories do not specify target settings, populations, times, or the like, so that external validity is of relatively little importance. In particular, it can be sacrificed for the statistical power that comes through having isolated settings, standardized procedures, and homogeneous respondent populations. Thus, for investigators with theoretical interests the rank-ordering of types of validity, in order of importance, is probably internal, construct, statistical conclusion, and external validity. (It is our impression that the construct validity of causes is more important for practitioners of such research than is the construct validity of effects. Think, for example, of how oversimply "attitude" is operationalized in many persuasion experiments, or "cooperation" in bargaining studies, or "aggression" in studies of interpersonal violence, and think how much care goes into demonstrating that the manipulation varied cognitive dissonance and not reactance. Might not the construct validity of effects come after statistical conclusion validity for most theory-testing researchers? If it does, it would be ironic in the sense that it is easier to achieve high construct validity of effects than of causes because multiple operationalization is easier with the former than the latter.)

Much applied research has a different set of priorities. It is often concerned with testing whether a particular specific problem has been alleviated (high construct validity of the effect), and it is critical that this demonstration be made in a setting and with persons that permit either wide generalization or generalization to specific targets (high interest in external validity). The research is relatively less concerned with whether the causal treatment is, for example, better lighting or a Hawthorne effect (low interest in construct validity of the cause). Thus, the priority-ordering for such researchers is something like internal validity, external validity, construct validity of the effect, statistical conclusion validity, and construct validity of the cause.

Though experiments are designed to test causal hypotheses, and though internal validity is the sine qua non of causal inference, there are nonetheless contexts where it would not be advisable to subordinate too much to internal validity. Someone commissioning research to improve the efficiency of his own organization might not take kindly to the idea of testing a proposed improvement in a laboratory setting with sophomore respondents. A necessary condition for meeting a client's needs is that the client could generalize any findings to his own organization and to the indicators of efficiency that he regularly uses for monitoring performance. Indeed, his need in this respect may be so great that he is prepared to sacrifice some gains in internal validity for a necessary minimum of external validity. However, he runs the risk because of this that he will not be able to answer his preliminary causal question with any confidence. Hence, while the sociology of doing research might sometimes incline one to rate external validity higher than internal validity, the logic of testing causal propositions suggests tempering this inclination lest the very hypothesis-testing rationale for conducting experiments be vitiated. "Common sense" is obviously called for in trading off internal and external validity in any research project, which is why we mentioned the general primacy of internal validity rather than its absolute primacy.

Disciplines like industrial and organizational research that have members with each of these different orientations would appear to have special difficulties of communication in that members share different systems of priorities. But at the same time such disciplines have a special advantage in that all four kinds of validity are represented at a high priority level in some persons. This may provide the potential for a fruitful integration of ideas and findings from both the theory-relevant and applied areas. Disciplines with no such mixture of persons with different validity priorities are likely never to know much about, say, external validity on the one hand or the construct validity of causes on the other hand.

REFERENCES

Ball, S., and Bogatz, G. A. *The First Year of Sesame Street: An Evaluation.* Princeton: Educational Testing Service, 1970.

Bogatz, G. A., and Ball, S. *The Second Year of Sesame Street: A Continuing Evalution.* Princeton: Educational Testing Service, 1971, two vols.

Bracht, G. H., and Glass, G. V. "The External Validity of Experiments," *American Educational Research Journal,* 1968, 5, 437–474.

Brannon, R., Cyphers, G., Hesse S., Hesselbart, S., Keane, R., Schuman, H., Viccaro, T., and Wright, D. "Attitude and Action: A Field Experiment Joined to a General Population Survey," *American Sociological Review,* 1973, 38, 625–634.

Campbell, D. T. "Leadership and Its Effects Upon the Group. In *Ohio Studies in Personnel.* Columbus: Ohio State University, Bureau of Business Research Monographs, 1956, No. 83.

Campbell, D. T. "Reforms as Experiments," *American Psychologist,* 1969, 24, 409–429.

Campbell, D. T., and Stanley, J. C. "Experimental and Quasi-experimental Designs for Research on Teaching. " In N. L. Gage (ed.), *Handbook of Research on Teaching.* Chicago: Rand McNally, 1963. (Also published as *Experimental and Quasi-experimental Designs for Research.* Chicago: Rand McNally, 1966.)

Cook, D. *The Impact of the Hawthorne Effect in Experimental Designs in Educational Research.* Washington, D.C.: U.S. Office of Education, No. 0726, June, 1967.

Cook, T. D. "The Potential and Limitations of Secondary Evaluations." In M. W. Apple, M. J. Subkoviak, and H. S. Lufler, Jr. (eds.), *Educational Evaluation: Analysis and Responsibility.* Berkeley, Calif.: McCutchan, 1974a.

Cook, T. D. "The Medical and Tailored Models of Evaluation Research." In J. G. Albert and M. Kamrass (eds.), *Social Experiments and Social Program Evaluation*. Cambridge: Ballinger, 1974b.

Cook, T. D., Appleton, H., Conner, R., Shaffer, A., Tamkin, G., and Weber, S. J. *Sesame Street Revisited: A Case Study in Evalution Research*. New York: Russell Sage Foundation, 1975.

Diamond, S. S. "Hawthorne Effects: Another Look." Unpublished manuscript, University of Illinois at Chicago, 1974.

Roethlisberger, F. J., and Dickson, W. J. *Management and the Worker*. Cambridge: Harvard University Press, 1939.

Rosenberg, M. J. "The Conditions and Consequences of Evaluation Apprehension." In R. Rosenthal and R. L. Rosnow (eds.), *Artifact in Behavioral Research*. New York: Academic Press, 1969.

Rosenthal, R. "On the Social Psychology of the Self-fulfilling Prophecy: Further Evidence for Pygmalion Effects and Their Mediating Mechanisms." Unpublished manuscript, Harvard University, Cambridge, 1972.

Rossi, P. H., Boeckmann, M., and Berk, R. A. "Some Ethical Implications of the New Jersey-Pennsylvania Income Maintenance Experiment." Unpublished manuscript, University of Massachusetts, Amherst, 1974.

Ryan, T. A. "Multiple Comparisons in Psychological Research," *Psychological Bulletin*, 1959, 56, 26–47.

Saretsky, G. "The OEO P.C. Experiment and the John Henry Effect," *Phi Delta Kappan*, 1972, 53, 579–581.

Schuman, H., and Duncan, O. D. "Questions About Attitude Survey Questions." In H. L. Costner (ed.), *Sociological Methodology, 1973–1974*. San Francisco: Jossey-Bass, 1974.

Snow, R. E. "Representative and Quasi-representative Designs for Research on Teaching," *Review of Educational Research*, 1974, 44, 265–291.

Weber, S. J., and Cook, T. D. "Subject Effects in Laboratory Research: An Examination of Subject Roles, Demand Characteristics, and Valid Inference," *Psychological Bulletin*, 1972, 77, 273–295.

Winch, R. F., and Campbell, D. T. "Proof? No! Evidence? Yes! The Significance of Tests of Significance," *American Sociologist*, 1969, 4, 140–143.

7 The Volunteer Subject

Robert Rosenthal
Ralph L. Rosnow

There is a growing suspicion among behavioral researchers that those human subjects who find their way into the role of research subject may not be entirely representative of humans in general. McNemar put it wisely when he said, "The existing sci-

From Robert Rosenthal and Ralph L. Rosnow, *The Volunteer Subject*. New York: Wiley, 1975. Reprinted by permission of John Wiley & Sons, Inc.

ence of human behavior is largely the science of the behavior of sophomores" (1946, p. 333). Sophomores are convenient subjects for study, and some sophomores are more convenient than others. Sophomores enrolled in psychology courses, for example, get more than their fair share of opportunities to play the role of the research subject whose responses provide the basis for formulations of the principles of human behavior. There are now indications that these "psychology sophomores" are not entirely representative of even sophomores in general (Hilgard, 1967), a possibility that makes McNemar's formulation sound unduly optimistic. The existing science of human behavior may be largely the science of those sophomores who both enroll in psychology courses and volunteer to participate in behavioral research. The extent to which a useful, comprehensive science of human behavior can be based upon the behavior of such self-selected and investigator-selected subjects is an empirical question of considerable importance. It is a question that has received increasing attention in recent years (e.g., Adair, 1973; Bell, 1961; Chapanis, 1967; Damon, 1965; Leslie, 1972; Lester, 1969; London and Rosenhan, 1964; Maul, 1970; Ora, 1965; Parten, 1950; Rosenhan, 1967; Rosenthal, 1965; Rosenthal and Rosnow, 1969; Rosnow and Rosenthal, 1970; Schappe, 1972; Silverman and Margulis, 1973; Straits and Wuebben, 1973; Wells and Schofield, 1972; Wunderlich and Becker, 1969).

Some of this recent interest has been focused on the actual proportion of human research subjects that are drawn from the collegiate setting. Table 1 shows the results of six studies investigating this question during the 1960s. The range is from 70% to 90%, with a median of 80%. Clearly, then, the vast majority of human research subjects have been sampled from populations of convenience, usually the college or university in which the investigator is employed. The studies in Table 1 span only an eight-year period, a period too short for the purpose of trying to discern a trend. Nevertheless, there is no reason for optimism based on a comparison of the earliest with the latest percentages. If anything, there may have been a rise in the percentage of human subjects who were college students. The concern over the use of college students as our model of persons in general is based not only on the very obvious differences between college students and more representative persons in age, intelligence, and social class but also on the suspicion that college students, because of their special relationship with the teacher-investigator, may be especially susceptible to the operation of the various mechanisms that together constitute what has been called the social psychology of

TABLE 1   College Students as a Percentage of Total Subjects Employed

Author	Source	Years	% College Students
Smart (1966) I	Journal of Abnormal and Social Psychology	1962–1964	73
Smart (1966) II	Journal of Experimental Psychology	1963–1964	86
Schultz (1969) I	Journal of Personality and Social Psychology	1966–1967	70
Schultz (1969) II	Journal of Experimental Psychology	1966–1967	84
Jung (1969)	Psychology Department Survey	1967–1968	90
Higbee and Wells (1972)	Journal of Personality and Social Psychology	1969	76
Median			80

behavioral research (e.g., Adair, 1973; Fraser and Zimbardo, n.d.; Haas, 1970; Lana, 1969; Lester, 1969; McGuire, 1969; Orne, 1969, 1970; Rosenberg, 1969; Straits and Wuebben, 1973; Straits, Wuebben, and Majka, 1972).

Although most of the interest in, and concern over, the problem of subject selection biases has been centered on human subjects, we should note that analogous interests and concerns have been developing among investigators employing animal subjects. Just as the college student may not be a very good model for the "typical" person, so the laboratory rat may not be a very good model for the typical rodent nor for a wild rat, nor even for another laboratory rat of a different strain (e.g., Beach, 1950, 1960; Boice, 1973; Christie, 1951; Ehrlich, 1974; Eysenck, 1967; Kavanau, 1964, 1967; Richter, 1959; Smith, 1969).

VOLUNTEER BIAS

The problem of the volunteer subject has been of interest to many behavioral researchers and evidence of their interest will be found in the . . . [sections] to follow. Fortunately for those of us who are behavioral researchers, however, mathematical statisticians have also devoted attention and effort to problems of the volunteer subject (e.g., Cochran, 1963; Cochran, Mosteller, and Tukey, 1953; Deming, 1944; Hansen and Hurwitz, 1946). Their work has shown the effects of the proportion of the population who select themselves out of the sample by not volunteering or responding, on the precision of estimates of various population values. These results are depressing to say the least, showing as they do how rapidly the margin of error increases as the proportion of nonvolunteers increases even moderately. In the present volume we shall not deal with the technical aspects of sampling and "nonresponse" theory, but it will be useful at this point to give in quantitative terms an example of volunteer bias in operation.

The basic data were presented by Cochran (1963) in his discussion of nonresponse bias. Three waves of questionnaires were mailed out to fruit growers, and the number of growers responding to each of the three waves was recorded, as was the remaining number of growers who never responded. One of the questions dealt with the number of fruit trees owned, and for just this question, data were available for the entire population of growers. Because of this fortunate circumstance, it was possible to calculate the degree of bias due to nonresponse, or nonvolunteering, present after the first, second, and third waves of questionnaires. Table 2 summarizes these calculations and gives the formal definition of volunteer bias. The first three rows of Table 2 give the basic data provided by Cochran: (1) the number of respondents to each wave of questionnaires and the number of nonrespondents, (2) the percentage of the total population represented by each wave of respondents and by the nonrespondents, and (3) the mean number of trees actually owned by each wave of respondents and by the nonrespondents. Examination of this row reveals the nature of the volunteer bias: the earlier responders owned more trees, on the average, than did the later responders. The remaining five rows of data are based on the cumulative number of respondents available after the first, second, and third waves. For each of these waves, five items of information are provided: (1) the mean number of trees owned by the respondents up to that point in the survey (Y_1); (2) the mean number of trees owned by those who had not yet responded up to that point in the survey (Y_2); (3) the difference between these two values ($Y_1 - Y_2$); (4) the percentage of the population that had not yet responded up to that point in the survey (P); and (5) the magnitude of the bias up to that point in the survey, defined as $P \times (Y_1 - Y_2)$. Examination of this last row shows that with each successive wave of respondents there was an appreciable decrease in the magnitude of the bias. This appears to be a fairly typical result of studies of this kind: increasing the effort to recruit the nonvolunteer decreases the bias in the sample estimates. Cochran gives considerable advice on how to minimize bias, given the usually greater cost of trying to recruit a nonvolunteer compared to the cost of recruiting a more willing respondent. Before leaving the present example of the calculation of bias, we should note again that in most circumstances of behavioral research we can compute the proportion of our population who fail to participate (P) and the statistic of interest for those who volunteer their data (Y_1); but we cannot compute the statistic of interest for those who do not volunteer (Y_2) so that it is often our lot to be in a position to suspect bias but to be unable to give an accurate quantitative statement about its magnitude.

TABLE 2   Example of Volunteer Bias in Survey Research

	Response to Three Mailings				
	First	Second	Third	Nonrespondents	Total Population
Basic data					
Number of respondents	300	543	434	1839	3116
% of population	10	17	14	59	100
Mean trees per respondent	456	382	340	290	329
Cumulative data					
Mean trees per respondent (Y_1)	456	408	385	—	—
Mean trees per nonrespondent (Y_2)	315	300	290	—	—
Difference $(Y_1 - Y_2)$	141	108	95	—	—
% of nonrespondents (P)	90	73	59	—	—
Bias $[(P) \times (Y_1 - Y_2)]$	127	79	56	—	—

Put most simply, then, the concern over the volunteer problem has had for its goal the reduction of bias, or unrepresentativeness, of volunteer samples so that investigators might increase the generality of their research results (e.g., Ferber, 1948-1949; Ford and Zeisel, 1949; Hyman and Sheatsley, 1954; Locke, 1954). The magnitude of the problem is not trivial. The potential biasing effects of using volunteer samples have been illustrated recently and clearly. At one large university, rates of volunteering varied from 100% down to 10%. Even within the same course, different recruiters visiting different sections of the course obtained rates of volunteering varying from 100% down to 50% (French, 1963). At another university, rates of volunteering varied from 74% down to 26% when the same recruiter, extending the same invitation to participate in the same experiment, solicited female volunteers from different floors of the same dormitory (Marmer, 1967). . . .

Some reduction of the volunteer sampling bias might be expected from the fairly common practice of requiring psychology undergraduates to spend a certain number of hours serving as research subjects. Such a requirement gets more students into the overall sampling urn, but without making their participation in any given experiment a randomly determined event (e.g., Johnson, 1973; King, 1970; MacDonald, 1972).

Students required to serve as research subjects often have a choice between alternative experiments. Given such a choice, will brighter (or duller) students sign up for an experiment on learning? Will better (or more poorly) adjusted students sign up for an experiment on personality? Will students who view their consciousness as broader (or narrower) sign up for an experiment that promises an encounter with "psychedelicacies"? We do not know the answers to these questions very well, nor do we know whether these possible self-selection biases would necessarily make any difference in the inferences we want to draw.

If the volunteer problem has been of interest and concern in the past, there is good evidence to suggest that it will become of even greater interest and concern in the future. Evidence of this comes from the popular press and the technical literature, and it says to us that in the future investigators may have less control than ever before over the kinds of human subjects who find their way into research. The ethical questions of humans' rights to privacy and to informed consent are more salient now than ever before (Adair, 1973; Adams, 1973; Bean, 1959; Clark et al., 1967; Etzioni, 1973; Katz, 1972; Martin, Arnold, Zimmerman, and Richart, 1968; May, Smith, and Morris, 1968; Miller, 1966; Orlans, 1967; Rokeach, 1966; Ruebhausen and Brim, 1966; Sasson and Nelson, 1969; Steiner, 1972; Sullivan and Deiker, 1973; Trotter, 1974; Walsh, 1973; Wicker, 1968b; Wolfensberger, 1967; Wolfle, 1960). One possible outcome of this unprecedented soul-searching is that the social science of the future may, because of internally and perhaps externally imposed constraints, be based upon propositions whose tenability will come only from volunteer subjects who have been made fully aware of the responses of interest to the investigator. However, even without this extreme consequence of the ethical crisis of the social sciences, we still will want to learn as much as we can about the external circumstances and the internal characteristics that bring any given individual into our sample of subjects or keep him out.

Our purpose in the . . . [sections] to follow will be to say something about the characteristics that serve to differentiate volunteers for behavioral research from nonvolunteers and to examine in some detail what is known about the motivational and situational determinants of the act of volunteering. Subsequently we shall consider the implications of what is now known about volunteers and volunteering for the representativeness of the findings of behavioral research. We shall give special attention to experimental research that suggests that volunteer status may often interact with the independent variables employed in a variety of types of research studies. There is increasing reason to believe that such interactions may well occur, although the effects will not always be very large (Cope and Kunce, 1971; Cox and Sipprelle, 1971; Marlatt, 1973; Oakes, 1972; Pavlos, 1972; Short and Oskamp, 1965). . . .

ASSESSING THE NONVOLUNTEER

How do researchers determine the attributes of those who do not volunteer to participate? Several procedures have been found useful, and they can be grouped into one of two types, the exhaustive and the nonexhaustive.

In the exhaustive method, all potential subjects are identified by their status on all the variables on which volunteers and nonvolunteers are to be compared. They may be tested first and then recruited, as when the investigator begins with an archive of data on each person and then, sometimes years later, makes a request for volunteers. For example, incoming freshmen are routinely administered a battery of tests in many colleges, and these data can then be drawn upon in future comparisons. Another variation is to recruit subjects and then test them. In this case, subjects for behavioral research are solicited, usually in a college classroom context, and the names of the volunteers and nonvolunteers are sorted out by using the class roster; shortly thereafter, a test or some other material is administered to the entire class by someone ostensibly unrelated to the person who recruited the volunteers.

In the nonexhaustive method, data are not available for all potential subjects, but they are available for those differing in likelihood of finding their way into a final sample. Thus, one variation of the method uses the easy-to-recruit subject, although, because true nonvolunteers are not available, it requires extrapolation on a gradient of volunteering. The procedure in this case is to tap a population of volunteer subjects repeatedly so as to compare second-stage volunteers with first-stage volunteers, and so on. If repeated volunteers, for example, were higher in the need for social approval than one-time volunteers, then by extrapolating these data roughly to the zero level of volunteering it could be tentatively concluded that nonvolunteers might be lower still in approval need. Another variation gets at the hard-to-recruit subject by repeatedly increasing the incentive to volunteer, a method frequently used in survey research to tease more respondents into the sampling urn. Still another variation focuses on the slow-to-reply subject. In this case only a single request for volunteers is issued, and latency of volunteering is the criterion for dividing up the waves of respondents, as well as the basis for extrapolating to nonrespondents.

VOLUNTEER CHARACTERISTICS

Examining studies that used these various procedures for assessing the nonvolunteers, we drew the following conclusions about characteristics that may reliably differentiate willing and unwilling subjects:

Conclusions Warranting Maximum Confidence

1. Volunteers tend to be better educated than nonvolunteers, especially when personal contact between investigator and respondent is not required.
2. Volunteers tend to have higher social-class status than nonvolunteers, especially when social class is defined by respondents' own status rather than by parental status.
3. Volunteers tend to be more intelligent than nonvolunteers when volunteering is for research in general but not when volunteering is for somewhat less typical types of research such as hypnosis, sensory isolation, sex research, small-group and personality research.
4. Volunteers tend to be higher in need for social approval than nonvolunteers.
5. Volunteers tend to be more sociable than nonvolunteers.

Conclusions Warranting Considerable Confidence

6. Volunteers tend to be more arousal-seeking than nonvolunteers, especially when volunteering is for studies of stress, sensory isolation, and hypnosis.
7. Volunteers tend to be more unconventional than nonvolunteers, especially when volunteering is for studies of sex behavior.
8. Females are more likely than males to volunteer for research in general, but

less likely than males to volunteer for physically and emotionally stressful research (e.g., electric shock, high temperature, sensory deprivation, interviews about sex behavior).

9. Volunteers tend to be less authoritarian than nonvolunteers.

10. Jews are more likely to volunteer than Protestants, and Protestants are more likely to volunteer than Catholics.

11. Volunteers tend to be less conforming than nonvolunteers when volunteering is for research in general but not when subjects are female and the task is relatively "clinical" (e.g., hypnosis, sleep, or counseling research).

Conclusions Warranting Some Confidence

12. Volunteers tend to be from smaller towns than nonvolunteers, especially when volunteering is for questionnaire studies.

13. Volunteers tend to be more interested in religion than nonvolunteers, especially when volunteering is for questionnaire studies.

14. Volunteers tend to be more altruistic than nonvolunteers.

15. Volunteers tend to be more self-disclosing than nonvolunteers.

16. Volunteers tend to be more maladjusted than nonvolunteers, especially when volunteering is for potentially unusual situations (e.g., drugs, hypnosis, high temperature, or vaguely described experiments) or for medical research employing clinical rather than psychometric definitions of psychopathology.

17. Volunteers tend to be younger than nonvolunteers, especially when volunteering is for laboratory research and especially if they are female.

Conclusions Warranting Minimum Confidence

18. Volunteers tend to be higher in need for achievement than nonvolunteers especially among American samples.

19. Volunteers are more likely to be married than nonvolunteers, especially when volunteering is for studies requiring no personal contact between investigator and respondent.

20. Firstborns are more likely than laterborns to volunteer, especially when recruitment is personal and when the research requires group interaction and a low level of stress.

21. Volunteers tend to be more anxious than nonvolunteers, especially when volunteering is for standard, nonstressful tasks and especially if they are college students.

22. Volunteers tend to be more extraverted than nonvolunteers when interaction with others is required by the nature of the research.

SITUATIONAL DETERMINANTS

What are the variables that tend to increase or decrease the rates of volunteering obtained? The answer to this question has implications both for the theory and practice of the behavioral sciences. If we can learn more about the situational determinants of volunteering, we will also have learned more about the social psychology of social-influence processes and, in terms of methodology, be in a better position to reduce the bias in our samples that derives from volunteers being systematically different from nonvolunteers on a variety of personal characteristics. As with the previous list of conclusions, our inventory of situational determinants was developed inductively, based on an examination of a fairly sizable number of research studies:

Conclusions Warranting Maximum Confidence

1. Persons more interested in the topic under investigation are more likely to volunteer.
2. Persons with expectations of being more favorably evaluated by the investigator are more likely to volunteer.

Conclusions Warranting Considerable Confidence

3. Persons perceiving the investigation as more important are more likely to volunteer.
4. Persons' feeling states at the time of the request for volunteers are likely to affect the probability of volunteering. Persons feeling guilty are more likely to volunteer, especially when contact with the unintended victim can be avoided and when the source of guilt is known to others. Persons made to "feel good" or to feel competent are also more likely to volunteer.
5. Persons offered greater material incentives are more likely to volunteer, especially if the incentives are offered as gifts in advance and without being contingent on the subject's decision to volunteer. Stable personal characteristics of the potential volunteer may moderate the relationship between volunteering and material incentives.

Conclusions Warranting Some Confidence

6. Personal characteristics of the recruiter are likely to affect the subject's probability of volunteering. Recruiters higher in status or prestige are likely to obtain higher rates of volunteering, as are female recruiters. This latter relationship is especially modifiable by the sex of the subject and the nature of the research.
7. Persons are less likely to volunteer for tasks that are more aversive in the sense of their being painful, stressful, or dangerous biologically or psychologically. Personal characteristics of the subject and level of incentive offered may moderate the relationship between volunteering and task aversiveness.
8. Persons are more likely to volunteer when volunteering is viewed as the normative, expected, appropriate thing to do.

Conclusions Warranting Minimum Confidence

9. Persons are more likely to volunteer when they are personally acquainted with the recruiter. The addition of a "personal touch" may also increase volunteering.
10. Conditions of public commitment may increase rates of volunteering when volunteering is normatively expected, but they may decrease rates of volunteering when nonvolunteering is normatively expected.

SUGGESTIONS FOR REDUCING VOLUNTEER BIAS

Our assessment of the literature dealing with the situational determinants of volunteering led us to make a number of tentative suggestions for the reduction of volunteer bias. Implementing these suggestions may serve not only to reduce volunteer bias but also to make us more thoughtful in the planning of the research itself. Our relations with potential subjects may become increasingly reciprocal and human and our procedures may become more humane. Our suggestions follow in outline form:

1. Make the appeal for volunteers as interesting as possible, keeping in mind the nature of the target population.
2. Make the appeal for volunteers as nonthreatening as possible so that potential volunteers will not be "put off" by unwarranted fears of unfavorable evaluation.
3. Explicitly state the theoretical and practical importance of the research for which volunteering is requested.
4. Explicitly state in what way the target population is particularly relevant to the research being conducted and the responsibility of potential volunteers to participate in research that has potential for benefiting others.
5. When possible, potential volunteers should be offered not only pay for participation but small courtesy gifts simply for taking time to consider whether they will want to participate.
6. Have the request for volunteering made by a person of status as high as possible, and preferably by a woman.
7. When possible, avoid research tasks that may be psychologically or biologically stressful.
8. When possible, communicate the normative nature of the volunteering response.
9. After a target population has been defined, an effort should be made to have someone known to that population make the appeal for volunteers. The request for volunteers itself may be more successful if a personalized appeal is made.
10. In situations where volunteering is regarded by the target population as normative, conditions of public commitment to volunteer may be more successful; where nonvolunteering is regarded as normative, conditions of private commitment may be more successful.

AN ETHICAL DILEMMA

The 1973 APA code of ethical guidelines for research with human subjects indirectly raises an issue as to whether compliance with the letter of the law might jeopardize the tenability of inferred causal relationships. A verbal-conditioning study by Resnick and Schwartz (1973) is illustrative of one horn of the dilemma in that volunteer subjects who were forewarned of the nature of the research along the lines of the APA standards showed a boomerang effect in the conditioning rate—a reaction quite contrary to our present laws of verbal learning. The ethnical dilemma results from the likelihood that fully informed voluntarism, while it may satisfy the moral concern of researchers, may be contraindicated for the scientific concern in many cases; and experimenters must weigh the social ethic against the scientific ethic in deciding which violation would constitute the greater moral danger.

Other research, by Sullivan and Deiker (1973), is reassuring at least from the point of view of the societal concern in implying that professional psychologists may be ultraconservative watchdogs because of their stringent ethical views. However, if the current social temper of the times persists, an already complicated issue may become further compounded in the future as greater restrictions are placed on the kinds of recruitment conditions that are ethically permissible.

ROBUSTNESS OF RESEARCH FINDINGS

In light of these developments emphasizing more use of fully informed consent procedures in recruiting subjects for behavioral research, it is important to be aware of the threat to the generalizability of data from using voluntary subjects exclusively. For example, to the extent that a pool of volunteers differed from the population at large, the resulting positive or negative bias would lead to overestimates or underestimates of certain population parameters. Suppose we relied entirely on volunteer subjects to standardize norms for a new test of social approval. Since volunteers tend to be higher in approval need than nonvolunteers, our estimated population mean would be artificially inflated by this procedure. Of course it is also possible to conceive of situations where population means were underestimated because only volunteers were used. The important point is that routinely sampling volunteer subjects could lead to estimates of population parameters that were seriously in error.

Another way in which volunteer status can affect the generalizability of inferences has to do with the naturalistic motivations of human beings. Insofar as volunteer status as an organismic variable was related to the dependent variable of an investigation, the study of voluntarism could be the substantive basis for the research. From this slightly different perspective, volunteer status can be seen as merely another organismic variable like all the myriad variables affecting human behavior. A good case in point was Horowitz's (1969) study on the effects of fear-arousal on attitude change. He noticed that research that used voluntary subjects tended to produce a positive relationship between fear-arousal and attitude change and that research using captive subjects tended toward the inverse relationship. Reasoning that volunteers and nonvolunteers may be differentially disposed to felt emotional-persuasive demands, he set about to demonstrate the difference in persuasibility of these two types of subjects by assigning them either to a condition of high or low fear-arousal. Consistent with his hypothesis, the attitude-change data clearly indicted that voluntarism was an important organismic variable for assessing the generality of the fear-arousal relationship. The important point in this case was the empirical emphasis on the fact that behavioral data must always be interpreted within the motivational context in which they occurred. . . .

REFERENCES

Adair, J. G. (1973). *The Human Subject: The Social Psychology of the Psychological Experiment.* Boston: Little, Brown.

Adams, M. (1973). "Science, Technology, and Some Dilemmas of Advocacy," *Science, 180,* 840–842.

Beach, F. A. (1950). "The Snark was a Boojum," *American Psychologist, 5,* 115–124.

Beach, F. A. (1960). "Experimental Investigations of Species Specific Behavior," *American Psychologist, 15,* 1–18.

Bean, W. B. (1959). "The Ethics of Experimentation on Human Beings." In S. O. Waife and A. P. Shapiro, eds., *The Clinical Evaluation of New Drugs*. New York: Hoeber-Harper, pp. 76–84.

Bell, C. R. (1961). "Psychological Versus Sociological Variables in Studies of Volunteer Bias in Surveys," *Journal of Applied Psychology, 45*, 80–85.

Boice, R. (1973). "Domestication," *Psychological Bulletin, 80*, 215–230.

Chapanis, A. (1967). "The Relevance of Laboratory Studies to Practical Situations," *Ergonomics, 10*, 557–577.

Christie, R. (1951). "Experimental Naïveté and Experiential Naïveté," *Psychological Bulletin, 48*, 327–339.

Clark, K. E. et al. (1967). "Privacy and Behavioral Research," *Science, 155*, 535–538.

Cochran, W. G. (1963). *Sampling Techniques*. 2nd ed. New York: Wiley.

Cochran, W. G., Mosteller, F., and Tukey, J. W. (1953). "Statistical Problems of the Kinsey Report," *Journal of the American Statistical Association, 48*, 673–716.

Cope, C. S., and Kunce, J. T. (1971). "Unobtrusive Behavior and Research Methodology," *Journal of Counseling Psychology, 18*, 592–594.

Cox, D. E., and Sipprelle, C. N. (1971). "Coercion in Participation as a Research Subject," *American Psychologist, 26*, 726–728.

Damon, A. (1965). "Discrepancies Between Findings of Longitudinal and Cross-sectional Studies in Adult Life: Physique and Physiology," *Human Development, 8*, 16–22.

Deming, W. E. (1944). "On Errors in Surveys," *American Sociological Review, 9*, 359–369.

Ehrlich, A. (1974). "The Age of the Rat," *Human Behavior, 3*, 25–28.

Etzioni, A. (1973). "Regulation of Human Experimentation," *Science, 182*, 1203.

Eysenck, H. J. (1967). *The Biological Basis of Personality*. Springfield, Ill.: Charles C. Thomas.

Ferber, R. (1948–1949). "The Problem of Bias in Mail Returns: A Solution," *Public Opinion Quarterly, 12*, 669–676.

Ford, R. N., and Zeisel, H. (1949). "Bias in Mail Surveys Cannot be Controlled by One Mailing," *Public Opinion Quarterly, 13*, 495–501.

Fraser, S. C., and Zimbardo, P. G. (n.d.) "Subject Compliance: The Effects of Knowing One is A Subject," Unpublished manuscript. New York University.

French, J. R. P. (1963). Personal communication. Aug. 19.

Haas, K. (1970). "Selection of Student Experimental Subjects," *American Psychologist, 25*, 366.

Hansen, M. H., and Hurwitz, W. N. (1946). "The Problem of Non-response in Sample Surveys," *Journal of the American Statistical Association, 41*, 517–529.

Hilgard, E. R. (1967). Personal communication. Feb. 6.

Horowitz, I. A. (1969). "Effects of Volunteering, Fear Arousal, and Number of Communications on Attitude Change," *Journal of Personality and Social Psychology, 11*, 34–37.

Hyman, H., and Sheatsley, P. B. (1954). "The Scientific Method." In D. P. Geddes, ed., *An Analysis of the Kinsey Reports*. New York: New American Library.

Johnson, R. W. (1973). "The Obtaining of Experimental Subjects," *Canadian Psychologist, 14*, 208–211.

Katz, J. (1972). *Experimentation with Human Beings: The Authority of the Investigator, Subject, Professions, and State in the Human Experimentation Process*. New York: Russell Sage Foundation (with the assistance of A. M. Capron and E. S. Glass).

Kavanau, J. L. (1964). "Behavior: Confinement, Adaptation, and Compulsory Regimes in Laboratory Studies," *Science, 143*, 490.

Kavanau, J. L. (1967). "Behavior of Captive White-footed Mice," *Science, 155*, 1623–1639.

King, D. J. (1970). "The Subject Pool," *American Psychologist, 25*, 1179–1181.

Lana, R. E. (1969). "Pretest Sensitization." In R. Rosenthal and R. L. Rosnow, eds., *Artifact in Behavioral Research*. New York: Academic Press.

Leslie, L. L. (1972). "Are High Response Rates Essential to Valid Surveys?" *Social Science Research, 1*, 323–334.

Lester, D. (1969). "The Subject as a Source of Bias in Psychological Research," *Journal of General Psychology, 81*, 237–248.

Locke, H. J. (1954). "Are Volunteer Interviewees Representative?" *Social Problems, 1*, 143–146.

London, P., and Rosenhan, D. (1964). "Personality Dynamics," *Annual Review of Psychology, 15*, 447–492.

MacDonald, A. P., Jr. (1972). "Does Required Participation Eliminate Volunteer Differences?" *Psychological Reports, 31*, 153–154.

Marlatt, G. A. (1973). "Are College Students 'Real People'?" *American Psychologist, 28*, 852–853.

Marmer, R. S. (1967). "The Effects of Volunteer Status on Dissonance Reduction." Unpublished master's thesis, Boston University.

Martin, D. C., Arnold, J. D., Zimmerman, T. F., and Richart, R. H. (1968). "Human Subjects in Clinical Research—A Report of Three Studies," *New England Journal of Medicine, 279*, 1426-1431.

Maul, R. C. (1970). "NCATE Accreditation." *Journal of Teacher Education, 21*, 47–52.

May, W. T., Smith, H. W., and Morris, J. R. (1968). "Consent Procedures and Volunteer Bias: A Dilemma," Paper read at Southeastern Psychological Association, Roanoke, April.

McGuire, W. J. (1969). "Suspiciousness of Experimenter's Intent." In R. Rosenthal and R. L. Rosnow, eds., *Artifact in Behavioral Research*. New York: Academic Press.

McNemar, Q. (1946). "Opinion-attitude Methodology," *Psychological Bulletin, 43*, 289–374.

Miller, S. E. (1966). "Psychology Experiments Without Subjects' Consent," *Science, 15*, 152.

Oakes, W. (1972). "External Validity and the Use of Real People as Subjects," *American Psychologist, 27*, 959–962.

Ora, J. P., Jr. (1965). "Characteristics of the Volunteer for Psychological Investigations," Technical Report, No. 27, November. Vanderbilt University, Contract Nonr 2149 (03).

Orlans, H. (1967). "Developments in Federal Policy Toward University Research," *Science, 155*, 665–668.

Orne, M. T. (1969). "Demand Characteristics and the Concept of Quasi-controls." In R. Rosenthal and R. L. Rosnow, eds., *Artifact in Behavioral Research*. New York: Academic Press.

Orne, M. T. (1970). "Hypnosis, Motivation, and the Ecological Validity of the Psychological Experiment," *Nebraska Symposium on Motivation, 18*, 187–265.

Parten, M. (1950). *Surveys, Polls, and Samples: Practical Procedures*. New York: Harper.

Pavlos, A. J. (1972). "Debriefing Effects for Volunteer and Nonvolunteer Subjects: Reactions to Bogus Physiological Feedback," Paper read at Southern Society for Philosophy and Psychology, St. Louis, March–April.

Resnick, J. H., and Schwartz, T. (1973). "Ethical Standards as an Independent Variable in Psychological Research," *American Psychologist, 28*, 134–139.

Richter, C. P. (1959). "Rats, Man, and the Welfare State," *American Psychologist, 14*, 18–28.

Rokeach, M. (1966). "Psychology Experiments without Subjects' Consent," *Science, 152*, 15.

Rosenberg, M. J. (1969). "The Conditions and Consequences of Evaluation Apprehension." In R. Rosenthal and R. L. Rosnow, eds., *Artifact in Behavioral Research*. New York: Academic Press.

Rosenhan, D. (1967). "On the Social Psychology of Hypnosis Research." In J. E. Gordon, ed., *Handbook of Clinical and Experimental Hypnosis*. New York: MacMillan, pp. 481-510.

Rosenthal, R. (1965). "The Volunteer Subject," *Human Relations, 18*, 389–406.

Rosenthal, R., and Rosnow, R. L. (1969). "The Volunteer Subject." In R. Rosenthal and R. L. Rosnow, eds., *Artifact in Behavioral Research*. New York: Academic Press.

Rosnow, R. L., and Rosenthal, R. (1970). "Volunteer Effects in Behavioral Research." In K. H. Craik, B. Kleinmuntz, R. L. Rosnow, R. Rosenthal, J. A. Cheyne, and R. H. Walters, *New Directions in Psychology*, Vol. IV. New York: Holt, Rinehart and Winston.

Ruebhausen, O. M., and Brim, O. G. (1966). "Privacy and Behavioral Research," *American Psychologist, 21*, 423–437.

Sasson, R., and Nelson, R. M. (1969). "The Human Experimental Subject in Context," *The Canadian Psychologist, 10*, 409–437.

Schappe, R. H. (1972). "The Volunteer and the Coerced Subject," *American Psychologist, 27*, 508–509.

Short, R. R., and Oskamp, S. (1965). "Lack of Suggestion Effects on Perceptual Isolation (Sensory Deprivation) Phenomena," *Journal of Nervous and Mental Disease, 141*, 190–194.

Silverman, I., and Margulis, S. (1973). "Experiment Title as a Source of Sampling Bias in Commonly Used 'Subject-pool' Procedures," *Canadian Psychologist, 14,* 197–201.

Smith, R. E. (1969). "The Other Side of the Coin," *Contemporary Psychology, 14,* 628–630.

Steiner, I. D. (1972). "The Evils of Research: Or What My Mother Didn't Tell Me About the Sins of Academia," *American Psychologist, 27,* 766–768.

Straits, B. C., and Wuebben, P. L. (1973). "College Students' Reactions to Social Scientific Experimentation," *Sociological Methods and Research, 1,* 355–386.

Straits, B. C., Wuebben, P. L., and Majka, T. J. (1972). "Influences on Subjects' Perceptions of Experimental Research Situations," *Sociometry, 35,* 499–518.

Sullivan, D. S., and Deiker, T. E. (1973). "Subject-Experimenter Perceptions of Ethical Issues in Human Research," *American Psychologist, 28,* 587–591.

Trotter, S. (1974). "Strict Regulations Proposed for Human Experimentation," *APA Monitor, 5,* 1–8.

Walsh, J. (1973). "Addiction Research Center: Pioneers Still on the Frontier," *Science, 182,* 1229–1231.

Wells, B. W. P., and Schofield, C. B. S. (1972). "Personality Characteristics of Homosexual Men Suffering From Sexually Transmitted Diseases," *British Journal of Venereal Diseases, 48,* 75–78.

Wicker, A. W. (1968a). "Overt Behaviors Toward the Church by Volunteers, Follow-up Volunteers, and Non-Volunteers in a Church Survey," *Psychological Reports, 22,* 917–920.

Wicker, A. W. (1968b). "Requirements for Protecting Privacy of Human Subjects: Some Implications for Generalization of Research Findings," *American Psychologist, 23,* 70–72.

Wolfensberger, W. (1967). "Ethical Issues in Research With Human Subjects," *Science, 155,* 47–51.

Wolfle, D. (1960). "Research With Human Subjects," *Science, 132,* 989.

Wunderlich, R. A., and Becker, J. (1969). "Obstacles to Research in the Social and Behavioral Sciences," *Catholic Educational Review, 66,* 722–729.

Field and Survey Methods

Clearly the majority of studies carried out in the area of organizational behavior are field studies. Field studies (as well as survey research) often represent a cost-effective compromise strategy for examining a given topic. They are typically easy to design and execute, do not unduly disturb the research site (as field experiments might), and are relatively inexpensive. In fact, there are many situations in which experimental methods are either not feasible or are not suitable as a research design. In such cases, field studies or survey research may be more appropriate.

For instance, some variables (e.g., sex, social class, age, job classification) cannot be experimentally varied, but may be important in the study of human behavior at work. Second, some variables (e.g., alcoholism, worker alienation) cannot be ethically manipulated. Third, it is not always feasible to set up a controlled field experiment (for example, to study the effects of different compensation systems on productivity) because of the inability to secure organizational cooperation. Finally, researchers often wish to do field studies in order to identify important variables that are then included in a model for subsequent experiments using more rigorous methods. In short, although nonexperimental methods may lack a certain degree of rigor and control, there are reasons why their choice as a research design is suitable.

The problem is not simply to examine the characteristics of field and survey methods in organizational research; instead, it is to review several unique aspects of methods that hitherto have received little attention, despite their potential value to researchers. Such methods include participant observation and phenomenology, whose underlying assumptions differ radically from the more common, "traditional" field methods. As Bruyn notes in this first reading selection: "The traditional empiricist sets up many preconceptions of his subject through his study of background materials, his definition of variables, his hypotheses, and the causal order he expects to find among his variables." In contrast, phenomenologists or participant observers typically "let the variables define themselves in the context of the research . . . and examine causal relations between these variables on the basis of the social perception of the subjects themselves." The selection by Bruyn cogently summarizes the major distinctions between these two approaches to field studies, as well as some of the more subtle differences between phenomenology and participant observation.

The second selection, by Kimberly, examines in detail the design and use of longitudinal research in organizations. Longitudinal research differs from cross-sectional research in that multiple data points are used across time; it is not an "organizational snapshot." As such, the researcher is provided with a unique opportunity to examine trends or changes in major study variables over time and develop a reasonable understanding concerning major processes in organizations. Based on this understanding, organizational interventions can be designed and then monitored. Several such advantages of longitudinal research (compared to cross-sectional research) are discussed. Kimberly then reviews several of the methodological problems inherent in such designs. Included here are the issues of appropriate time intervals for data collection, the duration of longitudinal studies, reliability problems, life cycle problems, and the selection of suitable analytic techniques. Kimberly points out that while problems exist with longitudinal designs (as they do with any design), such techniques provide for a richness of empirical findings not possible using more static designs. In his own words: "Longitudinal research in and on formal organizations is absolutely essential if we are to develop better theory and models and better strategies for interventions of various kinds" (p. 344).

Finally, Staw discusses a major problem that is endemic to many field studies, yet often goes unnoticed in our search for suitable models of organizational behavior. Specifically, Staw shows by way of example how causal inferences from correlational findings (such as those resulting from field studies) may in fact be the reverse of what is believed. Consider the following example: In many studies, it is hypothesized that increases in job scope (e.g., increased responsibility, autonomy, feedback, etc.) lead to increases in job performance. In most cases, job scope is measured by asking employees to describe their jobs (i.e., perceptual measures). Staw describes how basic attribution processes may cause subjects in such studies to describe their jobs *based upon* their existing knowledge of their own performance. In other words, performance causes perceptions of job scope rather than the opposite. People who perform well tend to like their jobs and describe them in favorable terms. On the other hand, people who perform poorly may need to "blame" their poor performance on something, including a poor job. Staw's findings from a study clearly support this attributional explanation, thus raising serious questions concerning the validity of perceptual measures of job scope or other such measures.

In all, the three readings push beyond the standard topics discussed in books or chapters on field studies and explore three major issues of importance in the study of organizational behavior.

REFERENCES AND SUGGESTED READINGS

Babbie, E. R. *Survey Research Methods.* Belmont, CA.: Wadsworth, 1973.

Bouchard, T. J. "Field Research Methods." In M. Dunnette (ed.). *Handbook of Industrial and Organizational Psychology.* Chicago: Rand McNally, 1976.

Buchwald, A. M. "Verbal Utterances as Data." In H. Feigl and G. Maxwell (eds.). *Current Issues in the Philosophy of Science.* New York: Holt, Rinehart & Winston, 1961.

Davis, J. A. *Elementary Survey Analysis.* Englewood Cliffs: Prentice-Hall, 1971.

Filstead, W. J. *Qualitative Methodology.* Chicago: Markham, 1970.

McCall, G. J., and Simmons, J. L. (eds.). *Issues in Participant Observation.* Reading, Mass.: Addison-Wesley, 1969.

Scott, W. R. "Field Methods in the Study of Organizations." In J. March (ed.). *Handbook of Organizations.* Chicago: Rand McNally, 1965.

8   The New Empiricists: The Participant Observer and Phenomenologist

Severyn T. Bruyn

Researchers in participant observation in the United States and researchers in phenomenology in Europe have been creating new procedures and perspectives in the study of man in society that break fundamentally with those of the older schools of scientific empiricism. The method of participant observation can be observed as developing in the works of American sociologists like Everett Hughes, Maurice Schwartz, Howard S. Becker, Herbert Gans, Anselm Strauss, and William Whyte. The method of phenomenology can be observed as developing in the works of such Europeans as George Gurvitch, Max Scheler, and Alfred Vierkandt. While studies in participant observation have been largely American in origin and studies in phenomenology have been largely European, they both exhibit a number of similarities, especially when they are seen in contrast to traditional empiricism. The similiarities are so marked that study of how ideas in these two new developments in research are related could produce the beginning of a rapprochement between the great opposing positions of American and European thought.

My purpose here is to suggest a few of the methodological features which participant observers and phenomenologists have in common when they are jointly compared to traditional scientific empiricism. The phenomenological method as described by Herbert Spiegelberg can serve as a useful model utilizing certain features of this model as a basis for making some comparisons with participant observation and with traditional empiricism.

Spiegelberg describes seven different steps in the phenomenological method which guide the researcher.[1] These steps are as follows:

1. Investigating particular phenomena
2. Investigating general essences
3. Apprehending essential relationships among essences
4. Watching modes of appearing
5. Watching the constitution of phenomena in consciousness
6. Suspending belief in the existence of the phenomena
7. Interpreting the meaning of phenomena

Certain subphases of these steps are especially notable for comparison. The first step contains three: (1) an intuitive grasp of the phenomena, (2) their analytic examination, and (3) their description. In this first subphase, the phenomenologist is required

From S. T. Bruyn, "The New Empiricists: The Participant Observer and Phenomenologist," *Sociology and Social Research*, 1967, 51(3), pp. 317–322. Reproduced by permission.

to become highly aware of his subject and its surroundings in order to obtain an accurate intuitive grasp of it. In this sense the phenomenologist is very much like the participant observer in so far as he approaches his subject with every effort to eliminate his preconceptions about it. He has no hypothesis to direct him; he takes special pains to conduct his research with a totally open mind, open in depth to all the stimuli that impinge upon his consciousness during his investigation.

This initial phenomenological rule of openness is reflected in the writings of participant observers who have found that theories or hypotheses can interfere with the accuracy of the findings. In their study of *Boys in White*, Becker, Geer, Hughes, and Strauss stress this rule as basic to their method. [2]

> This meant that we concentrated on *what* students learned as well as on *how* they learned it. Both of those assumptions committed us to working with an open theoretical scheme in which variables were to be discovered rather than with a scheme in which variables decided on in advance would be located and their consequences isolated and measured . . . .

The traditional empiricist sets up many preconceptions of his subject through his study of background materials, his definition of variables, his hypotheses, and the causal order he expects to find among his variables. The phenomenologist and the participant observer, on the other hand, tend to let the variables define themselves in the context of the research. And they examine causal relations between these variables on the basis of the social perception of the subjects themselves. The emphasis of the phenomenologist and the participant observer is upon following those procedures which best allow the subjects to speak for themselves in contrast to the traditional empiricist who emphasizes procedures which help explain the subjects from an independent standpoint.

The fourth step which Spiegelberg calls "watching modes of appearing" stresses the importance of seeing objects as they actually exist rather than as we imagine they exist. For example, if we look at a cube-like object we really see only one side of it with other sides shading off from our perception in a trapezoid-like form. One side, in fact, is totally invisible to us. And yet, when we observe the cube, our imagination normally immediately supplies the whole image. The process is so unconscious that we do not report it as we actually observe it. In field research of community life this experience is paralleled by what participant observers witness when participating only in the activities of one class level. When the observer participating in the upper class, for example, describes the lower classes, these lower classes visibly shade off, so to speak, into general categories. Lower class people are observed as "all wage-earners" or "the people on the other side of the tracks." If the observer were to participate in the life of the lower classes he would find considerable differentiation evident among the people themselves which he did not observe by taking the role of the members of the upper class. Lloyd Warner has already informed us of this experiential phenomenon. Class members of upper and lower extremes of a community cannot "see" the differences existing among the subclasses of those opposite to them. As a sociologist, however, the observer tends to supply the remaining image on the basis of his prior scientific conception of class structure (just as we normally supply the missing side of the cube and do not see the trapezoid-like shape of the sides as they appear to our eyes). The function of the phenomenologist and the participant observer in these cases is to record these dimensions of the object under study as they appear to the consciousness without supplying what the researchers conceive to be the whole object. Only later, are they privileged to supply the modes which complete the image when they finally appear through the total research process.

Edmund Husserl would contend that phenomenology is more fundamental than empiricism as a methodological effort to understand the world.[3] Phenomenology underlies traditional empiricism; it is a kind of foundation to the scientific method. (At one point Husserl called phenomenology the "true empiricism.") Therefore, it cannot be compared with traditional empiricism as though the two methods were polar types. Nevertheless, it is worthwhile summarizing some of the differences which appear evident in both approaches in order to gain insight into their character. The following are three points which both phenomenology and participant observation have in common in opposition to traditional empiricism.

First, the new researchers seek to investigate particular phenomena without preconception of their nature while the traditional empiricist is definitive in his preconceptions and his experimental design prior to his investigation. *Second*, the new researchers observe phenomena that appear symbolically in their consciousness and treat these symbols as data whereas the traditional empiricist observes first what immediately appears to his senses and often restricts his study solely to the realm of sense data. *Third*, the new researchers intuit essences and essential relations existing in the symbolic data they study whereas traditional empiricists operationally define variables which have visible reference and which can then be studied for their correspondence statistically.

The difference between knowing what appears to one's consciousness symbolically and knowing what appears immediately to one's senses by applying experimental controls, is basic here. The phenomenologist, like the participant observer, assumes that reliable knowledge can be gathered apart from sheer reason or sensory observation alone. Even though sense and reason enter the process of understanding at different stages to complement his findings, the observer finds that intuition which surrounds an adequate interpretation of symbolic data is also an important part of this process. While it is true that the traditional empiricist has occasionally recognized the useful role of intuition in field work by way of revelations which occur outside his legitimate logical-experimental procedure, he has never sought to explain the intuitive process in terms of a reliable process for gathering knowledge. I would suggest that the emerging methods of phenomenology and participant observation can now serve as an explanation of this intuitive process. What lies behind the sudden revelations in field research— or what Robert Merton has called the "serendipity pattern"[4]—are results of what is embodied in these new research procedures. What Merton calls surprising and unanticipated datum in traditional empirical studies is actually insight produced unintentionally through the researcher's unconscious encounter with the symbolic nuances of data— an encounter with a process which has become rationalized in the methods of phenomenology and participant observation. The researcher discovers new meanings in his data as he knowingly participates in the process of social communication which reflect the symbolic life of the people he studies. If he perceives this symbolic life accurately in his role as a participant observer he is rewarded by finding new perspectives cast on his data.

The method of phenomenology and the method of participant observation are not the same in spite of their common differences with traditional empiricism. The phenomenologist studies symbolic meanings as they constitute themselves in human consciousness.[5] The participant observer does this too but he is more concerned with how symbols are constituted in particular cultures and he studies these symbols through the process of taking the role of the people who normally experience these symbols. In the process of taking their role, he becomes personally involved in living with the culture he studies. He then has the problem of balancing his involvement with objective detachment in arriving at an accurate accounting of the culture. Personal involvement with cultural symbols is not a necessary factor entering into the method of phenomenology or the method traditional to empiricism. In fact, the traditional empiricist would condemn any involvement as alien to the values of the scientific process of gaining objective knowledge.

New empiricists, like the participant observer in America and like the phenomenologist in Europe, present a challenge to social scientists today who follow the older traditions of empiricism. A more thorough study of their approaches could provide a basis for resolving some of the problems which have long plagued social scientists without answers. For example, there is schism between what the phenomenologist calls "lived experience" (which is essentially what the participant observer studies) and scientific abstractions and reductionisms. There is also the schism between the moral and the natural worlds of man and the conflicting perspectives they have each engendered in relation to one another. The phenomenologist and the participant observer have been building new ground beneath these schisms. They are both taking man as he is given in his lived experience. They are placing the mechanical, organic, and functional images of man in their proper perspective—not negating their value to the formulation of theory but denying their supremacy in the explanation of society. They are giving supremacy to an inner perspective of man in society which ultimately could lead toward a more comprehensive sociological perspective. They are observing man in his concreteness and subjectiveness as opposed to the abstractness and objectiveness of the traditional empiricist and theorist; they are observing him as a social being with freedom and purpose as opposed to observing him deterministically as the product of external forces. In this process of seeing man from an inner perspective, these new researchers are creating a foundation for a human perspective of man. If this inner perspective were combined with the external perspective of the scientific tradition in the context of social research, the result could have a significant effect upon sociological theory in comprehending man in his wholeness during the latter third of the twentieth century.

NOTES

1. Herbert Spiegelberg, "The Essentials of the Phenomenological Method," *The Phenomenological Movement: A Historical Introduction* (2nd ed.; The Hague: Martinus Nijhoff, 1965), Vol. 2, pp. 655-70. The method of phenomenology is like participant observation and traditional empiricism in the sense that it is not restricted to the field of sociology by any means but rather exhibits a form which has an interdisciplinary character.

2. Howard S. Becker, Blanche Geer, Everett C. Hughes, and Anselm L. Strauss, *Boys in White* (Chicago: University of Chicago Press, 1961), p. 18.

3. Edmund Husserl, *Ideas*, trans. W. R. Boyce Gibson (London: George Allen & Univer., 1931). See also: E. Parl Welch, *The Philosophy of Edmund Husserl* (New York: Columbian University Press, 1941).

4. Robert K. Merton, *Social Theory and Social Structure* (New York: The Free Press, a Division of the MacMillan Co., 1949), p. 98.

5. A recent discussion of the nature of phenomenology in relation to sociological theory may be found in Edward A. Tiryakian, "Existential Phenomenology," *American Sociological Review*, 30 (October, 1965), 674-88. Critical appraisals of this article and a reply may be found in *American Sociological Review*, 31 (April, 1966), 258-64.

9 Issues in the Design of Longitudinal Organizational Research[1]

John R. Kimberly

The increase in the amount of empirical work in what might generally be called the area of organizational analysis in the last ten years is impressive indeed. While much of this work has been done by sociologists, individuals trained in other disciplines—notably psychology, economics, anthropology, and political science—have made important and extensive contributions as well. The result of these efforts, taken collectively, is a dramatic expansion of the empirical base of "organization theory." This expansion has not, however, been paralleled by a similar flowering of theory. Many explanations, of course, can be constructed to account for the apparent gap between data and theory; and although it is not the purpose of this paper to attempt to develop an elaborate argument on that issue, it does appear that at least part of the explanation lies in the fact that most of our data about organizations are cross-sectional while our nascent theories are, of necessity, dynamic.

This problem is not unique to the field of organizational research. Galtung (1970), for example, has argued that social science research in general is characterized by synchronic data and diachronic interpretations of those data. The nature of the problem, however, is becoming more widely recognized by organizational researchers, as the number of recent articles issuing clarion calls, by way of conclusion, for longitudinal research to pursue the implications of findings based on cross-sectional data suggests. That the problem is complex is evidenced by the mixed results coming from the few exemplars of longitudinal research which have appeared in the literature, such as the work of Hage and Dewar (1973) and Meyer (1972). Because of the increasing awareness in the field of the potential importance of longitudinal research and because of my own tentative efforts to undertake longitudinal research and the kinds of issues that have arisen as that work has proceeded, it appeared useful to attempt to consider seriously and somewhat systematically just what kinds of issues are involved in this enterprise. This paper, which has been written as much to raise questions as to provide answers, begins by trying to specify just what longitudinal organizational research is. Using the definition developed as a point of departure, a number of issues in this kind of research are raised, discussed, and illustrated with reference to an ongoing research project which is in the process of being redefined from a cross-sectional to a longitudinal study. Finally, the prospects for longitudinal organizational research are discussed briefly.

Source: "Issues in the Design of Longitudinal Organizational Research" by John R. Kimberly is reprinted from *Sociological Methods & Research* Vol. 4, No. 3 (February 1976) pp. 321–347 by permission of the Publisher, Sage Publications, Inc.

WHAT IS LONGITUDINAL RESEARCH?

The answer to this question does not come as easily as one might think. It is clearly not cross-sectional research; that is, it is not research based on data collected about an organization or organizations at a single point in time. It is not, therefore, an organizational snapshot. That said, however, it becomes more difficult to specify just what longitudinal organizational research is. Is it simply research involving a data collection strategy using more than one snapshot? Because of the difficulty encountered in answering this question directly, it seemed reasonable to examine the advantages generally thought to derive from longitudinal research and to work toward a definition inductively.

PRESUMED ADVANTAGES OF LONGITUDINAL RESEARCH

Review of available materials suggests five advantages generally thought to accompany longitudinal research. While there may be additional advantages, the five noted below appear to be the most frequently acknowledged.

1. *Longitudinal research facilitates attempts to establish causality.* Much has been written about the dangers inherent in drawing causal inferences from correlational analysis of cross-sectional data. Testing a causal hypothesis which predicts a relationship between two variables, A and B, requires several assumptions if the test is to be conducted using cross-sectional data. First, it must be assumed that the units of analysis are distributed across the range of the causal sequence. This means that some organizations must have low values for A, and others must have high values for A. If the causal hypothesis is correct, organizations with high values for A will have high values (or low values, depending on the hypothesis) for B. This will result in high correlations between the two variables. Absence of such correlations may be taken as evidence against the hypothesized relationship.

A second important assumption which must be met if a causal hypothesis is to be tested utilizing cross-sectional data is the assumption of causal priority. If it is hypothesized that variable A causes variable B when in fact variable B causes variable A, and the correlation between the two variables is high, then the causal hypothesis will not be rejected when in fact it is false. In many analyses the assumption of causal priority for one variable over another is not problematic. For example, if one hypothesized that performance in high school leads to performance in college, the causal priorities are relatively clear: it is not possible that performance in college can lead to performance in high school. Furthermore, if the causal priorities are clear, more sophisticated multivariate analyses may be employed to test for spurious relationships and for direct and indirect effects, all utilizing cross-sectional data.

Causal priorities between variables in most organizational research, however, are more problematic than was the relationship in the case of high school versus college performance, and in many cases it is possible to argue that the causal priorities are the reverse of the ones assumed. For example, it has been assumed in a study of hospital adoption of innovation which is described later in this paper that level of medical expertise is causally prior to amount of adoption behavior, because a new item is not likely to be adopted unless there is knowledge of it and the expertise required for its use. An alternative argument, however, may be made. It might be the case that hospitals would not be able to attract highly expert physicians unless they had modern technical equipment available for use. If this were the case, then the causal assumptions made above would be invalid, and the relationship observed between expertise and adoption would be a function of the causal priority of adoption over expertise rather than the reverse.

A second example of this problem involves the hypothesized causal priority between centralization of authority and adoption behavior. It was hypothesized on theoretical grounds in the original study that centralization would lead to lower adoption behavior. To the extent that physicians (e.g., department heads) had authority to purchase new equipment, it was expected that the hospital would be able to adopt technological innovations more rapidly and more often. But the reversed causal priority is perhaps equally plausible. To the extent that a hospital has modern technical equipment, it may be more dependent upon physician expertise. Not having the knowledge required to allocate resources for maintenance and additions, the administrator or the board might be compelled to decentralize discretion. So long as cross-sectional data are used to test the hypothesized relationship between centralization and responsiveness to change, the question of the causal priority between these two variables remains problematic. A major advantage of longitudinal research on formal organizations, therefore, is that temporal precedence can be established, at least within the constraints of available data. Although this clearly does not solve the considerable problems of the possible influence of other variables, or what Galtung (1970) has called the problem of invariance, it does decrease the margin of error in causal inference.

2. *Longitudinal research can help minimize the problems encountered when process is inferred from cross-sectional data.* Most of the kinds of questions that organizational researchers ask are process-oriented. Either implicitly or explicitly the questions focus on the interaction among variables in a setting which, whether the researchers' models are recursive or nonrecursive, unfolds in social time. It is difficult indeed to conceive of an interesting or important question about organizations which does not in some way involve a dynamic as opposed to static orientation. Furthermore, many of the variables that are used by organizational researchers actually represent information about organizations which is cumulative (i.e., which involves a temporal dimension) but which is viewed, for purposes of analysis, as cross-sectional. Indices of organizational (or individual) performance are perhaps the most obvious example. What results, therefore, is research activated by dynamic questions and concepts, implemented using some combination of cross-sectional, and dynamic converted to cross-sectional, variables, and then interpreted in many, if not most, cases in dynamic terms.

For purposes of illustration, consider the various studies of the interrelationships among structural characteristics of organizations. In particular, consider studies of the relationships between organizational structure and the size of the "supportive component" or the "administrative ratio." To cite but one example, Anderson and Warkov (1961) in their well-known, cross-sectional study of hospitals concluded that:

1. The relative size of the administrative component decreases as the number of persons performing identical tasks in the same place increases. 2. The relative size of the administrative component increases as the number of places at which work is performed increases. 3. The relative size of the administrative component increases as the number of tasks performed at the same place increases (or as roles become increasingly specialized and differentiated). [p. 27]

The problem here is that the data on which this interpretation is based are collected from a sample of organizations at a particular point in time, while the interpretation itself refers to processes within organizations over time. One is thus in the difficult position of having to assume, if the interpretation is to be accepted, that all organizations go through identical, or at least similar, processes of structural evolution and that environmental and/or contextual influences are either constant or random. Few organizational researchers would be prepared, I suspect, to accept this assumption, particularly in light of the differential dependence that different types of organizational economies have on various sectors of national economies. In addition, it is implicitly assumed that all organizations, when conceived, are the same size, and this is clearly not the case. While some organizations start out very small, others clearly do not, yet this empirical reality has not been taken into account theoretically and the question of what consequences, if any, variability in initial size may have for structural configuration has not been asked.

Longitudinal research can help minimize the problems encountered in inferring process from cross-sectional data in other kinds of organizational studies as well, or at least may make it more difficult to make incorrect inferences. One might be interested, for example, in determining the relative influence of individual abilities and organizational factors on student performance in schools. One strategy for making such a determination would be to regress performance on a standard year-end examination on a measure of individual ability such as IQ and measures of organizational experience such as hours in class and patterns of sociometric contact among students. The problem here is that there is no way of knowing how changes in the measures of organizational experience over time, such as increased or decreased attendance or change in performance during the school year, may relate to year-end performance. In other words, there is no indication of what processes led to the empirical relationships observed at the end of the year and one can only speculate about them. Were a longitudinal strategy employed in which measures of appropriate variables were made at various points in time throughout the year, the potential exists for developing a more complex but theoretically more interesting picture of the processes involved.

3. *Longitudinal research facilitates the development of better models of organizational growth and change.* There is a void in the literature in the development of comprehensive theories of organizational growth and change. There are numerous descriptive case studies of change (e.g., Gouldner, 1954; Schulman, 1969), a few conceptual discussions of growth (e.g., Starbuck, 1965; Matras, 1975), many comparative empirical studies where patterns of growth are inferred from cross-sectional data (e.g., Anderson and Warkov, 1961; Blau et al., 1966), and the beginnings of systematic theories of growth (e.g., Starbuck, 1968); there is little in the way of the empirical foundation necessary if better models of growth and change are to be built. Longitudinal data, it is often argued, will provide the necessary empirical foundation for such development. Such data are needed if we are to be able to pursue the promising work that has begun to emerge in this important area (e.g., Starbuck, 1971), although it is highly likely that this research will be confronted by a new set of problems all its own, as Harris (1963) has pointed out.

4. *Longitudinal research permits one to take contextual constraints into account in the research design.* A criticism frequently made of cross-sectional or "one-shot" organizational-research designs is that the researcher is unable to develop any real sensitivity for the setting being studied, and that there is little possibility for taking the effects of contextual constraints into account as a result. This, in turn, creates problems in comparing the results of studies using similar variables in different settings and may, as some have argued, explain at least partially why results often appear contradictory. The problem is complex, for the extreme case of focus on contextual constraints is

idiosyncratic description, while the extreme case of method and measurement comparability is quantitatively comparable results which lack substantive significance.

Without intending to minimize the complexity of the problems involved, it is often argued that longitudinal research can enhance the substantive significance of research outcomes by permitting the investigator to gain sufficient familiarity with the setting that modifications of either instruments or design can be made where appropriate to reflect important dimensions of the setting. Graen (1975), for example, argues that the potential costs of "getting too close" to the organization are more than offset by the kinds of new understandings that can emerge and that "through iterations of testing and refining measures throughout (a) study and attempt at each stage to understand more and to document this understanding, (b) study successively approximates the crucial set of variables." Such understanding is important if the theoretical underpinnings of organizational analysis are to be strengthened.

5. *Longitudinal research ultimately enhances the effectiveness of various strategies for organizational intervention.* If longitudinal research can help sort out questions of causality, if it can produce clearer understandings of process, if it can facilitate the development of better models of growth and change, and if it permits identification of contextual constraints, then it should aid in the design of more effective strategies for intervention, irrespective of the target of the intervention. Presumably, strategies for producing change in an organizational system would be more effective as would strategies intended to produce change across and/or between relatively large numbers of organizations at the interpersonal, sociotechnical, and structural levels. In addition, one might expect that more effective strategies for the design of entirely new organizations as well as the modification of existing ones would result.

The preceding discussion of its presumed advantages provides some leverage on the concept of longitudinal research in the context of organizational analysis, although a precise and specific definition appears impossible. Based on the points made thus far, the following definition is suggested:

> Longitudinal organizational research consists of those techniques, methodologies and activities which permit the observation, description and/or classification of organizational phenomena in such a way that processes can be identified and empirically documented.

While this definition is broad enough to apply to organizational research in general, there is sufficient diversity in the field to warrant some attempt at classification. At the risk of oversimplification, it seems useful to distinguish two general classes of questions which researchers have asked about organizations, questions which imply different units of analysis. The first class of questions has to do with patterns of relationships between variables within organizations in which, to use Blau's (1965) terminology, the units of analysis are individuals or groups. Examples of such questions might be the relationship between job satisfaction and performance (e.g., Wanous, 1974) or the relationship between organizational commitment and turnover (e.g., Porter et al., 1974). Research on these questions has been predominantly, although not exclusively, carried out by psychologists, social psychologists, and some sociologists and might be called research *in* organizations.

The second class of questions has to do with patterns of relationships between variables across organizations in which, following Blau, the units of analysis are characteristics of organizations per se. Within this general class of questions there are three reasonably distinct avenues of inquiry that have been developed: comparative analyses of the relationships among structural characteristics of organizations (e.g., Pugh et al., 1968; Pondy, 1969) and of the relationship between structure and performance (e.g., Blau, 1973; Heydebrand, 1973); analyses of interorganizational relationships (e.g., Paulson, 1974); and analyses of the relationships between organizational structure and social structure (e.g., Stinchcombe, 1965), or of the organization-environment interface. Within this general class of questions an example of the first avenue of inquiry might be the relationship between organizational size and the administrative ratio—or between size, formalization and differentiation. An example of the second avenue of inquiry might be the relationship between the extent of domain consensus and the amount of exchange between organizations, and of the third, the relationship between the point in time at which an organization was founded and its structure. Research on these questions has been predominantly, although again not exclusively, carried out by sociologists, economists, and political scientists, and might be called research *on* organizations.

The distinction between research *in* organizations and research *on* organizations may dichotomize research activity in the field in a way which makes some work difficult to classify and hence may oversimplify reality to a certain extent. It does appear that the distinction is generally valid, however, and that the definition of what longitudinal organizational research is (or should be) may depend on whether we are talking about research *in* organizations or research *on* organizations. While one consequence of the distinction may well be to suggest the importance of research which establishes the links between the two, it also strongly suggests that the strategies for longitudinal research that are developed are likely to be at least in part a function of the unit of analysis of concern to the researcher.

Cross-classifying the distinction between cross-sectional and longitudinal, or what Burns (1967) and others have called synchronic and diachronic, research and that between research *in* and *on* organizations yields the following four fold table:

If one were to order the cells in Table 1 based on the frequency of studies falling within each, cells 1 and 3 (those involving cross-sectional as opposed to longitudinal designs) would be clearly the highest and cell 4 (that involving longitudinal research on organizations) would be clearly the lowest. Cell 2 would include many diachronic case studies (e.g., Dalton, 1959; Seashore and Bowers, 1963; Schulman 1969; Hage, 1974, Part I), although their absolute number would be considerably smaller than those in cells 1 and 3.

TABLE 1   Organizational Research Strategies

	Design	
Type of Research	Cross-Sectional	Longitudinal
IN Organizations	1	2
ON Organizations	3	4

Each cell so defined actually represents a particular research strategy, and each has its own particular advantages and disadvantages, many of which were discussed above. Two additional observations are occasioned by this way of thinking about research that has been done to date. First, research *in* organizations is generally characterized by what Campbell and Dunnette (1968) have called the "n = 1" problem. Although relatively large numbers of individuals may be interviewed or surveyed, this activity is usually carried out in a single organization. Even when a longitudinal strategy is used, therefore, although it has considerable advantages over the "one-shot" approach, there are problems of generalizability that are inescapable.

A second observation is the fact that the major lacuna in contemporary organizational research is longitudinal research *on* organizations. If theory in this field is to be built, then, research *in* organizations has to be carried out in samples of organizations and research *on* organizations has to be carried out using longitudinal designs. Only then can problems of comparability and generalizability begin to be solved.

ISSUES IN LONGITUDINAL ORGANIZATIONAL RESEARCH

The preceding observations provide the background against which a number of issues likely to confront those who are or may become involved in longitudinal organizational research may be discussed. Because the issues are themselves somewhat general, each of them is discussed both in the abstract and in terms of a specific example. The example provides a concrete illustration of the implications of each issue for the design and execution of actual research.

The study used for purposes of illustration is an investigation of hospital responsiveness to technological innovation, and was begun in 1968 at Cornell University under the direction of Gerald Gordon. Hospitals are technology-based organizations (Perrow, 1965), that is, their primary function, the diagnosis and treatment of illness, is linked to and is dependent upon an external body of scientific knowledge. The body of knowledge which forms the core of its technology changes as research refines and extends the state of the art and/or produces new breakthroughs which enable it to carry out its primary function more efficiently or effectively. Technological obsolescence in hospitals cannot only mean poorer care for patients and competitive disadvantage in areas served by more than one, it can also present problems for attracting qualified staff and for accreditation.

The problem of responsiveness, therefore, has important policy implications. How can responsiveness be either facilitated or, in some cases, inhibited? And in a period of rapidly rising costs in the hospital industry there is the further question of the relationship between adoption of technological innovations and increasing costs. The problem is also important in a theoretical sense. What kinds of organizational characteristics are related to variability in responsiveness, and under what conditions?

The original design for the study was based on a cross-sectional strategy, and it therefore fell in cell 3 of Table 1, being a cross-sectional study *on*, as opposed to *in*, organizations. Extent of adoption of innovation, the dependent variable, was based on hospital responses to whether they had purchased, rented, or leased any or all of eleven pieces of equipment and/or drugs and whether they had used a particular surgical procedure. Each of these items was identified by a panel of leading experts as an innovation, and evidence of adoption used was written records as opposed to recall. Coughenour (1966) had pointed out the problems of reliability associated with the use of recall in adoption studies, and a quantitative indication of the efficacy of the use of records is the fact that the interrater/intermethod method of determining the reliability of the dependent variable yielded a correlation of .86.

Information on both the dependent variable and the independent variables—organizational characteristics of the hospitals such as authority patterns, staffing patterns, and communication patterns—was collected by a mailed survey. Further details on the design and content of the survey can be found in Gordon et al. (1975). Preliminary findings are presented in Gordon et al. (1974), Kimberly (1974), Moch (1974) and Morse et al. (1974). For present purposes, what is important is the fact that an effort is currently being made to move from a cross-sectional to a longitudinal design, from cell 3 to cell 4, for many of the reasons discussed above as presumed advantages of longitudinal research. Perhaps the most important among these is the additional leverage which diachronic data provide in helping to sort out questions of causality, an importance which derives primarily from the policy relevance of the research itself.

Longitudinal organizational research, however, is not a panacea, and a number of issues are likely to confront those designing and/or doing it. The following discussion identifies and elaborates on some of these issues, without attaching any particular priorities to any one.

1. *How long is longitudinal?* The question was raised earlier in the paper about whether anything which involved data collection at more than one point in time qualified as longitudinal research. The answer to this question has to be "yes, but . . . ." Part of the "but" of the response refers to the appropriateness of the interval between data collection points. The issue is hopefully more or less obvious. If we are studying the maturation process in fruit flies, for example, and if we know that the average life span of a fruit fly is six weeks, we do not want to collect data every six weeks. A more appropriate time interval might be every six days or perhaps every six hours.

Similarly, in the analysis of organizations, the nature of the problem and the nature of the theoretical framework brought to bear on the problem contains, or should contain, at least part of the response to the question of how long longitudinal is. Generally, in studies *in* organizations the intervals will not be as long as in studies *on* organizations, for the nature of the research question which animates these kinds of studies is typically centered on processes which unfold in *relatively* short periods of time. In Haga et al.'s (1974) longitudinal study of role-making processes in formal organizations, for example, the total amount of time covered by the research was one academic year, and four different interventions were undertaken to collect data during the period. By way of contrast, Heydebrand's (1973) study of change in hospitals covers a period of twenty-five years (1935–1960) with two different data collection points. Collection of data at too frequent intervals may result purely in description and in what Campbell and Stanley (1966) have called test effects, whereas if the intervals are too long important aspects of the process of interest will not be captured.

Prima facie, then, it would seem that longitudinal studies of change in patterns of structural interrelationships might require a substantially longer time frame than studies of patterns of individual/organizational adjustment. If, for example, we are interested in how observed relationships between size, centralization, and formalization evolve, we would probably agree that to collect a body of data on these variables from a sample of organizations in 1974 and again from the same sample in 1975 would be inappropriate. The time span is too short to permit the processes which give rise to changes in the configuration of these three variables a chance to unfold. In the study of hospital adoption of technological innovation, this question became even more difficult. On the one hand, we did not want to collect a second wave of data from our sample too soon, before the effects of time could be expected to be observable. This, in our judgment, meant waiting at least five years. On the other hand, waiting that long had at least two other consequences. First, and perhaps most important, in the time that passed since the initial survey it was entirely possible that certain of the innovations comprising the original dependent variable would have been supplanted by even newer developments, particularly in a field as volatile and as rapidly changing as that of medical technology. Thus, the dependent variable might have to be updated to reflect changes in the state of the art. Second, the longer we waited, the greater the possibility that variables not taken into account in the study design might be affecting the nature of the relationships among those that were. The increasingly salient role of the federal government in the health care industry is an example germane to this particular study.

Thus the question of how long longitudinal is has both theoretical and strategic dimensions. On the theoretical side, there is really a lack of information and/or theory suggesting just what the appropriate data collection intervals in organizational research might or should be. Since we apparently know a good deal more about fruit flies than about organizations, the problem of specifying appropriate time spans for data collection in the analysis of their maturation process is more easily solved. Theoretical work in this area is notably absent and sorely needed in the study of organizations.

Theoretical resolution, however, does not necessarily lead to practical solution, and it is apparent that even if more adequate theory is developed, there will be strategic issues of a decidedly nontrivial nature that will have to be dealt with. Because social phenomena do not march to the tune of the researcher, a certain amount of creativity will have to be applied to the solution of practical problems such as those noted in the example discussed above. Increasing use of quasi-experimental designs may be one partial solution, but new ways of thinking about the problem will have to develop as well.

In the immediate future, then, we will have to be guided primarily by intuition. In certain instances the question will answer itself, as when interest is in a critical episode in which the organizational system undergoes a dramatic transformation (e.g., Haga et al., 1974). In such a case, research from the "beginning" to the "end" of the episode would be mandated. While much can be learned from analysis of critical episodes, as Galtung (1970) has noted, preoccupation with them results in an oversampling of the discontinuous and an undersampling of the statistically normal, with consequent implications for the theories that are built.

2. *How many data collection points are necessary in longitudinal organizational research?* A second part of the "but" of the response to the question raised at the beginning of the preceding section has to do with whether two data points are "enough" in longitudinal research. In my own view, one of the basic problems in this area is the 'before-after" mentality which tends to accompany much of this research, a mentality which is born of the language and technology of experimental design but which may not be appropriate for many kinds of organizational research problems. In "pure" experimental research, where exogenous variables can theoretically be controlled and where endogenous variables can theoretically be manipulated singly and where the knowledge base is theoretically high, it makes sense to use treatment and control groups in order to isolate the effects of a particular intervention. The two-point, before-and-after measurement strategy is very compatible with this kind of research.

One of the presumed advantages of longitudinal organizational research, however, is that it helps one understand process, and it is questionable how well two data points help in this regard. There are two questions which need to be posed. First, is it reasonable to represent organizational reality in such a way that a "before-after" approach makes sense? My own best guess at this point is that perhaps it is reasonable under some conditions, particularly when we are interested in examining the consequences of a "critical episode," but under most it probably is not. Organizational life does not seem to me to be easily partitionable into finite segments for the most part, and while laboratory research can help illuminate certain limited aspects of organizational reality, life in the natural setting appears to resist "before-after" paradigms. Second, even in those instances in which a before-after approach appears to make sense, is it likely that data gathered only "before" and "after" will be sufficient? Here I would argue that they will probably not be sufficient if one is interested in process.

How many data points are then necessary? Obviously there are no easy answers, but those involved in longitudinal research should at least be aware of the advantages and disadvantages of multiple data points in developing strategies and building models. In some instances the theoretical perspective used may suggest both the appropriate intervals between points and the actual number of points that would be desirable. In most cases, however, the research will be operating very much on a trial-and-error basis with little in the way of substantive theory as a guide. In these cases the exigencies of the research process itself will probably dictate the number of data points to a large extent. If data collection involves human subjects (as it would, I suspect, in at least some organizational research), for example, too frequent intervention is likely to have negative consequences for the quality of data obtained (Campbell and Stanley, 1966). If it involves a large sample of organizations, as in the case of the hospital study described above, it may be prohibitively expensive to intervene too frequently. Decisions should not be made on wholly pragmatic grounds, however. In the absence of general theoretical guidelines, techniques for estimating the rates of change of various kinds of organizational variables may be helpful in suggesting answers to the general question of how many data points are necessary. Economists and demographers have had some success in this regard, and while their techniques are in most cases not directly applicable to organizational research, either because the data do not meet the necessary statistical assumptions or because they are simply not available, we can learn much from the form that their modes of inquiry have taken. The recent work of Matras (1975) in which the optique of the demographer is applied to organizational analysis is but one example of the kinds of benefits that are likely to result.

The answer, then, to how many data points are necessary is complex. Ideally, the number involved should be suggested by the nature of the problem being investigated and the theoretical perspective used. Practically, however, the number will most likely be determined by resource constraints, models of analysis used by the researchers and the urgency of the results, although the theoretical limitations of the two polar opposite strategies of over-collection (pure description) versus under-collection (underspecification) will have to be taken into account.

3. *How does one deal with "reliability" in longitudinal organizational research?* There is a very special problem confronting those who do longitudinal research *in* organizations, the problem of reliability. Basically, the problem is this: Traditional psychometric theory has heavily emphasized reliability in measurement, that is, the extent to which a given measure is stable and yields reproducible results. Traditionally, too, psychometricians have held that the validity of a measure is, in part, a function of its reliability; reliability has been held to be a necessary but not sufficient condition for validity. The problem comes when one moves from a cross-sectional to a longitudinal research mode. Here the possibility exists that repeated measures over time of a particular variable (e.g., satisfaction) on the same people can yield results which, by traditional measures, are "unreliable" but which, if what has occurred in the behavior setting is taken into account, reflect real change over time. Thus, there is an important ques-

tion of how the concept of reliability (or at least the way in which estimates of reliability are determined empirically) needs to be modified when longitudinal research *in*
organizations is being carried out and scaling of responses of individuals is involved.
How, in other words, do we distinguish between change and error in this sort of
research?

The problem is not new; it has been noted by Deutscher (1966) and Hirschi and
Selvin (1967) among others. Yet it seems that the psychometric paradigm is still dominant where research *in* organizations is concerned. Preoccupation with methodological
"rigor" often overshadows substantive import, and there is little evidence of the progress in this area so longingly envisioned by Hirschi and Selvin (1967, p. 213).

Research *on* organizations is also faced by problems of reliability although of a
somewhat different sort. One such problem is the fact that most of the variables used
to characterize organizational structure and performance are aggregated. But it is a fact
of organizational life that the individuals whose behavior is being aggregated move
about. They may move laterally or vertically to new positions or they may leave the
organization and be replaced (or not, as the case may be). New individuals may enter
the organization either as replacements or as new additions to the personnel. Thus, in
the case of any particular organization in a sample of organizations the referents of
aggregation may change considerably between measurement interventions. Does or
should this fact affect our measurement procedures?

Answers to this question do not come easily, and the standard measurement
responses of the psychometricians are notably absent. In my own view, the answer has
to be based primarily on the nature of the problem being examined. In the case of the
hospital study, for example, the time interval between initial and subsequent data collection is sufficiently long so that it would be safe to assume that considerable moving
about has taken place. I would also take the position that since we are primarily interested in the organizational system, the fact that that system may be populated with
different actors is only important insofar as the positions any of them occupy are felt
to be of theoretical consequence for adoption of innovation. I would be concerned,
therefore, with whether there has been a change in hospital administrators between the
initial and subsequent data collection interventions and whether there has been a net
increase or decrease in the personnel. Overall, however, I would not be concerned with
the fact of movement per se. It does not appear, in and of itself, to be a source of
measurement error.

A different sort of reliability problem is that associated with measurement of the
dependent variable, extent of adoption. As noted earlier, because of rapidly expanding
knowledge in the field it is possible, even likely, that certain of the original innovations
have been replaced by newer ones. For this reason, it would be inappropriate to use a
test-retest approach to estimating the measure's reliability. Instead, a more reasonable
approach, given the nature of the problem being studied, would be to update the
dependent variable making whatever changes appeared necessary and then to use the
same interrater-intermethod method of estimating reliability that was used in the original study. To repeat the original measure might yield highly reliable but only marginally valid results under these conditions.

There is a similar problem associated with the independent variables in the hospital
study. Using the interrater-common-method method, reliability analyses for the original
study reported elsewhere (Gordon et al., 1975) showed that "factual" questions were
much more reliable than "perceptual" questions. I would argue that on questions requiring perceptions, the extent of homogeneity in perceptions by different individuals of

the same stimulus is not a measure of reliability as some might contend, with close agreement taken as an indicator of high reliability, but rather is a measure of consensus or lack thereof about various aspects of the organization and may itself be used as an important predictor of various outcomes. Putting this argument aside, one of the presumed advantages of longitudinal research is that one can modify instruments and designs based on experience and increased familiarity with the context. Such modification, however, may do violence to some of the more prominent canons of scientific research. For example, a question which arises in the hospital study is which of the questions from the original study should be precisely replicated? Although the study itself is not intended as a replication, for purposes of comparability it would be important to have identical measures of identical variables. How much modification can take place, therefore, before there is essentially a different study? How does modification affect reliability? These are challenging questions, and at this point we are only beginning to try to deal with them conceptually and empirically.

4. *How does one deal with organizational "life cycles" in longitudinal theory and research?* This issue primarily confronts those who are interested in comparative longitudinal research on relatively large numbers of organizations. Comparative analyses of structural evolution, for example, would be best carried out using data from comparable periods in the organizations' life cycles, since we know that organizations have differing rates of survival and may go through a variety of metamorphoses as they are born, live, and die. Comparing data on the relationships between size, centralization, and formalization across a large sample of organizations, all of which data were collected in 1975, means that in all likelihood data from some very "young," some "middle-aged," and some "senior-citizen" organizations are included. Our data collection strategy is cross-sectional and even though we may run through several iterations of the process, we are still faced by the same fundamental dilemma, the fact that we are isolating the characteristics of organizations and drawing dynamic inferences from their interrelationships when they may be in different phases of the evolutionary process.

Partialling out the effects of age is, of course, one solution, and age as a variable is becoming increasingly used by organizational researchers who may have been stimulated to some extent by the work of Stinchcombe (1965). Even this strategy, while preferable to ignoring the problem, is not without its drawbacks, as there is no reason necessarily to expect that the effects of age in the process of evolution correspond to those which are assumed by treating years in operation as an interval-level variable. Such treatment cannot take different social, political, and economic-historical factors into account because it treats each year similarly. In addition we will normally be sampling, at least in part, on organizations that have survived, a fact which raises additional theoretical and empirical questions (Kimberly, 1975).

A further problem has to do with the fact that while there are some parallels between the life cycles of individuals and those of organizations, the analogy is far from perfect. In contrast to individuals, organizations have no finite, or even estimable, life expectancy. They may, in addition, undergo a variety of metamorphoses through mergers, changes in their fundamental mission and the like which substantially alter their identity. Thus, one challenge to longitudinal theory and research is to begin to consider the impact of these kinds of changes on the processes and outcomes that are of interest.

In the case of hospitals, for example, it is becoming increasingly common to find proprietary chains, that is, large numbers of hospitals owned by the same corporation but operating at different sites, often in different states. Because of the relative recency of this development, it is highly likely that at least some of the hospitals that were self-contained in the original survey have changed ownership and are now subsidiaries or branches of corporations, and this possibility will have to be taken into account because of its potential effects on adoption rates. It is also likely that at least some of the hospitals that were located in the same city have merged, and there is the difficult question of how to treat them in subsequent waves. Are they new organizations? If not, how should their responses be analyzed in relation to the earlier separate responses? These are very concrete examples of some of the kinds of questions relative to stages in organizational life cycles that are bound to arise in longitudinal research on organizations.

5. *What kinds of analytic techniques are appropriate for longitudinal organizational research?* Mathematical and statistical problems typically encountered in cross-sectional research appear to be exacerbated in longitudinal research. Apart from the problem of determining reliability discussed earlier, other problems exist as well. While path analysis, cross-lag correlational analysis, time-series analysis, repeated measures analysis of variance, and other more standard techniques may be used, each technique has its own particular drawbacks. For example, if organizations are nonrecursive systems, then unless time series data are available we are likely to have misspecified path diagrams. If there is a substantial amount of movement within an organization, repeated measures analysis of variance will be inappropriate because the samples measured will not be identical at multiple points in time. Although detailed discussion of specific techniques is beyond the scope of this paper, it should be pointed out that extreme care needs to be taken in analyzing longitudinal data because of the special problems that change poses for measurement. Use of raw-change scores may produce results which reflect regression effects rather than "true" change as Bohrnstedt (1969) has pointed out. And Land's (1975) criticism of Holdaway and Blowers' (1971) longitudinal analysis of the relationship between size and administrative-production ratios indicates that regression effects may account for much of the variability even when raw-change scores are residualized. Thoughtful discussions of some potentially helpful ways of thinking about the measurement of change can be found in Coleman (1964) and Galtung (1970).

In addition to the issues discussed above, longitudinal organizational research appears to pose somewhat unique problems of access and data collection. Longitudinal research *in* organizations requires substantial investment in obtaining entree and it may well be that those organizations which would permit such research have characteristics which differentiate them from those that would not. Longitudinal research *on* organizations, where the focus is primarily on structural attributes, is subject to problems of data availability and to the kinds of definitional issues described so well by Blau and Schoenherr (1971).

THE PROSPECTS FOR LONGITUDINAL ORGANIZATIONAL RESEARCH

What are the prospects for the kind of research discussed above? In my own view, longitudinal research in and on formal organizations is absolutely essential if we are to develop better theory and models and better strategies for interventions of various kinds. But there are barriers to this kind of research, barriers which are born of the expense in both time and money which it requires, of the problems of career advancement and the necessity of relatively rapid and prolific publication which do not make it terribly attractive to young researchers, of the reward structure in social science, and of the politics of research support. There are also technical problems of the sort described in this paper which need to be solved. On the other hand, there are some bright spots on the horizon. Much can be learned from the experiences of researchers in other areas. While some of the issues raised here are unique to the study of organizations, many have at least partial analogues in fields such as child development, education, and demography, fields which have a more firmly established tradition of longitudinal research. In addition, the implications of this sort of research for social policy are beginning to be demonstrated, and there appears to be increasing receptivity to funding longitudinal organizational research at the federal level.

On balance, therefore, while many problems remain I see the potential contributions of longitudinal research as extremely high and as justifying the considerable investments that it requires. The extent to which this potential is realized can be enhanced if increasing numbers of organizational researchers begin conceptualizing their research problems and interests in longitudinal terms. I have little doubt that reward structures and sources of support will begin to accommodate these interests.

NOTE

1.   This article is a revision of a paper presented at the 69th Annual Meeting of the American Sociological Association, Montreal, August 1974. I would like to acknowledge the helpful comments of William Evan, George Graen, Edward Morse, Louis Pondy, David Rottman, and David Whetten on the earlier version.

REFERENCES

Anderson, T. R. and S. Warkov (1961) "Organizational Size and Functional Complexity," *Amer. Soc. Rev.* 26: 23-28.

Blau, P. M. (1973) *The Organization of Academic Work.* New York: Wiley.

—— (1965) "The Comparative Study of Organizations," *Industrial and Labor Relations Review* 18: 323-338.

Blau, P. M. and R. A. Schoenherr (1971) *The Structure of Organizations.* New York: Basic Books.

Blau, P. M., W. V. Heydebrand, and R. E. Stauffer (1966) "The Structure of Small Bureaucracies," *Amer. Soc. Rev.* 31: 179-191.

Bohrnstedt, G. W. (1969) "Some Observations on the Measurement of Change," in E. Borgatta (ed.) *Sociological Methodology—1969.* San Francisco: Jossey-Bass.

Burns, T. (1967) "The Comparative Study of Organizations," in U. H. Broom (ed.) *Methods of Organizational Research.* Pittsburgh: Univ. of Pittsburgh Press.

Campbell, D. T. and J. C. Stanley (1966) *Experimental and Quasi-Experimental Designs for Research.* Chicago: Rand McNally.

Campbell, J. P. and M. D. Dunnette (1968) "Effectiveness of T-group Experiences in Managerial Training and Development," *Psych. Bull.* 70: 73-104.

Coleman, J. S. (1964) *Models of Change and Response Uncertainty.* Englewood Cliffs, N.J.: Prentice-Hall.

Coughenour, C. M. (1966) "The Problem of Reliability of Adoption Data in Survey Research," *Rural Sociology* 30: 43-56.

Dalton, M. (1959) *Men Who Manage.* New York: John Wiley.

Deutscher, I. (1966) "Words and Deeds: Social Science and Social Policy," *Social Problems* 13: 236-247.

Galtung, J. (1970) "Diachronic Correlation, Process Analysis and Causal Analysis," *Quality and Quantity* 4: 55-94.

Gordon, G., J. R. Kimberly, and A. MacEachron (1975) "Some Considerations in the Design of Effective Research Programs on the Diffusion of Medical Tehnology," in W. J. Abernathy, A. Sheldon and C. K. Prahalad (eds.) *The Management of Health Care*. Cambridge: Ballinger.

Gordon, G., E. V. Morse, S. M. Gordon, J. de Kervasdoue, J. R. Kimberly, M. K. Moch, and D. G. Swartz (1974) "Organizational Structure, Environmental Diversity, and Hospital Adoption of Medical Innovations," in A. D. Kaluzny, J. T. Gentry, and J. E. Veney (eds.) *Innovation in Health Care Organizations*. Chapel Hill, N.C.: University of North Carolina, Department of Health Administration.

Gouldner, A. W. (1954) *Patterns of Industrial Bureaucracy*. New York: Free Press.

Graen, G. (1975) "Role Making Processes in Complex Organizations," in M. D. Dunnette (ed.) *Handbook of Industrial and Organizational Psychology*. Chicago: Rand McNally.

Haga, W. J., G. Graen, and F. Dansereau (1974) "Professionalism and Role Making in a Service Organization: A Longitudinal Investigation," *Amer. Soc. Rev.* 39: 122-133.

Hage, J. (1974) *Communication and Control: Cybernetics in Health and Welfare Settings*. New York: John Wiley.

—— and R. Dewar (1973) "Elite Values Versus Organizational Structure in Predicting Innovation," *Admin. Sci. Q.* 18: 279-290.

Harris, C. W. (1963) *Problems in Measuring Change*. Madison, Wisconsin: Univ. of Wisconsin Press.

Heydebrand, W. V. (1973) *Hospital Bureaucracy: A Comparative Study of Organizations*. New York: Dunellen.

Hirschi, T. and H. C. Selvin (1967) *Delinquency Research: An Appraisal of Analytic Methods*. New York: Free Press.

Holdaway, E. A. and T. A. Blowers (1971) "Administrative Ratios and Organizational Size: A Longitudinal Examination," *Amer. Soc. Rev.* 36: 278-286.

Kimberly, J. R. (1975) "Environmental Constraints and Organizational Structure: A Comparative Analysis of Rehabilitation Organizations," *Admin. Sci. Q.* 20: 1-9.

—— (1974) "The Effects of Organizational Integration Into Informational Environments on Adoption of Innovation." Paper presented at the 69th Annual Meeting of the American Sociological Association. Montreal.

Land, K. C. (1975) "Comparative Statistics in Sociology," in H. M. Blalock, A. Aganbegian, Jr., F. M. Borodkin, R. Boudon and V. Capecchi (eds.) *Mathematics and Sociology*. New York: Academic Press.

Matras, J. (1975) "Models and Indicators of Organizational Growth, Changes and Transformations," in K. C. Land and S. Spilerman (eds.) *Social Indicator Models*. New York: Russell Sage.

Meyer, M. K. (1972) "Size and the Structure of Organizations: A Causal Analysis," *Amer. Soc. Rev.* 37: 434-440.

Moch, M. K. (1974) "Task Characteristics and Centralization in Formal Organizations." Paper presented at the 69th Annual Meeting of the American Sociological Association. Montreal.

Morse, E. V., G. Gordon, and M. K. Moch (1974) "Hospital Costs and Quality of Care: An Organizational Perspective," *Milbank Memorial Fund Q.* (Fall): 221-240.

Paulson, S. K. (1974) "Causal Analysis of Interorganizational Relations: An Axiomatic Theory Revised," *Admin. Sci. Q.* 19: 319-337.

Perrow, C. (1965) "Hospitals: Technology, Structure and Goals," in J. G. March (ed.) *Handbook of Organizations*. Chicago: Rand McNally.

Pondy, L. R. (1969) "Effects of Size, Complexity and Ownership on Administrative Intensity," *Admin. Sci. Q.* 14: 47-61.

Porter, L. W., R. M. Steers, R. T. Mowday, and P. V. Boulian (1974) "Organizational Commitment, Job Satisfaction and Turnover Among Psychiatric Technicians," *J. of Applied Pscyhology* 59: 603-609.

Pugh, D. S., D. J. Hickson, C. R. Hinings, and C. Turner (1968) "Dimensions of Organization Structure," *Admin. Sci. Q.* 13: 65-106.

Schulman, J. (1969) *Remaking an Organization: Innovations in a Specialized Psychiatric Hospital*. Albany, New York: SUNY Press.

Seashore, S. E. and D. G. Bowers (1963) "Changing the Structure and Functioning of an Organization," Monograph No. 33. Ann Arbor, Mich.: Institute for Social Research.

Starbuck, W. H. (1971) *Organizational Growth and Development*. Baltimore, Md.: Penguin Books.

—— (1968) "Organizational Metamorphosis," pp. 113-122 in R. W. Millman and M. P. Hottenstein (eds.) *Promising Research Directions*. Academy of Management.

—— (1965) "Organizational Growth and Development," pp. 451-522 in J. G. March (ed.) *Handbook of Organizations*. Chicago: Rand McNally.

Stinchcombe, A. L. (1965) "Social Structure and Organizations," pp. 142-193 in J. G. March (ed.) *Handbook of Organizations*. Chicago: Rand McNally.

Wanous, J. P. (1974) "A Causal-correlational Analysis of the Job Satisfaction and Performance Relationship," *J. of Applied Psychology* 59: 139-144.

10   Attribution of the "Causes" of Performance: A General Alternative Interpretation of Cross-Sectional Research on Organizations[1]

Barry M. Staw

Although much of the research in organizational behavior is devoted to understanding the causes of performance, the findings in the field are still largely based upon correlational data in which the direction of causation is unknown. At present, the research supporting most organizational theories contains hypothesized independent variables which can either be the causes of performance, the effects of performance, covariates of third variables, or the result of a network of reciprocal causation. Therefore, it could be argued strongly that, in terms of both theory and application, resolving ambiguity in causal inference is one of the field's most pressing issues.

Previously, there have been two empirical studies specifically designed to demonstrate problems in interpreting correlational data derived from cross-sectional surveys.[2] In the first of these studies, Lowin and Craig (1968) experimentally manipulated the performance of subordinates and measured the leadership style of persons hired to perform a real supervisory role. The results of this study showed that closeness of super-

Source: B. M. Staw, "Attribution of the 'Causes' of Performance: A General Alternative Interpretation of Cross-Sectional Research on Organizations," *Organizational Behavior and Human Performance* 1975, 13, pp. 414-432. Reproduced by permission.

vision may be a function of subordinate performance rather than a causal determinant of performance, as previously believed. In a somewhat parallel study, Farris and Lim (1969) compared the leadership style of work group supervisors after knowledge of subordinate performance had been experimentally manipulated. This research involved a role playing exercise in which one student was designated as a foreman and three other students acted as a three-person work group in an industrial conflict situation. Each group worked with its foreman toward the solution of the "Change in Work Procedure Case" (Maier, Solem, and Maier, 1957), and then completed a postexperimental questionnaire on the foreman's behavior. Knowledge of performance was manipulated by providing information to the foreman (before the work session) that his group was one of the highest or lowest groups in terms of previous performance. The results showed that, for high performing groups, the foreman was perceived to be more supportive of the workers, higher in goal emphasis, and more facilitative of interaction than was the foreman of low performing groups.

By showing that changes in performance can cause changes in other behavioral variables, both the Lowin and Craig (1968) and Farris and Lim (1969) studies represent efforts to stimulate more causal research on organizations. The approach represented by their research is a step-by-step demonstration of the plausibility of reversals in causal order. In fact, from this approach, one might advocate measuring the effects of performance upon an array of individual, group, and organizational variables, and the construction of a thorough inventory of plausible causal reversals. With this information, researchers eventually would know where to invest substantial resources on research with methods more conducive to causal inference (i.e., field experimentation, longitudinal analysis, and laboratory simulations of organizational processes).

The step-by-step demonstration of causal reversals is no doubt a worthwhile procedure to help budge the field of organizational behavior from its near total reliance on cross-sectional (correlational) data. However, it is believed that this procedure is neither sufficiently speedy nor now necessary to encourage a significant increase in causal research. The reason for this conjecture is a new alternative interpretation of cross-sectional data which is both parsimonious and of general applicability to correlational findings linking performance data to self-report measures of individual, group, and organizational characteristics. This alternative interpretation of correlational findings is derived from previous work on attribution theory.

Attribution theory is specifically concerned with how individuals assign enduring traits or dispositions to themselves and other persons (Heider, 1958; Jones and Davis, 1965; Kelley, 1971, 1973; Nisbett and Valins, 1971). It assumes that individuals have a need to understand and explain the events around them, and that based upon this need, individuals will develop a lay or "naive" psychology of behavior (Heider, 1958). To date, most of the research in attribution theory has studied the perception of personal characteristics under varied environmental conditions (e.g., Bem, 1965; Calder and Staw, 1975a, 1975b; Deci, 1971; Jones, Davis and Gergen, 1961; Jones and Harris, 1967; Schachter and Singer, 1962; Staw, 1974a, 1974b; Strickland, 1958). However, in its broadest context, attribution theory is concerned with the ascription of characteristics to any entity. As Kelley (1973) has noted, all of the judgments of the type, "Property X characterizes Entity Y" can be viewed as causal attributions. Thus, it seems reasonable to assume that the organizational participant, in a desire to understand and control his particular environment, may develop a lay psychology of individual, group, and organizational functioning. Just as individuals may possess an implicit personality theory to guide their impressions of others (Bruner and Tagiuri, 1954), the organizational participant may possess a theory of the relationships between organizational characteristics and subsequent performance.

The specific attribution hypothesis posited here is that individuals utilize knowledge of performance as a cue by which they ascribe characteristics to an individual, group, or organizational unit. The attribution hypothesis posits that performance is a potent independent variable, and that many of the correlations between performance and self-report data may be accounted for by the following causal sequence: Level of Performance → Attribution of Characteristics → Self-report of Characteristics. That is, performance data may cause persons to assign an entire set of characteristics (i.e., a stereotype) to individuals, groups, and organizations, and this attributed set of characteristics may underlie many of the correlations derived from cross-sectional studies of organizational processes.[3]

The attribution hypothesis can be illustrated by a questionnaire developed by Likert (1967) to support his System 4 theory of management. Likert asked several hundred managers to "think of the most productive department, division, or organization (they) have known well." The managers were then asked to rate this entity in terms of organizational processes such as motivation, influence, communication, and cooperation. Subsequently, these same managers were also asked to rate their least productive department, division, or organization on each of these dimensions. As expected, a high degree of motivation, mutual influence, cooperation, and communication were associated with the highest producing units. Although it is not yet clear whether the processes seen by managers as being associated with high performance actually contribute to performance, Likert's data do illustrate that, *perceptually*, individuals will distinguish between high and low producing units. Moreover, the existence of distinct stereotypes of successful versus unsuccessful organizations points to the very possibility that significant correlations between performance and self-report data may only be reflecting the respondents' "theories" of organizational performance rather than actual events. And as Heider (1958) has noted in his now classic analysis of interpersonal perception, a lay or "naive" psychology of behavior may or may not be correct.

Clearly, if knowledge of performance causes one to attribute particular characteristics to individuals, groups, or organizations, it may therefore be risky (and certainly unscientific) to posit that self-report data on these characteristics accurately represent the causal determinants of performance. In essence, questionnaire measures considered by organizational researchers to be indicators of the determinants of performance, may actually constitute the consequences of performance. This possibility is of substantial importance to organizational research since individual, group, and organizational characteristics are rarely observed directly, but are generally measured by respondents' perceptions within a field setting.

A laboratory experiment was conducted to test the relevance of the attribution interpretation to some important correlational findings. Specifically, it seemed desirable to test whether this alternative interpretation is applicable to Tannenbaum's (1968) replicated finding that high mutual influence is associated with high performance, Likert's (1961) finding that group cohesiveness is associated with high performance, and Evan's (1965) finding that interpersonal conflict (but not task conflict) is related to performance. In addition, the relationships of performance to motivation (Galbraith and Cummings, 1967), communication, and openness to change (Likert, 1961) were investigated by this research.

METHOD

Subjects. Subjects for this experiment were undergraduate students enrolled in the College of Commerce and Business Administration at the University of Illinois, Urbana-Champaign. Sixty students were randomly assigned to three-man groups and each group was asked to participate in a "Financial Puzzle Task." Group members were given copies of the 1969 annual report of a medium-sized (but not well-known) electronics company. The report contained a description of the company, a letter from the president on the firm's prospects, and five preceding years of financial data. The group members were told that their task was to estimate company sales and earnings per share for 1970, taking into consideration any knowledge they might have of the electronics industry or state of the economy at that time. Each group was given 30 minutes to discuss the issue and make any necessary calculations in formulating a group estimate of sales and earnings per share. Subjects were told that the purpose of the experiment was to evaluate the performance of groups of various sizes and that previous research had been conducted on three-, four-, and five-man groups.

Manipulation of performance. After each group presented its estimates of sales and earnings per share, the experimenter stated that "it would be interesting to see how well this group had performed relative to previous three-man groups." The experimenter then took the group's estimates of sales and earnings per share and searched through several file cabinets in the next room. On returning to the (randomly assigned) *High Performance* groups, the experimenter announced that the group had "done quite well," that their sales figure was off by only $10,000, earnings per share was accurate within $.05 a share, and that the group's overall performance was clearly in the top 20% of three-man groups. On returning to the (randomly assigned) *Low Performance* groups, the experimenter announced that they had "not done too well," that their estimate for sales was off by $10,000,000, their estimate for earnings per share was off by $1.00, and that the group's overall performance was in the lowest 20% of previous three-man groups. No subjects expressed strong doubts about their group's performance. However, it should be noted that the annual report used in this experiment was selected specifically on the basis of its ambiguity and could be interpreted in either a positive or negative manner.

Dependent variables. After being told of their group's performance, subjects were led to separate rooms and asked to complete a short questionnaire about "what went on in the group." On the questionnaire were items to measure group cohesiveness, influence, communication, task conflict, openness to change, motivation, ability, and clarity of instructions. Although the questions were randomly ordered on the questionnaire, they are listed below under the appropriate variable headings.

I. *Cohesiveness*
   a. To what extent did you enjoy working with your teammates?
      (11 point scale from "not at all" to "to a great extent")
   b. In working on the financial puzzle task, what were your personal feelings toward your teammates?
      (11 point scale from "I disliked them" to "I liked them")
   c. How would you rate the cohesiveness or group spirit of your team?
      (11 point scale from "extremely low" to "extremely high")

II. *Influence*
   a. How much influence did you have on final solution of the task?
      (11 point scale from "very little" to "a great amount")

      b. How much influence did your teammates have on the final solution of the task? (11 point scale from "very little" to "a great amount")

III. *Communication*

      a. How would you rate the quantity of communication between you and your teammates? (11 point scale from "very low" to "very high")

      b. How would you rate the quality of communication between you and your teammates? (11 point scale from "very low" to "very high")

IV. *Task Conflict*

      a. To what extent did you and your teammates each have different ideas about methods to solve the financial puzzle task? (11 point scale from "not at all" to "to a great extent")

      b. If you and your teammates had different ideas about solving the task, to what extent did you have an open confrontation of ideas? (11 point scale from "not at all" to "to a great extent")

V. *Openness to Change*

      a. How open were your teammates to your ideas and suggestions about solving the financial puzzle task? (11 point scale from "not open at all" to "extremely open")

      b. In solving the task, to what extent did your teammates ever attempt to impose or force their position(s) on you? (11 point scale from "not at all" to "to a great extent")

VI. *Satisfaction*

      a. To what extent did you enjoy working on the financial puzzle task? (11 point scale from "not at all" to "to a great extent")

VII. *Motivation*

      a. To what extent were you interested in performing well on the financial puzzle task? (11 point scale from "not at all" to "to a great extent")

      b. To what extent were your teammates interested in performing well on the financial puzzle task? (11 point scale from "not at all" to "to a great extent")

VIII. *Ability*

      a. In general, how would you rate your ability in solving financial puzzles? (11 point scale from "very low" to "very high")

      b. In general, how would you rate your teammates' ability in solving financial puzzles? (11 point scale from "very low" to "very high")

IX. *Role Clarity*

      a. Were the instructions for solving the financial puzzle made clear to you? (11 point scale from "not at all" to "very clear")

RESULTS

Check on the Performance Manipulation

    Subjects randomly assigned to High Performance groups rated their ability in solving financial puzzles as higher than did subjects in Low Performance groups ($t(58) = 5.64$,

$p < .001$). Subjects in the High Performance groups also rated their teammates' ability as higher than did those in Low Performance groups ($t(58) = 2.60$, $p < .01$). These data support the hypothesis that subjects believed the information provided by the experimenter on their group's performance.

It should be noted that, in actuality, the groups assigned to the High Performance condition performed no better than those assigned to the Low Performance condition (see Table 1). In fact, in terms of predicting corporate sales and earnings, groups told that they had performed well actually performed (nonsignificantly) worse than those told they had performed poorly (for sales: $t = -.48$, N.S.; for earnings: $t = -.23$, N.S.).

TABLE 1   Estimated 1970 Sales and Earnings Per Share for Low Performance Group, High Performance Group, and Actual Company Data for 1970

	Low Performance Group			High Performance Group			Actual Company Performance in 1970
	$\bar{x}$	SD	Range	$\bar{x}$	SD	Range	
Estimated 1970 sales (in millions of dollars)	44.93	3.21	39.50–49.00	45.63	3.22	40.00–50.00	40.45
Estimated 1970 earnings per shares (in dollars)	.69	.37	.10–1.25	.74	.44	.10–1.50	(Net Loss)

Thus, any reported differences in the perception of group characteristics are likely to be due to manipulated knowledge of performance rather than to any actual differences in the behavior of the groups. Again, it should be stressed that the financial data comprising the group task was specifically selected (in terms of ambiguity) so as to allow a credible manipulation of knowledge of performance.

Effect of Knowledge of Performance on Perceptions of Interpersonal Behavior

The perceptions of several dimensions of interpersonal behavior for subjects in both High and Low Performance groups are displayed in Table 2. One-tailed t tests are shown in the table since the statistical contrasts are based on a priori predictions. Where more than one item was used to measure a particular variable, and where these items were significantly intercorrelated, a combined score and resulting t value is also reported. As shown in Table 2, individuals who were randomly assigned to High Performance groups rated their groups as more cohesive ($t(58) = 1.68$, $p < .05$) and enjoyed working with their teammates to a greater extent ($t(58) = 1.81$, $p < .05$) than did individuals assigned to Low Performance groups. Persons in High Performance groups also rated their groups higher in quality and quantity of communication ($t(58) = 1.77$, $p < .05$), higher in total influence ($t(58) = 1.86$, $p < .05$), and marginally higher in openness to change ($t(58) = 1.49$, $p < .10$). It is interesting to note that the effect of performance on total influence was due primarily to the large effect of performance on the perception of one's own influence ($t(58) = 2.47$, $p < .01$), and that there was no effect of performance on the perception of teammates' influence on the group task. No clear relationship to performance was shown by the two indicators of task conflict and these two scales were not significantly intercorrelated.

TABLE 2   Effect of Knowledge of Performance Upon Individual
Perceptions of Intragroup Processes

		Low Performance	High Performance	t Value
Cohesiveness				
Cohesiveness of group	$\bar{x}$	6.70	7.83	1.68**
	SD	3.06	2.07	
Enjoy working with teammates	$\bar{x}$	7.23	8.28	1.81**
	SD	2.65	1.48	
Liking for teammates	$\bar{x}$	8.77	9.23	1.04
	SD	2.10	1.30	
Combined cohesiveness score	$\bar{x}$	7.57	8.43	1.72**
	SD	2.36	1.42	
Influence				
Teammates influence on task solution	$\bar{x}$	7.57	7.43	−.24
	SD	2.62	1.45	
Own influence on task solution	$\bar{x}$	6.00	7.73	2.47**
	SD	3.27	2.03	
Combined influence score	$\bar{x}$	6.78	7.58	1.86**
	SD	1.91	1.37	
Communication				
Quality of communication	$\bar{x}$	6.77	7.93	1.75**
	SD	3.11	1.91	
Quantity of communication	$\bar{x}$	6.47	7.30	1.33
	SD	2.71	2.12	
Combined communication score	$\bar{x}$	6.62	7.61	1.77**
	SD	2.49	1.82	
Task conflict				
Differences in ideas about methods to solve problems	$\bar{x}$	4.83	4.93	.17
	SD	2.38	2.03	
Confrontation of ideas with teammates	$\bar{x}$	5.34	7.03	1.97**
	SD	3.38	3.19	
Openness to change				
Openness of teammate to ideas and suggestions about solving problem	$\bar{x}$	7.73	8.55	1.52*
	SD	2.36	1.72	
Extent teammate attempted to force his position on you (scale reversed)	$\bar{x}$	8.53	9.21	1.02
	SD	2.84	2.19	
Combined openness score	$\bar{x}$	8.14	8.88	1.49*
	SD	2.12	1.69	

$*p < .10$, one-tailed test.
$**p < .05$, one-tailed test.
$***p < .01$, one-tailed test.

Effects of Knowledge of Performance on Satisfaction, Motivation, Ability, and Role Clarity

Table 3 shows that subjects assigned to High Performance groups enjoyed working on the experimental task to a greater extent than did subjects assigned to Low Perfor-

TABLE 3   Effect of Knowledge of Performance on Satisfaction,
Motivation, Ability, and Role Clarity

		Low Performance	High Performance	t Value
Motivation				
Teammates' interest in performing well	$\bar{x}$	4.97	7.47	3.87***
	SD	2.79	2.18	
Own interest in performing well	$\bar{x}$	4.73	7.90	5.33***
	SD	2.64	1.90	
Combined motivation score	$\bar{x}$	4.85	7.68	5.24***
	SD	2.26	1.91	
Ability				
Teammates' ability	$\bar{x}$	5.50	7.13	2.60***
	SD	3.01	1.65	
Own ability	$\bar{x}$	3.57	6.80	5.64***
	SD	2.33	2.11	
Combined ability score	$\bar{x}$	4.54	6.96	5.00***
	SD	2.03	1.72	
Satisfaction				
Enjoyed working on financial task	$\bar{x}$	3.47	7.20	5.93***
	SD	2.43	2.44	
Role clarity				
Clarity of instructions for the task	$\bar{x}$	7.23	8.70	2.20**
	SD	2.90	2.23	

*$p < .10$, one-tailed test.
**$p < .05$, one-tailed test.
***$p < .01$, one-tailed test.

mance groups ($t(58) = 5.93$, $p < .001$). In addition, subjects in High Performance groups rated their own interest in performing well on the task as greater than subjects assigned to Low Performance groups ($t(58) = 5.33$, $p < .001$). Similarly, these same subjects rated their teammates' interest in performing well on the task higher than did subjects in Low Performance groups. Finally, as previously reported, feedback on performance affected the subjects' rated ability ($t(58) = 5.64$, $p < .001$), his perception of his teammates' ability ($t(58) = 2.60$, $p < .01$), and also the rated clarity of instructions for the task ($t(58) = 2.20$, $p < .05$).[4]

DISCUSSION

As illustrated by the data of Tables 2 and 3, knowledge of performance had a marked effect on the self-report measures of intragroup processes. As expected, individuals who were told that they had participated in a high-performing group rated their groups higher in cohesiveness, influence, communication, openness to change (marginally significant) and motivation as compared to individuals who were told that they had participated in a low performing group. As a whole, these data provide support for the notion that individuals attribute one set of characteristics to a work group they believe is effective and another, different, set of characteristics to an ineffective work group. As a whole, these data also offer support for an attributional interpretation of correlations between self-report data and measures of group performance.

The data on cohesiveness and task conflict provide a particularly interesting test of the attribution hypothesis. Previously, Evan (1965) had hypothesized that the impact of intragroup conflict upon performance may not necessarily be negative, and that the effects of conflict might depend on the type of conflict involved. Specifically, Evan postulated that interpersonal conflict should have a negative effect on work group performance, while task conflict might prove beneficial. By correlating self-report measures of conflict to the performance of R and D groups, Evan's data showed a significant negative relationship between interpersonal conflict and performance, but no clear relationship between task conflict and performance. As shown in Table 1, quite similar results were obtained in this study when knowledge of high performance was the manipulated independent variable. Knowledge of high performance caused subjects to perceive less interpersonal conflict (as evidenced by greater interpersonal liking and cohesion), while there was a tendency (significant on one of two measures) to rate a high performing group higher in task conflict.[5] Evan's relatively complex relationship between conflict and performance was thus replicated when knowledge of performance was the manipulated independent variable.

A second test of the attribution hypothesis is provided by the data on intragroup influence. Within several organizational settings, Tannenbaum (1968) has found that the amount of total control or influence is significantly related to organizational effectiveness. In each of these studies (Smith and Tannenbaum, 1963; Tannenbaum, 1962, Tannenbaum, 1968), self-report measures of influence are correlated with objective measures of organizational performance. Although Tannenbaum has interpreted these findings as indicating that greater total influence causes improved performance, an attribution interpretation is also plausible. In fact, the hypothesis that individuals attribute greater influence to high rather than low producing groups is generally supported by the data of this experiment.

The data on quality and quantity of communication also provide support for the attribution hypothesis. Although communication has previously been found to correlate with organizational effectiveness (see Price, 1968), the direction of causation has not been clear. In this experiment, however, members of high producing groups inferred higher quality communication to their groups and tended also to infer a greater quantity of communication. In addition, persons with knowledge of high performance tended to rate their teammates as being more open to change (see Likert, 1961, 1967, for concomitant correlation), and perceived both themselves and their teammates as being higher in motivation (see Galbraith and Cummings, 1967, for concomitant correlation).

Although the data of this experiment are generally supportive of the attribution hypothesis, it should be noted that some of the data can be explained by alternative processes. For example, one indicator of group cohesiveness (enjoyed working with teammates) may have been higher among persons assigned to High Performance groups due to the reinforcement associated with task success. Although this explanation would also clearly apply to the measure of task satisfaction, it would not, however, be as applicable to other intragroup processes measured on the questionnaire (e.g., influence, conflict, communication, motivation, and openness to change).

A second alternative interpretation is suggested by the data on intragroup influence and motivation. Because persons assigned to Low Performance groups attributed less influence to themselves and rated themselves as lower in task motivation than persons in High Performance groups, an ego-defensive process is suggested (Weiner et al., 1971). One problem with the ego-defensive explanation, however, is that subjects also rated their teammates' motivation as lower under the Low Performance condition, and this result would not be predicted by an ego-defensive process. A second problem with the ego-defensive explanation is that subjects rated their own ability under Low Performance conditions as significantly lower than that of their teammates. Clearly, if an ego-defensive process were operating, one would expect subjects to depreciate their teammates' ability under low group performance, while keeping their own rated ability intact.

In sum, the results of this experiment support the contention that knowledge of performance is a relatively potent independent variable. Moreover, the overall pattern of results can be more parsimoniously explained by an attribution theory than by either a reinforcement or ego-defensive process. The attribution process posited here is that individuals hold distinct stereotypes of high versus low performing groups, and that persons will attribute these characteristics to a group based upon mere knowledge of its performance. So as to provide additional validation of this attribution process, an "interpersonal simulation" (Bem, 1965) was also performed.

An Interpersonal Simulation

In order to provide specific data on the stereotypes individuals hold and the attachment of these stereotypes to high and low performing groups, an "interpersonal simulation" was conducted. As described below, the study provided direct data on the attribution process in addition to replication of the previous experimental findings.

For the interpersonal simulation, 60 students were asked to participate in a study on perceptual accuracy. They were told that a large number of undergraduate business students had previously participated in a group problem-solving study in which measurements were taken of intragroup processes and performance. Subjects were told that the researchers were interested in seeing how accurately individuals could assess intragroup processes based upon a minimal amount of information, and that their assessments would be compared to "true" observational measures of group processes collected over the past year. The "Financial Puzzle Task" (as used in the above experiment) was then thoroughly described to the subjects in both written and oral form. Subsequently, subjects were asked to rate a typical group of business undergraduates who had performed in the lowest (or highest) 20% of all three-man groups. Via random assignment, 30 subjects were asked to rate a high performing group and 30 a low performing group. Efforts were made to keep the rating scales as similar as possible to those used in the previous experiment.

As shown in Table 4 the results of the interpersonal simulation followed closely those of the previous study. High performing groups were perceived to be higher in cohesiveness, total influence, quality and quantity of communication, motivation, and openness to change than low performing groups. As in the previous experiment, interpersonal conflict (i.e., low group cohesiveness) was negatively related to performance, while task conflict tended to be positively associated with performance.[6] Likewise, total influence was perceived to be greater in high rather than low performing groups. However, because persons in the interpersonal simulation did not actually participate in a problem-solving group, total influence was not measured by a combination of the rated influence of self and one's teammates. Instead, total influence was measured by, (1) combining the perceived influence scores for the "most influential" and "least influential" persons in the group, (2) by simply asking subjects to rate the influence of each group member. By either of these methods, total influence appeared to be positively associated with group performance.

TABLE 4   Effects of Knowledge of Performance for Interpersonal Simulation

		Low Performance	High Performance	t Value
Cohesiveness				
Cohesiveness of group	$\bar{x}$	3.00	8.67	17.18***
	SD	1.31	1.24	
Enjoyed working with teammates	$\bar{x}$	4.10	8.10	10.62***
	SD	1.52	1.40	
Liking for teammates	$\bar{x}$	4.93	7.50	7.17***
	SD	1.44	1.33	
Combined cohesiveness score	$\bar{x}$	4.01	8.09	15.46***
	SD	.94	1.10	
Influence				
Influence of each member	$\bar{x}$	5.17	6.97	3.49***
	SD	2.31	1.63	
Influence of "most influential" member	$\bar{x}$	8.90	8.90	.00
	SD	2.01	1.88	
Influence of "least influential" member	$\bar{x}$	2.60	4.03	2.74**
	SD	2.33	1.67	
Combined influence score	$\bar{x}$	5.75	6.47	2.21*
	SD	1.42	1.07	
Communication				
Quality of communication	$\bar{x}$	2.93	8.80	17.08***
	SD	1.33	1.32	
Quantity of communication	$\bar{x}$	4.50	8.37	8.22***
	SD	2.08	1.52	
Combined communication score	$\bar{x}$	3.72	8.58	14.47***
	SD	1.32	1.29	
Task conflict				
Difference in ideas about methods to	$\bar{x}$	6.80	6.50	−.53
solve problem	SD	2.48	1.89	
Confrontation of ideas with teammates	$\bar{x}$	5.30	7.03	2.98**
	SD	2.55	1.92	
Combined task conflict score	$\bar{x}$	6.05	6.77	1.53+
	SD	2.19	1.35	
Openness to change				
Openness to ideas and suggestions	$\bar{x}$	4.27	8.07	7.27***
about solving problem	SD	2.26	1.76	
Extent group members ever attempted to	$\bar{x}$	4.03	4.30	.40
force their positions (scale reversed)	SD	2.51	1.95	
Combined openness score	$\bar{x}$	4.65	6.68	5.04***
	SD	1.85	1.21	
Motivation				
Group members' interest in performing	$\bar{x}$	3.33	8.30	11.84***
well	SD	1.75	1.49	
Ability				
Rated ability of group on task	$\bar{x}$	2.90	8.93	19.13***
	SD	1.42	.98	
Role clarity				
Clarity of instructions for the task	$\bar{x}$	6.50	8.37	4.27***
	SD	1.85	1.52	

+$p < .10$, one-tailed test.   **$p < .01$, one-tailed test.
*$p < .05$, one-tailed test.   ***$p < .001$, one-tailed test.

CONCLUSIONS

The data of the true experiment and the interpersonal simulation, together, provide strong evidence for the attribution effect. The similarity of results from these two studies demonstrates that mere knowledge of performance may cause an individual to attribute one set of characteristics to a high performing group and a different set of characteristics to a low performing group. Supported by these data, the attribution effect thus constitutes a very plausible interpretation of correlations linking perceived group characteristics to work group performance. Moreover, though not yet specifically tested, this same attribution process may underlie many correlations between self-report data on individual characteristics (e.g., attitudes, perceived role conflict and ambiguity, perceived effort) and individual performance data, as well as many correlations between self-report data on organizational variables (e.g., openness, conflict, goal orientation, climate) and organizational performance data. In sum, the process by which individuals attribute the "causes" of performance may have important implications for the conduct of organizational research.

From the data presented here, the attribution effect can be viewed as potentially more threatening to the interpretation of correlational findings than the simple reversal of causal sequences. As noted by Lowin and Craig (1968) and Farris and Lim (1969), an assumed direction of causation may be incorrect since performance can affect actual interpersonal behavior. However, actual reversals in causation do not always occur and often it is possible for the researcher to discount the probability of their occurrence on logical and theoretical grounds. In essence, the more intuitively obvious or plausible is a particular causal sequence, the safer it is for researchers to discount its actual reversal. In direct contrast, the attribution interpretation posits that organizational participants possess theories of performance just as do organizational researchers. Thus, the more intuitively obvious or plausible is a theory of organizational behavior, the more likely is a correlation between self-report data and performance to be threatened by an attribution interpretation. Since there are no doubt a greater number of obvious than nonobvious findings in organizational research, the attribution effect may therefore be a greater threat to cross-sectional findings than actual reversals in causal order.

The attribution effect posited here is not unrelated to the notion of demand characteristics developed by experimental social psychologists (see Orne, 1962; Weber and Cook, 1972). Demand characteristics refer to the process by which experimental subjects may attempt to confirm a researcher's theoretical hypothesis by providing supporting empirical data. Although demand characteristics were originally conceived as a potential threat to the interpretation of experimental data, they are also applicable, like the attribution effect, to survey methodology. If a respondent can easily guess the researcher's hypothesis, any empirically derived relationship between two theoretical variables may be artifactual. The crucial element of demand characteristics, of course, is that the researcher's hypothesis be known or so obvious that most respondents will guess it correctly. In contrast, the attribution effect makes no such assumption. Instead of having to guess the *researcher's* hypothesis, it may only be necessary (as shown in the experiments above) that the majority of the respondents possess their *own* hypotheses linking individual, group, or organizational characteristics to performance.[7]

Clearly, a major problem still facing the field of organizational behavior is a dearth of firm causal findings. The results of this study, together with previous experiments on the effects of performance, underscore the need for methods more conducive to causal inference. Three primary solutions to this dilemma have already been posited, but not yet widely adopted. First, by conducting longitudinal studies using cross-lag correlation procedures (Pelz and Andrews, 1964; Vroom, 1966) there can be an improvement in our knowledge of causal order. (It should be noted, however, that the use of cross-lag correlational techniques implies equal time lags in the causal links $X_{t1} \rightarrow Y_{t2}$ and $Y_{t1} \rightarrow X_{t2}$). Second, by conducting true and (strong) quasi-experiments within organizations, we may be able to increase the internal validity of our findings without unduly sacrificing external validity (Campbell and Stanley, 1963; Cook and Campbell, 1975). Both as consultants to planned organizational changes and as documenters of naturally occurring organizational changes (Staw, 1974), there are many opportunities to obtain data from which causal inferences may be drawn. Third, it may be possible to combine constructively the advantages of laboratory and field methods in the investigation of organizational processes (McGrath, 1964; Evan, 1971). By coordinating laboratory and field studies (e.g., in terms of chosen variables and measurement instruments) the resultant findings could be high in both internal and external validity.

NOTES

1. The author is indebted to Greg R. Oldham for his comments on an earlier version of this paper, and to Ramamoorthi Narayan for serving as an experimenter in this research.

2. The term "cross sectional" is used in this paper to refer to survey data collected from one point in time (cf. Campbell and Katona, 1953) as opposed to longitudinal or panel studies in which there are several time-dependent measures.

3. Farris and Lim (1969) interpreted their data as knowledge of performance affecting actual supervisory behavior. However, these data can also be alternatively interpreted by an attribution effect. Persons playing subordinate roles in the study may have learned from their leaders that they were members of a high or low performing work group, attributed this past performance to the foreman's leadership capabilities, and then reported these characteristics on the postexperimental measures of perceived leadership behavior. It is therefore possible that knowledge of performance did not affect actual supervisory behavior but only subordinates' perceptions of it.

4. In each of the above analyses, the individual was regarded as the appropriate unit of analysis. This assumption was based on the fact that individuals were randomly assigned to high and low performance conditions, and that the theoretical hypotheses tested by this research lie at the individual level. Specifically, the research reported here deals with how individuals attribute particular characteristics to their work groups rather than the analytic properties of groups, *per se* (see Lazarsfeld and Menzel, 1969, for discussion of the relationship between individual and collective variables).

5. It should be noted that the questions used to measure interpersonal and task conflict in Evan's 1965 study were quite similar to those used to measure interpersonal cohesiveness and task conflict in this research.

6. Table 4 shows a combined task conflict score since, in the interpersonal simulation, the two indicators of task conflict were significantly intercorrelated. In contrast, Table 2 did not show a combined task conflict score since, in the earlier experiment, the two indicators of this variable were not significantly intercorrelated.

7. It could be argued that the experimental results presented here are, themselves, products of demand characteristics—that subjects attempted to confirm this experimenter's *a priori* hypotheses. Although it is impossible to totally disconfirm this alternative interpretation, it does not appear to be as plausible an explanation of the data as the attribution effect. Two factors decrease the likelihood of demand characteristics' accounting for the data presented here: (1) Since no hypotheses were related to the subjects, they would have had to guess the purpose of the study in *two quite different* experimental settings; (2) Subjects who participated in these studies did so in order to satisfy a course requirement of another university instructor. These subjects would be less motivated to confirm the experimenter's hypotheses than would subjects who were purely voluntary participants (see Rosenthal and Rosnow, 1969).

Although the attribution effect is a more parsimonious explanation of the present data than demand characteristics, it would be extremely difficult to devise an experiment which, in testing the attribution effect, would totally control for demand characteristics. For example, one might design a study in which subjects are specifically informed that the experimenter is testing a hypothesis which is the *opposite* of what most persons believe. This design would eliminate demand characteristics but might also severely weaken the test of the attribution effect, since *subjects'* initial theories of performance would probably be shaken by the conflicting information. Thus, providing an experimental context in which no research hypotheses are particularly salient (as in the present experiments) may be as close to an ideal test of the attribution effect as is currently feasible.

REFERENCES

Bem, D. J. "An Experimental Analysis of Self-persuasion," *Journal of Experimental Social Psychology*, 1965, 1, 199–218.

Bem, D. J. "Self-perception: The Dependent Variable of Human Performance," *Organizational Behavior and Human Performance*, 1967, 2, 105–121.

Bem, D. J. "Self-perception theory." In L. Berkowitz (ed.), *Advances in Experimental Social Psychology*. Vol. 6. New York: Academic Press, 1972, pp. 1–62.

Bruner, J. S. and Tagiuri, A. "The Perception of People." In G. Lindzey (ed.), *Handbook of Social Psychology*, 1954.

Calder, B. J. and Staw, B. M. "The Interaction of Intrinsic and Extrinsic Motivation: Some Methodological Notes," *Journal of Personality and Social Psychology*, 1975, 31, 76–80. (a)

Calder, B. J. and Staw, B. M. "The Self-perception of Intrinsic and Extrinsic Motivation," *Journal of Personality and Social Psychology*, April, 1975. (b)

Campbell, A. and Katona, G. "The Sample Survey: A Technique for Social Science Research." In L. Festinger and D. Katz (eds.), *Research Methods in the Behavioral Sciences*. New York: Holt, Rinehart, and Winston, 1953.

Campbell, D. T. and Stanley, J. C. *Experimental and Quasi-Experimental Designs for Research*. Chicago: Rand McNally, 1963.

Cook, T. D. and Campbell, D. T. "The Design and Conduct of Quasi-experiments and True Experiments in Field Settings." In M. D. Dunnette (ed.), *Handbook of Industrial and Organizational Psychology*, Chicago: Rand McNally, 1976.

Deci, E. L. "Effects of Externally Mediated Rewards on Intrinsic Motivation," *Journal of Personality and Social Psychology*, 1971, 18, 105–115.

Evan, W. M. "Conflict and Performance in R and D Organizations," *Industrial Management Review*, 1965, 7, 37–45; Also reprinted in B. L. Hinton and H. J. Reitz (eds.), *Groups and Organizations*. Belmont, California: Wadsworth, 1971.

Farris, G. F. and Lim, F. G. "Effect of Performance on Leadership, Cohesiveness, Influence, Satisfaction, and Subsequent Performance," *Journal of Applied Psychology*, 1969, 53, 490–497.

Galbraith, J. and Cummings, L. L. "An Empirical Investigation of the Motivational Determinants of Task Performance: Interactive Effects Between Instrumentality-valence and Motivation-ability," *Organizational Behavior and Human Performance*, 1967, 2, 237–257.

Heider, F. *The Psychology of Interpersonal Relations*. New York: Wiley, 1958.

Jones, E. E. and Davis, K. E. "From Acts to Dispositions: The Attribution Process in Person Perception." In L. Berkowitz (ed.), *Advances in Experimental Social Psychology*. Vol. 2. New York: Academic Press, 1965.

Jones, E. E., Davis, K. E., and Gergen, K. E. "Role Playing Variations and Their Informational Value for Person Perceptions," *Journal of Abnormal and Social Psychology*, 1961, 63, 302–310.

Jones, E. E. and Harris, V. A. "The Attribution of Attitudes," *Journal of Experimental Social Psychology*, 1967, 3, 1–24.

Kelley, H. H. *Attribution in Social Interaction*. Morristown, New Jersey: General Learning Press, 1971.

Kelley, H. H. "The Processes of Causal Attribution," *American Psychologist*, 1973, 28, 107–128.

Lazarsfeld, P. F. and Menzel, H. "On the Relation Between Individual and Collective Properties." In A. Etzioni (ed.), *A Sociological Reader on Complex Organizations*. New York: Holt, Rinehart and Winston, 1969.

Likert, R. "Measuring Organizational Performance," *Harvard Business Review*, March–April, 1958.

Likert, R. *New Patterns of Management*. New York: McGraw-Hill, 1961.

Likert, R. *Human Organization: Its Management and Value*. New York: McGraw-Hill, 1967.

Lowin, A. and Craig, J. R. "The Influence of Level of Performance on Managerial Style: An Experimental Object-lesson in the Ambiguity of Correlational Data," *Organizational Behavior and Human Performance*, 1968, 3, 440–458.

Maier, N. R. F., Solem, A. R., and Maier, A. *Supervisory and Executive Development: A Manual for Role Playing*. New York: Wiley, 1957.

McGrath, J. "Toward a 'Theory of Method' for Research on Organizations." In W. W. Cooper, H. J. Leavitt, and M. W. Shelly II (eds.), *New Perspectives in Organizational Research*. New York: Wiley, 1964.

Nisbett, R. E. and Valins, S. *Perceiving for Causes of One's Own Behavior*. Morristown, New Jersey: General Learning Press, 1971.

Orne, M. T. "On the Social Psychology of the Psychological Experiment: With Particular Reference to Demand Characteristics and Their Implications." *American Psychologist*, 1962, 17, 776–783.

Pelz, D. C. and Andrews, F. M. "Detecting Causal Priorities in Panel Study Data," *American Sociological Review*, 1964, 29, 836–848.

Price, J. L. *Organizational Effectiveness: An Inventory of Propositions*. Homewood, Ill.: Irwin, 1968.

Rosenthal, R. and Rosnow, R. L. "The Volunteer Subject." In R. Rosenthal and R. L. Rosnow (eds.), *Artifact in Behavior Research*. New York: Academic Press, 1969.

Schachter, S. and Singer, J. E. "Cognitive, Social and Physiological Determinants of Emotional State," *Psychological Review*, 1962, 69, 379–399.

Smith, C. G. and Tannenbaum, A. S. "Organizational Control Structure: A Comparative Analysis," *Human Relations*, 1963, 16, 299–316.

Staw, B. M. "Notes Toward a Theory of Intrinsic and Extrinsic Motivation." Paper presented at *Eastern Psychological Association*, 1974. (a)

Staw, B. M. "The Attitudinal and Behavioral Consequences of Changing a Major Organization Reward: A Natural Field Experiment," *Journal of Personality and Social Psychology*, 1974, 29, 742–751. (b)

Staw, B. M. *The Psychology of Intrinsic and Extrinsic Motivation*. Morristown, New Jersey: General Learning Press, 1975.

Strickland, L. H. "Surveillance and Trust," *Journal of Personality*, 1958, 26, 200–215.

Tannenbaum, A. S. "Control in Organizations: Individual and Organizational Performance," *Administrative Science Quarterly*, 1962, 7, 236–257.

Tannenbaum, A. S. *Control in Organizations*. New York: McGraw-Hill, 1968.

Vroom, V. H. "A Comparison of Static and Dynamic Correlational Methods in the Study of Organizations," *Organizational Behavior and Human Performance*, 1966, 1, 55–70.

Weber, S. J. and Cook, T. D. "Subject Effects in Laboratory Research: An Examination of Subject Roles, Demand Characteristics, and Valid Inference," *Psychological Bulletin*, 1972, 77, 273–295.

Weiner, B., Frieze, I., Kukla, A., Reed, L., Rest, S., and Rosenbaum, R. M. In E. E. Jones, D. E. Kanouse, H. H. Kelley, R. E. Nisbett, S. Valins, and B. Weiner (eds.), *Attribution: Perceiving the Causes of Behavior*. Morristown, New Jersey: General Learning Press, 1971.

Experimental and Quasi-Experimental Methods

The utility of empirical research is largely influenced by the quality, or rigor, of the research design. Several factors can be considered in evaluating this rigor: (1) the use of *a priori* hypotheses; (2) the use of *a priori* criteria for evaluating the extent to which the hypotheses are borne out; (3) the extent to which the researcher has successfully isolated and controlled the major study variables; and (4) the extent to which the measures employed are valid and reliable (Filley, House, and Kerr, 1976). It is generally believed that experimental methods more easily allow for these conditions to be met and hence, are more rigorous than nonexperimental techniques.

An experiment may be distinguished from other forms of scientific inquiry in that the researcher creates or instigates the conditions necessary for observation and measurement, instead of simply observing or measuring naturally-occurring phenomena. Because of this intervention, experimental designs have several advantages when compared to other less rigorous designs. First, and perhaps most important, experimental designs allow the researcher to draw clear cause-and-effect inferences. Second, experimental designs allow researchers to systematically vary the independent variables. In this way, researchers can be more precise in identifying variables for study and can examine how and to what extent such variables have an impact upon subsequent behavior. Finally, experimental designs allow for better control of extraneous variables that can influence study results. To the extent that such spurious influences can be minimized, greater confidence can be placed in the findings of the experiment. This increased rigor helps both researchers and *managers* who are interested in the effects of organizational change.

It must be recognized, however, that experimental designs also have several potential disadvantages. Experiments are time consuming and difficult to design. Often they make use of deception, and (in the case of laboratory experiments) may lack external validity. In the study of organizational behavior, such disadvantages must be weighed against the potential benefits of increased rigor in the selection of an appropriate design.

True experimental designs represent those situations whereby researchers intervene into a system and compare the results of this intervention with a control group. A *quasi-experimental* design is a design in which rigorous controls are not possible, but the researcher still intervenes in the system. As explained by Campbell and Stanley (1963,

p. 34): "There are many natural settings in which the research person can introduce something like experimental design into his scheduling of data collection procedures (e.g., the *when* and *to whom* of measurement), even though he lacks the full control over the scheduling of experimental stimuli (the *when* and *to whom* of exposure) and the ability to randomize exposures which make a true experiment possible. Collectively, such situations can be regarded as quasi-experimental designs." It is generally argued that such designs are desirable when better designs are not feasible.

The readings that follow examine several of the reasons for this increased rigor, as well as several problems associated with this approach to organizational research. In the first selection, Orne discusses some of the behavioral problems inherent in laboratory research. He distinguishes experimental methods in the behavioral sciences from those in the physical sciences and notes that behavioral research is complicated by the active presence of the subject in the study itself. We cannot assume that such subjects will be "passive responders to stimuli." Hence, it is important for researchers to be aware of the "social psychology" of the experiment itself—that is, the social dynamics that emerge in an otherwise pure experiment.

Orne attempts to identify many of the spurious influences of the subjects in an experiment. Of particular interest here is the concept of "demand characteristics," or those cues in the experimental environment that unintentionally tell subjects how to respond in the experiment. As Orne notes: "If a test is given twice with some intervening treatment, even the dullest college student is aware that some change is expected, particularly if the test is in some obvious way related to the treatment" (p. 779). It is therefore argued that a subject's response in an experiment is determined not only by the traditionally defined experimental variables, but also by those perceived demand characteristics of the particular situation. Possible mechanisms to overcome demand characteristics are discussed.

The second selection, by Weick, discusses the use of laboratory experiments in the study of organizations. Since the advantages of laboratory experiments in terms of increased experimenter control are well-known, Weick focuses his analysis on the problems that may be associated with the use of this method in studying organizational phenomena. He begins by identifying several "fictions" about research in the laboratory. These are "problems" commonly presumed to exist in laboratory research and upon closer analysis, can be shown to represent a misunderstanding of this methodology. Weick then proceeds to discuss a number of issues that must be considered by the researcher in deciding whether or not experimental laboratory research is an appropriate method of study for the research question. The advantages and disadvantages associated with research in the field and laboratory are highlighted by examining how a particular research question might be studied in both settings. While Weick suggests that laboratory studies have certain drawbacks not found in the more common field methods, the advantages associated with laboratory research indicate this method has considerable promise for extending our knowledge about organizations.

Next, Seashore focuses on field experiments as a viable research strategy in studying organizational behavior. First, a justification for the use of experimental (as opposed to correlational) methods is presented. Next, several examples of organizational experiments are reviewed in detail to provide a stage for a discussion of seven problems inherent in such experiments. These problems represent decision points (or trade-offs) for researchers who must balance diverse interests and practical realities in their pursuit or rigorous designs. Finally, several useful suggestions are offered concerning ways of implementing experimental designs in real organizations. As Seashore points out: "At this primitive stage of development in experimentation with formal organizations, it is probably desirable to emphasize simplicity of design and opportunism in execution as guides to research strategy" (p. 169).

In the fifteen years since Seashore's paper was written, little has changed as evidenced by Lawler's selection. Here too we see reference to the notions of simplicity and opportunism in field experiments. Lawler introduces the concept of "adaptive" experiments to be used in situations in which full field experimental methods are infeasible. An adaptive experiment "recognizes the realities of the field situation yet incorporates some of the key attributes of traditional experimental designs" (p. 578). As a quasi-experimental design, an adaptive experiment is particularly useful in assessing change in the ongoing quality of working life experiments in which changes evolve over time. In such instances, a single controlled intervention may not be possible; indeed, it may not even be desirable. Lawler discusses several of the requirements for adaptive experiments, including the use of standardized measures, several research sites for meaningful comparisons, a longitudinal design, third-party assessment, and careful consideration of the nature of the changes. Throughout the discussion, the point is made that such experimental methods may be superior to case studies of organizational change, which are now popular.

However, the reader should not conclude that experimental or quasi-experimental designs are necessarily superior in all cases. As noted by Homans (1949): "People who write about methodology often forget that it is a matter of strategy, not of morals. There are neither good nor bad methods, but only methods that are more or less effective under particular circumstances in reaching objectives on the way to a distant goal" (p. 330). Hence, it is necessary for the informed researcher to be familiar with divergent methods of research and to demonstrate analytic abilities in sizing up a particular research situation and selecting an appropriate strategy and design.

REFERENCES AND SUGGESTED READINGS

Barnes, L. B. "Organizational Change and Field Experimental Methods." In V. H. Vroom (ed.). *Methods of Organizational Research*. Pittsburgh: University of Pittsburgh Press, 1967.

Campbell, D. T. "Reforms as Experiments," *American Psychologist*, 24 (1969), pp. 409–429.

Campbell, D. T., and Stanley, J. C. *Experimental and Quasi-experimental Designs for Research*. Chicago: Rand McNally, 1963.

Caporaso, J. A., and Roos, L. L. (eds.). *Quasi-experimental Approaches: Testing Theory and Evaluating Policy*. Evanston: Northwestern University Press, 1974.

Cook, T. D., and Campbell, D. T. *The Design and Conduct of Quasi-experiments*. Chicago: Rand McNally, in press.

Cummings, L. L., and Harnett, D. L. "Managerial Problems and the Experimental Method," *Business Horizons*, 11 (1968), pp. 41–48.

Evans, M. G. "Opportunistic Organizational Research: The Role of Patch-up Designs," *Academy of Management Journal,* 18 (1975), pp. 98–108.

Filley, A. C., House, R. J., and Kerr, S. *Managerial Process and Organizational Behavior*. Glenview, Ill.: Scott, Foresman, 1976.

Fromkin, H. L., and Streufert, S. "Laboratory Experimentation." In M. Dunnette (ed.). *Handbook of Industrial and Organizational Psychology*. Chicago: Rand McNally, 1976.

Homans, G. C. "The Strategy of Industrial Sociology," *American Journal of Sociology*, 54 (1949), pp. 330–339.

Kirk, R. E. *Experimental Design: Procedures for the Behavioral Sciences*. Belmont, Calif.: Brooks/Cole, 1968.

Riecken, H. W., and Boruch, R. F. (eds.). *Social Experimentation: A Method of Planning and Evaluating Social Intervention*. New York: Academic Press, 1974.

Rosenthal, R., and Rosnow, R. L. (eds.). *Artifact in Behavioral Research*. New York: Academic Press, 1969.

11   On the Social Psychology of the Psychological Experiment[1]

Martin T. Orne[2]

It is to the highest degree probable that the subject[s] ... general attitude of mind is that of ready complacency and cheerful willingness to assist the investigator in every possible way by reporting to him those very things which he is most eager to find, and that the very questions of the experimenter ... suggest the shade of reply expected .... Indeed ... it seems too often as if the subject were now regarded as a stupid automaton ....

A. H. Pierce, 1908[3]

Since the time of Galileo, scientists have employed the laboratory experiment as a method of understanding natural phenomena. Generically, the experimental method consists of abstracting relevant variables from complex situations in nature and reproducing in the laboratory segments of these situations, varying the parameters involved so as to determine the effect of the experimental variables. This procedure allows generalization from the information obtained in the laboratory situation back to the original situation as it occurs in nature. The physical sciences have made striking advances through the use of this method, but in the behavioral sciences it has often been difficult to meet two necessary requirements for meaningful experimentation: reproducibility and ecological validity.[4] It has long been recognized that certain differences will exist between the types of experiments conducted in the physical sciences and those in the behavioral sciences because the former investigates a universe of inanimate objects and forces, whereas the latter deals with animate organisms, often thinking, conscious subjects. However, recognition of this distinction has not always led to appropriate changes in the traditional experimental model of physics as employed in the behavioral sciences. Rather the experimental model has been so successful as employed in physics that there has been a tendency in the behavioral sciences to follow precisely a paradigm originated for the study of inanimate objects, i.e., one which proceeds by exposing the subject to various conditions and observing the differences in reaction of the subject under different conditions. However, the use of such a model with animal or human subjects leads to the problem that the subject of the experiment is assumed, at least implicitly, to be a *passive responder* to stimuli—an assumption difficult to justify. Further, in this type of model the experimental stimuli themselves are usually rigorously defined in terms of what *is done* to the subject. In contrast, the purpose of this paper will be to focus

Source: M. T. Orne "On the Social Psychology of the Psychological Experiment: With Particular Reference to Demand Characteristics and Their Implications," *American Psychologist*, 1962, 17 (11), 776–783. Copyright (1962) by the American Psychological Association. Reprinted by permission. *Editor's note*: More recent work by Professor Orne on demand characteristics can be found in Orne (1969, 1970, 1972). See the additional references following this article.

on what the human subject *does* in the laboratory: what motivation the subject is likely to have in the experimental situation, how he usually perceives behavioral research, what the nature of the cues is that the subject is likely to pick up, etc. Stated in other terms, what factors are apt to affect the subject's reaction to the well-defined stimuli in the situation? These factors comprise what will be referred to here as the "experimental setting."

Since any experimental manipulation of human subjects takes place within this larger framework or setting, we should propose that the above-mentioned factors must be further elaborated and the parameters of the experimental setting more carefully defined so that adequate controls can be designed to isolate the effects of the experimental setting from the effects of the experimental variables. Later in this paper we shall propose certain possible techniques of control which have been devised in the process of our research on the nature of hypnosis.

Our initial focus here will be on some of the qualities peculiar to psychological experiments. The experimental situation is one which takes place within the context of an explicit agreement of the subject to participate in a special form of social interaction known as "taking part in an experiment." Within the context of our culture the roles of subject and experimenter are well understood and carry with them well-defined mutual role expectations. A particularly striking aspect of the typical experimenter-subject relationship is the extent to which the subject will play his role and place himself under the control of the experimenter. Once a subject has agreed to participate in a psychological experiment, he implicitly agrees to perform a very wide range of actions on request without inquiring as to their purpose, and frequently without inquiring as to their duration.

Furthermore, the subject agrees to tolerate a considerable degree of discomfort, boredom, or actual pain, if required to do so by the experimenter. Just about any request which could conceivably be asked of the subject by a reputable investigator is legitimized by the quasi-magical phrase, "This is an experiment," and the shared assumption that a legitimate purpose will be served by the subject's behavior. A somewhat trivial example of this legitimization of requests is as follows:

A number of casual acquaintances were asked whether they would do the experimenter a favor; on their acquiescence, they were asked to perform five push-ups. Their response tended to be amazement, incredulity and the question "Why?" Another similar group of individuals were asked whether they would take part in an experiment of brief duration. When they agreed to do so, they too were asked to perform five push-ups. Their typical response was "Where?"

The striking degree of control inherent in the experimental situation can also be illustrated by a set of pilot experiments which were performed in the course of designing an experiment to test whether the degree of control inherent in the *hypnotic* relationship is greater than that in a waking relationship.[5] In order to test this question, we tried to develop a set of tasks which waking subjects would refuse to do, or would do only for a short period of time. The tasks were intended to be psychologically noxious, meaningless, or boring, rather than painful or fatiguing.

For example, one task was to perform serial additions of each adjacent two numbers on sheets filled with rows of random digits. In order to complete just one sheet, the subject would be required to perform 224 additions! A stack of some 2,000 sheets was presented to each subject—clearly an impossible task to complete. After the instructions were given, the subject was deprived of his watch and told, "Continue to work; I will return eventually." Five and one-half hours later, the *experimenter* gave up! In general, subjects tended to continue this type of task for several hours, usually with little decrement in performance. Since we were trying to find a task which would be discontinued spontaneously within a brief period, we tried to create a more frustrating situation as follows:

Subjects were asked to perform the same task described above but were also told that when they finished the additions on each sheet, they should pick up a card from a large pile, which would instruct them on what to do next. However, every card in the pile read,

> You are to tear up the sheet of paper which you have just completed into a minimum of thirty-two pieces and go on to the next sheet of paper and continue working as you did before; when you have completed this piece of paper, pick up the next card which will instruct you further. Work as accurately and as rapidly as you can.

Our expectation was that subjects would discontinue the task as soon as they realized that the cards were worded identically, that each finished piece of work had to be destroyed, and that, in short, the task was completely meaningless.

Somewhat to our amazement, subjects tended to persist in the task for several hours with relatively little sign of overt hostility. Removal of the one-way screen did not tend to make much difference. The postexperimental inquiry helped to explain the subjects' behavior. When asked about the tasks, subjects would invariably attribute considerable meaning to their performance, viewing it as an endurance test or the like.

Thus far, we have been singularly unsuccessful in finding an experimental task which would be discontinued, or, indeed, refused by subjects in an experimental setting.[6,7] Not only do subjects continue to perform boring, unrewarding tasks, but they do so with few errors and little decrement in speed. It became apparent that it was extremely difficult to design an experiment to test the degree of social control in hypnosis, in view of the already *very high degree of control in the experimental situation itself.*

The quasi-experimental work reported here is highly informal and based on samples of three or four subjects in each group. It does, however, illustrate the remarkable compliance of the experimental subject. The only other situations where such a wide range of requests are carried out with little or no question are those of complete authority, such as some parent-child relationships or some doctor-patient relationships. This aspect of the experiment as a social situation will not become apparent unless one tests it; it is, however, present in varying degrees in all experimental contexts. Not only are tasks carried out, but they are performed with care over considerable periods of time.

Our observation that subjects tend to carry out a remarkably wide range of instructions with a surprising degree of diligence reflects only one aspect of the motivation manifested by most subjects in an experimental situation. It is relevant to consider another aspect of motivation that is common to the subjects of most psychological experiments: high regard for the aims of science and experimentation.

A volunteer who participates in a psychological experiment may do so for a wide variety of reasons ranging from the need to fulfill a course requirement, to the need for money, to the unvoiced hope of altering his personal adjustment for the better, etc. Over and above these motives, however, college students tend to share (with the experimenter) the hope and expectation that the study in which they are participating will in some material way contribute to science and perhaps ultimately to human welfare in general. We should expect that many of the characteristics of the experimental situation derive from the peculiar role relationship which exists between subject and experimenter. Both subject and experimenter share the belief that whatever the experimental task is, it is important, and that as such no matter how much effort must be exerted or how much discomfort must be endured, it is justified by the ultimate purpose.

If we assume that much of the motivation of the subject to comply with any and all experimental instructions derives from an identification with the goals of science in general and the success of the experiment in particular,[8] it follows that the subject has a stake in the outcome of the study in which he is participating. For the volunteer subject to feel that he has made a useful contribution, it is necessary for him to assume that the experimenter is competent and that he himself is a "good subject."

The significance to the subject of successfully being a "good subject" is attested to by the frequent questions at the conclusion of an experiment, to the effect of, "Did I ruin the experiment?" What is most commonly meant by this is, "Did I perform well in my role as experimental subject?" or "Did my behavior demonstrate that which the experiment is designed to show?" Admittedly, subjects are concerned about their performance in terms of reinforcing their self-image; nonetheless, they seem even more concerned with the utility of their performances. We might well expect then that as far as the subject is able, he will behave in an experimental context in a manner designed to play the role of a "good subject" or, in other words, *to validate the experimental hypothesis*. Viewed in this way, the student volunteer is *not* merely a passive responder in an experimental situation but rather he has a very real stake in the successful outcome of the experiment. This problem is implicitly recognized in the large number of psychological studies which attempt to conceal the true purpose of the experiment from the subject in the hope of thereby obtaining more reliable data. This maneuver on the part of psychologists is so widely known in the college population that even if a psychologist is honest with the subject, more often than not he will be distrusted. As one subject pithily put it, "Psychologists always lie!" This bit of paranoia has some support in reality.

The subject's performance in an experiment might almost be conceptualized as problem-solving behavior; that is, at some level he sees it as his task to ascertain the true purpose of the experiment and respond in a manner which will support the hypotheses being tested. Viewed in this light, the totality of cues which convey an experimental hypothesis to the subject become significant determinants of subjects' behavior. We have labeled the sum total of such cues as the *"demand characteristics of the experimental situation"* (Orne, 1959a). These cues include the rumors or campus scuttlebutt about the research, the information conveyed during the original solicitation, the person of the experimenter, and the setting of the laboratory, as well as all explicit and implicit communications during the experiment proper. A frequently overlooked, but nonetheless very significant source of cues for the subject lies in the experimental procedure itself, viewed in the light of the subject's previous knowledge and experience. For example, if a test is given twice with some intervening treatment, even the dullest college student is aware that some change is expected, particularly if the test is in some obvious way related to the treatment.

The demand characteristics perceived in any particular experiment will vary with the sophistication, intelligence, and previous experience of each experimental subject. To the extent that the demand characteristics of the experiment are clear-cut, they will be perceived uniformly by most experimental subjects. It is entirely possible to have an experimental situation with clear-cut demand characteristics for psychology undergraduates which, however, does not have the same clear-cut demand characteristics for enlisted army personnel. It is, of course, those demand characteristics which are perceived by the subject that will influence his behavior.

We should like to propose the heuristic assumption that a subject's behavior in any experimental situation will be determined by two sets of variables: (1) those which are traditionally defined as experimental variables and (2) the perceived demand characteristics of the experimental situation. The extent to which the subject's behavior is related to the demand characteristics, rather than to the experimental variable, will in large measure determine both the extent to which the experiment can be replicated with minor modification (i.e., modified demand characteristics) and the extent to which generalizations can be drawn about the effect of the experimental variables in nonexperimental contexts [the problem of ecological validity (Brunswik, 1947)].

It becomes an empirical issue to study under what circumstances, in what kind of experimental contexts, and with what kind of subject populations, demand characteristics become significant in determining the behavior of subjects in experimental situations. It should be clear that demand characteristics cannot be eliminated from experiments; all experiments will have demand characteristics, and these will always have some effect. It does become possible, however, to study the effect of demand characteristics as opposed to the effect of experimental variables. However, techniques designed to study the effect of demand characteristics need to take into account that these effects result from the subject's *active* attempt to respond appropriately to the *totality* of the experimental situation.

It is perhaps best to think of the perceived demand characteristics as a contextual variable in the experimental situation. We should like to emphasize that, at this stage, little is known about this variable. In our first study which utilized the demand characteristics concept (Orne, 1959b), we found that a particular experimental effect was present only in records of those subjects who were able to verbalize the experimenter's hypothesis. Those subjects who were unable to do so did not show the predicted phenomenon. Indeed we found that whether or not a given subject perceived the experimenter's hypothesis was a more accurate predictor of the subject's actual performance than his statement about what he thought he had done on the experimental task. It became clear from extensive interviews with subjects that response to the demand characteristics is not merely conscious compliance. When we speak of "playing the role of a good experimental subject," we use the concept analogously to the way in which Sarbin (1950) describes role playing in hypnosis: namely, largely on a nonconscious level. The demand characteristics of the situation help define the role of "good experimental subject," and the responses of the subject are a function of the role that is created.

We have a suspicion that the demand characteristics most potent in determining subjects' behavior are those which convey the purpose of the experiment effectively but not obviously. If the purpose of the experiment is not clear, or is highly ambiguous, many different hypotheses may be formed by different subjects, and the demand characteristics will not lead to clear-cut results. If, on the other hand, the demand characteristics are so obvious that the subject becomes fully conscious of the expectations of the experimenter, there is a tendency to lean over backwards to be honest. We are encountering here the effect of another facet of the college student's attitude toward science. While the student wants studies to "work," he feels he must be honest in his report; otherwise, erroneous conclusions will be drawn. Therefore, if the subject becomes acutely aware of the experimenter's expectations, there may be a tendency for biasing in the opposite direction. (This is analogous to the often observed tendency to favor individuals whom we dislike in an effort to be fair.)[9]

Delineation of the situations where demand characteristics may produce an effect ascribed to experimental variables, or where they may obscure such an effect and actually lead to systematic data in the opposite direction, as well as those experimental contexts where they do not play a major role, is an issue for further work. Recognizing the contribution to experimental results which may be made by the demand characteristics of the situation, what are some experimental techniques for the study of demand characteristics?

As we have pointed out, it is futile to imagine an experiment that could be created without demand characteristics. One of the basic characteristics of the human being is that he will ascribe purpose and meaning even in the absence of purpose and meaning. In an experiment where he knows some purpose exists, it is inconceivable for him not to form some hypothesis as to the purpose, based on some cues, no matter how meager; this will then determine the demand characteristics which will be perceived by and operate for a particular subject. Rather than eliminating this variable then, it becomes necessary to take demand characteristics into account, study their effect, and manipulate them if necessary.

One procedure to determine the demand characteristics is the systematic study of each individual subject's perception of the experimental hypothesis. If one can determine what demand characteristics are perceived by each subject, it becomes possible to determine to what extent these, rather than the experimental variables, correlate with the observed behavior. If the subject's behavior correlates better with the demand characteristics than with the experimental variables, it is probable that the demand characteristics are the major determinants of the behavior.

The most obvious technique for determining what demand characteristics are perceived is the use of postexperimental inquiry. In this regard, it is well to point out that considerable self-discipline is necessary for the experimenter to obtain a valid inquiry. A great many experimenters at least implicitly make the demand that the subject not perceive what is really going on. The temptation for the experimenter, in, say, a replication of an Asch group pressure experiment, is to ask the subject afterwards, "You didn't realize that the other fellows were confederates, did you?" Having obtained the required, "No," the experimenter breathes a sigh of relief and neither subject nor experimenter pursues the issue further.[10] However, even if the experimenter makes an effort to elicit the subject's perception of the hypothesis of the experiment, he may have difficulty in obtaining a valid report because the subject as well as he himself has considerable interest in appearing naive.

Most subjects are cognizant that they are not supposed to know any more about an experiment than they have been told and that excessive knowledge will disqualify them from participating, or, in the case of a postexperimental inquiry, such knowledge will invalidate their performance. As we pointed out earlier, subjects have a real stake in viewing their performance as meaningful. For this reason, it is commonplace to find a pact of ignorance resulting from the intertwining motives of both experimenter and subject, neither wishing to create a situation where the particular subject's performance needs to be excluded from the study.

For these reasons, inquiry procedures are required to push the subject for information without, however, providing in themselves cues as to what is expected. The general question which needs to be explored is the subject's perception of the experimental purpose and the specific hypotheses of the experimenter. This can best be done by an open-ended procedure starting with the very general question of, "What do you think that the experiment is about?" and only much later asking specific questions. Responses of "I don't know" should be dealt with by encouraging the subject to guess, use his imagination, and in general, by refusing to accept this response. Under these circumstances, the overwhelming majority of students will turn out to have evolved very definite hypotheses. These hypotheses can then be judged, and a correlation between them and experimental performance can be drawn.

Two objections may be made against this type of inquiry: (1) that the subject's perception of the experimenter's hypotheses is based on his own experimental behavior, and therefore a correlation between these two variables may have little to do with the determinants of behavior, and (2) that the inquiry procedure itself is subject to demand characteristics.

A procedure which has been independently advocated by Riecken (1958) and Orne (1959a) is designed to deal with the first of these objections. This consists of an inquiry procedure which is conducted much as though the subject had actually been run in the experiment, without, however, permitting him to be given any experimental data. Instead, the precise procedure of the experiment is explained, the experimental material is shown to the subject, and he is told what he would be required to do; however, he is not permitted to make any responses. He is then given a postexperimental inquiry as though he had been a subject. Thus, one would say, "If I had asked you to do all these things, what do you think that the experiment would be about, what do you think I would be trying to prove, what would my hypothesis be?" etc. This technique, which we have termed the pre-experimental inquiry, can be extended very readily to the giving of preexperimental tests, followed by the explanation of experimental conditions and tasks, and the administration of postexperimental tests. The subject is requested to behave on these tests as though he had been exposed to the experimental treatment that was described to him. This type of procedure is not open to the objection that the subject's own behavior has provided cues for him as to the purpose of the task. It presents him with a straight problem-solving situation and makes explicit what, for the true experimental subject, is implicit. It goes without saying that these subjects who are run on the preexperimental inquiry conditions must be drawn from the same population as the experimental groups and may, of course, not be run subsequently in the experimental condition. This technique is one of approximation rather than of proof. However, if subjects describe behavior on the pre-inquiry conditions as similar to, or identical with, that actually given by subjects exposed to the experimental conditions, the hypothesis becomes plausible that demand characteristics may be responsible for the behavior.

It is clear that pre and postexperimental inquiry techniques have their own demand characteristics. For these reasons, it is usually best to have the inquiry conducted by an experimenter who is not acquainted with the actual experimental behavior of the subjects. This will tend to minimize the effect of experimenter bias.

Another technique which we have utilized for approximating the effect of the demand characteristics is to attempt to hold the demand characteristics constant and eliminate the experimental variable. One way of accomplishing this purpose is through the use of simulating subjects. This is a group of subjects who are not exposed to the experimental variable to which the effect has been attributed, but who are instructed to act *as if* this were the case. In order to control for experimenter bias under these circumstances, it is advisable to utilize more than one experimenter and to have the experimenter who actually runs the subjects "blind" as to which group (simulating or real) any given individual belongs.

Our work in hypnosis (Damaser, Shor, and Orne, 1963; Orne, 1959b; Shor, 1959) is a good example of the use of simulating controls. Subjects unable to enter hypnosis are instructed to simulate entering hypnosis for another experimenter. The experimenter who runs the study sees both highly trained hypnotic subjects and simulators in random order and does not know to which group each subject belongs. Because the subjects are run "blind," the experimenter is more likely to treat the two groups of subjects identically. We have found that simulating subjects are able to perform with great effectiveness, deceiving even well-trained hypnotists. However, the simulating group is not exposed to the experimental condition (in this case, hypnosis) to which the given effect under investigation is often ascribed. Rather, it is a group faced with a problem-solving task: namely, to utilize whatever cues are made available by the experimental context and the experimenter's concrete behavior in order to behave as they think that hypnotized subjects might. Therefore, to the extent that simulating subjects are able to behave identically, it is possible that demand characteristics, rather than the altered state of consciousness, could account for the behavior of the experimental group.

The same type of technique can be utilized in other types of studies. For example, in contrast to the placebo control in a drug study, it is equally possible to instruct some subjects not to take the medication at all, but to act as if they had. It must be emphasized that this type of control is different from the placebo control. It represents an approximation. It maximally confronts the simulating subject with a problem-solving task and suggests how much of the total effect could be accounted for by the demand characteristics—assuming that the experimental group had taken full advantage of them, an assumption not necessarily correct.

All of the techniques proposed thus far share the quality that they depend upon the active cooperation of the control subjects, and in some way utilize their thinking processes as an intrinsic factor. The subject does *not* just respond in these control situations but, rather, he is required *actively* to solve the problem.

The use of placebo experimental conditions is a way in which this problem can be dealt with in a more classic fashion. Psychopharmacology has used such techniques extensively, but here too they present problems. In the case of placebos and drugs, it is often the case that the physician is "blind" as to whether a drug is placebo or active, but the patient is not, despite precautions to the contrary; i.e., the patient is cognizant that he does not have the side effects which some of his fellow patients on the ward experience. By the same token, in psychological placebo treatments, it is equally important to ascertain whether the subject actually perceived the treatment to be experimental or control. Certainly the subject's perception of himself as a control subject may materially alter the situation.

A recent experiment[11] in our laboratory illustrates this type of investigation. We were interested in studying the demand characteristics of sensory deprivation experiments, independent of any actual sensory deprivation. We hypothesized that the overly cautious treatment of subjects, careful screening for mental or physical disorders, awesome release forms, and, above all, the presence of a "panic (release) button" might be more significant in producing the effects reported from sensory deprivation than the actual diminution of sensory input. A pilot study (Stare, Brown, and Orne, 1959), employing preinquiry techniques, supported this view. Recently, we designed an experiment to test more rigorously this hypothesis.

This experiment, which we called Meaning Deprivation, had all the *accoutrements* of sensory deprivation, including release forms and a red panic button. However, we carefully refrained from creating any sensory deprivation whatsoever. The experimental task consisted of sitting in a small experimental room which was well lighted, with two comfortable chairs, as well as ice water and a sandwich, and an optional task of adding numbers. The subject did not have a watch during this time, the room was reasonably quiet, but not soundproof, and the duration of the experiment (of which the subject was ignorant) was four hours. Before the subject was placed in the experimental room, 10 tests previously used in sensory deprivation research were administered. At the completion of the experiment, the same tasks were again administered. A microphone and a one-way screen were present in the room, and the subject was encouraged to verbalize freely.

The control group of 10 subjects was subjected to the identical treatment, except that they were told that they were control subjects for a sensory deprivation experiment. The panic button was eliminated for this group. The formal experimental treatment of these two groups of subjects was the same in terms of the objective stress—four hours of isolation. However, the demand characteristics had been purposively varied for the two groups to study the effect of demand characteristics as opposed to objective stress. Of the 14 measures which could be quantified, 13 were in the predicted direction, and 6 were significant at the selected 10% alpha level or better. A Mann-Whitney U test has been performed on the summation ranks of all measures as a convenient method for summarizing the overall differences. The one-tailed probability which emerges is $p = .001$, a clear demonstration of expected effects.

This study suggests that demand characteristics may in part account for some of the findings commonly attributed to sensory deprivation. We have found similar significant effects of demand characteristics in accounting for a great deal of the findings reported in hypnosis. It is highly probable that careful attention to this variable, or group of variables, may resolve some of the current controversies regarding a number of psychological phenomena in motivation, learning, and perception.

In summary, we have suggested that the subject must be recognized as an active participant in any experiment, and that it may be fruitful to view the psychological experiment as a very special form of social interaction. We have proposed that the subject's behavior in an experiment is a function of the totality of the situation, which includes the experimental variables being investigated and at least one other set of variables which we have subsumed under the heading, demand characteristics of the experimental situation. The study and control of demand characteristics are not simply matters of good experimental technique; rather, it is an empirical issue to determine under what circumstances demand characteristics significantly affect subjects' experimental behavior. Several empirical techniques have been proposed for this purpose. It has been suggested that control of these variables in particular may lead to greater reproducibility and ecological validity of psychological experiments. With an increasing understanding of these factors intrinsic to the experimental context, the experimental method in psychology may become a more effective tool in predicting behavior in nonexperimental contexts.

NOTES

1. This paper was presented at the Symposium, "On the Social Psychology of the Psychological Experiment," American Psychological Association Convention, New York, 1961.
The work reported here was supported in part by a Public Health Service Research Grant, M-3369, National Institute of Mental Health.

2. I wish to thank my associates Ronald E. Shor, Donald N. O'Connell, Ulric Neisser, Karl E. Scheibe, and Emily F. Carota for their comments and criticisms in the preparation of this paper.

3. See reference list (Pierce, 1908).

4. Ecological validity, in the sense that Brunswik (1947) has used the term: appropriate generalization from the laboratory to nonexperimental situations.

5. These pilot studies were performed by Thomas Menaker.

6. Tasks which would involve the use of actual severe physical pain or exhaustion were not considered.

7. This observation is consistent with Frank's (1944) failure to obtain resistance to disagreeable or nonsensical tasks. He accounts for this "primarily by S's unwillingness to break the tacit agreement he had made when he volunteered to take part in the experiment, namely, to do whatever the experiment required of him" (p. 24).

8. This hypothesis is subject to empirical test. We should predict that there would be measurable differences in motivation between subjects who perceive a particular experiment as "significant" and those who perceive the experiment as "unimportant."

9. Rosenthal (1961) in his recent work on experimenter bias, has reported a similar type of phenomenon. Biasing was maximized by ego involvement of the experimenters, but when an attempt was made to increase biasing by paying for "good results," there was a marked reduction of effect. This reversal may be ascribed to the experimenters' becoming too aware of their own wishes in the situation.

10. Asch (1952) himself took great pains to avoid this pitfall.

11. Orne, M. T., and Scheibe, K. E. "The Contribution of Nondeprivation Factors in the Production of Sensory Deprivation Effects: The Psychology of the 'Panic Button.'" *J. Abnorm. Soc. Psychol.*, 1964, 68, 3–12.

REFERENCES

Asch, S. E. *Social Psychology*. Englewood Cliffs, N.J.: 1952.

Brunswik, E. *Systematic and Representative Design of Psychological Experiments With Results in Physical and Social Perception*. (Syllabus Series, No. 304) Berkeley: Univer. California Press, 1947.

Damaser, E. C., Shor, R. E., and Orne, M. T. "Physiological Effects During Hypnotically Requested Emotions," *Psychosom. Med.*, 1963, 25, 334–343.

Frank, J. D. "Experimental Studies of Personal Pressure and Resistance: I. Experimental Production of Resistance," *J. Gen. Psychol.*, 1944, 30, 23–41.

Orne, M. T. "The Demand Characteristics of an Experimental Design and Their Implications." Paper read at American Psychological Association, Cincinnati, 1959. (a)

Orne, M. T. "The Nature of Hypnosis: Artifact and Essence," *J. Abnorm. Soc. Psychol.*, 1959, 58, 277–299. (b)

Pierce, A. H. "The Subconscious Again, *J. Phil., Psychol., Scient. Meth.*, 1908, 5, 264–271.

Riecken, H. W. "A Program for Research on Experiments in Social Psychology." Paper read at Behavioral Sciences Conference, University of New Mexico, 1958.

Rosenthal, R. "On the Social Psychology of the Psychological Experiment: With Particular Reference to Experimenter Bias." Paper read at American Psychological Association, New York, 1961.

Sarbin, T. R. "Contributions to Role-taking Theory: I. Hypnotic Behavior," *Psychol. Rev.*, 1950, 57, 255–270.

Shor, R. E. "Explorations in Hypnosis: A Theoretical and Experimental Study." Unpublished doctoral dissertation, Brandeis University, 1959.

Stare, F., Brown, J., and Orne, M. T. "Demand Characteristics in Sensory Deprivation Studies." Unpublished seminar paper, Massachusetts Mental Health Center and Harvard University, 1959.

ADDITIONAL REFERENCES

Orne, M. T. "Demand Characteristics and the Concept of Quasi-Controls." In R. Rosenthal and R. Rosnow (eds.), *Artifact in Behavioral Research*. New York: Academic Press, 1969.

Orne, M. T. "Hypnosis, Motivation and the Ecological Validity of the Psychological Experiment." In W. J. Arnold and M. M. Page (eds.), *Nebraska Symposium on Motivation*. Lincoln: University of Nebraska Press, 1970.

Orne, M. T. "Communications by the Total Experimental Situation: Why It Is Important, How It Is Evaluated, and Its Significance for the Ecological Validity of Findings." In P. Pliner, L. Krames, and T. Alloway (eds.), *Communication and Affect*. New York: Academic Press, 1972.

12 Organizations in the Laboratory

Karl E. Weick

Eight people enter an experimental room and sit at separate desks. One of them silently reads through the following passage twice.

MODIFICATION OF SPECIES

One objection to the views of those who, like Mr. Gulick, believe isolation itself to be a cause of modification of species deserves attention, namely, the entire absence of change where, if·this were a *vera causa*, we should expect to find it. In Ireland we have an excellent test case, for we know that it has been separated from Britain since the end of the glacial epoch, certainly many thousand years. Yet hardly one of its mammals, reptiles or land molluscs, has undergone the slightest change, even though there is certainly a distinct difference of environment, both inorganic and organic. That changes have not occurred through natural selection is perhaps due to the less severe struggle for existence owing to the smaller number of competing species; but if isolation itself were an efficient cause, acting continuously and cum-

*The financial support of the National Science Foundation, Grant number GS–356, is gratefully acknowledged.

ulatively, it is incredible that a decided change should not have been produced in thousands of years. That no such change has occurred in this and many other cases of isolation seems to prove that it is not itself a cause of modification [Bartlett, 1932, p. 166].

After reading the excerpt, the subject spends a few minutes performing an unrelated task and then writes the story from memory. Next, his version of the story is given to the second subject who reads it twice, works at another task, and then reproduces it. Each subject responds similarly;

The story written by the last subject reads as follows:

Mr. Garlick says that isolation is the reason of modification. This has been proved by the fact that snakes and other reptiles were once in Ireland [ibid., p. 167].

Several things have happened to the story. The content has beem simplified rather than embellished. Conventional phrases have replaced unusual details. Details have been personalized. Titles have been dropped making it more difficult for persons to place the event. In short, the subjects have tried to "justify whatever impression may have been left by the original" (ibid., p. 176).

The important question here is what relevance, if any, does this experimental exercise have to the study of organizations? Do the eight men constitute an organization? Can we learn about organizations by studying the fate of stories as they are passed from person to person? What can be learned? Questions such as these, phrased in terms of the simple task of serial reproduction, point to several issues involved in learning about organizations through laboratory experiments.

Some persons might contend that experiments on serial reproduction *are* relevant to organizational research. Stogdill (1950) and Vroom (1964) argue that differentiation of positions and a division of labor are defining attributes of an organization. If the eight subjects have different assignments (e.g., one attends to grammar, another attends to plausibility) or if they differentiate themselves according to the responsibilities for accurate transmission of the story (e.g., the "first man" must be accurate, the "middle man" must add content because some will be lost), then it is conceivable that the situation of serial reproduction is like an organization. Guetzkow (1961) argues that mediated interaction distinguishes organization from small groups. Since interactions in serial reproduction are seldom face to face, the exercise qualifies as an organization by Guetzkow's standards. A related distinction is suggested by Bass (1964) who maintains that an organization consists of relations among positions, while small groups are relations among persons. It is unclear whether *Ss* perceive each other in positional or personal terms but, again, if positions are salient, serial reproduction has relevance to organizations.

Zelditch and Hopkins (1961) would probably describe the serial reproduction experiment as a "simply structured unit," meaning that it is neither complex nor does it have distinctive organizational properties. However, this type of unit still is relevant to organizations according to Zelditch and Hopkins because (1) it operates like a *subunit* in an organization, and (2) it has certain characteristics of a social system just as an organization does. It might also be argued that a serial reproduction exercise constitutes organizational research because it reproduces a common organizational phenomenon, "uncertainty absorption." March and Simon (1958, p. 165) comment that "uncertaintly absorption takes place when inferences are drawn from a body of evidence and the inferences, instead of the evidence itself, are then communicated." This process is much like that observed in serial reproduction.

In each of the preceding instances, the task was potentially an organizational exercise because it resembled a natural organization in some respect or because it tested a proposition of relevance in organizational theory. However, there are other reasons why serial reproduction may not be an organization experiment.

Some of these reasons are definitional. Serial reproduction does not include properties that several investigators regard as crucial to the definition of organization. It does not contain technology (Leavitt, 1964), multiple groups (Simon, 1960), an external environment (Becker, 1964; Krupp, 1961), hierarchy of authority (Schein, 1965), or formality of policies (Zelditch and Hopkins, 1961).

Aside from definitional shortcomings, the task also has the disadvantages of many contrived situations. The interactions between subjects are transitory (Lorge, Fox, Davitz, and Brenner, 1958) and there is little time or reason for group traditions, rituals, and norms to develop. The laboratory group probably is not of the subject's own choosing (Sherif and Sherif, 1964) although neither are many groups in natural organizations. Tasks may appear trivial (Mechanic, 1963), their performance may have few consequences for the subjects (Cook and Selltiz, 1964), and the subjects, if they are students, are probably excessively compliant (Proshansky and Seidenberg, 1965, p. 13).

This brief examination of serial reproduction suggests a few of the issues that arise when attempts are made to study organizations in the laboratory. These issues are especially sharp in the case of serial reproduction because the task is not conceived with organizations in mind. Yet even this task has some relevance, given certain definitions of an organization, and the exercise can be modified to make it more relevant. If eight persons are not enough to constitute an organization, more could be added. Participants could be supplied with selected information about the other communicators (e.g., one is ambitious, a newcomer, skilled, suspicious, trustworthy) and structural or status distinctions could be made explicit. Instead of stories, persons might reproduce communications about controversial issues within the organization. The first person in the chain might observe an event and report his observations rather than read an intact story. Subjects might be given access to earlier messages or spend the time interval prior to reproduction on some activity *related* to the content of the communication.

This introduction suggests three very general conclusions about laboratory studies of organizations.

1. Experimental Organizations are Simplified

The preceding review suggests that any laboratory experiment involving interacting persons contains both features that are typical of natural organizations and features that are not. Thus the same experiment can be seen by some investigators as relevant to the study of organizations, by others, as irrelevant. It all depends on which characteristics of organizations are regarded as crucial.

It is unlikely, however, that any experiment will fully satisfy the investigator who values fidelity between laboratory and natural events. Fidelity typically must be compromised to gain clarity and control. If a person wishes to use experiments, he probably will have to choose among the several characteristics of organizations that he regards as important. To gain control, simple tasks in simple settings are often required. Selectivity need not be detrimental, it may compel the investigator to be more explicit.

2. Tests of Organizational Theory Do Not Require Organizations

Experiments are often used to test propositions derived from organizational theory. When an experiment is used for this purpose, its content is determined by the theory, not the referent event. This is one of the reasons that a surface resemblance between laboratory organizations and natural organizations often is absent and unnecessary. The relationship between contrived and natural events in hypothesis testing is aptly summarized by Zigler (1963, p. 353).

> What the experimenter is saying is that if such and such holds in the real world because of the principles expounded in the particular theory under investigation, then such and such should hold in the world which the experimenter has created. This translatability is what gives theoretical import to experiments which involve phenomena which, taken in isolation, not only appear picayune but seem to have little relationship with what one observes in nature.

It should not be assumed that Zigler's description affords a blanket justification for all experiments. Instead, it sharpens those things for which an experimenter should be held accountable and those for which he should not. It is clear that the experimenter must be explicit about the "world that he has created." Recent research concerning the social psychology of experiments (Rosenthal, 1963) suggests that it is more difficult to be explicit about the world that one creates than many have expected. Only if an experimenter is explicit can an observer judge if the intended conditions have been created and whether equivalent opportunities exist for "real world" principles to operate. The experimenter's claim is that his design permits these same principles to operate and that the only changes in conditions are minor ones.

While it is probably true that the experimenter can muster a stronger argument for the generality of his findings if the experiment resembles the real world, all this really does is reduce the size of the deductive leap he must make and defend. Assuming that the principles from the real world are explicit, that the experimenter is rigorous in his deductions, and that he has intimate knowledge of the world he has created, he may be less concerned with creating a close replica of the natural event.

3. Organizations Can Be Created Experimentally in Several Ways

Although this point has some overlap with the first summary statement, it is included to indicate that organizational experiments assume many forms. For example, organizations can be created by appropriate choices of subjects. Any experiment that uses as subjects members of ongoing organizations (e.g., Bass, 1963; French and Snyder, 1959; Maier and Hoffman, 1961) may qualify as an organizational experiment. The subjects do not have to be members of organizations, they could be aspirants as in the case of students of journalism (Lyle, 1961), business (Bass, 1963), or international relations (Guetzkow, 1959). Even further removed from actual membership, but still potentially relevant, are experiments in which subjects either explicitly role play persons in organizations (Rosenberg and Abelson, 1960), engage in activities similar to those of persons in organizations (e.g., Cohen, 1958; Strickland, 1958), identify with one organizational member in a tape recorded interaction (Ring, 1964), or read about the activities of persons in organizations and react to what is read (DiVesta, Meyer, and Mills, 1964).

Organizational experiments also may be constituted by the inclusion of trappings found in actual organizations. Such experiments may range from actual organizations that are created in the laboratory and exist for several days (Wager and Palola, 1964), through partial organizations (Evan and Zelditch, 1961), down to experiments that have a plausible, but minimal set of props (Cyert, March, and Starbuck, 1961). It could also be argued that any experiment testing a proposition derived from or relevant to organization theory is an organizational experiment (as is one that is multi-person), permits interaction between groups, involves coalitions (Thibaut, 1964, p. 88), or exists for an extended period of time. Clearly, these criteria include most social psychological experiments.

In one sense, arguments over whether an experiment is organizational or not are unnecessary. This judgment depends on the extent to which the specific research promotes understanding of organizational processes. Our reason for illustrating various definitions of these experiments is to suggest some ways in which organizations can be studied in the laboratory and, indirectly, to suggest the flexibility of the laboratory.

Summary

At the outset, it is important to realize experimental organizations seldom resemble natural organizations. Experiments permit persons to look more closely at some problems, but not at others. However, it is the experimenter's theoretical preferences, his preconceptions about experiments and his ingenuity that define the range of problems that are susceptible to experimental inquiry. It is the purpose . . . [here] to detail how laboratory studies are created, and what they can and cannot accomplish.

The . . . [article] will contain the following sections. First, characteristics of experiments will be described in terms of the fictions and nonfictions that have emerged about laboratory experiments . . . . Then a comparison between field and laboratory studies of a common problem will introduce an extended discussion of the strengths and problems associated with conducting experiments. Primary emphasis will be placed on problems.

THE NATURE OF ORGANIZATIONAL EXPERIMENTS

Formally, it is possible to define experimentation as "experience carefully planned in advance" (R. A. Fisher, quoted in Kaplan, 1964, p. 147) or as "a process of observation, to be carried out in a situation especially brought about for that purpose" (Kaplan, 1964, p. 154). While these definitions do imply that experiments are intentionally structured "so that the effects of the independent variables can be evaluated unambiguously" (Underwood, 1957, p. 86), they do not hint at some of the controversial issues associated with experimentation. These issues are best portrayed by selections from the folklore about experiments:

> The social science laboratory with its sense of innovation, its mission of experimental proof and its direct, personal confrontation between subject and experimenter, is the highly charged home of chance, accident, hope, fear and danger [Mills, 1962, p. 24].
> What can be observed reliably is socially meaningless and what is socially meaningful cannot be observed reliably [Lewin, 1951, p. 155].
> No one believes an hypothesis except its originator but everyone believes an experiment except the experimenter [Beveridge, 1950, p. 47].
> Some social scientists will do any mad thing rather than study men at firsthand in their natural settings [Homans, 1962, p. 259].
> Man is evidently more efficient in his everyday life than in experimental rooms . . . . It is needless to point out how difficult it is for us to make threshold judgments, to not be tricked by an optical illusion, to remember nonsense syllables, and for a rat deprived of cues for proper discrimination to behave properly in a

maze. Man and rat are both incredibly stupid in an experimental room. On the other hand, psychology has paid little attention to the things they do in their normal habitats; man drives a car, plays complicated games, designs computers, and organizes society, and the rat is troublesomely cunning in the kitchen [Toda, 1962, p. 165].

While this folklore is rich, colorful, varied, at times polar, and often accurate, it also serves to perpetuate certain fictions about experiments. Generally these fictions suggest that experiments are more fallible, less conclusive, and apply to a more limited range of problems than need be true. Certain myths in the folklore about experiments are sufficiently compelling that, once persons are familiar with them, they shun experiments and thereby forego any opportunities to disconfirm these myths. Therefore, it seems relevant to look briefly at some beliefs about experiments that might otherwise deter the organizational theorist from working in the laboratory.

Fictions About Experiments

The four points that follow are not entirely fictions. Occasionally, they are problems in conducting experiments and in generalizing to the real world. However, their potency and disruptiveness are often overrated, hence they are not the deterrents to experimentation that persons believe they are.

1. Experiments Demonstrate the Obvious

A common belief is that laboratory experiments serve mainly "to demonstrate what you are already pretty sure of" (Homans, 1962, p. 264). While there is some support for this belief, it also represents a limited view of what can be accomplished in an experiment.

The impression that experiments amplify obvious phenomena arises from several sources. Experimental tasks often are sufficiently simple that the results appear straightforward and expected. Sometimes experiments are designed to produce a single phenomenon, no additional phenomena can occur in the same setting, therefore, the outcome seems obvious. Furthermore, when only a single variable is manipulated, observers often argue that an outcome is obvious because all the other crucial variables were controlled. It is also probable that the amount of work that precedes an experiment fosters the impression of obviousness. So much information is required to identify the variables, refine the predictions, and create the experimental situation, that it often seems that there is little more to be learned by actually executing the experiment. The important thinking about the problem has already occurred. The claim that obviousness pervades experiments also appears in conjunction with the argument that experiments test theory, but seldom generate hypotheses. As will be shown later, this view is too narrow.

There are several features of experimentation which suggest that obviousness is not as pervasive as many have imagined. And where experiments are obvious, this is often a strength rather than a weakness. Experiments furnish more occasions for hypothesis generation than is often realized. Seldom do the outcomes of an experiment unequivocally confirm a hypothesis. There are usually some measures or deviant cases that are inconsistent and require explanation. Attempts to account for these discrepant data often generate new hypotheses. But experiments can often generate hypotheses in a much more direct manner.

Discovery of hypotheses can be planned and it is in this sense that controls, hypotheses, contrived situations, and simple tasks—all prominent features of the laboratory—

can facilitate the discovery of new relationships. It is likely that many potentially important hypotheses go unnoticed in field studies because there are too many distractions. These distractions are reduced in the laboratory and, even though there may be fewer occasions for novel relationships to occur, those that do occur are more likely to be noticed. Thus controls may aid rather than hinder hypothesis generation, and the laboratory may be a more appropriate setting for this activity than the field.

Several examples of planned hypothesis generation can be cited. Each of these is a very general hypothesis that can be explored directly in the laboratory. March and Simon (1958, p. 169) propose that "the basic features of organization structure and function derive from the characteristics of human problem-solving processes and rational human choice." But, whether structure actually is constrained by human cognitive abilities is an empirical question. One way to explore this question is to vary systematically the composition of a group along some cognitive dimension (e.g., abstract-concrete) and observe differences in the structure and process of problem solving that emerge (Tuckman, 1964). If the problem is one of discovering the processes that perpetuate and disrupt group traditions when membership changes, a more explicit answer is likely to be found in the laboratory than in the field (Jacobs and Campbell, 1961; Kuethe, 1962). Frequently, the laboratory permits one to ask questions in an uncommon fashion and create conditions to arrive at the answers. In order to study what produces change, one could ask, "What does it take to keep an organization from changing?" The experimenter could allow experimental groups to have planning sessions (Shure, Rogers, Larsen and Tassone, 1962), could assign organizational structures that are intolerable and compel change (Bass, 1963, p. 152) or instruct participants to change their work structure every twenty minutes, and then determine what was required to *terminate* the changes that were instigated by these three procedures. A mechanism that terminates changes is apt to be a mechanism that also affects the adoption of change. Or, to study the relationship between organizational structure and motivational phenomena, such as inequity (Adams, 1963), the experimenter could vary organizational structure by creating different communication networks and determine in which kinds of networks participants experience greater and lesser inequity when payment differs from expectancy.

An additional sense in which experimentation aids discovery is implicit in the phrase, *experiment as metaphor*. By metaphor is meant "an implied comparison between things essentially unlike one another . . . . One image is superimposed upon another in order to provide a perspective or better understanding of the subject at hand" (Bruyn, 1964, pp. 101-102). Experiments often provide a means to visualize a complex event. Instead of trying to imagine the effects of different antecedents in the natural event, the experimenter visualizes what would happen if some feature of the experiment were changed. While in a sense such usage of experiments may be nothing more than the manipulation of a verbal model, it does have one important difference. If the experimenter's thinking does generate a potentially valuable observation concerning the real world, it is possible to verify this impression in the very situation where it was generated, the experiment. Errors in translation from one level of abstraction to another are thereby avoided.

Aside from the fact that experiments generate hypotheses, there are other reasons why obviousness is a fictitious shortcoming of experiments. Whether or not an outcome is obvious is a relative judgment. Findings that are obvious in terms of one set of beliefs are often unexpected in terms of another set. It is one of the truisms of experimentation that unequivocal support for one proposition seriously endangers other propositions.

However, many of these disconfirmations are unseen because premises are not made explicit. Intuition is a notoriously misleading basis for prediction, and criticism of obviousness often masks a failure to make intuitions explicit.

In short, the claim that experiments demonstrate the obvious may represent a confusion of explicitness with significance. As experimental operations are made more explicit, experimental outcomes often seem less surprising. This is desirable because it probably means that the findings are less ambiguous to interpret. Unfortunately lack of ambiguity is sometimes mistaken for lack of importance or significance. This is one of the reasons that experiments may appear to add little information.

Aside from the issue of mistaken interpretations of explicitness, there is the fact that experiments are not merely a means to demonstrate phenomena; they also aid hypothesis generation. Hypotheses may be suggested either indirectly by analysis of unexpected findings or directly by exploratory experimentation. The use of experiments for exploration has often been neglected, but this usage seems especially important given the continuing development of organization theory.

Whether or not one can make discoveries seems to depend less on where he looks than on how he looks. It is possible that during a given period of time less may happen in the laboratory than in the field. To some this means that laboratory events are less significant, to others it means that there are fewer distractions from observing the event.

2. Experiments Are Artificial

One of the most pervasive fictions about experiments is that they are artificial. This view often is held because novelty is confused with artificiality. Laboratory tasks and settings may be unfamiliar to the subject, but this has nothing to do with the significance of his responses. The laboratory situation is still real, the subject must make some adjustment to it, and there is no reason to believe that his responses will differ from those in other unfamiliar situations. As Kaplan (1964, p. 169) observes, "the experimental situation is not to be contrasted with 'real life' but at most only with everyday life."

It is also true that the novelty of experimental exercises is sometimes exaggerated. There are many organizational processes that have high "ecological validity" in the laboratory setting. Milgram (1964, p. 850), for example, stated that the laboratory "is one social context in which compliance occurs regularly" and, therefore, is an apt site in which to study obedience. Thus, whether the laboratory setting contains events that are novel or events that are expected, the settings coerce behavior and in this sense are not fictitious.

Artificiality, however, may become more of an issue when one considers the goals of people who participate in experiments. Subjects often are concerned with more than just the task assigned by the experimenter. It is this spread of concern to issues such as deciphering the purposes of the experiment and predicting what is a "healthy" or "safe" response, that many persons equate with artificiality.

Once again, however, artificiality is not the problem. The problem is one of control. The subject's motives are in no sense feigned, they simply encompass a larger portion of the experiment than the experimenter intended. The subject's plight is essentially that he knows he is being watched and evaluated while he does not know what is being observed. It is these doubts that lead to "evaluation apprehension" (Rosenberg, 1965) or the "deutero-problem" (Riecken, 1962). While the fact of being observed and evaluated in terms of unstated criteria is not uncommon in organizations, it does cause problems in the interpretation of experimental outcomes. It is sometimes difficult to disentangle the effects of trying to gain clarity from the effects of the experimenter's intended manipulations.

Apprehension, however, is not an unsolvable problem. One way to reduce its effects is to conceal the fact that data are being collected (e.g., Sherif and Sherif, 1964). Another way is to promise the subject *in advance* that information about the experiment, his responses, and those of others, will be provided at the conclusion of the exercise, and then to provide this information. Experiments are an unusually good chance for subjects to learn about themselves, about other people, and about research methods, and these learnings are typically regarded as a fair exchange for participation. Much of the difficulty in experiments occurs because the experimenter faults on his portion of the exchange.

A further characteristic of experiments that is often mistaken for artificiality is the population that is studied. It often appears as if college students are not people. A typical objection to the subject population found in experiments is voiced by Dill (1964, p. 52): "What college sophomores do, alas, may not be much more relevant than the behavior of monkeys for predicting how executives, nurses, or research scientists will perform."

Although college students differ from executives in many ways, they also have many similarities. Thus the question of appropriate subjects resolves to one of "are the ways in which he [the college student] differs from other people correlated with the effects investigated" (Zelditch and Evan, 1962, p. 59). In some studies college students do differ in relevant dimensions. Jensen and Terebinski (1963, p. 87), for example, report that in their simulation of a railroad system, "a PhD with system experience lost interest after four or five sessions in which he learned the . . . appropriate strategies. College sophomores used different heuristics and never seemed to understand the system in the same way as the others; they remained interested much longer." Thus, when system experience is a potential determinant of an effect, sophomores may be inappropriate *unless* the experimenter wishes to hold this variable at a value of zero. Also it is possible that the railroad simulation made demands unlike those of most "systems" which sophomores encounter. It is certainly true that sophomores have some "system experience." If they did not, they would be unlikely to survive in college.

It is unlikely that one could ever find a subject population that is equivalent to a typical organizational member. The reason is simply that there is no such thing as a typical member. Members vary just as subjects do. Observing executives to learn about foremen would be just as suspect as observing college students to learn the same information. Unless the experimenter is explicit about personal variables that moderate his phenomenon, and unless these variables assume quite different values in his subject population and his referent population, the use of a college student is not a serious limitation.

It is possible that most objections to the use of sophomores are really objections to recruitment procedures rather than to the abilities of this particular population. Conditions under which subjects participate in experiments often affect their behavior. Rosenthal (1963) and Hood (1964) detail the ways in which volunteer subjects respond differently than nonvolunteers. Gustav (1962) describes the resentment that occurs among subjects when they are required to participate in experiments. The form in which this resentment may be shown is interesting. Subjects often regard the requirement to serve in experiments as "one more harassment imposed by the university." To the extent that they equate experiments with waiting in line for meals and with restrictions on hours and automobiles, they probably exhibit a common response—rebellion and indifference. Thus, students may be less appropriate as subjects for experiments, *not* because of their skills and experiences or lack of them, but rather because the conditions under which they participate influence their reactions to laboratory events.

It can be concluded that even though there are many reasons why laboratory findings may not generalize to other settings, artificiality is not among these reasons. Furthermore, artificiality is a dangerous label to attach to experiments because it focuses attention on pseudo issues and suggests self-defeating solutions. If a situation seems artificial, the only thing to do is make it more real or natural. And this usually means that more "props" are added so that the setting *looks* more natural. But, as more props are added, controls founder and it becomes more difficult to observe what happens. The behavior that is evoked is made no more real by these additions and, in fact, the experimenter has probably made his propositions less accessible.

3.   Laboratory Contexts Are Oversimplified

Since natural events have multiple determinants, it may not seem helpful to study laboratory events that fail to retain this complex context. If a social system is the unit of analysis, then events "isolated" for study in the laboratory lack crucial properties. Dalton (1964, p. 56), in describing his preference for field methods, comments that "where the problem was inextricably inter-twined with others, I felt that too much injustice would be done to the whole to wrench it out for the sake of sampling and scaling theory. In such cases one might objectively relate the mutilated part to a subjectively established criterion and in doing so inflate the part out of all proportion to the interlinked parts discarded because of quantitative inadequacy."

Although few people would deny that behavior has multiple determinants or that it is embedded in a system, many would disagree about how to act once this fact is acknowledged. That an event has multiple determinants still remains a hypothesis, and whether "wrenching it out" will drastically alter its properties is at least a question that can be tested. It is not necessarily true that factors in close proximity to a natural event affect its course. Human perception is sufficiently affected by considerations of economy (Heider, 1944) that causal attributions made under field conditions may differ from those made in the laboratory.

Aside from the issue of how many determinants there are of natural events, and whether these judgments are susceptible to perceptual bias, it should be noted that laboratory exercises "create a context of their own which is not incompatible with what is being modeled" (Meier, 1961, p. 241). Assuming that laboratory events have some resemblance to natural events, it is not uncommon to find that subjects enrich the laboratory event and invest it with some of the meaning associated with the natural event. While this creates problems for the experimenter, it also indicates that context is not insufficient or unrepresentative.

Laboratory events often look simple because the experimenter has used simplifying assumptions in testing a theory or because a simple replica is an obvious place to launch an investigation. Blalock (1963, p. 402) notes that, even though a formulation or experiment may initially be unrealistic, "by beginning with grossly oversimplified models a cumulative process can be set in motion in which one successively modifies the model or theory until it becomes more and more complex and provides a better fit to reality." There is no implication that the experimenter will retain his simplification indefinitely. He may tarry in complicating the model and demand clear evidence that more variables are needed, but he can add them. And he has the further advantage that it is easier for him to observe the effects of these additions.

Simply because natural events exist in a system and have multiple determinants, they are not thereby disqualified as objects for laboratory experimentation. Laboratory events often generate their own systemic properties and, even when they do not, the experimenter can add them to his model and experimental operations *when he is ready to observe their effects*.

4. Hypotheses Induce Myopia

One reason experiments are avoided is that they all involve hypotheses. It is sometimes assumed that hypotheses retard rather than hasten understanding for they force selective attention toward events. In the quest for hypothesis confirmation, important relationships may be overlooked. Dalton (1964, p. 54) presents an especially colorful picture of this possibility: "A prematurely publicized hypothesis may bind both one's conscience and vanity . . . . A hypothetical statement is also one's attempt to be original. Having once made such a statement, one more easily overlooks negative findings or, on having them pointed out, one's emotional freight often limits creativity to ingenious counterarguments."

Hypotheses serve several functions, one of them being to structure observation. It is inconceivable that an observer can give undivided attention to everything that occurs. Selectivity intrudes in one form or other. And a hypothesis derived from a theory is one means to order observation. The order imposed by a hypothesis extends further than many persons realize. In many experiments incidental phenomena take on added meaning because, if the hypothesis is true, these secondary events should assume a particular form. Hypotheses, in other words, frequently direct attention to new areas rather than force a neglect of them.

The question of how an investigator responds when a hypothesis is not supported is important, but this question must be separated from the issue of whether or not hypotheses are helpful. Even if a hypothesis is retained longer than some observers think it should be, this is no reason for hypotheses to be avoided. Furthermore, it is much more difficult to judge when a hypothesis has outlived its usefulness than Dalton implies. There are numerous occasions when hypotheses have been dropped prematurely more for reasons of taste than of error or disconfirmation (Abelson, 1964; Boring, 1964; Weick, 1965a). And experimental results that do not support a hypothesis can occur for many reasons other than an error in the hypothesis. Incorrect independent variables may be chosen, manipulations may be unsuccessful, measurements may be insensitive, effects may be too weak to be observed, or the wrong outcomes may be observed. Even if a hypothesis receives continued negative evidence, it still may be useful to an investigator as a way to think about problems. However, one should not forget that seldom do good investigators propose just one hypothesis in a lifetime. Investments in any given idea tend to be less intense than Dalton suggests. And investigators also are mindful of "the cardinal principle of experimentation . . . that we must accept the outcome whether or not it is to our liking" (Kaplan, 1964, p. 145).

A conclusion about the value of hypotheses is advanced by Blau, a field worker who has used them: "It is all too easy to obtain impressionistic evidence for our broad theoretical speculations. Such evidence, therefore, helps us little in discriminating between diverse or even conflicting theoretical principles. My endeavor to stipulate hypotheses . . . and to collect at least some quantitative data served the purpose of furnishing a screening device for insight. Those ideas that survived this screening test, while still only hypotheses . . . were more apt to be correct than the original specula-tions" (Blau, 1964, p. 20). Hypotheses, in other words, may uncover problems as often as they obscure them.

Conclusion

Laboratory events are different from everyday events in many ways. But these dif-ferences do not always imply that the laboratory event is any less real or any less signif-icant as a means to learn about people. Relationships among variables are suggested in the laboratory just as they are in the field. Laboratory controls do not restrict the rich-ness of data; they frequently make it easier to detect the unexpected when it occurs. There are considerable problems in conducting laboratory studies. But the problems of incomplete knowledge of variables, artificiality, simplicity of events, and focused obser-vation are not among the major drawbacks even though they are often represented as such.

Nonfictions About Experiments

Once the investigator separates crucial from noncrucial issues in experimentation, he can concentrate on ways to cope with these more enduring features of experiments. The following discussion samples the "styles" of thinking associated with the use of the laboratory, styles often taken for granted by experimenters. When these stylistic features are made explicit, they provide a more complete view of demands imposed by experimentation and assumptions made by those who use the laboratory.

1.   *External Influences on Laboratory Events*

Experimenters sometimes overestimate the amount of control they have over the conditions of the experiment. Lewin, for example, propounded the view that the lab-oratory is an island. "Experimentation in the laboratory occurs, socially speaking, on an island quite isolated from the life of society. Although it cannot violate society's basic rules, it is largely free from those pressures which experimentation with 'life groups' has to face daily" (Lewin, 1951, p. 166). Experimenters currently are giving added attention to the fact that experiments are not as isolated as they would like. Experiments do exist in environments. The ways in which subjects act in experiments are frequently determined by the meaning of the experiment in the larger system. This can be an especially important issue in organizational experiments.

For example, an increasing number of organizational experiments are conducted at human relations training laboratories (e.g., Bass and Leavitt, 1963). Several rather explicit norms emerge in these laboratories and they undoubtedly affect the behavior of trainees when they participate in experiments. Egalitarian norms prevail, shared leadership is valued, status distinctions are discounted, previous experiences are irrelevant, and momentary feelings are expressed. In addition to being exposed to new and possibly unfamiliar norms, the trainees typically become more adept at working in groups.

Given these characteristics, it is not surprising that organization experiments con-ducted in training settings show that less highly structured organizations are superior to those with high structure. But the influence of the external system is not even this simple. Norms do not develop immediately; their clarification and acceptance take time. Thus it is probable that a person who has been in training for only a short time would feel more comfortable with a structured group since it closely resembles other groups with which he is familiar. As the training progresses, structured conditions probably create increased ambivalence, resentment, and frustration among participants because these conditions are contrary to those valued in the training sessions. Thus it is not surprising that experiments with the "link-pin organization" show superior results when they are conducted during the latter stages of training sessions. The important point is that this superiority may be the result, not of structural characteristics, but of uncertainty in the structured group concerning how they should act.

A further environmental influence in training laboratories is that most group exercises have a moral, and a task that "makes a point" is probably biased toward a particular outcome. If the results of the training exercise are then treated as experimental data, their significance should not be overestimated. It is probably safe to conclude that data collected during the early stages of a training laboratory are more representative of the population at large than are data collected later.

Experiments conducted at training laboratories are not the only ones susceptible to influence from the social system. Some effects of university settings have already been detailed. The point is that the experimenters must not ignore the setting in which experiments occur. The extent of this influence is suggested by Mills (1962, p. 22): "By examining the experiment's place within the institutional settings, its significance for the lives of the subjects, its operations as they represent interaction between observer and observed, by formulating the structure of role relationships and by interpreting the significance of events for this inclusive system, sociological analysis can . . . [help distinguish] that component in our raw data which should be charged to what experimenter and subject are doing to and for one another and that component which should be charged to the experimental group itself as an object of investigation."

2. Psychological Representation of Variables

The same feeling, belief, or perception can be created in several ways. For example, a person may experience uncertainty because he follows a bizarre and confusing route to arrive at the laboratory (Sherif and Harvey, 1952), is misinformed about physical symptoms that he experiences (Schachter and Singer, 1962), or meets persons who mistake his identity (Garfinkel, 1963). Experimenters typically exploit the fact that the same condition can be created in several ways and, as a result, they often expose subjects to contingencies that appear unusual and artificial. Experimenters assume that the critical problem in an experiment is to create the desired state in the subject. It is far less important what the manipulations that create this state look like.

Observers often believe that an event will be represented psychologically only if it unfolds in a manner familiar to the subject. In other words it is assumed that a physical resemblance between the laboratory and the real world is necessary if the input is to make a difference to the subject, i.e., to be represented psychologically. While it is a hypothetical question whether psychological representation can be created by unfamiliar stimuli, most experimenters assume that it can. This simplifying assumption is an important one.

Occasionally experimenters find that subjects become suspicious or at least more attentive when uncommon events are used to create common experiences. But the very uncommonness of these laboratory events prevents accurate labeling of their purpose, with the consequence that the suspicion tends to be "free-floating." As long as suspicion takes this form it is less likely to exert a *systematic* effect on the results.

The implication of these remarks is that any experimental manipulation is a theory. Manipulations represent an experimenter's hunch about the conditions necessary to create psychologically the phenomenon of interest. The manipulation also implies what the experimenter regards as the most important properties of the phenomenon. In the example involving uncertainty, each of the manipulations exploits a slightly different component of uncertainty. One exploits the desire for clear external frames of reference; another, the desire for consistent impressions of self; and the other, the desire for knowledge of the rules that guide the behavior of others. But always the criterion for choosing a manipulation is whether it makes a difference to the subject, not whether it is familiar to him. Lewin's concept of life space is a valuable caution to the person who believes that simulating the visible, physical components of a natural event is sufficient to induce psychological representation. "I do not consider as part of the psychological field at a given time those sections of the physical or social world which do not affect the life space of the person at that time. The food that lies behind doors at the end of a maze so that neither smell or sight can reach it is not a part of the life space of the animal" (Lewin, 1951, pp. 57-58). Unless the object makes a difference to the subject, it is not a part of the life space. And simply creating a physical likeness is not sufficient to insure that an object is included in the life space.

3. Parsimonious Explanations

Experimenters prefer simple explanations and they adopt more complex propositions only when the simple ones prove inadequte. This does not mean that experimenters refuse to study complex propositions. Demands for parsimony have nothing to do with hypothesis testing. As Marx (1963, p. 21) has stated, "the doctrine of parsimony is relevant only to the acceptance of propositions—not to their testing or development. As a matter of fact, it should serve as a spur to scientific advance, since it puts the burden of proof on those who prefer the more complex alternatives; let them find some evidence which *requires* it." Most experiments, therefore, attempt to study "fundamental processes which presumably underlie the behavior of humans in a broad range of organizational [and other] settings" (McGrath, 1964, p. 538).

A somewhat different (and less charitable) view of the experimenter's preference for simple explanations is expressed by Mills (1962, p. 23). He argues that experimenters are disenchanted because their experiments do not tell them more about groups and that, to defend against this disenchantment, they adopt simple models. The rationale for adoption is this: "The less there is to a group, the more we know about it. The more machine-like groups are, the more we can control them." Whether motivated by the strengths or the weaknesses of experiments, pressures toward parsimony are evident in the laboratory.

Among the basic organizational processes studied in the laboratory are delegation, decisions to participate, decisions to produce, and interdependence. Experimenters argue that if these processes are understood a great deal is known about organizations. Delegation is a good example. It is an important property of natural organizations (Selznick, 1948), it assumes several forms (Roby, 1962), and it can be studied in the laboratory (Solem, 1958).

Knowledge about the factors that led a person to join a firm is knowledge that helps predict what to expect from him. The decision to participate is a basic process in organizations, and the bases on which this decision is made can sometimes lead the person to exhibit high productivity (Weick, 1964) or low productivity (Adams and Rosenbaum, 1962). In a sense, any experiment can provide information about determinants of organizational productivity as long as the basis for participation is made explicit. Experiments involve the acceptance, performance and assessment of tasks just as do organizations. Conceivably a portion of the subject's performance is influenced by the conditions under which he accepted the task. At least this possibility can be examined if the bases of participation are known.

Interdependence (Miller and Hamblin, 1963) is also a basic fact of organizational life. Its effects are found everywhere. Events ramify widely, compensatory as well as retaliatory changes take place (Leavitt, 1964) and unanticipated consequences occur in unexpected places. Interdependence is a process that is especially well suited to exploration in the laboratory (e.g., Kelley, Condry, Dahlke, and Hill, 1965; Kelley, Thibaut, Radloff, and Mundy, 1962), and it can be created simply by putting each person's outcomes under at least the partial control of another person (e.g., Raven and Eachus, 1963; Weick and Penner, 1966).

One drawback in studies of basic processes is that they promote patchwork conceptions of organizations. The organization appears to be a set of independent processes or a set of dimensions. These properties are studied individually, and occasionally other dimensions serve as dependent variables. Although such an approach does not yield direct data on the interdependence of dimensions, this shortcoming is not serious at this stage of inquiry. The proposition that processes are complex is also subject to considerations of parsimony. It is probable that processes have multiple determinants; it is also probable that not all these determinants carry equal weight.

4.   Experimenter as Artisan

The creation of conditions that establish, control, measure, and disentangle variables requires resourcefulness and imagination. It is difficult to prescribe ways to attack these problems. Precedent is less important in experimental design than in many scientific activities. Although the experimenter examines earlier experiments to learn about factors that may confound the results, he typically must devise new procedures to deal with these sources of error.

Examples of procedural twists that aid measurement and control are plentiful. To combat problems of scoring open-ended remarks, the experimenter can have subjects select their remarks from a prepared list of comments (Pilisuk, 1962; Thibaut and Riecken, 1955). To insure that vacillation in making judgments is recorded, the experimenter can have subjects write their answers with pencils that have no erasers (Krugman, 1960). To help subjects see all the alternatives open to them in a coalition task, an accomplice of the experimenter can suggest different alternatives by his actions (Hoffman, Festinger, and Lawrence, 1954). To control impressions of mutual liking among group members, the experimenter can have subjects rate each other, can scan and then discard these ratings in a wastebasket, and finally retrieve a "planted" set of ratings which are returned to the subjects (Dittes and Kelley, 1956). Perhaps the most important skill of the experimenter-artisan is his ability to embed crucial manipulations and measures in an expected or plausible sequence of events. If embedding is successful, fewer suspicions are aroused and the manipulations may be more potent (Schachter, 1951). Surprises or irrelevant instructions may induce caution or indifference. Festinger (1953, p. 155) states that, unless experimental instructions "are plausible in the sense of being integrally related to the experimental activity in which the subjects are to engage," their impact will be slight. Potential implausibility occurs when "the subjects could have done everything the experimenter required of them without these instructions ever having been given" (ibid., p. 159). It may make little difference to subjects whether they are matched on intelligence, testing a new product, starting a new organization, generating normative data, or competing with other groups, if they can perform the experimental task without knowing this.

A good example of the importance of embedding is found in the methods used to obtain measurements of attitudes before and after attempted persuasion. Attempts to embed the postpersuasion measurement have included interpreting the premeasure as a "warmup" (Aronson, Turner, and Carlsmith, 1963), obtaining postmeasures in a different experiment (Rosenberg, 1965), obtaining postmeasures for an unrelated purpose (Festinger and Carlsmith, 1959), or presenting attitudinal items in different questionnaire formats (Hovland and Weiss, 1952). The crucial requirement is that the measurement not attract undue attention. Subjects must regard the event as a legitimate demand, i.e., they must see a rationale for its inclusion.

The consistency with which experimental events unfold affects subject behavior. Attention to subtle procedural details is necessary to maintain consistency. There are several examples in laboratory experiments where theoretically important contingencies were created, but aroused suspicion among subjects because of their implausibility. Ring (1964) varied status (high or low) and compliance (complies or fails to comply) and found that subjects were made uncomfortable by the high-status person who complied and the low-status person who did not comply. These contingencies were unexpected and, in *both* instances, the stimulus persons were regarded unfavorably. The compliant-high-status person was seen as timid and weak, the low-status-noncompliant person as brash and tactless. French and Snyder (1959) report that subjects in a work group found it difficult to comprehend why their supervisor in another room first sent them messages to slow down their work pace and, shortly thereafter, sent messages urging a speedup. Much of the suspicion may have occurred because the notes gave little explanation for the change in policy (e.g., "It's going fine. Forget about mistakes and try for speed"). The point is that tests of some propositions may impose considerable strains on plausibility. It should be noted that this argument does not contradict the earlier discussion of a confusion between novelty and artificiality. The earlier discussion dealt with unfamiliar events, whereas the present concern is more with incongruous events. It has been reasonably well demonstrated (e.g., Carlsmith and Aronson, 1963; Harvey, 1963) that mildly incongruous events are experienced as pleasurable but that marked incongruity evokes negative evaluations.

Demands for consistency and plausibility do not mean that the experimenter must forego important controls or measurements; but these demands do require ingenuity and revision of earlier procedures. It should be noted that requirements of consistency, plausibility, and embedding can be met in contrived situations. There is no implication that these ends are accomplished only in highly realistic experiments. It does not take an elaborate simulation to achieve satisfactory embedding. What is required is that subjects be given a rationale for the experimenter's demands and that this rationale be acceptable to them. The necessity for being an artisan arises from trying to provide subjects with legitimacy for experimental operations while retaining maximum control over what occurs.

Conclusion

Experiments are responsive to external influences. Experimenters acknowledge this fact when they try to integrate experimental demands with demands of the larger social system and when they legitimate experimental operations for subjects. If external influences are ignored, important sources of error are not controlled. Experimentalists, however, are concerned with problems other than confounding external sources. They are concerned with choosing experimental conditions that make a difference to the subject. These choices are not influenced by considerations of realism and artificiality. Concepts and propositions are continually reexamined for excessive simplicity or complexity. Frequently the act of translating a concept into experimental operations aids this conceptual refinement. Even though the experimenter may seem to dwell on simple methods to study simple explanations, in reality he examines continually the adequacy of these explanations and his methods to insure that they do not generate misleading data. These then represent some of the nonfictitious features of experiments . . . .

GAINS AND LOSSES IN THE LABORATORY

While laboratory experimentation as a method of investigation solves some problems, it creates others. The purpose of this section is to detail several problems that may plague the organizational researcher when he turns to the laboratory. These problems are not unsolvable, but they must be identified before anything can be done about them. The advantages of laboratory methods have been well documented elsewhere (e.g., Campbell and Stanley, 1963; Festinger, 1953; Weick, 1965a; Zigler, 1963). We will be content in this discussion to suggest some of these gains by means of an example comparing a laboratory and field experiment of the same organizational process. Although the example suggests some gains in the laboratory, it does so more by pointing to faults of the field than by pointing to strengths of the laboratory. After the two experiments have been compared, several problems will be described.

Emotional Disruption in the Field and Laboratory

Many investigators have puzzled over the question, "Why do changes in organizational procedure often disrupt activities for extended periods of time?" To learn more about changeovers, Schachter, Willerman, Festinger, and Hyman (1961) studied the effects of emotional arousal on the performance of manual tasks before and after the task had been changed. It was hypothesized that harassments would have little effect on habituated or stereotyped activities such as assembly-line work because these activities are executed with little concentration. Even if the harassment disturbs thinking processes, there should be no visible effects. However, when a change in activity occurs, the new task would require close attention until it is learned. A history of prior harassment would be likely to hinder the learning and performance of the new task. The purpose of the field experiment was to test these predictions.

Actually a relatively simple situation is required. "It was the intent of the manipulations to make one set of groups disturbed and upset and the other set as happy as possible" (Schachter et al., 1961, p. 203). The basic experiment was replicated three times using matched assembly lines. The "disfavored" groups received almost daily annoyances for periods ranging from two-to-four weeks before the changeover. Because of considerations of appropriateness, the content of the harassments differed markedly although they apparently had in common continual criticisms of the quality of work performance. Criticisms seldom involved problems unrelated to work. Favored groups were fussed over and sheltered from irritations during this period.

In the execution of the studies, problems were legion. As the authors modestly note, "the problems of attempting to keep tight control of the experimental situation in the hubbub of a major industrial operation forced us to abandon many of these [methodological] niceties if we were to have any experiment at all" (ibid. p. 205). To minimize plant-wide disruptions during the changeovers, rigid schedules were made and could not be changed. When a snowstorm occurred on the day of the planned changeover in one study, only a very few of the experimental subjects could get to work. Replacement operators filled in for the workers who were absent and thereby destroyed the harassment manipulation. Additional groups were lost because workers had instituted an informal job rotation system and, therefore, were not "habituated" prior to the changeover. To conceal the fact that an experiment was being conducted, workers were not interviewed, meaning that valuable data were lost. Favored and disfavored groups occasionally worked different shifts. It was impossible to control discussions among workers off the job. Although no information is given about how the changeover was explained to the workers, it is possible that the results were due to a subtle difference introduced here, and not to the previous harassments. For example, in one of the replications, the change involved "dropping one of the seven assembly workers from the line. Her job was redistributed among the remaining assemblers" (ibid. p. 206). Since all experimental groups had supposedly been together at least six months, it is conceivable that the choice of the person who was removed could have affected the reaction to the changeover. By chance, an informal leader might have been removed in the "disfavored" group, but not in the "favored" group.

Despite such problems, data were collected and the hypotheses seemingly were confirmed although no statistical tests were performed. The complications in this study make it more difficult to know what mechanism mediates these results, or even if there is a stable result that needs to be explained. Although the three studies were described as replications, the situations, tasks, and measures were sufficiently different to raise questions of comparability.

An attempt was made by Latané and Arrowood (1963) to test the identical hypothesis under laboratory conditions. Subjects were presented with a display containing three switches and three lights. Their initial task was to anticipate which light would turn on next by pressing the appropriate switch. The lights followed a simple repetitive sequence that was easily learned and that was paced by the subject. After the task changeover, subjects were to press the switch of the same *color* as the light which was to come on. Previously, they had responded to position.

Harassment occurred after twelve minutes on the first task and arrived in the form of a complaining, hostile female (subjects were male) who soundly criticized the subject for the way in which he had filled out a questionnaire at the start of the experiment. The nonharassment condition involved the same instigator, although now she mildly approved the subjects. After the unfriendly female left, the subjects continued the task for three minutes and then changed to the new task which they performed for eight minutes.

The results indicate that the female's harangue left the subjects significantly more tense, but not any more anxious, irritated, content, or happy than the control group. The differences in productivity following the changeover confirmed the predictions. The harassed group did significantly more poorly than the nonharassed group, although the effect was short-lived. Furthermore, the harassment did not affect performance before the changeover. Both groups performed equally well after the encounter but before the change to the new task.

These results are interesting, partly because they demonstrate similar findings in a field experiment and in a contrived laboratory situation. But even more strking is the fact that these similarities occur even though there are marked differences in time span.

"While Schachter et al. prolonged their emotional manipulation over 2–4 weeks, we used 2 minutes, while their subjects had become stereotyped on the same job for untold months, ours had to learn a task in 12 minutes. It is not inconsistent, then, that the emotion-produced decrement on nonstereotyped production which they observed lasted from 1 to 3 weeks after changeover, while we obtained effects for only 3 minutes" (Latané and Arrowood, 1963, p. 326). The experiment was not without its shortcomings. The performance curves for the first task were still increasing when the changeover occurred, thereby rendering more questionable the argument that stereotypy had developed. The lesser impact of the emotional disruption may have been due to a weaker manipulation, but it may also reflect stoicism among the male subjects. It will be recalled that the study by Schachter et al. involved mainly females.

It is worthwhile to speculate on how the laboratory findings would be regarded if the related field experiment did not exist. The outcomes are similar and the procedures in the laboratory experiment provide fewer bases for alternative explanations. Schachter et al. have some indication that the effect holds across industrial situations, across tasks, and with subjects who are probably older and more experienced than those in the laboratory. Juxtaposition of the two studies increases the plausibility of the hypothesis. It also indicates the distinct differences in time and financial costs between the laboratory and the field. Perhaps the most apparent fact from this comparison is that controls such as randomization and replication (Blalock, 1963, p. 401) are important and that they can be attained with more certainty when the experimenter can create the situation to his liking than when he is concerned about disrupting factory production.

It is also valuable to compare the question of motivation in the two populations of subjects. McGrath (1964, p. 537) contends that "one important feature of data obtained from a 'real-life' situation is that the humans in that situation are operating under natural (not necessarily stronger) motivational forces, since the phenomena being studied are a part of their actual lives." Our earlier discussion of similarities between the laboratory and the field would suggest that both situations create "natural motivational forces" that are "part of actual lives." It is possible that the harassments were more meaningful in the field because they occurred in a familiar context and because they had implications for the amount of money the worker would earn. It is not clear, however, that there was any less suspicion in the field than in the laboratory. A sudden upswing in harassments is just as apt to be unnatural in the field as in the sudden arrival of a bellowing female in the laboratory. The harassment may be dealt with in different ways. For example, subjects in the laboratory had to solve the problem themselves whereas the workers in the field study could talk with their fellow workers. To argue, however, that the subject's concern in the field is any more real or relevant is to deny that subjects ever get involved in laboratory exercises. And evidence suggests that they do and that experimenters can heighten this involvement.

Problems of Internal Validity

Having suggested some of the reasons why persons might wish to use the laboratory, we will describe some additional reasons why they might not. The problems to be discussed are some that are particularly bothersome in conducting organizational experiments. Using Campbell's (1957) classification, the errors will be divided crudely into those that affect internal validity and those that affect external validity. Internal validity is the basic minimum that any experiment must possess. The criterion by which it is evaluated is, "Did in fact the experimental stimulus make some significant difference in this specific instance?" (Campbell, 1957, p. 297). It is not infrequent for some variables other than the ones manipulated to influence systematically the results. If the experimenter fails to realize this, the findings he reports are incorrect in the sense that they are not a function of the manipulated antecedent. Internal validity is concerned with constructing experiments so that it is clear precisely what is controlling changes in the dependent variable. The problem of internal validity, in short, is to establish that the experimenter has actually found what he thinks he found.

Campbell (1957) discusses several quite general hindrances to internal validity. The present listing differs in that it is representative rather than comprehensive, specific rather than general, and, therefore, may apply only to certain kinds of experiments. The errors discussed below are intended to suggest the kinds of procedural subtleties in an organizational experiment that could render the results equivocal. It is anticipated that, with these few examples in mind, the reader will be alerted to a general kind of problem and will be able to locate many additional instances of such errors.

1. Esteem and Degradation

When a subject agrees to be looked at, he naturally wants to know what people see. If they withhold this information, require unpleasant activities, treat him as an object, or violate other social contracts, then it is likely that the subject will become concerned about his esteem as well as the experimenter's instructions. Subsequent behavior may be affected by either or both of these sources. An internally valid experiment exists only if instrumental behaviors are disentangled from those that are expressive.

Expressive behaviors are more likely, for example, when manipulations unintentionally threaten the status of subjects. Pepitone (1964) argues that experiments on aggression, consistency, and conformity often pose dilemmas for the subject in which he feels uncertain, incompetent, or belittled. The existence of these feelings constitutes an alternative explanation for the obtained results. For example, the requirements that subjects write strong arguments opposed to their private beliefs may generate something other than cognitive dissonance. "Inconsistent behavior increases the probability of social rejection. Since rational, intelligent behavior is highly valued by other people, the individual tries to reduce or at least conceal his irrationality for fear of losing status and power or even love and security" (Pepitone, 1964, p. 46). While this explanation seems more applicable to responses that are made in the presence of peers than those made in private, it does imply that persons worry about social censure and ridicule.

Concerns about esteem often undercut attempts to have subjects actually criticize each other or report to the experimenter that they dislike another person. Jones and DeCharms (1957) reported an unwillingness among subjects to dislike a person who obstructed progress. Jones (1964) found that subjects rate a disapproving interviewer quite favorably. Sampson and Insko (1964) used most of a two hour experimental session to get a subject angry. Mills (1962) suggested that the experimenter may have little difficulty creating dislike, but he may have considerable trouble directing it. He suggested that the well known experiment by Schachter (1951) on deviation can be interpreted as displacement onto a stooge of hostility actually felt toward the experimenter. The stooge became a scapegoat because the experimenter failed to fulfill his promises to the subjects concerning the agenda of their meetings.

While one implication of these remarks is that it is difficult to create dislike in the laboratory, the more important point is that the experimenter may get some indication that dislike is present but, overriding its effects, may be actions directed toward maintaining esteem.

Esteem also affects confederacy. Paid accomplices are often used to establish experimental conditions. If subjects are unwilling to be hostile or to deviate, the experimenter can hire someone to act this way in a group. Confederates, even when adequately trained (Efran, 1961), often find their antics costly and present a less explicit and compelling performance than the experimenter requires to test his predictions. Much of the discomfort felt by accomplices occurs because they forget that the attacks which their behavior elicits are directed at *the role*, not at them personally. Professional actors (Milgram, 1963) may be successful at making this distinction, but most amateurs are not. The stooge's discomfort may be increased even more if he has some doubts about his ability to play the role. Suppose he has been trained to be a belligerent manager in a simulation and, when he acts this way, his subordinates express strong resentment. If the stooge feels that he did not play the role well and yet provoked negative reactions in the other subjects, he may convince himself that he did a good job of role playing after all, *or* he may wind up believing that he really is an unattractive person. It is not the objective adequacy of the role playing so much as the stooge's feeling of adequacy that controls this process. It is difficult to institutionalize psychopathy. To insure reliability and intensity in stooge behavior, it is necessary to realize the costs of confederacy and to provide appropriate supports in the form of adequate pretraining, props, and scripts during the presentation, and decompression aimed at maintaining a separation of the role from the person.

Threats to esteem are often threats to internal validity. As long as these threats are randomized across treatments they are not a major problem. However, these threats can easily operate *differentially* within the same experiment because they are sensitive to slight differences in manipulations. When these differential effects occur, manipulated variables become clouded. Legitimation of instructions, the promise of an informative decompression, and foreknowledge of the general aims and value of experimentation may enable the subject to postpone concerns about esteem.

2. *Detachment in Dyads*

Field researchers report that when they become friendly with their informant, they are tempted to see the world solely from his point of view. If this occurs, the field man finds less and less that requires explanation. A related problem exists in the supposedly minimal and "programmed" contact between an experimenter and a subject. That this contact is not standardized has been suggested by several persons (Back, Hood, and Brehm, 1964; Criswell, 1958; Friedman, 1964). The problem of interest here is the way in which the number of subjects that an experimenter confronts at one time produces subtle differences in his behavior.

Schachter (1959) has discussed this problem. He noted that when subjects faced imminent electric shock, they were more anxious when this threat was made to groups of five to eight than when it was made to a single subject, even though the instructions were identical. The following is proposed as an explanation.

Despite the experimenter's deliberate attempt to behave identically in both experiments, inevitably a more personal relationship resulted in the two-person experiment. In this two-person study, the subjects felt free to ask questions and make comments and frequently did so, resulting in a relationship more informal than in the group setting, where almost no subject seemed to feel uninhibited enough to comment freely [p. 23].

Thus as the size or intimacy of the group changes, subjects may feel more or less comfort in seeking clarification of instructions, expressing dissatisfaction, or approving the experimenter. The experimenter also may act differently in small groups. He may express more interest, be more responsive, and provide more cues about the desired response. If he has any reservations about the reasonableness of demands made upon the subject, these doubts are apt to be sharpened in a dyad and the experimenter may feel greater pressure to weaken the demands.

Obviously several of these problems decrease if all comparisons involve groups of similar size. However, many organizational experiments, especially large-scale simulations, require the experimenter to give different instructions and feedback to small subgroups. When subgroups are instructed, this increases the chances that the experimental outcomes are due not so much to the manipulated variable, as to the fact that selected portions of the instructions were better understood, that distasteful requirements were made less painful, or that some of the hypotheses were more apparent. These influences may be partly countered in simulations simply because subjects have so much factual material to remember. Furthermore, in contrast to Schachter's study, the demands on the experimenter in a simulation are more complex and, therefore, individual requests are not as likely to receive undivided attention.

Aside from the simulations, organization theorists are interested in small groups. Frequently, groups of many differing sizes are lumped into this category, and comparisons are made among experiments in which size varies. The present argument is that size may be a subtle threat to internal validity because it mediates the ease with which the experimenter can remain detached from subjects. As intimacy increases, the number of alternative explanations for a finding also increases.

3. Task Substitution

Subjects frequently work on several problems in addition to the one they have been assigned; this problem has been discussed elsewhere as the problem of redefinition (Weick, 1965a). The present discussion focuses on a different aspect of the problem. It is concerned with this phenomenon solely as a problem of internal validity and seeks to avoid the implication that the subject accepts the experimenter's definition before he alters it. Sometimes the subject's task is totally different from the one assigned by the experimenter. Hence, the label "task substitution" is used. While task substitution takes many forms, some are more relevant to organizational research than others. For example, there are several reasons why the internal validity of studies of novel structures might be suspect. Persons who perform novel tasks in unfamiliar structures often feel uncomfortable. Unfortunately, they often interpret this discomfort as a sign of inefficiency, and they proceed to alter the task and/or structure "to make it more efficient." "Players will equate uncomfortable or strange relations with ineffective relations and fail to give innovative schemes a fair trial. Their behavior is quite rational. They want to win, and the game will last a short time. All the pressure is to convert the new scheme into the old, tried-and-true way of doing things." (Bass, 1964, p. 4). Alterations to increase efficiency do not have to be drastic. They may even go unnoticed. Nevertheless, if alterations are present, the intended structure is not and the experimental outcomes have different antecedents.

There are occasions when just the opposite problem occurs, when persons retain intact a task they are supposed to change. Persons may be given a task but not enough information to complete it (Evan and Zelditch, 1961), they may be placed in a structure that contains contradictory requirements, they may be placed with a partner who is ill suited for a job. The reason for these assignments is that the experimenter wants to force the subjects to make some changes. It is assumed that if persons are bothered by these circumstances, they will try to make them more acceptable. The experimenter wants to find out what is more acceptable and how it is adopted. Unfortunately, persons tend to invest their environment—whatever its content—with meaning, and typically they are reluctant to make changes. They may presume that the experimenter would not have assigned them a structure unless he thought it to be worthwhile. Guetzkow and Bowes (1957) suggest that subjects rarely revise imposed requirements because they are uncertain which revisions are within the rules of the game and which are not. This uncertainty is especially pronounced when lengthy instructions precede task performance.

In short, subjects often make sense out of experimental conditions when they are not supposed to. If subjects "rationalize nonrational requirements" internal validity is lessened. When a novel structure affects behavior, the effect may be due to the reasonableness of the structure instead of its novelty.

Task substitution may also originate in triviality. Many experimental tasks require little concentration and permit the subject to think about other things while he is working. These distractions often become more interesting than the task at hand and the outcomes of the experiment reflect a preoccupation with the substitute task. Rather than working on two tasks simultaneously, the subject may simply change the trivial task to make it more interesting. Schultz (1964, p. 397) argues that a considerable portion of a subject's behavior in experiments can be viewed as an attempt to vary the pattern of stimulation that reaches him. Thus a subject may alternate his responses in order to introduce a change in the number, nature, and temporal sequence of stimuli in his surroundings. Conditions that are especially prone to produce alternation behavior are (1) no reinforcement and/or knowledge of correctness of response, (2) great similarity between stimuli, (3) prolonged exercise of one response alternative, and (4) a short intertrial interval.

Thus, a simple cooperative game may be made competitive to increase its interest. Friedell (1964, p. 7) suggests that this is a common occurrence. "In many experimental games cooperation is boring and competition is interesting. Cooperative behavior may be represented by monotonous sameness of choice, while competition may involve variety. A structural reason for this is that effective competition often requires that one's opponent cannot predict one's strategy. In symmetrical games competition presents the attraction of testing oneself against a peer rather than a simple situation. Thus, subjects may actually cooperate by tacitly agreeing to compete."

Substitution because of triviality implies that simulations have an advantage because the subject has no time to make substitutions; too many things are going on. Herein lies one of the dilemmas in an organizational experiment. Presumably a simple task is preferable to a complex one and a simple environment is preferable to one with multiple happenings, because the subject can understand the assignment more quickly, there are fewer sources of distraction and, therefore, the independent variables should be less ambiguous. But, when these conditions exist, the subject also may have time on his hands and dream up variations of the basic task. A complex simulation leaves little time for fabrication, but it generates a different kind of substitution. The more an experimental setting resembles a real-life organization, the more an individual is prone to act as if the organization were real and not contrived. This may aid involvement, but it also means that the subject will impose constraints and definitions where none exist, ignore experimental requirements and definitions not in the actual organization, and redefine his position so that it accords with his position in natural organizations. In short, simulations encourage assimilation, simple settings encourage contrast. In both cases, substitutions make the experiment even less like an organization than it really is.

A substitute task is, by definition, not the task assigned by the experimenter or the one he wanted to study. If the substitution is undetected, the experiment has less internal validity.

4. Counter-Reference Demands

Experimental demands often require subjects to perceive or act in ways that are contrary to those which are valued in their reference groups. These contradictory demands may unintentionally produce ambivalence, uncertainty, or vacillation. When these conditions exist, they provide alternative explanations of experimental outcomes.

It may be argued that reference groups are not salient when a subject participates in experiments. However, it is probable that there are more cues that reinstate reference groups than are realized. For one thing, subjects are typically recruited from a homogeneous population. If they had not been members of a particular group, they would not have been contacted for the experiment. Thus, recruitment makes reference groups salient. Furthermore, the experimental instructions often remind the subject of a reference group. He is told that his responses are of interest because he is a typical college student, an engineer, a sophomore, a male, an adult, a psychology student, or an average human being. Although these instructions are usually intended merely to distract or heighten plausibility, they may lead the subject to act as if he is a member of that group. Relevance of a task or a dilemma to specific groups should also heighten their prominence as determinants of subsequent behavior. Jones and DeCharms (1957) report a study involving naval cadets where norms that were created experimentally clashed strongly with existing cadet norms. Subjects were asked to decide what disciplinary actions should be administered to a turncoat. In one condition, the subjects were told that the norms for judging whether or not a person was a turncoat were unclear. The cadets, however, simply could not accept this information. Undoubtedly the combination of recruitment of a specific group plus a relevant issue contributed to the weakening of this manipulation. Loyalties to the Navy may well have been pitted against felt obligations to the experimenter. Ambivalence was clearly the product. Demands that are inconsistent with reference groups probably can never be completely ruled out of experiments, especially vivid simulations. If experimental conditions are linked randomly with various reference groups, internal validity is not threatened. The implication is that the experimenter should assess whether a reference effect occurred, should examine manipulations to see if they make particular reference groups salient, and, in general, should look for uncertainty or ambivalence as competing explanations of experimental outcomes.

Summary

An apparent relationship among variables may actually reflect attempted solutions to maintenance problems, differential understanding of instructions and preferred behaviors, performance of unassigned tasks, or tenuous resolutions of contradictory demands. These threats to internal validity are common in organizational experiments, are difficult to randomize, and are sensitive to slight changes in an independent variable. They are also difficult to detect. Changes in realism reduce some problems, but create other ones. That the recognition and solution of these problems is mandatory can be seen if one looks at the next source of problems, external validity. External validity is concerned with generalization, and one needs to worry about generalization only when there is something to generalize from, namely a stable and valid relationship.

Problems of External Validity

Once an experimenter knows something about his laboratory subjects, he wants to know what he has also learned about other populations. This is the problem of external validity. External validity is concerned with the representativeness or generalizability of experimental findings. The criterion is, "To what populations, settings, and variables can this effect be generalized?" (Campbell, 1957, p. 297). External validity is restricted when conditions in the experiment are hard to find in everyday life. If the features of an experiment are rare, it is reasonable to conclude that the incidence of the demonstrated relationship will also be rare.

The following discussion describes five characteristics of experiments that hinder generalization.

1. Task Prominence

Experimental tasks differ from everyday tasks in several ways, the most obvious being that they command undivided attention from the subject. Even if the task is boring and the subject embellishes or makes substitutions for it, a single task is still involved. This contrasts with everyday life where attention is diffuse, where several tasks compete for attention (Atkinson and Cartwright, 1964), and where the existence of alternative tasks affects present productivity (Feather, 1963). Performance in the laboratory seldom reflects these competing demands on effort. As a result, laboratory findings may not hold up when replicated in the field where competing demands exist.

In addition to being prominent, laboratory tasks are also bounded. The subjects know that laboratory events will last for only a short time. Furthermore, many tasks have discrete trials and this may disrupt continuity, concentration, or the feeling that one is accomplishing a significant piece of work. The laboratory exercise, like assembly-line activity, is repetitive and movements become stereotyped (Schachter et al., 1961). These characteristics of tasks are relevant to external validity because they suggest what laboratory findings may obtain if the subject has circumscribed experiences and small exposure to the independent variable but that, as experiences lengthen and exposure becomes more intense and prolonged, relationships will change.

Laboratory tasks are often chosen for their sensitivity to independent variables (Hovland, 1959) and their openness to observation, not their representativeness. Unfortunately, not enough is known about tasks to be certain whether properties that promote sensitivity are also properties that materially affect a relationship when they are absent. The question of sensitivity is not to be confused with the argument that a highly sensitive task is "rigged" so that it amplifies what is, in reality, a trivial relationship. A sensitive task may magnify an insignificant effect. But that is not our concern here. Instead, assuming that some common elements are necessary for generalization, if features that aid sensitivity are features that also have to be present in the actual event for generalization to occur, then it may be difficult to obtain external validity.

A final task variable that may affect external validity is that of error prominence. When organizational activities are scaled down to fit the laboratory, it is seldom possible also to scale down the impact on the system of human errors. As a consequence, errors that would have only a slight effect on a natural system are a major disruption in a contrived system. Bass (1964, p. 5) describes the possible effects in a laboratory exercise of a minor managerial blunder. "As in real life, a manager may blurt out the wrong words resulting in a 'wildcat' strike, and production will close momentarily. In real life, this real effect may reduce industry-wide production by, say, 2 percent. In our game, it may reduce it by 35 percent for a given firm. Or, it might easily bankrupt a company in our game; it seldom does in real life." Errors frequently are handled in natural organizations with little enduring effect on the system. Experimental findings may have limited generality because they obtain only when errors have a marked impact on outcomes.

The preceding examples suggest that experimental tasks differ from everyday tasks along dimensions that may affect external validity. Simplicity itself does not necessarily threaten external validity. It depends on what is simplified, the rarity with which experimental task properties exist in everyday tasks, and the centrality of the property for generalization.

2.   Limited Alternatives

Just as it makes a difference in productivity whether a person is constrained to one task or several, so it also makes a difference whether a subject feels that he is a member of one group or several. The presence or absence of alternative tasks or groups often has a marked effect on a person's perception of his situation. Kiesler and Corbin (1965) report that conformity decreases linearly as group attractiveness decreases, *unless* the individual is committed to the group, i.e., has a high probability of continued future membership. When a commitment exists there is considerable discomfort if one learns that the group actually is unattractive. To resolve this discomfort, the subject could either devalue the group or enhance it by trying to conform to and be more like the other members. Since devaluation is not wholly satisfying given the prospect of continued membership, increased conformity should occur and Kiesler and Corbin (1965) found that it did.

The implication of these results is that perceived longevity of group membership and the feeling of volition in becoming a group member have a marked effect on subsequent behavior. Even when duration and commitment are not manipulated, the experimenter should assess the subject's conception of these features of group life since they may influence the results. The easiest solution to a discomforting situation is to disown one's acts, reject the group, or be indifferent. Furthermore, realignment of group ties is a common response in everyday life. When these alternatives are unavailable in the laboratory, relationships between variables may be affected. The implication is that it is important to know the extent to which a subject feels he must account for and resolve experimental occurrences. Less pressure for resolution should exist if the event or group is perceived to be fleeting, if alternatives are available, or if the problems are of minor importance. As pressures for resolution increase, the findings may be less applicable to situations where persons can choose among many alternatives, one of which is escape.

3.   Recruitment

Procedures to enlist subjects for an experiment may broaden or narrow the populations to which experimental findings can be generalized. Campbell (1957, p. 308) describes two principles that are relevant to recruitment as a source of bias. "The greater the cooperation required, the more the respondent has to deviate from the normal course of daily events, the greater will be the possibility of nonrepresentative reactions. . . . The longer the experiment is extended in time the more respondents are lost and the less representative are the groups of the original universe." Whenever impositions are considerable and subjects can refuse to participate, experimental results may apply only to a highly select population. By the time the experimenter has assembled a group of persons who are able to meet procedural requirements of the experiment (e.g., be free for three hours every day for a week), he may have constituted a highly select group thereby reducing external validity.

Even within a specific population, recruitment biases may appear. In academic environments, students who decide to fulfill their subject obligations early in the school year differ from those who postpone their participation until the last minute. Some manipulations are sensitive to these differences in motivation, others are not. Monetary incentives in experiments probably are more effective near the end of the month than at the start of the month. Extra credit for course grades is probably a stronger inducement after examinations are returned than before.

It is important to realize that experiments impose unique demands. Not everyone can or is willing to meet these demands. The more effort the experimenter has to exert to obtain subjects, the less representative his subjects will be.

4.   First-Day-at-Work Syndrome

It is possible that experiments tell us more about how a person will act on his first day at work than on his 400th day. A person who is in an experiment, like the newcomer on a job, often has low confidence in his judgments, is easily influenced, misunderstands instructions, is uninformed, finds the job novel and interesting, is cautious, and tolerates many demands that would anger him in more familiar settings. Many of these behaviors dissipate as he becomes more accustomed to the assignment. Thus data that are collected before a job becomes routinized and familiar may have limited generality. The implication is clear that subjects should be fully instructed about a task and should perform it long enough so that they are completely familiar with it. If it is not possible to produce this much familiarity, then the experimenter should assess the role that novelty and uncertainty play in the findings. If it appears that variations in uncertainty would not change the results, or that familiarity is unrelated to the outcomes, then external validity is not jeopardized.

5.   Multi-Determinants

Perhaps the most general problem of external validity concerns the fact that field events are affected by more variables than are present when laboratory events occur. These additional variables could increase the magnitude of a laboratory effect, or they could wash it out. The problem is essentially one of how to handle these additional variables in the laboratory so that both control and external validity are retained. For example, if an experimenter regards five dimensions to be important for characterizing an organization and he manipulates one of these five, what should be done with the other four? Should they be ignored for the moment and treated as potential variables that might affect a relationship? Should each of the four variables be set at a value greater than zero so that they are at least present when the relationship is studied?

Undoubtedly when a person becomes highly concerned with these problems he will go to the field rather than remain in the laboratory. However, it should be remembered that the many circumstances surrounding natural events are potential rather than actual influences. If a basic process is being studied, then the question of modifications from additional variables will change the appearance of the process but not its structure.

Summary

Organizational experiments are vulnerable to several threats to external validity. An organization experiment may be unrepresentative because experimental demands impose a high attrition rate on subjects, because tasks are excessively prominent or are performed when novelty and uncertainty are at their height, or because experimental settings provide few alternatives and only a limited number of influences. Simulations are not the complete solution to problems of external validity because they also have difficulties with recruitment, task familiarity, and task prominence. Since both organizational theory and research are in their early stages, it is reasonable to expect that more attention in the immediate future will be focused on internal validity rather than external validity.

CONCLUSION

Despite the recent interest in organizational behavior on the part of behavioral scientists and the large amount of empirical data that has been collected on this problem, there are surprisingly few well-supported causal propositions about the determinants of organizational behavior. The data and methods have often been unsuited to stating propositions of this kind. Most of the investigators who have studied organizations have been concerned chiefly with problems of external validity. The point . . . is that we are unlikely to learn much about organizations unless we give just as much attention to questions of internal validity.

Laboratories often seem insignificant as a means to learn about organizations because they are judged against criteria established for the more common field investigation. Laboratory experiments often are structured quite differently from natural organizations and, for this reason, questions of generalization can be sizeable, as has been noted throughout. But there are ways in which the investigator can cope with the problem of external validity and can, therefore, benefit from the strength of the laboratory to show unambiguous causal linkages between events.

External *and* internal validity can be achieved if the experimenter moves back and forth between the laboratory and field as in the example of emotional disruption, if he moves between abstract and simulated organizations in the laboratory, or if he structures a field study so that it contains more of the controls found in the laboratory. Instead of changing his setting, the investigator may change his activities. He may establish a stable relationship in a tightly controlled situation and then lessen these constraints to see what variables condition the relationship, or he may find an interesting phenomenon and then tighten the constraints to see why it occurred. *Either* strategy is pointed toward the same eventual conclusion.

Laboratory experiments also seem useful because they press investigators to be explicit. The most common objection to the laboratory is that it does not contain several "obviously" important features of organization, e.g., a complex environment. This objection is well founded. But, when the investigator thinks in terms of building an organization in the laboratory, he has to explicate these variables, and he usually has to state why these variables must be included. It often happens that he finds that a variable really makes no difference to his problem whether it is included or not.

A final problem in laboratory experiments is that it is difficult to tell what the referent reality is for an organizational study. It is unclear what dimensions of a natural organization should be modeled in the laboratory or even what the dimensions are. It is clear that laboratories and natural organizations differ, but it is unclear which of the differences may be crucial because they condition a causal relationship. Nonobvious differences may turn out to be crucial. The point is that, until these crucial differences become clearer, considerable trial and error approximation between the two settings must occur.

Experiments have numerous shortcomings but they are also somewhat more versatile than existing folklore would suggest. As more and more of the shortcomings of the laboratory and it seems clear that imaginative investigators will be able to increase the research. Furthermore, an increasing number of phenomena can now be created in the laboratory and it seems clear that imaginative investigators will be able to increase the phenomena that can be brought under laboratory control. Although there is little history of organizations in the laboratory, the promise seems considerable.

REFERENCES

ABBREVIATIONS

ASR   *American Sociological Review*
HR   *Human Relations*
JAP   *Journal of Applied Psychology*
JASP   *Journal of Abnormal and Social Psychology*
MS   *Management Science*
SSR   *Sociology and Social Research*

Abelson, P. "Bigotry in Science," *Science*, 1964, 144, 371.
Adams, J. S. and Jacobsen, P. R. "Effects of Wage Inequities on Work Quality," *JASP*, 1964, 69, 19-25.
Adams, J. S. and Rosenbaum, W. B. "The Relationship of Worker Productivity to Cognitive Dissonance About Wage Inequities," *JAP*, 1962, 46, 161-164.
Ammons, R. B. and Ammons, C. H. "A Standard Anagram Task," *Psychological Reports*, 1959a, 5, 654-656.
——. "Rational Evaluation of the 'Standard Anagram Task' as a Laboratory Analogue of 'Real-Life' Problem Solving." *Psychological Reports*, 1959b, 5, 718-720.
Aronson, E., Turner, J. A., and Carlsmith, J. M. "Communicator Credibility and Communication Discrepancy as Determinants of Attitude Change." *JASP*, 1963, 67, 31-36.
Atkinson, J. W. and Cartwright, D. "Some Neglected Variables in Contemporary Conceptions of Decision and Performance." *Psychological Reports*, 1964, 14, 575-590.
Back, K. W., Hood, T. C., and Brehm, Mary L. "The Subject Role in Small Group Experiments," *Social Forces*, 1964, 43, 181-187.
Bartlett, F. C. *Remembering*. Cambridge: Cambridge U. Press, 1932.
Bass, B. M. "Experimenting With Simulated Manufacturing Organizations." In S. B. Sells (ed.), *Stimulus Determinants of Behavior*. New York: Ronald, 1963, 117-196.
——. "Some Methodological Issues in Experimenting with Human Simulations of Business Firms." Paper prepared for 3rd Seminar in Social Science of Organizations, U. of Pittsburgh, 1964.
Bass, B. M. and Leavitt, H. S. "Some Experiments in Planning and Operating," *MS*, 1963, 9, 574-585.
Bass, B. M. and Vaughan, J. A. "Experimenting With the Man-in-the-Middle." Paper presented at 1st Seminar in Social Science of Organizations, U. of Pittsburgh, 1962.
——. "Production Organization Exercise IV." Pittsburgh: U. of Pittsburgh, Graduate School of Business, 1963.
Becker, S. W. "Organizations in the Laboratory." Paper prepared for 3rd Seminar in Social Science of Organizations, U. of Pittsburgh, 1964.
Beveridge, W. I. B. *The Art of Scientific Investigation*. New York: Norton, 1950.
Blalock, H. M. "Some Important Methodological Problems for Sociology," *SSR*, 1963, 47, 398-407.

Blau, P. M. "The Research Process in the Study of *The Dynamics of Bureaucracy*." In P. E. Hammond (ed.), *Sociologists at Work*. New York: Basic Books, 1964, 16–49.

Boring, E. G. "Cognitive Dissonance: Its Use in Science," *Science*, 1964, 145, 680–685.

Bruyn, S. "Rhetorical Devices in Sociological Analysis." *Sociological Qtly.*, 1964, 5, 101–112.

Burns, T. "The Communication Exercise." Paper presented at 3rd Seminar in Social Science of Organizations, U. of Pittsburgh (Pa.), 1964.

Campbell, D. T. "Factors Relevant to the Validity of Experiments in Social Settings," *Psychological Bull.*, 1957, 54, 297–312.

Campbell, D. T. and Stanley, J. C. "Experimental and Quasi-Experimental Designs for Research on Teaching." In N. L. Gage (ed.), *Handbook of Research on Teaching*. Chicago: Rand McNally, 1963, 171–246.

Carlsmith, J. M. and Aronson, E. "Some Hedonic Consequences of the Confirmation and Disconfirmation of Expectancies," *JASP*, 1963, 66, 151–156.

Cohen, A. R. "Upward Communication in Experimentally Created Hierarchies," *HR*, 1958, 11, 41–53.

Cook, S. W. and Selltiz, C. "A Multiple-Indicator Approach to Attitude Measurement," *Psychological Bull.*, 1964, 62, 36–55.

Cottrell, N. B. "Means-Interdependency, Prior Acquaintance, and Subsequent Competition," *HR*, 1963, 16, 249–262.

Criswell, J. H. "The Psychologist as Perceiver." In R. Taguiri and L. Petrullo (eds.), *Person Perception and Interpersonal Behavior*. Stanford: Stanford U. Press, 1958, 95–109.

Cyert, R. M., March J. G., and Starbuck, W. H. "Two Experiments on Bias and Conflict in Organizational Estimation," *MS*, 1961, 7, 254–264.

Dalton, M. "Preconceptions and Methods in *Men Who Manage*." In P. E. Hammond (ed.), *Sociologists at Work*. New York: Basic Books, 1964, 50–95.

Delbecq, A. "Managerial Leadership Styles in Problem Solving Conferences, II," *J. Academy of Management*, 1965, 8, 32–43.

Dill, W. R. "Desegregation or Integration?: Comments About Contemporary Research on Organizations." In W. W. Cooper, H. J. Leavitt, and M. W. Shelly (eds.), *New Perspectives in Organization Research*. New York: Wiley, 1964, 39–52.

Dittes, J. E. and Kelley, H. H. "Effects of Different Conditions of Acceptance Upon Conformity to Group Norms," *JASP*, 1956, 53, 100–107.

DiVesta, F. J., Meyer, D. L., and Mills, J. "Confidence in an Expert as a Function of His Judgments," *HR*, 1964, 17, 235–242.

Dubin, R. "Business Behavior Behaviorally Viewed." In C. Argyris et al., *Social Science Approaches to Business Behavior*. Homewood, Ill.: Dorsey, 1962, 11–55.

Efran, J. S. "Descriptive Account of Training Procedures." In P. Pepinsky (ed.), *Studies of the Effects of Sponsorship and Strategy Upon the Actor's Independence and Upon the Social Assessment of His Productivity*. Columbus, Ohio: Ohio State U. Research Foundation, 1961, C37–C46.

Enke, S. "On the Economic Management of Large Organizations: A Laboratory Study," *J. Business*, 1958, 31, 280–292.

Evan, W. M. and Zelditch, M. "A Laboratory Experiment on Bureaucratic Authority," *ASR*, 1961, 26, 883–893.

Feather, N. T. "Persistence at a Difficult Task With Alternative Task of Intermediate Difficulty," *JASP*, 1963, 66, 231–238.

Festinger, L. "Laboratory Experiments." In L. Festinger and D. Katz (eds.), *Research Methods in the Behavioral Sciences*. New York: Holt, Rinehart & Winston, 1953, 136–172.

Festinger, L. and Carlsmith, J. M. "Cognitive Consequences of Forced Compliance," *JASP*, 1959, 58, 203–210.

Fiedler, F. E. "A Contingency Model of Leadership Effectiveness." In L. Berkowitz (ed.), *Advances in Experimental Social Psychology*, New York: Academic, 1964, I, 149–190.

French, J. R. P., Jr. and Snyder, R. "Leadership and Interpersonal Power." In D. Cartwright (ed:), *Studies in Social Power*. Ann Arbor: U. of Michigan Press, 1959, 118–149.

Friedell, M. F. "The Experimental Game as an Instrument for the Study of Social Behavior." Paper presented at Midwestern Psychological Assn., 1964.

Friedman, N. "The Psychological Experiment as a Social Interaction." Unpublished Doctoral Dissertation, Harvard U., 1964.

Garfinkel, E. "A Conception of, and Experiments With 'Trust' as a Condition of Stable Concerted Actions." In O. J. Harvey (ed.), *Motivation and Social Interaction*. New York: Ronald, 1963, 187–238.

Guetzkow, H. "A Use of Simulation in the Study of Inter-Nation Relations," *Behavioral Science*, 1959, 4, 183–191.

Guetzkow, H. "Organizational Leadership in Task-Oriented Groups." In L. Petrullo and B. M. Bass (eds.), *Leadership and Interpersonal Behavior*. New York: Holt, Rinehart & Winston, 1961, 187–200.

Guetzkow, H. and Bowes, A. E. "The Development of Organizations in a Laboratory," *MS*, 1957, 3, 380–402.

Gustav, A. "Students' Attitude Toward Compulsory Participation in Experiments," *J. Psychology*, 1962, 53, 119–125.

Harvey, O. J. (ed.), *Motivation and Social Interaction*. New York: Ronald, 1963.

Heider, F. "Social Perception and Phenomenal Causality," *Psychological Rev.*, 1944, 51, 358–374.

Hoffman, L. R., Harburg, E., and Maier, N. R. F. "Differences and Disagreement as Factors in Creative Group Problem Solving," *JASP*, 1962, 64, 206–214.

Hoffman, P. J., Festinger, L., and Lawrence, D. H. "Tendencies Toward Group Comparability in Competitive Bargaining," *HR*, 1954, 7, 141–159.

Homans, G. C. "The Strategy of Industrial Sociology." In G. C. Homans (ed.), *Sentiments and Activities*. New York: Free Press, 1962, 257–268.

Hood, T. "The Decision to Participate in Small Group Experiments: Patterns of Self Disclosure and the Volunteer." Technical Report 14, Durham, N.C.: Duke University, Dept. of Psychology, 1964.

Hovland, C. I. "Reconciling Conflicting Results Derived From Experimental and Survey Studies of Attitude Change," *American Psychologist*, 1959, 14, 8–17.

Hovland, C. I. and Weiss, W. "The Influence of Source Credibility on Communication," *Public Opinion Qtly.*, 1952, 15, 635–650.

Hutte, H. "Decision-Taking in a Management Game," *HR*, 1965, 18, 5–20.

Jacobs, R. C. and Campbell, D. T. "The Perpetuation of an Arbitrary Tradition Through Several Generations of a Laboratory Microculture," *JASP*, 1961, 62, 649–658.

Jensen, B. T. "Instructions for 'The Railroad Game.'" Technical Memorandum 608, Santa Monica, Calif.: System Development Corp., 1961.

Jensen, B. T. and Terebinski, S. J. "'The Railroad Game': A Tool for Research in Social Sciences," *J. Social Psychology*, 1963, 60, 85–87.

Jones, E. E. *Ingratiation*. New York: Appleton-Century, 1964.

Jones, E. E. and DeCharms, R. "Changes in Social Perception as a Function of the Personal Relevance of Behavior," *Sociometry*, 1957, 20, 75–85.

Joyner, R. C. "SIN-Simulation of Interaction in Communication Networks, II: Experiments With the Common Target Game." Unpublished MS, Carnegie Institute of Technology, 1965.

Kaplan, A. *The Conduct of Inquiry*. San Francisco: Chandler, 1964.

Kelley, H. H. "Communication in Experimentally Created Hierarchies," *HR*, 1951, 4, 39–56.

Kelley, H. H., Condry, J. C., Jr., Dahlke, A. E., and Hill, A. H. "Collective Behavior in a Simulated Panic Situation," *J. Experimental Social Psychology*, 1965, 1, 20–54.

Kelley, H. H., Thibaut, J. W., Radloff, R., and Mundy, D. "The Development of Cooperation in the 'Minimal Social Situation,'" *Psychological Monographs*, 1962, 76, (19, Whole No. 538).

Kennedy, J. L. "Experimenters Manual: Research and Development Game." Unpublished MS, Princeton University, 1963.

Kiesler, C. A. and Corbin, L. H. "Commitment, Attraction, and Conformity," *J. Personality and Social Psychology*, 1965, 2, 890–895.

King, D. C. "Summary of Intergroup Exercise I." Unpublished MS, Purdue University, 1964.

Krugman, H. E. "The 'Draw a Supermarket' Technique," *Public Opinion Qtly.*, 1960, 24, 148-149.

Krupp, S. "Pattern in Organization Analysis." New York: Holt, Rinehart & Winston, 1961.

Kuethe, J. L. "Social Schemas," *JASP*, 1962, 64, 31-38.

Latané, B. and Arrowood, A. J. "Emotional Arousal and Task Performance," *JAP*, 1963, 47, 324-327.

Leavitt, H. J. "Task Ordering and Organizational Development in the Common Target Game," *Behavioral Science*, 1960, 5, 233-239.

——. "Applied Organization Change in Industry: Structural, Technical, and Human Approaches." In W. W. Cooper, H. J. Leavitt, and M. W. Shelly (eds.), *New Perspectives in Organization Research*. New York: Wiley, 1964, II, 55-71.

Lewin, K. *Field Theory in Social Science*. New York: Harper, 1951.

Lorge, I., Fox, D., Davitz, J., and Brenner, M. "A Survey of Studies Contrasting the Quality of Group Performance and Individual Performance," *Psychological Bull.*, 1958, 55, 337-370.

Lyle, J. "Communication, Group Atmosphere, Productivity, and Morale in Small Task Groups," *HR*, 1961, 14, 369-379.

Maier, N. R. F. and Hoffman, L. R. "Organization and Creative Problem Solving," *JAP*, 1961, 45, 277-280.

March, J. G. and Simon, H. A. *Organizations*. New York: Wiley, 1958.

Marx, M. H. "The General Nature of Theory Construction." In M. H. Marx (ed.), *Theories in Contemporary Psychology*. New York: Macmillan, 1963, 4-46.

McGrath, J. E. "Toward a 'Theory of Method' for Research on Organizations." In W. W. Cooper, H. J. Leavitt, and M. W. Shelly (eds.), *New Perspectives in Organization Research*. New York: Wiley, 1964, 533-556.

Mechanic, D. "Some Considerations in the Methodology of Organizational Studies." In H. Leavitt (ed.), *The Social Science of Organizations*. Englewood Cliffs: Prentice-Hall, 1963, 139-182.

Meier, R. C. "Explorations in the Realm of Organization Theory IV: The Simulation of Social Organization," *Behavioral Science*, 1961, 6, 232-248.

Milgram, S. "Behavioral Study of Obedience," *JASP*, 1963, 67, 371-378.

Milgram, S. "Issues in the Study of Obedience: A Reply to Baumrind," *American Psychologist*, 1964, 19, 848-852.

Miller, L. K. and Hamblin, R. L. "Interdependence, Differential Rewarding, and Productivity," *ASR*, 1963, 28, 768-778.

Mills, T. M. "A Sleeper Variable in Small Groups Research: The Experimenter," *Pacific Sociological Rev.*, 1962, 5 (1), 21-28.

Orne, M. T. "On the Social Psychology of the Psychological Experiment: With Particular Reference to Demand Characteristics and Their Implications," *American Psychologist*, 1962, 17, 776-783.

Pepitone, A. *Attraction and Hostility*. New York: Atherton, 1964.

Pilisuk, M. "Cognitive Balance and Self-Relevant Attitudes," *JASP*, 1962, 65, 95-103.

Proshansky, H. and Seidenberg, B. (eds.), *Basic Studies in Social Psychology*. New York: Holt, Rinehart & Winston, 1965.

Raven, B. H. and Eachus, H. T. "Cooperation and Competition in Means-Interdependent Triads," *JASP*, 1963, 67, 307-316.

Riecken, H. W. "A Program for Research on Experiments in Social Psychology." In N. F. Washburne (ed.), *Decisions, Values, and Groups*. New York: Macmillan, 1962, II, 25-41.

Ring, K. "Some Determinants of Interpersonal Attraction in Hierarchical Relationships: A Motivational Analysis," *J. Personality*, 1964, 32, 651-665.

Roby, T. B. "Subtask Phasing in Small Groups." In J. H. Criswell, H. Solomon, and P. Suppes (eds.), *Mathematical Methods in Small Group Processes*. Stanford: Stanford U. Press, 1962, 263-281.

Roby, T. B. and Lanzetta, J. T. "Considerations in the Analysis of Group Tasks," *Psychological Bull.*, 1958, 55, 88-101.

Rosenberg, M. J. "When Dissonance Fails: On Eliminating Evaluation Apprehension from Attitude Measurement," *J. Personality and Social Psychology*, 1965, 1, 28-42.

Rosenberg, M. J. and Abelson, R. P. "An Analysis of Cognitive Balancing." In M. J. Rosenberg et al., *Attitude Organization and Change*. New Haven: Yale U. Press, 1960, 112–163.

Rosenthal, R. "On the Social Psychology of the Psychological Experiment: The Experimenter's Hypothesis as Unintended Determinant of Experimental Results," *American Scientist*, 1963, 51, 268–283.

Sampson, E. E. and Insko, C. A. "Cognitive Consistency and Performance in the Autokinetic Situation," *JASP*, 1964, 68, 184–192.

Schachter, S. "Deviation, Rejection, and Communication," *JASP*, 1951, 46, 190–207.

———. *The Psychology of Affiliation*. Stanford: Stanford U. Press, 1959.

Schachter, S. and Singer, J. E. "Cognitive, Social, and Physiological Determinants of Emotional State." *Psychological Rev.*, 1962, 69, 379–399.

Schachter, S., Willerman, B., Festinger, L., and Hyman, R. "Emotional Disruption and Industrial Productivity," *JAP*, 1961, 45, 201–213.

Schein, E. H. *Organizational Psychology*. Englewood Cliffs: Prentice-Hall, 1965.

Schein, E. H. and King, D. C. "The House Building and Community Planning Intergroup Exercise." Unpublished MS, Massachusetts Institute of Technology, 1964.

Schultz, D. P. "Spontaneous Alternation Behavior in Humans: Implications for Psychological Research," *Psychological Bull.*, 1964, 62, 394–400.

Selznick, P. "Foundations of the Theory of Organization," *ASR*, 1948, 13, 25–35.

Sherif, M. and Harvey. O. J. "A Study in Ego Functioning: Elimination of Stable Anchorages in Individual and Group Situations," *Sociometry*, 1952, 15, 272–305.

Sherif, M. and Sherif, C. W. *Reference Groups*. New York: Harper, 1964.

Shure, G. H., Rogers, M. S., Larsen, I. M., and Tassone, J. "Group Planning and Task Effectiveness," *Sociometry*, 1962, 25, 263–282.

Simon, H. A. "Comments on the Theory of Organizations." In A. H. Rubenstein and C. J. Haberstroh (eds.), *Some Theories of Organization*. Homewood, Ill: Dorsey, 1960, 157–167.

Solem, A. R. "An Evaluation of Two Attitudinal Approaches to Delegation," *JAP*, 1958, 42, 36–39.

Stogdill, R. "Leadership, Membership, and Organization," *Psychological Bull.*, 1950, 47, 1–14.

Strickland, L. H. "Surveillance and Trust," *J. Personality*, 1958, 26, 200–215.

Thibaut, J. "The Motivational Effects of Social Dependence on a Powerful Agency of Control." In W. W. Cooper, H. J. Leavitt, and M. W. Shelly (eds.), *New Perspectives in Organization Research*. New York: Wiley, 1964, 87–96.

Thibaut, J. and Riecken, H. W. "Some Determinants and Consequences of the Perception of Social Causality," *J. Personality*, 1955, 24, 113–134.

Toda, M. "The Design of a Fungus-Eater: A Model of Human Behavior in an Unsophisticated Environment," *Behavioral Science*, 1962, 7, 164–183.

Tuckman, B. W. "Personality Structure, Group Composition, and Group Function," *Sociometry*, 1964, 27, 469–487.

Underwood, B. J. *Psychological Research*. New York: Appleton-Century, 1957.

Vroom, V. H. "A Working Paper on Laboratory Experiments on Organization." Paper prepared for 3rd Seminar in the Social Science of Organizations, U. of Pittsburgh, 1964.

Wager, L. W. and Palola, E. G. "The Miniature Replica Model and Its Use in Laboratory Experiments of Complex Organizations," *Social Forces*, 1964, 42, 418–429

Weick, K. E. "Reduction of Cognitive Dissonance Through Task Enhancement and Effort Expenditure," *JASP*, 1964, 68, 533–539.

———. "Laboratory Experimentation with Organizations." In J. G. March (ed.), *Handbook of Organizations*. Chicago: Rand McNally, 1965a.

———. "When Prophecy Pales: The Fate of Dissonance Theory," *Psychological Reports*, 1965b, 16, 1261–1275.

Weick, K. E. and Penner, D. D. "Triads: a Laboratory Analogue," *Organizational Behavior and Human Performance*, 1966, 1 (2).

Zajonc, R. B. "The Requirements and Design of a Standard Group Task," *J. Experimental Social Psychology*, 1965, 1, 71–78.

Zand, D. E. and Costello, T. W. "Effect of Problem Variation on Group Problem Solving Efficiency Under Constrained Communication," *Psychological Reports*, 1963, 13, 219–224.

Zelditch, M. "Some Methodological Problems of Field Studies," *American J. Sociology*, 1962, 67, 566–576.

Zelditch, M. and Evan, W. M. "Simulated Bureaucracies: A Methodological Analysis." In H. Guetzkow (ed.), *Simulation in Social Science: Readings.* Englewood Cliffs: Prentice-Hall, 1962, 48–60.

Zelditch, M. and Hopkins, T. K. "Laboratory Experiments with Organizations." In A. Etzioni (ed.), *Complex Organizations.* New York: Holt, Rinehart & Winston, 1961, 464–478.

Zigler, E. "Metatheoretical Issues in Developmental Psychology." In M. Marx (ed.), *Theories in Contemporary Psychology.* New York: Macmillan, 1963, 341–369.

13 Field Experiments with Formal Organizations*

Stanley E. Seashore

A recent effort at describing a field experiment concerning organizational structure and process (Seashore and Bowers, 1963) has led us to make a review of some other studies of a similar kind, and to formulate some general thoughts on the dilemmas and strategies in such research. This chapter is a first attempt at organizing these thoughts. It seems worth doing because: (1) few people have had any direct experiences in conducting field experiments with complex organizations, (2) with increasing financial and methodological resources we are likely to see more work of this kind, and (3) compared with experiments of other kinds, certain issues of strategy and method become of crucial importance and deserve examination.

Let us first state the universe of discourse. We will consider here experiments done in natural settings where the experiment is incidental to the main purposes of the organizations. We will consider as a formal organization any relatively stable social system that is complex in the sense of including two or more component groups coordinated through two or more hierarchical levels of leadership. What constitutes an experiment is less easy to state. Obviously, there are alternative designs and a continuum of conformance with ideal experimental design. Let us settle, for the moment, on minimum criteria of: (1) definable and measurable change in organizational environment, struc-

*Some of the work leading to this paper was supported by a grant from the Air Force Office of Scientific Research, Contract AF 49 (638)–1032.

Source: S. E. Seashore, "Field Experiments with Formal Organizations." Reproduced by permission of the Society for Applied Anthropology from *Human Organization*, 23(2): 164–170, 1964.

ture, or process, (2) some means for quantification of variables, and (3) some provision for testing of causal hypotheses through the method of difference.

These definitions exempt from consideration *simulation experiments* (such as the work of Sidney and Beatrice Rome with a computer model of an organization), *case studies* (such as the Tavistock Institute's work at the Glacier metals factory), *correlational* studies (such as those of the Survey Research Center done in many organizations), and most *ex post facto comparison studies* (such the work of Mann and Hoffman comparing two power plants with differing degrees of automation). These are all highly productive and valuable classes of research effort, but they are not experiments even by our suggested minimal standards. Also excluded from discussion are the many *group experiments* that have been conducted within organizations (such as the classic Hawthorne Test Room and Harwood Rate Change experiments). Exclusion is on the grounds that such field experiments concern small groups rather than larger, more complex social organizations, and that the location of the subject groups within complex organizations is, in such cases, only incidental to the purposes, design and conduct of the work.

The reader will recognize that these exclusions are arbitrary, and have no purpose other than to narrow attention to the special problems that arise or become accentuated when one attempts field studies of relatively large and complex organizational units with methods that approach those of classical experimental design.

WHY EXPERIMENTS?

The justification for conducting experiments must rest on grounds of effectiveness and efficiency in generating information and testing hypotheses. The advantages must be sufficient to offset the added costs, which may be great. Two considerations seem relevant.

It is difficult to establish unequivocally a causal relationship between variables without a controlled experiment spanning the period of change in both variables. Organizational theory is becoming sufficiently complex and sophisticated to bring to the fore issues of causality. Therefore, on certain theoretical issues, no other research approach is effective.

The second consideration is one of efficiency and economy. A single well-designed experiment can, in principle, produce information of such unequivocal nature that it outweighs any number of case studies or demonstrations.[1]

Other reasons one might invoke to justify attempts to use the experimental method are of a different order. For example, an experiment in a natural setting with real organizations is likely to produce results that seem acceptable and persuasive to action-oriented people and therefore to encourage application of the results.

Literature on the Methodology of Field Experiments

The otherwise rich literature on methodology of research on human social behavior is barren when it comes to experiments with formal organizations. The two primary works in the field from the early Fifties (Festinger and Katz, 1953; Jahoda et al., 1951) contain sections on experimental design and on field procedures, but no special reference to experiments with formal organizations, and only one example is mentioned— possibly the only one that existed at the time. A later book by Argyle (1957) includes an excellent critical review of methodological designs and principles, arguing strongly for the use of experimental methods, but has no reference to the special case of experiments with formal organizations. Etzioni's recent collection of articles (1961) similarly is void of examples or discussion in this area.

A scanning of five recent major works on research design in the behavioral sciences uncovered not a single example of experimental work with formal human organizations, and no reference to the problems of conducting such research in field settings.

The picture looks very different when one turns from sources that focus on experimental design to those that focus on field research methods generally. Here one finds a rich fund of example and analytic discussion of procedures for obtaining information about complex social organizations, for inducing change in organizations, and for drawing tentative conclusions from field data. There are numerous reports of anthropological methods in the study of formal organizations, descriptions of participant-observer techniques and of survey techniques, and the like (Adams and Preiss, 1960). All these have great merit and are highly relevant to the conduct of field experiments, but do not deal systematically with the special problems of experimental design in conjunction with these methods.

Dimensions for Describing and Evaluating Experiments

A general and inclusive set of dimensions for describing and evaluating field experimental designs would be a very long and complicated one, and probably not very useful at the present time. However, some dimensions of evident importance can be suggested as a start:

1. *Choice of populations*: Number and size of organizational units; pre-experimental homogeneity and differences as to membership, structure, function; provision for control populations and for contrasting or variable treatment of experimental units; provision for control of potential confounding variables through randomization, purposive selection, measurement, and statistical treatment of population variables not part of the theory.
2. *Approach to change*: Natural vs. purposeful change; if purposeful, is the point-of-change at the level of individual members, general organizational policy, internal structure and process, or in the organization's environment?
3. *Variables for manipulation or measurement*: Are the point-of-change variables part of the theory? How many independent variables are there and what are the provisions for treating their relationship? How many are the dependent variables, and do they include both internal and output variables? What causal chains and interactions are implied if not specified by the design?
4. *Level of theory*: Does the theory refer to institutional, organizational, social-psychological, or psychological phenomena? What is the level of abstraction on a continuum from the highly specific and restricted to the highly general and universal?
5. *Duration in time*.
6. *Analysis plan*: Assessment of results through before-after comparisons, through difference between experimental and control units, through analysis of variance, etc. Is analysis at the individual, the group, or the organizational level?

EXAMPLES OF EXPERIMENTS WITH
FORMAL ORGANIZATIONS

The total number of research ventures that might be reasonably considered to be field experiments with formal organizations is very small, perhaps from five to ten, depending upon how generous one chooses to be in tolerating deviations from ideal experimental conditions. None of these fulfills the canons of experimental design to the degree ordinarily expected in laboratory or field experiments on small groups. One must view them as rather primitive, pioneering ventures. Three of the better examples are summarized briefly here.

Experiment I concerns the relationship between level of decision-making in an organization and the effectiveness of work performance (Morse and Reimer, 1956). The population included four parallel divisions (about 500 employees) of a large business firm, all performing similar clerical work under similar conditions. Data on work force composition, past performance, and the like were used to estimate and maximize preexperimental homogeneity. Divisions were paired for contrasting experimental treatment. The experimental changes involved policy clarification and change, training of individual supervisors and employees, alteration of certain organizational structures and processes. These actions were intended to produce contrasting effects on the independent variable, and measurements were obtained to confirm the success of the change program. Dependent variables included both variables descriptive of internal organizational processes and also output variables such as cost of production and member satisfaction. The theory was at the level of social-psychology, in the sense of treating the psychological consequences of social structure and processes. The experimental period extended over a full year, with measurements before and after, and with active change program interventions conducted during the six months preceding the experimental period. Results: increasing the amount of involvement in decision-making of rank and file employees led to reduced cost of work performance, increased employee satisfaction, and increased sense of responsibility for work performance. Increasing the amount of involvement in decision-making by higher-level staff and supervisors also reduced cost of work performance, but otherwise led to reduced employee satisfaction, a lowering of individual responsibility for production and other similar changes.

Experiment II concerns the feedback of employee attitude survey data as a means for inducing beneficial changes in the attitudes and morale of employees. The population included six departments (about 1,000 employees) of the accounting division of a large utility firm, with two departments serving as control units and four having differential amounts of change treatment. The method and amount of feedback activity was voluntary for each department and hence the experimental units were self-selected. The several departments were of varying size and membership composition, and performed somewhat different functions. The experimental change program was a combination of natural and purposeful procedures; the units electing to undertake the feedback of survey data did so to the extent possible in ways that expressed their normal policies and work processes but the managers and supervisors received coaching and counseling in feedback procedures and encouragement toward extensive and intensive use of the process. Higher-level management support was obtained to legitimize the experiment. The point of change therefore was internal to the organization, and included policy clarification and change, as well as individual training and alteration of organizational processes.

The independent variable was the amount of feedback activity over a one-year span of time and the dependent variables represented numerous aspects of employee satisfaction and morale, treated as separate variables and also summed to obtain an overall index of attitudes favorable to the achievement of the organization's goals. The theory underlying the experiment was social-psychological in character and assumed that unspecified but adaptive changes in the attitudes and overt behavior of supervisors were the principal intervening variables. The elements of the theory were not differentiated or measured separately in the experimental plan. The experiment had a total duration of four years, including two pre-experimental measurements of dependent variables (to set base rates), an active feedback period of about one year followed by a year of time, and a final measurement after the fourth year. Analysis consisted of the comparison of experimental and control departments on the dependent variables at the end of the period, and also before-after change measurements for each department. Results: the amount of the improvements in employee attitudes and "morale" were roughly proportional to the amount of effort allocated to the feedback process.[2]

Experiment III concerns the induction of change in four variables central to Likert's management theory (1961) and the consequences with respect to output criteria of work efficiency, waste, absence, and employee satisfaction. The population included five production departments (about 500 employees) of a packaging materials firm. One of the experimental departments was selected by the research team, two others volunteered for experimental change treatment, and the remaining two were used as control units. The departments varied in size and in productive function but were similar in composition of work force, and exposure to a common plantwide policy and history. The change procedures included policy change to legitimize the experiment and to permit certain structural changes in the organization, training of supervisory and staff people, and changes in various organizational processes concerning communications and decision-making. The change program was intended to induce, in the experimental units: (1) more employee involvement in decision-making, (2) more use of work groups as a medium for organizational activity, (3) more supportiveness in supervisor-employee relationships, and (4) more mutual interaction and influence within work groups. Measurements before and after the change program in both experimental and control units confirmed the successful induction of the desired changes. Criterion variables were also measured before, at one point during, and again after the change period. The change program extended over a three-year period. The theory was social-psychological in character, and (for purposes of this experiment) treated the independent variables as a set, not attempting to differentiate their separate effects. The dependent variables were treated separately. Assessment of results provided for before-after comparisons for each unit, and for comparison of experimental and control departments before and again after the experimental period. Results: changes in the four independent variables are associated with increased employee satisfaction, reduction in waste, increase in productive efficiency, and dampening of a trend toward increased absenteeism.

SOME DILEMMAS IN EXPERIMENTAL DESIGN

The design and conduct of field experiments with formal organizations involve the same methodological, theoretical, and ethical considerations that apply to any research with human subjects, but some are particularly bothersome. Some comments follow on several dilemmas that are apparent from a review of the experiments that have been reported thus far.

1. Control vs. Representativeness

The most common forms of organization tend to be exactly those most difficult to perform experiments upon. Experiment I, above, achieved a fairly high degree of control over unknown confounding variables by restricting its scope to four parallel divisions matched in a number of respects. Experiment III, by contrast, involved a much more commonly prevailing situation with organizational units differing in a number of respects (size, population mix, nature of work, etc.) in such a way as to leave some question whether the experimental results derived from the experimental variables or from other unknown sources. The added precision of Experiment I must be weighed against the possibility that its results derive from some feature of the restricted and exceptional population. There are at least two guides toward resolving this dilemma. Until more is known about confounding factors in field experiments there is great merit in emphasizing control through the selection of an initially homogeneous population. Those choosing to emphasize representativeness might well compensate for loss of homogeneity by using a larger number of cases, thus allowing randomization of some intruding variables. No experiment known to us so far has an N of organizational units greater than six.

2. Short-term vs. Long-term Experiments

Of five cases of field experiments with formal organizations which have been examined most closely, three required a span of time (years, not months) considerably greater than originally intended, and this permitted the intrusion of personnel changes, technological changes, and other events that may well have confounded the results. The problem appears to be that significant changes in organizational structure and process come about rather slowly; at the same time, the longer an experiment continues in a natural organization, the more likely that there will be some loss of control over experimental conditions. In Experiment III, for example, some organizational units present at the beginning of the experiment simply disappeared under the press of technological change in the course of a three-year change program, and there took place a considerable but normal turnover of membership in the experimental units. The advantages of short-term experimental plans are very great, but rest upon having powerful change methods and upon excluding variables not subject to change in a short time. Long-term experimental plans permit the utilization of natural changes and changes induced with less risk of stressful side-effects which might themselves introduce confounding effects.

3. Small, Explicit Theories vs. Global, Syndromatic Theories

Theoretical development, especially during early years of experimentation, is likely to be optimized to the extent that experiments focus upon small segments of organizational theory and deal precisely with a limited number of variables having a high degree of generality. This assertion argues for experiments designed around small, explicit theories (but, note that these may be small theories about large phenomena). On the other hand, preliminary theory testing is likely to be accomplished more easily on a global or syndromatic basis. Natural organizations function not in segments but as totalities, and it is likely that larger theoretical systems, necessarily coupled with reduced precision of conceptualization and measurement, are needed to capture the main phenomena that occur. All of the experiments examined by the writer chose the latter course, and in translating theory into design ended by making large and risky assumptions about the interrelations among the elements of theory and by using syndromatic assessments. Experiment II, for example, bypassed entirely the details of its theory and measured only the change input, and also the output at the level of individual behavior. Experiment III deliberately treated, as a syndrome, four independent variables which in theory are separate and not of the same order; this forceable simplification of theory can be justified only on grounds of experimental expediency. The researchers' choice in this dilemma may well be based on grounds of convenience or esthetics until enough progress is made to permit some better judgment of relative effectiveness of the two approaches.

4. Massive vs. Controlled Change

The dilemma here arises from the conflict between the need to obtain change great enough to sustain measurement while at the same time preserving the possibility of differentiating among change sources and avoiding unintended and uncontrolled change. The experiments conducted thus far appear without exception to have called into play virtually all of the change resources available to the experimenters, and none has attempted to separate in analysis the effects of different sources or kinds of change activities. This dilemma is the counterpart, at the level of change induction, of the preceding point regarding specificity of theory. One known experiment was initially designed to differentiate among three change strategies, but this feature of the initial design failed of realization. Considering the difficulty of inducing a significant intentional change in organizational process, it appears likely that the first successful attempts to differentiate and control the sources of change will take the form of "natural" experiments (which exploit powerful singular events and conditions) or changes induced through modifications of organizational environment and/or formal structure (which require less direct intervention within the organizations).

5. Near vs. Distant Criteria

Organizational theories of the dynamic variety all involve chains of causal linkages between variables. The differentiation between independent and dependent variables accordingly becomes arbitrary except for their relative position in the causal sequence. One man's independent variables is another's criterion. The dilemma for the designer of experiments lies in weighing the advantages of near and distant criteria. His theoretical interests press toward criteria of organizational structure or process that are presumed to be immediately dependent upon his independent variables; at the same time his concerns for enlarging the conceptual scheme press toward criteria representing the output of the organizational system. The first choice maximizes his chances of getting significant relationships and is more likely to illuminate and add precision to this theory. The second choice offers the important gain of proving some link between his independent variables and the ultimate criteria by which the organizations are judged by society. Of the three examples given earlier, all involved output or distant criteria, and Experiment I also provided for assessment of certain near criteria. An example may be needed to clarify the point: a researcher changing the number of hierarchical levels in his experimental organizations might use a near dependent variable such as change in communication rates within the organizations, or he might choose to use a distant criterion such as change in productivity rates. In principle, of course, one can account for all elements in the theoretically specified causal chains, together with their interactions, but this would be a truly formidable and presently impossible task.

6.   Self- vs. Independent Selection of Subjects

A problem that has not been treated as yet in any experimental investigation on organizations, but which needs attention concerns the consequences of self-selection of the subject organizations. The dilemma for the researcher is to balance the advantages of working with organizations that are accessible and compliant against the hazard that these qualities may themselves interfere with control and representativeness in the research operations. Having a manager willing to expose his organization to experimentation is hardly a typical organizational condition, and implies that the outcome may be prejudiced in unforeseen ways. The same dilemma arises in experiments with individuals and small groups, but in a less disruptive degree.

7.   Scientific vs. Ethical and Practical Considerations

All of the organizational experiments reported thus far involved a degree of collaboration between the subjects and the researchers which is greater than commonly holds for other experiments with human subjects. This collaboration typically includes a rather great financial investment by the subjects with some corresponding expectation of benefit, and the scale of the work means that any harm that inadvertently may be incurred will affect many people. It is the nature of useful experiments that they tend to go beyond our confident knowledge and established experimental skills, with consequent risk, and in the case of organizational experiments these risks are on a large scale. The course of experimentally induced changes is not likely to remain in the immediate control of the experimenter, and he must depend upon many others who may misunderstand or take advantage of the experimental situation. A protection is often available in the way of making the design and conduct of the experiment a truly collaborative matter with responsibility for consequences located in ways compatible with the structure of the organization, but this in turn limits the change program to matters known to and understood by the participants. A few instances are on record where organizations or members have been harmed by organizational-level intervention for research purposes, and more are bound to occur if experimentation proceeds in a vigorous and venturesome way.

RESEARCH STRATEGIES

At this primitive stage of development in experimentation with formal organizations it is probably desirable to emphasize simplicity of design and opportunism in execution as guides to research strategy. Some suggestions follow:

1.   Search for Optimum Research Sites

This writer is much impressed by the difficulties of establishing control over variables which are not components of the research design. The practical approach will ordinarily involve a deliberate search for subject organizations which are stable in their environment, technology, and membership,[3] and which are accessible in large numbers. Homogeneity of subject organizations has evident advantage; large N's allow randomization, matching or sampling techniques for removal of some potentially confounding effects. Where will such populations be found? Mainly in activities relatively uncomplicated by changing machine technology (e.g., sales, service, government, education, etc.) and in fields having very large parent organizations with many similar decentralized field units (e.g., armed forces, large corporations, communities, government agencies, etc.).

2.   Availability of Criterion Data

In instances when the research design rests upon hard criteria of organizational performance, a great value must be placed on locating subject organizations that offer reliable differences in performance. Since high reliability and comparability of organizational performance criteria are *very* rare, it is likely that other considerations in choice of research site will yield to this essential one, or else the research designs will need to be modified in ways to avoid the problem entirely. The chief way to avoid the problem is to settle for criteria of organizational structure and process, rather than criteria of organizational output; these are often relatively easy to measure, are less contaminated, and for many theoretical purposes equally or even more useful than the hard criteria.

3.   Induction of Change

A general principle of experimental design is to avoid introducing any changes in conditions other than those absolutely essential for obtaining the desired modification of the independent variables. The organizational experiments reported so far have all involved a rather large amount of loosely-controlled intervention by outside change agents, and this risks the introduction of "Hawthorne effects" and other effects not accounted for in the design. There appears to be great merit in designs which introduce changes in ways that involve little or no contact between experimenter and subject organization. How is this likely to be managed? (1) Through policy and structural changes introduced via persuasion at the top levels of the organizations, (2) by intervention into allocative processes (e.g., assignment of funds, people, tasks) which purposefully affect the subject organizations without direct intervention into the organizations themselves, (3) by altering the environment of the subject organizations.[4]

4.   Pre-Experimental Assessment of Confounding Variables

One way of coming to terms with potentially confounding conditions is to make in advance a realistic assessment of what they are and then provide some control through population selection or statistical adjustment of the experimental variables.

To do this appears to require a more thorough scouting and preparatory operation than is typically done, and in any case it is a procedure dependent on the insight and judgment of the experimenters rather than upon replicable methods. An ideal situation would be that in which the subject organizations (or others like them) were subjected to a series of preliminary investigations allowing the research team to become intimately familiar with the total situation and thus to have a chance, at least, of knowing the surroundings of the experiment. In Experiment II, described earlier, this was done, and the experiment itself followed after several years of prior research within the organization. In Experiment III, there was a full year of preliminary scouting, but crucial factors were overlooked which later revealed their potency in disrupting the experimental plan. A useful guide in this preliminary work would be the formulation of explicit conditional assumptions implied by the proposed research design, so that points of hazard can more readily be discerned and treated.

5.   Skills in Change Induction

Some variables of importance in organizational theory present special problems with respect to the introduction of purposeful change and probably have to be dealt with through direct and intensive interventions. An example would be a variable such as consideration (a variable referring to a style of supervisory behavior believed to be conditioned by the actor's organizational climate) which has its variance sources in individual personality, local group norms, and formal organizational policy, as well as in the climate and traditions of the organization (Fleishman, 1953). To attempt to change such a variable experimentally through indirect, sanitary means would probably require a great span of time and considerable uncertainty of outcome. To change it directly through intervention by change agents at the personal contact level is also difficult (failures have been reported) but is known to be feasible. To accommodate the requirements of both experimental change and practical application ventures, there is likely to arise a new professional group devoted to change agentry, different in important respects from their professional colleagues in the fields of training and management consulting. The researcher himself is not likely to have the qualifications or time to perform this essential research function, and in the interests of objectivity he probably should not be involved in it. For such practical reasons, the research plans in field experiments should in many cases provide for some kind of division of labor between those who do the theoretical, analytic, and interpretive work, on the one hand, and those who engage in active and personal interventions in the subject organizations.

6.   Creating New Organizations

One potential means for avoiding many of the foregoing problems has, to our knowledge, never been tried. This is the procedure of linking an experimental plan with the growth of an organization in such a way that new organizational units may be designed from their initiation with contrasting characteristics that permit testing of theoretical propositions. Some lucky researcher will one day be permitted to impose such a plan upon, say, the formation of 100 new welfare agencies, retail outlets, or military units.[5]

7. Utilization of Natural Change

A prime practical problem in experiments with larger organizations is the induction of a change that is sufficiently great to permit hypothesis-testing even after the consequences of the change are dampened and confounded by the unavoidable surrounding noise. This calls for an enhanced alertness on the part of both researchers and organization managers so that instances of impending natural change can be exploited. In this manner the experimenter may have the use of change events far greater (for reasons of competence and ethics) than those he could introduce on his own initiative. However, optimum use of such situations requires advance knowledge in order that population controls and pre-measures may be instituted.

NOTES

1. An example of the failure of nonexperimental method comes to mind. Marriott's review (1957) of the research on the efficacy of incentive payment plans in raising individual and organizational work performance led to the conclusion that, in spite of many hundreds of successful introductions of incentive pay plans, one cannot know whether the reported effects are produced by the pay plans or by other concomitant factors. There have been a total of three experiments on the matter, but all were done about thirty years ago and all involved N's of less than ten individuals. The amount of useful information from this vast amount of work is remarkably small.

2. This study was conducted by Floyd Mann. See (Likert and Hayes, 1957) pages 103–108 for a summary description of this study.

3. Unless, of course, these enter directly into the experimental design.

4. Alteration of the environment or allocative processes of organizations may at first seem an impossible accomplishment for a researcher, but consider these hypothetical possibilities as examples: Through home-office intervention, field (subject) organizations could be subjected temporarily to different degrees of work overload; through home-office intervention some subject units and not others could be subjected to conditions of inter-unit competition or cooperation.

5. This paper has excluded consideration of laboratory experiments, which may involve creation of new complex organizations and may in degree of realism approach field conditions. An example is described in "A Laboratory Experiment on Bureaucratic Authority," by William M. Evan and Morris Zelditch, Jr., *American Sociological Review*, XXVI (1961), 883–893.

REFERENCES

Adams, R. N. and J. J. Preiss (eds.), *Human Organization Research*, Dorsey, Homewood, Ill., 1960.

Argyle, M. *The Scientific Study of Social Behavior*, Philosophical Library, New York, 1957.

Etzioni, A. *Complex Organizations: A Sociological Reader*, Holt, Rinehart and Winston, New York, 1961.

Festinger, L. and D. Katz (eds.), *Research Methods in the Behavioral Sciences*, Holt, Rinehart and Winston, New York, 1953.

Fleishman, E. A. "Leadership Climate, Human Relations Training and Supervisory Behavior," *Personnel Psychology*, VI (1953), 205–222.

Jahoda, M., M. Deutsch, and S. Cook. *Research Methods in Social Relations*, Dryden Press, New York, 1951.

Likert, R. *New Patterns of Management*, McGraw-Hill, New York, 1961.

Likert, R. and S. Hayes (eds.), *Some Applications of Behavioral Research*, UNESCO, New York, 1957.

Marriott, R. *Incentive Payment Systems*, Staples Press, London, 1957.

Morse, N. and E. Reimer. "The Experimental Change of a Major Organizational Variable," *J. Abnormal and Social Psychology*, LII, 1956, 120–129.

Seashore, S. E. and D. G. Bowers, *Changing the Structure and Functioning of an Organization*, Survey Research Center, Ann Arbor, 1963.

14 Adaptive Experiments: An Approach to Organizational Behavior Research

Edward E. Lawler III

The behavioral science and management literature suggests many ways in which organizations can be changed to increase their effectiveness and to provide a better quality of work life for employees. Job enrichment, autonomous work groups, the Scanlon Plan and participative management are but a few suggested approaches. Unfortunately little systematic evidence indicates the effectiveness of any of these approaches to organizational design and management. Available research consists primarily of poorly documented case studies, and correlational studies which show the relationship between certain practices and a limited number of measures of organizational effectiveness (Katzell and Yankelovich, 1975). In the absence of evidence on their effectiveness, it is hard to make a convincing case for adopting these practices. In addition, their improvement and further development are retarded because feedback on effectiveness is lacking. Thus, it is imperative that information about the effects of a wide variety of managerial practices and organization designs be developed. How can this be done? What kinds of research designs are appropriate?

EXPERIMENTS

Questions about the effects of organization designs and practices are questions of causality. The need for causal information has important implications for the kinds of research to be done. Since case studies and correlational studies do not provide convincing causal evidence, some other research design is needed. At first glance, carefully controlled experimental designs which follow the physical science model, including control groups and random assignment, seem called for, since they can produce convincing causal evidence and can be utilized in field settings (Campbell, 1969). The few field experiments which have been done enjoy wide visibility (Coch and French, 1948; Morse and Reimer, 1956) and provide graphic testimony of their value.

Given the obvious value of field experiments, why have there been so few? A number of explanations are given: organizations do not allow them, they are too expensive, organizational researchers are not willing to do the necessary hard work, and researchers are not aware of these designs. Although these explanations have some validity,

*Preparation of this article was supported by a grant from the Ford Foundation and the Economic Development Administration of the Department of Commerce.

Source: E. E. Lawler III, "Adaptive Experiments: An Approach to Organizational Behavior Research," *Academy of Management Review*, 1977, 2, pp. 576–585. Reproduced by permission.

they fail to highlight the basic reason why so few experiments are done in organizations: the methodological requirements of traditional experiments fail to mesh with the realities of life in organizations.

Stated another way, the demands of all experimental designs are unrealistic in light of how organizations actually operate. Among other things, all designs require random assignment of subjects to conditions, a control group, a limited carefully defined experimental treatment, and control over variables which might confound the experiment. These conditions are all difficult, if not impossible, to obtain in ongoing organizations.

Random assignment is hard to obtain because people and organizational units want to have a say in how they are treated, and indeed some psychologists argue that they should have a say (Argyris, 1971). This is both an ethical issue of informed consent and a practical issue of what people are willing to accept simply because someone says it will be so.

It is also unclear in many cases whether individual or organizational units should be randomly assigned. In many cases, it probably should be organizational units, since the changes affect whole units in a similar manner, but there often are too few of them. In addition, management for its own reasons frequently favors doing experiments in particular parts of the organization and as a result is not willing to accept random assignment.

Control groups are often difficult to set up in organizations because few have units that are comparable in relevant ways. Different parts of organizations and different organizations always seem to differ in important ways, even though they exist in the same environment and have the same purpose. It is virtually impossible to impose comparability just for the purpose of having a control group and an experimental group which differ in only one respect. Such an intrusion into an organization would be hard to justify in terms of either an improved quality of work life or increased organizational effectiveness.

Finally, even if a control group can be established, it is often contaminated by what is going on in the experimental group because of intraorganization communication. Campbell (1969) suggested several strategies for justifying the establishment and maintenance of a control group; they can work under some conditions, but the basic point remains that the establishment and maintenance of a control group in an organization is a precarious undertaking.

It is not easy to introduce a limited, carefully defined, experimental treatment. The introduction of any change into an ongoing organizational setting is a complex process—so complex that it is difficult to define in advance just how and when the change will be introduced. To a substantial degree, the introduction process has to be modified as it evolves, which means that it can be described only after it has occurred. Similarly, the actual change may have to be modified as the introduction process evolves in order to gain acceptance. Thus, the idea of a carefully predefined intervention with a defined introduction process is usually unrealistic in organizational change research.

The situation is further complicated by the fact that organizational environments are always changing and organizations must change in order to cope with them. Thus, unlike the laboratory where other factors can be controlled, it is hard in a field setting to study the effects of a single change in isolation. In most situations, organizations simply cannot stop introducing change; in addition, the environment is often changing in ways that interfere with the experiment. Thus, the researcher is faced with a series of changes, some planned and others unplanned.

Given the problems of doing traditional experiments in organizations, it seems unlikely that enough can ever be done to fill the large need for information on the effectiveness of different organizational designs and practices. One possible approach is laboratory experiments, since the requirements of a traditional experiment can be met in the laboratory. But they raise real questions of external validity which center on the difficulty of capturing the essence of a complex organization in a laboratory setting. Organizations cannot be simulated easily. This is not to say that laboratory experiments shouldn't be done, but rather that there are enough questions about their external validity that we cannot depend on them. Thus, alternatives to traditional laboratory and field experiments must be developed.

ADAPTIVE EXPERIMENTS

One plausible approach is to do research which recognizes the realities of the field situation yet incorporates some of the key attributes of traditional experimental designs. By taking the right approach to evaluating changes which take place in organizations, researchers often can do just this. These changes may be either naturally occurring or introduced as part of the experiment. The crucial research issues do not involve the source of the change, but which measures are taken and how they are analyzed. By establishing a broad measurement net and a control or comparison group or groups before the change is introduced, much can be learned.

Perhaps the best term for describing the type of experiments suggested here is *adaptive*: they are adaptive in the sense that although data gathering begins before the change is introduced, the final form is likely to be known only after the change has been completed and all the data have been collected. Adaptive experiments are not substitutes for traditional experiments as far as assessing causality is concerned. But they are a definite improvement over static, one-time correlational studies. They typically make it possible to rule out certain spurious causes for the existence of a relationship that cannot be ruled out with a correlational study. Adaptive experiments fit what Campbell and Stanley (1966) call the nonequivalent control group design which they classify as quasi-experimental. This involves before and after measures, a control group and nonrandom assignment of subjects.

Campbell and Stanley (1966) make the point that this is a preferred design in many ways and one that in many field situations is superior to the pure experimental designs because of greater external validity. It does a good job of controlling for the effects of history, maturation, testing, instrumentation regression (one of the groups picked because it is extreme), and mortality. All of these can be dismissed as causes of any changes in the experimental group because of the existence of the comparison or control group. This is important because organizational researchers often are apologetic for their inability to do traditional experiments. They need not be, for adaptive experiments can do many of the same things and they fit better with the realities of organizational life.

Because they lack random assignment, adaptive experiments cannot do everything a true experiment can. The possibility cannot be ruled out that the change had the effects it did because of some characteristic of the particular population or situation where it was carried out. This problem can be dealt with to some extent if it can be demonstrated that the experimental and control groups are comparable on such things as age, education, production, etc. even though they were not randomly selected. It is also difficult to rule out the possibility that a third variable caused the change. But if a good job is done of monitoring changes in possible third variables (e.g., changes in pay during a job design experiment) it is possible to rule out many potential third variables and thus increase the possibility that the intervention is responsible for the change. In effect, all third variables that change in ways that do not fit the change in the dependent variable can be ruled out, as can all those that do not change at all (Vroom, 1966).

The key to any adaptive experiment lies in skillful application of the measurement package before the change is introduced, so that it will be in place to "capture" the change and its effects. An ideal measurement package should have five characteristics: (1) it should be longitudinal, usually covering several years; (2) it should cover all parts of the organization where the change will be implemented, as well as some other roughly comparable areas where it is expected the change will not be introduced; (3) it should involve a broad range of economic and behavioral measures; (4) it should be performed by an individual who is not actively involved in the change process; and (5) it should incorporate measures which will specify the nature of the changes as it evolves and suggest hypotheses about the effects of the change. Because of the crucial importance of measurement, the remainder of this article considers each of these five elements which need to be built into measurement packages for adaptive experiments.

LONGITUDINAL

The limited amount of longitudinal research which has been done in OB suggests that a number of the outcomes from organizational change efforts appear considerably after the introduction of the change, as Likert (1961) pointed out. Apparently, changes directed toward improving the quality of work life first impact on organizational process, employee satisfaction, and motivation. These in turn affect such things as absenteeism, turnover, quality of decision making, employee skill levels, and product quality.

These factors in turn influence costs, but often their influence is not immediate or direct, and thus the impact on costs and therefore profit is delayed. For example, changes in job design seem to affect job satisfaction and absenteeism almost immediately. But their impact on turnover often does not appear for six or more months, and their impact on operating costs may not appear for a year or longer. This delay occurs since savings from absenteeism come from being able to reduce the number of extra employees who are hired to fill in for absentees, and this cannot be done until it is clear that absenteeism has been reduced permanently. The situation is further complicated because the time lag between the actual change and changes in the measures of organizational effectiveness may not be the same for all measures. The only solution seems to be to collect data for a considerable period of time after the change has been introduced.

CONTROL OR COMPARISON GROUPS

It is always desirable to compare changes in the experimental situation with those in a similar situation where no such change has been attempted, so as to determine what improvements or problems in the experimental situation may have been due to factors other than the change effort. But this may not be possible because similar situations are not available. Like random assignment, it is highly desirable but difficult to obtain in field settings. Still it often can be approximated if data are collected on a variety of sites, some of which are not expected to be changed. If this turns out to be true, then they can be treated as comparison sites. Where no obvious comparable sites exist, all that can be done is to collect data everywhere that the change is expected to impact and wait to see if it does impact everywhere. If it does not, then a post hoc comparison group can be established. If it does impact everywhere, then an effort should be made to find an area where no change has occurred or a group that has been less affected by the change.

Lawler, Hackman, and Kaufman (1973) successfully used one approach to establishing a post hoc control group. In their job redesign study, the employees changed their jobs only half time; the researchers compared subjects' attitudes during the two different periods, so that the subjects served as their own control. If no post hoc control group can be established, the study must be interpreted as an interrupted time series design. As Campbell and Stanley (1966) point out, even though this design is inferior to the noncomparable control group design, it can yield useful data.

TYPES OF MEASURES

The comparisons required by adaptive experiments can be done only if comprehensive standardized measures are used in all situations. Without standardization, valid comparisons cannot be made among groups. Without comprehensive measures, the crucial change areas may be missed. Figure 1 shows one view of the causes of organizational effectiveness and quality of work life and illustrates some areas that need to be measured. The characteristics of individuals combine with the characteristics of the work

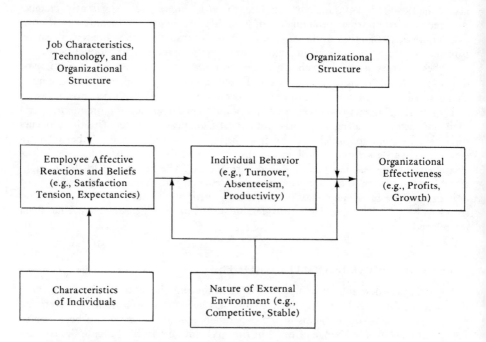

FIGURE 1   Model of the Determinants of Organizational Effectiveness

environment to produce attitudes and beliefs. Job, technology, and organizational structure are the crucial aspects of the environment. In turn, organizational effectiveness is a function of the combined behavior of individuals as modified by the kind of organization structure and control system that is used to coordinate their behaviors. The external environment is an important influence on both the kind of behavior which results from attitudes and the effectiveness of organizations. This model argues that six different kinds of variables need to be measured. Much is known about how to measure some variables, but in other areas little is known. A brief review of the state of measurement in each area will illustrate this point and introduce the kind of measures available.

Characteristics of Individuals

Relatively speaking, a great deal is known about measuring the characteristics of individuals, particularly with respect to what individuals can do. Standardized tests have been shown to predict behavior. Less is known about how to measure aspects of individuals' willingness to perform a job once they accept it (Ghiselli, 1966). Such qualities as motivation and personality are difficult to measure, but useful measures of need strength do exist (Hackman and Lawler, 1971). The Human Resource Accounting approach represents one attempt to quantify the characteristics of individuals—a promising approach, but not of proven utility (Flamholtz, 1974; Rhode and Lawler, 1973). At this time, the best approach is to measure those things which have been shown by previous research to affect the reactions of employees to different management practices and organization designs. Essentially this means measuring individuals' demographic characteristics, some personality characteristics (e.g., self-esteem), and the strength of employees' desires for such things as pay, autonomy, and interesting work.

Job, Technology, and Organization Structure

Some work has been done on measuring the characteristics of the individual's work situation. An adequate assessment of the work situation should include examination of the nature of the technology, design of jobs, and structure of the organization. An adequate measure of technology should look at issues of work flow, adequacy of standards, type of technology, degree of technological development, and appropriateness of technology. Because little OB work has been done on how to measure technology, the researcher who wishes to measure it must do a considerable amount of development work first.

Significant advances have been made in looking at job characteristics from the point of view of their potential impact on the person (Hackman and Lawler, 1971; Hackman and Oldham, 1975; Jenkins et al., 1975). Much effort in sociology has gone into measuring the structural characteristics of organizations. Reasonably good measures exist for such factors as degree of bureaucracy and how the organization is shaped (Price, 1972). Good measures of job and organization structure as well as technology must be used in adaptive experiments, because they are often the major things that are altered in planned change programs. Unless they are measured accurately, it is difficult to identify exactly how the functioning of the organization has changed as a result of a change effort.

Attitudes and Beliefs

Thousands of questionnaire and interview forms have been used to try to measure employee attitudes and beliefs. An infinity of questionnaire items are available for use in assessing attitudinal change. But no questionnaire is comprehensive in the sense that it measures all attitudes and beliefs likely to be affected by membership in an organization. Attitudes concerned with individual, group, intergroup, and organization level factors need to be treated. We need to know how individuals feel about things such as their pay and jobs, as well as their work group and how the organization as a whole functions and deals with them. Measures which look at all of these and which can be used in a number of sites are needed.

Individual Behavior

Performance is difficult to measure at the individual level because objective indicators frequently are not present. It is almost impossible to develop standardized measures that can be used in all sites. But standardized measures of accidents, absenteeism, turnover, and tardiness can and need to be developed. There is little agreement on what these terms mean. In the literature, one person's tardiness is another's absenteeism. As a recent paper points out, it is possible and necessary to move toward greater agreement (Macy and Mirvis, 1976).

Also missing are well-developed methods to evaluate the costs of individual behavior. Results of recent work in this field are encouraging (Macy and Mirvis, 1976). It appears possible through cost accounting techniques to measure the costs of such counter-productive behaviors as absenteeism, turnover, and tardiness in dollar terms. Further developments here are important in assessing the impact of different job designs and management styles, since these are factors that they affect directly.

Organizational Effectiveness

Organizational performance is normally measured quite well with respect to financial indicators. Such data provide a readily available but incomplete criterion for assessment. They are incomplete in the sense that they fail to measure the total effect of organizations on the communities in which they operate, or on their employees. Some have suggested that organizations do social accounting (Dierkes and Bauer, 1973) in order to measure their full impact. Development of a generally applied social accounting system would help in efforts to evaluate different organizational designs and management practices. Unfortunately it is not yet developed well enough to be used. Thus, research must focus on traditional measures of organizational effectiveness and on a broad array of measures which tap the impact of the organization on the individual (e.g., satisfaction, turnover, accidents).

External Environment

Considerable evidence shows that the nature of the external environment influences how effective different organization structures are and how individuals react to new organization designs. For example, the labor market has a strong influence on employee reactions to feelings of job dissatisfaction; when jobs are plentiful, they are more likely to quit. The cultural environment influences employee reaction to participative decision making practices and enriched jobs. Other studies show that market factors such as stability and competitiveness influence the effectiveness of different organization stuctures (Lawrence and Lorsch, 1967).

Finally, unions and collective bargaining influence what changes can be initiated and how successful they will be. Certain changes in management practices and organization design may affect the nature of the union and the union-management relationship; thus they must be viewed as factors which may be altered, just like profits, individual behavior, and individuals' attitudes. In some areas there are readily available measures (e.g., labor market), but in others such as the nature of the union and the union-management relationship, work needs to be done to develop appropriate measures.

Overview—Types of Measures

No discipline or set of disciplines has all the measures needed to assess organizational change. Measures suggested by Figure 1 draw upon engineering, accounting, economics, sociology, and psychology. Thus the measures of organizations used in adaptive experiments need to be done by interdisciplinary teams or at least to draw upon the products of such teams, and a rather extensive measurement program is needed. It is not practical in most studies to collect all the measures suggested by Figure 1; the cost is too great. But it represents an ideal, which can be used to test the breadth of measurement in future studies.

Planned change efforts often involve multiple changes and almost all changes affect multiple outcomes. In the end only part of the data collected may need to be analyzed. In some ways, this is inefficient since it involves collecting more data than are "needed." But at the beginning of the study it is often impossible to specify what data are needed, so the only safe approach is to collect enough data that the design of the study can be adapted to the intervention as it unfolds. To do less is to risk missing the effect of the intervention. As the study progresses, certain measures may be dropped, but at the beginning a broad data collection approach is the only efficient method. This point highlights an important difference between lab experiments—where a careful, limited and defined change can be introduced and the results captured by a few measures—and field situations where this is almost impossible.

THIRD PARTY RESEARCH ROLE

The study of an organization change by a group which is not an active part of the change program offers advantages over a study done by the person(s) doing the change. There is always a credibility problem when the person doing the change reports on its effectiveness. People are particularly suspicious of reports of a large success, and data suggest that this suspicion has a basis in reality. A recent review of evaluation research projects not concerned with organizational problems found that significantly more successes are reported when affiliated researchers (the change agent or a colleague at the same institution) do evaluations than when they are done by a third party with a vested interest in doing the research well and not in the success of the change effort (Gordon and Morse, 1975). But one problem with third party evaluators is that they may be too motivated to find fault.

When a person is engaged in both change and measurement, there is often a conflict between what is good for research and what is good for the change. This can take the form of competing demands for time and energy, or problems about whether particular measures should be collected. Having a separate assessor should improve the quality of evaluation research, by reducing these role conflicts. Gordon and Morse (1975), in their review of evaluation research, found that evaluations done by third parties are better methodologically than those done by affiliated researchers.

Research on new organization practices and designs is often criticized because failures are never reported. The change agent has little reason to report a failure even though others might learn from it, but having a third party involved might stimulate the reporting of failures. Presumably, the assessor would be interested in reporting failures because professional credit would come to him or her as long as the assessment was done well.

Finally, having a third party involved means a different, perhaps more objective, description of what has happened. Organization change efforts often are criticized because they are not described in a way that allows an outsider to understand and replicate the change process. The person doing the change often is in a poor position to assess what a naive outsider needs to know about the effort and to describe it. As a result of personal involvement, the change agent often sees the situation in a quite different light than does the outsider. It is possible to argue about who has the more accurate view of the actual change program—the outsider or the person doing the change—but certainly it would be informative to have *both* their views.

MEASUREMENT OF THE CHANGE

One reality of organizational change is that most interventions change as they are implemented. Although they start out to be one thing, they often end up being another. This means that any adaptive experiment must concentrate on measuring the intervention as it evolves. To some extent this can be captured by questionnaires and more traditional methodologies but there is a risk that these will miss the essence of the intervention. For one thing they are poor at recording the day-to-day events which surround implementation of the change and they often are not broad enough to capture all aspects of the change.

This suggests that it is important to utilize the change agent (if one exists) and to build into the experimental design someone who will act as an observer of the change. Both the change agent and the observer should be charged with writing a history of the change. They should not be limited to simply recording the events around the change, but both should be important sources of insight about what the impact of the change actually is. They can be invaluable in suggesting how the data should be analyzed to best capture the effects of the change, and they can suggest adaptations as the measurement program develops. The observer and the change agent probably will have different views of what changes have occurred, and thus are likely to be complementary rather than overlapping data sources. The role of the observer is particulary important since change agents are notorious for not adequately describing their efforts (Weiss, 1972).

In traditional experiments, describing the change usually is not a problem, but in experiments discussed here, it can be. For one thing, they involve collection of a tremendous amount of data, and help is needed in hypothesis generating when the data are analyzed. They also involve changes which often cannot be specified until after they have occurred. Thus, the expected impact can be specified only after the experiment is over. But it is crucial that this be done, even if it is post hoc; otherwise the experiment will end up as a massive data processing exercise. Finally, many of the changes probably will be unexpected and thus will go undetected if a sensitive observer is not present to record them and to suggest how they may impact on other measures.

SUMMARY AND CONCLUSIONS

A strong case can be made for the vital importance of assessing the relative effectiveness of different management practices and organization designs by studying what happens when they are introduced into organizations. Failure to do this dooms us to repeating the use of ineffective methods and to the slow development of better approaches to organizational design and theory. Although this kind of research does not allow the frequent use of traditional experimental designs, research can be done which allows for assessing causality if adaptive research designs are used. Adaptive research requires a comprehensive set of standardized measures, a number of sites so that meaningful comparisons can be made, a long time period, a third party, and careful assessment of the nature of the change. Research that meets these requirements is feasible and can come to conclusions about causation. It takes a large investment of time and effort, but this investment seems small in comparison to the importance of the questions which can be addressed.

REFERENCES

Argyris, C. *Intervention Theory and Method*. Reading, Mass.: Addison-Wesley, 1971.

Campbell, D. T. "Reforms as Experiments," *American Psychologist*, Vol. 24 (1969), 409–429.

Campbell, D. T., and J. C. Stanley. *Experimental and Quasi-Experimental Designs for Research*. Chicago: Rand McNally, 1966.

Coch, L., and J. R. P. French. "Overcoming Resistance to Change," *Human Relations*, Vol. 1 (1948), 512–532.

Dierkes, M., and R. A. Bauer (eds.), *Corporate Social Accounting*. New York: Praeger, 1973.

Flamholtz, E. *Human Resource Accounting*. Encino, Calif.: Dickenson, 1974.

Ghiselli, E. E. *The Validity of Occupational Aptitude Tests*. New York: John Wiley and Sons, 1966.

Gordon, G., and E. U. Morse. "Evaluation Research: A Critical Review," in *The Annual Review of Sociology*, Vol. 1 (1975), 339–361.

Hackman, J. R., and E. E. Lawler. "Employee Reactions to Job Characteristics," *Journal of Applied Psychology*, Vol. 55 (1971), 259–286.

Hackman, J. R., and G. R. Oldham. "Development of the Job Diagnostic Survey," *Journal of Applied Psychology*, Vol. 60 (1975), 159–170.

Jenkins, G. D., D. A. Nadler, E. E. Lawler, and C. Cammann. "Standardized Observations: An Approach to Measuring the Nature of Jobs," *Journal of Applied Psychology*, Vol. 60 (1975), 171–180.

Katzell, R. A., and D. Yankelovich. *Work, Productivity, and Job Satisfaction*. New York: Psychological Corporation, 1975.

Lawler, E. E., J. R. Hackman, and S. Kaufman. "Effects of Job Redesign: A Field Experiment," *Journal of Applied Social Psychology*, Vol. 3 (1973), 49–62.

Lawrence, P. R., and J. W. Lorsch. *Organization and Environment*. Boston: Division of Research, Graduate School of Business Administration, Harvard University, 1967.

Likert, R. *New Patterns of Management*. New York: McGraw-Hill, 1961.

Macy B. A., and P. H. Mirvis. "A Methodology for Assessment of Quality of Work Life and Organizational Effectiveness in Behavioral-Economic Terms," *Administrative Science Quarterly*, Vol. 21 (1976), 212–226.

Morse, N., and E. Reimer, "The Experimental Change of a Major Organizational Variable," *Journal of Abnormal and Social Psychology*, Vol. 52 (1956), 120–129.

Price, J. L. *Handbook of Organizational Measurement*. Lexington, Mass.: Heath, 1972.
Rhode, J. G., and E. E. Lawler. "Human Resource Accounting: Accounting Systems of the Future?" in M. Dunnette (ed.), *Work and Nonwork in the Year 2001*. Belmont, Calif.: Wadsworth, 1973.
Vroom, V. H. "A Comparison of Static and Dynamic Correlation Methods in the Study of Organizations," *Organizational Behavior and Human Performance*, Vol. 1 (1966), 55–70.
Weiss, C. H. *Evaluating Action Programs*. Boston: Allyn and Bacon, 1972.

Special Topics in Data Analysis

Discussions of statistical methods of data analysis are generally not found in introductory textbooks on research methodology. With one or two exceptions (e.g., Kerlinger, 1973), most methodology texts, by implication, treat statistics as a separate area of study existing largely independent of strategic choices about how a research problem is to be studied. Although statistics are often referred to in the discussion of various aspects of methodology, it is rarely a topic which receives major attention.

The tendency to neglect statistical issues of data analysis in discussions of research methodology is probably attributable to several factors. First, from a pedagogical standpoint, statistics is often taught as a separate course, frequently in a department other than the one in which the students receive their research training. The intellectual gap that often exists between researchers and statisticians may also compound this separation. To the researcher without extensive training in statistics, statisticians often appear to be distant and interested more in the theoretical questions about statistics than their application to messy research questions.

The way in which researchers have historically been trained may also contribute to the absence of statistical issues in methodology texts. As Lundberg (1976) has noted, training for research in organizational behavior in the past involved an apprenticeship spent in the field doing cases and/or clinical observation. Training for research involved a thorough empirical grounding in one's chosen area of study and it was only after this was completed that questions about research methods and data analysis were raised. Substantive grounding in a field of study appears to have been considered more important than methodological questions of how data were to be analyzed.

Finally, the research process is most often considered a creative act involving the identification of important research questions and the design of appropriate strategies for answering those questions. Considerations of data analysis are clearly secondary in importance. Once a method of study has been devised and data collected, statistical techniques can almost mechanically be applied in answering the research question. The choice of an appropriate statistic requires the guidance of a technician rather than the creativity of a researcher.

As research on organizations has matured, the problems which are commonly addressed have increased in complexity. Although research questions in the past could most often be analyzed within a bivariate framework, the number of variables involved in current research and the complexity of the interactions postulated between variables suggest that simple statistical approaches may no longer be sufficient. The inappropriate application of statistical techniques in data analysis is increasingly being recognized as a problem in research. In a paper in this section, Bakan discusses Type III errors—errors resulting from the inappropriate application of statistical techniques. Some think these errors to be more severe than the Type I and II errors with which researchers usually concern themselves. The importance of data analysis techniques is also reflected in the Cook and Campbell paper (Section 2) on threats to validity in research. While threats to validity in the past were most often confined to discussions of internal and external validity, statistical conclusion validity is currently considered a major area for concern for the researcher.

Inadequate training in the methods of data analysis may prove to be a serious handicap to the researcher. The researcher may often be forced to view complex multivariate research problems within a bivariate analytical framework dictated by his or her knowledge of available statistical techniques. Another problem occurs when the researcher gains familiarity with one or two more powerful statistical techniques. Similar to the problem identified by Kaplan's (1964, p. 28) Iron Law of the Instrument ("give a small boy a hammer, and he will suddenly discover that everything he encounters needs pounding"), the researcher may apply a particular technique to any and all research problems, whether it is appropriate or not. For example, the researcher familiar with factor analysis may find the need to factor analyze all the data that are collected. There are obvious problems associated with the failure to carefully consider various statistical methods of data analysis and choose the method that is most appropriate for a given research question.

The selections in this section discuss several important and often controversial issues in the analysis of data. The paper by Bakan provides a careful review of the use of statistical inference by psychological researchers. He argues that the manner in which researchers commonly apply statistics and interpret the results of their data analyses often constitute a serious misuse of statistical techniques and the logic of inference. Bakan identifies and discusses the more common abuses in the use of statistics in research.

The second paper, by Peters and Champoux, highlights a current controversy in the analysis of organizational research data. As contingency approaches to the study of organizations have become more popular, variables which moderate the relationship between two other variables have been identified and analyzed. Subgroup correlational analysis is the method most often chosen by organizational researchers to analyze the effects of these moderator variables. Peters and Champoux suggest, however, that the appropriateness of this technique is dependent upon the theory underlying the relationships studied. In many cases, subgroup correlational analysis may not provide the information desired by the researcher. Moderated regression analysis is presented in this paper as an alternative method of analyzing the existence of moderator variables. The important point of this article is that the researcher must select the method of analyzing moderator variables that is most appropriate for the research question being studied.

Questions of causality underlie much of the research conducted in organizations. Researchers are frequently interested, for example, in whether a certain behavior on the part of a supervisor will result in predicted responses on the part of subordinates. When survey methods are used in organizational research to test relationships between variables, however, the direction of causality found in the relationships is difficult to detect. The paper by Clegg, Jackson, and Wall and the one by Pfaffenberger present two approaches to the analysis of causal relationships in survey data. Clegg et al. discuss cross-lag panel correlations, an approach particularly suited to longitudinal research. Pfaffenberger focuses on the uses and abuses of path analysis. Both papers present clear explanations of these techniques and their possible application to organizational research. Both papers examine the assumptions underlying the use of these techniques and the possible consequences of violating these assumptions for interpretation of the results.

REFERENCES AND SUGGESTED READING

Cohen, J., and Cohen, P. *Applied Multiple Regression/Correlation Analysis in the Behavioral Sciences*. Hillsdale, N.J.: Lawrence Erlbaum, 1975.

Heise, D. R. *Causal Analysis*. New York: Wiley, 1975.

Kaplan, A. *The Conduct of Inquiry*. San Francisco: Chandler, 1964.

Kerlinger, F. N. *Foundations of Behavioral Research* (2nd ed.). New York: Holt, Rinehart and Winston, 1973.

Kirk, R. E. *Statistical Issues: A Reader for the Behavioral Sciences*. Monterey, Calif.: Brooks/Cole, 1972.

Kish, L. "Some Statistical Problems in Research Design," *American Sociological Review*, 24 (1959), pp. 328–337.

Lundberg, C. C. "Hypothesis Creation in Organizational Behavior Research," *Academy of Management Review*, 1 (1976), 5–12.

Nunnally, J. "The Place of Statistics in Psychology," *Educational and Psychological Measurement*, 20 (1960), 641–650.

Willemsen, E. W. *Understanding Statistical Reasoning*. San Francisco: Freeman, 1974.

Winer, B. J. *Statistical Principles in Experimental Design* (2nd ed.). New York: McGraw-Hill, 1971.

15   The Test of Significance in Psychological Research

David Bakan

That which we might identify as the "crisis of psychology" is closely related to what Hogben (1958) has called the "crisis in statistical theory." The vast majority of investigations which pass for research in the field of psychology today entail the use of statistical tests of significance. Most characteristically, when a psychologist finds a problem he wishes to investigate he converts his intuitions and hypotheses into procedures which will yield a test of significance; and will characteristically allow the result of the test of significance to bear the essential responsibility for the conclusions which he will draw.

The major point of this paper is that the test of significance does not provide the information concerning psychological phenomena characteristically attributed to it; and that, furthermore, a great deal of mischief has been associated with its use. What will be said in this paper is hardly original. It is, in a certain sense, what "everybody knows." To say it "out loud" is, as it were, to assume the role of the child who pointed out that the emperor was really outfitted only in his underwear. Little of that which is contained in this paper is not already available in the literature, and the literature will be cited.

Lest what is being said in this paper be misunderstood, some clarification needs to be made at the outset. It is not a blanket criticism of statistics, mathematics, or, for that matter, even the test of significance when it can be appropriately used. The argument is rather that the test of significance has been carrying too much of the burden of scientific inference. Wise and ingenious investigators can find their way to reasonable conclusions from data because and in spite of their procedures. Too often, however, even wise and ingenious investigators, for varieties of reasons not the least of which are the editorial policies of our major psychological journals, which we will discuss below, tend to credit the test of significance with properties it does not have.

LOGIC OF THE TEST OF SIGNIFICANCE

The test of significance has as its aim obtaining information concerning a characteristic of a *population* which is itself not directly observable, whether for practical or more intrinsic reasons. What is observable is the *sample*. The work assigned to the test of significance is that of aiding in making inferences from the observed sample to the unobserved population.

Source: D. Bakan, "The Test of Significance in Psychological Research," *Psychological Bulletin*, 1966, 66(6), pp. 423–437. Copyright (1966) by the American Psychological Association. Reprinted by permission.

The critical assumption involved in testing significance is that, if the experiment is conducted properly, *the characteristics of the population have a designably determinative influence on samples drawn from it*, that, for example, the mean of a population has a determinative influence on the mean of a sample drawn from it. Thus if P, the population characteristic, has a determinative influence on S, the sample characteristic, then there is some license for making inferences from S to P.

If the determinative influence of P on S could be put in the form of simple logical *implication*, that P implies S, the problem would be quite simple. For then we would have the simple situation: if P implies S, and if S is false, P is false. There are some limited instances in which this logic applies directly in sampling. For example, if the range of values in the population is between 3 and 9 (P), then the range of values in any sample must be between 3 and 9 (S). Should we find a value in a sample of, say, 10, it would mean that S is false; and we could assert that P is false.

It is clear from this, however, that *strictly speaking*, one can only go from the denial of S to the denial of P; and not from the assertion of S to the assertion of P. It is within this context of simple logical implication that the Fisher school of statisticians have made important contributions—and it is extremely important to recognize this as the context.

In contrast, approaches based on the theorem of Bayes (Bakan, 1953, 1956; Edwards, Lindman, and Savage, 1963; Keynes, 1948; Savage, 1954; Schlaifer, 1959) would allow inferences to P from S even when S is not denied, as S adding something to the credibility of P when S is found to be the case. One of the most viable alternatives to the use of the test of significance involves the theorem of Bayes; and the paper by Edwards et al. (1963) is particularly directed to the attention of psychologists for use in psychological research.

The notion of the null hypothesis[1] promoted by Fisher constituted an advance *within this context* of simple logical implication. It allowed experimenters to set up a null hypothesis complementary to the hypothesis that the investigator was interested in, and provided him with a way of positively confirming his hypothesis. Thus, for example, the investigator might have the hypothesis that, say, normals differ from schizophrenics. He would then set up the *null hypothesis* that the means in the population of all normals and all schizophrenics were *equal*. Thus, the rejection of the null hypothesis constituted a way of *asserting* that the means of the populations of normals and schizophrenics *were different*, a completely reasonable device whereby to affirm a logical antecedent.

The model of simple logical implication for making inferences from S to P has another difficulty which the Fisher approach sought to overcome. This is that it is rarely meaningful to set up any simple "P implies S" model for parameters that we are interested in. In the case of the mean, for example, it is rather that P has a determinative influence on the *frequency* of any specific S. But one experiment does not provide many values of S to allow the study of their frequencies. It gives us *only one* value of S. The *sampling distribution* is conceived which specifies the relative frequencies of all possible values of S. Then, with the help of an adopted *level of significance*, we could, *in effect*, say that S was false; that is, any S which fell in a region whose relative theoretical frequency under the null hypothesis was, say, 5% would be *considered* false. If such an S actually occurred, we would be in a position to declare P to be false, still within the model of simple logical implication.

It is important to recognize that one of the essential features of the Fisher approach is what may be called the *once-ness* of the experiment; the inference model takes as critical that the experiment has been conducted *once*. If an S which has a low probability under the null hypothesis actually occurs, it is taken that the null hypothesis is false. As Fisher (1947, p. 14) put it, why should the theoretically rare event under the null hypothesis actually occur to "us"? If it does occur, we take it that the null hypothesis is false. Basic is the idea that "the theoretically unusual does not happen to me."[2] It should be noted that the referent for all probability considerations is neither in the population itself nor the subjective confidence of the investigator. It is rather in a hypothetical population of experiments all conducted in the same manner, but *only one of which is actually conducted*. Thus, of course, the probability of falsely rejecting the null hypothesis if it were true is exactly that value which has been taken as the level of significance. Replication of the experiment vitiates the validity of the inference model, unless the replication itself is taken into account in the model and the probabilities of the model modified accordingly (as is done in various designs which entail replication, where, however, the total experiment, including the replications, is again considered as *one* experiment). According to Fisher (1947), "it is an essential characteristic of experimentation that it is carried out with limited resources [p. 18]." In the Fisher approach, the "limited resources" is not only a making of the best out of a limited situation, but is rather an integral feature of the inference model itself. Lest he be done a complete injustice, it should be pointed out that he did say, "In relation to the test of significance, we may say that a phenomenon is experimentally demonstrable when we know how to conduct an experiment which will rarely fail to give us statistically significant results [1947, p. 14]." However, although Fisher "himself" believes this, it is *not* built into the inference model.[3]

DIFFICULTIES OF THE NULL HYPOTHESIS

As already indicated, research workers in the field of psychology place a heavy burden on the test of significance. Let us consider some of the difficulties associated with the null hypothesis.

1. *The a priori reasons for believing that the null hypothesis is generally false anyway*. One of the common experiences of research workers is the very high frequency with which significant results are obtained with large samples. Some years ago, the author had occasion to run a number of tests of significance on a battery of tests collected on about 60,000 subjects from all over the United States. Every test came out significant. Dividing the cards by such arbitrary criteria as east versus west of the Mississippi River, Maine versus the rest of the country, North versus South, etc., all produced significant differences in means. In some instances, the differences in the sample means were quite small, but nonetheless, the p values were all very low. Nunnally (1960) has reported a similar experience involving correlation coefficients on 700 subjects. Joseph Berkson (1938) made the observation almost 30 years ago in connection with chi-square:

> I believe that an observant statistician who has had any considerable experience with applying the chi-square test repeatedly will agree with my statement that, as a matter of observation, when the numbers in the data are quite large, the P's tend to come out small. Having observed this, and on reflection, I make the following dogmatic statement, referring for illustration to the normal curve: "If the normal curve is fitted to a body of data representing any real observations whatever of quantities in the physical world, then if the number of observations is

extremely large—for instance, on an order of 200,000—the chi-square P will be small beyond any usual limit of significance."

This dogmatic statement is made on the basis of an extrapolation of the observation referred to and can also be defended as a prediction from *a priori* considerations. For we may assume that it is practically certain that any series of real observations does not actually follow a normal curve *with absolute exactitude* in all respects, and no matter how small the discrepancy between the normal curve and the true curve of observations, the chi-square P will be small if the sample has a sufficiently large number of observations in it.

If this be so, then we have something here that is apt to trouble the conscience of a reflective statistician using the chi-square test. For I suppose it would be agreed by statisticians that a large sample is always better than a small sample. If, then, we know in advance the P that will result from an application of a chi-square test to a large sample, there would seem to be no use in doing it on a smaller one. But since the result of the former test is known, it is no test at all [pp. 526–527].

As one group of authors has put it, "in typical applications . . . the null hypothesis . . . is known by all concerned to be false from the outset [Edwards et al., 1963, p. 214]." The fact of the matter is that *there is really no good reason to expect the null hypothesis to be true in any population*. Why should the mean, say, of all scores east of the Mississippi be *identical* to all scores west of the Mississippi? Why should any correlation coefficient be *exactly* .00 in the population? Why should we expect the ratio of males to females to be *exactly* 50:50 in any population? Or why should different drugs have *exactly* the same effect on any population parameter (Smith, 1960)? *A glance at any set of statistics on total populations will quickly confirm the rarity of the null hypothesis in nature.*

The reason why the null hypothesis is characteristically rejected with large samples was made patent by the theoretical work of Neyman and Pearson (1933). The probability of rejecting the null hypothesis is a function of five factors: whether the test is one- or two-tailed, the level of significance, the standard deviation, the amount of deviation from the null hypothesis, *and the number of observations*. The choice of a one- or two-tailed test is the investigator's; the level of significance is also based on the choice of the investigator; the standard deviation is a given of the situation, and is characteristically reasonably well estimated; the deviation from the null hypothesis is what is unknown; and the choice of the number of cases is in psychological work characteristically arbitrary or expeditious. Should there be any deviation from the null hypothesis in the population, *no matter how small*—and we have little doubt but that such a deviation usually exists—a sufficiently large number of observations will lead to the rejection of the null hypothesis. As Nunnally (1960) put it,

> if the null hypothesis is not rejected, it is usually because the N is too small. If enough data are gathered, the hypothesis will generally be rejected. If rejection of the null hypothesis were the real intention in psychological experiments, there usually would be no need to gather data [p. 643].

2. *Type I error and publication practices.* The Type I error is the error of rejecting the null hypothesis when it is indeed true, and its probability is the level of significance. Later in this paper we will discuss the distinction between *sharp* and *loose* null hypotheses. The sharp null hypothesis, which we have been discussing, is an exact value for the null hypothesis as, for example, the difference between population means being precisely zero. A loose null hypothesis is one in which it is conceived of as being *around* null. Sharp null hypotheses, as we have indicated, rarely exist in nature. Assuming that

loose null hypotheses are not rare, and that their testing may make sense under some circumstances, let us consider the role of the publication practices of our journals in their connection.

It is the practice of editors of our psychological journals, receiving many more papers than they can possibly publish, to use the magnitude of the p values reported as one criterion for acceptance or rejection of a study. For example, consider the following statement made by Arthur W. Melton (1962) on completing 12 years as editor of the *Journal of Experimental Psychology*, certainly one of the most prestigious and scientifically meticulous psychological journals. In enumerating the criteria by which articles were evaluated, he said:

> The next step in the assessment of an article involved a judgment with respect to the confidence to be placed in the findings—confidence that the results of the experiment would be repeatable under the conditions described. In editing the *Journal* there has been a strong reluctance to accept and publish results related to the principal concern of the research when those results were significant at the .05 level, whether by one- or two-tailed test. This has not implied a slavish worship of the .01 level, as some critics may have implied. Rather, it reflects a belief that it is the responsibility of the investigator in a science to reveal his effect in such a way that no reasonable man would be in a position to discredit the results by saying that they were the product of the way the ball bounces [pp. 553-554].

His clearly expressed opinion that nonsignificant results should not take up the space of the journals is shared by most editors of psychological journals. It is important to point out that I am not advocating a change in policy in this connection. In the total research enterprise where so much of the load for making inferences concerning the nature of phenomena is carried by the test of significance, the editors can do little else. The point is rather that the situation in regard to publication makes manifest the difficulties in connection with the overemphasis on the test of significance as a principal basis for making inferences.

McNemar (1960) has rightly pointed out that not only do journal editors reject papers in which the results are not significant, but that papers in which significance has not been obtained are not submitted, that investigators select out their significant findings for inclusion in their reports, and that theory-oriented research workers tend to discard data which do not work to confirm their theories. The result of all of this is that "published results are more likely to involve false rejection of null hypotheses than indicated by the stated levels of significance [p. 300]," that is, published results which are significant may well have Type I errors in them far in excess of, say, the 5% which we may allow ourselves.

The suspicion that the Type I error may well be plaguing our literature is given confirmation in an analysis of articles published in the *Journal of Abnormal and Social Psychology* for one complete year (Cohen, 1962). Analyzing 70 studies in which significant results were obtained with respect to the power of the statistical tests used, Cohen found that power, the probability of rejecting the null hypothesis when the null hypothesis was false, was characteristically meager. Theoretically, with such tests, one should not often expect significant results even when the null hypothesis was false. Yet, there they were! Even if deviations from null existed in the relevant populations, the investigations were characteristically not powerful enough to have detected them. This strongly suggests that there is something additional associated with these rejections of the null hypotheses in question. It strongly points to the possibility that the manner in which studies get published is associated with the findings; that *the very publication practices themselves are part and parcel of the probabilistic processes on which we base our conclusions concerning the nature of psychological phenomena.* Our total research enterprise is, at least in part, a kind of scientific roulette, in which the "lucky," or constant player, "wins," that is, gets his paper or papers published. And certainly, going from 5% to 1% does not eliminate the possibility that it is "the way the ball bounces," to use Melton's phrase. It changes the odds in this roulette, but it does not make it less a game of roulette.

The damage to the scientific enterprise is compounded by the fact that the publication of "significant" results tends to stop further investigation. If the publication of papers containing Type I errors tended to foster further investigation so that the psychological phenomena with which we are concerned would be further probed by others, it would not be too bad. But it does not. Quite the contrary. As Lindquist (1940, p. 17) has correctly pointed out, the danger to science of the Type I error is much more serious than the Type II error—for when a Type I error is committed, it has the effect of stopping investigation. A highly significant result appears definitive, as Melton's comments indicate. In the 12 years that he edited the *Journal of Experimental Psychology*, he sought to select papers which were worthy of being placed in the "archives," as he put it. Even the strict repetition of an experiment and not getting significance in the same way does not speak against the result already reported in the literature. For failing to get significance, speaking strictly within the inference model, only means that that experiment is inconclusive; whereas the study already reported in the literature, with a low *p* value, is regarded as conclusive. Thus we tend to place in the archives studies with a relatively high number of Type I errors, or, at any rate, studies which reflect small deviations from null in the respective populations; and we act in such a fashion as to reduce the likelihood of their correction.

PSYCHOLOGIST'S "ADJUSTMENT"
BY MISINTERPRETATION

The psychological literature is filled with misinterpretations of the nature of the test of significance. One may be tempted to attribute this to such things as lack of proper education, the simple fact that humans may err, and the prevailing tendency to take a cookbook approach in which the mathematical and philosophical framework out of which the tests of significance emerge are ignored; that, in other words, these misinterpretations are somehow the result of simple intellectual inadequacy on the part of psychologists. However, such an explanation is hardly tenable. Graduate schools are adamant with respect to statistical education. Any number of psychologists have taken out substantial amounts of time to equip themselves mathematically and philosophically. Psychologists as a group do a great deal of mutual criticism. Editorial reviews prior to publication are carried out with eminent conscientiousness. There is even a substantial literature devoted to various kinds of "misuse" of statistical procedures, to which not a little attention has been paid.

It is rather that the test of significance is profoundly interwoven with other strands of the psychological research enterprise in such a way that it constitutes a critical part of the total cultural-scientific tapestry. To pull out the strand of the test of significance would seem to make the whole tapestry fall apart. In the face of the intrinsic difficulties that the test of significance provides, we rather attempt to make an "adjustment" by attributing to the test of significance characteristics which it does not have, and overlook characteristics that it does have. The difficulty is that the test of significance can, especially when not considered too carefully, do *some* work; for, after all, the results of the test of significance *are* related to the phenomena in which we are interested. One may well ask whether we do not have here, perhaps, an instance of the phenomenon that learning under partial reinforcement is very highly resistant to extinction. Some of these misinterpretations are as follows:

1. *Taking the* p *value as a "measure" of significance.* A common misinterpretation of the test of significance is to regard it as a "measure" of significance. It is interpreted as the answer to the question "How significant is it?" A p value of .05 is thought of as less significant than a p value of .01, and so on. The characteristic practice on the part of psychologists is to compute, say, a t, and then "look up" the significance in the table, taking the p value as a *function of* t, and thereby a "measure" of significance. Indeed, since the p value is inversely related to the magnitude of, say, the difference between means *in the sample*, it can function as a kind of "standard score" measure for a variety of different experiments. Mathematically, the t is actually very similar to a "standard score," entailing a deviation in the numerator, and a function of the variation in the denominator; and the p value is a "function" of t. If this use were explicit, it would perhaps not be too bad. But it must be remembered that this is using the p value as a *statistic descriptive of the sample alone*, and does not automatically give an inference to the population. There is even the practice of using tests of significance in studies of total populations, in which the observations cannot by any stretch of the imagination be thought of as having been randomly selected from any designable population.[4] Using the p value in this way, in which the statistical inference model is even hinted at, is completely indefensible; for the single function of the statistical inference model is making inferences to populations from samples.

The practice of "looking up" the p value for the t, which has even been advocated in some of our statistical handbooks (e.g., Lacey, 1953, p. 117; Underwood, Duncan, Taylor, and Cotton, 1954, p. 129), rather than looking up the t for a given p value, violates the inference model. The inference model is based on the presumption that one *initially* adopts a level of significance as the specification of that probability which is too low to occur to "us," as Fisher has put it, in this one instance, and under the null hypothesis. A purist might speak of the "delicate problem . . . of fudging with a posteriori alpha values [levels of significance. Kaiser, 1960, p. 165]," as though the levels of significance were initially decided upon, but rarely do psychological research workers or editors take the level of significance as other than a "measure."

But taken as a "measure," it is only a measure of the sample. Psychologists often erroneously believe that the p value is "the probability that the results are due to chance," as Wilson (1961, p. 230) has pointed out; that a p value of .05 means that the chances are .95 that the scientific hypothesis is correct, as Bolles (1962) has pointed out; that it is a measure of the power to "predict" the behavior of a population (Underwood et al., 1954, p. 107); and that it is a measure of the "confidence that the results of the experiment would be repeatable under the conditions described," as Melton put it. Unfortunately, none of these interpretations are within the inference model of the test of significance. Some of our statistical handbooks have "allowed" misinterpretation. For example, in discussing the erroneous rhetoric associated with talking of the "probability" of a population parameter (in the inference model there is no probability associated with something which is either true or false), Lindquist (1940) said, "For most practical purposes, the end result is the same as if the 'level of confidence' type of interpretation is employed [p. 14]." Ferguson (1959) wrote, "The .05 and .01 probability levels are descriptive of our degree of confidence [p. 133]." There is little question but that sizable differences, correlations, etc., in *samples*, especially samples of reasonable size, speak more strongly of sizable differences, correlations, etc., in the population; and there is little question but that if there is real and strong effect in the population, it will continue to manifest itself in further sampling. However, these are inferences which *we* may make. They are outside the inference model associated with the test of significance. The p value within the inference model is only the value which we take to be as how improbable an event could be under the null hypothesis, which we judge will not take place to "us," in this one experiment. *It is not a "measure" of the goodness of the other inferences which we might make.* It is an a priori condition that we set up whereby we decide whether or not we will reject the null hypothesis, not a measure of significance.

There is a study in the literature (Rosenthal and Gaito, 1963) which points up sharply the lack of understanding on the part of psychologists of the meaning of the test of significance. The subjects were 9 members of the psychology department faculty, all holding doctoral degrees, and 10 graduate students, at the University of North Dakota; and there is little reason to believe that this group of psychologists was more or less sophisticated than any other. They were asked to rate their degree of belief or confidence in results of hypothetical studies for a variety of p values, and for n's of 10 and 100. That there should be a relationship between the average rated confidence or belief and p value, as they found, is to be expected. What is shocking is that these psychologists indicated substantially greater confidence or belief in results associated with the larger sample size for the same p values! According to the theory, especially as this has been amplified by Neyman and Pearson (1933), the probability of rejecting the null hypothesis for any given deviation from null and p value *increases* as a function of the number of observations. The rejection of the null hypothesis when the number of cases is small speaks for a more dramatic effect in the population; and if the p value is the same, the probability of committing a Type I error remains the same. Thus one can be more confident with a small n than a large n. The question is, how could a group of psychologists be so wrong? I believe that this wrongness is based on the commonly held belief that the p value is a "measure" of degree of confidence. Thus, the reasoning behind such a wrong set of answers by these psychologists may well have been something like this: the p value is a measure of confidence; but a larger number of cases also increases confidence; therefore, for any given p value, the degree of confidence should be higher for the larger n. The wrong conclusion arises from the erroneous character of the first premise, and from the failure to recognize that the p value is a function of sample size for any given deviation from null in the population. The author knows of instances in which editors of very reputable psychological journals have rejected papers in which the p values and n's were small on the grounds that there were not enough observations, clearly demonstrating that the same mode of thought is operating in them. Indeed, rejecting the null hypothesis with a small n is indicative of a strong deviation from null in the population, the mathematics of the test of significance having already taken into account the smallness of the sample. Increasing the n increases the probability of rejecting the null hypothesis; and in these studies rejected for small sample size, that task has already been accomplished. These editors are, of course, in some sense the ultimate "teachers" of the profession; and they have been teaching something which is patently wrong!

2. *Automaticity of inference.* What may be considered to be a dream, fantasy, or ideal in the culture of psychology is that of achieving complete automaticity of inference. The making of inductive generalizations is always somewhat risky. In Fisher's *The Design of Experiments* (1947, p. 4), he made the claim that the methods of induction could be made rigorous, exemplified by the procedures which he was setting forth. This is indeed quite correct in the sense indicated earlier. In a later paper, he made explicit what was strongly hinted at in his earlier writing, that the methods which he proposed constituted a relatively *complete* specification of the process of induction:

> That such a process induction existed and was possible to normal minds, has been understood for centuries; it is only with the recent development of statistical science that an analytic account can now be given, about as satisfying and complete, at least, as that given traditionally of the deductive processes [Fisher, 1955, p. 74].

Psychologists certainly took the procedures associated with the *t* test, *F* test, and so on, in this manner. *Instead* of having to engage in inference themselves, they had but to "run the tests" for the purpose of making inferences, since, as it appeared, the statistical tests were analytic analogues of inductive inference. The "operationist" orientation among psychologists, which recognized the contingency of knowledge on the knowledge-getting operations and advocated their specification, could, it would seem, "operationalize" the inferential processes simply by reporting the details of the statistical analysis! It thus removed the burden of responsibility, the chance of being wrong, the necessity for making inductive inferences, from the shoulders of the investigator and placed them on the tests of significance. The contingency of the conclusion upon the experimenter's decision of the level of significance was managed in two ways. The first, by resting on a kind of social agreement that 5% was good, and 1% better. The second in the manner which has already been discussed, by not making a decision of the level of significance, but only reporting the *p* value as a "result" and a presumably objective "measure" of degree of confidence. But that the probability of getting significance is also contingent upon the number of observations has been handled largely by ignoring it.

A crisis was experienced among psychologists when the matter of the one- versus the two-tailed test came into prominence; for here the contingency of the result of a test of significance on a decision of the investigator was simply too conspicuous to be ignored. An investigator, say, was interested in the difference between two groups on some measure. He collected his data, found that Mean A was greater than Mean B in the sample, and ran the ordinary two-tailed *t* test; and, let us say, it was not significant. Then he bethought himself. The two-tailed test tested against *two* alternatives, that the population Mean A was greater than population Mean B and vice versa. But then, he really wanted to know whether Mean A was greater than Mean B. Thus, he could run a one-tailed test. He did this and found, since the one-tailed test is more powerful, that his difference was now significant.

Now here there was a difficulty. The test of significance is not nearly so automatic an inference process as had been thought. It is manifestly contingent on the decision of the investigator as to whether to run a one- or a two-tailed test. And somehow, making the decision *after* the data were collected and the means computed, seemed like "cheating." How should this be handled? Should there be some central registry in which one registers one's decision to run a one- or two-tailed test before collecting the data? Should one, as one eminent psychologist once suggested to me, send oneself a letter so that the postmark would prove that one had pre-decided to run a one-tailed test? The literature on ways of handling this difficulty has grown quite a bit in the strain to somehow overcome this particular clear contingency of the results of a test of significance on the decision of the investigator. The author will not attempt here to review this literature, except to cite one very competent paper which points up the intrinsic difficulty associated with this problem, the *reductio ad absurdum* to which one comes. Kaiser (1960), early in his paper, distinguished between the *logic* associated with the test of significance and other forms of inference, a distinction which, incidentally, Fisher would hardly have allowed: "The arguments developed in this paper are based on logical considerations in statistical inference. (We do not, of course, suggest that statistical inference is the only basis for scientific inference) [p. 160]." But then, having taken the position that he is going to follow the logic of statistical inference relentlessly, he said (Kaiser's italics): "*we cannot logically make a directional statistical decision or statement when the null hypothesis is rejected on the basis of the direction of the difference in the observed sample means* [p. 161]." One really needs to strike oneself in the head! If Sample Mean A is greater than Sample Mean B, and there is reason to reject the null hypothesis, in what other direction can it reasonably be? What kind of logic is it that leads one to believe that it could be otherwise than that Population Mean A is greater than Population Mean B? We do not know whether Kaiser intended his paper as a *reductio ad absurdum*, but it certainly turned out that way.

The issue of the one- versus the two-tailed test genuinely challenges the presumptive "objectivity" characteristically attributed to the test of significance. On the one hand, it makes patent what was the case under any circumstances (at the least in the choice of level of significance, and the choice of the number of cases in the sample), that the conclusion is contingent upon the decision of the investigator. An astute investigator, who foresaw the results, and who therefore pre-decided to use a one-tailed test, will get one *p* value. The less astute but honorable investigator, who did not foresee the results, would feel obliged to use a two-tailed test, and would get another *p* value. On the other hand, if one decides to be relentlessly logical within the logic of statistical inference, one winds up with the kind of absurdity which we have cited above.

3. *The confusion of induction to the aggregate with induction to the general.* Consider a not atypical investigation of the following sort: A group of, say, 20 normals and a group of, say, 20 schizophrenics are given a test. The tests are scored, and a *t* test is run, and it is found that the means differ significantly at some level of significance, say 1%. What inference can be drawn? As we have already indicated, the investigator could have insured this result by choosing a sufficiently large number of cases. Suppose we overlook this objection, which we can to some extent, by saying that the difference between the means in the population must have been *large enough* to have manifested itself with only 40 cases. But still, what do we know from this? The *only* inference which this allows is that the mean of all normals is different from the mean of all schizophrenics in the populations from which the samples have presumably been drawn at random. (Rarely is the criterion of randomness satisfied. But let us overlook this objection, too.)

The common rhetoric in which such results are discussed is in the form "Schizophrenics differ from normals in such and such ways." The sense that both the reader and the writer have of this rhetoric is that it has been justified by the finding of significance. Yet clearly it does not mean *all* schizophrenics and *all* normals. All that the test of significance justifies is that *measures of central tendency of the aggregates* differ in the populations. The test of significance has *not* addressed itself to anything about the schizophrenia or normality which characterizes *each* member of the respective populations. Now it is certainly possible for an investigator to develop a hypothesis about the nature of schizophrenia *from which he may infer* that there should be differences between the means in the populations; and his finding of a significant difference in the means of his sample would add to the credibility of the former. However, that 1% which he obtained in his study bears only on the means of the populations, and is not a "measure" of the confidence that he may have in his hypothesis concerning the nature of schizophrenia. There are *two* inferences that he must make. One is that of the sample to the population, for which the test of significance is of some use. The other is from his inference concerning the population to his hypothesis concerning the nature of schizophrenia. The *p* value does not bear on this second inference. The psychological literature is filled with assertions which confound these two inferential processes.

Or consider another hardly atypical style of research. Say an experimenter divides 40 subjects at random into two groups of 20 subjects each. One group is assigned to one condition and the other to another condition, perhaps, say, massing and distribution of trials. The subjects are given a learning task, one group under massed conditions, the other under distributed conditions. The experimenter runs a *t* test on the learning measure and again, say, finds that the difference is significant at the 1% level of significance. He may then say in his report, being more careful than the psychologist who was studying the difference between normals and schizophrenics (being more "scientific" than his clinically-interested colleague), that "the mean in the population of learning under massed conditions is lower than the mean in the population of learning under distributed conditions," feeling that he can say this with a good deal of certainty because of his test of significance. But here too (like his clinical colleague) he has made *two* inferences, and not one, and the 1% bears on the one but not the other. The statistical inference model certainly allows him to make his statement for the population, but only for *that* learning task, and the *p* value is appropriate only to that. But the generalization to "massed conditions" and "distributed conditions" beyond that particular learning task is a second inference with respect to which the *p* value is not relevant. The psychological literature is plagued with any number of instances in which the rhetoric indicates that the *p* value does bear on this second inference.

Part of the blame for this confusion can be ascribed to Fisher who, in *The Design of Experiments* (1947, p. 9), suggested that the mathematical methods which he proposed were exhaustive of scientific induction, and that the principles he was advancing were "common to all experimentation." What he failed to see and to say was that after an inference was made concerning a population parameter, *one still needed to engage in induction* to obtain meaningful scientific propositions.

To regard the methods of statistical inference as exhaustive of the inductive inferences called for in experimentation is completely confounding. When the test of significance has been run, the necessity for induction has hardly been completely satisfied. However, the research worker knows this, in some sense, and proceeds, as he should, to make further inductive inferences. He is, however, still ensnarled in his test of significance and the presumption that *it* is the whole of his inductive activity, and thus mistakenly takes a low *p* value for the measure of the validity of his *other* inductions.

The seriousness of this confusion may be seen by again referring back to the Rosenthal and Gaito (1963) study and the remark by Berkson which indicate that research workers believe that a large sample is better than a small sample. We need to refine the rhetoric somewhat. Induction consists in making inferences from the particular to the general. It is certainly the case that as confirming particulars are added, the credibility of the general is increased. However, *the addition of observations to a sample is*, in the context of statistical inference, *not the addition of particulars* but the modification of what is *one particular* in the inference model, the sample aggregate. In the context of statistical inference, it is not necessarily true that "a large sample is better than a small sample." For, as has been already indicated, obtaining a significant result with a small sample suggests a larger deviation from null in the population, and may be considerably more meaningful. Thus more particulars are better than fewer particulars on the making of an inductive inference; but not necessarily a larger sample.

In the marriage of psychological research and statistical inference, psychology brought its own reasons for accepting this confusion, reasons which inhere in the history of psychology. Measurement psychology arises out of two radically different traditions, as has been pointed out by Guilford (1936, pp. 5 ff.) and Cronbach (1957), and the matter of putting them together raised certain difficulties. The one tradition seeks to find propositions concerning the nature of man in *general*—propositions of a general nature, with each *individual a particular* in which the general is manifest. This is the kind of psychology associated with the traditional experimental psychology of Fechner, Ebbinghaus, Wundt, and Titchener. It seeks to find the laws which characterize the "generalized, normal, human, adult mind [Boring, 1950, p. 413]." The research strategy associated with this kind of psychology is straightforwardly inductive. It seeks inductive generalizations which will apply to *every* member of a designated class. A single particular in which a generalization fails forces a rejection of the generalization, calling for either a redefinition of the class to which it applies or a modification of the generalization. The other tradition is the psychology of individual differences, which has its roots more in England and the United States than on the continent. We may recall that when the young American, James McKeen Cattell, who invented the term *mental test*, came to Wundt with his own problem of individual differences, it was regarded by Wundt as *ganz Amerikanisch* (Boring, 1950, p. 324).

The basic datum for an individual-differences approach is not anything that characterizes *each* of two subjects, but the *difference between them*. For this latter tradition, it is the *aggregate* which is of interest, and not the general. One of the most unfortunate characteristics of many studies in psychology, especially in experimental psychology, is that the data are treated as aggregates while the experimenter is trying to infer general propositions. There is hardly an issue of most of the major psychological journals reporting experimentation in which this confusion does not appear several times; and in which the test of significance, which has some value in connection with the study of aggregates, is not interpreted as a measure of the credibility of the general proposition in which the investigator is interested.

The distinction between the aggregate and the general may be illuminated by a small mathematical exercise. The methods of analysis of variance developed by Fisher and his school have become techniques of choice among psychologists. However, at root, the methods of analysis of variance do not deal with that which any two or more subjects may have in common, but consider only *differences between* scores. This is all that is analyzed by analysis of variance. The following identity illustrates this clearly, showing that the original total sum squares, of which everything else in any analysis of variance is simply the partitioning of, is based on the literal difference between each pair of scores (cf. Bakan, 1955). Except for n, it is the only information used from the data:

$$\sum_{i=1}^{n} (X_i - \overline{X})^2 = \frac{1}{2}\left[\frac{(X_1 - X_2)}{1}\right]^2$$

$$+ \frac{2}{3}\left[\frac{(X_1 - X_3) + (X_2 - X_3)}{2}\right]^2 + \cdots$$

$$+ \frac{n-1}{n}\left[\frac{(X_1 - X_n) + \cdots + (X_{n-1} - X_n)}{n-1}\right]^2.$$

Thus, what took place historically in psychology is that instead of attempting to *synthesize* the two traditional approaches to psychological phenomena, which is both possible and desirable, a syncretic combination took place of the methods appropriate to the study of aggregates with the aims of a psychology which sought for general propositions. One of the most overworked terms, which added not a little to the essential confusion, was the term "error," which was a kind of umbrella term for (at the least) variation among scores from different individuals, variation among measurements for the same individual, and variation among samples.

Let us add another historical note. In 1936, Guilford published his well-known *Psychometric Methods*. In this book, which became a kind of "bible" for many psychologists, he made a noble effort at a "Rapprochement of Psychophysical and Test Methods" (p. 9). He observed, quite properly, that mathematical developments in each of the two fields might be of value in the other, that "Both psychophysics and mental testing have rested upon the same fundamental statistical devices [p. 9]." There is no question of the truth of this. However, what he failed to emphasize sufficiently was that mathematics is so abstract that the same mathematics is applicable to rather different fields of investigation without there being any necessary further identity between them. (One would not, for example, argue that business and genetics are essentially the same because the same arithmetic is applicable to market research and in the investigation of the facts of heredity.) A critical point of contact between the two traditions was in connection with scaling in which Cattell's principle that "equally often noticed differences are equal unless always or never noticed [Guilford, 1936, p. 217]" was adopted as a fundamental assumption. The "equally often noticed differences" is, of course, based on aggregates. By means of this assumption, one could collapse the distinction between the two areas of investigation. Indeed, this is not really too bad if one is alert to the fact that *it is* an assumption, one which even has considerable pragmatic value. As a set of techniques whereby data could be analyzed, that is, as a set of techniques whereby one could *describe* one's findings, and then make inductions about the nature of the psychological phenomena, that which Guilford put together in his book was eminently valuable. However, around this time the work of Fisher and his school was coming to the attention of psychologists. It was attractive for several reasons. It offered advice for handling "small samples." It offered a number of eminently ingenious new ways of organizing and extracting information from data. It offered ways by which several variables could be analyzed simultaneously, away from the old notion that one had to keep everything constant and vary only one variable at a time. It showed how the effect of the "interaction" of variables could be assessed. But it also claimed to have mathematized induction! The Fisher approach was thus "bought," and the psychologists got a theory of induction in the bargain, a theory which seemed to exhaust the inductive processes. Whereas the question of the "reliability" of statistics had been a matter of concern for some time before (although frequently very garbled), it had not carried the burden of induction to the degree that it did with the Fisher approach. With the "buying" of the Fisher approach the psychological research worker also bought, and then overused, the test of significance, in the largest sense of the word, of his research efforts.

SHARP AND LOOSE NULL HYPOTHESES

Earlier, a distinction was made between sharp and loose null hypotheses. One of the major difficulties associated with the Fisher approach is the problem presented by sharp null hypotheses; for, as we have already seen, there is reason to believe that the existence of sharp null hypotheses is characteristically unlikely. There have been some efforts to correct for this difficulty by proposing the use of loose null hypotheses; in place of a single point, a region being considered null. Hodges and Lehmann (1954) have proposed a distinction between "statistical significance," which entails the sharp hypothesis, and "material significance," in which one tests the hypothesis of a deviation of a stated amount from the null point instead of the null point itself. Edwards (1950, pp. 30-31) has suggested the notion of "practical significance" in which one takes into account the meaning, in some practical sense, of the magnitude of the deviation from null together with the number of observations which have been involved in getting statistical significance. Binder (1963) has equally argued that a subset of parameters be equated with the null hypothesis. Essentially what has been suggested is that the investigator make some kind of a decision concerning "How much, say, of a difference makes a difference?" The difficulty with this solution, which is certainly a sound one technically, is that in psychological research we do not often have very good grounds for answering this question. This is partly due to the inadequacies of psychological measurement, but mostly due to the fact that the answer to the question of "How much of a difference makes a difference?" is not forthcoming outside of some particular practical context. The question calls forth another question, "How much of a difference makes a difference *for what*?"

DECISIONS VERSUS ASSERTIONS

This brings us to one of the major issues within the field of statistics itself. The problems of the research psychologist do not generally lie within practical contexts. He is rather interested in making assertions concerning psychological functions which have a reasonable amount of credibility associated with them. He is more concerned with "What is the case?" than with "What is wise to do?" (cf. Rozeboom, 1960).

It is here that the decision-theory approach of Neyman, Pearson, and Wald (Neyman, 1937, 1957; Neyman and Pearson, 1933; Wald, 1939, 1950, 1955) becomes relevant. The decision-theory school, still basing itself on some basic notions of the Fisher approach, deviated from it in several respects:

1. In Fisher's inference model, the two alternatives between which one chose on the basis of an experiment were *reject* and *inconclusive*. As he said in *The Design of Experiments* (1947), "the null hypothesis is never proved or established, but is possibly disproved, in the course of experimentation [p. 16]." In the decision-theory approach, the two alternatives are rather *reject* and *accept*.

2. Whereas in the Fisher approach the interpretation of the test of significance critically depends on having one sample from a *hypothetical* population of experiments,

the decision-theory approach conceives of, is applicable to, and is sensible with respect to numerous repetitions of the experiment.

3. The decision-theory approach added the notions of the Type II error (which can be made only if the null hypothesis is accepted) and power as significant features of their model.

4. The decision-theory model gave a significant place to the matter of what is concretely lost if an error is made in the practical context, on the presumption that accept entailed one concrete action, and reject another. It is in these actions and their consequences that there is a basis for deciding on a level of confidence. The Fisher approach has little to say about the consequences.

As it has turned out, the field of application par excellence for the decision-theory approach has been the sampling inspection of mass-produced items. In sampling inspection, the acceptable deviation from null can be specified; both accept and reject are appropriate categories; the alternative courses of action can be clearly specified; there is a definite measure of loss for each possible action; and the choice can be regarded as one of a series of such choices, so that one can minimize the overall loss (cf. Barnard, 1954). Where the aim is only the acquisition of knowledge without regard to a specific practical context, these conditions do not often prevail. Many psychologists who learned about analysis of variance from books such as those by Snedecor (1946) found the examples involving log weights, etc., somewhat annoying. The decision-theory school makes it clear that such practical contexts are not only "examples" given for pedagogical purposes, but actually are essential features of the methods themselves.

The contributions of the decision-theory school essentially revealed the intrinsic nature of the test of significance beyond that seen by Fisher and his colleagues. They demonstrated that the methods associated with the test of significance constitute not an assertion, or an induction, or a conclusion calculus, but a decision- or risk-evaluation calculus. Fisher (1955) has reacted to the decision-theory approach in polemic style, suggesting that its advocates were like "Russians [who] are made familiar with the ideal that research in pure science can and should be geared to technological performance, in the comprehensive organized effort of a five-year plan for the nation." He also suggested an American "ideological" orientation: "In the U.S. also the great importance of organized technology has I think made it easy to confuse the process appropriate for drawing correct conclusions, with those aimed rather at, let us say, speeding production, or saving money [p. 70] ."[5] But perhaps a more reasonable way of looking at this is to regard the decision-theory school to have explicated what was already implicit in the work of the Fisher school.

CONCLUSION

What then is our alternative, if the test of significance is really of such limited appropriateness as has been indicated? At the very least it would appear that we would be much better off if we were to attempt to *estimate* the magnitude of the parameters in the populations; and recognize that we then need to make other inferences concerning the psychological phenomena which may be manifesting themselves in these magnitudes. In terms of a statistical approach which is an alternative, the various methods associated with the theorem of Bayes which was referred to earlier may be appropriate; and the paper by Edwards et al. (1963) and the book by Schlaifer (1959) are good starting points. However, that which is expressed in the theorem of Bayes alludes to the more general process of inducing propositions concerning the nonmanifest (which is what the population is a special instance of) and ascertaining the way in which that which is manifest (which the sample is a special instance of) bears on it. This is what the scientific method has been about for centuries. However, if the reader who might be sympathetic to the considerations set forth in this paper quickly goes out and reads some of the material on the Bayesian approach with the hope that thereby he will find a *new basis for automatic inference*, this paper will have misfired, and he will be disappointed.

That which we have indicated in this paper in connection with the test of significance in psychological research may be taken as an instance of a kind of essential mindlessness in the conduct of research which may be, as the author has suggested elsewhere (Bakan, 1965), related to the presumption of the nonexistence of mind in the subjects of psychological research. Karl Pearson once indicated that higher statistics were only common sense reduced to numerical appreciation. However, that base in common sense must be maintained with vigilance. When we reach a point where our statistical procedures are substitutes instead of aids to thought, and we are led to absurdities, then we must return to the common sense basis. Tukey (1962) has very properly pointed out that statistical procedures may take our attention away from the data, which constitute the ultimate base for any inferences which we might make. Robert Schlaifer (1959, p. 654) has dubbed the error of the misapplication of statistical procedures the "error of the third kind," the most serious error which can be made. Berkson has suggested the use of "the interocular traumatic test, you know what the data mean when the conclusion hits you between the eyes [Edwards et al., 1963, p. 217]." We must overcome the myth that if our treatment of our subject matter is mathematical it is therefore precise and valid. Mathematics can serve to obscure as well as reveal.

Most importantly, we need to get on with the business of generating *psychological* hypotheses and proceed to do investigations and make inferences which bear on them; instead of, as so much of our literature would attest, testing the statistical null hypothesis in any number of contexts in which we have every reason to suppose that it is false in the first place.

NOTES

1. There is some confusion in the literature concerning the meaning of the term *null hypothesis*. Fisher used the term to designate any exact hypothesis that we might be interested in disproving, and "null" was used in the sense of that which is to be nullified (cf., e.g., Berkson, 1942). It has, however, also been used to indicate a parameter of zero (cf., e.g., Lindquist, 1940, p. 15), that the difference between the population means is zero, or the correlation coefficient in the population is zero, the difference in proportions in the population is zero, etc. Since both meanings are usually intended in psychological research, it causes little difficulty.

2. I playfully once conducted the following "experiment": Suppose, I said, that every coin has associated with it a "spirit"; and suppose, furthermore, that if the spirit is implored properly, the coin will veer head or tail as one requests of the spirit. I thus invoked the spirit to make the coin fall head. I threw it once, it came up head. I did it again, it came up head again. I did this six times, and got six heads. Under the null hypothesis the probability of occurrence of six heads is $(\frac{1}{2})^6 = .016$, significant at the 2% level of significance. I have never repeated the experiment. But, then, the logic of the inference model does not really demand that I do! It may be objected that the coin, or my tossing, or even my observation was biased. But I submit that such things were in all likelihood not as involved in the result as corresponding things in most psychological research.

3. Possibly not even this criterion is sound. It may be that a number of statistically significant results which are *borderline* "speak for the null hypothesis rather than against it [Edwards et al., 1963, p. 235]." If the null hypothesis were really false, then with an increase in the number of

instances in which it can be rejected, there should be some substantial proportion of more dramatic rejections rather than borderline rejections.

4. It was decided not to cite any specific studies to exemplify points such as this one. The reader will undoubtedly be able to supply them for himself.

5. For a reply to Fisher, see Pearson (1955).

REFERENCES

Bakan, D. "Learning and the Principle of Inverse Probability," *Psychological Review*, 1953, 60, 360–370.

Bakan, D. "The General and the Aggregate: A Methodological Distinction," *Perceptual and Motor Skills*, 1955, 5, 211–212.

Bakan, D. "Clinical Psychology and Logic," *American Psychologist*, 1956, 11, 655–662.

Bakan, D. "The Mystery-Mastery Complex in Contemporary Psychology," *American Psychologist*, 1965, 20, 186–191.

Barnard, G. A. "Sampling Inspection and Statistical Decisions," *Journal of the Royal Statisical Society* (B), 1954, 16, 151–165.

Berkson, J. "Some Difficulties of Interpretation Encountered in the Application of the Chi-square Test," *Journal of the American Statistical Association*, 1938, 33, 526–542.

Berkson, J. "Tests of Significance Considered as Evidence," *Journal of the American Statistical Association*, 1942, 37, 325–335.

Binder, A. "Further Considerations on Testing the Null Hypothesis and the Strategy and Tactics of Investigating Theoretical Models," *Psychological Review*, 1963, 70, 101–109.

Bolles, R. C. "The Difference Between Statistical Hypotheses and Scientific Hypotheses," *Psychological Reports*, 1962, 11, 639–645.

Boring, E. G. *A History of Experimental Psychology*. (2nd ed.) New York: Appleton-Century-Crofts, 1950.

Cohen, J. "The Statistical Power of Abnormal-social Psychological Research: A Review," *Journal of Abnormal and Social Psychology*, 1962, 65, 145–153.

Cronbach, L. J. "The Two Disciplines of Scientific Psychology, *American Psychologist*, 1957, 12, 671–684.

Edwards, A. L. *Experimental Design in Psychological Research*. New York: Rinehart, 1950.

Edwards, W., Lindman, H., and Savage, L. J. "Bayesian Statistical Inference for Psychological Research," *Psychological Review*, 1963, 70, 193–242.

Ferguson, L. *Statistical Analysis in Psychology and Education*. New York: McGraw-Hill, 1959.

Fisher, R. A. *The Design of Experiments*. (4th ed.) Edinburgh: Oliver & Boyd, 1947.

Fisher, R. A. "Statistical Methods and Scientific Induction," *Journal of the Royal Statistical Society* (B), 1955, 17, 69–78.

Guilford, J. P. *Psychometric Methods*. New York: McGraw-Hill, 1936.

Hodges, J. L., and Lehman, E. L. "Testing the Approximate Validity of Statistical Hypotheses," *Journal of the Royal Statistical Society* (B), 1954, 16, 261–268.

Hogben, L. *The Relationship of Probability, Credibility and Error: An Examination of the Contemporary Crisis in Statistical Theory From a Behaviourist Viewpoint*. New York: Norton, 1958.

Kaiser, H. F. "Directional Statistical Decision," *Psychological Review*, 1960, 67, 160–167.

Keynes, J. M. *A Treatise on Probability*. London: Macmillan, 1948.

Lacey, O. L. *Statistical Methods in Experimentation*. New York: Macmillan, 1953.

Lindquist, E. F. *Statistical Analysis in Educational Research*. Boston: Houghton Mifflin, 1940.

McNemar, Q. "At Random: Sense and Nonsense," *American Psychologist*, 1960, 15, 295–300.

Melton, A. W. Editorial, *Journal of Experimental Psychology*, 1962, 64, 553–557.

Neyman, J. "Outline of a Theory of Statistical Estimation Based on the Classical Theory of Probability," *Philosophical Transactions of the Royal Society* (A), 1937, 236, 333–380.

Neyman, J. "Inductive Behavior as a Basic Concept of Philosophy of Science," *Review of the Mathematical Statistics Institute*, 1957, 25, 7–22.

Neyman, J., and Pearson, E. S. "On the Problem of the Most Efficient Tests of Statistical Hypotheses," *Philosophical Transactions of the Royal Society* (A), 1933, 231, 289–337.

Nunnally, J. "The Place of Statistics in Psychology," *Education and Psychological Measurement*, 1960, 20, 641–650.

Pearson, E. S. "Statistical Concepts in Their Relation to Reality," *Journal of the Royal Statistical Society* (B), 1955, 17, 204–207.

Rosenthal, R., and Gaito, J. "The Interpretation of Levels of Significance by Psychological Researchers," *Journal of Psychology*, 1963, 55, 33–38.

Rozeboom, W. W. "The Fallacy of the Null-Hypothesis Significance Test," *Psychological Bulletin*, 1960, 57, 416–428.

Savage, L. J. *The Foundations of Statistics*. New York: Wiley, 1954.

Schlaifer, R. *Probability and Statistics for Business Decisions*. New York: McGraw-Hill, 1959.

Smith, C. A. B. Review of N. T. J. Bailey, *Statistical Methods in Biology. Applied Statistics*, 1960, 9, 64–66.

Snedecor, G. W. *Statistical Methods*. (4th ed.; orig. publ. 1937) Ames, Iowa: Iowa State College Press, 1946.

Tukey, J. W. "The Future of Data Analysis," *Annals of Mathematical Statistics*, 1962, 33, 1–67.

Underwood, B. J., Duncan, C. P., Taylor, J. A., and Cotton, J. W. *Elementary Statistics*. New York: Appleton-Century-Crofts, 1954.

Wald, A. "Contributions to the Theory of Statistical Estimation and Testing Hypotheses," *Annals of Mathematical Statistics*, 1939, 10, 299–326.

Wald, A. *Statistical Decision Functions*. New York: Wiley, 1950.

Wald, A. *Selected Papers in Statistics and Probability*. New York: McGraw-Hill, 1955.

Wilson, K. V. "Subjectivist Statistics for the Current Crisis," *Contemporary Psychology*, 1961, 6, 229–231.

16 The Role and Analysis of Moderator Variables in Organizational Research*

William S. Peters
Joseph E. Champoux

As evidenced by a review of journals which publish organizational research, moderator variables are being incorporated more frequently in data analysis. The long line of research dealing with different responses to characteristics of jobs due to differences in personal and organizational variables is probably the most notable (Adams, Laker, and Hulin, 1977; Brief and Aldag, 1975; Dunham, 1977; Hackman and Lawler, 1971;

*This article was written especially for this book.

Hackman and Oldham, 1976; Hulin and Blood, 1968; O'Reilly, 1977; Robey, 1974; Sims and Szilagyi, 1976; Steers and Spencer, 1977; Stone, 1975, 1976; Turner and Lawrence, 1965; Umstot, Bell, and Mitchell, 1976; Wanous, 1974). Other examples can be found in the studies of the moderating effect of organizational and personal characteristics on employee attitudes, stress, tension, role ambiguity, and role conflict (Arvey, Dewhirst, and Boling, 1976; Beehr, Walsh, and Taber, 1976; Herman, Dunham, and Hulin, 1975; Herman and Hulin, 1972; Johnson and Stinson, 1975; O'Connell and Cummings, 1976; Organ, 1975; Schuler, 1977a, 1977b, 1977c; Siegel and Ruh, 1973).

The term *moderator variable* was apparently coined by Saunders (1956). Though he did not provide an explicit definition of the term, it appeared to be referring to conditions under "which the predictive validity of some psychological measure varies systematically in accord with some other independent psychological variable" (p. 209).

Zedeck (1971) has described the analytical procedures for moderator variables as falling into three major categories. The first category referred to the search for different validity coefficients (correlations) between a predictor and criterion variable within different subgroups of individuals formed from the moderator variable. The moderator variable could be either qualitative or quantitative. Subgroups are formed either by the categories of the qualitative variable, or by partitioning the quantitative variable. Correlations are computed between the predictor and criterion variable within each subgroup. If they differ significantly from each other, a moderating influence is said to exist. An example from the recent organizational literature is the study by Siegel and Ruh (1973). They found a moderating effect of community size on the correlation between job involvement and participation in decision making. The correlation was significantly higher for individuals from large communities than for those from small communities.

The second use of moderator variable was found in studies focusing on the differential predictability of individuals. In this use, one searches for a third variable which will predict whether individual observations will lie close to or far from the regression line for the relationship between the predictor and criterion variables. Ghiselli was the first to develop procedures for finding differences in accuracy of prediction (1956, 1960a, 1960b, 1963). More recently, there have been extensions of his work as well as discussions of the pitfalls in using his procedures (Abrahams and Alf, 1972a, 1972b; Dunnette, 1972; Ghiselli, 1972; Hobart and Dunnette, 1967; Pinder, 1973).

The third category contained what Zedeck called the *moderated regression techniques.* These techniques use multiple regression equations incorporating the predictor, criterion, and moderator variables. The use of this technique does not require the subgrouping of individuals on the moderator variable. Several regression equations are calculated and statistically compared to determine whether the hypothesized moderating effect on the predictor-criterion relationship occurred.

Two observations may be made from the above discussion. First, there appears to be some semantic confusion in the use of the term *moderator.* It has been used in the literature to describe variables from which subgroups of individuals are formed within which an investigator may find different predictor-criterion validities. It also describes the use of variables that identify individuals who differ in predictive accuracy with respect to some predictor variable. Finally, the term applies to continuous variables used in moderated regression equations to improve the predictive effectiveness of a predictor variable.

The second observation is that the treatment of moderator variables has been primarily in the context of validity. This was true of both Saunders's original description of the moderator variable and Zedeck's review of moderator variables (Saunders, 1956; Zedeck, 1971). The validity context was especially true of Zedeck's description of moderated regression techniques and we feel this has led to some confusion in their application and interpretation (Peters and Champoux, 1977).

In many instances, investigators may be interested in using moderator variables to examine their "interaction" with independent variables in determining levels of a dependent variable. Interaction refers to differences in the form and degree of relationship between two variables due to a third variable (Cohen and Cohen, 1975). For example, an investigator may be interested in the relationship between job attitudes (y) and ethnicity (x) as moderated by age (z). In analysis of variance terms, the investigator is interested in the interaction of ethnicity and age ($x \times z$) as a determinant of different *levels* of job attitudes. Note that the investigator is interested in different attitude response levels and *not* different correlations between job attitudes and ethnicity.

In the following we take the position that many investigators are interested in using moderator variables to find interactions. These moderator variables may be continuous quantitative variables as well as categorical variables such as sex, ethnicity, or residency. We shall show that serious errors may be made by the investigator who approaches his analysis of continuous moderator variables with subgroup analyses similar to those described earlier. Furthermore, we shall show that through the formulation of appropriate multiple regression models, the investigator can readily accommodate different types of moderator variables and in increasing complexity.

THE GENERAL LINEAR MODEL
AND MODERATED REGRESSION

We have argued that many investigators may be concerned with moderator variables in the analysis of variance sense of interaction. It may be tempting, therefore, to incorporate such moderator variables into conventional analysis of variance procedures. It has been shown, however, that both multiple regression and analysis of variance are subsumed by the "general linear model" of mathematical statistics (Cohen, 1968; Cohen and Cohen, 1975). Furthermore, the additional power and flexibility of multiple regression argues strongly for treating moderator variables—either qualitative or quantitative—in the context of multiple regression.

In this section we shall illustrate the formulation of moderated regression models and show how to interpret the results of these models. To show how this subject fits in the broader one of linear models, we will carry a single example through several models which are identical to the conventional statistical tests for differences between means and analysis of variance. We then proceed to models that represent conventional multiple regression, subgroups regression, and conventional moderated regression. With this background we then make extensions to more complex moderated regression situations.

Categorical Effects Models

The first set of models we shall examine is designed to handle categorical effects (independent) and moderator variables. Such variables may have natural categories such as sex and ethnicity, or may be formed from continuous variables by partitioning the distribution of values into two or more categories.

Linear Model for Difference between Two Subgroup Means

Consider our data (Table 1) to represent hours of training (x), motivation (z), and task achievement (y) for sixteen randomly selected employees. Should one ask if achievement is different for those with three or more hours of training than for those with one or two hours of training, the usual analysis would be a Student t test for difference between means. The exact equivalent, using a linear model, is achieved by encoding a "dummy" variable (Cohen, 1968) to represent the two levels of training.

TABLE 1   Illustrative Data—Training, Motivation and
Task Achievement for Sixteen Employees

Employee	Training x	Motivation z	Achievement y	(See Equations 1 to 9)			
				x'	z'	xz	xz'
1	1	1	10	0	0	1	0
2	1	2	13	0	0	2	0
3	1	3	16	0	1	3	1
4	1	4	19	0	1	4	1
5	2	1	14	0	0	2	0
6	2	2	18	0	0	4	0
7	2	3	22	0	1	6	2
8	2	4	26	0	1	8	2
9	3	1	18	1	0	3	0
10	3	2	23	1	0	6	0
11	3	3	28	1	1	9	3
12	3	4	33	1	1	12	3
13	4	1	22	1	0	4	0
14	4	2	28	1	0	8	0
15	4	3	34	1	1	12	4
16	4	4	40	1	1	16	4

We let $x' = 0$ for each employee who does *not* have three or more hours of training, and $x' = 1$ for each employee with three or more hours of training.[1] Then, the ordinary least squares regression is calculated as follows:

$$\hat{y} = a + bx'. \tag{1}$$

The results for our data are $y = 17.25 + 11.0x'$, and the ANOVA (analysis of variance) table with F test for significance of the regression is

Source	Sum of Squares	Degrees of Freedom	Mean Square	F
Regression	484	1	484	12.3
Error	551	14	39.4	
Total	1035	15		

The F ratio (484/39.4), with 1 and 14 degrees of freedom, is highly significant ($p < 0.01$). The estimated mean achievement for $x' = 0$ (1 and 2 weeks training) is $a = 17.25$, and for $x' = 1$ (3 and 4 weeks training), mean achievement is $a + b = 28.25$. These are the subgroup sample means, and the F value from the regression ANOVA table is equal to the square of the conventional t statistic for significance of the difference between the subgroup means.

Linear Model for 2 × 2 Analysis of Variance—Additive Effects

An investigator may then be interested in examining differences in task achievement for high and low motivation as well as for high and low training levels. Once again, with appropriate "dummy" variables, the investigator can perform a simple two-way analysis of variance with multiple regression. The linear model is

$$\hat{y} = a + bx' + cz' \qquad (2)$$

where, in our example, $z' = 0$ for $z \leqslant 2$ (low motivation), and $z' = 1$ for $z \geqslant 3$ (high motivation). The results of this regression, produced by any standard regression package, are $y = 12.75 + 11.0x' + 9.0z'$, and the regression ANOVA table:

Source	Sum of Squares	Degrees of Freedom	Mean Square	F
Regression	808	2	404	23.1
Error	227	13	17.5	
Total	1035	15		

The significance of the F statistic indicates that the additive effects model yields significant differences among means. The estimated group means are

Training	Achievement	
	Low ($z' = 0$)	High ($z' = 1$)
Low ($x' = 0$)	$a = 12.75$	$a + c = 21.75$
High ($x' = 1$)	$a + b = 23.75$	$a + b + c = 32.75$

Linear Model for 2 × 2 Analysis of Variance with Interaction

Our investigator might now question whether the effect of high versus low training is the same for employees with high as it is for those with low motivation. Here the investigator is asking whether there is an interaction between training time and motivation in determining levels of task achievement. The linear model now includes an interaction term,

$$\hat{y} = a + bx' + cz' + d(x'z'). \qquad (3)$$

For our data, this regression yields $y = 13.75 + 9x' + 7z' + 4x'z'$. The ANOVA for this regression is

Source	Sum of Squares	Degrees of Freedom	Mean Square	F
Regression	824	3	274.7	15.6
Error	211	12	17.6	
Total	1035	15		

The F statistic is significant, and the estimated means are

	Achievement	
Training	Low ($z' = 0$)	High ($z' = 1$)
Low ($x' = 0$)	$a = 13.75$	$a + c = 20.75$
High ($x' = 1$)	$a + b = 22.75$	$a + b + c + d = 33.75$

The increment in achievement from low to high training at low motivation is $b = 9.0$, while the corresponding effect at high motivation is $b + d = 9.0 + 4.0 = 13.0$. Motivation could be said to moderate the relation between achievement and training, provided our interaction model withstood the significance tests described in the next section.[2]

Incremental Significance of Increasingly Complex Models

While our interaction, or moderator model was judged significant on its own, one should test whether it is a significant *improvement* over the simpler additive effects model. In fact, this kind of test can and should be done for our sequence of three models. The relevant sums of squares are contained in our previous three regression ANOVA tables.

Model	Regression Sum of Squares	Incremental Sum of Squares	Error Sum of Squares
$\hat{y} = a + bx'$	484	484	551
$\hat{y} = a + bx' + cz'$	808	324	227
$\hat{y} = a + bx' + cz' + d(x'z')$	824	16	211

The general form of an F test for the incremental contribution of Model (2) over Model (1), with Model (2) being the more complex model, is

$$F = \frac{(\Delta \text{ Regression SS})/(\Delta \text{ Regression Parameters})}{\text{Mean Squared Error of Model (2)}}$$

Thus, the incremental significance of the two-way additive effects model over the model postulating only training differences is

$$F = \frac{324/1}{227/13} = \frac{324}{17.5} = 18.5,$$

which is highly significant at 1 and 13 degrees of freedom. The incremental significance of the interaction model is

$$F = \frac{16/1}{211/12} = \frac{16}{17.6} = 0.9,$$

and we lack substantial evidence that the more complex moderator model is any better than the simpler additive effects model. In each of our increasingly complex models, there was one more parameter, or regression coefficient to be estimated, and thus one more degree of freedom used to improve the regression sum of squares. In other instances, a more complex model may entail several additional parameters.

Summary and Extensions thus Far

To this point we have:

1. Shown how to apply regression methods to analyze differences among subgroups. The {0, 1} variables that were used are often called "dummy" variables (Cohen, 1968).
2. Introduced the concept of a moderator as equivalent to the analysis of variance term interaction.
3. Introduced the F test for incremental contribution of a more complex model.

Two practical extensions should be noted. The first is that more than two categories of a nominal variable can be handled by the dummy variable technique. As an example, a three-fold classification would be handled by encoding *two* dummy variables, as follows:

Group 1	Group 2	Group 3
$x' = 1$	$x' = 0$	$x' = 0$
$v' = 0$	$v' = 1$	$v' = 0$

A one-way analysis of variance would be done by fitting the equation

$$\hat{y} = a + bx' + dv'.$$

A 2 × 3 analysis of variance with interaction terms would be handled by fitting the least squares equation

$$\hat{y} = a + bx' + dv' + cz' + e(x'z') + f(v'z').$$

By substituting the dummy values for the various subgroups, the estimates for subgroup means can be seen to be

	Group 1	Group 2	Group 3
$z' = 0$	$a + b$	$a + d$	a
$z' = 1$	$a + b + c + e$	$a + d + c + f$	$a + c$

The second extension is to note that a sequence of incremental significance tests can be produced by packaged stepwise regression programs where the order of entry of additional variables can be controlled.

Continuous Effects Models

In the preceding section, both the effects (x) variable and the moderator (z) variable were treated as categorical. In our example, the categories were high and low, although in other data contexts there need not even be a rank connotation. An example would be an ethnic effect moderated by sex. We now consider first, the case where the effects variable is continuous and the moderator discrete, and second, the case where both the effects and moderator variables are continuous.

Linear Models for Categorical Moderator

Where the proposed moderator variable is categorical (or so treated), and the effects variable continuous, the three models of increasing complexity are:

Single effect $\hat{y} = a + bx$ (4)

Additive effects	$\hat{y} = a + bx + cz'$
Moderator model	$\hat{y} = a + bx + cz' + d(xz')$

(5)
(6)

The incremental regression sums of squares from fitting these models to our illustrative data are:

Model	Regression Sum of Squares	Incremental Sum of Squares	Error Sum of Squares
$\hat{y} = 9.0 + 5.5x$	605	605	745
$\hat{y} = 4.5 + 5.5x + 9.0z'$	929	324	106
$\hat{y} = 7.0 + 4.5x + 4.0z' + 2.0(xz')$	949	20	86

The incremental significance of the additive effects model is indicated by the significance of $F = 324/(106/13) = 39.7$, and the lack of incremental significance, in this case, of the moderator model by $F = 20/(86/12) = 2.8$, insignificant at the 0.05 level for 1 and 12 degrees of freedom.

In the additive effects model, a regression of y (achievement) on x (training) with a common slope for both high and low motivation groups is postulated. This can be seen from the regressions expressed as

$$\hat{y} = a + bx, \text{ for } z' = 0$$
$$\hat{y} = (a + c) + bx \text{ for } z' = 1,$$

which differ only as to intercept, or level.

In the moderator model, different regressions are postulated for each subgroup. The estimates of these regressions are:

$$\hat{y} = a + bx, \text{ for } z' = 0$$
$$\hat{y} = (a + c) + (b + d)x, \text{ for } z' = 1.$$

The moderator model says that the way y changes with x is different for the two categories of the moderator variable.

Linear Models for Continuous Moderators

When both the effects (x) and potential moderating (z) variables are continuous measures, the sequence of models we have been illustrating becomes:

Single effect	$\hat{y} = a + bx$
Additive effects	$\hat{y} = a + bx + cz$
Moderator model	$\hat{y} = a + bx + cz + d(xz)$

(7)
(8)
(9)

For our data, these models yield the following:

Model	Regression Sum of Squares	Incremental Sum of Squares	Error Sum of Squares
$\hat{y} = 9.0 + 5.5x$	605	605	745
$\hat{y} = -2.25 + 5.5x + 4.5z$	1010	405	25
$\hat{y} = 4 + 3x + 2z + 1(xz)$	1035	25	0

The F statistic for incremental signficance of the additive effects model is 211, with 1 and 13 degrees of freedom. The moderator model results reveal what the reader may have suspected all along—that we made these data up! We generated the data according to the formula $y = 4 + 3x + 2z + 1(xz)$ and, for simplicity, did not include any error component. An independent investigator would properly discover from an incremental F test that this model fits "infinitely better" than the additive effects model. However, it would not be fair for us to make that test.

The continuous moderator model says that the way y changes with x (the slope of $\hat{y}$ with respect to x) is a continuous function of z. This is emphasized by writing the model as

$$\hat{y} = (a + cz) + (b + dz)x$$

Thus, both the intercept and the slope are linear functions of the moderator variable (z). Figure 1 illustrates this moderating effect in our data by showing the different regressions at $z = 1, 2, 3,$ and 4. While these are the only values for motivation in our data, we can certainly imagine a continuous interval measure and corresponding regression for other values of z in the range $z = 1$ to $z = 4$. Note that when we employed the model with a categorical moderator (high and low motivation) we lost a certain amount of explanatory power compared with taking full account of the interval measure. If a potential moderator is inherently categorical, for example sex, ethnic group, and department, then the categorical moderator model takes full account of the data.

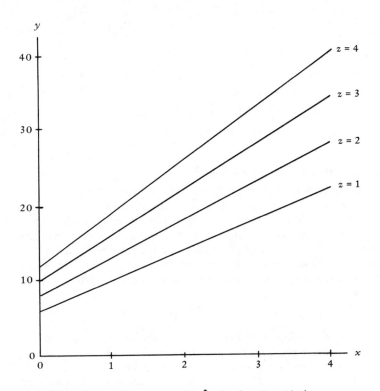

FIGURE 1   The moderated regression $\hat{y} = 4 + 3x + 2z + 1(xz)$

Correlations among Model Variables

The reader may have noticed another peculiarity in our illustrative data. Amount of training (x) and motivation (z) are uncorrelated. To illustrate the consequences of correlation between the effect and moderator variables, we modified the example to obtain the data in Table 2. Here, the distributions of x and z remain the same, and again the y values were determined according to $y = 4 + 3x + 2z + 1(xz)$. However, the correlation between x and z is 0.80 rather than zero. This has no effect on the ability of the continuous moderator model Equation (9) to recover the original formula. Neither does it have any effect on the estimated regression parameters for the categorical (high versus low motivation) moderator model in Equation (6). The reader is encouraged to run these models for both sets of data with a regression package to verify these statements.

TABLE 2   Illustrative Data With x and z Correlated

Employee	Training x	Motivation z	Achievement y
1	1	1	10
2	1	2	13
3	1	1	10
4	1	2	13
5	2	1	14
6	2	2	18
7	2	1	14
8	2	2	18
9	3	3	28
10	3	4	33
11	3	3	28
12	3	4	33
13	4	3	34
14	4	4	40
15	4	3	34
16	4	4	40

Extensions of Continuous Moderator Models

In the continuous moderator model of Equation (9) and Figure 1 there are two elements of linearity. First, the regression of y on x at any level of z is linear. Second, the effect of z on the level of the regressions is linear. One may wish to test a theory that encompasses nonlinearity in either of these respects. Continuing with our illustrative variables, an investigator might well entertain the hypothesis that at any level of motivation, task achievement could be related to training by a second degree, or parabolic equation whose level and average slope depends on motivation level. The model can be seen in the form

$$\hat{y} = a + bx + cz + d(xz) + e(x^2). \tag{10}$$

Thus, the model is Equation (9) with the addition of the variable, x^2, and its coefficient. The slope with respect to x at any level of x and z is $b + 2ex + dz$. A stepwise regression with variables entered in order (alphabetical) of their coefficients in Equation (10) will produce output from which an incremental significance test of Model (10) compared with Model (9) can be made.

Nonlinearity of the effect of z in moderating the regression of y on x is accommodated by

$$\hat{y} = a + bx + cz + d(xz) + f(xz^2). \tag{11}$$

in which the slope with respect to x at any level of x and z is $b + dz + f^2z^2$. If one wants to consider both elements of nonlinearity, one fits the model

$$\hat{y} = a + bx + cz + d(xz) + e(x^2) + f(xz^2). \tag{12}$$

An incremental test of the effect of f in Equation (11) could be made as well as a test of the incremental effects of e and f combined in Equation (12) compared to Equation (9).

Thus far we have considered the moderated model in the context of a regression of y on x as modified by a second explanatory variable, z. The moderator variable can also have an effect on y apart from its moderator (interaction) role. Restatement of Equation (9) as

$$\hat{y} = a + (b + dz)x + cz$$

emphasizes these two effects of z.

Consider now the introduction of a third explanatory variable, v. An example might be pretraining aptitude in the illustration we have been using. The complete model is

$$\hat{y} = a + bx + cz + d(xz) + ev + f(vx) + g(vz) + h(vxz). \tag{13}$$

Interpretation in terms of the xy relation is emphasized by rewriting Equation (13) as

$$\hat{y} = a + [b + dz + fv + h(vz)]x + (c + gv)z + ev.$$

In this model the achievement-training relation is potentially moderated by both motivation (z) and aptitude (v), as well as by the interaction between motivation and aptitude. Further, the separate effect of motivation on achievement is potentially moderated by aptitude, as indicated by the vz interaction. When a model reaches this level of complexity in the absence of strong *a priori* theory, one can let a stepwise regression program select the order of inclusion of variables, discarding elements of the complete model that do not attain significant incremental F levels.[3]

Often a third explanatory variable will be categorical. Examples are sex, ethnicity, and department within a firm. The model formulation is similar to the above. However, there can be several "v" coefficients depending on the number of classes of the categorical variable, and interaction terms will have to be generated involving each of these. The model can be written as

$$\hat{y} = a + \Sigma_i e_i v_i + [b + \Sigma_i f_i v_i]x + [d + \Sigma_i h_i v_i]xz + [c + \Sigma_i g_i v_i]z \tag{14}$$

where $i = 1, 2, \ldots, k - 1$ with k classes of the categorical variable. Equation (14) emphasizes differentials associated with the categorical variable. For example, with k departments in a firm the regression for department k (all $v_i = 0$) is

$$\hat{y} = a + bx + d(xz) + cz,$$

which is the same as Equation (9) discussed earlier. For department 1, $v_i = 1$ and $v_2, v_3, \ldots, v_{k-1} = 0$, and

$$\hat{y}_{i=1} = (a + e_1) + (b + f_1)x + (d + h_1)xz + (c + g_1)z.$$

In general,

$$\hat{y}_i = (a + e_i) + (b + f_i)x + (d + h_i)xz + (c + g_i)z.$$

Again, a stepwise regression program would include only the significant coefficients among b, c, d, and e_i as judged by an incremental F value specified by the investigator. The insignificant coefficients are replaced by zeros in the above expressions.

MODERATED REGRESSION VERSUS SUBGROUPS ANALYSIS

In the introduction to this paper, the three contexts in which the term "moderator" has been used were identified. Two of these are of interest to us in this section.

The first use was in identifying subgroups for which the relation between a predictor and a criterion variable led to different validity (correlation) coefficients. The third use, which has been the focus of the paper, employs multiple regression to show whether and how a third variable moderates the regression between a predictor and criterion variable of interest. In this use, the focus is on regression coefficients indicating the *response* of predicted y to changes in x at different levels of z. In the linear moderator model of Equation (9),

$$\hat{y} = a + (b + dz)x + cz,$$

one would examine the slope coefficients, $b + dz$ for selected values of z. In the parabolic model of Equation (10),

$$\hat{y} = a + (b + dz + ex)x + cz,$$

the slope with respect to x is $b + dz + 2ex$. Here, differences in response of predicted y to changes in x can be examined for selected values of z and x within the range of the data.

The difference in focus between these two uses of the term *moderator* is fairly characterized as *validities* versus *responses*. An investigator should be clear about which of these concepts lies at the heart of his research question.

An example of confusion between differential validities and differential responses has occurred in the studies dealing with the theory of job design set forth by Hackman and Oldham (1976). It seems clear that the theory is couched in regression (response) rather than correlation (validities) terms. For example, Hackman, Oldham, Janson, and Purdy (1975) state

. . . responses to jobs high in motivating potential are more positive for people who have strong growth needs than for people with weak needs for growth. (p. 66)

The statement is accompanied by a graphic illustration that the authors describe as follows:

While both groups of employees show increases in internal motivation as MPS increases, the *rate* of increase is significantly greater for the group of employees who have strong needs for growth. (p. 67)

It appears to us that subgroup analysis with emphasis on differential correlation coefficients among subgroups is not directed at the theory as stated (e.g., Brief and Aldag, 1975; Hackman and Lawler, 1971; Hackman and Oldham, 1976). This is not to say that differential validity is not an important question, but rather to plead for careful statements of the questions to be answered.

In order to obtain differential validities (correlation coefficients), one must deal with subgroups even in the case where the moderator is a continuous variable. Cutoff points of the moderator variable (z) would be established to form the subgroups. Then, the subgroup correlation coefficients would be determined and compared. In the case of linear regression between y and x, the subgroup r's obtained are related to the subgroup slope coefficients of a multiple regression moderator model similar to Equation (6). Where $i = 1, 2, \ldots, k - 1$, and there are k subgroups,

$$\hat{y}_i = (a + c_i) + (b + d_i)x$$
$$\hat{y}_k = a + bx.$$

Now the jth subgroup slope coefficient ($j = 1, 2, \ldots, k$) is

$$P_j = \begin{cases} b + d_i, j = i \\ b \quad\quad , j = k \end{cases}$$

and the jth subgroup correlation coefficient is

$$r_j = P_j \frac{\sigma(x_j)}{\sigma(y_j)} , \tag{15}$$

where $\sigma(x_j)$ and $\sigma(y_j)$ are the standard deviations of x and y respectively in the jth subgroup. Equation (15) embodies the relation that a correlation coefficient is a slope coefficient expressed in standardized units (Neter and Wasserman, 1974, pp. 91–92). It is clear from Equation (15) that the comparative magnitudes of r_j can differ from the slope coefficients, P_j, depending on the ratios of $\sigma(x_j)$ to $\sigma(y_j)$ in the subgroups. This has two consequences. First, in an investigation concerned with validities, it should be realized that the validity measures (r's) can vary depending on the cutoff points used to define subgroups.[4] Second, one should not attempt to answer a question calling for *response* comparisons with comparisons of subgroup correlation coefficients. We believe that discussion of the relative merits of subgroup analysis using r's versus moderated regression analysis (e.g., Zedeck, 1971) has been muddied by an understandable confusion over the different uses of the moderator concept combined with a failure to distinguish clearly between the research goals of validity versus response.

SUMMARY

This paper shows the development of a number of moderated regression models beginning with an elementary model and progressing to models of considerable complexity. The models were presented in the context of the general linear model and with the view that moderator variables may be usefully conceptualized in the analysis of variance sense of interaction.

A comparison was made between subgroup analysis and moderated regression. We also discussed the conditions under which a subgroup analysis is appropriate and the pitfalls that face an investigator who uses this procedure.

NOTES

1. Throughout this paper, primes will be used for categorical variables that have been constructed by combining values of a continuous variable. For illustrating a "dummy variable" regression, we could as well have used sex (male, female) here, a true categorical variable.

2. Equally, training could be said to moderate the relation between achievement and motivation. Usually, the focus of the investigation, or the theory being examined, dictates the point of view.

3. Moderated, of course, by cautions about capitalizing on chance relations in the sample data (Type I error). Confirmation in another study or in a reserved sample of the main study is desirable.

4. For further discussion, see Peters and Champoux, 1977.

REFERENCES

Abrahams, N. M. and Alf, E., Jr. "Pratfalls in Moderator Research," *Journal of Applied Psychology*, 56 (1972), pp. 245-251. (a)

Abrahams, N. M. and Alf, E. Jr. Reply to Dunnette's "Comments on Abrahams and Alf's 'Pratfalls in Moderator Research,'" *Journal of Applied Psychology*, 56 (1972), pp. 257-261. (b)

Adams, E. F., Laker, D. R. and Hulin, C. L. "An Investigation of the Influences of Job Level and Functional Specialty on Job Attitudes and Perceptions," *Journal of Applied Psychology*, 62 (1977), pp. 335-343.

Arvey, R. D., Dewhirst, H. D., and Boling, J. C. "Relationships Between Goal Clarity, Participation in Goal Setting, and Personality Characteristics on Job Satisfaction in a Scientific Organization," *Journal of Applied Psychology*, 61 (1976), pp. 103-105.

Beehr, T. A., Walsh, J. T., and Taber, T. D. "Relationships of Stress to Individually and Organizationally Valued States: Higher Order Needs as a Moderator," *Journal of Applied Psychology*, 61 (1976), pp. 41-47.

Brief, A. P. and Aldag, R. J. "Employee Reactions to Job Characteristics: A Constructive Replication," *Journal of Applied Psychology*, 60 (1975), pp. 182-186.

Cohen, J. "Multiple Regression as a General Data Analytic System," *Psychological Bulletin*, 70 (1968), pp. 426-443.

Cohen, J. and Cohen P. *Applied Multiple Regression/Correlation Analysis for the Behavioral Sciences*. Hillsdale, New Jersey: Lawrence Erlbaum Associates, Publishers, 1975.

Dunham, R. B. "Reactions to Job Characteristics: Moderating Effects of the Organization," *Academy of Management Journal*, 20 (1977), pp. 42-65.

Dunnette, M. D. Comments on Abrahams and Alf's "Pratfalls in Moderator Research," *Journal of Applied Psychology*, 56 (1972), pp. 252-256.

Ghiselli, E. E. "Differentiation of Individuals in Terms of Their Predictability," *Journal of Applied Psychology*, 40 (1956), pp. 374-377.

Ghiselli, E. E. "Differentiation of Tests in Terms of the Accuracy With Which They Predict for a Given Individual," *Educational and Psychological Measurement*, 20 (1960), pp. 675-684. (a)

Ghiselli, E. E. "The Prediction of Predictability," *Educational and Psychological Measurement*, 20 (1960), pp. 3-8. (b)

Ghiselli, E. E. "Moderating Effects and Differential Reliability and Validity," *Journal of Applied Psychology*, 47 (1963), pp. 81-86.

Ghiselli, E. E. "Comment on the Use of Moderator Variables," *Journal of Applied Psychology*, 56 (1972), p. 270.

Hackman, J. R. and Lawler, E. E., III. "Employee Reactions to Job Characteristics," *Journal of Applied Psychology Monograph*, 55 (1971), pp. 259-286.

Hackman, J. R. and Oldham, G. R. "Motivation Through the Design of Work: Test of a Theory," *Organizational Behavior and Human Performance*, 16 (1976), pp. 250-279.

Hackman, J. R., Oldham, G. R., Janson, R., and Purdy, K. "A New Strategy for Job Enrichment," *California Management Review*, 17 (1975), pp. 57-71.

Herman, J. B., Dunham, R. B., and Hulin, C. L. "Organizational Structure, Demographic Characteristics, and Employee Responses," *Organizational Behavior and Human Performance*, 13 (1975), pp. 206-232.

Herman, J. B. and Hulin, C. L. "Studying Organizational Attitudes From Individual and Organizational Frames of Reference," *Organizational Behavior and Human Performance*, 8 (1972), pp. 84-108.

Hobart, R. D. and Dunnette, M. D. "Development of Moderator Variables to Enhance the Prediction of Managerial Effectiveness," *Journal of Applied Psychology*, 51 (1967), pp. 50-64.

Hulin, C. L. and Blood, M. R. "Job Enlargement, Individual Differences, and Worker Responses," *Psychological Bulletin*, 69 (1968), pp. 41-55.

Johnson, T. W. and Stinson, J. E. "Role Ambiguity, Role Conflict, and Satisfaction: Moderating Effects of Individual Differences," *Journal of Applied Psychology*, 60 (1975), pp. 329-333.

Neter, J. and Wasserman, W. *Applied Linear Statistical Models*. Homewood, Illinois: Richard D. Irwin, Inc., 1974.

O'Connell, M. J. and Cummings, L. L. "The Moderating Effect of Environment and Structure on the Satisfaction-tension-influence Network," *Organizational Behavior and Human Performance*, 17 (1976), pp. 350-366.

O'Reilly, C. A. "Personality-job Fit: Implications for Individual Attitudes and Performance," *Organizational Behavior and Human Performance*, 18 (1977), pp. 36-46.

Organ, D. W. "Effects of Pressure and Individual Neuroticism on Emotional Responses to Task-Role Ambiguity," *Journal of Applied Psychology*, 60 (1975), pp. 397-400.

Peters, W. S. and Champoux, J. E. "Moderated Regression in Job Design Research: Some Issues and Answers," *American Institute for Decision Science Proceedings*, Justin D. Stolen and James J. Conway (eds.), October 19-21, 1977.

Pinder, C. C. "Statistical Accuracy and Practical Utility in the Use of Moderator Variables," *Journal of Applied Psychology*, 57 (1973), pp. 214-221.

Robey, D. "Task Design, Work Values, and Worker Response: An Experimental Test," *Organizational Behavior and Human Performance*, 12 (1974), pp. 264-273.

Saunders, D. R. "Moderator Variables in Prediction," *Educational and Psychological Measurement*, 16 (1956), pp. 209-222.

Schuler, R. S. "The Effects of Role Perceptions on Employee Satisfaction and Performance Moderated by Employee Ability," *Organizational Behavior and Human Performance*, 18 (1977), pp. 98-107. (a)

Schuler, R. S. "Role Conflict and Ambiguity as a Function of the Task-structure-technology Interaction," *Organizational Behavior and Human Performance*, 20 (1977), pp. 66-74. (b)

Schuler, R. S. "Role Perceptions, Satisfaction and Performance Moderated by Organization Level and Participation in Decision Making," *Academy of Management Journal*, 20 (1977), pp. 159-165.

Siegel, A. L. and Ruh, R. A. "Job Involvement, Participation in Decision Making, Personal Background and Job Behavior," *Organizational Behavior and Human Performance*, 9 (1973), pp. 318-327.

Sims, H. P. and Szilagyi, A. D. "Job Characteristics Relationships: Individual and Structural Moderators," *Organizational Behavior and Human Performance*, 17 (1976), pp. 211-230.

Steers, R. M. and Spencer, D. G. "The Role of Achievement Motivation in Job Design," *Journal of Applied Psychology*, 62 (1977), pp. 472-479.

Stone, E. F. "Job Scope, Job Satisfaction, and the Protestant Ethic: A Study of Enlisted Men in the U.S. Navy," *Journal of Vocational Behavior*, 7 (1975), pp. 215-234.

Stone, E. F. "The Moderating Effect of Work-related Values on the Job Scope-Job Satisfaction Relationship," *Organizational Behavior and Human Performance*, 15 (1976), pp. 147-167.

Turner, A. N. and Lawrence, P. R. *Industrial Jobs and the Worker*, Boston: Harvard Graduate School of Business Administration, 1965.

Umstot, D. D., Bell, C. H., Jr., and Mitchell, T. R. "Effects of Job Enrichment and Task Goals on Satisfaction and Productivity: Implications for Job Design," *Journal of Applied Psychology*, 61 (1976), pp. 379-394.

Wanous, J. P. "Individual Differences and Reactions to Job Characteristics," *Journal of Applied Psychology*, 59 (1974), pp. 616-622.

Zedeck, S. "Problems With the Use of 'Moderator' Variables," *Psychological Bulletin*, 76 (1971), pp. 295-310.

17   The Potential of Cross-Lagged Correlation Analysis in Field Research

C. W. Clegg
P. R. Jackson
T. D. Wall

The search for causal relationships is central to occupational psychology just as it is to other areas of the discipline. Information about such relationships gives the psychologist a better understanding of work environments. For example he may be interested in whether certain job characteristics are in part responsible for job holders' mental health and well-being; whether orientations to work determine levels of absence; or whether technological complexity has an impact on supervisory style. No matter what the particular focus of interest, both researcher and practitioner are explicitly or implicitly concerned with causality.

When investigating such relationships an initial decision has to be made about the research setting. For many areas of inquiry a field study is especially attractive. Given the objective of understanding individuals in their normal work environment the alternative, laboratory investigation, is often inappropriate since the transfer of a problem to this artificial environment may change its very nature. But, having chosen a field setting the researcher faces constraints over and above those typically encountered in the laboratory. More specifically he cannot exert the same degree of control over the environment and the individuals involved, and this affects his choice of research design and techniques.

A useful way of looking at the field researcher's methodological problems is in terms of *commitment* and *logical interpretability. Commitment* refers to the demand a study makes of the participants. The academic occupational psychologist has no intrinsic right to carry out any particular field project but is reliant on the cooperation of the organization and its employees. As a result, the lower the commitment required of the organization, in terms of risk and disruption to normal working practices, the more likely it is that cooperation will be forthcoming. From a purely pragmatic perspective the pressure is on the researcher to select a methodology which minimizes the costs to the host population. *Logical interpretability*, in contrast, concerns the scientific properties of the methodology chosen. It refers to the extent to which on the basis of research design alone the researcher is justified in drawing causal inferences. One way of conceptualizing this is in terms of "plausible rival hypotheses" (Campbell, 1963). A

Source: C. W. Clegg, P. R. Jackson, and T. D. Wall, "The Potential of Cross-Lagged Correlation Analysis in Field Research," *Journal of Occupational Psychology* 50, 1977, pp. 177–196. Published by Cambridge University Press. Reproduced by permission.

methodology which yields evidence compatible with a large number of plausible explanations is weak, whereas one which restricts the feasible alternatives is stronger.

The situation facing the field researcher is often one of a "trade-off" between commitment and logical interpretability. This is well illustrated by a consideration of three general types of research strategy. By far the most commonly used has been the correlational or cross-sectional approach. One does not have to look far to account for its popularity. It is a pragmatic response to the realities of field research in that it demands the minimum of commitment. Access to the organization and its employees is required on one occasion only and by careful planning can be achieved with little disruption to everyday work. But this advantage of the simple correlational approach is offset by its low logical interpretability: as Simon states (1954, p. 467), "correlation is no proof of causation." A correlation between two variables may signify a causal link in either or both directions or may be attributable to a third factor. We may conclude with Kenny (1975b) that this approach provides a useful start in research but has low interpretability with respect to causal relationships.

The second general approach involves the use of simple longitudinal studies requiring access to the host organization on at least two separate occasions thus making greater demands in terms of commitment. This decrement in acceptability, however, results in some gain in logical interpretability. By obtaining measures of the same variables at different points in time the researcher strengthens the basis from which to draw causal inferences. Not only can he see whether a pattern of cross-sectional relationships is replicated, but he can also look at the association between changes in variables over time. This provides greater control over intra-individual sources of variability in the findings. Nevertheless, the logical interpretability of simple longitudinal studies is not particularly high since observed relationships are still open to a number of alternative explanations (e.g., third factors changing over time and jointly affecting both variables).

The third general approach involves experimental and those quasi-experimental studies which embody the introduction of deliberate change. This feature alone places the approach in an entirely different league from those previously considered since it requires an extremely high level of commitment. In essence the researcher asks the organization not only for access to measure the variables of interest on one, two, or more occasions, but also to intervene more fundamentally in the working lives of the participants. Moreover, the researcher may wish to be involved in the process of change over a considerable period of time. It is in the nature of such research that the outcomes are unknown. Thus it is not surprising that most organizations find the risk too great, with the result that few such studies are undertaken. In contrast to its relatively low acceptability in terms of commitment, the logical interpretability of this form of field experiment is good.

Whilst some commentators express some reservations about experiments in general (e.g., Howard and Krause, 1970), most agree that they enable one to rule out a large number of plausible rival hypotheses. Of course the level of logical interpretability varies from one design to another. That generally regarded as the most powerful is the "true experiment" which "controls for spuriousness by random assignment" (Kenny, 1975b, p. 887)—what Campbell (1963) calls the "magic of randomization" (p. 213). This is often not possible in field settings since a random allocation procedure to different experimental groups may be unacceptable to the participants or undesirable because of other factors such as the availability of skills and experience. Alternative designs, for example those using a group which acts as its own control, or those using nonequivalent control groups, nevertheless provide a strong basis for causal inference.

It is only a slight caricature to say that on the one hand there is the much used correlational approach which is relatively easy to implement in field settings but provides at best only weak evidence concerning causality; and on the other hand there is the experimental approach which is much higher in logical interpretability but demands a level of organizational commitment which it is difficult if not impossible to obtain.

In the light of this, cross-lagged correlation analysis is potentially of immense importance. This technique demands relatively low commitment but at the same time, according to its proponents (e.g. Cook and Campbell, 1976), has high logical interpretability. As such it appears to offer the 'best of both worlds' and thus warrants serious consideration by occupational psychologists with an interest in field research. Furthermore it has other advantages. Being based on natural changes it may be used to explore causal variables which, for practical, logical, or ethical reasons cannot be manipulated and thereby examined within the framework of experiments based on deliberate change. The purpose of this paper is to examine the value of cross-lagged correlation analysis as an addition to the researcher's methodological armory. The scene is set by describing the technique and some assumptions and issues which affect its interpretability. Then its use in occupational psychology is examined with particular reference to the extent to which these assumptions and issues have been explicitly recognized in the interpretation of empirical results. Finally an approach for providing a comprehensive evaluation of the technique is described and some preliminary findings presented.

CROSS-LAGGED CORRELATION ANALYSIS: ITS RATIONALE

The direct ancestor of cross-lagged correlation analysis is the 16-fold table method developed by Lazarsfeld (1948). He was examining the 1940 Presidential election in the United States and was interested in whether the voter's attitudes to a political party determined his opinion of the party leader or vice versa. Campbell (1963) and Pelz and Andrews (1964) independently adapted Lazarsfeld's approach for use with continuous data, using the title of cross-lagged correlation analysis to describe their reformulations.

The rationale behind cross-lagged correlation analysis may be best understood by considering a simple example involving two variables X and Y (as shown in Figure 1). Assume that X causes Y and that Y has no reciprocal influence on X. Assume also that the influence of X on Y takes some time to have an effect; in other words that there is a causal time-lag. By measuring X and Y on two separate occasions (time 1 and time 2) one can derive six correlation coefficients (or other measures of association). The *simultaneous correlations*, those between X and Y at each time period (shown as 1 and 2 in Figure 1) are ordinary cross-sectional measures of association which can be positive or negative and should be of approximately the same magnitude. The *autocorrelations*, those between X at time 1 and X at time 2 and between Y at time 1 and Y at time 2 (shown as 3 and 4 in Figure 1), reflect the consistency of each variable over time. The remaining relationships are the *cross-lagged correlations* between X at time 1 and Y at time 2 and between Y at time 1 and X at time 2 (shown as 5 and 6 in Figure 1). Assuming that the interval between the time periods used corresponds to the "true" causal lag, then the maximum effect of X at time 1 will be evident in Y at time 2. Conversely, Y at time 1 will have little or no effect on X at time 2. Hence one

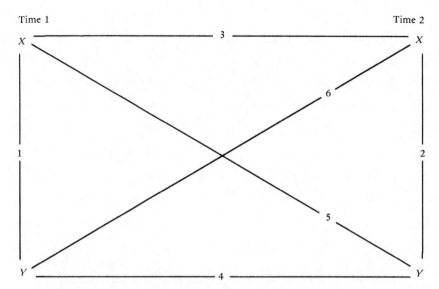

FIGURE 1   Diagrammatic representation of cross-lagged correlation analysis.

would expect correlation 5 to be greater than both correlation 6 and the simultaneous correlations (1 and 2), and correlation 6 to be smaller than the two simultaneous correlations. Thus, under the simple condition of monocausality, cross-lagged correlation analysis predicts the following ordering:

$$r_{X_1 Y_2} > r_{X_1 Y_1} \doteq r_{X_2 Y_2} > r_{Y_1 X_2},$$

which in terms of the numbered relationships in Figure 1 is

$$5 > 1 \doteq 2 > 6.$$

An illustration from the literature serves to put flesh on this rather abstract skeleton. Lawler (1968) was concerned to uncover the nature of the relationship between job performance and reward expectancy attitudes at work. He chose a group of 55 managers for his investigation and measured both variables with a time-lag of one year. Some of his findings are given in Figure 2 where it can be seen the pattern of relationships, as follows, approximates to the expected ordering:

$$0.55 > 0.44 \doteq 0.52 > 0.39$$
$$5 \quad > \quad 1 \quad \doteq \quad 2 \quad > \quad 6.$$

From this analysis (and others, including a test for "third factoredness"—an issue we take up later in the paper) Lawler concluded that "expectancy attitudes can best be thought of as causing performance" (p. 467). In parenthesis it is worth noting that the cross-lagged correlation analysis which encouraged this relatively strong conclusion involved only a small commitment on the part of the participants. Moreover, it is doubtful whether the research question itself could have been explored within an experimental framework since to manipulate subjects' reward expectancies and job performance would raise practical, logical and ethical issues.

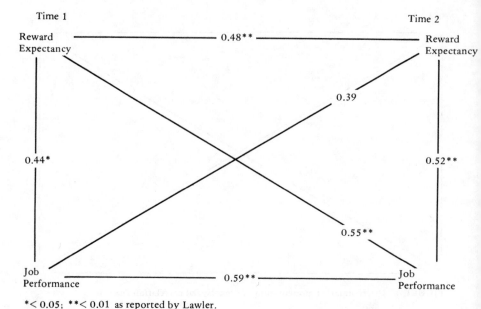

Time 1   Time 2

*< 0.05; **< 0.01 as reported by Lawler.

FIGURE 2   Some cross-lagged correlation analysis results from Lawler (1968) relating reward expectancy attitudes to job performance with a time-lag of one year.

The rationale described above is only a part of the picture in that it has described a monocausal relationship (i.e. where X causes Y and not vice versa). Two other sorts of relationship are also relevant: the first where the two variables are reciprocally related (i.e., where X causes Y and Y causes X), and the second where a third variable causes two variables which are otherwise unrelated (i.e. where C causes both X and Y). The logic of cross-lagged correlation analysis can be used to generate predictions for both types of relationship. In the case of reciprocal causation it would predict:

$$r_{X_1Y_2} \doteq r_{Y_1X_2} > r_{X_1Y_1} \doteq r_{X_2Y_2},$$

which in terms of the notation in Figure 1 becomes

$$5 \doteq 6 > 1 \doteq 2.$$

In the case of a third factor it would predict:

$$r_{X_1Y_1} \doteq r_{X_2Y_2} > r_{X_1Y_2} \doteq r_{Y_1X_2},$$

which in terms of the notation in Figure 1 becomes

$$1 \doteq 2 > 5 \doteq 6.$$

At first sight, then, the inference process from cross-lagged analysis seems clear and straighforward. However a number of assumptions underpin the technique and several issues need to be raised with respect to its validity in relation to differing causal structures.

CROSS-LAGGED CORRELATION ANALYSIS: SOME ASSUMPTIONS AND ISSUES RELEVANT TO ITS INTERPRETABILITY

In this section some assumptions and issues pertinent to cross-lagged correlation analysis which have attracted the attention of those developing the technique (e.g., Heise, 1970; Pelz and Lew, 1970) are outlined. In particular the focus is on four areas. These concern: generality assumptions, time-lag assumptions, external sources of variation in the measured variables, and the criteria used to identify cross-lagged differences.

Generality Assumptions

Two basic assumptions necessarily underpin the generality of findings obtained from cross-lagged correlation analysis. The first is that the same model holds for all subjects. This is, of course, an assumption common to all empirical studies of causal relationships. Moreover, should it be violated, it can in principle be overcome by finding a moderating variable which allows identification of subgroups to which the model applies. The other assumption is that the causal model is constant over the period of investigation. Again, this is an assumption common to all methods of analyzing longitudinal data.

Time-Lag Assumptions

More specific to cross-lagged correlation analysis itself are two assumptions regarding timing. The first of these is that the measurement interval is equivalent to the true causal interval. Since in most situations the investigator is likely to be unaware of the real interval he must make a guess about the appropriate measurement interval. Clearly, cross-lagged correlation analysis will fail under two extreme circumstances: either if the causal lag is so short that it operates after one variable has been measured but before the other can be recorded under the notional category of a single time period; or if the causal lag is so long that it falls completely outside the timespan of the investigation. If one assumes that most researchers are sufficiently informed to avoid these pitfalls then the question becomes one of identifying the extent to which deviations of the measurement interval from the causal interval affect the interpretability of the technique. Pelz (1968) explored this issue and concluded: "the introduction of known causal connections in fact generated clear-cut differences in the cross-lagged correlations even where the lag (measurement interval) departed from the interval of causation" (p. 71). Thus some degree of violation of this assumption does not necessarily render the technique uninterpretable.

The second assumption related to the problem of timing applies to the situation where the variables of interest are reciprocally causally related. If one wishes to draw inferences about the causal priority of two such variables on the basis of two measurements only, one must assume that their causal lags are equal. If they are not, and the chosen measurement interval approximates the shorter lag of one variable rather than the longer lag of the other, then misleading results may be obtained. Nevertheless, the investigator who interprets his findings only in terms of a selected measurement interval will not be drawing unjustified conclusions. Should he continue his investigation to a further measurement interval the effect of the longer causal lag may become apparent. Thus, under conditions of unequal causal lags, cross-lagged correlation analysis (and also any other technique based on measures taken at two points in time) cannot provide definitive evidence of causal priorities among variables, but it does allow inferences concerning such priorities within the chosen measurement interval.

External Sources of Variation

There are several assumptions relevant to the interpretability of the technique relating to sources of variation in the variables under study which are not simply a function of the variables themselves. These include the effects of a third factor which is causally related to both variables being studied, the linearity of the data obtained, the effects of independent errors and the stability of variables during the period of the investigation, and the influence of correlated residuals.

Several authors have identified "third-factoredness" as an occurrence which raises problems of interpretation with cross-lagged correlation analysis. Lawler (1968), for example, states that "the one weakness in this approach is that it cannot rule out the possibility that a third variable causes the other two variables to covary" (p. 463). The assumption is that cross-lagged correlations operate exactly like cross-sectional correlations, where the classical correlation-regression framework requires the residual influences on a variable to be unrelated to any other variable in the system. In order to avoid misinterpretations due to the violation of this assumption, users of cross-lagged analysis used the complementary technique of *dynamic correlations* introduced by Vroom (1966). This relates changes in one variable to changes in the other, and a high dynamic correlation is taken to signify the absence of a third factor.

However, "third-factoredness" is not necessarily as disruptive to inference as it might appear, though under certain conditions (such as reciprocal causality) it can lead to interpretational problems, as Rozelle and Campbell (1969) point out. The effect of third factors on the interpretability of the technique and the use of dynamic correlations as a complementary technique are taken up again later in the paper.

The second assumption in this section concerns the scaling of variables and in particular the assumption of linearity, which is common to all forms of analysis based on product moment correlations. This is not particularly restrictive since the distributional properties of the data can readily be made explicit, and transformations applied or alternative measures of association used. Thus the violation of this assumption does not necessarily render cross-lagged correlation analysis uninterpretable.

The third assumption under the heading of external sources of variation concerns the two concepts of stability and reliability. Stability refers to the relationship between two measures of a variable taken at separate points in time (correlations 3 and 4 in Figure 1), while reliability refers to the relationship between measured and true scores. In practice, reliability is often estimated by the association between two measures of a variable under the assumption that nothing has changed during the interval between measurements. However, the two concepts are distinct: the former is a measure of actual change, the latter one of measurement accuracy. Pelz (1968) has shown that, with high stability, the cross-lagged correlation technique fails to unmask causal relationships. Taken to its extreme this makes sense on purely logical grounds, since a variable that does not change over time cannot be influenced by another variable which itself does not change. The issue becomes one of practical importance when the variables in question have differing stabilities, though evidence to date suggests that this occurrence in itself does not necessarily invalidate causal inferences drawn from cross-lagged correlation analysis. The same conclusion may be reached concerning the effect of unreliability or independent measurement errors, which is known to attenuate the size of correlations. It may be expected that cross-lagged correlation analysis will become less sensitive as reliability decreases, but it is not necessarily uninterpretable on these grounds alone.

Potentially more serious is the final assumption in this section which refers to correlated residuals. The earlier discussion of reliability assumed that errors were independent over time and classical test theory has been laregly concerned with this condition. However, in longitudinal studies it is much more likely that the same errors, or sources of residual variation, will be at least moderately stable over time. For example, distortions in the way a scale is used will recur at each administration of a measurement instrument thus producing correlations between error terms over time. While independent errors will reduce the sensitivity of cross-lagged analysis, the effect of correlated errors is less certain, for they may increase correlations as well as reduce them. Pelz (1968) has considered some aspects of this problem and has shown that at least in some circumstances cross-lagged correlation analysis is still interpretable in the presence of correlated errors.

Criteria Issues

A final problem associated with cross-lagged correlation analysis concerns the criteria for attributing a causal interpretation to the correlations obtained. The issue centers on whether one should focus simply on the direction of differences between lagged correlation coefficients, or require one to be statistically significant and the other not, or require a statistically significant difference between the correlations. Little comment has yet been offered in the literature on this question, but it is clear that some difficulties are involved since the magnitude of cross-lagged correlations is affected both by the simultaneous correlations and the auto-correlations. Thus an assumption of zero correlation is unlikely to be an appropriate baseline.

Overview

What then are the implications of the several issues raised in this section for the usefulness of cross-lagged correlation analysis as an aid to causal inference? In general there seem to be few grounds on which the technique would have to be rejected for use in applied studies. Its requirements are compatible both with important scientific questions and the nature of data often obtained in field research. Thus the investigator interested in relatively enduring causal structures, where the causal lag is not excessively short or long, where the variables in question show a degree of change over time, and who wishes to generalize only to the time-lag under scrutiny, will not be violating the technique in such a way as to invalidate the inference process. Moreover, should he encounter problems due to the causal model applying only to a subsample of the population, or to the existence of nonlinear data, the researcher can handle them in much the same way as he would using other approaches. What has been argued is that *by itself* no single assumption, or particular kind of causal relationship, will necessarily invalidate the causal inference process.

CROSS-LAGGED CORRELATION ANALYSIS AS USED IN OCCUPATIONAL PSYCHOLOGY

The use to which cross-lagged correlation analysis has been put in occupational psychology is of interest in its own right, but more so because its consideration complements the previous discussion by illustrating the nature of the problems to which researchers have applied the technique, and the guidelines they have in practice adopted in drawing inferences from it.

The earliest use of cross-lagged correlation analysis in the occupational psychology literature was that by Lawler (1968) (described earlier in this paper). A further 12 papers have since been published and these are outlined briefly in Table 1 where they are listed in chronological order.

An initial point of interest concerns the increasing popularity of the technique. In the five years after its introduction into occupational psychology three uses were reported, while the subsequent four years witnessed a further nine, six of which were published in the last two years. Given that a similar trend is evident in other areas of psychology (papers by Crano, Kenny and Campbell, 1972; Schmidt and Crano, 1974; Quicker, 1975; Arlin, 1976, illustrate the use of the technique in educational/social psychology) one is justified in describing cross-lagged correlation analysis as a technique which is becoming assimilated into the methodological culture of the discipline.

The kind of problem to which cross-lagged correlation analysis has been applied illustrates another aspect of its potential contribution to occupational psychology. Most of the authors using the technique have been concerned to reach a decision about *causal priority* between two variables believed to be reciprocally causally related. Thus it has been applied to those perennial problems of whether satisfaction determines performance or vice versa (e.g., Siegel and Bowen, 1971; Wanous, 1974), and whether leadership style causes subordinate satisfaction or vice versa (Taylor, 1971; Greene, 1975). For this kind of question cross-lagged correlation analysis would appear to be particularly appropriate. An experimental alternative would involve the use of parallel studies where each variable was manipulated in turn to observe its effects on the other. Not only would this require extremely high commitment from the participants, but it would still be difficult to interpret. To draw any conclusions about causal priorities one would need to raise (and lower) each of the variables by equivalent amounts. This gives rise to insoluble problems about the comparability between levels of satisfaction and performance or leadership style. In any case, how does one manipulate employees' satisfaction, and has the experimenter any right to so do? Moreover, the experimental approach involves randomizing other variables as a means of controlling "extraneous" influences. Whilst this serves to put the spotlight on the causal relationship of interest it may at the same time influence the size of the experimental effect obtained, since it excludes those factors which in practice operate to reduce or enhance the causal potency of the variable of interest. In summary, the literature reveals how cross-lagged correlation analysis has been chosen in order to study relationships the existence of which would not be readily identifiable using other approaches. This is an advantage of the technique over and above the low level of commitment it demands.

Many users have been prepared to draw causal inferences of some strength from their results, as can be seen in Table 1. For example, Wanous (1974) concludes: "The data suggest that performance causes intrinsic satisfaction and that extrinsic satisfaction causes performance" (p. 139). Only some of the researchers however referred to the issue of the criterion to be used for making such inferences. Most, in fact, adopted

TABLE 1 A Review of the Uses of Cross-Lagged Correlation Analysis in Occupational Psychology

Author(s)	Variables	Population	Length of Lag	Type of Change (N = Natural, I = induced)	Dynamic Correlation Used	Author(s)' Conclusions
Lawler (1968)	Job performance Expectancy attitudes	55 managers	1 year	N	yes	"Expectancy attitudes could best be thought of as causing the job performance" (p. 462)
Taylor (1971)	Sophistication of technology Supervisory leadership Work group activities Satisfaction with work group	1000 nonsupervisors	1 year*	I	no	e.g., "suggests satisfaction takes a key place in the causal matrix" (p. 118)
Siegel and Bowen (1971)	Performance Satisfaction with self Self-esteem Satisfaction with group	86 students	3 weeks**	N	no	"The data presented provide strong support for viewing satisfaction as dependent upon performance and little support for viewing performance as an outcome of satisfaction" (p. 267)
Lawler and Suttle	Need satisfaction and need importance— security, social, esteem, autonomy, and self-actualization needs	132 managers	6 and 12 months	N	yes	"The data offered little support for the view set forth by Maslow and others that human needs are arranged in a multi-level hierarchy" (p. 265)
Greene (1973)	Merit pay Job satisfaction Performance	62 managers	1 year	N	no	"The results indicated that merit pay caused satisfaction; satisfaction was found to be an effect and not a cause of performance" (p. 95)
Wanous (1974)	Performance Intrinsic and extrinsic satisfaction	80 female telephone operators	2 months	N	yes	"The data suggest that performance causes intrinsic satisfaction and that extrinsic satisfaction causes performance" (p. 139)

TABLE 1 (continued)

Author(s)	Variables	Population	Length of Lag	Type of Change (N = Natural, I = Induced)	Dynamic Correlation Used	Author(s)' Conclusions
Greene (1975)	Leader behavior (consideration and initiating structure) Subordinate performance	103 first-line managers 206 subordinates	1 month*	N	yes	"The results strongly suggest that (1) consideration caused subordinate performance; (2) subordinate performance caused changes in leader emphasis on both consideration and structure; and (3) consideration moderated the initiating structure-performance relationship such that with highly considerate leaders emphasis on structure caused higher subordinate performance" (p. 187)
Sheridan and Slocum (1975)	Job satisfaction Performance	35 managers 59 machine operators	1 year	N	yes	"Affective measures of job satisfaction were linked to managers' performance in a lagged performance-satisfaction relationship. Need deficiency measures of job satisfaction were linked to the machine operators' performance in a lead dissatisfaction-performance relationship" (p. 15)
Bakeman and Helmreich (1975)	Group cohesiveness Performance	40 scientists 8 engineers	2 days	N	no	"It was concluded at least in the context of this study that cohesiveness was not an important determinant of performance, but that good performance may well have been a cause of cohesiveness" (p. 478)

TABLE 1 (continued)

Author(s)	Variables	Population	Length of Lag	Type of Change (N = Natural, I = Induced)	Dynamic Correlation Used	Author(s)' Conclusions
Miles (1975)	Role conflict Role ambiguity Job related tension Job satisfaction Attitudes to role senders	202 R and D professionals	4 months	N	yes	"They (the variables) meet the static and dynamic criteria necessary to infer a causal basis for the relationship, but direction of causality is indeterminate because of failure to meet the cross-lagged criterion" (p. 338)
Tosi et al. (1976)	7 variables (e.g., satisfaction with job, orientation toward MBO)	190 managers 53 managers	18 months 18 months*	N	yes	"Most studies that have used either a cross-sectional correlation methodology or even a two time cross-lagged methodology have drawn invalid conclusions as to the causal relationships between the variables studied" (p. 302)
Bechtold, Sims and Szilagyi (1976)	Job characteristics Expectancy Satisfaction Performance	191 hospital administrators and professionals	18 months	N	yes	"The results indicated that job characteristics tend to cause satisfaction rather than the converse" (p. 1)
Sims (1976)	Job characteristics Satisfaction Performance Expectancy	61 young professionals	6 months	N	yes	"In summary, this research has generally supported the conclusion that perceptions of job characteristics tend to cause employee intrinsic expectancies and satisfaction" (p. 13)

Note: *indicates 3 measurement occasions; **indicates 5 measurement occasions.

the view that one cross-lagged correlation need be significant and the other not (e.g., Siegel and Bowen, 1971). Only Miles (1975) adopted the stronger criterion that the two cross-lagged correlations should be significantly different. None questioned the implicit use of a zero correlation baseline, even though significant cross-lagged correlations may be obtained simply as a result of the effects of moderately large simultaneous and auto-correlations. In nine studies dynamic correlations were calculated. In seven of these the explicit aim was to examine the possibility of "third factoredness"—which in six instances was excluded as an explanation of the findings.

Of the other issues affecting the interpretability of cross-lagged analysis raised in the previous section, little explicit consideration is evident in the empirical literature drawn from the area of occupational psychology. Most authors reported information on the reliability of the measures employed but none attempted to evaluate the implications of this for interpretability. Stability was not considered except by Miles (1975) whose account did not show how it was to be distinguished from reliability. Little attention was paid to alternative causal explanations of the findings presented (see, for example, those proposed by Rozelle and Campbell, 1969), nor was evidence presented to justify the use of linear statistics. Finally, no users reported on the possible problem of correlated residuals.

Thus one can see a growing recognition of the potential of cross-lagged correlation analysis both because of its low requirements in terms of research commitment and its applicability to questions of dual causality. Also evident is a developing consensus about the guidelines for judging differences between cross-lagged correlations and for establishing whether or not these are likely to be a function of a "third variable." There is, however, little consideration of other issues which bear on the interpretability of the technique.

Given the evidence presented in the previous section which showed that the assumptions are not too restrictive, investigators may not be entirely unjustified in pushing ahead in this way and their interpretations are not necessarily invalid. Nevertheless they may be accused of preempting the issue. The accuracy of the criterion in practice adopted for assessing cross-lagged differences, and the adequacy of dynamic correlation for detecting third factors, are still in dispute. Additionally, the extent to which the data obtained may deviate from each of the assumptions before rendering the technique uninterpretable is unknown. Of particular importance is the interpretability of the technique when confronted with different *combinations* of violation of assumptions. For example, the researcher needs to know how robust his technique is when dealing with variables that are only moderately stable, the measurement of which is only moderately reliable and which contain correlated errors. Should the technique become insensitive with such data (Type II error), or—worse—lead to false interpretations (Type I error), it is to be discarded.

It will be appreciated that an evaluation of cross-lagged correlation analysis in these terms represents a complex and large scale enterprise. Each type of causal model must be examined within the context of varying degrees of violation of assumptions both alone and in combination. This results in an extremely large number of conditions. Nevertheless, such an evaluation is a worthwhile exercise since the potential of cross-lagged correlation analysis is so great. The next section describes an approach to this problem based on simulation and presents the initial findings to which it has given rise.

ASSESSING CROSS-LAGGED CORRELATION ANALYSIS
THROUGH SIMULATION

The principal advantage of using simulated data as a basis for evaluating cross-lagged correlation analysis is that the investigator knows the 'truth' and thus always has a criterion against which to assess the performance of the technique. Such is usually not the case with "real" data since the underlying causal structure is rarely self-evident. Moreover, even where logical considerations allow but a single causal model to apply to "real" data (as the instance considered by Pelz and Andrews, 1964—but disputed by Rozelle and Campbell, 1969), it is still of limited value for our present purposes. This is because the performance of the technique can be assessed only against the particular instance and not as parameters of the process are systematically varied.

Using an algorithm, such as that implemented by Heise (1970) and Pelz and Lew (1970), data may be generated for any number of subjects for specified causal models which may vary both in complexity and strength of relationships. These data may then be changed in quality, for example by introducing different levels and kinds of measurement error, or varying levels of stability. Cross-lagged correlation analysis can be applied to the resultant data, and its performance under different conditions assessed. This is the rationale behind the evaluative program we are currently undertaking, details of which are described in the remainder of this paper along with some preliminary findings.

The Present Simulation Exercise: Parameters

In starting out on the simulation exercise an initial decision had to be made about the complexity of the causal structures and measurement characteristics to be considered. It was decided to start with relatively straightforward conditions on the assumption that if the technique fails under these circumstances there is little need to continue to more complicated configurations. More specifically, three causal structures were selected: a simple monocausality model; a dual causality model with one variable having priority over the other; and a model in which two variables were independent but both caused by a third variable. For each of these the performance of cross-lagged correlation analysis was examined under different measurement conditions: two levels of measurement reliability (high = 81 percent and low = 36 percent); and three levels of stability (0.9, 0.6 and 0.3—where 1.0 represents no change over time). These we considered to be levels particularly relevant to applied research. In each case the values chosen for these parameters were the same for all variables within the system being modeled for both time periods. In certain instances the effects of correlated measurement errors were also examined.

A sample size of 100 was selected for each simulation since this is representative of the numbers studied by psychologists who have so far used the technique. Moreover, 12 independent runs were made for each set of conditions in order to gain information about the effects of sampling variability on the distribution of values obtained. (A description of the technical aspects of the procedure used to generate the data along with details of the computer program may be obtained from the second author.)

A final decision concerned the choice of criterion for assessing the performance of cross-lagged correlation analysis. As discussed earlier this has raised problems for the interpretation of empirical data and there is little reason on a priori grounds for adopting one criterion over another. Rather, it is an issue requiring empirical investigation by examining how alternative criteria succeed or fail against data with known causal properties. For our present purposes, however, a weak criterion was adopted. Cross-lagged correlation differences were classified into three main groups: *misses*, where the difference was less than 0.05 (but a true causal relationship existed); *hits*, where the difference was greater than 0.05 in the "true" direction; and *false alarms*, where the difference was greater than 0.05 in the "wrong" direction. These admittedly arbitrary criteria provide a stable baseline for highlighting the problem areas for the technique and enable direct comparison to be made across differing conditions.

The Present Simulation Exercise: Preliminary Findings

The amount of computer output generated by 12 runs for each of the 18 conditions, resulting from three causal models, two levels of reliability, and three levels of stability, is too great to be described in detail here. So, by way of example, we present the results for the simplest causal model, that of monocausality, and summarize our findings with respect to dual causality with causal priority and "third-factoredness."

The rationale for cross-lagged correlation analysis gives the prediction that where X causes Y but not vice versa, $r_{X_1 Y_2}$ (correlation 5 in Figure 1) will be greater than $r_{Y_1 X_2}$ (correlation 6 in Figure 1). Table 2 presents the results for 12 independent runs of the simulation program for each of the six combinations of values selected for reliability and stability. The errors are independent over time and the criteria for "hits," "misses" and "false alarms" are as described above. The size of the causal parameter was set at 0.3 prior to introducing error into the data, an effect statistically significant beyond the 0.001 level of confidence and representing a moderately strong causal influence. (The causal parameters, as well as the stability coefficients, are path coefficients in the models described here, rather than correlations. Details of the definition of models may be obtained from the second author.)

Considering reliability first, it is clear that the technique performs better under conditions of high (81 percent) rather than low reliability (36 percent). There are no false alarms with measures characterized by high reliability, a large proportion of hits, and few misses (all except one, that under the condition of low stability, being in the predicted direction). With low reliability, however, the performance of the technique is substantially worse. The hits decrease in number, the misses correspondingly increase, and false alarms are also evident. The evidence presented in Figure 3 underlines these results by showing the average magnitude of the cross-lagged coefficients obtained and the differences between them.

Table 2 and Figure 3 also show the effects of varying levels of stability for the performance of cross-lagged analysis on a monocausal model. The most obvious feature of both sets of results is the contrast between the high stability conditions and the other two. The only false alarms (essentially the worst kind of error) occur where stability is high, and there are also fewer hits. Under conditions of medium and low stability the technique's performance is much superior.

As long as the data are highly reliable, therefore, cross-lagged correlation analysis appears to perform reasonably well, though the differences between cross-lagged correlations (as shown in Figure 3) are not particularly large. There is also some suggestion that with highly reliable data, lower levels of stability make the technique more sensitive. The main problems arise with data of low reliability but high stability. Under these circumstances the technique is not only insensitive but also often misleading. These conclusions apply equally to findings obtained when using a dual-causality model with causal priority.

TABLE 2 The Performance of Cross-Lagged Correlation Analysis on Twelve Runs with Simulated Data Where X Causes $Y(0.3)$ Under Different Conditions of Reliability and Stability.

	High Stability				Medium Stability				Low Stability			
		Misses in:				*Misses in:*				*Misses in:*		
	Hits	*predicted direction*	*opposite direction*	*False alarms*	*Hits*	*predicted direction*	*opposite direction*	*False alarms*	*Hits*	*predicted direction*	*opposite direction*	*False alarms*
High reliability	8	4	0	0	9	3	0	0	10	1	1	0
Low reliability	4	0	4	4	8	0	4	0	6	3	3	0

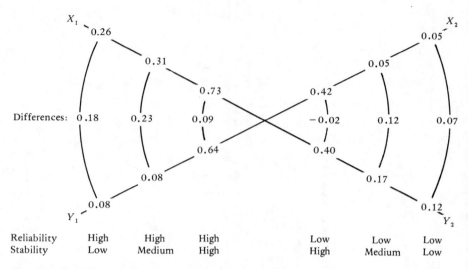

FIGURE 3 Mean cross-lagged correlations from the simulation exercise where X_1 causes Y_2 (0.3) under different conditions of reliability and stability.

Note: Means are taken over 12 independent runs for samples of 100 cases under each condition.

The causal model based on a third factor posed few problems for the technique in that cross-lagged correlations obtained were close to zero as were the differences between them. In addition, the use of dynamic correlations failed to discriminate between this "third factor" model and the other two, being largely insignificant whether a third factor was present or not. In this context, therefore, the use of dynamic correlation seems redundant.

One feature of the present findings compared with those reported in the psychological literature is that the cross-lagged correlation coefficients are smaller. However, this was not the case when correlated errors over time were introduced into the data. The effect of this was to raise all the correlations by about the same amount. But, this did not affect the interpretation of the technique since the differences remained constant. Nevertheless, it does have implications with respect to the use of traditional levels of statistical significance for interpreting cross-lagged correlations.

CONCLUSIONS

The findings from the simulation exercises paint a generally encouraging picture for cross-lagged correlation analysis, but this must be tempered by two caveats. First, only a restricted number of relatively simple conditions were examined. The next task is to consider more complex, and thereby more realistic, configurations of causal models and data, varying the strength of the causal influences, as well as introducing further combinations of measurement error of different strengths. Under these conditions it may turn out that the current optimism is unfounded. Secondly, the criterion to be used to identify cross-lagged differences must be developed in order to maximize the technique's sensitivity whilst minimizing its tendency to give false alarms. An additional point should be raised. The work described here has focused exclusively on whether cross-lagged correlation differences are consistent with the known causal properties of sets of data. A more stringent test would be whether or not the technique can be used to derive unique causal interpretations.

Finally, it is evident that the general strategy behind the simulation exercise is also appropriate for evaluating alternative techniques for inferring causality from panel data. Thus it may be used to compare cross-lagged correlation analysis with such approaches as those proposed by Lazarsfeld (1948) and Yee and Gage (1968), and with path analysis (Duncan, 1966).

REFERENCES

Alwin, D. F. and Tessler, R. C. (1974) "Causal Models, Unobserved Variables, and Experimental Data," *Am. J. Sociol. 80*, 58–86.

Arlin, M. (1976). "Causal Priority of Social Desirability Over Self-concept: A Cross-lagged Correlation Analysis," *J. Person. Soc. Psychol. 33*, 267–272.

Bakeman, R. and Helmreich, R. (1975). "Cohesiveness and Performance: Covariation and Causality in an Undersea Environment," *J. Exp. Soc. Psychol. 11*, 478–489.

Bechtold, S., Sims, H. P., Jr. and Szilagyi, A. D. (1976). "A Causal Analysis of Job Characteristic Relationships." Paper presented at Midwest Association of Decision Sciences, Detroit.

Blalock, H. M., Jr. (1974). *Measurement in the Social Sciences*. London: Macmillan.

Blalock, H. M., Jr. (1975). *Quantitative Sociology*. New York: Academic Press.

Campbell, D. T. (1963). "From Description to Experimentation: Interpreting Trends as Quasi-Experiments. In C. W. Harris (ed.), *Problems in Measuring Change*. Madison: University of Wisconsin Press.

Campbell, D. T. and Stanley, J. C. (1963). *Experimental and Quasi-experimental Designs for Research*. Chicago: Rand-McNally.

Cook, T. D. and Campbell, D. T. (1976). "The Design and Conduct of Quasi-experiments and True Experiments in Field Settings. In M. D. Dunnette (ed.), *Handbook of Industrial and Organizational Psychology*. Chicago: Rand-McNally.

Crano, W. D., Kenny, D. A. and Campbell, D. T. (1972). "Does Intelligence Cause Achievement: A Cross-lagged Panel Analysis," *J. Educ. Psychol. 63*, 238–275.

Duncan, O. D. (1966). "Path Analysis: Sociological Examples," *Am. J. Sociol. 72*, 1–16.

Duncan, O. D. (1969). "Some Linear Models for Two-wave, Two Variable Panel Analysis," *Psychol. Bull. 70*, 177–182.

Feldman, J. (1975). "Consideration in the Use of Causal-Correlational Techniques in Applied Psychology," *J. Appl. Psychol. 60*, 663–670.

Goldberger, A. (1971). "Econometrics and Psychometrics: A Survey of Commonalities," *Psychometrika 36*, 83–107.

Goldberger, A. and Duncan, O. D. (1973). *Structural Models in the Social Sciences*. New York: Seminar Press.

Goodman, L. A. (1973). "Causal Analysis of Data From Panel Studies and Other Kinds of Surveys," *Am. J. Sociol. 78*, 1135–1191.

Greene, C. N. (1973). "Causal Connections Among Managers' Merit Pay, Job Satisfaction, and Performance," *J. Appl. Psychol. 58*, 95–100.

Greene, C. N. (1975). "The Reciprocal Nature of Influence Between Leader and Subordinate," *J. Appl. Psychol. 60*, 187–193.

Heise, D. R. (1970). "Causal Inference From Panel Data." In E. F. Borgatta and G. W. Bohrnstedt (eds.), *Sociological Methodology 1970*. San Francisco: Jossey-Bass.

Hilton, G. (1972). "Causal Inference Analysis: A Seductive Process," *Admin. Sci. Q. 17*, 44–57.

Howard, K. I. and Krause, M. S. (1970). "Some Comments on 'Techniques for Estimating the Source and Direction of Influence in Panel Data'," *Psychol. Bull. 74*, 219–224.

Howard, K. I., Krause, M. S. and Orlinsky, D. E. (1969). "Direction of Affective Influence in Psychotherapy," *J. Consult. Clin. Psychol. 33*, 614–620.

Kenny, D. A. (1975a). "A Quasi-experimental Approach to Assessing Treatment Effects in the Nonequivalent Control Group Design," *Psychol. Bull. 82*, 345–362.

Kenny, D. A. (1975b). "Cross-lagged Panel Correlation: A Test for Spuriousness," *Psychol. Bull. 82*, 887–903.

Lawler, E. E. (1968). "A Correlational-causal Analysis of the Relationship Between Expectancy Attitudes and Job Performance," *J. Appl. Psychol. 52*, 462–468.

Lawler, E. E. and Suttle, J. L. (1972). "A Causal Correlational Test of the Need Hierarchy Concept," *Organiz. Behav. Hum. Perf. 7*, 265–287.

Lazarsfeld, P. F. (1948). "Mutual Effects of Statistical Variables." Bureau of Applied Social Research, Columbia University (mimeo).

Miles, R. H. (1975). "An Empirical Test of Causal Inference Between Role Perceptions of Conflict and Ambiguity and Various Personal Outcomes," *J. appl. Psychol. 60*, 334–339.

Pelz, D. C. (1968). "Correlational Properties of Simulated Panel Data With Causal Connections Between Two Variables." Interim Report no. 1, Causal Analysis Project. Survey Research Center, University of Michigan.

Pelz, D. C. and Andrews, F. M. (1964). "Detecting Causal Priorities in Panel Study Data," *Am. Sociol. Rev. 29*, 836–848.

Pelz, D. C. and Faith, R. E. (1970). "Some Effects of Causal Connections in Simulated Time Series Data." Interim Report no. 2, Causal Analysis Project. Survey Research Center, University of Michigan.

Pelz, D. C. and Faith, R. E. (1973). "Detecting Causal Connections in Panel Data: January 1971–December 1972." Interim Report no. 3, Causal Analysis Project. Survey Research Center, University of Michigan.

Pelz, D. C. and Lew, R. A. (1970). "Heise's Causal Model Applied." In E. F. Borgatta and G. W. Bohrnstedt (eds.), *Sociological Methodology, 1970*. San Francisco: Jossey-Bass.

Quicker, J. C. (1975). "The Effect of Goal Discrepancy on Delinquency," *Soc. Problems 22*, 76–86.

Rozelle, R. M. and Campbell, D. T. (1969). "More Plausible Rival Hypotheses in the Cross-lagged Panel Correlation Technique," *Psychol Bull. 71*, 74–80.

Sandell, R. G. (1971). "Notes on Choosing Between Competing Interpretations of Cross-lagged Panel Correlations," *Psychol. Bull. 75*, 367–368.

Schmidt, F. L. and Crano, W. D. (1974). "A Test of the Theory of Fluid and Crystallized Intelligence in Middle and Low Socioeconomic Status Children," *J. Educ. Psychol. 66*, 255–261.

Sheridan, J. E. and Slocum, J. W. (1975). "The Direction of Causal Relationship Between Job Satisfaction and Work Performance," *Organiz. Behav. Hum. Perf. 14*, 159–172.

Siegel, J. P. and Bowen, D. (1971). "Satisfaction and Performance: Causal Relationships and Moderating Effects," *J. Voc. Behav. 1*, 263–269.

Simon, H. A. (1954). "Spurious Correlation: A Causal Interpretation," *J. Am. statist. Ass. 49*, 467–479.

Sims, H. P., Jr. (1976). "A Longitudinal Study of Job Characteristics Relationships." Working paper, Department of Administrative and Behavioral Studies, Indiana University.

Taylor, J. C. (1971). "Some Effects of Technology in Organizational Change," *Hum. Relat. 24*, 105–123.

Tosi, H., Hunter, J., Chesser, R., Tarter, J. R. and Carroll, S. (1976). "How Real Are Changes Induced by Management by Objectives?" *Admin. Sci. Q. 21*, 276–306.

Vroom, V. H. (1966). "A Comparison of Static and Dynamic Correlational Methods in the Study of Organizations," *Organiz. Behav. Hum. Perf. 1*, 55–70.

Wanous, J. P. (1974). "A Causal-correlational Analysis of the Job Satisfaction and Performance Relationships," *J. Appl. Psychol. 59*, 139–144.

Yee, A. H. and Gage, N. L. (1968). "Techniques for Estimating the Source and Direction of Causal Influence in Panel Data," *Psychol. Bull. 70*, 115–126.

18   Using and Abusing Path Analysis as a Research Tool in the Behavioral Sciences

Roger Pfaffenberger

INTRODUCTION

The purpose of this paper is to provide organizational science researchers using path analysis a better understanding and perspective for what this technique can and cannot do in the analysis of data. The paper was motivated by an increasing awareness that some who are using path analysis do not have a true appreciation of its limitations (i.e., the necessary assumptions for its correct use), the statistical estimation problems associated with its use and the interpretational intricacies associated with the underlying theory. The suspicion that abuses of path analysis are on the increase is at least partially borne out by perusing the literature in the behavioral and social sciences.

The occurrence of inappropriate applications of path analysis has been facilitated by the exuberant acceptance of the tool as a "solution" to the problem of quantitatively analyzing sociological or behavioral data[1] and the widespread availability of statistical computer programs to perform the analysis.[2] The availability of computer codes tends to promote the abuse of path analysis by enabling virtually anyone to run computer programs that perform sophisticated tests and manipulations of the data, even though they may lack a true understanding of the quantitative methods being employed.

Perhaps the ultimate abuse of path analysis is partially attributable to the "publish or perish" syndrome. Once a "new" and sophisticated quantitative tool is introduced into a literature, there is a precedent set for others to follow. Unless the literature is fortunate to have a plentiful supply of reviewers who are competent to review quantitative research (few are), the introduction of a new quantitative technique can place considerable pressure on the reviewing process with the all too frequent consequence that papers of questionable quantitative competence are published. When papers using the technique begin to appear in mass, it becomes a fad—indeed, often a necessity—to use the quantitative method to analyze data in submitted papers to the literature. The result is an inevitable increase in the abuse of the method evidenced by researchers who use it without fully understanding its limitations and by those who do understand its limitations, but use it in questionable circumstances to increase the likelihood of the publication of their work. This process, involving the use of path analysis, has clearly occurred in some behavioral science literatures (as will be shown) and will likely occur in other literatures shortly as the path analysis "gospel" spreads.

It is hoped that this paper may diminish the abuses of path analysis in the òrganizational science literatures. The principal contribution of the paper is to synthesize

Source: Paper presented at The American Institute for Decision Sciences, Sixth Annual Meeting, October 30–November 2, 1974, Atlanta, Georgia. Reproduced by permission.

and organize the important literature on path analysis so as to make it easier for researchers using the tool to competently familiarize themselves with its methods and limitations.

A REVIEW OF PATH ANALYSIS

History

Path analysis was developed by a geneticist, Sewall Wright (1921). The method used standard regression and correlation techniques to study linear, additive and causal systems of variables in which the direction of causal relationships was generally accepted on the bases of genetic theory. Wright promoted the use of path analysis in genetics research for a number of years, but suffered the misfortune of competing with R. A. Fisher, the famous British statistician, who had developed a quantitative genetic theory based on probability. Fisher's approach prevailed and, consequently, path analysis became buried in the literature for a period of approximately thirty years.

In the fifties, path analysis was unearthed from the genetics literature graveyard by Wright and others who appreciated its utility. Interestingly, it was the path diagram that principally resulted in the renewed interest in path analysis. Fisher's probability approach to quantitative genetics is mathematically rigorous and requires a prolonged learning curve before it can be productively employed. Path analysis is certainly no easier to master mathematically, but the path diagram does enable a researcher to come to an understanding of the relationships among the functions and variables much easier than does a set of Fisherian probability equations.

By the mid-fifties, path analysis found wide applicability in the biological sciences. Interest in path analysis in this area continues today as evidenced by the growing number of articles that have drawn upon it. In the past three years, the method has been extensively used to analyze the yield of grains and other grasses (e.g., see Mishra et al., 1973 and Shasha et al., 1973).

Path analysis found its way into the social science literature in the mid-sixties, principally due to the paper on sociological examples of its use by Duncan (1966). Since then, the method has been employed to analyze data arising in a variety of disciplines. Recent research efforts include the disciplines of anthropology (see Hadden and Dewalt, 1974), library science (see Kronus, 1973) and social work (see Lyden and Lee, 1973). The application of path analysis in the organizational sciences is, perhaps, the latest discipline entry (e.g., Aldrich, 1972, Anderson and Pfaffenberger, 1974). It would appear that path analysis has a significant place in organizational analysis if researchers in this area continue to develop and test causal models. Further applications could include the analysis of the performance and satisfaction models of Cummings and Schwab (1973) and Porter and Lawler (1968). Models of individual motivation and decision making appear to readily lend themselves to this type of analysis as well.

Basic Readings in Path Analysis

Since path analysis was developed in the genetics discipline, it should come as no surprise that much of the developmental research has been associated with the genetics literature. A highly readable and elementary presentation of path analysis (only a limited statistical background is required) can be found in the Li (1955) text on population genetics. Chapter 13 in Wright's book (1968) covers the theory of path analysis as developed by its founder, but one should have read an introduction to path analysis elsewhere (e.g., Li, 1955) before attempting to comprehend this material. Chapter 14 is on the interpretation of path coefficients; it is an excellent and informative presentation, but the examples are exclusively in genetics.

A "must" reading by researchers in the behavioral sciences is *Causal Models in the Social Sciences*, edited by Blalock (1971). The *Sociological Methodology* series is also highly recommended, particulary the first edited by Borgatta (1969). It contains the important papers by Land (1969), entitled "Principles of Path Analysis," and by Heise (1969), entitled "Problems in Path Analysis and Causal Inference." Two additional important papers are those by Tukey (1954) and Turner and Stevens (1959). Others will be discussed in the remainder of this paper.

The Path Analysis Technique

It is not the purpose of this paper to develop the technique of path analysis. But, to discuss fully the abuses of path analysis, it is necessary to review the basic tenets of the method. For those who are unfamiliar with path analysis, it is a method used to analyze causal systems of variables. The causal system typically is an oversimplification of reality that is represented by a set of structural equations. In the system of relationships, a subset of the variables is considered to be linearly dependent on the remaining variables. Exogenous variables are those determined by factors outside the system under consideration while the endogenous variables are determined by one or more exogenous or endogenous variables within the system. In other words, exogenous variables are treated as predetermined while endogenous variables result from interactions (dependence) within the system.

The analysis of the structural system of variables is typically based on partial regression methodology. Path coefficients are partial regression coefficients that may be standardized or unstandardized. The square of the path coefficient is a measure of the fraction of variability in the dependent variable which is accounted for by the set of independent variables in a single equation model.

As developed by Wright, path diagrams play an important function in path analysis. In the diagrams, certain conventions must be followed:

1. The causal relationships of the variables are indicated by unidirectional arrows.
2. Pairwise correlations among exogenous variables are indicated by bidirectional arrows.
3. Residual variables are represented by unidirectional arrows connected to the appropriate dependent variables and are denoted by unsubscripted letters.
4. Path coefficients, denoted by p_{ij}, are given on the causal connections between pairs of variables.

For example, in Figure 1, the two exogenous variables x_1 and x_2 have a product moment correlation coefficient r, p_{13} and p_{23} are the path coefficients relating x_1, x_3 and x_2, x_3, respectively, and e is the residual variable.

In the simple model illustrated in Figure 1, standard regression techniques could be used to determine p_{13}, p_{23} and the amount of variability in the dependent variable x_3 that is absorbed by the independent variables x_1 and x_2.

The analysis of complex path models requires a fundamental understanding of multiple correlation and regression techniques and the methods used to analyze simultaneous systems of equations subject to the estimation problems of the identification of parameters. A prerequisite for the use of path analysis by a researcher is, therefore,

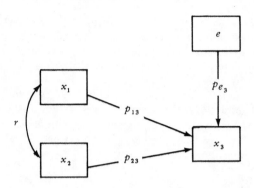

FIGURE 1   A Simple Path Diagram

the working knowledge of linear models theory and multivariate estimation methods. For those without this training, path analysis should not be undertaken without consulting and working with one who has the necessary statistical training. To do otherwise is an invitation to join the growing list of abusers of path analysis.

Objectives of Path Analysis

The objectives of the path analysis of data have generally been postulated as falling in one or more of the following areas:

1. Determination of the relative importance of each path of causation. Given a situation in which multiple independent units affect the value of a dependent unit, path analysis allows the researcher to assign a "weight" to the causal effects of such independent units.
2. Pictorial representation of relationships among variables. The "picture is worth a thousand words" effect applies to path analysis, through clarity of the resulting causal diagram. Concomitantly, criticism of the framework is facilitated through this representation.
3. "Teasing out" the nature of causal relationships among variables. Although misuses of the technique have occurred in this sense (model construction from the data rather than analysis of a predetermined causal model), the technique can aid in model formation in cases in which the causal relationships among the model units are ambiguous.

PATH ANALYSIS ASSUMPTIONS

The Heise (1969) paper identifies the crucial assumptions that must be met by the researcher and his data for the proper use of path analysis. These are:

1. *In the structural system of variables, change in one variable is always a linear function of changes in other variables.* This linearity assumption eliminates the explicit use of multiplicative terms, such as $x_1 x_2$, in the model. Those familiar with multiple regression techniques know that multiplicative terms can be "linearized" by introducing new variables into the model. However,

it may not be easy, or indeed, possible to linearize the model if complex nonlinear terms exist in it.

2. *One way causation.* The system contains no reciprocal causations or feedback loops. That is, if x causes y, then y cannot affect x either directly or through a chain of other variables.

3. *A clearly defined causal system.* The causal laws governing the system are established so as to specify causal relationships that are "undebatable." This assumption is perhaps the most important assumption and, concomitantly, the most difficult to satisfy. In the early genetics applications, the causal systems were widely accepted based upon "hard science" genetics theory. In the "soft science," satisfying this assumption may be difficult, if not impossible, in many applications of path analysis. At the least, a strong conviction that the model is "correct" is required together with persuasive powers to deal with adversaries, who may not be able to suggest better models, but certainly can envisage multiple faults in the posited model.

4. *Dependent variables are uncorrelated with one another.* This requires that all system inputs must be explicitly delineated in the path diagrams. When constructs are used in the model, it is difficult to assess if this assumption is satisfied, for often the construct variables are unmeasurable. Who knows if all proper system inputs have been accounted for in these instances?

5. *A higher degree of measurement reliability and validity.* In many genetic applications, it is relatively easy to satisfy this assumption, for the measurements may be weights, heights, yields, etc. But, how does one know if, say, IQ is being measured reliably?

6. *The usual multivariate regression assumptions must be met by the data.* This assumption leads to a host of assumptions that are rarely, if ever, completely satisfied in applications of path analysis to behavioral research data. Among these are:
   i.   Interval scale measurements on all variables.
   ii. Homoscedasticity—the variances of exogenous variables in each equation are homogeneous.
   iii. The exogenous variables are not highly correlated with one another.
   iv. The effects among variables are linear and additive.
   v.   Residuals are uncorrelated with any independent variables directly affecting the dependent variable upon which it acts.
   vi. The independent variables are fixed effects.

For those of you who have used regression in your research with perhaps justified misgivings, think of now using path analysis in which the regression assumptions form by one portion of a larger set of assumptions. If the letter of the law were obeyed, path analysis would have few applications in the analysis of data and these could be found mostly in the biological sciences. It is not surprising, therefore, that considerable attention has been recently devoted to studying the effects of "relaxing assumptions" in regression and path analysis methods.

A number of papers have been written concerning problems in employing regression analysis, since it has become one of the most important statistical techniques in analyzing data. A paper by Box (1966) was one of the first to point out abuses of regression analysis that began appearing in the scientific literature in the early and mid-sixties. Bohrnstedt and Carter (1971) discussed the robustness of regression to the relaxation of assumptions with particular attention given to applications of regression in behavioral science research. The limitations of using R^2, the multiple correlation coefficient, as a measure of absorbed variability in a dependent variable by a set of independent variables, has been addressed by Barrett (1974), Morrison (1972) and Toy and Hayya (1974). It is apparent that some users of regression do not understand that R^2 is a *statistic*, an estimate of the population multiple correlation coefficient, ρ^2. As an estimator of ρ^2, R^2 is subject to variability as a function of the sample set of data used in the regression analysis. As pointed out by Toy and Hayya (1974), the value of R^2 in a particular experiment may depart radically from ρ^2 due to a number of causes. Its value may be inflated due to the least squares fitting process which guarantees an increased R^2 as new independent variables are added to the regression, regardless of the magnitude of their correlations with the dependent variables. A corrected R^2 that more truly reflects the portion of explained variance is given by

$$\hat{R}^2 = 1-(1-R^2)[(n-1)/(n-1-p)],$$

where n is the sample size and p is the number of fitted coefficients in the regression. Additionally, the sample multiple correlation coefficient R^2 is a *biased* estimator of the true multiple correlation coefficient ρ^2. The magnitude of the bias can become large, particularly if certain regression assumptions are not satisfied. Morrison (1972) has shown the bias can become quite severe if the dependent variable is discrete instead of being continuously distributed, for example.

The bias in R^2 when $\rho^2 = 0$ is given by:

$$E(R^2/\rho^2 = 0 = \frac{p}{n-1}$$

Thus, if the sample size is slightly larger than p, the number of fitted coefficients, then the sample R^2 is likely to be artificially high. Examples of falling into this trap abound in the literature. For example, in a study by Clawson (1974), a regression with 24 coefficients was fitted with a sample of 26 observations—the bias in R^2 is 24/25 = .96. The fact that the R^2 in this study was greater than .90 becomes quite meaningless in the light of the magnitude of the bias in R^2!

Recognizing that R^2 is biased is important for users of path analysis, since this measure is commonly used to indicate the "strength of causality" in causal relationships among variables. Notice that the bias goes to zero as n, the sample size, increases. Large sample sizes are necessities in most applications of regression to behavioral science research, since many regression properties will hold asymptotically when most assumptions are not satisfied. The key question is, of course, how large a sample is large enough? The Toy and Hayya (1974) paper reviews most of the relevant sample size research, but the answer depends upon so many considerations that it is usually advisable to consult a statistician who is able to familiarize himself with the specific nuances of the sampling experiment.

Swindel (1974) has shown the instability of the estimated regression coefficients as a function of relaxing assumptions. Hayya, Pfaffenberger, and Chan (1974) have studied the robustness of classic least squares regression to relaxing assumptions on the continuity of the dependent variable. This study has shown that very large sample sizes (in excess of 150 for simple linear regression) are required before the distributions of the estimated coefficients begin to converge to the normal distribution, the theoretically exact distribution of the estimated coefficients *if* all regression assumptions are satisfied.

It is evident that more work is required on the effects of relaxing regression assumptions, since the tool is and will continue to be popular among researchers. As an alternative to regression, analytic methods are being devised to analyze data when not all of the regression assumptions are satisfied. Goodman (1972a,b) has suggested contingency table based methods for analyzing a discrete dependent variable. Cox (1970) has written a book on dichotomous dependent variable analysis.

The problem of estimating parameters in structural equations has been the subject of a collection of papers, edited by Goldberger and Duncan (1973). This set of papers is required reading for users of path analysis. In one of these papers, Joreskog (1969) has suggested maximum likelihood based methods for estimating parameters in structural equations that appear to lead to estimators with properties that are at least as good as those produced by least squares. The Joreskog method is particularly suitable for use in path analysis wherein the model is generally identified by a system of structural equations.

Researchers are beginning to write on the relaxation of path analysis assumptions, beyond the regression assumption subset. Hauser and Goldberger (1970) and Werts et. al. (1973) have developed and discussed methods of dealing with unmeasured variables that frequently arise in the path analysis of behavioral research data. Blalock et. al. (1970) and Klemmack et. al. (1970) have studied the effects of measurement error on path analysis.

A frequent concern is the use of variables in path analysis that are ordinally measured. Boyle (1970) has studied this problem in some detail. He has investigated what can go wrong if a "true" equal-interval scale is distorted into unequal intervals, discusses the use of dummy variables when the independent variables are ordinally measured, and empirically compares results obtained for path analysis with dummy variables for path analysis with equal intervals assumed and with nonparametric analysis. He concluded that the dangers of assuming equal intervals is not great and suggests the use of the dummy variable technique as a way of improving sociological measurement.

The analysis of ordinal data is also discussed by Hawkes (1971), Somers (1962, 1970), Werts and Linn (1971, 1973) and Wilson (1971). In a paper by Smith (1972), a path analysis involving ordinal data is developed together with a discussion of the appropriateness of using the Boyle (1970) methods of dealing with ordinal variables.

The important problem of model selection is the subject of a Blalock (1968) paper. A good example of the application of the process to determine a correct model is given by Goldberger (1971) in an example concerning voting behavior.

It is apparent that much more work is required on assessing the consequences of relaxing path analysis assumptions. If in doubt, consultation with a statistician is highly recommended.

EXAMPLES

In this section, two examples are given in which path analysis has been used under questionable circumstances. The salient features of the papers and the published critiques are given, but for a full appreciation of the difficulties of using path analysis in behavioral research, the reader is urged to study the referenced papers below.

In the Lyden and Lee (1973) paper, an evaluation by path analysis of a program designed to vitalize local communities is reported. The intent of the authors is to demonstrate that federal agencies can effectively monitor such programs, even though the agencies must "measure both direct and indirect effects on hundreds of organizations, many of which have little or no contact with the monitoring agency." Regarding path analysis, the authors write, "The power of path analysis to explain findings, which was exemplified in this study, suggests that this technique may be a valuable analytic tool for the emerging field of program evaluation. Although path analysis has been used for many years in the biological sciences, its application to the social sciences is quite recent and consequently still in a developmental state. *It should therefore be used with due caution.* But today's administrators, inundated with computer print-out data, desperately need analytic tools to help them organize and interpret this supraabundant information. Path analysis shows promise of becoming such a tool."

It is apparent that the authors have not heeded their own advice. In their use of path analysis, they violate the following assumptions as pointed out by Nolle (1973):

1. *A clearly defined causal system.* Lyden and Lee state, "Path analysis examines *all possible* relationships and arranges them in order according to their logical relationships." Of course, it does no such thing. As Nolle points out, "it is only the analyst who can arrange the variables. Path analysis gives the implications of a particular arrangement which has already specified the causal ordering and the nature of the causal connections according to the theoretical predilections of the researchers." Lyden and Lee additionally fail to give "undebatable" reasons for the path diagram they use. This is consistent with their error, since they apparently let path analysis "select" the diagram. No structural equations are given and nothing is said about how the parameters in the model were estimated.
2. *Path diagram conventions are not followed.* No residual terms are used and correlations, if any, are not indicated. Therefore, it is impossible to determine what the structural equations are.
3. *Estimation inadequacies.* Although the estimation procedures are unclear, it is apparent that standard linear model techniques were not correctly employed. Specifically, in the model, zero-order correlations were used when it seems obvious that partial correlations of some sort should have been used.

In summary, Nolle makes the following points:

1. "Path analysis does show promise as a tool in social work, but it requires a strong theoretical base to provide equations that can be used to estimate parameters than can be used to describe the relative effects of a collection of variables in a complex system of causality."
2. "The authors (Lyden and Lee) ignore the fundamental point made above and consequently they do social work and path analysis a severe disservice. They exemplify the point that the worst enemies of a faddish technique are its uninformed advocates. The editors of *Social Work* and future users of path analysis can be spared this type of commentary by forwarding future manuscripts to persons who are knowledgeable in this area."
3. "My best estimate is that it will take five years to correct some of the harmful effects of Lyden and Lee's article. This estimate is based on the fact that it took five years for O. D. Duncan, the man who popularized path analysis in sociology, to place into print his revisions to his original article."

While Nolle's last two points may appear to be rather harsh, they are well-taken. The abuse of a technique can snowball by its continued misuse and it may take a literature at least five years to set the record straight.

The tragedy of committing the type of error discussed in connection with the Lyden and Lee paper is that policy may well be formulated on the inferences made in the study, when in fact the inferences are based on questionable applications of a quantitative technique. This concern is best exemplified by a major and sensitive research effort such as the Jencks et. al. (1972) study, "Inequality: A Reassessment of the Effects of Family and Schooling in America." The study has received considerable publicity in the literature and press, since among its findings is that the number of years of education has little effect upon later occupational and income attainment. Thus, the person's inherited intelligence, IQ, family background, and so on are the main determinants of occupation and income. Obviously, this finding has potentially dramatic policy implications.

It turns out that most of the findings in the Jencks study are based on path analysis, when, in fact, most of the path analysis assumptions are not supported by the data. Taylor (1973a) has pointed this out in a paper that is must reading for path analysis users. Borrowing from Taylor, consider the primary path diagram used in the Jencks study shown in Figure 2.

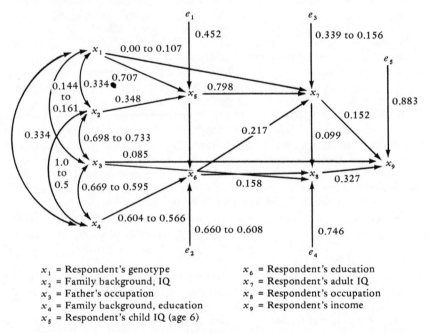

x_1 = Respondent's genotype
x_2 = Family background, IQ
x_3 = Father's occupation
x_4 = Family background, education
x_5 = Respondent's child IQ (age 6)

x_6 = Respondent's education
x_7 = Respondent's adult IQ
x_8 = Respondent's occupation
x_9 = Respondent's income

FIGURE 2   A Path Model of Effects Upon Income and Occupation (Native, white non-farm males)

From Figure 2, the variability in the respondent's income is explained by occupation, adult IQ, father's occupation, and other factors—e_5. The "other factors" account for 78% of the variability! Thus, the model explains only 22% of the variability in income attainment. Also, notice that IQ heritability $(x_1 \rightarrow x_5)$ is taken to be roughly 50% $(.707^2)$. It is clear that a great deal of weight is given to R^2 in drawing conclusions about the model, and as was pointed out earlier, R^2 is susceptible to large biases if certain "regression" assumptions are not met.

Now consider the Heise (1969) assumptions in context with the Jencks model for income attainment.

1. *Change in one variable is always a linear function of change in other variables.* Jencks does assume linear effects in the model and argues that it is an acceptable assumption. The consequences, if it is not, are significant. As Taylor points out, "Any multiple correlation R^2 assuming linearity is *necessarily always* less than or equal to a comparable multiple correlation, say R^2, using a technique not requiring linearity." Thus, if nonlinear relationships exist among the variables, the computer R^2 will be biased downwards. It seems likely that this occurs given the variables in the Jencks model.

2. *One way causation.* The model does appear to satisfy this assumption. For example, IQ in school (x_5) can affect later occupation (x_8), but the reverse is not possible. As Taylor points out, it may well be that Jencks *selected* the variables that would conform to this assumption and dropped those that did not, even though they may have been important variables. In any event, it would seem necessary for Jencks to present a discussion of why no recursive variables were included. No such explanations appear. It is possible, of course, to include recursive variables in path analysis when the appropriate modifications are made (see Wright, 1960; Henry and Hummon, 1971).

3. *A clearly defined causal system.* This is the crux of the matter. Who is to say that the system illustrated in Figure 2 is "best"? According to Jencks, this is the investigators' "best effort at describing the determinants of adult success in America." It appears, however, that variables were chosen with an eye towards using path analysis, an eye that could have possibly been in need of corrective lenses. As mentioned above, it is questionable whether a careful analysis of model construction was undertaken. They did not use the well-known methods proposed by Blalock (1971) to eliminate implausible causal models nor those proposed by Heise (1969). Taylor points out that they did not bother to cite the relevant literature on model construction.

4. *Dependent variables are uncorrelated with one another.* This is difficult to assess in the model. The assumption is not precisely satisfied, but it rarely is— it is a matter of degree. How seriously is this assumption violated? Jencks does not address this issue.

5. *A high degree of measurement reliability and validity.* Reliable estimates of correlations are required for path analysis. In the model, certain variables are constructs (child's genotype, family IQ and family education) and are, therefore, measured indirectly. Thus, guesses must be made as to what the correlations between unmeasured constructs are. The study did not use original data, but rather borrowed correlations from previous experiments. Taylor suggests that this resulted in some "pretty wild" guesses of some correlations and much faith in accepting others. He cites, for example, the correlation between x_2-family IQ and x_4-family education, stated as being between .5 and 1.00. Since the path coefficients are functions of the correlations, variability in the "guesses" of the correlations will send waves in the estimates of the path coefficients through the entire model. It is clear that guesses of certain correlations had to be made since some are inherently unmeasurable. This should have been made patently clear and the consequences expounded upon.

6. *The usual multivariate regression assumptions must be met.* As pointed out earlier, this assumption is, in fact, a set of important and necessary assump-

tions. First, the variables must be measured on an interval scale. This is questionable regarding occupational prestige rank and IQ scores. But, why are there no variables that clearly are ordinal measures? In a complex system such as this, it is surprising to not find a larger class of variables. Taylor suggests that this may have been by design; that is, variables were selected that were only interval or quasi-interval measurable. It is possible, however, to include ordinal data in path analysis, if done with care, as pointed out by Boyle (1970), among others. Second, the model assumes additivity. No interactions are included and there is little evidence that appropriate tests of additivity were conducted. It is well known that interactions terms can be used in multiple regression by forming new variables that represent the products of two or more variables in the set. Since Jencks did not have the original data, the additivity of the model could not be tested, nor could interaction terms be included in the model. In a study of such importance, it is surprising that the investigators did not obtain the original data for these purposes. Third, the analysis did not acknowledge that explained variance is dependent upon variable ordering. As pointed out by Jencks, "It is well understood that if one relates any x_1 to y with x_2 constant, and then relates x_1 to y with x_2 and x_3 held constant, and then relates x_1 to y with x_2, x_3 and x_4 held constant and so on, then usually (though not necessarily), the proportion of total variance in y that will be explained by x_1 will become progressively less and less. At each stage, less residual variance in y is left to be explained." Taylor suggests that Jencks may have "stacked the deck" by choosing the ordering scheme. For example, "the effect of schooling (x_6) on income (x_9) is substantially reduced simply because adult IQ, child IQ, respondent's occupation, and father's occupation are held constant simultaneously."

In summary, Taylor suggests that "path analysis restrictions on interval measurement, linearity, additivity and variable ordering all point to the conclusion that the effects of various factors on occupational and income inequality in American society, particularly the effects of education, are actually *underestimated* in the report. Higher estimates would necessarily result from the techniques employing noninterval measurement, nonlinearity, nonadditivity and experimentation with variable ordering."

CONCLUDING REMARKS

The abuses of path analysis abound in the literature. This has led to the publication of erratum on papers, rebuttals, and in some instances, rather heated exchanges between authors, reviewers, and readers. Will the organizational sciences follow this path? Not if certain precautions are taken. For the user of path analysis, make certain that you understand the correct use of the technique. For the reviewer of path analysis research papers, if you do not understand the techniques and concepts being used, decline to review the paper. A good editor will respect and appreciate your professionalism.

NOTES

1.   Quoting Boyle (1970), "The recent introduction of path analysis to sociology is an event of almost revolutionary importance. In company with other advances in multiple regression analysis, we now have available procedures which are more powerful statistically, and also more directly

relevant to sociological theory. Rather than leaving data analysis and theory construction as two separate steps, these techniques provide a model in terms of which the theory is expressed, and then directly evaluated through the statistical procedures."

2. Computer codes are available from Nygreen (1971) and Srivasta et. al. (1973).

REFERENCES

Aldrich, H. O. (1972). "Technology and Organization Structure: A Reexamination of the Findings of the Aston Group," *Administrative Science Quarterly* 19, 26.

Anderson, C. and Pfaffenberger, R. (1974). "Path Analysis as a Research Tool in the Study of Organizations," *Proceedings*, Eastern Academy of Management Science Meeting, May 10-11, University of Maryland, College Park, Maryland.

Barrett, J. P. (1974). "The Coefficient of Determination—Some Limitations," *The American Statistician* 28, 19.

Blalock, H. M. (1968). "Theory Building and Causal Inferences." In *Methodology in Social Research*, ed. H. M. Blalock. New York: McGraw-Hill.

Blalock, H. M. (1971) (ed.) *Causal Models in the Social Sciences*. Chicago: Aldine-Atherton.

Blalock, H. M., Wells, C. S. and Carter, L. F. (1970). "Statistical Estimation With Random Measurement Error." In *Sociological Methodology*, eds. E. F. Borgatta and G. W. Bohrnstedt. San Francisco: Jossey-Bass.

Bohrnstedt, G. W. and Carter, T. M. (1971). "Robustness in Regression Analysis." In *Sociological Methodology*, ed. H. L. Costner. San Francisco: Jossey-Bass.

Borgatta, E. F. (1969) (ed.) *Sociological Methodology*. San Francisco: Jossey-Bass.

Borgatta, E. F. and Bohrnstedt, G. W. (1970) (eds.) *Sociological Methodology*. San Francisco: Jossey-Bass.

Box, G. E. P. (1966). "Use and Abuse of Regression," *Technometrics* 8, 625.

Boyle, R. P. (1966). "Causal Theory and Statistical Measures of Effect: A Convergence," *American Sociological Review* 31, 843.

Boyle, R. P. (1970). "Path Analysis and Ordinal Data," *American Journal of Sociology* 75, 461.

Clawson, C. J. (1974). "Fitting Branch Locations, Performance Standards and Marketing Strategies to Local Conditions," *Journal of Marketing* 38, 8.

Costner, H. L. (1972) (ed.) *Sociological Methodology*. San Francisco: Jossey-Bass.

Cox, D. R. (1970). *The Analysis of Binary Data*. London: Methuen.

Cummings, L. L. and Schwab, D. P. (1973). *Performance in Organizations*. Glenview, Ill.: Scott, Foresman and Co.

Duncan, O. D. (1966). "Path Analysis: Sociological Examples," *American Journal of Sociology* 72, 1.

Duncan, O. D. (1970). "Partials, Partitions and Paths." In *Sociological Methodology*, eds. E. F. Borgatta and G. W. Bohrnstedt. San Francisco: Jossey-Bass.

Duncan, O. D. (1971). "Path Analysis: Sociological Examples (Addenda)." In *Causal Models in the Social Sciences*, ed. H. M. Blalock. Chicago: Aldine-Atherton.

Goldberger, A. S. (1971). "Discerning a Causal Pattern Among Data on Voting Behavior." In *Causal Models in the Social Sciences*, ed. H. M. Blalock. Chicago: Aldine-Atherton.

Goldberger, A. S. and Duncan, O. D. (1973) (eds.) *Structural Equation Models in the Social Sciences*. New York: Seminar Press.

Goodman, L. A. (1972a). "A General Model for the Analysis of Surveys," *American Journal of Sociology* 77, 1035.

Goodman, L. A. (1972b). "The Analysis of Multidimensional Contingency Tables When Some Variables are Posterior to Others," (abs.), *Biometrics* 28, 1169.

Hadden, K. and Dewalt, B. (1974). "Path Analysis—Some Anthropological Examples," *Ethnology* 13, 105.

Hauser, R. M. and Goldberger, A. S. (1970). "The Treatment of Unobservable Variables in Path Analysis." In *Sociological Methodology*, eds. E. F. Borgatta and G. W. Bohrnstedt. San Francisco: Jossey-Bass.

Hawkes, R. J. (1971). "The Multivariate Analysis of Ordinal Measures," *American Journal of Sociology* 76, 908.

Hayya, J., Pfaffenberger, R. and Chan, H. (1974). "On Some Considerations in Discrete Regression." In *Proceedings*, American Statistical Association Business and Economics Section, St. Louis, Missouri.

Heise, D. R. (1969). "Problems in Path Analysis and Causal Inference." In *Sociological Methodology*, ed. E. F. Borgatta. San Francisco: Jossey-Bass.

Heise, D. R. (1970). "Causal Inference From Panel Data." *Sociological Methodology*, eds. E. F. Borgatta and G. W. Bohrnstedt. San Francisco: Jossey-Bass.

Henry, N. W. and Hummon, N. P. (1971). "An Example of Estimation Procedures in a Nonrecursive System," *American Sociological Review* 36, 1099.

Jencks, C., Smith, M., Acland, H., Bane, J. J., Cohen, D., Gintis, H., Heyns, B. and Michelson, S. (1972). *Inequality: A Reassessment of the Effects of Family and Schooling in America*. New York: Basic Books.

Joreskog, K. G. (1969). "A General Method for Analysis of Covariance Structures," *Biometrika* 57, 239.

Joreskog, K. G., Gruveaus, G. T. and Van Thillo, M. (1970). "A General Computer Program for Analysis of Covariance Structures," *Educational Testing Service Research Bulletin* 70, 15.

Klemmack, D. L., Wells, C. S. and Carter, L. F. (1970). "Statistical Estimation With Random Measurement Error." In *Sociological Methodology*, eds. E. F. Borgatta and G. W. Bohrnstedt. San Francisco: Jossey-Bass.

Kronus, C. L. (1973). "Patterns of Adult Library Use—Regression and Path Analysis," *Adult Education—Washington* 23, 115.

Land, K. C. (1969). "Principles of Path Analysis." In *Sociological Methodology*, ed. E. F. Borgatta. San Francisco: Jossey-Bass.

Li, C. C. (1955). *Population Genetics*. Chicago, Ill.: University of Chicago Press.

Loebner, H. and Driver, E. (1973). "Differential Fertility in Central India—A Path Analysis," *Demography* 10, 329.

Lyden, F. J. and Lee, L. K. (1973). "Evaluating Program Change," *Social Work* 18, 87.

Mapes, R. (1973). "Path Analysis—A Cautionary Note," *Sociological Review* 21, 137.

Miller, A. D. (1971). "The Logic of Causal Analysis: From Experimental to Nonexperimental Designs." In *Causal Models in the Social Sciences*, ed. H. M. Blalock. Chicago: Aldine-Atherton.

Mishra, K. N., Nanda, J. S. and Chaudhar, R. C. (1973). "Correlation Path Coefficients and Selection Indices in Dwarf Rice," *Indian Journal of Agricultural Sciences* 43, 306.

Morrison, D. G. (1972). "Regressions With Discrete Dependent Variables: The Effect on R^2," *Journal of Marketing Research* 9, 338.

Nolle, D. B. (1973). "Using Path Analysis," *Social Work* 18, 110.

Nygreen, G. T. (1971). "Interactive Path Analysis," *The American Sociologist* 6, 37.

Porter, L. W. and Lawler, E. E. (1968). *Managerial Attitudes and Performance*. Homewood, Ill.: Richard D. Irwin.

Schoenberg, R. (1972). "Strategies for Meaningful Comparison." In *Sociological Methodology*, ed. H. L. Costner. San Francisco: Jossey-Bass.

Seibel, H. D. (1972). "Path Analysis: Statistical Method for Investigating Causal Models," *Zeitschrift fur Sociol Psychologie* 3, 5.

Shasha, N. S., Nye, W. P. and Campbell, W. F. (1973). "Path Coefficient Analysis of Correlation Between Honey Bee Activity and Seed Yield in Allium-Cepa L," *Journal of the American Society for Horticulture Science* 98, 341.

Smith, R. B. (1972). "Neighborhood Context and College Plans: An Ordinal Path Analysis," *Social Forces* 51, 199.

Somers, R. H. (1962). "A New Asymmetric Measure for Ordinal Variables," *American Sociological Review* 27, 799.

Somers, R. H. (1970). "A Partitioning of Ordinal Information in Three-Way Cross-Classification," *Multivariate Behavior Research* 5, 217.

Srivasta, V. K., Peter, K. V., Rai, B. and Jain, R. C. (1973). "A TDC-12 Computer Program for Estimating Path-Coefficients, Partial Regressions and Multiple Correlations," *Current Science* 42, 842.

Swindel, B. G. (1974). "Instability of Regression Coefficients Illustrated," *American Statistician* 28, 63.

Taylor, H. F. (1973a). "Linear Models of Consistency: Some Extensions of Blalock's Strategy," *American Journal of Sociology* 78, 1192.

Taylor, H. F. (1973b). "Playing Dozens With Path Analysis: Methodological Pitfalls in Jencks, et. al., Inequality," *Sociology of Education* 46, 433.

Toy, D. and Hayya, J. (1974). "On the Appropriate Use of Regression Analysis in Marketing Research," *Working Series in Marketing Research*, No. 24; Department of Marketing, The Pennsylvania State University.

Tukey, J. (1954). "Causation, Regression and Path Analysis." In *Statistics and Mathematics in Biology*, ed. O. Kempthorne. Ames, Iowa: Iowa State University Press.

Turner, M. E. and Stevens, C. D. (1959). "The Regression Analysis of Causal Chains," *Biometrics* 15, 236.

Ward, J. H., Jennings, E. and Bottenberg, R. (1970). "A New Vector Approach to Regression Analysis and Computers in Research." Manuscript. Washington, D.C. Control Data Corporation.

Werts, C. E., Joreskog, K. G. and Linn, R. L. (1973). "Identification and Estimation in Path Analysis With Unmeasured Variables," *American Journal of Sociology* 78, 1469.

Werts, C. E. and Linn, R. L. (1971). "Comment on 'Path Analysis and Ordinal Data' (Boyle, 1970)," *American Journal of Sociology* 76, 1109.

Werts, C. E. and Linn, R. L. (1973). "Erratum to the Werts-Linn Comments on Boyle's 'Path Analysis and Ordinal Data,'" *American Journal of Sociology* 78, 689.

Wilson, T. P. (1971). "A Critique of Ordinal Variables," *Social Forces* 49, 432.

Wright, S. (1921). "Correlation and Causation," *Journal of Agricultural Research* 20, 557.

Wright, S. (1943). "The Method of Path Coefficients," *Annals of Mathematical Statistics* 5, 161.

Wright, S. (1954). "The Interpretation of Multivariate Systems." In *Statistics and Mathematics in Biology*, ed. O. Kempthorne. Ames, Iowa: Iowa State University Press.

Wright, S. (1960). "The Treatment of Reciprocal Interactions, With or Without Lag, in Path Analysis," *Biometrics* 16, 425.

Wright, S. (1968). *Genetic and Biometric Foundations*: Volume 1. Chicago: University of Chicago Press.

Conflicts and Controversies in Behavioral Research

One of the first lessons learned by researchers in organizational behavior is that there is typically no one best way to design or carry out a study. Instead, there are research questions for which experimental designs are most appropriate and times when surveys or field studies are in order. Hence, a major aspect of research centers around the investigator's ability to understand the advantages and disadvantages associated with various designs and to be able to make difficult decisions concerning an appropriate research strategy given existing constraints.

In order to better understand the nature of these problems, this chapter deals with several of the conflicts and controversies involved in organizational research. A major conclusion to be drawn from these readings is the fact that researchers do not always agree on the most appropriate research strategy. Instead, choices among alternative strategies must be made based on the research questions raised and in full recognition of the constraints placed on a particular investigation.

The readings that follow deal not only with such constraints, but in addition, focus on what may best be described as tunnel vision by researchers in their investigations. Hopefully, these selections will clearly identify several of the major obstacles to substantive and creative research in work organizations.

In the first selection, Argyris discusses several unintended problems that arise from the use of human subjects in experiments and field studies. Problems inherent in the use of research assistants are also discussed. Argyris points out that, as a result of a researcher's desire for a "rigorous" design, subjects and assistants may engage in defensive and collaborative behavior that negatively influences the results. In particular, he discusses such problems as overdependency on the researcher, overt and covert withdrawal, aggression toward the researcher, and the banding together of subjects to protect their interests. Illustrations of each of these dysfunctional consequences of rigorous research are provided and several useful techniques are identified that may help to overcome such problems.

Second, Dunnette takes a "clinical" as well as provocative look at the "games psychologists play" in doing behavioral research. As Dunnette notes, "Somewhat to my surprise, I experienced no difficulty slipping into the role of a medical clinician—intent on describing fully and completely the behavioral symptomatology of psychology's distress in terms of the games we all play—many of which may reflect underlying pathologies leading us down the primrose path to nonscience" (p. 344). He identifies six "games," each dealing with one problem encountered in behavioral research. Based on this discussion, Dunnette goes on to speculate about the causes of such "nonscience" and to suggest several reasonable alternative courses of action for researchers. These suggestions, in part, represent a case for being more realistic and straightforward in designing, executing, *and reporting* investigations. He argues for increasing the use of eclecticism and multiple working hypotheses, and at the same time reducing pretense in academic environments. Such actions, although not necessarily resulting in a utopian situation, should at the very least lead to a more enriched (and less burdensome) intellectual climate for serious research.

Third, McGuire discusses the evolution of research paradigms in social psychology. Initially, the traditional and "emerging" paradigms are examined and critically evaluated. McGuire rejects both of these paradigms as being inadequate and instead suggests directions for a "new social psychology." Specifically, seven koan (or propositions) are proposed which call for a more creative, synergistic approach to research design and methodology. For instance, McGuire calls for greater emphasis on hypothesis *formation*—that is, how to identify important research questions. Moreover, McGuire argues for more comprehensive models (and studies) of human behavior and against the continued proliferation of simple linear process models. The argument is made throughout that investigators must step back from their research periodically and attempt to see and understand their own activities and how they relate to the larger issues of social sciences. Although McGuire focuses on experimental social psychology for his examples, it is easy to understand how the principles suggested here relate to the study of organizational behavior.

In the final selection, Staw questions the way in which behavioral science research can most effectively contribute to administrative practice in organizations. The traditional role of the researcher vis-à-vis practitioner is viewed as one in which the researcher is in possession of valid knowledge about organizational behavior—knowledge that is then disseminated to administrators. In this model, the researcher becomes an advocate of a particular theory or finding in dealing with practitioners. Staw casts doubt on the utility of this model in view of the serious threats to validity that exist in most research in organizations. Staw then suggests an alternative model in which the administrator is viewed as the center of innovation and evaluation of behavioral science theory applied to organizational practices. The role of the researcher in this model is to make available to administrators alternative theories and findings that might be applied to organizations and to train administrators in evaluating innovations in organizations. This latter model recognizes the inherent limitations associated with organizational research and suggests the need for administrators to become more willing to experiment with various administrative practices. Staw also discusses the types of quasi-experimental designs that may be appropriate in evaluating organizational innovations and the problems that may be encountered if administrators take a more experimental orientation in organizations.

REFERENCES AND SUGGESTED READINGS

Argyris, C. "Problems and New Directions for Industrial Psychology." In M. Dunnette (ed.), *Handbook of Industrial and Organizational Psychology*. Chicago: Rand McNally, 1976.

Becker, H. S. "Whose Side Are We On?" *Social Problems*, 14 (1967), pp. 239-249.

Harlow, H. F. "Fundamental Principles for Preparing Psychology Journal Articles," *Journal of Comparative and Physiological Psychology*, 55 (1962), pp. 893-896.

Kelman, H. C. *A Time to Speak*. San Francisco: Jossey-Bass, 1968.

Kelman, H. C. "Human Use of Human Subjects," *Psychological Bulletin*, 67 (1967), pp. 1-11.

Maier, N. R. F. "Maier's Law," *American Psychologist*, 15 (1960), pp. 208-212.

Ring, K. "Experimental Social Psychology: Some Sober Questions About Some Frivolous Values," *Journal of Experimental Social Psychology*, 3 (1967), pp. 113-123.

Silverman, I. "Nonreactive Measures and the Law," *American Psychologist*, 30 (1975), pp. 764-769.

Sommer, R. "On Writing Little Papers," *American Psychologist*, 14 (1959), pp. 235-237.

Stern, C. "Thoughts on Research," *Science*, 148 (1964), pp. 772-773.

Wollins, L. "Responsibility for Raw Data," *American Psychologist*, 17 (1962), pp. 657-658.

19 Some Unintended Consequences of Rigorous Research[1]

Chris Argyris

Rigorousness is to a researcher what efficiency is to an executive: an ideal state that is always aspired to, never reached, and continually revered. Much literature exists regarding the best ways to approach both rigorousness and efficiency. In the case of efficiency, executives have traditionally assumed that when organizations are not efficient it is usually because the members have not been adhering to an efficient organizational strategy. One of the contributions of organizational behaviorists has been to study how executives and employees actually behave (not limit themselves to how they say they behave). One major result of these studies has been to show that a good deal of inefficiency may occur precisely when and because the members are following closely the most accepted strategies for efficiency.

Recently a new literature has been, and continues to be, developed by scholars studying the research situation (Friedman, 1967; Rosenthal, 1966). They too have not limited themselves to what researchers say they do in conducting research. They have studied research in terms of how it is actually carried out. As a result, they have reported dysfunctions and opened up important new questions.

An exploration of this literature from the viewpoint of an organizational theorist suggests that his field may be able to make a modest contribution in terms of a theoretical framework to organize the existing findings and suggest other possible conclusions that have yet to be documented systematically. This framework conceives of the researcher-subject relationship as a systemic one, be it temporary. By borrowing from the established literature on research methodology, we shall attempt to show that the properties of this temporary system are remarkably similar to the properties of formal organizations. Moreover, many of the dysfunctions reported between experimenter and subject are similar to the dysfunctions between management and employee.

THE UNDERLYING ASSUMPTIONS ABOUT RIGOROUS RESEARCH

Let us begin by asking what are the underlying assumptions for conducting rigorous research. The first is that rigorousness is an ideal state which one can only approximate. The second assumption is that rigorousness is more closely approximated as the researcher is able to define unambiguously his problem and the relevant variables.

Source: C. Argyris, "Some Unintended Consequences of Rigorous Research," *Psychological Bulletin*, 1968, *70*(3), pp. 185–197. Copyright (1968) by the American Psychological Association. Reprinted by permission.

Moreover, the more easily the variables can be observed and measured, the greater the reliability, the greater the probability for future public verifiability, the more rigorous will be the research. The third assumption is that the more control a researcher has over his variables, the more rigorous will be his research.

THE NATURE OF THE RELATIONSHIP
BETWEEN RESEARCHER AND SUBJECT

These assumptions provide the basis for elegant research designs. Like management principles, the designs are expected to work if subjects cooperate. It is precisely at the point when people are brought into the picture that the difficulties arise. Why is this so?

In order to answer this question let us examine the basic qualities of rigorous research. Most methodologists agree with Edwards (1954) that rigorous research tends to occur when:

1. The research is deliberately undertaken to satisfy the needs of the researcher and where the pace of activity is controlled by the researcher to give him maximum possible control over the subjects' behavior.
2. The setting is designed by the researcher to achieve his objectives and to minimize any of the subjects' desires from contaminating the experiment.
3. The researcher is responsible for making accurate observations, recording them, analyzing them, and eventually reporting them.
4. The researcher has the conditions so rigorously defined that he or others can replicate them.
5. The researcher can systematically vary the conditions and note the concomitant variation among the variables.

These conditions are remarkably similar to those top management defines when designing an organization. Top management (researcher) defines the worker's (subject's) role as rationally and clearly as possible (to minimize error) and as simply as possible (to minimize having to draw from a select population, thereby reducing the generalizability of the research findings); provides as little information as possible beyond the tasks (thereby minimizing the time perspective of the subject); and defines the inducements for participating (e.g., a requirement to pass a course, a plea for the creation of knowledge, or money). Indeed, if Edwards's description is valid, the rigorous research criteria would create a world for the subject in which his behavior is defined, controlled, evaluated, manipulated, and reported to a degree that is comparable to the behavior of workers in the most mechanized assembly-line conditions.

THE UNINTENDED CONSEQUENCES OF
RIGOROUS RESEARCH DESIGNS

If this similarity between conditions in organizations and those in research systems does exist, then the unintended consequences found in formal organizations should also be found, in varying degree, in the temporary systems created by research. These consequences have been discussed in detail elsewhere (Argyris, 1964). Briefly they are:

1. Physical withdrawal which results in absenteeism and turnover.

2. Psychological withdrawal while remaining physically in the research situation. Under these conditions the subject is willing to let the researcher manipulate his behavior, usually for a price. The studies that show subjects as all too willing to cooperate are, from this point of view, examples of subject withdrawal from involvement and not, as some researchers suggest, signs of subjects' high involvement. To give a researcher what he wants in such a way that the researcher does not realize that the subject is doing this (a skill long ago learned by employees and students) is a sign of nonresponsibility and of a lack of commitment to the effectiveness of the research.

3. Overt hostility toward the research. Openly fighting the research rarely occurs, probably because the subjects are "volunteers." If they are not volunteers, they may still feel pressured to participate. If so, they would probably not feel free to fight the researcher openly.

4. Covert hostility is a safer adaptive mechanism. It includes such behavior as knowingly giving incorrect answers, being a difficult subject, second-guessing the research design and trying to circumvent it in some fashion, producing the minimally accepted amount of behavior, coercing others to produce minimally, and disbelief and mistrust of the researcher.

5. Emphasis upon monetary rewards as the reason for participation.

6. Unionization of subjects.

Organizational theory would suggest that the exact degree to which any of these conditions would hold for a given subject would be, in turn, a function of:

1. The degree to which being dependent, manipulated, and controlled is "natural" in the lives of the subjects (e.g., research utilizing children or adults in highly authoritarian cultures may be more generalizable).

2. The length of time that the research takes and the degree of subject control it requires.

3. The motivations of the subjects (e.g., for the sake of science, to pass a course, to learn about self, for money).

4. The potency of the research (the involvement it requires of the subject).

5. The possible effect participation in research or its results could have on the subject's evaluation of his previous, and perception of his future, life.

6. The number of times the subject participates in other research.

7. The degree to which the research situation is similar to other situations in which the subject is immersed, about which he has strong feelings, few of which he can express. For example, in the case of students, the role in a lecture class is similar to the role of a subject in a psychological experiment. (The teacher controls, has the long-range perspective, defines the tasks, etc.) To the extent that he is unable to express his frustration in relation to the class, he may find it appropriate, if indeed he does not feel himself inwardly compelled, to express these pent-up feelings during the research.

Some may question if these feelings would come out in such research situations because participating in an experiment, being interviewed, filling out a questionnaire tend to take a short time. This view may be questioned. Has not the reader watched how quickly people become involved in parlor games and noted how easy it is for them to surface competitive needs, power aspirations, and fears of failure? Indeed, is it not the fundamental assumption of the researcher that an experiment is genuinely involving? Is it not accepted that the data would hardly be generalizable if the subjects could be shown to be involved only peripherally because of the shortness of time? As Sales (1966), a proponent of experimentation pointed out, the

> "brevity" argument is not valid . . . the entire science of experimental social psychology rests upon the assumption that experimental periods are sufficiently lengthy for treatments to "take," an assumption which is supported in every significant finding obtained in the experimental laboratory [p. 28].

If experimental conditions "take" in short periods, then why should not the psychological conditions implicit in the researcher-subject relationship also "take"?

ILLUSTRATION OF THE EXISTENCE OF ADAPTIVE STRATEGIES

The next question is, to what extent are subjects beginning to adapt in ways suggested by the theoretical framework? Orne (1962), Mills (1962), and Rosenthal (1963) have presented evidence that subjects are willing to become dependent upon and submissive to the experimenter and, as Kiesler (1969) suggested, overcooperative with the researcher. Unfortunately, little systematic research exists beyond these studies. Some anecdotal evidence was collected by the writer at his own institution. The students have increasingly emphasized the importance of being paid for participating in research. This trend can be predicted by an organizational theory. The "market orientation" (so common among lower level employees in industry) is an inevitable consequence of being in a formal organization (Argyris, 1964).

Second-guessing and beating the researcher at his own game may also be becoming commonplace, especially in dissonance experiments. Many experiments have been reported where it was crucial to deceive the students. Naturally, in many cases the students were carefully debriefed (although to the writer's knowledge few, if any, researchers have provided evidence which was collected as rigorously for this assertion as were the data directly related to the goal of the experiment). One result that has occurred is that students now come to experiments expecting to be tricked. The initial romance and challenge of being subjects has left them and they are now beginning to behave like lower level employees in companies. Their big challenge is to guess the deception (beat the management). If one likes the experimenter, then he cooperates. If he does not, he may enjoy botching the works with such great skill that the experimenter is not aware of this behavior. This practice is frequent enough for Burdick (1957) to make it the subject matter of an entire chapter in his best seller, *The Ninth Wave*. He describes the hero who outguessed the experimenters and was eventually rejected by them. He also describes another subject who pleased the experimenters but who, it turned out, hated the experimenters deeply. In one major university a formal evaluation was made of the basic psychology course by nearly 600 undergraduates. They were given three topics from which they could choose one to evaluate thoroughly. The senior professor responsible for the course reported an overwhelming majority of the students focused on the requirement, in the course, that they had to participate as subjects. The students were very critical, mistrustful, and hostile to the requirement. In many cases they identified how they expressed their pent-up feelings by "beating the researcher" in such a way that he never found out (an activity frequently observed among frustrated employees).

These examples, incidentally, also serve to illustrate that students can generate strong feelings about experimentation in a very short time. They also raise the question, Do we need systematic data showing that the briefing each subject received actually generated not only the correct cognitive maps but the proper psychological set upon which the experiment depends (Friedman, 1967)?

Another example of how students are beginning to react like employees is illustrated by a request received by the writer recently from a senior social psychologist at Yale. He had concluded that to identify an experiment openly and honestly would lead to a set of attitudes among students that would be harmful to the experiments. He wanted to know if a place could be found for him to conduct his experiment in an organizational setting. He assumed that people in an organizational setting are not so contaminated as students (especially along the dimension of expecting to be tricked). As we shall see, this assumption is not necessarily valid.

A graduate student was recently able to design an experiment with no deception and one in which he could honestly advertise (as he did) that the students might learn about themselves as a result of participating in the research. His experiment was a 10-hour T group. In the first four sessions at least 3 hours were spent by the members trying to deal with the students' deep beliefs that the ad was phony, that they were to be tricked, and that the researcher didn't really mean what he had said.

Recently, Kelman (1967) raised similar issues. He doubts that the subjects will remain naive. He quoted one subject as saying, "Psychologists always lie!" He also suggested, and this would be predicted by an organizational theory, that the subjects may come to resent the experimenter and throw a monkey wrench in the experiment.

Brock and Becker (1966) attempted to prove that deception may not have the harmful effects suggested by Kelman (1967). Their work is open to serious question. Nowhere do they provide evidence that the subjects were not dutifully playing the role of subject and doing everything asked of them. One could argue that they signed the petition, after being told they had just ruined the experimenter's mechanical box (which was contrived to blow up when a button was pressed), because they saw through the hoax and went along with the game. An explanation for those who refused to sign the petition could be that since they did not blow up the box they saw little reason to go along with the researchers. One would predict that the subjects might openly resist if they were given a rational opportunity to do so. This turned out to be the case. There was high resistance to the experimenter when it was possible to connect the massive debriefing with participation in the second experiment.

Two points require emphasis at this juncture. First, these adaptive strategies are predictable by organizational theory because the relationship between the researcher and the subject is similar to the one between the manager and the employee in formal organizations. Moreover, the adaptive strategies may well lead to internal psychological states, on the part of the subjects, that can significantly alter their perception of the research and their response to it. If this is the case, then the generalizability of the results may be seriously limited unless the researcher can show "rigorously" that he has been able to control the existence of subjects' adaptive strategies.

One way a researcher may respond to the problem of controlling these adaptive strategies is to obtain a large sample of subjects. He may assume that these kinds of behavior are "noise" that can be partialed out. If our theoretical view is valid, then any increase in the sample may simply tend to increase the difficulties, not decrease them. Moreover, as the "noise" increases it may eliminate any "real" effect that might be there. Another response may be to increase the controls over the subjects' behavior. According to this analysis, the problems would then be compounded.

As another illustration of dysfunctions, some enterprising students at two major universities have begun to think about starting a student organization that would be similar to Manpower or, if this were resisted by the university, similar to a union. Instead of secretaries, they would offer subjects. They believe that they can get students to cooperate because they would promise them more money, better debriefing, and more interest on the part of the researcher (e.g., more complete feedback). When this experience was reported to some psychologists their response was similar to the reactions of businessmen who have just been told for the first time that their employees were considering the creation of a union. There was some nervous laughter, a comment indicating surprise, then another comment to the effect that every organization has some troublemakers, and finally a prediction that such an activity would never succeed because "the students are too disjointed to unite."

To continue the comparison with businessmen, is there not a strong similarity of the attitudes held by the early lumber kings and those held presently by many researchers? The lumber kings consumed trees without worrying very much about the future supply. Researchers (field and experimental) seem to consume subjects without worrying very much about their future supply. For example, as was shown above, simple debriefing may not be enough. Students who serve as subjects talk about their experiences with other students; they may even magnify them as they are prone to do a fraternity initiation rite. The impact upon future subjects can be deadly and difficult to overcome.

An experience the writer had several years ago illustrates how much the formal, authoritarian, pyramidal relationships are endemic in many social science generalizations even though they are never made explicit.

A world-renowned learning theorist met with a group of executives. To his surprise, one of these, a senior corporate officer, had attempted to utilize the learning theorist's views in his workplace. For example, he wanted to see what would happen if he related to his subordinates in a more systematic way, that is, by following a carefully thought-through reinforcement schedule of rewards. He reported the following difficulties:

First, it was difficult to infer any guidelines or criteria as to what would be a valid schedule. Nevertheless, with the help of an advanced graduate student, one was developed. It was not too long before the executive found that he spent the majority of his time simply monitoring the schedules and giving the appropriate rewards according to schedule.

Although all subordinates seemed to respond favorably, there was an unexpected differential reaction. Many men, unlike the subjects in the experiment, reacted positively to their boss and to his rewards. They would say in effect, "Thank you, sir. I certainly appreciate your thoughtfulness." This genuine response tended to complicate matters for two reasons. First, being able to show gratitude toward a superior may in itself be gratifying. Second, such a warm response normally calls for an equally positive response from the recipient, such as "It's always a pleasure, Smith, to reward excellent behavior." In either case the subject is experiencing rewards that would not be in the reinforcement schedule.

The executive, although pleased with the "subject's" reaction, strove to minimize the pleasure so that the original reinforcement schedule would not be confounded. In doing this he found that he was creating a world where his subordinates had a relationship to him that was similar to the one rats (or children) have to an experimenter. This relationship was one in which the subordinate was dependent and had a short time perspective. The schedule, if it were to work, required a fundamentally authoritarian relationship!

To make matters worse, the "subjects" were constantly having their lives bombarded with meaningful rewards and penalties from other employees as well as from such administrative procedures as budgets. The executive began to realize that if these were to be systematically controlled, he would have to become a little Hitler, control the world of his subordinates completely, to the point that they would be isolated from the system in which they were embedded.

It is important to note that nowhere did the learning theorist state these conditions in his generalizations. For example, he had concluded that a specified reinforcement schedule seemed to lead to a specific level of learning. He failed to specify that this generalization held only if the subject was in a specified relationship to the one doing the rewarding and penalizing, namely, one that is similar to that of an experimenter with a rat. Thus, we see that the nature of person-to-person relationships and the nature of the research situation can serve as potent moderators of the variable relationships we often study. If this is the case, the generalizations from rigorous research studies of the types described above ought to "work" (in the sense that they account for substantial portions of the nonrandom variance) only in life situations which are analogous to the experimental situations in which the original data were collected. The analogous situations are those that contain authoritarian relationships and provide for social isolation of the participants. These generalizations ought not to hold up (and indeed ought not to be expected to hold up), however, in those cases where a controlling party and the object of control are engaged in a relationship which is of a qualitatively different type than that of the experimenter and subject in the experimental situation which gave rise to the data, and where the characteristics of the situation (i.e., of the task and social environment) are substantially different in the life situation than in the experimental situation.

RESEARCH IN FIELD SETTINGS

The problems discussed above also hold true for the researcher-subject relationship in field settings; indeed, in some cases the problems are compounded.

During the past several years, while conducting field research, the writer has interviewed 35 lower level employees and 30 upper level executives on the subject of how they heard about the research, how they felt coming to be interviewed or filling out the questionnaire, and how they felt while being interviewed or filling out a questionnaire.

The most consistent finding was the unanimity of responses. Apparently research conducted in organizations may create even deeper problems for subjects. Although the data are admittedly anecdotal, it seems appropriate to use them as suggestive of the problem. In doing so, it is important to keep in mind that in all the field studies from which these data were developed, the management at all levels had been briefed by the researcher in small groups with ample time for questions, and letters of explanation had gone to each employee from the president, as well as being displayed on all the bulletin boards.

Although the managers at the lower levels felt they understood the research program and were in favor of it, when it came to telling the employee such a seemingly simple thing as that he was scheduled to be interviewed the next day, many felt uncomfortable in doing so. They did not feel they could honestly describe the research, nor did they feel they could answer employee anxieties, and more importantly, they reported, they did not want to try. This attitude is understandable because most managers tend to emphasize "getting the job done"; they rarely inquire about their interpersonal impact on the employees, nor about interpersonal problems (Argyris, 1962; 1965). Thus to discuss a research project that could arouse emotional responses would place the manager in an interpersonal situation that would be uncomfortable for him.

Instead of running the risk of engaging in possible difficult conversation with an employee, most managers reported (and employees confirmed) that they simply went up to the employee and notified him that he would be interviewed the next day at a particular time. Over 75% of the employees reported that their superiors either ordered them to go to be interviewed or said it in such way that they implied that they did not want any "noise." Thus, most employees felt they (the employees) knew very little about the research. Few reported open resentment (after all, they were always being ordered to do something). Many reported feeling anxious.

The reasons for anxiety seemed to vary enormously. "Why did they pick me? Who picked me? Are they going to ask personal questions? Are they trying to get rid of me? Whose crazy idea was this? Will I be able to understand a professor or a researcher? Will the questions be too difficult? Will they ask me to write? How open should I be? Will it get anyone (including me) in trouble? What effect will this have on my wages earned for the day? What effect will my absence have upon others who are working and depend on me?" In some cases the anxiety was compounded by informal employee kidding and discussion about the research. "Who goes to see the headshrinkers first?" "I hear they place a hot towel on your head and send electrical currents through you to make sure you don't lie." "They have a guy who can read your mind."

Few of these anxieties were openly stated and fewer were dealt with. Many employees, who came to be interviewed or to fill out the questionnaire with varying degrees of anxiety, attempted to cope with their feelings by becoming resigned ("They do things to me unilaterally all the time"), or by mild hostility and cautious withdrawal or noninvolvement.

The feelings of being controlled, or being pushed around, and of anxiety were reduced more quickly in the interview situation because the interviewer was able to answer many of their questions (without their having to raise them), helped them to feel that they did not have to participate, and encouraged them to alter the questions or the sequence in which they were asked, as well as to feel free to refuse to answer any questions. The negative feelings, reported the subjects, persisted over a longer period in the questionnaire situation. They reported that they felt more controlled, pushed around, and dealt with at a distance, while filling out the questionnaire. For example, many reported questions that arose in their minds but they hesitated to discuss them openly.

The reported feelings of being controlled, being dependent, and submissive to a researcher tended to decrease as one went up the hierarchy and with more participation people had in learning about the research and in deciding if permission was to be granted for its execution. Moreover, the fear of intellectual incompetence to participate was almost negligible. However, there were some anxieties about how open to be, how much risk to take, and how much to level with the interviewer. As in the case of the lower level employees, the (properly executed) questionnaire situation irritated a significantly higher proportion of the managers than did a (properly executed) interview. The executives reported that they resented the unilateral dependence that they experienced in filling out a questionnaire.

It seems that the research process, in a field setting, tends to place subjects in a situation vis-à-vis the researcher that is similar to the superior-subordinate relationship. This is not a neutral encounter for most people, especially for employees of organizations, and especially if the research is being conducted within the organization and during working time.

There is another impact that the research process tends to have upon people that has the effect of creating a double bind. Bennis (1966) has summarized the position of many scientists and philosophers of science that the underlying spirit of scientific research is the spirit of inquiry. It is the irresistible need to explore, the hypothetical spirit. The norm to be open, to experiment, is also crucial in the spirit of inquiry. Also there is a fundamental belief in the gratification derived from gaining knowledge for its own sake as well as the sharing of knowledge with all.

If we compare these conditions with those found in the living systems of organizations we find that the organizations tend to create the opposite conditions. For example, it has been shown that interpersonal openness, experimentation, and trust tend to be inhibited in organizations (Argyris, 1962). The same may be said for the concern for truth for its own sake. The sharing of knowledge is not a living value since that could lead to one's organizational survival being threatened. Thus, the subject is in a double bind. He is expected to be open, manifest a spirit of inquiry, and take risks when he is placed in a situation that has many of the repressive characteristics of formal organizations, which he has long ago learned to adapt to by not being open or taking risks.

The degree to which this double bind exists probably varies enormously with the living system of the organization, the personal and organizational security of the subjects, their intellectual competence, their position in the system as well as the research methods, research style, and the interpersonal skills of the researcher. However, the position being taken here is that these forces and binds should be taken into account by the researchers in designing, introducing, executing, analyzing, and feeding back the data to the subjects.

To complete the picture we should mention the relationship between the senior researcher and the junior members of a research team. After all, they too form a system in which superior-subordinate relationships exist. If our model is valid, we would expect that some of the adaptive mechanisms predicted above would be found in these relationships. Unfortunately, little systematic data exist on this subject. Recently, Roth (1966) presented some data that illustrate the writer's predictions. He presented evidence that the graduate students saw much of their work as being boring and tedious. In several cases the students adapted by withdrawing from work and by cheating. Observation time was cut, the number of observations reduced, and finally fake observations were submitted for full time periods. In other cases Roth suggests that guilt was reduced by becoming less able to hear what the people said and by reducing the richness of the observations on the (conscious) grounds that there was less going on. In still other cases, researchers who missed appointments or skipped questions, filled out their forms later by putting down what they thought the respondent should have answered. Of course, none of these informal behaviors was ever revealed to the senior researcher. As Roth correctly points out, the researchers acted pretty much like lower level employees in plants who perform repetitive tasks.

Recently, Rosenthal (1964) suggested another possibility which, if confirmed, is even more serious. He suggested that, in some cases, the junior investigator may be in such a dependency relationship to the senior investigator that he may, unknowingly, be more sensitized to instances that confirm his superior's views than to those that do not. These data raise serious questions about the standards usually accepted for checks on reliability and validity (i.e., the use of friends, colleagues, wives).

Before this discussion is ended, it may be helpful to note an important problem identified by research in organizations that social scientists may be faced with when conducting research in ongoing systems. The problem stems from the fact that in organizations, at the higher and lower levels, openness, concern for feelings, self-awareness, interpersonal experimentation, and trust tend to be suppressed. The reason for this, at the lower levels, is the technology which ties an employee to a highly molecularized and specialized job permitting little expression of self. At the upper levels, the technology decreases as a causal factor and the values executives hold about effective interpersonal relationships become dominant causal factors. In both cases therefore, organizational theory predicts, and to date the data support the prediction, that employees (lower and upper) will tend to be programmed to behave interpersonally more incompetently than competently, and to be unaware of this fact.

For example, in 35 different groups, with 370 participants, in 265 problem-solving and decision-making meetings, tackling issues ranging from investments, production, engineering, personnel, foreign policy, case discussions, new products, sales promotion, to physical science research discussions, it was found that the participants were unable to predict their interpersonal behavior accurately. Ninety-two percent predicted that the *most frequently* observed categories would be owning up, concern, trust, individuality, experimentation, helping others, and openness to feelings. The actual scores (in a sample of 10,150 units) showed that their prediction was accurate only in the case of owning up to ideas. The prediction was moderately accurate in the case of concern for ideas. Trust, experimentation, individuality, helping others, and the expression of positive or negative feelings—all behaviors that they predicted would be frequent—were rarely observed. Conformity, a category which they predicted would be low in frequency, was the second most frequently observed category (Argyris, 1966). These data have been replicated with groups of students, clergy, nurses, teachers, and physical scientists. If these data continue to be replicated, then the researchers who are studying interpersonal relationships may have to include observational data of the subject's actual behavior because the interview or questionnaire data could be highly (but unknowingly) distorted.

To summarize up to this point: Organizational theory is an appropriate theory to use to understand the human system created by rigorous research designs. The theory predicts that the correct use of rigorous designs, in experimental or field settings, will tend to place subjects in situations that are similar to those organizations create for the lower level employees. Also predicted is that the research assistants may be placed in situations that are similar, at worst, to the low-skill and, at best, to the high-skill employees in organizations.

These conditions lead to unintended consequences. The subjects may adapt by becoming dependent. They may also fight the research by actively rejecting a positive contributive role or by covertly withdrawing this involvement and thereby provide minimally useful data. The subjects may also band together into an organization that may better represent their interest. Finally, an organized society may unintentionally program people who may be asked to be interpersonally incompetent and unaware of the fact.

SUGGESTIONS TO OVERCOME THE PROBLEMS

If the unintended consequences of rigorous research reside in the degree of control the researcher has over the subject and the subject's resultant dependence, submissiveness, and short time perspective, then theoretically it would make sense to reduce the researcher's control over the subject. It would also follow from the theoretical framework that it would make sense to provide the subject with greater influence, with longer time perspective regarding, and greater involvement in, the research project.

It is understandable that researchers resist these action suggestions. They argue that all research could be ruined if subjects had greater influence.

These arguments are almost identical with the reactions of many executives when asked to consider giving greater influence to their employees in administration of the firm. However, after much research the executives have begun to learn that the situation is not as bleak as they pictured it would be. They have learned that workers do not demand nor desire complete control. They do not want to manage the entire plant. They wish greater influence, longer time perspective, and an opportunity for genuine participation at points and during time spans where it makes sense.

The same may be true of subjects. They would not tend to see the issue as one of complete versus no involvement. They would be willing to react reasonably if the researchers could show, by their behavior, that they assumed the subjects could be reasonable and are to be trusted.

Managers have developed from research an increasing number of guideposts regarding the conditions under which employee participation is helpful and harmful to the employee and to the organization. Unfortunately similar research is lacking in the area of conducting research. We have few data regarding when it is in the interests of the researcher and of the subject to invite the subject to participate in the design and execution of the research. It may be that, as a first step, much can be accomplished by having worker representative groups (in organizations) and student representative groups (in universities) to help in the design and execution of research as well as in the attraction and involvement of subjects in the research.

The most important fear expressed by researchers when considering subject influence is the fear of contamination of research. This is a legitimate fear. As we have seen, if subjects know what the research is about they may give the researcher what he wants. However, it should be noted in the studies where these results have been found they were *not* studies where the subject was to gain personally from participating (e.g., voting or marketing studies, Hyman, Cobb, Feldman, Hart, and Stember, 1954). One must be careful in generalizing from these studies to situations where the subject feels genuinely involved in the research.

There are further two points that may be worth considering about this position. Subjects *are* trying to please the researcher even when they are not told what the research is about. This means that much time and energy is being spent by the subject in second-guessing the researcher. If this is so, the researcher runs the risk of compounding the problem of unintended contamination.

The second point to be made about contamination is that it is inevitable. The issue therefore is *not* contamination versus no contamination. *The issue is under what conditions can the researcher have the greatest awareness of, and control over, the degree of contamination.*

Is it possible to create a psychological set on the part of the subject so that he is involved in giving as accurate replies as he can *and* in keeping the researcher informed as to when he (subject) is becoming defensive or could become defensive? Can the subject be helped to become as objective and verbal as he can about his subjectivity? Under what conditions can subjects be motivated to be so involved in the research that they strive to give valid data and warn the researcher when they (or others) may not be giving valid data?

Perhaps subjects will be motivated when they believe that it is in their interests to be so. Perhaps researchers may wish to consider designing research in such a way that the subject can gain from participating in the research (a gain that goes beyond simple feedback of results).

Motivating subjects by offering some possible help could make the situation more threatening rather than less threatening. For example, there are studies to show that people lie to their physicians when they describe their problems if they fear that there is something seriously wrong with them and they may be asked to undergo some stressful therapy like surgery. This is most certainly the case with employees who mistrust their management and would fear participation in research feedback and cooperating with management. In no case will valid research data be obtained where the subjects are fearful of the research or its consequences. If they are fearful, however, would it not be better to know this early in the relationship? Decisions could be made to drop the research or somehow account for the influence the fear would have upon the subjects' participation.

In field research, the biggest fear that we have discovered is that the research will not be relevant to their lives. They tend to see the researcher as a "long-hair" who wants to use them as guinea pigs and who, at most, promises a feedback session to give them the results and leaves them with the more difficult problem (for them) of what to do about their feelings. For example, the writer interviewed about 50 employees in a bank to test certain hypotheses. As an expression of gratitude he wrote a nontechnical report to the officers, who liked it so much that they provided the support to enlarge the study. In enlarging the number interviewed, 25 of the original sample were reinterviewed. The results showed that many of their answers were drastically different from their original answers to the same questions. When the subjects were confronted they replied as follows: During the first study they saw the writer as a researcher who wanted to use them as guinea pigs; during the second study the officers had described the research as helping them to make the bank a more effective system. "Now," they continued, "you could really make a difference in our lives, so we had to tell you the truth!"

In our experience the more subjects are involved directly (or through representatives) in planning and designing the research, the more we learn about the best ways to ask questions, the critical questions from the employees' views, the kinds of resistances each research method would generate, and the best way to gain genuine and long-range commitment to the research (Argyris, 1968). Moreover, subjects have told interviewers why they felt the interviewers were biasing their answers, so that they wondered if giving an answer during an interview might not bias an interviewer in his observations (which they expected since they had participated in the design of the research). Or, they have hesitated to tell the researcher certain information in the interview because they thought it might bias his observations. In reading protocols of interviews where feedback and help in exploring their problems is promised to subjects, one can find a great number of comments that indicate the subject is trying to be very careful not to distort his responses. For example, subjects have told the writer when they were not certain about an answer, or when they were biased, or how we should check their views with certain individuals.

Researchers are also concerned about telling subjects about the research lest such feedback influence them to change their behavior. In our experience this fear is more valid when the subject does *not* perceive the feedback of the results as relevant to his life or when he is asked to provide data that he perceives as inconsequential and nonrelevant. Also, the degree to which a subject can vary his response is much less if one is studying his behavior through observations rather than his reports of his behavior (either through interviews or questionnaires). For example, telling the subjects the plan of a study did not alter their behavior. The subjects were unable to alter their behavior even when asked, told, cajoled, required to do so (Argyris, 1965). In one case 10 executives were observed for 3 months without telling them the variables that were being studied or the results. Their behavior showed no change during this period. Two men were then asked to alter their behavior in the direction that would make them more effective group members. They agreed to try and both were unable to do so. One man became so frustrated with himself that he wrote a large note to keep in front of himself with appropriate reminders (e.g., to listen more, to cut people off less, etc.). In the first 10 minutes of a meeting a topic was raised that centrally involved him and he returned immediately to his original style.

In another case (Argyris, manuscript in preparation) feedback was given to a group of executives about their behavior. After the feedback session, they spent 3 hours deciding what behavior they wanted to change. Three of them committed themselves to work together to change their behavior. The researcher acknowledged their constructive intent but told them he doubted they could change their behavior. They became annoyed and insisted they could. Subsequent research showed that their behavior patterns never changed.

These observations should not be surprising to anyone who has to help people change behavior that is internalized, highly potent, and related to their feelings of intellectual and interpersonal competence, as well as to their career survival. Put in another way, the more researchers study such behavior, the less they may need to worry about such contamination.

Even if this were not the case, the researcher still has many ways to check as to whether involving the subject and offering help contaminate the research. For example, if the analysis is valid, predictions can be made as to how subordinates will respond on a superior's behavior (or vice versa), or how people will behave under particular conditions. If these predictions are not confirmed, then one can doubt the validity of the diagnosis.

It should be emphasized that we are not suggesting that we must swing from little subject influence and control to total subject influence and control. The major suggestion is that research needs to be conducted to learn more about the conditions where subject influence and control are possible and under what conditions more rigorous research (in the sense that the researcher has greater awareness and control over contamination) can be accomplished.

We may also have to reexamine the meaning of our present concepts of rigorousness and preciseness. They may imply a degree of precision about the nature of our universe which may not be the case. Is not the universe of human behavior more accurately characterized by redundancy and overdeterminedness? Human beings may design and build their interpersonal relationships the way engineers design and build bridges. The latter usually figure out precisely the stresses and strains and then triple their figures as a safety factor. Bridges are "over-built"; and behavior may be overdetermined. Human beings build their interpersonal relationships with the use of many imprecise and overlapping units. As Herbert A. Simon has pointed out, people's problem-solving processes may be quite sloppy; they neither maximize nor optimize; they satisfice.

However, he has also shown that these sloppier processes are subject to systematic understanding.

This view is similar to von Neumann's (1958) thesis that one of the crucial differences between the computer and the brain is the brain's capacity to be accurate with a lot of noise going on in its circuits. The brain can operate relatively accurately with a calculus that, for the computer, is relatively sloppy. Indeed, the computer would probably break down if it had to use the calculus characteristic of the brain. Perhaps what social science methodology needs to do is take on more of the characteristics of human problem solving. It would then enter a realm of overlapping redundant concepts and thus be able to operate and predict in the world in which we live even though it is full of noise.

In closing, it may be worth noting that high validity and reliability scores with these concepts are best obtained with observers who manifest a relatively high degree of competence in the variables being studied. For example, in the development of a system of categories in organization and innovation, observers with relatively high degree of interpersonal openness and trust were able to develop interobserver reliability scores with these variables ranging from 80% to 94% within 8 hours of scoring. Two of these observers were able within 2 hours to reproduce the score of 74% agreement after 1 year of not using the scoring system. However, two observers with relatively low capacity to be open and trusting were never able to reach a higher observer interreliability score than about 50%. The possession of the higher level of interpersonal competence made it possible for the first pair to see the interpersonal world more accurately and reliably. These findings are similar to Meehl's (1965) and Barron's (1965). They have suggested that the most reliable and valid raters of "creativity" were people who themselves were creative. Reliable and valid observation of interpersonal phenomena may also require a certain level of interpersonal competence.

Research is needed to help us understand more precisely how social scientists can develop valid theories and rigorous operational measures in a universe which may be composed of overlapping and redundant parts; where interrelationships are so complex that concepts of steady state are needed to conceptualize them; where objective observations may be limited to researchers who already manifest a relatively high competence in the phenomena under study.

NOTE

1. The author wishes to express his appreciation to his colleagues Douglas Hall, Richard Hackman, Edward Lawler, Lyman Porter, and Betty Ann Nunes for their many helpful suggestions.

REFERENCES

Argyris, C. "Today's Problems with Tomorrow's Organizations," *Journal of Management Studies*, 1967, 4(1), 31–55.

Argyris, C. *Interpersonal Competence and Organizational Effectiveness.* Homewood, Ill.: Irwin, 1962.

Argyris, C. *Integrating the Individual and the Organization.* New York: Wiley, 1964.

Argyris, C. *Organization and Innovation.* Homewood, Ill.: Irwin, 1965.

Argyris, C. "Interpersonal Barriers to Decision Making," *Harvard Business Review*, 1966, 44(2), 84–97.

Argyris, C. "Today's Problems with Tomorrow's Organizations," *Journal of Management Studies*, 1967, 4(1), 31–55.

Barron, F. "Some Studies of Creativity at the Institute of Personality Assessment and Research," In H. A. Steiner (ed.), *The Creative Organization*. Chicago: University of Chicago Press, 1965.

Bennis, W. *Changing Organizations*. New York: McGraw-Hill, 1966.

Brock, C., and Becker, L. A. "'Debriefing' and Susceptibility to Subsequent Experimental Manipulation," *Journal of Experimental Social Psychology*, 1966, **2**, 314–323.

Burdick, E. *The Ninth Wave*. New York: Dell, 1957.

Edwards, A. L. "Experiments: Their Planning and Execution." In G. Lindzey (ed.), *Handbook of Social Psychology*. Reading, Mass.: Addison-Wesley, 1954.

Friedman, N. *The Social Nature of Psychological Research*. New York: Basic Books, 1967.

Hyman, H. H., Cobb, W. J., Feldman, J. J., Hart, C. W., and Stember, C. H. *Interviewing in Social Research*. Chicago: University of Chicago Press, 1954.

Kelman, H. C. "The Problem of Deception in Social Psychological Experiments," *Psychological Bulletin*, 1967, **67**, 1–11.

Kiesler, C. "Group Pressure and Conformity." In J. Mills (ed.), *Advanced Experimental Social Psychology*. New York: Macmillan, 1969.

Meehl, P. E. "The Creative Individual: Why It Is Hard to Identify Him." In H. A. Steiner (ed.), *The Creative Organization*. Chicago: University of Chicago Press, 1965.

Mills, T. M. "A Sleeper Variable in Small Groups Research: The Experimenter," *Pacific Sociology Review*, 1962, **5**, 21–28.

Orne, M. T. "On the Social Psychology of the Psychology Experiment; With Particular Reference to Demand Characteristics and Their Implications," *American Psychologist*, 1962, **17**, 776–783.

Rosenthal, R. "On the Social Psychology of the Psychological Experiment: The Experimenter's Hypotheses as Unintended Determinants of Experimental Results," *American Scientist*, 1963, **51**, 268–283.

Rosenthal, R. "Experimenter Outcome-Orientation and the Results of the Psychological Experiment," *Psychological Bulletin*, 1964, **61**, 405–412.

Rosenthal, R. *Experimenter Effects in Behavioral Research*. New York: Appleton-Century-Crofts, 1966.

Roth, J. A. "Hired Hand Research," *American Sociologist*, 1966, **1**, 190–196.

Sales, S. M. "Supervisory Style and Productivity: Review and Theory," *Personnel Psychology*, 1966, **19**, 281–282.

von Neumann, J. *The Computer and the Brain*. New Haven: Yale University Press, 1958.

20 Fads, Fashions, and Folderol in Psychology [1]

Marvin D. Dunnette

When I chose this title, it seemed *very* clever, and I looked forward to venting my spleen a bit and to saying sage things about what is wrong with psychology and how its ills might be cured.

It was not long, however, before I felt misgivings about the whole enterprise and doubted whether I could meet the challenge to put up or to shut up that my own fool-hardiness had cast upon me. At first I thought I knew the things in psychology that bothered *me*, but would there be consensus about this? Suddenly, I had the sobering thought that I might be the only one out of step and that, really, all was well with psychology.

So—seizing upon one of my own pet types of methdological folderol—I decided to run a survey! I contacted older or wiser heads,[2] to inquire what, if anything, was currently bothering them. Their responses might conservatively be described as a vast outpouring. The volume and intensity of their replies caused me to give up my speculations about joining the French Foreign Legion and show up here today after all.

With their suggestions, however, I was faced suddenly with a plethora of fads, fashions, and folderol and the need to make some systematic sense of them. Let me give you the flavor of my survey results by simply mentioning some of the things listed by me and by my respondents.

Fads—those practices and concepts characterized by capriciousness and intense, but short-lived interest—included such things as brainstorming, Q technique, level of aspiration, forced choice, critical incidents, semantic differential, role playing, need theory, grids of various types, adjective checklists, two-factor theory, Theory X and Theory Y, social desirability, response sets and response styles, need hierarchies, and so on and so on.

Fashions—those manners or modes of action taking on the character of habits and enforced by social or scientific norms defining what constitutes the "thing to do"—included theorizing and theory building, criterion fixation, model building, null hypothesis testing, sensitivity training, being productive at work, developing authentic relationships, devising "cute" experiments, simulation, using "elegant" statistics, and so on.

Finally, folderol—those practices characterized by excessive ornamentation, non-sensical and unnecessary actions, trifles and essentially useless and wastefull fiddle-faddle—included tendencies to be fixated on theories, methods, and point of view, conducting "little" studies with great precision, attaching dramatic but unnecessary trappings to experiments, asking unimportant or irrelevant questions, grantsmanship,

Source: M. D. Dunnette, "Fads, Fashions, and Folderol in Psychology," *American Psychologist*, 1966, *21*(4), pp. 343-352. Copyright (1966) by the American Psychological Association. Reprinted by permission.

coining new names for old concepts, fixation on methods and apparatus, seeking to "prove" rather than "test" theories, and myriad other methodological ceremonies conducted in the name of rigorous research.

But, even armed with my list, about all I could say is that there are many things going on in psychology that reasonably responsible people were willing to label faddish folderol. It accomplished the aim of identifying some of the less honorable things we all are doing, but it seemed rather sterile as a source of prescriptive implications. What was needed was a better taxonomy for listing psychology's ills than the rather artificial trichotomy established by my title.

One approach might be through some form of cluster analysis—but my data did not prove amenable to any of the widely used methods such as Pattern Analysis, Elementary Linkage Analysis, Hierarchical Linkage Analysis, Hierarchical Syndrome Analysis, Typal Analysis, Rank Order Typal Analysis, Comprehensive Hierarchical Analysis, or even Multiple Hierarchical Classification.

Just when I was facing this impasse, I received the best-selling book by Eric Berne (1964) titled *Games People Play*. I was stimulated by this magnificent book to give thought to the games psychologists play. Somewhat to my surprise, I experienced no difficulty slipping into the robes of a medical clinician—intent on describing fully and completely the behavioral symptomatology of psychology's distress in terms of the games we all play—many of which may reflect underlying pathologies leading us down the primrose path to nonscience.

The games can be discussed under six broad headings—The Pets We Keep; The Names We Love; The Fun We Have; The Delusions We Suffer; The Secrets We Keep; and The Questions We Ask.

THE PETS WE KEEP

Subtitled "What Was Good Enough for Daddy Is Good Enough for Me," this game is characterized by an early and premature commitment to some Great Theory or Great Method. One major effect is to distort research problems so that they fit the theory or the method. The theory, method, or both can be viewed as pets inherited by fledgling psychologists and kept and nurtured by them, in loving kindness, protecting them from all possible harm due to the slings and arrows and attacks from other psychologists who, in turn, are keeping their own menageries.

At a general level, the premature commitment to a theory is usually accompanied by the set to *prove* rather than to modify the theory. The problem and its potentially bad outcome was outlined by T. C. Chamberlin (1965), a well-known geologist. He stated:

> The moment one has offered an original explanation for a phenomenon which seems satisfactory, that moment affection for his intellectual child springs into existence; . . . there is an unconscious selection and magnifying of the phenomena that fall into harmony with the theory and support it, and an unconscious neglect of those that fail of coincidence. . . . When these biasing tendencies set in, the mind rapidly degenerates into the partiality of paternalism. . . . From an unduly favored child, it [the theory] readily becomes master, and leads its author withersoever it will [p. 755].

It is not difficult in psychology to recognize the sequence of events described by Chamberlin. A pessimist might, in fact, find it difficult to identify any psychological theories which do *not* currently enjoy this form of affectionate nurturing. On the other hand, a more optimistic view might accord to theories the important function of ordering and systematizing the conduct of research studies. What is to be avoided, of course, is the kind of paternal affection and closed mind described by Chamberlin.

The problem in psychology is made more severe, however, by the inexplicitness (Fiegel, 1962) and, as Ritchie[3] has called it, the "incurable vagueness' with which most theories are stated—but then, it should be clear that vagueness in theory construction may simply be part of the game, insuring higher likelihood of a pet theory's long life.

Methodologically, our favored *pets* include factor analysis, complex analysis of variance designs, the concept of statistical significance, and multiple-regression analyses. It is common for psychologists to apply so-called sophisticated methods of analysis to data hardly warranting such careful attention. I shall not try to enumerate the nature of the painstaking activities included in the game of statistical pet keeping. I refer those of you who are interested to excellent papers by McNemar (1964) and by Guilford (1960). The net effect, however, is that attention to relevant and important scientific questions is diminished in favor of working through the subtle nuances of methodological manipulation. As my colleague, David Campbell remarked,[4]

> We seem to believe that TRUTH will be discovered somehow through using more and more esoteric techniques of data manipulation rather than by looking for it in the real world.

Or, as Platt (1964) has said:

> Beware of the man of one method or one instrument, either experimental or theoretical. He tends to become method-oriented rather than problem oriented; the method oriented man is shackled [p. 351].

THE NAMES WE LOVE

An alternate title for this game is "What's New Under the Sun?" Unfortunately, an undue amount of energy is devoted to the Great Word Game—the coining of new words and labels either to fit old concepts or to cast new facts outside the ken of a theory in need of protection.

Just one from among many possible examples is the great emphasis in recent years on Social Desirability—a new label for a phenomenon in test-taking behavior dealt with extensively by Meehl and Hathaway (1946), Jurgensen, and others many years previously, but which did not create much interest because they failed at the time to coin a label sufficiently attractive to "grab" other psychologists.

As Maier (1960) has so aptly pointed out, one major effect of the Name Game is to sustain theories even if the facts seem to refute them. If facts appear that cannot be ignored, relabeling them or renaming them gives them their own special compartment so that they cease to infringe upon the privacy of the theory.

Perhaps the most serious effect of this game is the tendency to apply new names in psychological research widely and uncritically before sufficient work has been done to specify the degree of generality or specificity of the "trait" being dealt with. Examples of this are numerous—anxiety, test-taking anxiety, rigidity, social desirability, creativity, acquiescence, social intelligence, and so on—*ad infinitum*.

THE FUN WE HAVE

A suitable title for this game would be—quite simply—"Tennis Anyone?" But the game has many variants, including My Model Is Nicer than Your Model!, Computers I Have Slept With!, or the best game of all—A Difference Doesn't Need to Make a Difference if It's a Real Difference.

As should be clear, the underlying theme of the game—Tennis Anyone?—is the compulsion to forget the problem—in essence to forget what we are really doing—because of the fun we may be enjoying with our apparatus, our computers, our models or the simple act of testing statistical null hypotheses. Often, in our zest for this particular game, we forget not only the problem, but we may even literally forget to look at the data!

The most serious yet most common symptom of this game is the "glow" that so many of us get from saying that a result is "statistically significant." The song and dance of null hypothesis testing goes on and on—apparently endlessly. In my opinion, this one practice is as much responsible as anything for what Sommer (1959) has called the "little studies" and the "little papers" of psychology.

As so many others have pointed out (Binder, 1963; Grant, 1962; Hays, 1964; Nunnally, 1960; Rozeboom, 1960), the major difficulty with psychology's use of the statistical null hypothesis is that the structure of scientific conclusions derived thereby is based on a foundation of triviality. When even moderately small numbers of subjects are used nearly all comparisons between means will yield so-called "significant" differences. I believe most psychologists will agree, in their more sober and less fun-loving moments, that small differences and inconsequential correlations do not provide a sufficient yield either for accurately predicting other persons' behavior or for understanding theoretically the functional relations between behavior and other variables. Yet, most of us still remain content to build our theoretical castles on the quicksand of merely rejecting the null hypothesis.

It may seem that my criticism of this particular game is unduly severe. Perhaps the differences reported in our journals are not really all that small. In order to examine this question, I asked one of my research assistants, Milton Hakel, to sample recent issues of four APA Journals—the *Journal of Applied Psychology, Journal of Abnormal and Social Psychology, Journal of Personality and Social Psychology, and Journal of Experimental Psychology.* He selected randomly from among studies employing either *t* tests or complex analysis of variance designs, and converted the *t* and *F* values to correlation ratios (eta) in order to estimate the strength of association between independent and dependent variables.

The distribution of the 112 correlation ratios ranged from .05 to .92 with a median value of .42. Five percent of the studies showed values below .20; over one-sixth were below .25; and nearly one-third failed to reach .30. The only encouragement I derive from these data stems from my identification with industrial psychology. At a time when many in industrial psychology are worried because predictive validities rarely exceed .50, it is at least reassuring—though still disconcerting—to note that our brethren in social and experimental psychology are doing little better.

It is particularly informative to note the conclusions made by the authors of the articles sampled by Hakel. Authors of the study yielding the eta of .05 concluded "that rating-scale format is a determiner of the judgment of raters in this sample [Madden and Bourdon, 1964]." In an investigation yielding an eta of .14, the authors concluded "that highly creative subjects give the greatest number of associations and maintain a relatively higher speed of association throughout a 2 minute period [Mednick, Mednick, and Jung, 1964] ."

Surprisingly, these rather definite conclusions differ little in tone from those based on studies yielding much stronger relationships. For example, a study yielding an eta of .77 is summarized with "Highly anxious subjects tended to give sets of word associates higher in intersubject variability than nonanxious subjects [Brody, 1964] ." In like manner, the conclusion stated for a study yielding an eta of .63 was simply "It was found that reinforcement affected subjects' verbalizations [Ganzer and Sarason, 1964] ."

It seems abundantly clear that our little survey provides convincing and frightening evidence that playing the game of null hypothesis testing has led a sizeable number of psychologists to lose sight of the importance of the strength of relationships underlying their conclusions. I could not agree more fully with Nunnally (1960), who has said:

> it would be a pity to see it (psychology) settle for meager efforts . . . encouraged by the use of the hypothesis testing models. . . . We should not feel proud when we see the psychologist smile and say "the correlation is significant beyond the .01 level." Perhaps that is the most that he can say, but he has no reason to smile [p. 650] .

THE DELUSIONS WE SUFFER

This is probably the most dangerous game of all. At the core, it consists of maintaining delusional systems to support our claims that the things we are doing *really* constitute good science. The game develops out of a pattern of self-deceit which becomes more ingrained and less tractable with each new delusion. Thus, an appropriate subtitle is "This Above All, to Thine Ownself Be *False!*"

The forms of these delusions are so numerous and so widespread in psychology that time permits only brief mention of a few.

One common variant of the game can be called, "Boy, Did I Ever Make Them Sit Up and Take Notice!" The argument is often made and seemingly almost always accepted that if a new theory or method stimulates others to do research, it *must* be good. Although I greatly dislike analogic arguments, I am compelled to suggest that such reasoning is very similar to stating that accidental fire must be good simply because it keeps so many firemen busy. Unfortunately, an inestimable amount of psychological research energy has been dissipated in fighting brush fires spawned by faddish theories—which careful research might better have refuted at their inception.

It is probably far too much to hope that we have seen the last of the studies "stimulated" by Sheldon's notions about physique and temperament, or by the overly simplified but widely popular two-factor theory of job motivation (Herzberg, Mausner, and Snyderman, 1959).

A second common delusion seems to arise out of the early recognition that gathering data from real people emitting real behaviors in the day-to-day world proves often to be difficult, unwieldy, and just plain unrewarding. Thus many retreat into the relative security of experimental or psychometric laboratories where new laboratory or test behaviors may be concocted to be observed, measured, and subjected to an endless array of internal analyses. These usually lead to elaborate theories or behavioral taxonomies, entirely consistent within themselves but lacking the acid test of contact with reality . . . McNemar (1964) summarized once more for us the evidence showing the pathetic record of factor analytically derived tests for predicting day-to-day behavior. A former professor at Minnesota used to say—when describing a lost soul—"He disappeared into the Jungle of Factor Analysis—never to be heard from again." Psychologists who choose to partake of the advantages of the more rigorous controls possible in the psychometric or experimental laboratories must also accept responsibility for assuring the day-to-day behavioral relevance of the behavioral observations they undertake.

A third unfortunate delusion rationalizes certain practices on the grounds that they are intrinsically good for humanity and that they need not, therefore, meet the usual standards demanded by scientific verification. In this regard, Astin (1961) has done an effective job of analyzing the functional autonomy of psychotherapy and offers a number of reasons why it continues to survive in spite of a lack of evidence about its effectiveness. In industrial psychology, a most widespread current fashion is the extensive use by firms of group-process or sensitivity-training programs; the effectiveness of such programs is still proclaimed solely on the basis of testimonials, and a primary rationale for their inadequate evaluation is that they are a form of therapy and must, therefore, be good and worthwhile.

Finally, yet another pair of delusions, representing polar opposites of one another, were discussed by Cronbach (1957) in his American Psychological Association Presidential Address. One extreme, shown chiefly by the experimentalists, treats individual differences as merely bothersome variation—to be reduced by adequate controls or treated as error variance in the search for General Laws. Such assumptions cannot help but lead to an oversimplified image of man, for the simplification is introduced at the very beginning. We cannot expect a science of human behavior to advance far until the moderating effects of individual variation on the functional relationships being studied are taken fully into account. People do, after all, differ greatly from one another and they differ even more from monkeys, white rats, or pigeons. It should not *really* be too heretical to suggest that many of the lawful relations governing the behavior of lower organisms may be inapplicable to the human species and, moreover, that laws describing the behavior of certain selected human subjects—such as psychology sophomores—may upon examination prove only weakly applicable to many other individuals. It should be incumbent upon the experimentalist or the theorist either to incorporate a consideration of individual differences into his research and theorizing or to define explicitly the individual parameters or population characteristics within which he expects his laws to be applicable.

The other extreme, actually extending considerably beyond the correlational psychology discussed by Cronbach, is just as delusory and even more detrimental to the eventual development of psychology than the one just discussed. Differences between individuals are regarded as so pervasive that it is assumed *no* laws can be stated. The likely outcome of a strong commitment to this point of view must ultimately be an admission that the methods of science cannot be applied to the study of human behavior. Yet, this outcome is not often openly recognized or honestly accepted by those believing in the ultimate uniqueness of each individual. Instead, they speak of "new approaches," less "mechanistic emphases," and a more "humanistic endeavor."

Cronbach, nearly a decade ago, sounded an urgent call for his fellow psychologists to cast aside the delusions represented by these two extremes. Unfortunately, today we seem no closer to achieving this end than we were then.

THE SECRETS WE KEEP

We might better label this game "Dear God, Please Don't Tell Anyone." As the name implies, it incorporates all the things we do to accomplish the aim of looking better in public than we really are.

The most common variant is, of course, the tendency to bury negative results. I only recently became aware of the massive size of this great graveyard for dead studies when a colleage expressed gratification that only a third of his studies "turned out"— as he put it.

Recently, a second variant of this secrecy game was discovered, quite inadvertently, by Wolins (1962) when he wrote to 37 authors to ask for the raw data on which they had based recent journal articles. Wolins found that of 32 who replied, 21 reported their data to be either misplaced, lost, or inadvertently destroyed. Finally, after some negotiation, Wolins was able to complete seven reanalyses on the data supplied from 5 authors. Of the seven, he found gross errors in three—errors so great as to clearly change the outcome of the results already reported. Thus, if we are to accept these results from Wolins's sampling, we might expect that as many as one-third of the studies in our journals contain gross miscalculations. In fact, this variant of the secrecy game might well be labeled "I Wonder Where the Yellow (data) Went." In commenting on Wolins's finding, Friedlander (1964), impressed by the strong commitments psychologists hold for their theories, tests and methods, suggests that "Hope springs eternal— and is evidently expressed through subjective arithmetic"—a possibility which is probably too close to the truth to be taken lightly.

Another extremely vexing and entirely unnecessary type of secrecy is clearly apparent to anyone who takes but a moment to page through one of our current data-oriented psychological journals. I chose a recent issue of the *Journal of Personality and Social Psychology*. It was very difficult to find such mundane statistics as means or standard deviations. Instead, the pages abounded with analysis of variance tables, charts, F ratios, and even t tests in the absence of their corresponding means and SDs. The net effect of this is to make very difficult and often impossible any further analyses that a reader might want to undertake. The implication of this, it seems to me, is that many authors have actually failed to bother computing such statistics as means or SDs and that, further, they probably have not examined their data with sufficient care to appreciate in any degree what they may really portray.

Other examples of the secrecy game abound. They include such practices as dropping subjects from the analyses—a practice discussed at some length in the critical review of a sampling of dissonance studies by Chapanis and Chapanis (1964), experimenter-biasing factors, incomplete descriptions of methodology, failure to carry out or to report cross-validation studies, and the more general problem of failure to carry out or to report replication studies.

I believe you will agree that these tactics of secrecy can be nothing but severely damaging to any hopes of advancing psychology as a science. It seems likely that such practices are rather widely applied in psychology by psychologists. I suggest that we vow here and now to keep these secrecy games secret from our colleagues in the other sciences!

THE QUESTIONS WE ASK

There are many titles that might be appropriate for this last game that I shall discuss. One might be, "Who's on First?"—or better yet, "What Game Are We In?"—or a rather common version in these days of large Federal support for research, "While You're Up, Get Me a Grant." My major point here is quite simply that the other games we play, the pets we keep, our delusions, our secrets, and the Great Name Game interact to cause us to lose sight of the essence of the problems that need to be solved and the questions that need answers. The questions that get asked are dictated—all too often—by investigators' pet theories or methods, or by the need to gain "visibility" among one's colleagues. One of my respondents—a younger but undoubtedly wiser head than I—summed it up nicely.[5] He said:

> Psychologists seem to be afraid to ask really important questions. The whole Zeitgeist seems to encourage research efforts that earn big grants, crank out publications frequently and regularly, self-perpetuate themselves, don't entail much difficulty in getting subjects, don't require the researchers to move from behind their desks or out of their laboratories except to accept speaking engagements, and serve to protect the scientist from all the forces that can knock him out of the secure "visible circle."

Another of my respondents, a verbal behavior researcher, illustrated the dilemma by mentioning a fellow researcher who phrased his research question as: "How do the principles of classical and instrumental conditioning explain the learning of language?" This sort of question is clearly illustrative of the tendency to defer too readily to existing popular points of view and to allow them to distort the direction of research activities. It would be better simply to ask "What is learned?" rather than making the premature assumptions that (1) language is learned in the sense that the term *learning* is usually used or (2) *all* learning is of only two types.

An even more serious and, unfortunately, probably more common form of the question-asking game is the game of "Ha! Sure Slipped That One Past You, Didn't I?" Here, the investigator shrewdly fails to state the question he is trying to answer, gathers data to provide answers to simpler questions, and then behaves as if his research has been relevant to other unstated but more important and more interesting problems. The vast majority of studies devoted to measuring employee attitudes have committed this error. It is no trick to develop questionnaires to gather systematically the opinions of workers about their jobs. It is quite something else, however, suddenly to begin talking about measures of employee *motivation* and to suggest that the employee responses have direct relevance to what they may actually do on the job. The literature on response set and response style is another clear case of new questions being designed to fit existing answers. Showing high correlations between scores on empirically developed scoring keys and the numbers of items keyed *True* or some other item index should not be taken as having any bearing on the empirical validities of these keys. Yet for over a decade, our literature has been burdened with all sorts of set and style studies characterized by seemingly endless factor analyses and silly arguments between persons committed to acquiescence and those committed to social desirability.

Thus, we all are far too eager to ask such questions as: "What problems can be *easily* answered?" "What else can I do with my test?" "What problems or questions does my theory lead to?" "What aspects of behavior can I study with my computer or with my apparatus?" or "What problems can I find that I can fit this method to?"

Certainly, as psychologists—as scientists presumably interested in the subject matter of human behavior—we should be able to do better than this!

THE CAUSES

You may have inferred by now that I feel some sense of pessimism about the current state of psychology. Based on what you have heard so far, such an inference is probably appropriate. I *do* believe that the games I have described offer little that can be beneficial for psychology in the long run. The behaviors underlying the games represent enormous and essentially wasteful expenditures of our own research energy.

Even so, my mood is not basically pessimistic. In fact, we should be able to emerge from this soul searching with a constructive sense of discontent rather than one of destructive despair. The description of our condition carries with it a number of implications for corrective action. Moreover, we may infer from the condition some possible causes, and listing them should also suggest possible correctives.

To this end, let me consider briefly what I believe to be the major causes of psychology's fads, fashions, and folderol.

The most important, I believe, is related quite directly to the relative insecurity of being a scientist, a problem that is particularly acute in psychology where we must cope with such complex phenomena as those involved in the study of human behavior. The scientist's stance includes the constant need to doubt his own work. Moreover, the long-range significance of his work cannot often be forecast, and rarely can the scientist—least of all, perhaps, the psychologist—preplan his inspirations and his ideas. It is little wonder, then, that many seek, through their theories, methodologies, or other of the games we have discussed, to organize, systematize, and regularize their creative output. When viewed against the backdrop of publication pressures prevailing in academia, the lure of large-scale support from Federal agencies, and the presumed necessity to become "visible" among one's colleagues, the insecurities of undertaking research on important questions in possibly untapped and unfamiliar areas become even more apparent. Stern (1964) has recently very effectively stated the case for the desirability of moving from research into equally fulfilling careers of teaching and administration. But we cannot forget that the value system of science places research and publication at the peak, and it should, therefore, be no surprise that the less able researchers in psychology—learning early that no great breakthrough is in the offing—simply seek to eat their cake and have it too, by playing the games and the song and dance of scientific research, usually convincing even themselves that the games are "for real" and that their activities really "make a difference."

The perpetuation of this state of affairs is related to our present system of graduate education. Many psychology graduate students today find themselves under the tutelage of a faculty member who has bought the system wholeheartedly. Such students live for a period of from 3 to 8 years in an environment that enforces and reinforces the learning of a particular approach, a narrow point of view or a set of pet methodologies which come to define for them the things they will pursue as psychologists.

THE REMEDY

But here I am—sounding pessimistic and noxious again, and getting farther out on the limb than I really want to be.

In order to convince you of my good intentions and my hope for the future, I had better get on with some constructive suggestions. My suggested remedy—if it can be called that, for indeed it may be more painful than the disease—can be summarized in five imperative statements:

1. Give up constraining commitments to theories, methods, and apparatus!
2. Adopt methods of multiple working hypotheses!
3. Put more eclecticism into graduate education!
4. Press for new values and less *pretense* in the academic environments of our universities!
5. Get to the editors of our psychological journals!

Let me elaborate briefly on each of these recommendations.

First, I advocate a more careful and studied choice of research questions. As should be apparent, I believe research energy should be directed toward questions that contain as few as possible of any prior unproven assumptions about the nature of man. We must be constantly alert to the narrowing of research perspectives due to prior theoretical or methodological commitments. I am calling for less premature theorizing—particularly that which leads to vaguely stated "wide-band" theories that are often essentially incapable of disproof.

I am not advocating the abandonment of deduction in psychology; in fact, psychology needs stronger and more specific deductions rather than the weak and fuzzy ones so typical of so many current theories. What I am advocating is the more systematic study of lawful relationships *before* interpretations are attempted. When explanation *is* attempted, the data should be sufficient to allow hypotheses to be stated with the clarity and precision to render them directly capable of disproof. As the philosopher Karl Popper has said, there is no such thing as proof in science; science advances only by disproofs.

This leads directly to my second recommendation which is to state and systematically test multiple hypotheses. Platt recently advocated this approach which he calls *Strong Inference* (Platt, 1964). The approach entails devising multiple hypotheses to explain observed phenomena, devising crucial experiments each of which may exclude or disprove one or more of the hypotheses, and continuing with the retained hypotheses to develop further subtests of sequential hypotheses to refine the possibilities that remain. This process does not seem new; in fact it is not. It simply entails developing ideas or leads, stating alternative possibilities, testing their plausibility, and proceeding to develop predictive and explanatory evidence concerning the phenomena under investigation. One might say that the research emphasis is one of "studying hypotheses" as opposed to "substantiating theories." The difference seems slight, but it is really quite important. However, in psychology, the approach is little used, for, as we have said, the commitments are more often to *a* theory than to the process of *finding out*.

The method of multiple hypotheses takes on greatly added power when combined with greater care in the analysis and reporting of research results. Instead of serving as the sole statistical test of hypotheses, the statistical null hypothesis should always be supplemented by estimates of strength of association. The psychologist owes it to himself to determine not only whether an association exists between two variables—an association which may often be so small as to be trivial—but also to determine the probable magnitude of the association. As Hays (1964) has suggested, if psychologists are content to adopt conventions (such as .05 or .01) for deciding on statistical significance, they should also adopt conventions concerning the strength of association which may be sufficiently large to regard as worthy of further investigation. Obviously, such conventions cannot be the same for all areas and for all research questions, but it should be clear that an emphasis on magnitude estimation will demand that researchers give much more careful thought than they now do to defining ahead of time the actual magnitudes that will be regarded as possessing either theoretical or practical consequence.

By now, it is apparent why my fifth recommendation has to do with our journals. It will require a new kind of surveillance from both the editors and their consultants if we are to implement the greater care in research conception and in data analysis and reporting that I am advocating. When and if null-hypothesis testing is accorded a lower position in the status hierarchy and comes to be supplemented by emphases on Strong Inference and magnitude estimation, I would predict that the bulk of published material will, for a time, greatly diminish. That which does appear, however, will be guaranteed to be of considerably greater consequence for furthering our understanding of behavior.

One of the possible loopholes in the method of Strong Inference, it should be clear, is the great difficulty of designing and carrying out crucial experiments. Recently Hafner and Presswood (1965) described how faulty experiments had led physicists astray for several decades as they sought to explain the phenomenon of beta decay. We must broaden our conception of multiple hypotheses to include as one quite plausible hypothesis the possibility of poorly conceived or poorly conducted experiments. This, of course, simply speaks to the need for more replication in psychology of crucial experiments, a practice which undoubtedly would become more widespread if psychologists possessed fewer of their own theoretical pets and stronger motivation to examine systematically whole sets of contending hypotheses and alternative explanations.

My third and fourth recommendations need not be elaborated extensively. Both are intended to foster less pretense in the conduct of psychological research by enabling those scholars who may be ill fitted for the research enterprise to gain rewards in other endeavors. The change in the academic atmosphere would need to take the form of according more status to good teaching and to good administration. Perhaps this change would be most rapidly fostered if the scientific games I have described would be more readily recognized for what they are and appropriately devalued in the scheme of things within academia.

Obviously, greater eclecticism in graduate education is crucial to the successful outcome of my other suggestions. It is difficult to know how this can be implemented. But, at least, the goals seem clear. We desire to teach the core of psychology's knowledge and methods, its subject matter and its questions, the statistical methods and their appropriate applications—but most of all, through selection or training or both, we should seek to turn out persons with intense curiosity about the vast array of psychological questions and problems occurring everywhere in the world around us, with a willingness to ask *open* questions unhampered by the prior constraints of a particular point of view or method. Let us hope that graduate education, in the years ahead, will become more eclectic and that even the Great Men in our field may adopt a sense of humility when transmitting knowledge to the fledglings of our science.

THE OUTCOME: UTOPIA

How do I envision the eventual outcome if all these recommendations were to come to pass? What would the psychologizing of the future look like and what would psychologists be up to?

Chief among the outcomes, I expect, would be a marked lessening of tensions and disputes among the Great Men of our field. I would hope that we might once again witness the emergence of an honest community of scholars all engaged in the zestful enterprise of trying to describe, understand, predict, and control human behavior.

Certainly our journals would be more meaty and less burdensome. There would be more honesty in publishing the fruits of one's labors. Negative results—the disproof of theoretical formulations and the casting aside of working hypotheses—would be a more important part of the journals' contents. In consequence, the journals would contribute more meaningfully to the broad effort to achieve understanding, and we should expect to witness a sharp decline in the number of disconnected little studies bearing little or no relation to each other.

Moreover, I expect that many present schisms in psychology would be welded. The academic-professional bipolarity described by Tryon (1963) would be lessened, for the advantages to both of close association between basic researchers and those practicing the art of psychology should become more apparent. The researchers would thereby establish and maintain contact with the real world and real problems of human behavior, and the professional practitioners would be more fully alert to the need for assessing their methods by generating and testing alternate deductions and hypotheses growing out of them.

Thus, in the long run we might hope for fewer disputes, a spirit of more open cooperation, greater innovation in the generation and testing of working hypotheses, greater care and precision in the development of theoretical formulations, and increased rigor in specifying the magnitude of outcomes such that they have both practical and theoretical importance.

Does this sound like Utopia? Indeed it does. But is it too much to expect of a science now well into its second 100 years? I think not. Let us get on then with the process of change and of reconsolidation.

NOTES

1. Invited Address presented to Division 14 at American Psychological Association, Chicago, September 1965.

2. I should like to thank the following persons for their readiness to come to my aid, but please understand that I do so only because of a strong sense of gratitude and with no thought of having them join me out at the end of the limb. They are: David P. Campbell, John P. Campbell, Alphonse Chapanis, Edwin E. Ghiselli, Mason Haire, James Jenkins, Quinn McNemar, Paul Meehl, William A. Owens, Jr., Bernard Rimland, Auke Tellegen, Rains Wallace, and Karl Weick.

3. B. F. Ritchie, unpublished work.

4. Personal communication, 1965.

5. J. P. Campbell, personal communication, 1965.

REFERENCES

Astin, A. W. "The Functional Autonomy of Psychotherapy," *American Psychologist*, 1961, **16**, 75-78.

Berne, E. *Games People Play*. New York: Grove Press, 1964.

Binder, A. "Further Considerations on Testing the Null Hypothesis and the Strategy and Tactics of Investigating Theoretical Models," *Psychological Review*, 1963, **70**, 107-115.

Brody, N. "Anxiety and the Variability of Word Associates," *Journal of Abnormal and Social Psychology*, 1964, **68**, 331-334.

Chamberlin, T. C. "The Method of Multiple Working Hypotheses," *Science*, 1965, **148**, 754-759.

Chapanis, N., and Chapanis, A. "Cognitive Dissonance: Five Years Later," *Psychological Bulletin*, 1964, **61**, 1-22.

Cronbach, L. J. "The Two Disciplines of Scientific Psychology," *American Psychologist*, 1957, **12**, 671-684.

Fiegel, H. "Philosophical Embarrassments of Psychology," *Psychologishe Beitrage*, 1962, 6, 340-364.

Friedlander, F. "Type I and Type II Bias," *American Psychologist*, 1964, 19, 198-199.

Ganzer, V. J., and Sarason, I. G. "Interrelationships Among Hostility, Experimental Conditions, and Verbal Behavior," *Journal of Abnormal and Social Psychology*, 1964, 68, 79-84.

Grant, D. A. "Testing the Null Hypothesis and the Strategy and Tactics of Investigating Theoretical Models," *Psychological Review*, 1962, 69, 54-61.

Guilford, J. P. "Psychological Measurement a Hundred and Twenty-five Years Later." Invited address presented at American Psychological Association, Chicago, September 1960.

Hafner, E. M., and Presswood, S. "Strong Inference and Weak Interactions," *Science*, 1965, 149, 503-510.

Hays, W. L. *Statistics for Psychologists*. New York: Holt, Rinehart & Winston, 1964.

Herzberg, F., Mausner, B., and Snyderman, B. *The Motivation to Work*. New York: Wiley, 1959.

Madden J. M., and Bourdon, R. D. "Effects of Variations in Rating Scale Format on Judgment," *Journal of Applied Psychology*, 1964, 48, 147-151.

Maier, N. R. F. "Maier's Law," *American Psychologist*, 1960, 15, 208-212.

McNemar, Q. "Lost Our Intelligence? Why?" *American Psychologist*, 1964, 19, 871-882.

Mednick, M., Mednick, S. A., and Jung, C. C. "Continual Association as a Function of Level of Creativity and Type of Verbal Stimulus," *Journal of Abnormal and Social Psychology*, 1964, 69, 511-515.

Meehl, P. E., and Hathaway, S. R. "The K Factor as a Suppressor Variable in the MMPI," *Journal of Applied Psychology*, 1946, 30, 525-564.

Nunnally, J. "The Place of Statistics in Psychology," *Educational and Psychological Measurement*, 1960, 20, 641-650.

Platt, J. R. "Strong Inference," *Science*, 1964, 146, 347-352.

Rozeboom, W. W. "The Fallacy of the Null-Hypothesis Significance Test," *Psychological Bulletin*, 1960, 57, 416-428.

Sommer, R. "On Writing Little Papers," *American Psychologist*, 1959, 14, 235-237.

Stern, C. "Thoughts on Research," *Science*, 1964, 148, 772-773.

Tryon, R. C. "Psychology in Flux: The Academic-Professional Bipolarity," *American Psychologist*, 1963, 18, 134-143.

Wolins, L. "Responsibility for Raw Data," *American Psychologist*, 1962, 17, 657-658.

21 The Yin and Yang of Progress in Social Psychology: Seven Koan[1]

William J. McGuire

THE PARADIGM RECENTLY GUIDING EXPERIMENTAL SOCIAL PSYCHOLOGY

When the XIXth Congress met 3 years ago in London, and certainly a half-dozen years back at the Moscow Congress, social psychology appeared to be in a golden age. It was a prestigious and productive area in which droves of bright young people, a sufficiency of middle-aged colonels, and a few grand old men were pursuing their research with a confidence and energy that is found in those who know where they are going. Any moments of doubt we experienced involved anxiety as to whether we were doing our thing well, rather than uncertainty as to whether it needed to be done at all.

The image of these golden boys (and a few, but all too few, golden girls) of social psychology, glowing with confidence and chutzpah only 6 years back at the Moscow Congress, blissfully unaware of the strident attacks which were soon to strike confusion into the field, brings to mind a beautiful haiku of Buson that goes

> Tsurigane-ni
> Tomarite nemuru
> Kochō kana

which I hasten to translate as follows

> On a temple bell
> Settled, asleep,
> A butterfly.

We social psychology researchers know all too well that the peaceful temple bell on which we were then displaying ourselves has now rudely rung. During the past half-dozen years, the vibrations which could be vaguely sensed at the time of the Moscow meeting have gathered force. Now the temple bell has tolled and tolled again, rudely disturbing the stream of experimental social psychological research and shaking the confidence of many of us who work in the area.

The first half of this paper is devoted to describing the three successive waves of this current history. First, I shall describe the experimental social psychology paradigm that has recently guided our prolific research. Second, I shall discuss why this recent

Source: W. J. McGuire, "The Yin and Yang of Progress in Social Psychology," *Journal of Personality and Social Psychology*, 1973, *26*(3), pp. 446–456. Copyright (1973) by the American Psychological Association. Reprinted by permission.

paradigm is being attacked and what, superficially at least, appears to be emerging in its place. Third, I shall say why I feel the seemingly emerging new paradigm is as inadequate as the one we would replace. Then, in the second half of this paper I shall offer, in the form of seven koan, my prescriptions for a new paradigm, more radically different from the recent one, but more in tune with the times and the march of history than is the variant that is supposedly emerging.

The Old Paradigm

What was the experimental social psychology paradigm which until recently had been unquestioningly accepted by the great majority of us but which now is being so vigorously attacked? Like any adequate paradigm it had two aspects, a creative and a critical component (McGuire, 1969, pp. 22-25). By the creative aspect, I mean the part of our scientific thinking that involves hypothesis generation, and by the critical aspect, I mean the hypothesis-testing part of our work.

The creative aspect of the recent paradigm inclined us to derive our hypotheses from current theoretical formulations. Typically, these theoretical formulations were borrowed from other areas of psychology (such as the study of psychopathology or of learning and memory), though without the level of refinement and quantification which those theories had reached in their fields of origin.

The critical, hypothesis-testing aspect of the recent paradigm called for manipulational experiments carried out in the laboratory. The experimental social psychologist attempted to simulate in the laboratory the gist of the situation to which he hoped to generalize, and he measured the dependent variable after deliberately manipulating the independent variable while trying to hold constant all other factors likely to affect the social behavior under study. In brief, the recent paradigm called for selecting our hypotheses for their relevance to broad theoretical formulations and testing them by laboratory manipulational experiments. McGuire (1965) presented an emphatic assertion of this recent paradigm in its heyday.

Assaults on the Old Paradigm

During the past several years both the creative and the critical aspects of this experimental social psychology paradigm have come under increasing attack. The creative aspect of formulating hypotheses for their relevance to theory has been denounced as a mandarin activity out of phase with the needs of our time. It has been argued that hypotheses should be formulated for their relevance to social problems rather than for their relevance to theoretical issues. Such urgings come from people inside and outside social psychology, reflecting both the increasing social concern of researchers themselves and the demands of an articulate public for greater payoff from expensive scientific research. While many of us still insist with Lewin that "There is nothing so practical as a good theory," the extent to which the pendulum has swung from the theoretically relevant toward the socially relevant pole is shown in the recent upsurge of publications on socially important topics of ad hoc interest, such as bystander intervention, the use of local space, the mass media and violence, the determinants of love, responses to victimization, nonverbal communication, etc.

At least as strong and successful an assault has been launched on the critical aspect of the recent paradigm, namely, the notion that hypotheses should be tested by manipulational laboratory experiments. It has been urged that laboratory experiments are full of artifacts (such as experimenter bias, demand character, evaluation apprehension, etc.) which make their results very hard to interpret. Ethical questions also have been raised against the laboratory social experiments on the grounds that they expose the participants to an unacceptable amount of deception, coercion, and stress.

In place of the laboratory manipulational experiment, there has been a definite trend toward experiments conducted in field settings and toward correlational analysis of data from naturalistic situations. A variety of recent methodological advances (which we shall list under Koan 5) has made alternative hypothesis-testing procedures more attractive.

The attacks on the old paradigm of theory-derived hypotheses tested in laboratory manipulational experiments have certainly shaken confidence in that approach. At the same time, there is some suggestion of an emerging new paradigm which has as its creative aspect the derivation of new hypotheses for their ad hoc interest and social relevance. And in its critical aspect, this new paradigm involves testing these hypotheses by field experiments and, where necessary, by the correlational analysis of naturalistic data. McGuire (1967, 1969) described in more detail the worries about the recent paradigm and the nature of the purportedly emerging one. Higbee and Wells (1972) and Fried, Gumpper, and Allen (1973) suggested that reports by McGuire, by Sears and Abeles (1969), etc., of the demise of the recent paradigm may be exaggerated, but perhaps they have underestimated the time that must intervene before a change of vogue by the leaders shows up in mass analysis of the methods used in published research.

MORE BASIC QUESTIONS REGARDING BOTH THE RECENT AND EMERGING PARADIGMS

My own position on the relative merits of the recent paradigm and this supposedly emerging new paradigm is a complex and developing one which I have detailed in print (McGuire, 1965, 1967, 1969) so the reader will be spared here a recital of my Byzantine opinions on this issue. Instead, I am raising the more fundamental issue of whether or not both the recent and the seemingly emerging paradigms which I have just described fail to come to grips with the deeper questions which lie behind our present unease. It seems to me that any truly new paradigm that ultimately arises from the present unrest is going to be more radically different from the recent one than is the supposedly emerging paradigm I have just depicted. It will represent a more fundamental departure on both the creative and the critical sides.

Inadequacies on the Creative Side

The switch from theory relevance to social relevance as the criterion in the creative, hypothesis-generating aspect of our work seems to me to constitute only a superficial cosmetic change that masks rather than corrects the basic problem. Socially relevant hypotheses, no less than theoretically relevant hypotheses, tend to be based on a simple linear process model, a sequential chain of cause and effect which is inadequate to simulate the true complexities of the individual's cognitive system or of the social system which we are typically trying to describe. Such simple a-affects-b hypotheses fail to catch the complexities of parallel processing, bidirectional causality, and reverberating feedback that characterize both cognitive and social organizations. The simple sequential model had its uses, but these have been largely exploited in past progress, and we must now deal with the complexities of systems in order to continue the progress on a new level.

The real inadequacy of the theory-derived hypotheses of the recent paradigm is not, as those now advocating socially relevant hypotheses insist, that it focused on the wrong variables (those that were theory rather than problem relevant). Rather, the basic shortcoming of the theory-relevant and the socially relevant hypotheses alike is that they fail to come to grips with the complexities with which the variables are organized in the individual and social systems.

Inadequacies of the Critical Aspect of the Recent Paradigm

The critical, hypothesis-testing aspect of the purportedly emerging paradigm also has the defect of being but a minor variant of the recent experimental social psychology paradigm rather than the fundamental departure which is called for. Let me first describe some of the deep epistemological uneasiness some of us have been expressing about the manipulational laboratory experiment that was the hypothesis-testing procedure of the recent paradigm. The crux of this objection is that we social psychologists have tended to use the manipulational laboratory experiment not to test our hypotheses but to demonstrate their obvious truth. We tend to start off with an hypothesis that is so clearly true (given the implicit and explicit assumptions) and which we have no intention of rejecting however the experiment comes out. Such a stance is quite appropriate, since the hypothesis by its meaningfulness and plausibility to reasonable people is tautologically true in the assumed context. As Blake said, "Everything possible to be believ'd is an image of truth."

The area of interpersonal attraction will serve to illustrate my point. The researcher might start off with a *really* obvious proposition from bubba-psychology, such as "The more someone perceives another person as having attitudes similar to his own, the more he tends to like that other person." Or a somewhat more flashy researcher, a little hungrier for novelty, might hypothesize the opposite. That is, he could look for certain circumstances in which the generally true, obvious hypothesis would obviously be reversed. He might hypothesize exceptional circumstances where attitudinal similarity would be anxiety arousing and a source of hostility; for example, if one loves one's wife, then one might actually dislike some other man to the extent that one perceives that other as also loving one's wife. Or another exceptional reversal might be that some people may think so poorly of themselves that they think less well of another person to the extent that the other person is like themselves. If the negative relationship is not found, we are likely to conclude that the person did not have a sufficiently low self-image, not that the hypothesis is wrong. Both the original obvious hypothesis and the obvious reversed hypothesis are reasonable and valid in the sense that if all our premises obtained, then our conclusion would pretty much have to follow.

Experiments on such hypotheses naturally turn out to be more like demonstrations than tests. If the experiment does not come out "right," then the researcher does not say that the hypothesis is wrong but rather that something was wrong with the experiment, and he corrects and revises it, perhaps by using more appropriate subjects, by strengthening the independent variable manipulation, by blocking off extraneous response possibilities, or by setting up a more appropriate context, etc. Sometimes he may have such continuous bad luck that he finally gives up the demonstration because the phenomenon proves to be so elusive as to be beyond his ability to demonstrate.

The more persistent of us typically manage at last to get control of the experimental situation so that we can reliably demonstrate the hypothesized relationship. But note that what the experiment tests is not whether the hypothesis is true but rather whether the experimenter is a sufficiently ingenious stage manager to produce in the laboratory conditions which demonstrate that an obviously true hypothesis is correct. In our graduate programs in social psychology, we try to train people who are good enough stage managers so that they can create in the laboratory simulations of realities in which the obvious correctness of our hypothesis can be demonstrated.

It is this kind of epistemological worry about manipulational laboratory experiments that a half-dozen years back caused a number of observers (e.g., McGuire, 1967) to urge social psychology to search for interrelations among naturally varying factors in the world outside the laboratory. Out of these urgings has come the critical aspect of the apparently emerging paradigm which I have described above, calling for research in the field rather than in the laboratory.

Inadequacies of the Critical Aspects of the Purportedly Emerging New Field-Experiment Paradigm

Recently, I have come to recognize that this flight from the laboratory manipulational experiment to the field study, which I myself helped to instigate, is a tactical evasion which fails to meet the basic problem. We would grant that in the field we put the question to nature in a world we never made, where the context factors cannot be so confounded by our stage management proclivities as they were in the laboratory. But in this natural world research, the basic problem remains that we are not really testing our hypotheses. Rather, just as in the laboratory experiment we were testing our stage-managing abilities, in the field study we are testing our ability as "finders," if I may use a term from real estate and merchandising. When our field test of the hypothesis does not come out correctly, we are probably going to assume not that the hypothesis is wrong but that we unwisely chose an inappropriate natural setting in which to test it, and so we shall try again to test it in some other setting in which the conditions are more relevant to the hypothesis. Increasing our own and our graduate students' critical skill will involve making us not better hypothesis testers or better stage managers but rather better finders of situations in which our hypotheses can be demonstrated as tautologically true. Though I shall not pursue the point here, other objections to the laboratory experiment, including ethical and methodological considerations, that have been used (McGuire, 1969) to argue for more field research could similarly be turned against experiments conducted in the natural environment.

What I am arguing here is that changing from a theory-relevant to a socially relevant criterion for variable selection does not constitute a real answer to the basic problem with the creative aspect of our recent social psychology paradigm. And again, the switch from laboratory to field manipulation does not meet the basic objection to the critical aspect of the old paradigm. Neither the recent paradigm nor the supposedly emerging one really supplies the answer to our present needs. The discontent is a quite healthy one, and we should indeed be dissatisfied with the recent paradigm of testing theory-derived hypotheses by means of laboratory manipulational experiments. But our healthy discontent should carry us to a more fundamentally new outlook than is provided by this supposedly emerging variant paradigm of testing socially relevant hypotheses by experiments in natural settings.

SOURCES OF THE NEW SOCIAL PSYCHOLOGY

The Ultimate Shape of the New Paradigm

What I have written in the previous section suggests my general vision of what the more radically different new paradigm for social psychology will look like. On the creative side, it will involve theoretical models of the cognitive and social systems in their true multivariate complexity, involving a great deal of parallel processing, bidirectional relationships, and feedback circuits. Since such complex theoretical formulations will be far more in accord with actual individual and social reality than our present a-affects-b linear models, it follows that theory-derived hypotheses will be similar to hypotheses selected for their relevance to social issues. Correspondingly, the critical aspect of this new paradigm involves hypothesis testing by multivariate time series designs that recognize the obsolescence of our current simplistic a-affects-b sequential designs with their distinctions between dependent and independent variables.

But I feel somewhat uncomfortable here in trying to describe in detail what the next, radically different paradigm will look like. It will be hammered out by theoretically and empirically skilled researchers in a hundred eyeball-to-eyeball confrontations of thought with data, all the while obscured by a thousand mediocre and irrelevant studies which will constitute the background noise in which the true signal will be detected only gradually. Trying to predict precisely what new paradigm will emerge is almost as foolish as trying to control it.

But there is a subsidiary task with which I feel more comfortable and to which I shall devote the rest of this paper. I have come to feel that some specific tactical changes should be made in our creative and critical work in social psychology so as to enhance the momentum and the ultimate sweep of this wave of the future, whatever form it may take. I shall here recommend a few of these needed innovations and correctives, presenting them as koans and commentaries thereon, to mask my own uncertainties.

Koan 1: The Sound of One Hand Clapping ... and the Wrong Hand

One drastic change that is called for in our teaching of research methodology is that we should emphasize the creative, hypothesis-formation stage relative to the critical, hypothesis-testing stage of research. It is my guess that at least 90% of the time in our current courses on methodology is devoted to presenting ways of testing hypotheses and that little time is spent on the prior and more important process of how one creates these hypotheses in the first place. Both the creation and testing of hypotheses are important parts of the scientific method, but the creative phase is the more important of the two. If our hypotheses are trivial, it is hardly worth amassing a great methodological arsenal to test them; to paraphrase Maslow, what is not worth doing, is not worth doing well. Surely, we all recognize that the creation of hypotheses is an essential part of the scientific process. The neglect of the creative phase in our methodology courses probably comes neither from a failure to recognize its importance nor a belief that it is trivially simple. Rather, the neglect is probably due to the suspicion that so complex a creative process as hypothesis formation is something that cannot be taught.

I admit that creative hypothesis formation cannot be reduced to teachable rules, and that there are individual differences among us in ultimate capacity for creative hypothesis generation. Still, it seems to me that we have to give increased time in our own thinking and teaching about methodology to the hypothesis-generating phase of research, even at the expense of reducing the time spent discussing hypothesis testing. In my own methodology courses, I make a point of stressing the importance of the hypothesis-generating phase of our work by describing and illustrating at least a dozen or so different approaches to hypothesis formation which have been used in psychological research, some of which I can briefly describe here, including case study, paradoxical incident, analogy, hypothetico-deductive method, functional analysis, rules of thumb, conflicting results, accounting for exceptions, and straightening out complex relationships.

For example, there is the intensive case study, such as Piaget's of his children's cognitive development or Freud's mulling over and over and over of the Dora or the Wolf Man case or his own dreams or memory difficulties. Often the case is hardly an exceptional one—for example, Dora strikes me as a rather mild and uninteresting case of hysteria—so that it almost seems as if any case studied intensively might serve as a Rorschach card to provoke interesting hypotheses. Perhaps an even surer method of arriving at an interesting hypothesis is to try to account for a paradoxical incident. For example, in a study of rumors circulating in Bihar, India, after a devastating earthquake, Prasad found that the rumors tended to predict further catastrophes. It seemed paradoxical that the victims of the disaster did not seek some gratification in fantasy, when reality was so harsh, by generating rumors that would be gratifying rather than further disturbing. I believe that attempting to explain this paradox played a more than trivial role in Festinger's formulation of dissonance theory and Schachter's development of a cognitive theory of emotion.

A third creative method for generating hypotheses is the use of analogy, as in my own work on deriving hypotheses about techniques for inducing resistance to persuasion, where I formulated hypotheses by analogy with the biological process of inoculating the person in advance with a weakened form of the threatening material, an idea suggested in earlier work by Janis and Lumsdaine. A fourth creative procedure is the hypothetico-deductive method, where one puts together a number of commonsensical principles and derives from their conjunction some interesting predictions, as in the Hull and Hovland mathematico-deductive theory of rote learning, or the work by Simon and his colleagues on logical reasoning. The possibility of computer simulation has made this hypothesis-generating procedure increasingly possible and popular.

A fifth way of deriving hypotheses might be called the functional or adaptive approach, as when Hull generated the principles on which we would have to operate if we were to be able to learn from experience to repeat successful actions, and yet eventually be able to learn an alternative shorter path to a goal even though we have already mastered a longer path which does successfully lead us to that goal. A sixth approach involves analyzing the practitioner's rule of thumb. Here when one observes that practitioners or craftsmen generally follow some procedural rule of thumb, we assume that it probably works, and one tries to think of theoretical implications of its effectiveness. One does not have to be a Maoist to admit that the basic researcher can learn something by talking to a practitioner. For example, one's programmed simulation of chess playing is improved by accepting the good player's heuristic of keeping control of the center of the board. Or one's attitude change theorization can be helped by noting the politician's and advertiser's rule that when dealing with public opinion, it is better to ignore your opposition than to refute it. These examples also serve to remind us that the practitioner's rule of thumb is as suggestive by its failures as by its successes.

A seventh technique for provoking new hypotheses is trying to account for conflicting results. For example, in learning and attitude change situations, there are opposite laws of primacy and of recency, each of which sometimes seems valid; or in information integration, sometimes an additive or sometimes an averaging model seems more appropriate. The work by Anderson trying to reconcile these seeming conflicts shows how provocative a technique this can be in generating new theories. An eighth creative method is accounting for exceptions to general findings, as when Hovland tried to account for delayed action effect in opinion change. That is, while usually the persuasive effect of communications dissipates with time, Hovland found that occasionally the impact actually intensifies over time, which provoked him to formulate a variety of interesting hypotheses about delayed action effects. A ninth creative technique for hypothesis formation involves reducing observed complex relationships to simpler component relationships. For example, the somewhat untidy line that illustrates the functional relationship between visual acuity and light intensity can be reduced to a prettier set of rectilinear functions by hypothesizing separate rod and cone processes, a logarithmic transformation, a Blondel-Rey-type threshold phenomenon to account for deviations at very low intensities, etc.

But our purpose here is not to design a methodology course, so it would be inappropriate to prolong this list. Let me say once again, to summarize our first koan, that we have listened too long to the sound of one hand clapping, and the less interesting hand at that, in confining our methodology discussion almost exclusively to hypothesis testing. It is now time to clap more loudly using the other hand as well by stressing the importance of hypothesis generation as part of psychological methodology.

Koan 2: In This Nettle Chaos, We Discern
This Pattern, Truth

I stress here the basic point that our cognitive systems and social systems are complex and that the currently conventional simple linear process models have outlived their heuristic usefulness as descriptions of these complex systems. In our actual cognitive and social systems, effects are the outcome of multiple causes which are often in complex interactions; moreover, it is the rule rather than the exception that the effects act back on the causal variables. Hence, students of cognitive and social processes must be encouraged to think big, or rather to think complexly, with conceptual models that involve parallel processing, nets of causally interrelated factors, feedback loops, bidirectional causation, etc.

If we and our students are to begin thinking in terms of these more complex models, then explicit encouragement is necessary since the published literature on social and cognitive processes is dominated by the simple linear models, and our students must be warned against imprinting on them. But our encouragement, while necessary, will not be sufficient to provoke our students into the more complex theorizing. We shall all shy away from the mental strain of keeping in mind so many variables, so completely interrelated. Moreover, such complex theories allow so many degrees of freedom as to threaten the dictum that in order to be scientifically interesting, a theory must be testable, that is, disprovable. These complex theories, with their free-floating parameters, seem to be adjustable to any outcome.

Hence, we have to give our students skill and confidence and be role models to encourage them to use complex formulations. To this end we have to give greater play to techniques like computer simulation, parameter estimation, multivariate time series designs, path analysis, etc. (as discussed further in Koan 5 below), in our graduate training programs.

Koan 3: Observe. But Observe People, Not Data

In our father's house there are many rooms. In the total structure of the intelligentsia, there is a place for the philosopher of mind and the social philosopher, as well as for the scientific psychologist. But the scientific psychologist can offer something beside and beyond these armchair thinkers in that we not only generate delusional systems, but we go further and test our delusional systems against objective data as well as for their subjective plausibility. Between the philosopher of mind and the scientific psychologist, there is the difference of putting the question to nature. Even when our theory seems plausible and so ingenious that it deserves to be true, we are conditioned to follow the Cromwellian dictum (better than did the Lord Protector himself) to consider in the bowels of Christ that we may be wrong.

But I feel that in our determination to maintain this difference we have gone too far. In our holy determination to confront reality and put our theory to the test of nature, we have plunged through reality, like Alice through the mirror, into a never-never land in which we contemplate not life but data. All too often the scientific psychologist is observing not mind or behavior but summed data and computer printout. He is thus a self-incarcerated prisoner in a platonic cave, where he has placed himself with his back to the outside world, watching its shadows on the walls. There may be a time to watch shadows but not to the exclusion of the real thing.

Perhaps Piaget should be held up as a role model here, as an inspiring example of how a creative mind can be guided in theorizing by direct confrontation with empirical reality. Piaget's close observation of how the developing human mind grapples with carefully devised problems was much more conducive to his interesting theorizing than would have been either the armchair philosopher's test of subjective plausibility or the scientific entrepreneur's massive project in which assistants bring him computer printout, inches thick.

The young student typically enters graduate study wanting to do just what we are proposing, that is, to engage in a direct confrontation with reality. All too often, it is our graduate programs which distract him with shadows. Either by falling into the hands of the humanists, he is diverted into subjectivism and twice-removed scholarly studies of what other subjectivists have said; or, if he falls under the influence of scientific psychologists, he becomes preoccupied with twice-removed sanitized data in the form of computer printout. I am urging that we restructure our graduate programs somewhat to keep the novice's eye on the real rather than distracting and obscuring his view behind a wall of data.

Koan 4: To See the Future in the Present, Find the Present in the Past

One idea whose time has come in social psychology is the accumulation of social data archives. Leaders of both the social science and the political establishments have recognized that we need a quality-of-life index (based perhaps on trace data, social records, self-reports obtained through survey research, etc.). Such social archives will also include data on factors which might affect subjective happiness, and analyses will be done to tease out the complex interrelations among these important variables. The need for such archives is adequately recognized; the interest and advocacy may even have outrun the talent, energy, and funds needed to assemble them.

In this growing interest in social data archives, one essential feature has been neglected, namely, the importance of obtaining time series data on the variables. While it will be useful to have contemporaneous data on a wide variety of social, economic, and psychological variables, the full exploitation of these data becomes possible only when we have recorded them at several successive points in time. Likewise, while a nation-wide survey of subjective feelings and attitudes is quite useful for its demographic break-downs at one point in time, the value of such a social survey becomes magnified many times when we have it repeated at successive points in history. It is only when we have the time series provided by a reconstructed or preplanned longitudinal study that we can apply the powerful methodology of time series analyses which allow us to reduce the complexity of the data and identify causality.

Hence, my fourth koan emphasizes the usefulness of collecting and using social data archives but adds that we should collect data on these variables not only at a single contemporaneous point in time, but also that we should set up a time series by recon-structing measures of the variables from the recent and distant past and prospectively by repeated surveys into the future.

Koan 5: The New Methodology Where Correlation Can Indicate Causation

If we agree that the simple linear sequence model has outlived its usefulness for guiding our theorizing about cognitive and social systems, then we must also grant that the laboratory manipulational experiment should not be the standard method for test-ing psychological hypotheses. But most graduate programs and most of the published studies (Higbee and Wells, 1972) focus disproportionately on descriptive and inferential statistics appropriate mainly to the linear models from the recent paradigm. The meth-ods taught and used are characterized by obsolescent procedures, such as rigorous dis-tinction between dependent and independent variables, two-variable or few-variable designs, an assumption of continuous variables, the setting of equal numbers and equal intervals, etc.

It seems to me that we should revise the methodology curriculum of our graduate programs and our research practice so as to make us better able to cope with the dirty data of the real world, where the intervals cannot be preset equally, where the subjects cannot be assigned randomly and in the same number, and where continuous measures and normal distributions typically cannot be obtained. In previous writings in recent years, I have called attention to advances in these directions which I mention here (McGuire, 1967, 1969), and Campbell (1969) has been in the forefront in devising, assembling, and using such procedures.

Our graduate programs should call the student's attention to new sources of social data, such as archives conveniently storing information from public opinion surveys, and to nonreactive measures of the unobtrusive trace type discussed by Webb and his colleagues.

Our students should also be acquainted with the newer analytic methods that make more possible the reduction of the complex natural field to a manageable num-ber of underlying variables whose interrelations can be determined. To this end, we and our students must have the opportunity to master new techniques for scaling qual-itative data, new methods of multivariate analysis, such as those devised by Shepard and others, and the use of time series causal analyses like the cross-lag panel design. More training is also needed in computer simulation and techniques of parameter estimation.

Mastery of these techniques will not be easy. Because we older researchers have already mastered difficult techniques which have served us well, we naturally look upon this retooling task with something less than enthusiasm. We have worked hard and endured much; how much more can be asked of us? But however we answer that question regarding our obligation to master these techniques ourselves, we owe it to our students to make the newer techniques available to those who wish it, rather than requiring all students to preoccupy themselves with the old techniques which have served us so well in reaching the point from which our students must now proceed.

Koan 6: The Riches of Poverty

The industrial countries, where the great bulk of psychological research is conducted, have in the past couple of years suffered economic growing pains which, if they have not quite reduced the amount of funds available for scientific research, at least have reduced the rate at which these funds have been growing. In the United States, at least, the last couple of years have been ones of worry about leveling scientific budgets. It is my feeling that the worry exceeds the actuality. In the United States' situation, psychology has in fact suffered very little as compared with our sister sciences. As an irrepressible optimist I am of the opinion that not only will this privileged position of psychology continue but also that the budgetary retrenchment in the other fields of science is only a temporary one and that, in the long run, the social investment in scientific research will resume a healthy, if not exuberant, rate of growth. I recognize that this optimism on my part will do little to cheer scientists whose own research programs have been hard hit by the financial cuts. To my prediction that in the long run social investment in science will grow again after this temporary recession, they might point out (like Keynes) that in the long run we shall all be dead.

I persist in my Dr. Pangloss optimism that things are going to turn out well and even engage in gallows humor by saying that what psychological research has needed is a good depression. I do feel that during the recent period of affluence when we in the United States could obtain government funds for psychological research simply by asking, we did develop some fat, some bad habits, and some distorted priorities which should now be corrected. While we could have made these corrections without enforced poverty, at least we can make a virtue of necessity by using this time of budgetary retrenchment to cut out some of the waste and distraction so that we shall emerge from this period of retrenchment stronger than we entered it.

The days of easy research money sometimes induced frenzies of expensive and exhausting activity. We hired many people to help us, often having to dip into less creative populations, and to keep them employed the easiest thing to do was to have them continue doing pretty much what we had already done, resulting in a stereotyping of research and a repetitious output. It tended to result in the collection of more data of the same type and subjecting them to the same kinds of analyses as in the past. It also motivated us to churn out one little study after another, to the neglect of the more solitary and reflective intellectual activity of integrating all the isolated findings into more meaningful big pictures.

Affluence has also produced the complex research project which has removed us from reality into the realm of data as I discussed in Koan 3. The affluent senior researcher often carried out his work through graduate assistants and research associates, who, in turn, often have the actual observations done by parapsychological technicians or hourly help, and the data they collect go to cardpunchers who feed them into computers, whose output goes back to the research associate, who might call the more meaningful outcome to the attention of the senior researcher, who is too busy meeting the payrolls to control the form of the printout or look diligently through it when it arrives. A cutback in research funds might in some cases divert these assistants into more productive and satisfying work while freeing the creative senior researcher from wasting his efforts on meeting the payroll rather than observing the phenomena.

I am urging here, then, that if the budgetary cutbacks continue instead of running ever faster on the Big-Science treadmill, we make the best of the bad bargain by changing our research organization, our mode of working, and our priorities. I would suggest that rather than fighting for a bigger slice of the diminishing financial pie, we redirect our efforts somewhat. We should rediscover the gratification of personally observing the phenomena ourselves and experiencing the relief of not having to administer our research empire. Also, I think we should spend a greater portion of our time trying to interpret and integrate the empirical relationships that have been turned up by the recent deluge of studies, rather than simply adding new, undigested relationships to the existing pile.

Koan 7: The Opposite of a Great Truth is Also True

What I have been prescribing above is not a simple, coherent list. A number of my urgings would pull the field in opposite directions. For example, Koan 1 urges that our methodology courses place more emphasis on the creative hypothesis-forming aspect of research even at the cost of less attention to the critical, hypothesis-testing aspect, but then in Koan 5 I urged that we, or at least our students, master a whole new pattern of hypothesis-testing procedures. Again, Koan 3 urges that we observe concrete phenomena rather than abstract data, but Koan 4 favors assembling social data archives that would reduce concrete historical events to abstract numbers. My prescriptions admittedly ride off in opposite directions, but let us remember that "consistency is the hobgoblin of little minds."

That my attempt to discuss ways in which our current psychological research enterprise could be improved has led me in opposite directions does not terribly disconcert me. I remember that Bohr has written, "There are trivial truths and great truths. The opposite of a trivial truth is plainly false. The opposite of a great truth is also true." The same paradox has appealed to thinkers of East and West alike since Sikh sacred writings advise that if any two passages in that scripture contradict one another, then both are true. The urging at the same time of seemingly opposed courses is not necessarily false. It should be recognized that I have been giving mini-directives which are only a few parts of the total system which our psychological research and research training should involve. Indeed, I have specified only a few components of such a total research program. Any adequate synthesis of a total program must be expected to contain theses and antitheses.

I have asserted that social psychology is currently passing through a period of more than usual uneasiness, an uneasiness which is felt even more by researchers inside the field than by outside observers. I have tried to analyze and describe the sources of this uneasiness as it is felt at various levels of depth. I have also described a few of the undercurrents which I believe will, or at any rate should, be part of the wave of the future which will eventuate in a new paradigm which will lead us to further successes, after it replaces the recent paradigm which has served us well but shows signs of obsolescence.

A time of troubles like the present one is a worrisome period in which to work, but it is also an exciting period. It is a time of contention when everything is questioned, when it sometimes seems that "the best lack all conviction, while the worst are full of passionate intensity." It may seem that this is the day of the assassin, but remember that "it is he devours death, mocks mutability, has heart to make an end, keeps nature new." These are the times when the "rough beast, its hour come round at last, slouches toward Bethlehem to be born." Ours is a dangerous period, when the stakes have been raised, when nothing seems certain but everything seems possible.

I began this talk by describing the proud and placid social psychology of a half-dozen years back, just before the bell tolled, as suggesting Buson's beautiful sleeping butterfly. I close by drawing upon his disciple, the angry young man Shiki, for a related but dynamically different image of the new social psychology which is struggling to be born. Shiki wrote a variant on Buson's haiku as follows:

Tsurigane-ni
Tomarite hikaru
Hotaru kana.

Or,

On a temple bell
Waiting, glittering,
A firefly.

NOTE

1. This paper is based on an address given at the Nineteenth Congress of the International Union of Scientific Psychology at Tokyo in August 1972.

REFERENCES

Campbell, D. T. "Reforms as Experiments," *American Psychologist*, 1969, **24**, 409-429.

Fried, S. B., Gumpper, D. C., and Allen, J. C. "Ten Years of Social Psychology: Is There a Growing Commitment to Field Research?" *American Psychologist*, 1973, **28**, 155-156.

Higbee, K. L., and Wells, M. G. "Some Research Trends in Social Psychology During the 1960s," *American Psychologist*, 1972, **27**, 963-966.

McGuire, W. J. "Learning Theory and Social Psychology." In O. Klineberg and R. Christie (eds.), *Perspectives in Social Psychology*. New York: Holt, Rinehart & Winston, 1965.

McGuire, W. J. "Some Impending Reorientations in Social Psychology," *Journal of Experimental Social Psychology*, 1967, **3**, 124-139.

McGuire, W. J. "Theory-oriented Research in Natural Settings: The Best of Both Worlds for Social Psychology." In M. Sherif and C. Sherif (eds.), *Interdisciplinary Relationships in the Social Sciences*. Chicago: Aldine, 1969.

Sears, D. O., and Abeles, R. P. "Attitudes and Opinions," *Annual Review of Psychology*, 1969, **20**, 253-288.

22 The Experimenting Organization: Problems and Prospects

Barry M. Staw

The last decade has seen a burgeoning of interest in the evaluation of social programs. Social scientists have increasingly focused their attention upon conceptual definitions of evaluation (e.g., Bennet and Lumsdaine, 1975; Campbell, 1969; Scriven, 1967; Wortman, 1975), the development of evaluation research methodologies (e.g., Campbell and Stanley, 1966; Cook and Campbell, 1976; Riecken and Boruch, 1974), and the political dynamics of evaluating various action programs (e.g., Banner, 1974; Berk and Rossi, 1976; Weiss, 1973, 1975). In short, there appears to be good progress toward what Campbell (1974) has labeled as "the experimenting society."

Although evaluation research has heightened in popularity during recent years, it is important to recognize that most of this activity has been centered on the evaluation of externally visible health, education, and welfare programs introduced by public sector organizations. Few evaluation research studies are conducted *within* public or private organizations to test whether internal innovations are effective or not. Rarely are persons trained in social research assigned to internal evaluation tasks. Instead, research-oriented staff are generally confined to established organizational functions, such as personnel selection, testing, and market research. Even the academic discipline of organizational behavior, whose function it is to study the internal workings of organizations, has largely ignored evaluation research as an important input to administrative decision making or the assessment of various programs *within* organizations. The purpose of the present paper is therefore to explore some of the implications of evaluation research for organizational decision processes and to discuss the problems as well as the prospects for the "experimenting organization."

THE CURRENT STATE OF ADMINISTRATIVE DECISION MAKING

Most organizational decisions are, by necessity, formulated within a context of uncertainty. For example, when deciding to start a new employee compensation scheme, a new program for task redesign, or a new training procedure, an administrator is often quite uncertain whether it will prove effective or not. In facing these kinds of decisions, the administrator usually comes armed only with a "lay psychology of organizational effectiveness." That is, through personal trial and error experiences in organizational settings, and both direct and indirect observations of the previous experiences of others, the administrator may have constructed his own theory to explain the internal

Source: B. M. Staw, *Psychological Foundations of Organizational Behavior* (Santa Monica, Calif.: Goodyear, 1977), pp. 466–486. Reproduced by permission.

workings of organizations (Staw, 1975). The administrator may have constructed his own personality theory to explain the relative productivity of different individuals (Bruner & Taguiri, 1954), his own interpersonal theory to explain what makes some groups more effective than others (Staw, 1975), and his own organizational theory to explain the chief determinants of an efficient administrative unit (Likert, 1967). The problem that remains, however, is that these lay theories may or may not be correct.

The major shortcoming of lay theories of organizational effectiveness is the methodological weakness of their supporting data. The administrator, for example, may construct a theory merely from the static observation of two groups differing in both performance and some other property A. If the differences between the two groups on both performance and property A are substantial, the individual is likely to conclude that A is a cause of performance. Moreover, if several groups are observed with the same pattern of data, the individual's confidence in this causal inference is likely to increase. Unfortunately, neither of these sources of cross-sectional data provides a highly valid basis for causal inference. In the case of the two-group comparison, statistical instability may have accounted for the result; in the comparison of many such groups, the threat of statistical instability is lessened, but the accuracy of causal inference is not greatly increased. The problem with drawing causal inference from a static-group comparison is that any other factor may have caused both property A and performance to vary together, and the direction of causation may merely be reversed.

The individual, in constructing his own theory of organizational effectiveness, may also utilize longitudinal data. Rather than relying solely upon static differences between individuals or groups, a person may look for covariation over time. A number of laboratory studies (e.g., Bavelas et al., 1965; Heider and Simmel, 1944; Michotte, 1963) have shown, for example, that causal inferences are most likely to be drawn when two variables covary over time and a change in one variable closely follows a change in another. Unfortunately, however, one's causal experience in observing covariation over time generally consists of only the weakest of longitudinal designs. For example, using Campbell and Stanley's (1966) notation in which X represents a change in an independent variable or treatment (e.g., a new job procedure) and O represents an observation of a dependent variable (e.g., work performance), the typical administrator has probably experienced some of the following "pre-experimental" designs:

1. $O \; X_1 \; O$
2. $O \; X_1 \; X_2 \; O$
3. $X_1 \; X_2 \; X_3 \; O$

As shown in the first example, the administrator may have changed X and then observed a change in the observation O from time 1 to time 2. In the second example, the administrator may have made multiple changes and observed a complex effect. Finally, in the third case, the administrator may have made multiple changes with only one post-treatment observation. Unfortunately, in none of these data-gathering instances can one be very confident of valid causal inference, regardless of the level or apparent change in the dependent variable(s).

THE ATTRIBUTION OF A CAUSAL RELATIONSHIP

The study of how individuals draw causal inferences from the data around them is the chief focus of attribution theory (Kelley, 1967). In general, empirical data has shown individuals to follow a relatively rational procedure of induction. Individuals look for salient differences or covariation from which to draw inferences and they employ a "discounting principle" in which confidence in causal inference is decreased when there exist salient alternative causes of the same phenomena (e.g., Bem, 1976; Calder and Staw, 1975; Deci, 1971; Jones et al., 1961; Jones and Harris, 1967; Kruglanski et al., 1971; Lepper et al., 1973; Staw, 1976a; Strickland, 1958; Thibaut and Riecken, 1955). More recently, Kelley (1973) has expanded this "discounting principle" in causal inference to encompass both inhibitory and facilitative causes. For example, if a new work training program accomplishes a goal in the face of an inhibitory cause (e.g., a strike or raw materials shortage) the new program would likely be given more credit as a causal factor than if such inhibitory forces were not present. Likewise, if the same new training program accomplishes a goal when other facilitative forces are present (e.g., an influx of more educated workers or improved physical surroundings), the impact of the new program would likely be discounted.

Methodologists in the evaluation area have also been concerned with facilitative and inhibitory causes that are external to a new program or experimental treatment. Campbell (1969), for instance, has systematically outlined a number of threats to the internal validity of experimental results. Because threats to internal validity are factors that can either hide a true effect of a treatment or make it appear overly robust, they are actually quite similar to Kelley's facilitative and inhibitory causes of a phenomenon. In Table 1, for example, are listed nine possible threats to the internal validity of experimental results. When any of them are judged to be present, one's confidence that a given treatment has caused a change in a dependent variable *ought* to be lessened. Also in Table 1 is a list of threats to external validity. These rival hypotheses limit the confidence one has in generalizing the results found in one situation to that of a new setting. The closer situation *A* resembles situation *B*, the more confidence one *should* have in an *A*-to-*B* generalization. Obviously, it would be useful to know if uninitiated observers of social phenomena also take these threats to internal and external validity into consideration and whether they are judged to be equally or differentially weighted in importance.

Given the present trend of research findings in the attribution area (c.f. Kelley, 1973), it is not unlikely for researchers to find individuals drawing causal inferences and making generalizations in much the same fashion as do social researchers. Although their terminology would no doubt be different, individuals are probably aware of threats to both internal and external validity. Thus, the principal shortcoming of lay theories of effectiveness is not likely to be the administrator's *innate* capacity for drawing causal inferences and generalizing from them, but the difficulty of being accurate given the incomplete and confounded data with which he must work. Because most administrative experiences conform to neither sound experimental or quasi-experimental designs, the administrator is forced to draw inferences from only the weakest of data sets.

DATA GENERATED BY 'EXPERTS'

In facing a decision to start a particular innovation, an administrator may sometimes attempt to go beyond his lay psychology of effectiveness and turn to behavioral scientists for help. Behavioral scientists have laid claim to a relatively objective view of persons and things (e.g., technology, structure) within organizational settings, and have amassed a very large body of research findings. Moreover, researchers in organizational behavior frequently view their role as one of providing practicing administrators with theories that are an improvement over the commonly held lay theories of practitioners (e.g., Behling and Schriesheim, 1976; Filley et al., 1976). It must be noted, however, that many of the "expert" theories are based upon research designs that are not far in advance of those used by the lay observer of behavior.

TABLE 1

Threats to Internal Validity	Threats to External Validity
1. *History:* events, other than the experimental treatment, occurring between pretest and posttest and thus providing alternate explanations of effects.	1. *Interaction effects of testing:* the effect of a pretest in increasing or decreasing the respondent's sensitivity or responsiveness to the experimental variable, thus making the results obtained for a pretested population unrepresentative of the effects of the experimental variable for the unpretested universe from which the experimental respondents were selected.
2. *Maturation:* processes within the respondents or observed social units producing changes as a function of the passage of time per se, such as growth, fatigue, secular trends, etc.	2. *Interaction of selection and experimental treatment:* unrepresentative responsiveness of the treated population.
3. *Instability:* unreliability of measures, fluctuations in sampling persons or components, autonomous instability of repeated or "equivalent" measures. (This is the only threat to which statistical tests of significance are relevant.)	3. *Reactive effects of experimental arrangements:* "artificially"; conditions making the experimental setting atypical of conditions of regular application of the treatment: "Hawthorne effects."
4. *Testing:* the effect of taking a test upon the scores of a second testing. The effect of publication of a social indicator upon subsequent readings of that indicator.	4. *Multiple-treatment interference:* where multiple treatments are jointly applied, effects atypical of the separate application of the treatments.
5. *Instrumentation:* in which changes in the calibration of a measuring instrument or changes in the observers or scores used may produce changes in the obtained measurements.	5. *Irrelevant responsiveness of measures:* all measures are complex, and all include irrelevant components that may produce apparent effects.
6. *Regression artifacts:* pseudo-shifts occurring when persons or treatment units have been selected upon the basis of their extreme scores.	6. *Irrelevant replicability of treatments:* treatments are complex, and replications of them may fail to include those components actually responsible for the effects.
7. *Selection:* biases resulting from differential recruitment of comparison groups, producing different mean levels on the measure of effects.	
8. *Experimental mortality:* the differential loss of respondents from comparison groups.	
9. *Selection-maturation interaction:* selection biases resulting in differential rates of "maturation" or autonomous change.	

Note: *Internal validity* refers to the level of confidence one has in whether a change in variable *X* actually caused a change in variable *Y*.

External validity refers to the level of confidence one has in whether such a causal relationship can be generalized.

From D. T. Campbell, "Reforms as Experiments," *American Psychologist* 24 (1969): 409-29.

One problem with data generated in the field of organizational behavior is that it merely feeds back to administrators their own lay theories of effectiveness. This problem stems from the fact that most data are based on cross-sectional surveys that relate various self-report measures to measures of performance. Research data, for example, show that questionnaire responses to items on influence, openness to change, cohesiveness, and so on correlate significantly with organizational performance. However, research has shown (see Staw, 1975) that beliefs about performance *also* influence one's beliefs about other processes that occur in social situations. Once one knows that an individual, group, or organization is a high or low performer, one is likely to make consistent attributions along many other dimensions. For example, regardless of the actual processes that may have occurred in a group, it has been shown that knowledge that the group was effective will lead to the attribution that it was also cohesive, high in communication, and high in mutual influence. Thus, when the organizational researcher attempts to show that various self-report measures are the causes of performance, he may merely be tapping a preexisting, lay theory of effectiveness.

In addition to the attributional problem in interpreting cross-sectional data, there are also recognized difficulties of reversed or reciprocal causation. As an example of some high quality cross-sectional research which may still be subject to these difficulties, let us examine the work of Hackman and Oldham (1976). These researchers measured job characteristics using both observer and self-rating forms and correlated these data with measures of work performance. Several characteristics of job enrichment (e.g., task variety, significance, identity) correlate significantly with performance and would seem to be determinants of task behavior in organizations. However, caution must be exercised in drawing such causal inferences since the best performers in an organization are likely to be given the most enriched and responsible jobs. And, although the Hackman and Oldham data show that the relationship between task characteristics and performance is strongest for persons with potent high-order needs, this moderated relationship could also be causally reversed. That is, high performance may not only generally lead supervisors to assign enriched jobs to subordinates, but this effect may be especially strong for those with high needs for autonomy and self-actualization. These persons may not merely wait for challenging jobs to be assigned; they may *actively lobby* for them.

Because of the difficulties of interpreting cross-sectional survey data, many researchers have resorted to laboratory experimentation. Laboratory experimentation provides much greater confidence in causal inference (i.e., internal validity) because changes in one variable are introduced and effects observed in a second variable, while extraneous factors are controlled. However, with each addition of experimental control, the laboratory situation becomes more and more divorced from everyday behavior. Hence, laboratory experiments often rank low in external validity, and one cannot often generalize their results to the organization with confidence. The greater the difference in research participants, experimental treatments, and setting from that of the real world, the lower is the external validity.

The organizational researcher often faces a dilemma in attempting to increase both internal and external validity. Those techniques that aid the interpretability of cause-effect relationships often decrease external validity, while efforts to make effects more generalizable often reduce internal validity. What is needed, therefore, are coordinated efforts tying together both laboratory and field research, and also field studies that utilize methods with greater internal validity. To date, there are few findings that have been tested in both the laboratory and field settings, or through a series of controlled field experiments.

Aside from the traditional concerns for internal and external validity of research data, there are several additional factors that may limit the applicability of research findings. First, within the behavioral sciences as a whole, there is a serious under-reporting of negative results (Notz et al., 1976). Data that are statistically significant and easily interpreted with a preexisting hypothesis are much more likely to be published than negative or inconsistent data. While this practice substantially reduces the volume of material for members of the field to process, it also limits the representativeness of published research results.

A second limitation is the frequent use of reconstructed logic in the presentation of research studies. As Notz et al. (1976) have noted, theories are often either fitted to data *post facto* or are amplified in those aspects that are consistent with the reported findings. Hypotheses and research designs are seldom as explicitly *a priori* as they are presented in published form. In large part, this bias is due to the fact that the author is judged professionally in the role of *advocate*—that is, on the basis of the consistency of his argument as well as the strength of his data. Because of the use of reconstructed logic, undue faith is often awarded to a particular theory, especially if its author is an articulate advocate.

A third, and perhaps most serious, problem in applying organizational research findings stems from a common misunderstanding of normative versus descriptive research. Most descriptive studies endeavor to report on cause-effect relationships found in the behavior of groups, individuals or organizations. The documentation of such findings can comprise a science of behavior and lead to a more accurate description of the social world. However, from a normative perspective, some authors have used these descriptive data to posit what *should* be done in a given situation. For example, Vroom and Yetton (1973) posit conditions when leaders should be participative or authoritarian in order to achieve maximum results. Their theoretical model is based upon a large amount of descriptive research in small group behavior and is likely to be accurate. But, as Argyris (1976) has cogently noted, Vroom and Yetton have implicitly accepted and made the status quo a desirable state by building it into their normative model. Argyris would argue that knowledge of individuals' reactions to participative or authoritarian management does not mean these reactions cannot be changed in the future. Thus, in deriving prescriptive statements from descriptive data, the researcher should be aware of his tacit role of either defender of tradition or change agent. As Gergen (1973) has noted, knowledge of cause-effect relationships is basically historical knowledge. Not only can one never be totally confident of effects in future situations (Campbell, 1975), but, even when there is high external validity, specific actions can often be taken to change future states.

THE CONTRIBUTION OF BEHAVIORAL SCIENCES TO ADMINISTRATION

It may seem that we have painted a dark outlook for the contribution of behavioral science to practicing administrators. We have noted that research findings may be questionable in terms of either internal or external validity and are seldom high on both dimensions. We have noted that there is bias in the selection of published research to favor both statistically significant results and reconstructed logic. Finally, we have noted that what should exist need not be the same as what currently exists, and prescriptive statements need not be totally consistent with previous descriptive research. What is the purpose of these caveats and where do they lead the practicing administrator?

At present, the behavioral sciences utilize what Schon (1971) has labeled a center-periphery model of dissemination. As shown in Figure 1, the model rests on the assumption that internally and externally valid findings are held by behavioral researchers (who are presumably at the center of knowledge), and that the primary job is to disseminate the expertise to users at the periphery. Obviously, as we have seen, this is an erroneous view of the applicability of behavioral research. Because there are few behavioral principles that can be readily applied in a formula-like fashion, potential users might well be cautious of the zealous purveyor of such research findings.

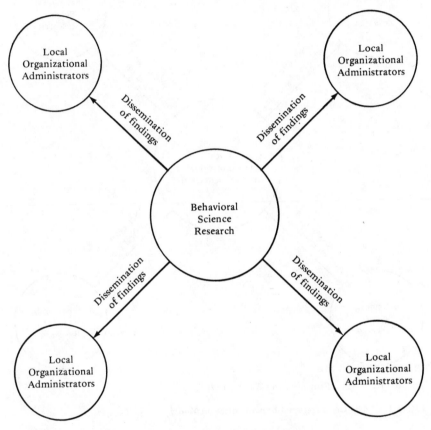

Adapted from Schon, 1971 and Notz, Salipante, and Waters, 1976.

FIGURE 1   The Center-Periphery Model of the Dissemination of Knowledge

A more realistic view is to acknowledge the uncertainty present in the social sciences and to accept the source of innovation at a more local level. From the administrator's point of view, behavioral findings should be appraised in terms of *best guesses*; what is most likely, and least likely to work. Once the existing research literature is assessed in terms of its internal and external validity, the administrator should *experimentally* undertake the seemingly best course of action. As shown in Figure 2, the administrator can be the focus of innovation utilizing the social science community as peripheral resources. The practitioner can be the one who ultimately tests the usefulness of any given theory or set of research findings (Notz et al., 1976).

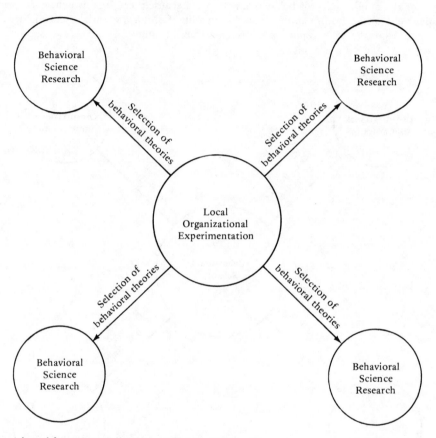

Adapted from Notz, Salipante, and Waters, 1976

FIGURE 2   The Organizational Experimentation Model

When the role of behavioral science shifts from center to periphery, its educational task also shifts. Instead of persuading practitioners to adopt one particular theory and reject another, it may expend more energy to training practitioners in evaluation skills— skills needed to ascertain whether a particular program is working or not. These evaluation skills can be viewed as tools that improve upon those normally available to the lay administrator in assessing cause-effect relationships. Because there are already entire volumes devoted to the development of appropriate evaluation techniques, we will mention only a few methods that are especially applicable to organizational administrators.

Methods of Evaluating Change in Large Organizations

When an organization is large it is often possible to introduce a change (e.g., job redesign, participation system, incentive scheme) on a truly experimental basis. That is, individuals or intact work groups may be assigned randomly to experimental and control conditions and measures taken both before and after the experimental treatment or change. Such an experimental design is shown below:

$R \quad O \quad X \quad O$
$R \quad O \qquad O$

In the above design, the existence of a cause-effect relationship can be assessed with relative confidence. If job enlargement is introduced by random assignment, for example, then any increase in job satisfaction over the control group (those for whom jobs were left unchanged) can be attributed to the enlargement. Randomization controls for history, maturation, selection, selection-maturation, and regression by equalizing experimental and control groups on all dimensions except the treatment. Instrumentation and testing can also be readily controlled by administering the same measures to both experimental and control groups. Mortality can present a problem for interpretation if it is treatment-induced (e.g., job enlargement causes greater or lesser turnover in the experimental than in the control group), but this threat can be easily measured and assessed. Finally, statistical instability may confound results if the sample size of the experimental and control groups are small or variability extremely large, but this is readily assessed through standard statistical tests of significance.

As Cook and Campbell (1976) have noted, there are several conditions that are especially conducive to true experimentation in organizations. The most common are when demand outstrips supply or when an innovation cannot be delivered to all individuals or units at once. In such situations, the most equitable way of distributing an improvement (e.g., job change) is through random assignment. Moreover, even when a basis can be firmly established for need priority, experimentation is frequently still possible. If the population is large enough, individuals (or groups) can be ranked in terms of their need priority. Those who clearly need the treatment can be given it immediately, and those who definitely do not need it can be denied the opportunity. However, within a range of "need ambiguity" individuals or groups can be randomly assigned to experimental and control groups. If this subgroup is large enough, a true experiment may result.

Perhaps the most important factor that is conducive to true experimentation is uncertainty over the results of an innovation. If it is not clear whether a change is helpful, the most reasonable procedure from a managerial point of view is to administer the treatment through random assignment. And, when a change is thought almost certainly to be costly to individuals or groups, random assignment removes the onus from the administrator. When lotteries are expected in a field setting, they provide data especially high in internal as well as external validity (see, e.g., the draft lottery studies conducted by Notz et al., 1971; Staw, 1974; and Staw et al., 1974).

Though true experimentation ranks highest in valid causal inference, it is not always the most practical course of action in administrative settings. Individuals cannot always be randomly assigned to experimental and control groups because such a procedure might disrupt normal production systems (e.g., in the case of job enlargement) or produce inequities between experimental and control groups (e.g., in the case of incentive or reward changes). In addition, there may be too few intact work groups for randomization to work effectively in equating the experimental and control groups. In such cases, the best procedure is to employ a time-series design. A time-series design basically utilizes a large number of observations before and after an experimental change and may or may not involve a comparison group. Shown below is a time-series design using two intact groups, one of which has received an experimental treatment.

O O O X O O O
O O O   O O O

The groups shown above are not randomly assigned and may not be perfectly comparable. However, by taking numerous measures of a dependent variable before and after a change, one can rule out such common threats to internal validity as testing, maturation, regression, and instrumentation. History remains the most problematic aspect of the time-series design. One must ask whether any other external event (other than the experimental change) could have caused a substantial shift in the dependent variable. For example, has production changed due to new job standards, plant modernization, leadership changes or any other factor in addition to the introduction of job enlargement? A control group that is measured before and after the change will aid in this inference process, if these two groups are believed to be subject to similar exogenous forces.

Time-series designs are the most easily implemented within organizational settings, because they involve little or no disruption of ongoing operations. What they demand, however, is extensive use of archival data. It is rarely possible to gather enough questionnaire data to construct a time-series of before and after observations of attitudes toward various aspects of organizational life. However, it is possible to utilize routinely collected behavioral observations such as absenteeism, turnover and production. In addition, an administrator can creatively collect data on many surrogates of attitudinal variables (Webb et al., 1966). For example, how early in the day a worker starts his cleanup may be indicative of his attitude toward the job; the number of cigarette butts found in the ashtrays during departmental meetings may be representative of intradepartmental conflict or tension; the number of employees using company's product (e.g., in an automobile plant) may relate to organizational loyalty or identification.

Although the time-series design explicitly demands nothing more than careful documentation and observation, its power can also be improved by an administrative attitude of tentativeness. That is, if an innovation is first implemented on an experimental basis to a small sample within an organization, it may be subsequently administered on an increasingly inclusive basis. Such a replicated time-series design offers both a powerful basis from which to infer cause-effect relations and a great deal of generalizability. A replicated time-series design is shown below:

O O O X O O O O O O O O
O O O O O O X O O O O O
O O O O O O O O X O O O

By staging the introduction of a change at several different points in time, one can readily rule out history as an alternative explanation of the change in a dependent variable. In addition, one can be relatively more certain that the observed change was not due to mere statistical instability, and can be more confident that the change will be applicable to multiple units in the organization.

The major requirement of a replicated time-series design is separation of the various treatment groups. If the groups can communicate and/or observe each other, the change in one group may spill over or diffuse to the others. This could result in either interunit jealousy resulting in deterioration in attitudes or the expression of rivalry, which could improve morale. Obviously under these conditions, the introduction of an innovation to an observing group differs from the initial innovation and does not constitute a true replication. A second and more serious problem for interpreting time-series designs, however, is the requirement of a relatively quick, high-impact treatment. If a change is slow and incremental (as in many O.D. interventions) it is often difficult to separate treatment-induced change from statistical error and other internal influences. Still, irrespective of these limitations, time-series techniques are a powerful tool in the evaluation of large-scale administrative changes. (For discussion of the data analysis techniques available for time-series studies, see Glass et al., 1975; McCain and McCleary, 1976; Nelson, 1973).

Methods of Evaluating Change in Small Administrative Units

We have seen that it is often possible for the administrator to make large-scale changes and to use these changes to infer cause-effect relationships. Does the administrator of a small unit (e.g., imagine one is supervising four people on a face-to-face basis) also have the capacity to make such valid causal inferences?

An immediate response to the above query is, "no, the small unit administrator is armed merely with theory rather than method." The administrator of a small, face-to-face unit cannot readily assign two people to a job-enlargement condition while leaving two others' jobs alone. Moreover, a random assignment with such small samples (coupled with the high degree of interaction among all the individuals involved) would provide little improvement in internal validity. A time-series analysis is possible with few subjects (see Chassan, 1967), although obviously changes will be more difficult to infer due to the statistical instability of such a small sample.

Must we then conclude that our only real leverage in improving decision-making skills of the small-unit administrator is in theory transmission? Certainly, in its role of training future administrators, the field of organizational behavior is chiefly involved in transmitting "expert" theories of leadership, motivation and group process and dispelling "lay" theories. Yet, there is room for methodological skills at this level, also. When sample size is small and statistical power weakened, one should turn to more qualitative research techniques. Training for the evaluation of small-unit changes should concentrate upon interviewing and observational techniques. Administrators can be trained to recognize facial expressions, physical distance and other nonverbal cues in evaluating the attitudes and beliefs of others. In addition, administrators can be trained to conduct clinically oriented interviews to discover the source and possible remedies of problems. Related techniques of interaction analysis and sensitivity training are already available and are used in professional school programs. What is necessary is to recognize these tools as data-gathering devices and couple them with other less obtrusive forms of measurement (Webb et al., 1966). For example, if the administrator changes the jobs of several of his employees, he should look for behavioral indicators of changes in attitude and performance in addition to those that result from direct questioning and interviewing. Unfortunately advocates of qualitative and quantitative research techniques have not recognized the special role and utility of each other's methodology. Proponents of qualitative techniques are often more interested in promoting new forms of human interaction than using their techniques in objective data gathering. Meanwhile, proponents of quantitative analysis have tended to restrict their attention to the testing of theory rather than to how practitioners can measure and evaluate their own changes. Needless to say, there is a great deal to be gained by a practitioner's synthesis of both forms of analysis.

Formative versus Summative Evaluation

To this point our discussion has centered on how behavioral science might improve causal inference in administrative settings. However, the evaluation techniques elaborated so far attack only part of the problem. Although tools such as experimental and quasi-experimental design help one to gather internally valid data, they presume a clearly formulated or at least explicitly chosen program of action. It is assumed, for example, that in evaluating the results of job enlargement, administrators know what job enlargement is and have chosen a particular aspect of it (e.g., increased task variety) to implement. The process of inferring whether a treatment "worked" or has had a positive effect is referred to as *summative evaluation*. The process of selecting program goals and building a treatment is referred to as *formative evaluation*. Formative evaluation resembles the pilot study stage of a research project in which the researcher gathers information about how he should proceed with a full-scale test of his hypothesis. As Wortman (1975) notes, the procedures involved in formative evaluation remain more of an art than a science. There is no convenient list of threats to validity, techniques, and methods for conducting a formative evaluation. Presumably, however, the successful "builder" of treatments must search for the correct blend of expert and lay theories of organizational effectiveness, be able to evaluate their prospects of success in his own situation, and conduct some inquiry (e.g., through interviews with other administrators, subordinates, search of prior records) into the likely consequences of his actions.

Wortman (1975) has described how formative and summative evaluation can be effectively combined in program evaluation. His basic point is that the qualitative and quantitative techniques used in formative and summative evaluations can be complementary rather than competing forms of evaluation. Thus, one might imagine an administrator first making small-scale changes (as in a pilot study) and using primarily qualitative analysis techniques. Then, once the administrator has a greater source of knowledge and has built what he thinks is a good treatment, he may implement this change on a larger-scale basis. The large-scale change can be evaluated using experimental and/or time-series research designs.

Problems in Moving from Formative to Summative Evaluation

Though the sequential use of formative and summative evaluation makes intuitive sense, is it realistic in most administrative settings? The principal problem seems to be when, and if, one can move from formative to summative evaluation. At what stage is the administrator willing to regard his change as "in place" and ready for testing? As Lindblom (1959) has noted, the answer may be *never!*

The administrative process, as Lindblom notes, may be a perpetual sequence of making incremental changes or "tinkering with the treatment." Lindblom describes the public administrator, for example, as one who makes a number of successive limited goals, and implement solutions. In Lindblom's view, incrementalism is the most rational comparisons rather than attempting to comprehensively analyze problems, set specific way to address any complex social problem, and he labels this process as "the science of muddling through."

The incrementalism explicit in Lindblom's "science of muddling through" is not inconsistent with the concept of the experimenting organization. In fáct, an administrator's willingness to change policy or course of action on the basis of data is the *essence* of social experimentation. However, there may be important differences between the administrator's and the organization's *preferred* form of incrementalism. From the organization's point of view, it would seem generally preferable to build a treatment through formative evaluation and then subject it to a rigorous test through summative evaluation. This procedure would be quite consistent with an evolutionary model of organizations in which evaluation research functions as a device to aid selection and retention processes (Pondy, 1977; Weick, 1969). But, from the individual administrator's point of view, it may seem preferable to forge an acceptable treatment through a succession of limited comparisons without ever being subjected to a summative evaluation. By remaining at the formative evaluation stage, administrators may continuously revise a program (or even its goals) to meet the demands of clients and other administrators. Lindblom would argue that this process of revision never ends for administrators, especially in the public sector. Of necessity, the administrator may have to continuously shape and reshape a program to retain the support of shifting coalitions of power within organizations and their environments. Obviously, such political considerations will often determine the nature and scope of any evaluation effort, and must be seriously examined in the initial design of a program evaluation.

The Trapped Administrator

Although administrators are often willing to make incremental changes in a treatment, they are frequently hesitant to "backtrack" or make changes that can be construed as an admission of previous error. In fact, there are some visible cases, such as the U.S. intervention in the Indochina War, that seem to indicate that decision makers will even escalate their commitment following negative results rather than undertake any major shifts in policy. The Indochina War effort was similar to an investment decision context in which it was possible to recoup an initial loss by increasing one's subsequent investment. Similar situations might also exist in organizations, such as when one must decide how much advertising is needed to successfully launch a new product or how much R&D expenditure is needed to build a new or improved product. Each of these situations poses a dilemma when negative results occur. Does one accept one's losses and scuttle the program or escalate one's investment in an effort to turn the situation around?

Using a simulated business decision case, Staw (1976b) experimentally tested for the tendency to escalate following the receipt of negative consequences. In his study, business school students were asked to allocate research and development funds to one of two operating divisions of a company. They were then given the results of their initial decisions and asked to make a second allocation of R&D funds. In this study, some subjects also were assigned to a condition in which they did not make the initial allocation decision *themselves*, but were told that it was made earlier by another financial officer of the firm. The results of the experiment were as follows: (1) there was a main effect of responsibility such that subjects allocated more money when *they*, rather than another financial officer, had made the initial decision; (2) there was a main effect of consequences such that subjects allocated more money to the declining rather than improving division; and (3) there was a significant interaction of responsibility and consequences. That is, subjects allocated even more money when they were responsible for negative consequences than would be expected by the two main effects acting alone. Personal responsibility for negative consequence, therefore, may lead to the greatest likelihood of escalation behavior.

From the experimental results described above and observational evidence of real-world escalations (see, e.g., *The Pentagon Papers*), it seems possible that administrators can become trapped by their own previous mistakes. It seems that a key problem the administrator faces is knowing when it is appropriate to accept one's losses or enlarge the stakes. Hindsight yields examples of leaders who are perceived as strong and coura-geous following *either* of these two strategies. For example, Lyndon Johnson's leader-ship ability was assailed for following the escalation route. However, if Johnson had succeeded in "winning the war" in Indochina, he no doubt would have been hailed widely as a wise and bold leader. Unfortunately, from the administrator's perspective, there are no available statistical techniques that will substitute for qualitative judgment on this classic investment problem.

Staw and Fox (1977) found that many decision makers attempt to "test the system" by allocating a substantial amount of resources to the problem and then, if no effect results, reduce their commitment substantially. This strategy would seem appropriate for treatments that require a large, immediate expenditure of resources to create an impact (e.g., advertising a new product), but quite inappropriate for treatments that require a slow, building commitment (e.g., many O.D. interventions). As mentioned earlier, the latter treatments not only pose difficulties in judgment, but are especially troublesome for detecting changes using statistical techniques such as time-series anal-ysis (Glass et al., 1975).

In addition to the problem of knowing how much investment is enough to create a change, there is likely to be a second and even more important cause of the trapped administrator. From the administrator's point of view, a program must sometimes be *made to work at almost any cost*. A program that fails is frequently treated as an admin-istrative failure and can be cause for demotion or dismissal. Few organizations have assimilated an experimental philosophy in which ineffective programs are merely replaced by other more promising programs. Instead, programs are advocated and imple-mented by ambitious administrators who, in case of failure, are replaced by other more promising candidates. Thus, evaluation apprehension (Rosenberg, 1969) is a likely cause of administrative defense and advocacy of programs that appear to others as obvi-ous failures. Moreover, because evaluation in organizations is frequently *ad hominem* there may also be pressure throughout the system to bias the data forming the basis of program evaluation. Close associates of administrative heads may be hesitant to relay negative information (Janis, 1972; Tesser and Rosen, 1975), and lower level officials may be selective in the information they pass upward (Cohen, 1958; Read, 1962). As Thompson (1967) has noted, there may be enormous pressure at the individual, group and organizational levels to report successes and deemphasize any information that can be construed as a failure. Clearly, a great deal of work needs to be done to design an organizational system that can effectively monitor, feed back, and utilize negative as well as positive data.

Some Organizational Solutions to Evaluation Apprehension

The most obvious solution to the apprehension that often accompanies evaluation research is to take specific measures to insure that one is evaluating *programs* and not *people*. As Campbell has noted (personal communication, 1976), decisions about the salary, grade, or promotions of program administrators should be divorced from program evaluation and reporting procedures. Campbell also goes so far as to state that program funding decisions should be removed from evaluation research activities. Taken literally, this solution is quite similar to that frequently advocated (e.g., Porter et al., 1975) for other kinds of performance evaluation systems within organizations. For example, in the personnel evaluation context, it is not in the employee's best interest to present any negative information to his superior. However, it is precisely such weaknesses that need to be communicated in order for the supervisor to properly counsel and guide the employee for improvement. Hence, it is sometimes recommended that performance evaluation be temporally (and even functionally) separated for salary review and employee development sessions. The only hitch is that, even when there is temporal spacing or some other form of separation, any perceived relationship between communicated negative information and salary decisions is likely to lead to future defensiveness and data filtering.

In the contexts of both program evaluation and personnel evaluation, there is a very real conflict between the organizational functions of feedback and resource allocation. The desire to know what programs are working well and to allocate money to the most effective is similar to the need to know who are the best performing workers in order to allocate rewards as a consequence of performance. From the organization's point of view, rewards that are not contingent upon behavior will lead to a decrease in task motivation (Hamner, 1974; Nord, 1969); likewise, resources that are not allocated to the most effective programs (or perhaps program administrators) may be misspent or wasted. However, from the individual employee or program administrator's point of view, efforts will be taken to insure that reports are positive, show improvement, or closely follow *whatever criteria* is utilized in resource allocation decisions.

Given the inherent conflict between resource allocation and feedback processes, program evaluation will no doubt always retain some aspects of a "police function." Teams of evaluators may be viewed warily, and data may continue to be made available only selectively. At the same time, evaluators will attempt to find unobtrusive and seemingly uncorrupted measures of program effectiveness. If organizations opt to recognize such conflict as intractable, they may concentrate on developing structures to manage the conflict. One possibility is that of building a quasi-legal system within organizations in which advocacy (both pro and con) is voiced, evidence is presented, and then resource allocation decisions are made by a single authority or unbiased panel. Although Wolf (1974) has discussed such a possibility within educational organizations, there have as yet been no known attempts to implement such a aystem.

A second and apparently more popular way of dealing with the conflict between resource allocation and feedback is to attempt to reduce it by decoupling these organizational processes. Summative or outcome evaluation can be deemphasized, and instead efforts can be made to concentrate on formative evaluation in which the program is changed. Formative evaluation is less likely to be threatening than summative evaluation because it is focused upon improving the program rather than evaluating its impact vis-à-vis other uses for resources. Unfortunately, deemphasis of summative evaluation may also drastically reduce organizational efficiency or cost effectiveness. A better strategy for decoupling feedback and allocation processes is for the organization to guarantee continued funding of a particular organizational unit, but to encourage that unit to experiment among various programs. Carried to its extreme, the organization could reward organizational units and administrators, not on their overall results, but on the quality of their experimentation and program evaluation techniques.

A third solution to evaluation apprehension is to design organizational reward systems so that resources are highly contingent upon performance. However, at the same time, one might also institute an evaluation research group as an in-house consulting unit. The idea here is to actually *increase* pressure upon individuals and work units to perform, but also to offer free evaluation consulting as an aid to improve local performance. Obviously, for this solution to work, the in-house consulting group must be perceived to be politically neutral and the data offered to program evaluators held confidential. If such a system functioned successfully, organizational units might be encouraged to experiment in order to increase their own monitored effectiveness. Organizational units might simultaneously utilize two methods and then choose the best, or sequentially explore new program tools and procedures.

Operationalism versus Goal Accomplishment

In addition to the problem of data biasing, one other key difficulty with program evaluation merits attention in this paper. Within organizations, program evaluation may often be troubled by a confusion between measured improvement and goal accomplishment. That is, there may tend to be undue emphasis upon a particular indicator or operationalization of effectiveness at the expense of the construct of effectiveness itself. The problem is best illustrated in the context of performance contracting for education. When private contractors are paid on the basis of improvement in students' reading or math scores, they tend to "teach for the test," giving repeated examples of old test materials and spending most of the class time on tested skills (Stake, 1971). Although tested scores may improve, educational effectiveness of the program may thus be low. Similarly, organizational units may spend an undue amount of effort on those behaviors that are measured and weighted heavily within a program evaluation (Ridgeway, 1956; Thompson, 1967). Patients may not be referred to hospitals in order to keep a mental health program's hospital recidivism rate low; poor workers may be encouraged to stay on the job to keep employee turnover down, and work quantity may be emphasized at the expense of quality.

One solution to this problem is to use multiple indicators or operationalizations of the construct of effectiveness (Campbell, 1974). For example, in addition to measuring the number of absences before and after a program of applied reinforcement for work attendance (e.g., Lawler and Hackman, 1969), one should also measure work quality, quantity, and satisfaction. As shown by Staw and Oldham (1976), it is possible that there are some positive consequences of absenteeism, and that strong inducements for attendance could actually lead to decrements in work performance. The crucial point is that program evaluators should try to avoid concentrating upon single indicators of success.

Of course, even with multiple operationalizations of the effectiveness criterion, there may still be some focusing of local effort upon a presumed hierarchy of results. Regardless of the number of indicators of success, program administrators may attempt to discern which are *the* most important indicators in a final judgment affecting resource allocation decisions (Pfeffer, 1977). The weighting of effectiveness indicators should thus be made an *explicit and public aspect* of the evaluation process so that local organizational units can legitimately focus their attention on the most important criteria. No doubt, it will frequently be necessary for an evaluation team to get higher level management to specify clearly what their criteria for effectiveness are. This process, not unlike the setting of organizational objectives (Drucker, 1954; Odiorne, 1965), may even prove to be one of the most valuable aspects of program evaluation. For example, when administrators and participants of a program disagree on what criteria a program should be evaluated, such disagreement can often be translated into a positive program of participative goal setting. And, participation of program administrators, participants, and higher level management in criteria selection may turn out to be one of the most important necessary conditions of successful program evaluation within organizations.

CONCLUSIONS

In this paper, we have discussed several of the difficulties facing evaluation research within organizations. We have offered some suggestions to minimize problems such as evaluation apprehension, biasing of data, and over-focusing upon operationalized measures of effectiveness. Still, we do not wish to promote the naive impression that program evaluation is easy, foolproof, or necessarily accurate. Some problems such as those discussed here may be endemic to any attempt to assess the effectiveness of an organizational program.

Our main purpose has been to promote a cautious optimism about evaluation activities within organizations. Administrators have been viewed here as having the innate capacity to make relatively rational causal inferences and to be able to evaluate both large and small unit changes. In fact, the chief difficulty confronting organizational administrators in our view is the lack of appropriate data and research design capability *within* organizations. Instead of merely proffering new or revised theories for administrators to use in an "across the board" fashion, behavioral scientists should therefore concentrate more on transferring methodological skills to practicing administrators so that they can experimentally test the usefulness of various theories, including their own. In this way, organizational researchers may provide the greatest contribution to the organizations they study.

REFERENCES

Argyris, C. "Problems and New Directions for Industrial Psychology." In *Handbook of Industrial Organizational Psychology*, edited by M. D. Dunnette. Chicago: Rand McNally, 1976.

Banner, D. K. "The Politics of Evaluation Research," *Omega* 2 (1974): 736-74.

Bavelas, A., Hastorf, A. H., Gross, A. E., and Kite, W. R. "Experiments in Alteration of Group Structure," *Journal of Experimental Social Psychology* 1 (1965): 199-218.

Behling, O., and Schriesheim, C. *Organizational Behavior: Theory, Research, and Application.* Boston: Allyn and Bacon, 1976.

Bem, D. J. "Self-perception: The Dependent Variable of Human Performance," *Organizational Behavior and Human Performance* 2 (1976): 105-21.

Bennett, C. A., and Lumsdaine, A. A. "Social Program Evalution: Definitions and Issues." In *Evaluation and Experiment: Some Critical Issues in Assessing Social Programs*, edited by C. A. Bennett and A. A. Lumsdaine. New York: Academic Press, 1975.

Berk, R. A., and Rossi, P. H. "Doing Good or Worse: Evaluation Research Politically Reexamined," *Social Problems* 23 (1976): 337-49.

Bruner, J. S., and Taguiri, A. "The Perception of People." In *Handbook of Social Psychology*, edited by G. Lindzey. Reading, Massachusetts: Addison-Wesley, 1954.

Calder, B. J., and Staw, B. M. "Self-perception of Intrinsic and Extrinsic Motivation," *Journal of Personality and Social Psychology* 31 (1975): 599-605.

Campbell, D. T. "Reforms as Experiments," *American Psychologist* 24 (1969): 409-29.

——. "Methods for the Experimenting Society," *Evaluation Research Program Paper Series, No. 5.* Evanston, Illinois: Northwestern University, 1974.

——. "Assessing the Impact of Planned Social Change." In *Social Research and Public Policies*, edited by G. M. Lyons. Hanover, New Hampshire: University Press of New England, 1975.

——, and Stanley, J. C. *Experimental and Quasi-Experimental Designs for Research*. Chicago: Rand McNally, 1966.

Chassan, J. B. *Research Designs in Clinical Psychology and Psychiatry*. New York: Appleton-Century-Crofts, 1967.

Cohen, A. R. "Upward Communication in Experimentally Created Hierarchies," *Human Relations* 11 (1958): 41-53.

Cook, T. D., and Campbell, D. T. "The Design and Conduct of Quasi-Experiments and True Experiments in Field Settings." In *Handbook of Industrial and Organizational Psychology*, edited by M. D. Dunnette. Chicago: Rand McNally, 1976.

Deci, E. L. "The Effects of Externally Mediated Rewards on Intrinsic Motivation," *Journal of Personality and Social Psychology* 18 (1971): 105-15.

Drucker, P. *The Practice of Management*. New York: Harper & Row, 1954.

Filley, A. C.; House, R. J.; and Kerr, S. *Managerial Process and Organizational Behavior*. Glenview, Illinois: Scott, Foresman, & Co., 1976.

Gergen, K. V. "Social Psychology as History," *Journal of Personality and Social Psychology* 26 (1973): 309-20.

Glass, G. V., Willson, V. L., and Gottman, J. M. *Design and Analysis of Time-Series Experiments*. Boulder, Colorado: Colorado Associated University Press, 1975.

Hackman, J. R., and Oldham, G. R. "Motivation Through the Design of Work," *Organizational Behavior and Human Performance*, 1976.

Hamner, W. C. "Reinforcement Theory and Contingency Management in Organizational Settings." In *Organizational Behavior and Management: A Contingency Approach*, edited by H. L. Tosi and W. C. Hamner. Chicago: St. Clair Press, 1974.

Heider, F., and Simmel, M. "An Experimental Study of Apparent Behavior," *American Journal of Psychology* 57 (1944): 243-59.

Janis, I. L. *Victims of Groupthink: A Psychological Study of Foreign Policy Decisions and Fiascos*. Boston: Houghton Mifflin Co., 1972.

Jones, E. E., Davis, K. E., and Gergen, K. E. "Role Playing Variations and Their Informational Value for Person Perception," *Journal of Abnormal and Social Psychology* 63 (1961): 302-10.

——, and Harris, V. A. "The Attribution of Attitudes," *Journal of Experimental Social Psychology* 3 (1967): 1-24.

Kelley, H. H. "Attribution Theory in Social Psychology." In *Nebraska Symposium on Motivation*, edited by D. Levine. Lincoln: University of Nebraska Press, 1967.

——. "The Processes of Causal Attribution." *American Psychologist* 28 (1973): 107-28.

Kruglanski, A. W., Freedman, I., and Zeevi, G. "The Effects of Extrinsic Incentives on Some Qualitative Aspects of Task Performance," *Journal of Personality* 39 (1971): 606-17.

Lawler, E. E., and Hackman, J. R. "Impact of Employee Participation in the Development of Pay Incentive Plans: A Field Experiment," *Journal of Applied Psychology* 53 (1969): 467-71.

Lepper, M. R., Greene, D., and Nisbett, R. E. "Undermining Children's Intrinsic Interest with Extrinsic Rewards: A Test of the Over-justification Hypothesis," *Journal of Personality and Social Psychology* 28 (1973): 129-37.

Likert, R. *Human Organization: Its Management and Value*. New York: McGraw-Hill, 1967.

Lindblom, C. E. "The Science of Muddling Through," *Public Administration Review* 19 (1959): 79-88.

McCain, L. J., and McCleary, R. "The Statistical Analysis of Interrupted Time Series Quasi-Experiments." In *The Design and Analysis of Quasi-Experiments in Field Settings*, edited by T. D. Cook and D. T. Campbell. Chicago: Rand McNally, 1976.

Michotte, A. *The Perception of Causality*. New York: Basic Books, 1963.

Nelson, C. R. *Applied Time Series Analysis for Managerial Forecasting*. San Francisco: Holden Day, 1973.

Nord, W. R. "Beyond the Teaching Machine: The Neglected Area of Operant Conditioning in the Theory and Practice of Management," *Organizational Behavior and Human Performance* 4 (1969): 375-401.

Notz, W. W., Salipante, P. E., and Waters, J. A. "Innovation in Situ: A Contingency Approach to Human Resource Development." Working paper, Department of Administrative Sciences, University of Manitoba, Winnepeg, Canada, 1976.

———, Staw, B. M., and Cook, T. D. "Attitude Toward Troop Withdrawal from Indochina as a Function of Draft Number: Dissonance or Self-Interest?" *Journal of Personality and Social Psychology* 20 (1971): 118-26.

Odiorne, G. S. *Management by Objectives*. New York: Pitman Publishing Co., 1965.

Pentagon Papers, The New York Times (based on investigative reporting of Neil Sheehan). New York: Bantam Books, 1971.

Pfeffer, J. "Power and Resource Allocation in Organizations." In *New Directions in Organizational Behavior*, edited by B. M. Staw and G. R. Salancik. Chicago: St. Clair Press, 1977.

Pondy, L. R. "Two Faces of Evaluation." In *Accounting for Social Goals and Social Organization*, edited by H. W. Metton and D. Watson. Columbus, Ohio: Grid Publishing Co., 1977.

Porter, L. W., Lawler, E. E., and Hackman, J. R. *Behavior in Organizations*. New York: McGraw-Hill, 1975.

Read, W. "Upward Communication in Industrial Hierarchies," *Human Relations* 15 (1962): 3-16.

Ridgeway, V. "Dysfunctional Consequences of Performance Measures," *Administrative Science Quarterly* 1 (1956): 240-47.

Riecken, H. W., and Boruch, R. F., eds. *Social Experimentation: A Method for Planning and Evaluating Social Intervention*. New York: Academic Press, 1974.

Rosenberg, M. J. "The Conditions and Consequences of Evaluation Apprehension." In *Artifact in Behavioral Research*, edited by R. Rosenthal and R. L. Rosnow. New York: Academic Press, 1969.

Schon, D. A. *Beyond the Stable State*. New York: Random House, 1971.

Scriven, M. "The Methodology of Evaluation." In *Perspectives of Curriculum Evaluation*, edited by R. W. Tyler, R. M. Gagné, and M. Scriven. Chicago: Rand McNally, 1967.

Stake, R. E. "Testing Hazards in Performance Contracting," *Phi Delta Kappan* 52 (1971): 583-88.

Staw, B. M. "Attitudinal and Behavioral Consequences of Changing a Major Organizational Reward: A Natural Field Experiment," *Journal of Personality and Social Psychology* 29 (1974): 742-51.

———. "Attribution of the 'Causes' of Performance: A General Alternative Interpretation of Cross-Sectional Research on Organizations," *Organizational Behavior and Human Performance* 13 (1975): 414-32.

———. *Intrinsic and Extrinsic Motivation*. Morristown, N.J.: General Learning Press, 1976. (a)

———. "Knee-Deep in the Big Muddy: A Study of Escalating Commitment to a Chosen Course of Action," *Organizational Behavior and Human Performance* 16 (1976): 27-44. (b)

———, and Fox, F. W. "Escalation: Some Determinants of Commitment to a Previously Chosen Course of Action," *Human Relations* 30 (1977): 431-50.

———, Notz, W. W., and Cook, T. D. "Vulnerability to the Draft and Attitudes Toward Troop Withdrawal from Indochina: Replication and Refinement." *Psychological Reports* 34 (1974): 407-17.

———, and Oldham, G. R. "Some Functional Consequences of Absenteeism." Working paper, Northwestern University, 1976.

Strickland, L. H. "Surveillance and Trust." *Journal of Personality* 26 (1958): 200-15.

Tesser, A., and Rosen, S. "The Reluctance to Transmit Bad News." In *Advances in Experimental Social Psychology*, edited by C. Berkowitz. New York: Academic Press, 1975.

Thibaut, J. W. and Riecken, H. W. "Some Determinants and Consequences of the Perception of Social Causality," *Journal of Personality* 24 (1955): 113–33.

Thompson, J. D. *Organizations in Action*. New York: McGraw-Hill, 1967.

Vroom, V. H., and Yetton, P. W. *Leadership and Decision Making*. Pittsburgh: University of Pittsburgh Press, 1973.

Webb, E. J., Campbell, D. T., Schwartz, R. D., and Sechrest, L. *Unobtrusive Measures: Non-Reactive Research in the Social Sciences*. Chicago: Rand McNally, 1966.

Weick, K. E. *The Social Psychology of Organizing*. Reading, Mass.: Addison-Wesley, 1969.

Weiss, C. H. "Where Politics and Evaluation Research," *Evaluation* 1 (1973): 37-45.

——. "Evaluation Research in the Political Context." In *Handbook of Evaluation Research*, edited by E. L. Struening and M. Guttentag. Beverly Hills, California: Sage Publications, 1975.

Wolf, R. L. *The Application of Select Legal Concepts to Educational Evaluation*. Ph.D. dissertation, University of Illinois at Urbana-Champaign, School of Education, 1974.

Wortman, P. M. "Evaluation Research: A Psychological Perspective," *American Psychologist* 30 (1975): 562-75.